CW00835905

INFORMATION MANAGEMENT DECISIONS
Briefings and Critical Thinking

The management of information technology has attracted many theories and techniques, but how should the *general ideas* of consultants and professors affect *decisions in specific organisations*? That question dominates this book.

By contrast, the author's earlier *Demands and Decisions, Briefings on Issues in Information Technology Strategy*, discussed management issues as rationally as possible, without the distractions of ideas proposed by other people:

> 'Clear style and easily understood lines of argument . . frequent pearls of wisdom' *Computer Weekly*

> 'One word which occurs throughout is 'tradeoff', and this could be said to epitomise the entire philosophy of decision-making.' *Computing*

> ' . . raises more questions than it answers. But they are certainly interesting questions. So, recommended.' *Informatie Management*

> 'takes a different approach . . very readable . . particularly if you are involved in strategic decisions about the use of IT' *IDPM Journal*

> 'practical, challenging and sometimes controversial . . strongest of all on presentation of useful frameworks for systematic and rational approaches to difficult areas of decision-making. The wonder is that, in a book . . about the very volatile areas of IT strategy. . the author has managed to write at a useful level of detail in a manner which will not age rapidly . . Overall, this book is strongly recommended.' *Journal of Strategic Change*

O'Brien's other book, just published by Pitman, is *Database Decisions, Briefings on the Management of Technology*. This tackles an important question on a different plane: How can you know what is worth knowing about the *facts* of information technology?

Information Management Decisions

Briefings and Critical Thinking

Bart O'Brien

PITMAN PUBLISHING
128 Long Acre, London WC2E 9AN

A Division of Longman Group Limited

First published in Great Britain 1995

© Bart O'Brien 1995

British Library Cataloguing in Publication Data
A CIP catalogue record for this book can be obtained fom the British Library.

ISBN 0 273 60288 8

All rights reserved; no part of this publication may be reproduced, stored in a retrieval system, or transmitted in any form or by any means, electronic, mechanical, photocopying, recording, or otherwise without either the prior written permission of the Publishers or a licence permitting restricted copying in the United Kingdom issued by the Copyright Licensing Agency Ltd, 90 Tottenham Court Road, London W1P 9HE. This book may not be lent, resold, hired out or otherwise disposed of by way of trade in any form of binding or cover other than that in which it is published, without the prior consent of the Publishers.

10 9 8 7 6 5 4 3 2 1

Printed and bound in Great Britain by Clays Ltd, St Ives plc

The Publishers' policy is to use paper manufactured from sustainable forests.

Henk and Walter Baghuis of
Compubest BV, Rotterdam, the Netherlands
helped the author by generously providing
image-scanning, image-editing and
PostScript printing facilities.

Contents

Introduction

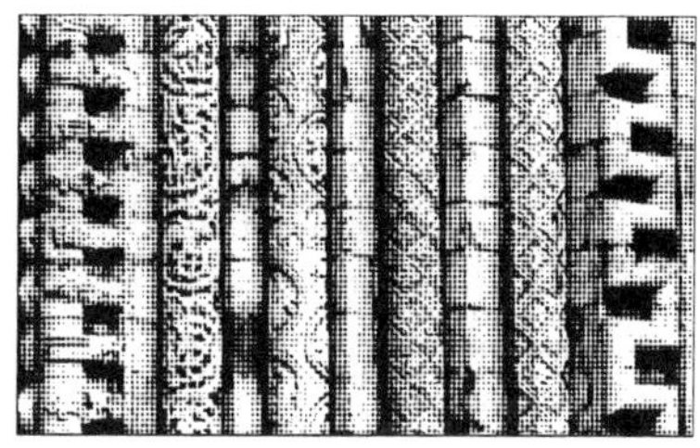

'You ask me to treat information as a key corporate strategic resource. But what do those words actually mean?'

'As you say, close integration of IT systems with re-engineered and more effective business processes probably will achieve far greater benefits than merely using IT to improve the efficiency of existing processes. Are you asking me to nod at a platitude or have you some concrete decision in mind?'

'Certainly our IT planning should make full allowance for our company's culture, and for the sensitivities and values of key individuals and groups. But, if anybody can bring in intangible factors to support or oppose any proposal how can we ever arrive at well-reasoned decisions?'

'End-user computing is a vital issue for us, with far-reaching implications. Very well then; what, in clear, jargon-free terms, are the real options we have to choose between?'

These questions belong to a field that can be roughly demarcated as the management of the organisation's information technology — in a wide sense, not merely the management of IT projects or IT departments. *Information management* has come to be regarded as the least misleading term for this field.

Information management (IM) is unavoidably concerned with inter-disciplinary and inter-departmental matters, and its problems are often slippery ones. As the questions hint, it may be difficult to define just what a certain problem is without being either too vague or too specific, or difficult to see quite how one problem interacts with others, or difficult to know what kind of evidence and reasoning should carry weight, or difficult to distinguish between a genuine solution and a fudged one, or difficult to debate the issues without lapsing into obscure abstractions.

Established Knowledge

If a field abounds in slippery problems, a good start is to ask: What reliable, established knowledge is there to be found?

A student of engineering (or a qualified engineer who wants to brush up on a certain part of the subject) can consult a textbook that sets out a massive body of established knowledge. The same applies to cost accountancy, medicine, economics and many other disciplines. A textbook of (say) bridge-building contains many items of knowledge that are *fundamental* (on matters central to the job of building a bridge) *and substantial* (needing plenty of brainpower and concentration to master) *and widely accepted* (known and used by most competent bridge-builders) *and well-proven* (the bridges don't fall down). That is the justification for textbooks that recommend, in effect: 'To be successful at building bridges use the following well-accepted principles, techniques etc: . . '

But with IM there is currently no great body of ideas that deserve to be counted as fundamental and substantial and widely accepted and well-proven.[1] Certainly, professors and consultants have produced many generalisations about IM — about IT and business strategy, about the special characteristics of IT, about its organisational impact, about the significance of certain technologies and applications, and so on. Some of these ideas are accorded considerable reverence, but, as the questions at the beginning insinuate, it may still be difficult to apply them usefully to specific cases. Some even turn out to be mere platitude, tautology or exhortation.[2]

Plainly, this state of affairs is associated with the theme of slippery problems. If the problems were less slippery, established knowledge would develop more quickly; conversely, as established knowledge does gradually develop, some of the problems should become less slippery. But, for the moment, the question is: What kind of books about IM are worth writing and reading?

There is something unsatisfactory about a textbook that provides a review of the best-known ideas about IM, implying that this is a body of established knowledge, as useful and reliable as that found in other more mature fields. Some books, it is true, offer a more selective mixture of widely-known and original prescriptions for IM. But this book takes a different approach altogether.

This Book's Approach

If you follow a recommended diet it may not be the optimum possible, given all the specific details of your physical health; also, you may find all kinds of plausible reasons to deviate from the diet. Indeed, the diet's main benefit may not be the actual food it recommends, but the fact that it induces you to think carefully about everything you eat. Many items of IM lore are valuable in a similar indirect sense: they can help you think carefully about the issues of IM they raise.

Most books that present (say) the Ives and Learmonth 'customer resource life-cycle' do so uncritically, with the implicit recommendation that this is a technique of IM worth knowing and using. But this book presents that technique (and dozens of others) with an entirely different claim: 'Here is a representative example of a technique; by examining its aims, assumptions, limitations and shortcomings, and by discussing them with colleagues, you will probably gain useful insight into certain characteristic IM issues; this in turn will help you get a better grip on the slippery problems you come across in practice.'

This somewhat disrespectful attitude also helps in spotting certain parts of the subject that are important but have received little attention from other authors. Here the book sets out some original ideas and analysis, but still its purpose is to stimulate insight into the issues that are really at stake, rather than to lay down knowledge to be learnt or procedures to be followed.

In short, the test of any passage picked at random out of this book is not 'Is this an adequate representation of a piece of established knowledge?', but 'Is this useful material for stimulating insight into characteristic IM issues?'

Using This Book

This book rejects the notion of setting out a body of established IM knowledge. Instead, it suggests ways of refining general ideas about the subject in order to think clearly about IM's slippery problems, both at organisation and at project level.[3]

That should interest many non-IT managers, IT managers, consultants, modellers and analysts of various types — and, of course, all those who study the way such people operate.

A substantial book about IM can easily become a procession in near-arbitrary sequence of drab abstractions, giving little sense of how the different ideas fit together. This book has been designed as something a good deal more elaborate than a procession. The main features of its structure are sketched out in the diagrams over the page.

Whole Book

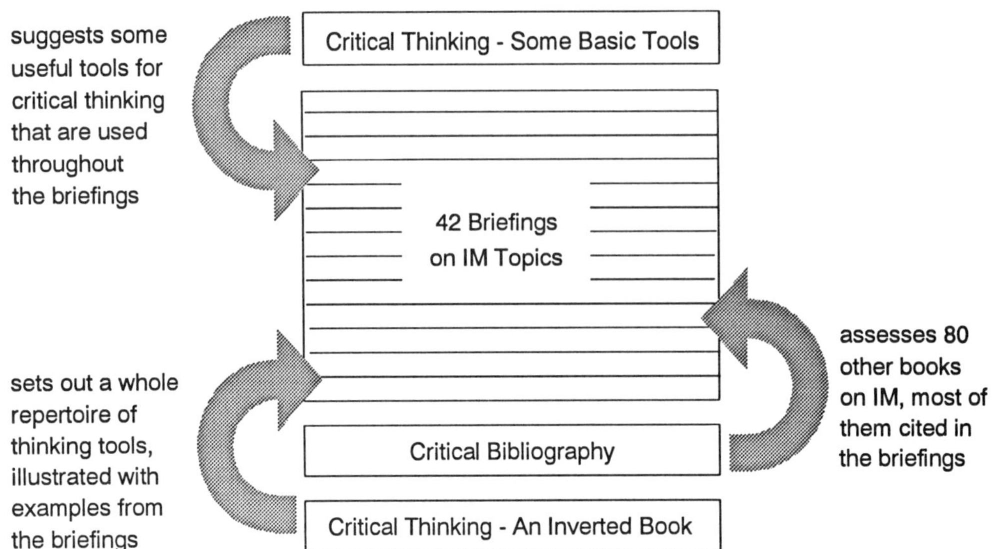
suggests some useful tools for critical thinking that are used throughout the briefings
Critical Thinking - Some Basic Tools
42 Briefings on IM Topics
assesses 80 other books on IM, most of them cited in the briefings
sets out a whole repertoire of thinking tools, illustrated with examples from the briefings
Critical Bibliography
Critical Thinking - An Inverted Book

Briefings and Planes

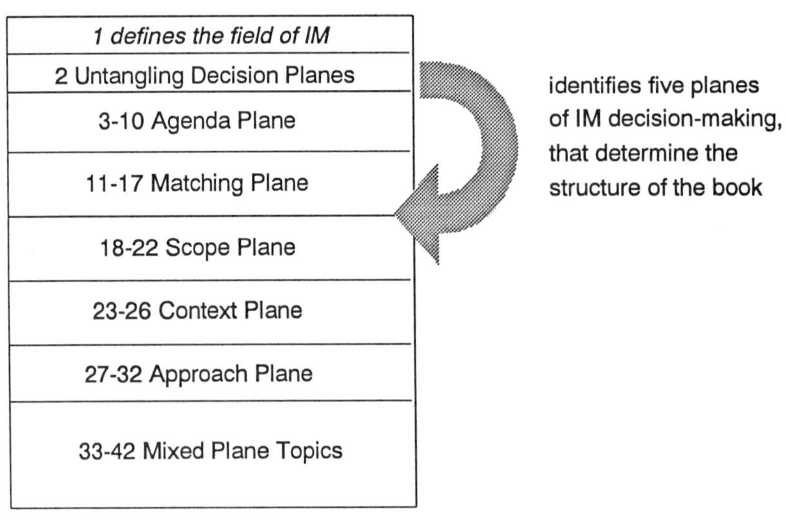
1 defines the field of IM
2 Untangling Decision Planes
3-10 Agenda Plane
11-17 Matching Plane
18-22 Scope Plane
23-26 Context Plane
27-32 Approach Plane
33-42 Mixed Plane Topics
identifies five planes of IM decision-making, that determine the structure of the book

Briefings - Maps of Continent and Country

'Untangling' briefings are like the world and continent maps of an atlas, showing how the countries/topics of the other briefings fit together

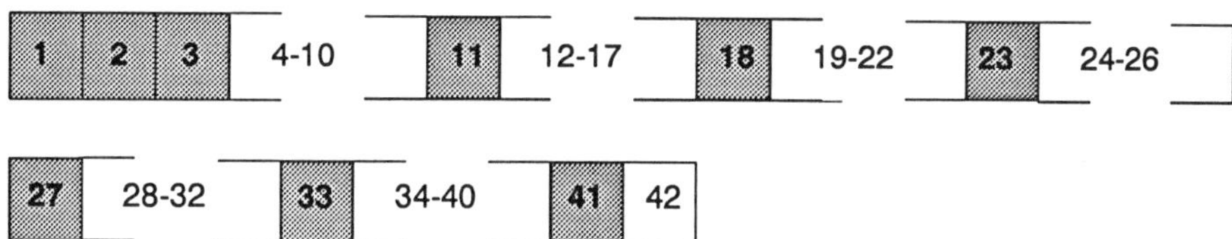

Structure of each Briefing

Main text:
always some combination of these three sections;
if a much-discussed topic, then mainly rep. ideas; but if not, mainly suggested fresh ideas

Extra level of rebuttals, justifications, disclaimers, corollaries; discussion of related, important matters; some of the most feisty arguments

Pointers to other briefings on related topics

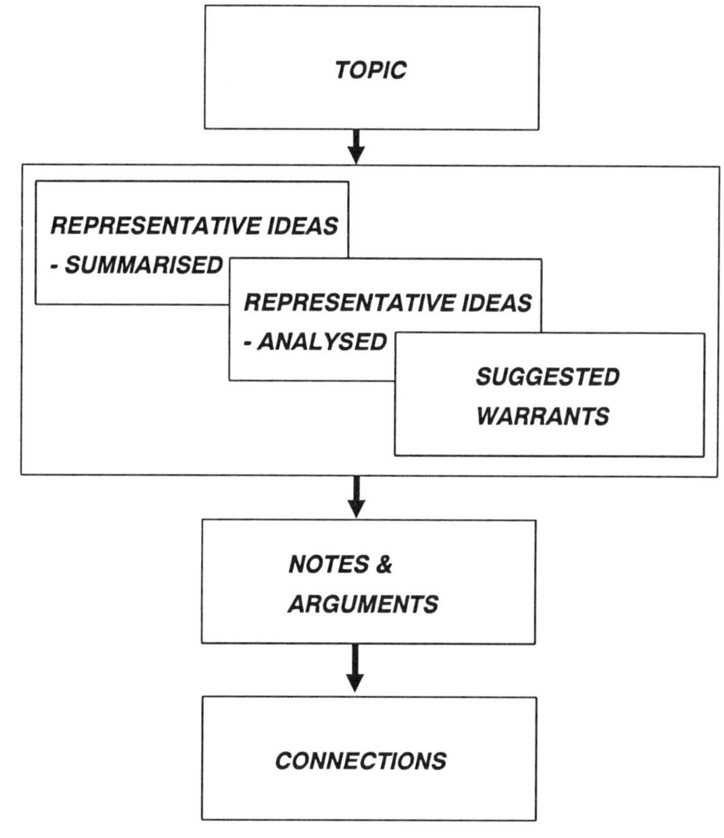

NOTES & ARGUMENTS

1 But, it may be objected, a computer system differs from a physical artefact such as a bridge, in being a complex combination of technology and people; therefore IM knowledge can't be assessed by the same criteria as knowledge of civil engineering. This is a correct premise but a false conclusion. IM, like civil engineering or economics or medicine, but unlike literary criticism or art appreciation, is concerned with getting certain things done successfully in practice. Therefore any knowledge about IM deserving to count as useful and well-established really has to be fundamental, substantial, widely accepted and well-proven.

2 This may seem an arrogant view. How can it be substantiated? *First*, consider the case for the proposition that IM is an immature field:

- In a mature field there is general agreement on some kernel of ideas that are both well-proven and non-trivial. In IM most of the ideas people agree on are just platitudes (eg 'Information systems are assuming critical importance for the success of many enterprises').
- In a mature field most of the main terms used stand for clear concepts, and the main concepts are described by clear terms. In IM terms like 'competitive advantage', 'open system', 're-engineering' and so on are employed so loosely that they are more of a hindrance than a help in rational debate.
- In a mature field, there are generally some fascinating battles of ideas in progress on the frontiers of established knowledge. But it is very rare to find a journal article about IM raising stimulating arguments against the plausible-sounding concepts of another authority. Shots at fish in a barrel (eg 'Unfortunately, many boards still regard IT as a technical issue rather than a business weapon') don't count.
- In a mature field detailed ideas from different corners of the subject can be related together in a framework based on some unifying principles. Books on IM rarely attempt this; they usually offer little more than a procession of different ideas.

Second, if still unconvinced of the fragility of most current ideas about IM, check out the rest of this book.

3 It may reasonably be said that knowing how to refine ideas and facts, and how to think clearly about IM, won't get you very far in real situations, unless you possess certain interpersonal qualities, that are quite distinct from rational thought: the intuition to sense how the feelings of other people are camouflaged by their words, the charm to make people want to help you, the courage to push through unwelcome innovations, the charisma to inspire other people to think positively, the networking skills to have contacts all over the organisation, the self-confidence to bluff convincingly about dubious claims, the cunning to thwart obstreperous opponents, and so on. This point is entirely correct. In fact anybody who ignores or underestimates it is pretty sure to fail at IM.

But this is a book. For developing personal qualities, such as charm, courage and so on, the book is not a good medium. Were this a videocassette or a computer-aided instruction product, the emphasis could be different: techniques for developing intuition or cunning might perhaps be shown. But since this is a book, it concentrates on something books can be good at: stimulating careful thought about a subject. The claim is that, however strong or weak your interpersonal skills may be, you are bound to operate somewhat more effectively if your thinking is clear and rational, as opposed to muddled.

Even this modest claim may not be acceptable to all. In some quarters 'rational' is a term of abuse. The justification for this strange use of language runs something like this: a rational approach relies on hard data, but in many cases factors impossible to measure are vital; a rational approach stresses logical reasoning, but in many cases creativity is also important; a rational approach aims for consistency and co-ordination, but in many cases loosely related, inconsistent actions are desirable; a rational approach uses clear step-by-step methods, but in many cases a variety of approaches from different angles, including awkward confusion-creating feedback are more effective.

This is a good example of the disreputable technique of setting up a straw man for attack. Of course, an approach that takes account of nothing but absolutely certain quantified data, that spends no time whatsoever in hunting for new ideas etc, will be worthless. But this merely shows that an absurd travesty of rationality is a bad thing. It doesn't discredit rationality itself.

What would be a good description of an approach that aimed to give appropriate weight to all factors of relevance, that identified certain areas where bright new ideas were needed and tried to stimulate them, that consciously assessed how much co-ordination and how much flexibility the situation required, and carefully designed the decision-process to maintain a sense of direction while encouraging some, but not too much, brainstorming, reassessment and feedback? Isn't that approach rational?

Critical Thinking — Some Basic Tools

'I believe the information systems architecture must always reflect the strategic vision of the business.'

'Agreed; but any well designed architecture provides the flexibility to introduce new functions required by rapidly changing business conditions.'

'Absolutely; that's why the design of core systems should always lay the accent on data structures rather than process structures.'

These are representative generalisations about information management (IM). Since they are rather abstract, the questions arise: Do they mean anything useful? How could anyone decide? Are there perhaps some neat ways of thinking to cut through to the essence of *any* such generalisations?

Critical thinking is the study of real-life arguments.**1** It leads to no profound and difficult truths, but it does encourage you to think about the way you think. This essay suggests how to apply critical thinking to IM.

Different Decision-making Activities

One useful insight from critical thinking is that the processes of debating and deciding can encompass a great variety of different activities. This is particularly true in an area such as IM, where many issues cross organisational boundaries.

As a thought experiment, take the hypothetical Antarctic Beech Corporation (ABC).**2** It is trying to work out a strategy for the use of IT to develop innovative products and services. The diagram suggests how a director participating in this process may have to engage in any of a dozen or more different kinds of activity where rational thought is one component.

Plainly, these are not all cerebral activities calmly performed in a quiet office. Moreover, it would surely be naive to draw up a schedule of all activities or even a detailed structure, before the decision-making process started. A neat, methodical approach of (say) first collecting data about all relevant factors, and only then reasoning from it to arrive at

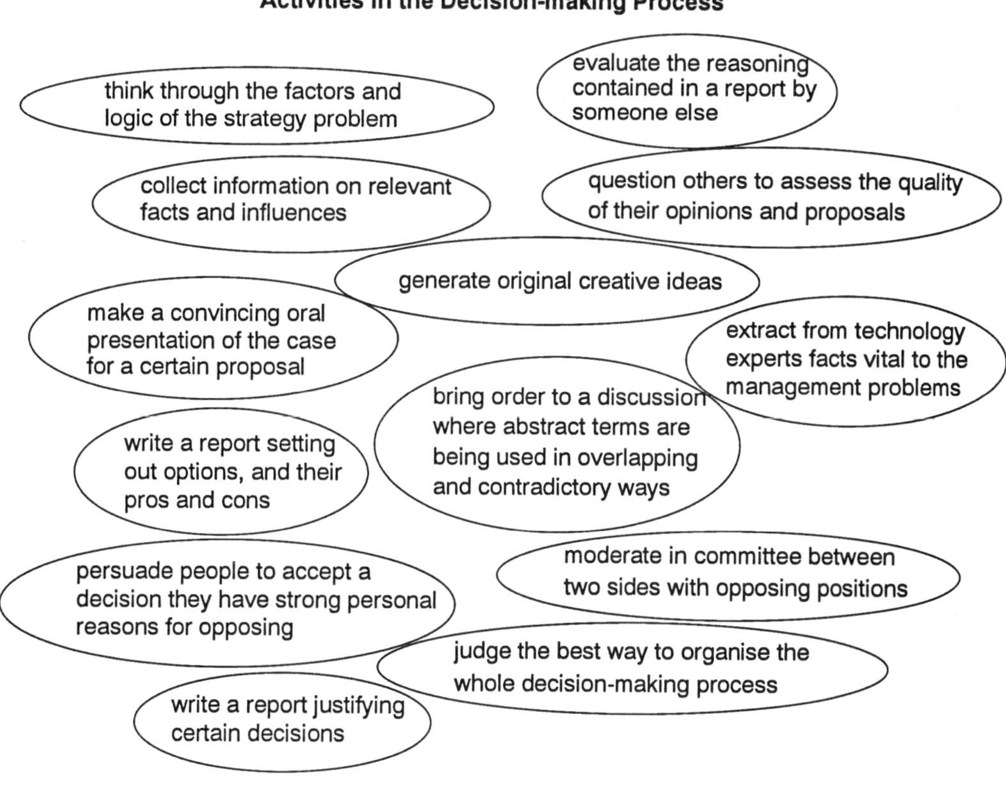

decisions, will not do justice to the richness of ABC's problems — nor to many less complex IM problems either.

It seems a hopeless task to devise any generally valid format to organise IM decision-making — except by making all manner of unacceptable simplifying assumptions. A much more promising endeavour is to develop general tools for thinking about IM matters, that are nimble and flexible enough to use in *any* of the activities listed, no matter how they happen to crop up in any particular case.[3]

Generalisations and Knowledge

The three statements at the beginning of this essay are generalisations. It is an unavoidable fact that debate about any practical matter entails combining statements about the specific case ('This particular picture needs to be hung') with generalisations ('A nail can be used for hanging a picture') to arrive at decisions for action ('We will hang this picture with a nail').

In a mature field such as engineering or medicine there is an enormous stock of useful generalisations available, and an expert is a person who can pick the right items from this store of knowledge to be useful in a particular case. The trouble with IM is that many of the generalisations commonly found don't deserve to be regarded as reliable knowledge.

ABC is a conglomerate with a range of interests in entertainment, travel, employment agencies, communications and other information-intensive businesses. ABC managers are sure that promising opportunities exist to develop innovative IT-based products and services. Moreover, it seems sensible to have some group-wide strategy to co-ordinate these developments. This is easy to say; the real questions are: *Which particular opportunities* for innovative investment should they choose? *What matters* should a co-ordinating strategy cover, what should it say about them, and what matters should not be co-ordinated but left to the initiative of individual business units?

To arrive at sound decisions economically, ABC needs:

- to combine **particular facts**, about ABC's situation and opportunities;
- with **generalisations**, eg principles for appraising innovative projects that have difficult-to-measure risks and benefits, generic options for stimulating and controlling innovation in an organisation, etc — in other words, IM knowledge;
- to arrive at **particular decisions**, eg which innovative opportunities ABC should invest in, and what its co-ordinating strategy should contain.

As the diagram suggests, a great deal depends on ABC applying generalisations that help move the decision-making process along in a useful direction. These may range from ideas found in the latest *Harvard Business Review*, through carefully considered personal views and principles about the management of IT, to habits, approaches and assumptions that are scarcely articulated. Since the quality of the generalisations will affect the quality of the decisions, the question arises: What is the test of a worthwhile generalisation that deserves to be regarded as part of IM knowledge?

An Example of the Decision Question

In the early stages of discussions at ABC, somebody comes across a brochure which describes 'five levels of application of IT that support or induce Business Transformation to enhance the competitive capability of the organisation'. The five levels are: 1, localised exploitation; 2, internal integration; 3, business process redesign; 4, business network redesign; 5, business scope redefinition. Levels 1 and 2 are said to be evolutionary levels, and levels 3, 4 and 5 revolutionary levels.

This analysis is introduced into debates among the ABC decision-makers. After studying the verbal descriptions of the five levels, one person is fairly sure that ABC currently has no applications higher than level 2. Someone else believes that ABC already has more level-3 applications than any of its rivals. Somebody else sees possible new applications at all five levels. Others are not sure what to think.

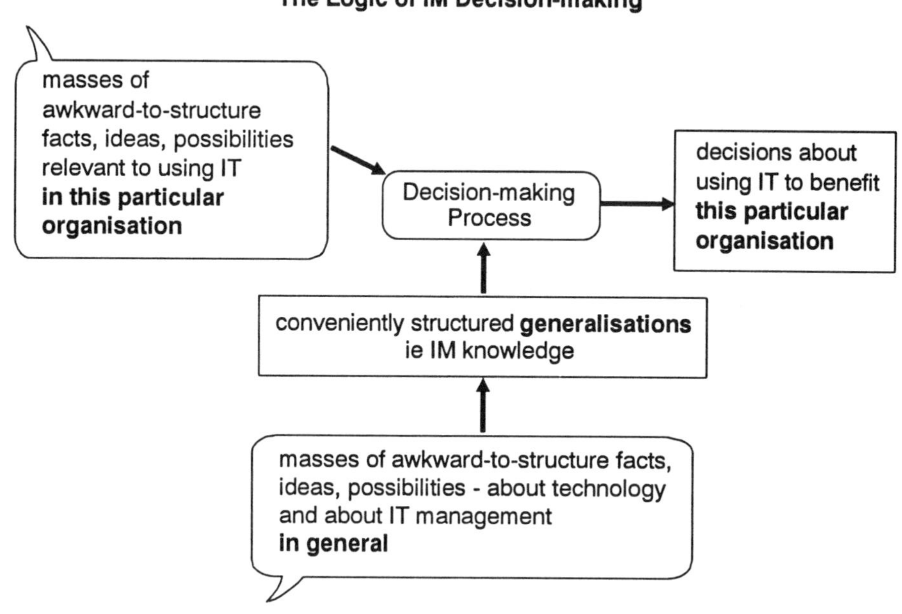

After a while it becomes clear that such discussion is pointless. Even if they all agreed what level each application should be placed at, what advantage would they gain? Would they be in a better position to decide which innovations to approve and which to reject? Would they be able to decide the right balance between co-ordination and local initiative within an overall strategy? Or decide anything else of importance? They are certainly not prepared to drift into the assumption that the higher the level the better the application, since they have no reason to believe that this is a sensible rule.

If this model of the five levels is of no help in any of their decision-making, then the managers of ABC can decide quite rationally that it is simply not worth knowing about. If any proposed generalisation has any practical value, it ought to pass a test that this book will call the *Decision Question:*

Even if true, how could this generalisation assist a decision of information management in any particular case?

This is rather a fundamental test. If a generalisation (such as one about five levels of business transformation) offers the prospect of helping some organisation (such as ABC) arrive at some decisions, then it has at least a chance of counting as useful knowledge in the field of information management. But if a certain generalisation cannot ever be relevant to any sensible person's decision about anything of consequence, then it can be consigned to the flames. There isn't even any point in asking whether it is soundly supported by research data or is of good quality in any other ways.[4]

Decision Question and Warrants

The Decision Question is quite a powerful tool. For some candidate generalisations, no satisfactory answer is forthcoming. If the answer is that the generalisation certainly can assist decisions, at least to some degree, then new questions arise, but first it is worthwhile to introduce a new term.

This book uses the term *warrant* for any generalisation that passes the test of the Decision Question to at least the degree that it promises to influence some identifiable IM decisions.[5] For example:

- A piece of analysis beginning: 'In general, the tradeoffs between having one large data centre and several are . . .' is probably a warrant assisting a decision on how many data centres to have.
- 'The differences between CD-ROM and WORM as storage media for high-volume databases are . . ' is probably a warrant assisting a decision on the storage medium to use for a certain application.
- 'The structure of an experimental project differs from that of a prototype project in the following fundamental ways . . .' is probably a warrant assisting a decision on the structure of a particular project.

Articles, books and consultants' presentations can often seem barren of warrants. It is worthwhile to do the best you reasonably can to reorganise such material in a way as warrant-like as possible, but in some cases, this procedure may reveal quite starkly that the material is next to valueless. Here are some examples of this kind of critical thinking in action:[6]

- 'In (some) companies, information, although perhaps not being the backbone of the organization, is at least its blood supply.' If you suspect that this is an excessively vague metaphor, pose the Decision Question: How could knowing about this distinction between backbone and blood supply help anyone make better decisions?
- 'Case studies repeatedly show that CSFs (critical success factors) can only be achieved optimally if a conscious effort is made to streamline and direct information resources and activities to the specific goals of managing the underlying critical tasks and processes effectively.' This statement is one of many that don't usefully assist decision-making, because they are tautology or platitude or a mixture of the two.
- Useful warrants often break an area down into several categories; but not all categorising statements are useful warrants. One book distinguishes between data (eg the quantity of an item on the supermarket shelf), information (eg the total value of current stock in the supermarket), knowledge (eg that the stock level needs to be higher than normal because of Christmas) and wisdom (no example provided). This may sound interesting, but would it help a manager reach decisions

better? Would somebody unaware of this four-way breakdown be in danger of making bad decisions? How? On what subjects? Unless there are some good answers, the analysis is just an imposing signpost leading to a blank wall.

● Sometimes a text fails the test of the Decision Question because it is too specific and descriptive to yield any clear insight that is generally applicable. Many case studies describe a company that gained some advantage through IT, but often the only decision-supporting generalisation that can be extracted is either absurd ('Every organisation should do exactly the same as the company in the case study') or banal ('Competitive advantage through IT is a good thing'). 7,8

Decision-making Force

Some warrants are more *decision-forcing* than others. Compare these two:

● 'The three main tradeoff points between CD-ROM and WORM as storage media for high-volume databases are . . .'

● 'This table sets out in a neutral way the main characteristics of all types of disk storage from diskette, through conventional hard disk up to CD-ROM, WORM and videodisk . . .'

The first has more decision-making force than the second. It encourages you to assess the relevance to your own particular case of the tradeoff points it mentions. For example: 'CD-ROM is cheaper than WORM if you want to distribute many copies of the same information'; that could be decisive to your choice for a particular application, or irrelevant or perhaps relevant but outweighed by some other factor. The material in the second warrant will assist decision-making by showing options to consider, but it will leave more to be done before a decision is reached about the choice in a particular case.

Warrants on matters other than technology choice may differ in force too:

● 'Setting up a separate innovation group to stimulate innovative use of IT tends to have the following advantages and disadvantages and thus suit certain generic situations . . but not others . . '

● 'Here is a description of the role played by a separate, elite innovation group at one particular go-ahead organisation . . '

The first warrant has great force. If a certain case corresponds to one of the situations where the typical advantages of an innovation group seem great and the typical disadvantages relatively unimportant, then a clear decision is strongly suggested. The second warrant leaves more to be done before a decision is reached

But it isn't true that the more decision-force a warrant has, the better it is. A strong warrant may well achieve its strength by simplifying the issues — perhaps too much. In some decision-making activities, particularly early on, it may not be appropriate to force the pace. Warrants that help summarise and prune factors and possibilities, or that help in

Warrant Forms and Decision-making

	Warrant Form	*Illustration of Use*
	**Comparison.** The most forceful; exposes two or more clear, mutually exclusive options, and compares their pros and cons in general. By seeing how these factors weigh in your specific case, you can arrive at a decision.	A comparison warrant giving the pros and cons of different interface devices (mouse, tablet, touch screen etc) could help you decide which to choose for a certain system.
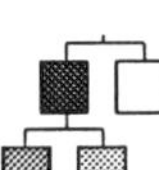	**Distinctions.** Exposes clear, mutually exclusive possibilities, but gives little explicit guidance on pros and cons; helps establish main generic options for consideration in your case.	A warrant giving distinctions between different types of standard methodology for IM planning could help clarify the most relevant options open to you: a methodology that collects quantitative data about the business, one more concerned with human factors, etc.
	**Gradations.** Plays a similar role to a distinctions warrant; establishes options in areas where possibilities are best seen as gradations along a scale.	A warrant sketching out five gradations of (de)centralisation of software development in any organisation could help you see the main options on that issue in your own case.
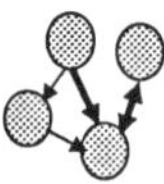	**Chart.** A degree less decision-forcing, but can be very useful; charts out (logically, not necessarily as a diagram) how certain concepts are related to each other.	A chart warrant of how the terms strategic system, end-user computing, re-engineering and several others relate to each other could reduce confusion in making policy about these matters.
	**Aspects.** As decision-forcing as a chart warrant, but less complicated; funnels detail into a few broad aspects; an orientation device that helps you get a grip on the whole debate.	A warrant explaining the three main aspects of the large subject of integration (context integration, data integration and process integration) could make it easier to debate what kind and degree of integration to go for in your own case.
	**Example.** Lowest on the decision-forcing scale, but has its place; not just anecdotal; must have general relevance; does more than exemplify an idea that could be expressed economically as another form of warrant; helps form an instinct about some concept.	An example warrant about an expert system application could help a group of decision-makers develop sound instincts about the kind of applications that fit this technology neatly and those that don't.

Thinking in Warrant Forms
ABC, a Conglomerate

'This distinctions warrant exposes the main generic options in structuring an experimental project. Now we can see the main options we have in planning an innovative attempt to use artificial intelligence in our travel agency company.'

'This detail about the issues in building our corporate telecoms infrastructure is thoroughly confusing. Could you perhaps sketch out three or four generic gradations of telecoms network sophistication — perhaps one simple, one complex and one or two in between.'

'That case study about neural networks in a manufacturing business is a poor one, because its general relevance is obscure. I'm sure we could find a better example warrant to help us form sound instincts for the possibilities of neural network technology in our organisation.'

'The confusion over our policy on data centre security has gone on long enough. I'm going to make a chart warrant, spelling out the main issues and concepts in this field and how they are inter-related.'

'This warrant defines three different possibilities for organising end-user computing, and spells out their implications under different circumstances. It looks like a comparison warrant, but I don't think its three possibilities are the only important options, and they also seem to be overlapping rather than distinct. In fact, it is nothing more than a weak aspects warrant.'

understanding the real issues and their interactions, may be more useful than warrants that suggest immediate decision between discrete choices.

Warrant Forms

The decision-making force of a warrant is related to its form. A warrant comparing two possibilities has great decision-making force. One that makes distinctions between possibilities or describes a representative example can assist decision-making, but in a less direct way.

There are not all that many distinct ways of forming a useful warrant. The table 'Warrant Forms and Decision-making' sets out six basic forms. In summary: example warrants help form instincts about matters likely to be relevant to the case; aspects and chart warrants help organise the debate in directions likely to cross the most important ground; distinctions and gradations warrants help establish what the options are in a given area; comparison warrants help in evaluating specific options. **9**

The questions must be faced: 'What is the value of analysing the forms of warrants?' and 'How could this promote better information management?'

Some general ideas expressed by authorities on IM may seem perceptive and plausible, yet difficult to get hold of; it is worthwhile to have techniques for extracting what is good and relevant to decisions. As the table 'Thinking in Warrant Forms' shows, a keen analysis of the characteristics of different forms of warrant can help both in warrant-fashioning and in warrant-appraisal. In other words, the different warrant forms can be regarded as a set of intellectual tools, widely applicable to different problems in IM decision-making. Thus equipped, you can make good use of generalisations about the main IM topics and reach sound decisions economically.

NOTES & ARGUMENTS

1 Strictly speaking, *critical thinking*, *argumentation analysis* and *informal logic* are three related and overlapping terms, not synonyms. Since this is a book about IM, such nuances are ignored and one term, *critical thinking*, is used throughout.

Here is an updated version of a logical conundrum once put by Bertrand Russell: 'The MD doesn't know whether Microsoft is the supplier of Excel. Microsoft *is* the supplier of Excel. Therefore the MD doesn't know whether Microsoft is Microsoft.' This argument with a nonsensical conclusion raises subtle points about the use of words like 'the' and 'know' and 'is'. That kind of analysis belongs to the province of *academic logic*.

Critical thinking, by contrast, examines the reasoning of every-day debates far away from the philosophy department: 'The most successful companies spend more on IT than the average for their market sector. Therefore we should spend more on IT than our competitors.' Is this argument valid, persuasive, worthless, circular, incomplete . . ?

The subject may sound dry, but most books on critical thinking are more lucid than most on IM; eg:

Monroe C Beardsley, *Thinking Straight; Principles of Reasoning for Readers and Writers* (Prentice Hall, 4th ed., 1975)

Irving M Copi and K Burgess-Jackson, *Informal Logic* (Macmillan, 2nd ed., 1992)

Douglas Ehninger and Wayne Brockriede, *Decision by Debate* (Harper & Row, 2nd ed., 1978)

Alec Fisher, *The Logic of Real Arguments* (Cambridge University Press, 1988)

Robert J Fogelin, *Understanding Arguments* (Harcourt Brace Jovanovich, 1987)

C A Missimer, *Good Arguments; An Introduction to Critical Thinking* (Prentice Hall, 1986)

Michael Scriven, *Reasoning* (McGraw-Hill, 1976)

2 Many of the examples in this book are fabricated, because a fabricated example is generally more incisive than a real case. Real-life, situation-specific details blur the general points illustrated by the example — and if the case is edited drastically to avoid this, then it is no longer a real case.

Hardly any other book on IM takes this point of view. Writers on management usually cite real not imaginary examples, but if a book's aim is to go beyond anecdote into generally useful ideas, there is no logic in this preference. Geometry books discuss triangles and spheres that don't actually exist. Books about economics use artificial examples to illustrate macro-economic concepts. Books about taxation use simple, made-up examples. Why should a book on IM be any different?

3 Many academic authorities offer a standard structure for decisions:

- *five steps:* appraising the challenge; surveying alternatives; weighing alternatives; deliberation about commitment; and adhering despite negative feedback; in *Decision Making* by Irving L Janis and Leon Mann (The Free Press, 1977), pp. 171ff.;
- *alternative breakdown:* problem definition; choosing alternatives; implementation; control; and evaluation; in *Managerial Decision Making* by Alan J Rowe and James D Boulgarides (Maxwell Macmillan, 1992), pp. 12-14.

This is tame stuff. For one thing, it structures just one decision. Real-life IM decision-making defies such structures, because a number of decisions are required, and they are inter-related in awkward ways: how much stress to put on innovation as a matter of business policy, which specific innovating opportunities to invest in, whether to set up an innovation department as an organisational entity etc.

4 The ideas mentioned in the briefing text are from *A Window on the Future*, pp. 11-16 (ICL, 1990).

Beaumont and Sutherland (pp. 269ff.) describe how ICL was one of twelve sponsors of the $5m MIT90s research programme. Some senior ICL managers were not impressed by the product of their investment. This motivated some other ICL people to summarise the findings in seminars and a brochure (*A Window on the Future*).

Beaumont and Sutherland write: 'The real problem was that the material was not presented in a way which helped managers to see how to act.' This is like saying that the real problem with a certain menu is that it is not presented in a way that helps anyone see what food the restaurant serves, or the real problem with a certain newspaper is that it is not presented in a way that helps anyone read the news, or the real problem with a certain musical score is that it is not presented in a way that helps anyone perform it. It is tantamount to saying that the MIT90s research programme was a waste of $5m.

The Scott Morton book presents the MIT90s findings much more fully; Chapter 5 by N Venkatraman is about the five levels discussed in the text. This material is like certain texts in sociology or literary criticism that seem designed to exhaust the reader into submission. You strongly suspect that, given the time and patience, anyone who scrutinised thoroughly all the abstractions set up and the claims made could show that most were platitudinous, circular or arbitrary, and thus not of much value.

But perhaps all the above is unfair to the MIT90s product. According to the *Financial Times* (30 April 1990), 'There has never been . . such a complete prescription of the measures companies must adopt if they are to stay afloat in the uncharted waters of today's fiercely competitive global marketplace.' The main point here is not to judge this particular material, but to suggest that the test of worth for *any* generalision put forward — Venkatraman's 'five levels of application of IT that support or induce Business Transformation' or any other — is whether or not it can help people reach sensible decisions on specific matters in particular cases. Generalisations that are obscure or arbitrary or platitudinous or circular are bad because they don't help people reach decisions.

Wang Shou-Jen, a sage, went as far as: 'There is no such thing as knowledge which cannot be carried into practice, for such knowledge is really no knowledge at all.' As an argument this is circular, but then it is intended less as an argument than a suggested way of deciding what is worth knowing. Some such starting-point is needed. If Wang Shou-Jen's criterion and the Decision Question in the briefing text don't suit you, can you propose some other test that seems more acceptable?

5 The term *warrant* is used by Stephen Toulmin in his books *The Uses of Argument* (Cambridge University Press, 1958) and (with Richard Rieke and Allan Janik) *An Introduction to Reasoning* (Macmillan, 1979). Toulmin provides the insight that the only way to make progress in real-life arguments is to inject a powerful, summarising generalisation (which he calls a *warrant*) into debate from time to time. If challenged, a warrant can be backed up by more detailed facts or other evidence, but in practice, the parties to any substantial debate need to accept the validity of at least some warrants without calling for very much backing; otherwise the process will be interminable. This is an unavoidable feature of human arguments outside the philosophy department. Thus an expert on a certain field is somebody who can inject fruitful, reliable warrants into debates about that field.

Toulmin's warrant is always a simple statement, whereas this book uses the term for whole chunks of decision-supporting generalisation, perhaps a page or two in length. Toulmin discusses several types of argument, but says almost nothing about arguments leading to decisions — the focus of this book. He also puts forward a generic format for arguments, with six components: claim, warrant, backing and so on — which this book ignores.

In this book a warrant is a generalisation that helps in arriving at a decision. Whether the decision promoted is sensible or not is another matter. Daft statements can be warrants too; eg 'Every organisation should have five data centres' or 'A computer made by a company whose name is a three-letter acronym is never a good buy.'

6 Blood supply: Jackson, p. 24; CSFs: Hochstrasser and Griffiths, p. 134; data to wisdom: Knight and Silk, pp. 22-3, and similar ideas in Frenzel, p. 10; case studies: most of those in Keen (1992), Williams, and Feigenbaum, McCorduck and Nii.

7 Here are some more. Books about organisational structure and IT tend to fare badly. One by Harrington analyses such things as: resource-driven and perception-driven paradigms for viewing information; different generic perspectives (sociological, political, economic) on technology; theories of organisations as machines, organisms or processes. Representative section headings are: 'the implications of bounded rationality'; 'the dimensions of socialisation'; 'interaction as a function of perception'. The whole discussion within these headings turns out to be just too obscure to yield any warrants that would help anyone decide anything.

Sometimes methods are described too vaguely to yield any value. One approach to IT planning (in Scott Morton, Appendix E, The Strategic Alignment Process by K Hugh Macdonald) is based on the concept that each 'problem domain' has three components: 'domain anchor', 'domain pivot' and 'impacted domain'. Then: 'In a generalized form, the process is taking account of the constraints and contributions of the domain anchor on the domain pivot; noting any unacceptable constraints or unneeded contributions from the domain anchor; and, after taking account of limitations on the freedom to change the impacted domain, resolving and confirming the content of the domain pivot and determining the changes to be considered in the impacted domain.' As it stands this is too obscure to have any value. It might become a useful warrant to support decisions, if brought to life by examples, showing how to deal with some particular tricky issue: eg helping an organisation decide how to use artificial intelligence technology, or decide how to develop innovative products, or decide how to recover from a disastrous situation.

By contrast, some material may be too specific for effective decision-making. A table showing the characteristics of several different options can often make a big contribution to decision-making debate, but a huge matrix comparing 55 different word processing packages together against a list of 250 possible features may be too detailed to have much decision-making force; eg *PC Magazine*, 7/4, pp. 166-205.

8 Using the Decision Question to examine the ideas of other people raises one unavoidable issue: Isn't critical thinking negative, destructive and sterile, and thus a rather inferior kind of activity?

No. In a field like IM critical thinking is often the same as the processing of facts and ideas to develop knowledge — surely a positive thing. Here is an example. Jackson (pp. 11ff.) declares that the central mission of information resource management (IRM) is 'the achievement of cost-effective management of the corporate information processing resources'. This may seem vulnerable to charges of being too obscure or a platitude or a tautology, but before passing judgement, it is only fair to consider what lines of defence may be open:

- Could it be argued that IRM should work for *cost-effective* management of information as opposed to some other kind of management; eg quality management or human values-oriented management, entrusted perhaps to a staff department? If the case for such a distinction is made plausible, then that could be a useful decision-influencing warrant.
- Or is there an argument that IRM should work with *corporate* information processing resources, as opposed to other, more narrowly defined, information resources? Again, if plausible, that could be at least the outline sketch of a warrant.

Exploring these and similar avenues helps assess the quality of what is offered by the original generalisation. Even if the final verdict is unfavourable, the thinking itself develops a better awareness of the topic. You may very well find that you can fashion a useful warrant about IRM of your own. In a field like IM where the subject-matter to be known consists largely of ideas rather than facts, critical thinking and knowledge processing are much the same thing.

9 Are these six warrant forms in any sense true or real? Could you prove there were just these six forms and not (say) seven or ten? Certainly not. There are many plausible ways of classifying warrants. You could, if you preferred, break the distinction form into several discrete types, or lump aspects and chart together as varieties of one form. It can't be shown that any one analysis is correct and all others false. The issue here isn't truth but convenience. The six warrant forms proposed provide a handy set of intellectual tools —

not too crude and not too complicated either.

The pure imperative is of course another decision-forcing form. 'Ensure that the organisation structure is in a constant state of change!' or 'Always choose packaged software!' But in practice, most advice in this form is either bad or trivial or both.

What kind of warrant form is the *quadrant-diagram*? If you ask two either/or questions (eg Is this technology hard or soft? Is this process new or traditional?), then four combinations of answers are possible (eg hard technology used to support a new process, soft technology used . . . etc), and they can be shown as quadrants in a diagram. Plainly this general technique can be applied to analyse almost anything: guns, religions, folk dances etc.

Not all analysis in quadrant form is the same kind of analysis, to be interpreted in the same way. Sometimes the four quadrants are meant as discrete pigeon-holes (ie the important claim is that most particular cases can be placed firmly in one or the other); if so, this is a distinctions warrant. But sometimes the claim is that the diagram forms a kind of grid for measurement (eg the claim is not that all technologies are either entirely hard or entirely soft, but rather that any technology should be assessed on some hardness-softness continuum, and similarly any process on a new-traditional continuum); in this case the diagram is an aspects warrant. Sometimes the claim is more ambitious, such as that the four quadrants, taken in a clockwise direction, form a natural progression of ascending complexity (eg from soft-new round to soft-traditional); if so, this is a gradations warrant.

It pays to ask of any quadrant-diagram: Just what is being claimed here? Relating it to the six warrant forms is an effective way of getting at the answer.

Strassmann, one of the most sensible writers on IM, is sceptical about quadrant-diagrams (pp. 418-20, 433): 'Several (quadrant) frameworks have achieved widespread popularity precisely because of their vagueness.' 'The skillful use of a good thesaurus is the only limitation on the invention of new typologies.' Almost uniquely among other authors, he touches on the central idea of *Information Management Decisions*: 'I find that the increasing size and proliferation of various frameworks stimulate thinking. It ultimately leads frustrated executives to the awareness that real systems problems do not have solutions in the form of simple tables containing terse phrases.'

1. Untangling Information Management

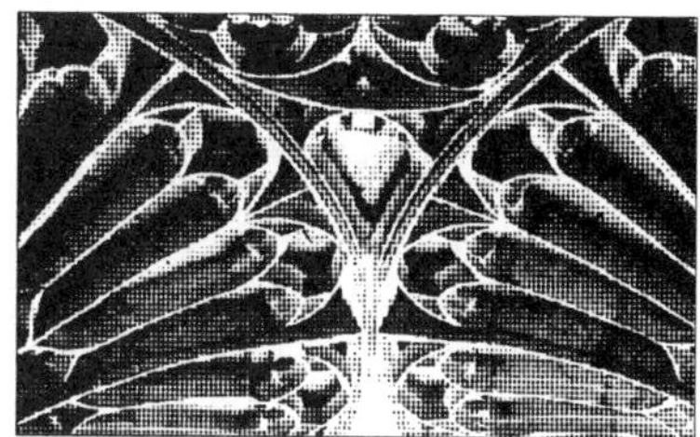

TOPIC

A book like this needs some defined territory, if it is to be coherent. But rigorous definitions easily end up as mere patterns of abstractions. This briefing suggests some boundaries for the field of information management (IM), and also untangles several closely associated themes that can otherwise confuse matters: Are all IM issues strategic? What counts as strategic anyway? Where does technology fit in? Should IM decisions be taken without reference to the facts of technology?

To justify the luxury of such high-level discussion, this briefing aims to spark some insights that, worked up in subsequent briefings, can help in getting to grips with the IM decisions that arise in practice.

REPRESENTATIVE IDEAS — SUMMARISED

Information management (from now on usually IM) has emerged as the most common brief name for the management of the use of information technology in an organisation.**1**

In this context *information technology* (from now on usually IT) refers to the hardware and software of computing and telecoms, and associated resources (eg professional staff such as programmers). *Management of the use of IT* refers only in part to such things as the day-to-day management of a project or a computer installation or an IT department; it is mainly concerned with managing the *application* of IT in the organisation as a whole.

To bring these abstractions to life the table gives a selection of representative IM issues. Most people active in the field of IM would probably agree that these issues fall within the scope of the above defining notes.**2**

REPRESENTATIVE IDEAS — ANALYSED

Given a working definition of the field as judgement-free as possible, the

Sycamore Supplies, Wholesalers of Office Equipment
Representative Information Management Issues

'Should we adopt an 18-month plan to get the company's (rather poor) systems for order processing and invoicing up to a reasonable standard, or go for much more sophisticated systems that could take three years?'

'How can we stimulate people at the four regional offices to use PCs imaginatively on their own initiative, without creating problems of inconsistency and incompatibility?'

'What are the main opportunies for new applications of IT that, as wholesalers of office equipment, we should be considering?'

'Should we introduce a new chargeback system where the IT department acts as a profit centre, charging commercial rates to user departments?'

'What, if anything, should we do about document imaging technology?'

'A consultancy has proposed to carry out an information planning exercise for us; do we need one, and, if so, how can we guard against paralysis by analysis?'

'Three different options have been put up for a company-wide telecoms network; how do we choose?'

'Our business strategy is to be cheaper than most of our rivals — as opposed to (say) offering a greater range of products. How do we make our IT activities consistent with that?'

next step is to expose potential boundary disputes or areas of vagueness and possible confusion.[3] Here disagreements can't be avoided. Most of the rest of the briefing presents clarifications, suggestions and arguments; it doesn't claim to report on any established usage. Here are five issues concerning the frontiers of the IM field:

- How important or strategic must issues or decisions be to count as IM? Or is that irrelevant?
- How do the general knowledge, principles and techniques of wider management matters and the decisions they produce relate to IM?
- To what extent do technology matters enter into IM?
- Do all or most IM matters, by their very nature, cross boundaries between departments or different specialities within a department?
- How does IM in the sense of decision-making relate to management in the sense of taking day-to-day actions to run things efficiently?

Debating such boundary disputes is worthwhile, because it sheds light on the way different topics and themes are interconnected. This helps ensure that the right people are involved in decision-making, organised in the right way to do justice to the issues.

SUGGESTED WARRANTS

Rather than follow an order of importance or a strict chain of logic, this section takes the path that offers the easiest tour of the frontier issues.

Charting the Frontier with Wider Business Issues

Debates and decisions about an organisation's business strategy at the very top level *may* call for consideration of IM factors. If so, there is no option but to regard these debates as occurring in a heterogeneous area where IM is mixed with other matters.

What about general ideas such as value chain analysis and critical success factors and the Boston Consulting Group's famous quadrant-diagram? They are by no means uniquely relevant to IM, but they often come into it. And what of less glamorous things such as the principles of DCF (discounted cashflow), alternative ways of depreciating assets, and techniques of linear programming? The answer is in several parts:

- People who discuss any management matters — whether IM, distribution management, quality management or cost accountancy — need a minimum basic knowledge of certain management concepts (eg the Boston Consulting Group's quadrant-diagram) just as they need *some* knowledge of geography and English grammar. That doesn't mean that any of these things are *per se* part of IM, distribution management or anything else.
- However, certain aspects of certain general management concepts are so strongly relevant to IM, that they really have to be counted as a necessary part of IM knowledge. For example, business modelling, including value chain analysis, is part of IM.
- Moreover, on some topics that, in principle, belong to general management, an expert on IM may need to be specially knowledgeable. For instance, certain subtle issues with DCF are much more relevant to IM investments than to any other; eg technology obsolescence, negative price changes through technology advances, appraisal of investment in 'enabling' infrastructure.

Charting the Technology Frontier

The relationship between IM and technology itself is more contentious. Sometimes the following argument is put (though not always quite so baldly): Technology is only a means to an end. The only important decisions are about ends. Therefore the only genuine IM decisions are about ends. Therefore technology decisions are not really IM decisions. Therefore they can be left to technical people. Therefore the people involved in IM decisions don't need to take account of (or perhaps even know about) technology facts.

This is as nonsensical as saying that an architect ought to finalise the design for an office block without taking any account of such technical matters as the properties of steel girders and concrete, since these are mere means to ends, that can be left for the builders to worry about later. In any decision-making about any technology, the relation between ends and means is fairly subtle: considering the means carefully can lead to new ideas of the appropriate ends — by exposing constraints, but also by improving awareness of possibilities.

Of course this does not mean that every single technology-related issue belongs under the heading of IM. That could lead to endless wanderings in a labyrinth of technology detail. Some rough boundary line has to be drawn somewhere. Here is an example to sharpen this discussion:

- At Sycamore Supplies clerks take orders from customers over the phone, and key the data into terminals connected to a large computer system. A Sycamore manager commissions a consultant to recommend ways of *improving* this system.
- The manager and the consultant interpret this as: 'consider ways of tuning or replacing the existing hardware and software, in order to reduce costs or allow larger volumes of orders to be handled or improve system reliability, *without any other major repercussions*.'
- With this understanding, the consultant's task, though challenging, is primarily technological. It starts out from a clear problem to be solved by technological means. It seems natural to regard this as a technology matter, just outside the frontier of IM — even if large sums of money are involved.

But suppose the manager and consultant take a broader view, and consider whether to develop a completely new system, automating additional functions, requiring considerable investment, but perhaps reducing labour costs or improving response to customer demand or having other desirable effects on the business. This is surely an IM matter. There is no clearly defined problem to be solved by technological means; instead there is a problem-area where technology and wider issues *interact*:

- 'Using expert system technology, we could make the order-entry process much more efficient. But some order-entry clerks might be unhappy that the most interesting and most responsible parts of the job had been shifted from human to machine (eg handling cases where the customer has special delivery or batch-size requirements, applying intricate discount structures, substituting similar products for out-of-stock products etc). But other clerks with a different outlook might be glad to be clear of such things. So, how can we make our plans for IT systems consistent with our policy on the kind of people we employ as order entry clerks, and the responsibilities we give them?'
- *Or* 'There is a fine opportunity here for a new system, using document imaging technology to improve the service to customers. But Sycamore's general business policy is to offer its customers lower prices than competitors — not necessarily better service. So investing in that new system would be inconsistent with business policy. Does this matter? If so, how should the inconsistency be resolved?'

This suggests criteria for technology matters that deserve to count as IM: rule into IM those discussions where technology factors interact with broader factors; exclude from IM those discussions mainly concerned with using technology competently (ie cost-effectively, reliably etc) for purposes that are already well defined.

Charting Strategy and Related Concepts

The other major issue of definition is *level of importance*. Take these four decisions:

- 'We will put 5% of our total IT spend into projects of a purely experimental character.'
- 'The Sundry Products Promotion (SPP) project will be planned and carried out as an experiment. The objective is to gain experience, rather than to build a robust, full-scale system.'
- 'On the SPP project public holidays will be treated as working days.'
- 'There will be a meeting of members of the SPP project team next Wednesday.'

It is surely desirable to count the first and very probably the second as IM decisions, and to exclude the last two. But are they not merely points on an infinitely graded scale between the strategic and the mundane? And isn't this rather unsatisfactory?

There is no complete answer to these difficulties. It is best to regard 'strategic' as a relative term like 'tall' or 'sweet'.[4] What is strategic enough to count as IM is then a matter of judgement. Still, there are some natural criteria that help in forming the judgement:

- **Implications.** The more far-reaching the implications and more intricate their interconnections with other matters, the more a decision deserves to be called strategic. If the decision not only affects but guides other decisions in a coherent way, then so much the more strategic.
- **Options.** The more a decision is a choice between several plausible and significantly different options, the more it deserves to be called strategic.
- **Leap in the dark.** Most decisions are based on imperfect knowledge, since it is not practical to study every conceivable factor, combination of circumstances, possible outcome and implication. The more a decision has this property, the more it deserves to be called strategic.
- **Cross-boundary.** The more a decision requires the involvement of people at several levels of a hierarchy or across departmental boundaries (and the less it can be seen as a decision within the responsibility of one person or department), the more it deserves to be called strategic.

These criteria can help in looking at the issues of any particular case more carefully. The issues that really count don't always get the discussion they deserve, while other issues may occupy management attention more than their strategic trickiness deserves.[5]

NOTES & ARGUMENTS

1 Some people talk of 'information resource management', stress the notion of a resource, and imply something more exciting than the sober definition of IM in this briefing: eg 'Information is a resource just like capital, manpower, and equipment.' (Synnott, p. 46) 'Information resource management is a management approach that treats the management of information as a value-added asset of the firm.' (Synnott, p. 14) Peevish questions: What is a value-added asset as opposed to an ordinary asset? How can the *management* of X (as opposed to X itself) be an asset?

Jackson (pp. 5ff., pp. 11ff.) talks of information as a resource and uses vivid language such as 'wealth of information', 'mining information', and information as the organisation's 'blood supply'. He sees information resource management as a 'direction-setting concept, the idea being to use technology to focus on the use of information' and a 'bridge between the managers of the enterprise and those charged with the responsibility for the implementation of information technology'. Burk and Horton compare the discoverer of information resources with the geologist finding gold-bearing rocks or oil reserves (pp. 1-3).

What does it mean to call information a resource? Should information be likened to a traditional economic resource, such as land, labour and capital? If information were comparable to those resources, then many concepts in economics (eg about elasticity of demand, market-clearing prices, perfect and imperfect competition etc) could be applied to it — an exciting prospect.

But information is not much like these other resources. True, information is sometimes bought and sold, it can benefit a business, and it has diminishing returns. But information can't readily be quantified; it is non-exclusive (ie can be passed from supplier to recipient and still be retained by the supplier); it doesn't deteriorate with use, but with age; and it is very heterogeneous (facts, judgements, advice, propaganda etc). On balance, information is too different from resources such as land, labour and capital to be subject to the same laws and theories. Therefore information seems to be only a resource in a poetic, impressionistic sense — not in any useful sense. (This is based on arguments in the book by Angell and Smithson, pp. 122-3.)

This discussion demonstrates a certain general-purpose tool for critical thinking: the *Trivial-False Fork*. Check any assertion by asking: Can this be interpreted in a way that is both useful (ie not trivial) and true (ie not false)? The meaning 'information is analogous to resources like land, capital etc, and is governed by similar laws' is non-trivial but it is false. The meaning 'information is important stuff' is true but trivial. Unless 'information is a resource' can be interpreted in a way both true and non-trivial, the slogan can be discarded as useless.

2 The claim here is that most people active in IM would agree that these issues count as IM. Generally held views should not be accepted without question, but in this case the field marked out is indeed a fairly coherent one. The set of issues given is meant to be a representative, but not necessarily an accurately weighted, sample of IM issues.

3 Sometimes emotive slogans creep into definitions of IM: 'aligning IT with strategic objectives', 'integrating IT and business planning' etc. This runs into a hazard that lurks in the defining of anything: how X ought to be defined (ie what should count as an X and what should not) is one thing, and what distinguishes a good X from a bad X is something else. To mix definition and quality judgements together in one statement promotes confusion without any compensatory advantage. Things are much clearer if you say first what you mean by an X (any X good, bad or indifferent), and then, separately, discuss what qualities make an X good rather than bad.

How well do the defining notes and examples in this briefing pass this test? Admittedly they do imply that sensible use of IT should be consistent with some other things within the organisation — but only to some degree, which is left open. But this is scarcely a fault; it is impossible to see how anyone could mount any rational argument against such a mild assumption.

4 If that is 'strategic', then a 'strategy' is just a statement of the points that seem, relatively speaking, the most important. This way of looking at it bypasses tedious stuff such as: 'Business strategy is the broad collection of decision rules and guidelines that define a business's scope and growth direction' and 'Strategy formulation involves the interpretation of the environment and the development of consistent patterns in streams of organisational decisions.' Why put in a portentous way what can be put simply?

Also, those statements beginning: 'Every organisation should have an IT strategy because . . ' are pointless, since it is self-evidently a good idea to pick out the important points on IT, as on any other complicated matter. And a statement beginning 'Every organisation's IT strategy should contain . . ' only makes sense if it is true that the same things are important to every organisation, irrespective of time and circumstances: an improbable assertion.

The discussions often found in management literature about whether strategy is a good or a bad thing often turn out to use 'strategy' in the very odd sense of 'formal, centralised, detailed planning.' Whether the latter is good or bad is a different issue altogether.

5 Warning! Before accepting all these criteria as natural and self-evident, note some of their implications:

- They help dispose of the dull recommendations, found in some IM textbooks, about the importance of good backup procedures, not allowing smoking in the computer room and so on. In particular, the cross-boundary test is very effective. If it can be said of issue X: 'Any competent departmental manager ought to handle X, without holding special consultations with managers from other parts of the organisation', then that is an argument for excluding X from the canon of IM issues.
- They suggest strongly that IM (or at least the difficult parts) must be resistant to generalised techniques. Predefined, detailed checklists and standard step-by-step procedures can never determine reliably how to take a leap in the dark — which large areas can safely be glossed over in broad summary, which complexities really ought to be unravelled thoroughly, and which apparently insignificant details are potentially critical to later developments.
- They exclude the notion that a large-scale *descriptive activity* (as opposed to a decision) should be labelled as 'strategic' or

regarded as an IM activity. The work of developing a 200-page document, providing a data architecture for a whole family of systems in a large company may be labelled 'strategic information planning', but this is deceptive. The decision to set up the activity and the choice of method are strategic IM decisions; strategic IM decisions may follow once people have studied the product. But it is usually misleading to call a 200-page document a strategic document.

● They contradict any assumption that IM decisions are necessarily decisions that top people are involved in. Boards of directors often discuss and apparently decide matters where in fact there are no plausible, different options to choose between. Factory foremen may well be asked for judgements on possible system features where the options available have subtle and far-reaching implications.

● By the same token, there is no good reason to regard IM as something that is only for big organisations, because small ones hardly need it.

CONNECTIONS

2. Untangling Decision Planes	Decisions within the field of IM marked out by this briefing, analysed across planes
3. Untangling Agenda Decisions	Much the most discussed, though far from the only, general issues in information management
42. Unifying Theories	Some fundamental ideas about the field of information management

2. Untangling Decision Planes

TOPIC

Suppose that IM decisions could be sorted into categories. What value would such analysis have? How could it promote better management of IT? A schematic answer is that distinguishing different types of decision could help clarify what is at stake in many cases:

'We are muddling together matters calling for two quite different types of decision; our first step should be to disentangle them.'

'The decisions we have taken on this topic only make sense if you assume that a certain decision has already been taken on another dimension altogether — but it hasn't.'

'We have assumed that the main problem is to reach a decision of a certain type; we put all our effort into getting that right, and drifted into an important decision of another type, without even debating it.'

Some authors present a long list or a hierarchy of IM topics, begging many questions about the way the topics are inter-related. Others offer diagrams with so many items and interconnecting arrows that they yield no clear message. Analysis gets a much sharper edge if vague things such as 'challenges' and 'problem areas' and 'implications' and 'management concerns' are avoided and the focus is directed at the actual *decisions* that people take.1

This briefing suggests that it is worth recognising five different *planes of IM decision-making*. The five planes play a large role in structuring the rest of the book.

SUGGESTED WARRANTS

This section is one large warrant — a chart of the planes of IM decision-making. It begins with a body of representative IM decisions, and gradually sorts them out.

Decisions at Murray Pine Organisation

The hypothetical Murray Pine Organisation publishes books and

Murray Pine Organisation, Publishers
Representative Information Management Decisions

'Each business unit of the organisation will have its own IT director.'

'In future MIS will charge departments in the organisation for all its services at full commercial rates.'

'The experimental hypertext project will have the following review points . . '

'To choose the new presentation graphics package we will send out questionnaires to all users and weight their preferences by their amount and type of use.'

'We will build a process model of our newspaper publishing division, as the main input to decision-making.'

'We will have a separate innovation group, containing experts on advanced technology for publishing, and it will have the following terms of reference . . '

'We will shift the balance of spend between our three main business units — now roughly 50-25-25 — to more like 40-40-20.'

'We will have a system to provide a new publishing product: technical abstracts supplied to library customers on CD-ROM.'

'We will introduce IT-based facilities for our office workers at least as good as those of our most sophisticated competitors.'

'We will concentrate on using IT to develop innovative publishing products and services.'

'We will set up several independent projects to try out new products in the market for IT-based reference works (eg encyclopaedia, dictionary etc).'

'We will have a standard company-wide system for document production.'

'We will use expert system technology as the basis for a new system to send out mailshots marketing our books.'

'We will use the IEF methodology to produce an organisation-wide information architecture.'

'We will use the software products WordPerfect, FrameMaker and Harvard Graphics to meet our requirements for document production.'

newspapers and magazines. As the table suggests, its IM decisions may vary in character considerably.**2**

Three Useful Tools

Several tools for critical thinking will be useful in analysing these decisions.

● Decisions are sometimes difficult to appraise because it isn't clear what they are deciding. Apply the **as-opposed-to** tool. 'We will concentrate on using IT to develop innovative products and services' seems rather bland; how could anybody object to it? But if it really means 'We will use IT to develop innovative products and services, *as opposed to* other plausible things such as redesigning our core financial and order fulfilment systems, or extending our existing systems to handle the business of another publisher we intend to take over, or . . ', then it is clearly a decision with powerful implications.

● 'We will use the following combination of software products — WordPerfect, FrameMaker and Harvard Graphics — as the basis for a standard company-wide system for document production' is really two decisions masquerading as one. The **decision-breakdown** tool shows that one of the two is: 'We will have a standard company-wide system for document production — *as opposed to* (say) allowing each unit to decide its document production arrangements for itself', and the other is: 'We will use WordPerfect, FrameMaker etc — *as opposed to* (say) Microsoft Word, Quark Xpress etc.'

● The decision to have a new publishing product based on CD-ROM seems to be on a **different plane** altogether from the decision to charge departments for MIS services at full commercial rates. Anyone justifying the CD-ROM decision would try to show that such a system could bring benefits making Murray Pine a more successful business. But the payoff from the decision to recharge MIS services in a certain way is indirect. It will affect discussions about any future projects, because it will determine how any work done by MIS people will be costed. It should help people make better decisions (ie decisions based on better awareness of costs and benefits) about the things with a more direct effect, such as CD-ROM projects. Thus the main point of this decision on one plane is to affect decisions on another plane.[3]

Decisions of Matching

Now begin with some relatively straightforward decisions. Many decisions explicitly match *demand* — functions intended to benefit the business — with *supply* — the technology and associated means for achieving them. For instance, the following are *matching decisions:*

● the decision to supply technical abstracts to library customers on CD-ROM (as opposed to using WORM or videodisk technology, or supplying some other types of data on CD-ROM);

● the decision to use WordPerfect etc for the body of document production work (as opposed to using some other software products, or matching different products to different types of documents);

● the decision to use expert system technology for a mailing system (as opposed to using some other technology for mailing).

Decisions like these on the *same plane* can still be be regarded as being at *different levels of detail*: a decision to use expert system technology is at a higher, less detailed level, than a decision to use the software product VP-Expert.

Decisions of Scope

The next step is to expose a different plane of decision-making — that sets the scope for matching. Murray Pine has the requirements for word processing and desktop publishing typical of any large company, but there are also more specialised requirements for preparing some text in-house that will eventually be published in magazines and books. A committee studies the matter; its report recommends using the combination of WordPerfect, FrameMaker and Harvard Graphics as the basis for a new standard company-wide document production system. But a huge assumption has crept in here unnoticed. The breakdown tool shows that the committee is really recommending two decisions: a *matching* decision to favour certain software products (as opposed to others) to produce certain documents (as opposed to others); and a *scope* decision to have standard company-wide document production systems (as opposed to (say) encouraging each unit to decide its document production arrangements for itself).4

The second of these is itself a far-reaching decision that may be good or bad, wise or unwise. It decides the scope of the whole matching problem. With a different scope decision a different matching decision might be appropriate.

Scope decisions typically cover three main types of question, often entangled together:

- Do you make organisation-uniform choices or provide freedom for different units to make different choices?
- Where do you draw the boundary around your functional area for decision (since it is usually possible to wonder whether some additional function ought to be regarded as part of the problem too)?
- Do you develop a robust system methodically, or experiment and cut corners for quick feedback?

Given this analysis, the following decisions can be recognised as being on the scope plane too:

- 'We will set up several independent projects to try out new products in the market for IT-based reference works, as opposed to having a master plan that co-ordinates our product designs and technology choices in the area of IT-based reference works.'
- 'The experimental hypertext project will have the following review points . . (breakdown: the hypertext system will be experimental, not a solid, durable system built in a methodical, step-by-step way; *and* the particular points in the project's structure where the experiment will be reviewed are . . as opposed to any number of other possible review points that might be chosen).'

The as-opposed-to tool shows that these decisions are not concerned with proposing any particular match of supply and demand. They set the scope within which supply and demand are matched.

Decisions of Context

Now take the decision to have a separate innovation group, with certain terms of reference (as opposed to one with some other terms of reference, or some different way of stimulating and controlling innovation). Matching and scope decisions are all concerned with some specific applications of IT that can be stated, but the as-opposed-to tool shows that the decision about the innovation group is independent of particular applications. It may have some relevance to systems already under development, and rather more to systems currently being considered, but its main impact will probably be on *systems that nobody has even yet conceived.*

The decision to organise in this way sets up a context that will shape future decisions of matching and scope. Decisions about innovation will take place in an arena where the innovation group is one of the players. Here are some other *context decisions:*

- the decision that each business unit should have its own IT director (as opposed to having one IT chief for the whole organisation, or concentrating power in a co-ordinating committee of board members);
- the decision that MIS should charge departments at full commercial rates (as opposed to charging at rates intended to recover costs, or distinguishing between fixed and marginal costs, or some other principle).

Decisions of Approach

Another type of decision affects decisions on other planes even more explicitly — but for a specific one-off purpose, rather than as a context for an indefinite period. When major decisions have to be taken, it is often best to start by agreeing how to organise the decision-making and what methods to use. This may sound a pedantic point, but the choice of (say) James Martin's IEF (as opposed to (say) Arthur Andersen's Method/1 or PA's IT Strategy methodology) for a multi-phase, multi-month planning study is surely a significant decision, with many implications.

Here are some more examples on this plane of *approach decisions* that decide about the decision-making process:

- the decision to choose the new presentation graphics package on the basis of questionnaire data (as opposed to using discounted cash-flow techniques to analyse costs and benefits, or trying first to get a consensus on essential and desirable features before considering specific products);
- the decision to make a detailed model of the newspaper publishing division and derive strategic decisions from that (as opposed to resolving the key issues of strategy first, thus eliminating many options and leaving modelling with a more restricted role).[5]

Decisions of Agenda

Each of the four categories set out so far can contain decisions at different levels of generality. But some IM decisions are certainly high-level and yet not obviously high-level matching, high-level scope or any of the others; eg the decision to use IT to develop innovative products and

Planes of Decision-making

Agenda: deciding broad policy affecting decisions on any of the other planes	eg 'The policy principles that will affect some more specific decisions are *these* (as opposed to some other principles).'
Matching: deciding how to match supply and demand	eg 'To serve *this* function, we will use *that* technology (as opposed to some other match of function and technology).'
Scope: deciding the terms of reference of matching decisions	eg 'We will choose the best match of supply-demand for *that* business unit (as opposed to the whole, or some other slice, of the company).'
Context: deciding on the management environment that will influence decisions on any of the other planes	eg 'The ongoing procedures and responsibilities will be like *this* (as opposed to some other way).'
Approach: deciding on the process for taking specific one-off decisions on any of the other planes	eg 'For this particular problem decision-making will be organised like *this* (as opposed to some other way).'

services (as opposed to redesigning the core financial and order fulfilment systems). Such an *agenda decision* is something of an agenda-setting statement of intent that may influence debates around decisions on several different planes:

- **matching**: what matches of innovative new products and technology to choose;
- **scope**: how to set up nimble, limited projects that will test out innovative ideas;
- **context**: how to organise responsibilities best to stimulate and exploit innovation;
- **approach**: how to set up a planning process that will generate ideas for innovative applications.

An agenda decision is at a fairly high level of abstraction, but is not so abstract that it fails to count as a decision at all. 'We will make information a management asset' is a platitude, not a decision.[6]

Other representative agenda decisions are the decision to introduce IT-based facilities for office workers at least as good as those of competitors, and the decision to alter the balance of spend on IT between business units.

Analysing Murray Pine Decisions

The table above gives the five planes of IM decision-making and charts the relations between them.

Murray Pine Decisions, Analysed by Plane

Agenda	'We will concentrate on using IT to develop innovative publishing products and services.' 'We will introduce IT-based facilities for our office workers at least as good as those of our most sophisticated competitors.' 'We will shift the balance of spend between our three main business units — now roughly 50-25-25 — to more like 40-40-20.'
Matching	'We will have a system to provide a new publishing product: technical abstracts supplied to library customers on CD-ROM.' 'We will use the products WordPerfect, FrameMaker and Harvard Graphics to meet our requirements for document production.' 'We will use expert system technology as the basis for a new system to send out mailshots marketing our books.'
Scope	'We will have a standard company-wide system for document production.' 'We will set up several independent projects to try out new products in the market for IT-based reference works (eg encyclopaedia, dictionary etc).' 'The experimental hypertext project will have the following review points . . '
Context	'We will have a separate innovation group, containing experts on advanced technology for publishing, and it will have the following terms of reference . . ' 'Each business unit of the organisation will have its own IT director.' 'In future MIS will charge departments in the organisation for all its services at full commercial rates.'
Approach	'We will use the IEF methodology to produce an organisation-wide information architecture.' 'To choose the new presentation graphics package we will send out questionnaires to all users and weight their preferences by their amount and type of use.' 'We will build a process model of our newspaper publishing division, as the main input to decision-making.'

As the other table shows, these concepts can be used to bring order to the body of decisions from the Murray Pine Organisation.

Warrants for IM Decisions

So far this briefing has analysed *decisions*. What about *warrants*, the generalisations that can help in reaching good decisions?

Many of the best warrants in the literature of IM fit in fairly well.

Representative Warrants

Warrant	*How does it help you reach decisions?*
Agenda 'The following seven generic possibilities exist for any business to profit from IT. . '	'Choose one (eg develop new products and services) and you have made a decision setting the agenda for more detailed IT decisions.'
Matching 'The tradeoffs between CD-ROM and WORM as storage media for high-volume databases are . . '	'Decide whether to use CD-ROM or WORM for any particular application (eg an encyclopaedia published on disk) by weighing the tradeoff factors . . '
Scope 'The advantages of choosing the same PC software organisation-wide are . . . but the disadvantages are . . '	'See how these factors weigh in each particular case; eg when deciding whether to have the same word processing software across the organisation.'
Context 'Having a separate innovation group can stimulate innovative use of IT, but also has the following dangers . . '	'See how the pros and cons weigh up in your case before deciding whether to have an innovation group, or to handle innovation some other way.'
Approach 'Standard methodologies for developing an information architecture can be divided over three broad categories . . '	'Use these distinctions to contrast different approaches while deciding which is most appropriate for the situation.'

Posing the Decision Question can clarify both *whether* the warrant can assist decision-making, and also the *plane* of decision-making where it plays a role: agenda, matching . . and so on.

The next table shows how a warrant is often directly relevant to one particular plane: a warrant about the tradeoffs between two types of technology will normally support matching decisions, so it can reasonably be called a matching warrant. But this isn't a firm rule. One warrant can be relevant to several different planes of decision.

Take a simple warrant asserting that there is a distinction between two types of business re-engineering: that which *streamlines* administration, eg reducing processing steps and paper; and that which *enables* people to collaborate better on things that are not really administration, eg designing a new product. This warrant could help in reaching an agenda decision: 'We will concentrate on the enabling type of re-engineering (as opposed to the streamlining type).' It could also lead to a context decision: 'Our accounting system will treat the costing of the different types of re-engineering somewhat differently.' And it could influence debate about an approach decision: 'In our multi-stage planning exercise the two types of re-engineering will be discussed at different points and in different ways.'

Value of the Chart of IM Decision Planes

The main claim made by the chart is that all IM decisions can be placed on one of the five planes, or else decomposed into two or more decisions which can. What is the value of that? As in any complex field, a framework that identifies the main areas of interest and fits them together is an aid to orientation. Thinking in terms of the five planes can bring other benefits, too:

- Plunging into detail without making any agenda decisions is a common weakness in IM decision-making. Another is taking decisions that may look like agenda decisions at first glance, but are really decisions on other planes in disguise. Another is taking agenda decisions couched in such abstract terms that they don't in fact set any meaningful agenda for decisions on the other planes.
- Another common failing is to overlook issues of scope. Managers sometimes assume that you should *always* standardise organisation-wide as much as possible, integrate as much as possible and develop systems as methodically as possible. That, if valid, would remove the need for any separate plane of scope decisions. But it isn't valid; experience shows that disastrous projects are often the result of undebated assumptions about scope.
- These distinctions between planes can sometimes be the key to defining an organisation's whole IM strategy. In some situations it may be quite correct to focus on the issue: 'What new systems should be developed?'; but in others, 'What new context arrangements should be introduced?' may be the more crucial question.[7]

Several other analyses of types of decisions could be made, but the chart of the five planes is adequate for its purpose of maintaining a sense of direction across the whole field of IM.[8,9]

NOTES & ARGUMENTS

1 Business-school textbooks offer ways of categorising management decisions in general: some decisions are about long-term matters, others medium-term, and others short-term; some are semi-programmed, whereas others offer freedom for initiative, and there are gradations here too. Applying this traditional analysis to IM decisions brings no particular insight. This briefing aims for something more illuminating.

Gerstein (pp. 135-171) offers an interesting breakdown of 'requirements for the effective management of information technology and . . recommendations to fulfill them.' About 40 items are grouped under five headings:

- general **managerial** requirements: eg change management skills;
- implications for the **chief executive (CEO)**: eg selecting a chief technology officer, revamping planning processes to fit together IT and strategic planning;
- implications for operational, ie **non-IT, managers**: eg IT affects organisation and job design within the department, the manager has to carry out planning and budgeting for IT;
- implications for senior **MIS managers**: eg supporting 'distributing' computing, developing a strategic systems plan;
- implications for the **human resources function**: eg changes in compensation resulting from new jobs after system redesign, different skills relevant in staff selection for more-IT-based work.

This is certainly more thoughtful than most breakdowns of the field of IM into topics, but it is ultimately unsatisfactory. The identification and *classification* of IM issues is dominated by generalised *recommendations* about them. For instance, a number of topics are given on which, it is said, the CEO should explicitly formulate policy; key steps are given that the CEO should take. You might easily agree with all Gerstein says about one topic; agree that a second topic belongs in any list of the main IM issues, but disagree that it should be handled by the CEO; agree with the inclusion of some third topic too, and agree also that it should be handled by the CEO, but not in the way suggested. Moreover, since some of the items are formulated in rather detailed terms, you might well hold that one topic, though important in some cases, doesn't really belong in any general classification, especially since another topic, which isn't included, can also be important in some cases.

Gerstein's analysis stands or falls by its quality as a set of recommendations; as a neutral map of the subject of IM it doesn't compete. Briefing 2, by contrast, aims for a recommendation-free, situation-independent, first-order breakdown of IM matters, to provide a sense of direction in investigating the subject. It charts out the *kind* of IM matters that organisations have to decide about, without the distractions of recommending *what* their decisions should be or *how* the decisions should be taken.

2 The list is a representative sample of the kinds of decisions typically made or considered within a large organisation. The challenge is to sort them into robust, plausible categories. 'Representative' doesn't mean 'recommended'. These may or may not be *wise* decisions for MPO; they may or may not form an entirely *coherent* set of decisions. These points are not germane here, because the aim is to classify *all* IM decisions (other than manifestly absurd ones, perhaps), not merely excellent IM decisions. The same riders apply to the representative decisions listed in other 'Untangling' briefings later in the book.

Here is another disclaimer. To classify decisions is not to suggest how or in what sequence decisions should be taken. It is usually wise to take broader decisions before more detailed ones. But not always; sometimes a broad decision is no more than a summary — a way of showing that several specific decisions already taken are indeed consistent and based on implicit common ground. Therefore in *classifying* the decisions people take, it is best to avoid the distraction of assumptions about the sequence of the decisions.

3 *Plane* is a better term than *level.* Two decisions are often said to be on different *levels,* when they differ in degree of detail. 'We will use word processing software here, as opposed to presentation graphics software' is less detailed than 'we will use WordPerfect here, as opposed to Microsoft Word.' But a decision on a different *plane,* such as 'each business unit may choose its PC software without reference to the MIS department' differs in a more subtle way than just degree of detail.

Were it possible to arrange most IM issues and decisions on branches at different levels in just one hierarchy, everything would be simpler, and the problems far less slippery. This briefing asserts fairly emphatically that it is not possible.

4 Here are some other scope options that MPO might find worth considering:

- 'We will replace existing systems throughout the company with one new, standard system for WP and straightforward work, but exclude arrangements for the more sophisticated work, such as colour graphics and mathematical typesetting; decisions on these will be taken by other people at other times.'
- 'We will give each of the company's divisions the freedom to make its own decisions in the area of document production systems, but only subject to certain requirements that will be specified for interchanging text (not graphics) in a standard format.'
- 'We will select several attractive technology components and several promising new styles of work organisation; try them out in selected locations for six months; learn from this experience; only then take major company-wide decisions.'
- 'We will treat document production as part of a total office automation problem, embracing not only well known matters such as electronic mail and electronic diaries for appointment scheduling, but also financial modelling, time recording for project accounting, and on-line databases for access to archive and reference information. We will regard this entire area throughout the company as one whole, and our decisions will be solutions to that large problem.'

5 Someone who believed that a certain standard methodology was: a, supreme, b, universally applicable and c, comprehensive, would always take exactly the same approach decision: follow the methodology. The less you believe that any standard methodology can have all these three qualities, the more interested you will be in the variety of decisions on the approach plane.

6 To have any power an agenda decision needs some meaningful as-opposed-to component. The decision to shift the balance of spend between the three business units to about 40-40-20 may be wise or foolish, but at least it is easy to see what plausible possibilities are rejected: equal shares, *laissez faire* etc.

Sager (pp. 225-6, after J Pinghera and H Phills) quotes an information policy consisting of eight statements: 'AT&T's information and data are corporate resources; data will be safeguarded; data will be shared according to company policies; data will be managed as a corporate resource; corporate data will be identified and defined; databases will be developed on business needs; information will be managed actively; information will be used to enhance current offerings and pursue new business opportunities.' These are surely not tough, incisive decisions that reject plausible alternatives. It is difficult to imagine (say) an articulate minority on the AT&T board putting up a convincing case that data *should not* be shared according to company policies.

Agenda decisions tend to say more about business objectives than about technology choices. But not all are so high-level that they ignore technology completely. 'We will develop expertise in neural network technology and use it intensively for a variety of applications (as yet undefined)' could be a plausible agenda decision.

But what about demand-driven decisions, that decide in detail what is to be done without taking any account of technology constraints, or supply-driven decisions, that say a lot about technology without explaining what it is to be used for? Often these are less decisions than working hypotheses (analogous to 'let's just assume for the moment that there is oil there') or, worse, unsubstantiated hopes (as in 'I intend to discover a new chemical element').

Conversely, a high-level decision may be so focused that it isn't agenda, but belongs on one of the other planes: 'We will make a five-year plan to co-ordinate the whole organisation's IT activities' is a high-level scope decision.

7 Suppose the ideas in this briefing are valid, or even more-or-less valid. Aren't they too *abstract* for practical use in the hurly-burly of debate with the managers of real organisations? Wouldn't many managers have an instinctive antagonism to fancy ideas about planes of decision-making? And if these ideas are valid in principle but useless in practice, then they are, well, useless. And if useless, they are not worth knowing about. This argument might threaten other ideas in this book too — as well as some other books, of course. It needs to be tackled.

If valid, or even more-or-less valid, then (given the insights they claim to offer) the five planes of IM decision-making must be important and relevant. *If important and relevant,* then it must be desirable to make practical use of them. But *how* to make practical use of any general idea is a tactical matter. An idea is best expressed in different ways to different audiences. You might say to one person: 'to get better health care, we will have to pay more'; to another: 'the financing of health care is essentially a kind of insurance, where the money we pay in when healthy goes to pay for the care we need when sick'; and to a third: 'now let d_1 be the demand for health care in community c_1 . . '

There may be some organisations where it would be appropriate to set up a day's seminar for all key managers, and hold semi-theological debates about whether a certain decision should count as context or scope. But in other organisations, the sensible way to use these ideas could be to hide abstract terms and ideas from most decision-makers, and have just a few people consciously watching out for major confusions of plane: decisions of matching that beg questions of scope, or decisions of context inconsistent with other decisions of agenda etc. Even when such things are spotted and discussed, it isn't compulsory to use abstract names to explain what is wrong.

In summary: clear thinking about the interactions between decisions is desirable, and, carefully used, abstract terms and concepts can further it. But the proper objective is good, coherent decisions; the vocabulary used is a subordinate, tactical matter.

8 What about *problems* as opposed to decisions? Are there matching problems, scope problems and so on. Plainly, there are. But the trickiness of many problems lies in the very fact that they call for several related decisions on different planes. A company's policy on (say) end-user computing may have to be a coherent blend of decisions on matching, scope and context planes. Recognising how the issues on different planes fit together may well be the key to sound decisions.

9 *Knowledge and Decisions* (Basic Books, 1980) by Thomas Sowell gives some neat distinctions between *types of decision* (pp. 18ff.). Since any of them could be relevant to IM matters, they are paraphrased here:

- A decision may be *binary* (eg peace or war, guilty or innocent) or *continuously variable* (using more or less petrol, living a more relaxed or hectic life).
- A decision may be *once-and-for-all* (suicide, burning a Rembrandt) or *readily reversible* (cancelling a subscription, switching off a TV programme).
- A decision may be *individual* (buying onions, bread etc in separate stores according to price) or *package deal* (voting for a candidate).
- A decision may be *instantaneous*, even if preceded by lengthy consideration (declaring war) or *sequential*, ie piecemeal and based on initially incomplete knowledge (appeasement).

These distinctions can throw light on some IM decisions. It might seem that the level of use of an electronic mail service in an organisation was a *continuously variable* decision. But, it might be argued, this decision is, in practice, *binary*, since an electronic mail service is not worth having unless most people use it. Or perhaps that can be disputed. The point is that recognising the distinction could make for a better focused discussion of possible decisions.

CONNECTIONS

Briefings 3-10	**Agenda**: deciding the broad policy affecting decisions of other types
Briefings 11-17	**Matching**: deciding how to match supply and demand
Briefings 18-22	**Scope**: deciding terms of reference of matching decisions: whole company, experiment etc
Briefings 23-26	**Context**: deciding on the application-independent management environment within which the other types of decisions are taken
Briefings 27-32	**Approach**: deciding the method of taking specific decisions of any of the other types
Briefings 33-40	**Grand Topics**: deciding about things that mix several planes of decision-making
Briefings 41-42	**Meta-topics**: other ways of looking at the foregoing ideas

3. Untangling Agenda Decisions

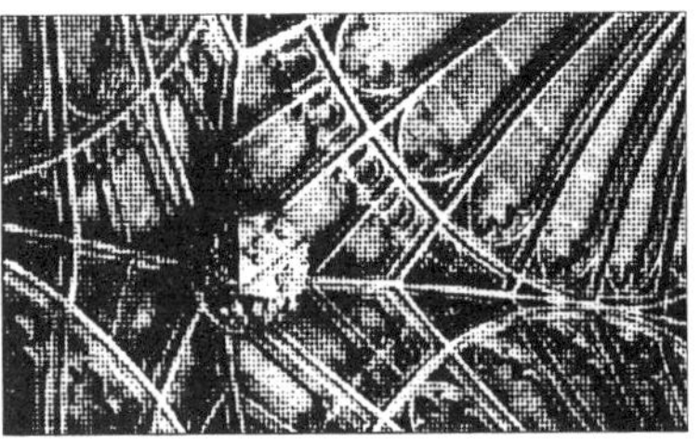

TOPIC

This briefing concentrates on issues and ideas on one of the five planes of decision — agenda. Agenda decisions are broad, top-level decisions. Good agenda decisions make it easier to find a way through the thicket of plausible options available to an organisation on more specific matters. They channel attention, reduce the possibilities to be scrutinised and help attain consistency between more detailed decisions.

IM lore holds an abundance of advice relevant to such decisions — probably as much as on all other matters put together. The trouble is that the subject attracts abstractions and platitudes and thus confusion. Suppose one person insists on aligning business and IT strategy, and another wants to make IT a strategic weapon. Are they saying much the same thing, only with different words? Or is there a genuine difference of principle? Or are they making distinct points that are complementary? Or is one describing what to do and the other how to do it? It can be frustratingly difficult to clarify such basic things.

The task for this briefing is to find ways of sifting through the mass of generalisations relevant to agenda decisions.

SUGGESTED WARRANTS

As the table shows, agenda decisions can cover quite a variety of matters. At first glance, it may seem best to separate out decisions, and the warrants that support them, according to what is decided: identifying some broad application area as a priority for attention seems a different kind of decision from changing the balance of IT spending between different units of the company, or concentrating on applications to support a certain business strategy rather than some other.

Unfortunately, such plausible categories of agenda decision tend to blur hopelessly into each other: deciding to give priority to the broad application area of production automation may be much the same thing as deciding to spend more on IT in those departments associated with

Yellow Carbeen, Manufacturers of Vending Machines
Representative Agenda Decisions

'Our IT decisions will be guided by two big business objectives: one is to improve customer service dramatically; the other to earn at least 25% of revenue within three years from new types of product (as opposed to other possible objectives, eg increase total turnover, slash production costs, double export sales etc).'

'We will concentrate new investment on automating production in the factory (rather than on management and administration systems).'

'We will invest heavily in building up our expertise in CAD/CAM, so that we can use the technology more widely and intensively than any other company in our industry.'

'Our new investment will be targeted towards bringing all our systems up to average standards of database and telecoms network use (as opposed to trying to be industry-leaders).'

'We will redevelop major systems X and Y (but not . .)."

'We will develop an inter-organisational system for our inbound logistics function (one of three chosen out of ten candidates for major investment we considered).'

In general, we will make large investments in new systems to match the innovations of our competitors (as opposed to investing and risking enough to try and dominate the industry through our own innovation).'

---

production, or concentrating on applications that support the business strategy of more-efficient, low-cost production.**1**

A more fruitful approach is to categorise the generalisations and advice available rather than the decisions — and do so by examining the different *roles* that generalisations can play in decision-making on the agenda plane.**2**

Aspects of Agenda Generalisations

The key to sorting out all the generalising items — theories, quadrant-diagrams, techniques and so on — possibly relevant to agenda decisions is to examine their *role* in decision-making. There are three main questions:

- Does this suggest conventions for business **modelling**, to describe a specific organisation in a useful way? A descriptive model, like a map, doesn't recommend or reason; it just describes — though only those features thought to be relevant. It is a source of material (preferably rich and insight-forming, but also elegant) to be drawn on in debates. Different people may seize on different features depicted by the model to support different reasoning. The model entails no presuppositions about how debate is organised.**3**
- Does this provide **generic analysis**, helpful in relating the specific

organisation to some set of general possibilities? For instance: 'there are essentially four strategies open to any business . . ' or 'there are six generic ways of relating IM strategy to business strategy.' This is much more decision-forcing than modelling, since the generalisation implies that one out of the generic possibilities should be adopted, and the others explicitly rejected. This, like modelling, is a way of generating ideas that can be thrown into the hurly-burly of debate. One person may support a certain policy by arguing 'There are four generic business strategies . . ' Another may respond 'Yes, but if we look at the Boston Consulting Group's famous four categories of product . .' Items like these don't presuppose organising debate in any particular format of steps.

- Does this recommend a **procedure** that formats the process of decision-making: 'In stage 1, ask the following fundamental questions . . Carry the answers forward to stage 2, and then ask the following slightly more precise questions . . '?

Distinctions between Generalisations

The three questions suggest three different roles that an item may play in decision-making. However, they set up three *aspects* rather than firm distinctions. Though many generalisations play one and only one of the roles, others have traces of more than one aspect. Here are some examples:

First, the critical success factors technique — at least, as widely practiced — has as end-product a kind of business model. But the technique is really an instance of the *modelling-procedure* combination of aspects. The end-model has several levels of detail: you model what seems important at one level, and then move on to the next more detailed level. As you progress you are making decisions about what is important. Thus the technique implies a procedure for both modelling and decision-making.

Second, suppose someone asserts that a certain company is in the 'factory' situation (out of the four situations defined by the strategic grid of Cash, McFarlan and McKenney). This only becomes useful when another piece of generic analysis is switched into the line of reasoning; eg for a company in the factory situation, a certain style for organising IT is appropriate; this leads to the recommendation that IT costs should be tightly controlled and justified by financial benefits (as opposed to spent on experimental innovations, or on projects to improve the company's image). Thus the strategic grid is essentially a starting-point for a multi-step generic analysis. This kind of *extended generic analysis* unavoidably has a procedural aspect.

The other important type is the *combination* of all three aspects. The 'customer resource life-cycle' (CRLC) of Ives and Learmonth proposes a certain generic analysis (13 types of activity in a business), partly as a basis for modelling organisation-specific data, but also as the impetus for a procedure in several steps to generate new ideas.

Bringing all this analysis together produces a six-way distinction warrant:

- **Pure modelling**: eg value chain analysis;
- **Modelling-procedure**: eg critical success factors;
- **Pure generic analysis**: eg Porter's generic business strategies;
- **Extended generic analysis**: eg the strategic grid of Cash, McFarlan and McKenney;
- **Combination**: eg the 'customer resource life-cycle' (CRLC) of Ives and Learmonth;
- **Less tractable material**: generalising material where a satisfactory answer to the Decision Question is not immediately obvious — either because the material is practically worthless, or because effort is needed to get the ideas into a form that will support decisions; eg theories about eras and stages in the development of IT; surveys of management concerns; and metrics and benchmarking.[4,5]

Using This Analysis

The purpose of this analysis? It helps in getting a grip on the hundreds of ideas tangled together in this area:

- 'The vocabulary and diagrams of Idea A and Idea B are entirely different. But analysed carefully in terms of their role in decision-making they come out similar. Therefore we should probably make use of one or the other, but not both.'
- 'Ideas C and D may sound much the same superficially, but on examination of their possible role in decision-making, they belong to different categories. Bear that in mind when deciding whether to use both, either or neither.'
- Idea E is very impressive, but we don't need an idea to play that role in our case. We do need an idea of the category that Idea F belongs to, but unfortunately the idea itself seems rather feeble.

In other words, the categorisation helps you choose what you need *in your particular case.* The need can vary considerably. In some cases an organisation dedicates most effort to the descriptive work of business modelling, and subsequent agenda decisions can be regarded as natural outcomes of the situation depicted in the model, without much additional debate. In other cases, there is little use of model-like description but much debate; eg if the intention is to change things radically, description of the old methods is relatively unimportant, but there may be great controversy about the options for change, and a variety of different generic analyses may be thrown into the debate. And in other cases again, describing and debating may be more evenly balanced.

Relation of Agenda to the Other Planes

As the name suggests agenda decisions set the scene for other decisions on other planes. Many of the cruder generalisations offered are primarily concerned with opportunity-spotting, which is another name for taking decisions that set the agenda for more specific matching decisions to follow: eg 'we could gain competitive advantage with a new system to do this new thing' or, less glamorously, 'we ought to redevelop systems in that area.' However, some of the more sophisticated generalisations concerned with establishing the place of IT in the organisation are a source of agenda decisions affecting issues of scope, context and approach.

The relationship between agenda and approach can be a little tricky. In a strict sense, the decision to use any particular generalisation whatsoever is an approach decision, that will lead in due course to some agenda decision. This is well worth remembering, particularly with those generalisations that recommend or imply multi-step procedures. However, at some point the analysis has to stop; otherwise a vicious regress of decisions about decisions will ensue.

NOTES & ARGUMENTS

1 Priority-setting is an agenda theme with nuances. For instance: Is a list of priorities a list of things all of which you will definitely do, arranged in order of importance? Or will those items lower down the list only be done in so far as this is possible after the higher ones have been done? Or, again . . This is one of those topics well worth thinking about carefully, but not explored in detail in this book. The book doesn't lay down knowledge that ought to be known on every IM topic; it aims to stimulate careful thought on *any* IM topic. That is why some topics are debated quite fully, others sketched out and others just suggested. That said, there is a discussion of priorities to be found in O'Brien (*Demands*), Briefing 24.

2 Earl (pp. 39-61) suggests a classification of 'frameworks . . to guide practitioners in exploiting IT for strategic advantage':

- awareness (sub-divided into refocusing, impact and scoping);
- opportunity (sub-divided into systems analysis, applications search, technology fitting and business strategy);
- positioning (sub-divided into scaling, spatial and temporal).

Thus, for example, value chain analysis is classed as systems analysis (within opportunity) and the strategic grid of Cash, McFarlan and McKenney as scaling (within positioning). The trouble with such abstract labels is that many items seem to go just as well in any three or four out of the ten pigeon-holes. The critical success factors technique isn't mentioned. Where would it go? Or doesn't it count as a framework?

3 But what have modelling techniques and conventions to do with warrants for decision-making? This is mixed up with the question of appraising modelling techniques: Why use one rather than another?

Different styles of business modelling rest on different premises and expose different features of the organisation modelled. One will expose features that are *more helpful* than another, ie more relevant to understanding the key issues of a particular case. Anyone who advocates general use of one particular modelling technique is asserting 'The most helpful way of depicting an organisation is generally *this* way: . . '

This statement is in effect a chart warrant about the nature of organisations. It can be appraised, by asking the kind of questions that apply to all chart warrants: Does this way of seeing things obscure or distort some dimensions or factors that should really be in the centre of the picture? Is it an over-complex way of gaining insight into what is important? Do the items and relations inherent in the warrant seem plain and natural, or obscure and arbitrary?

4 Surveys of agenda-setting matters such as concerns, key issues and so on are quite common. One survey (Sager, p. 218) of key issues recognised by managers placed 'strategic planning' top, 'IS's role and contribution' fourth, 'end-user computing' sixth etc. Similar material is given by Earl (p. 26) and Frenzel (pp. 24ff.) and in numerous issues of the magazine *Datamation*.

One journal article reported on a survey of 600 firms, with tables of results, showing that 47% of manufacturing and 75% of service businesses thought IT had a significant overall impact on corporate strategy, and that of those in the distribution sector, 54% thought IT reduced product cost in general, of which 36% thought IT led to strategic advantage. (Tor Guimeraes, Crumpton Farrell, Jae Song, 'Computing Technology as a Strategic Business Tool', *SAM Advanced Management Journal*, Summer 1988, pp. 25ff.)

Hochstrasser and Griffiths build on survey results ('Currently, 36% of company managers find in IT an essential tool for improving after-sales services, but only 18% of managers have used IT to strengthen the links with their customers') (p. 58) to form conclusions and recommend methods. Grindley's book is also based on a large-scale survey of opinions, but contains a considerable degree of personal interpretation.

How could such material affect anybody's decision-making? The immediate problem with most surveys of IM concerns is that the standard of the surveying is so poor. Take the survey cited by Sager above:

- 'Data as a corporate resource' came seventh and 'information architecture' eighth. The two seem so closely related that if the supporters of both had agreed on a joint candidate ('information architecture as a corporate resource', perhaps), it might have come much higher than seventh.
- 'IS's role and contribution' came fourth and 'end-user computing' came sixth. These are different but not independent. You can scarcely say much about one that does not have implications for the other. Treating them as if they were independent items is like asking: Which are you most worried about: the rise in sea level or the flooding of low-lying land?
- 'Strategic planning' came top and 'integrating data processing, office automation, factory automation, and telecoms' only tenth. But these two are broad and narrow terms: strategy includes much else besides integration but you can't discuss integration at all without discussing strategy. You might as well say that people's main worry is the disastrous economic situation and that the complete absence of food in the shops is only their tenth worry.

Muddled material like this surely can't help anybody to take good IM decisions. But could an impeccably conducted survey of concerns help? Knowing that other people believe something to be very important and some other thing less important doesn't really get you very far. And those books that develop general concepts about IM from the starting-point of survey research don't produce anything more convincing than books that don't.

These comments are negative but necessary. Surveys are often accorded respect that they simply don't deserve.

5 The notion of IM metrics is popular in some quarters. The aim is certainly attractive. Suppose you knew the spend-per-head on IT (and various other averages and ratios) in your organisation, and also the figures for your industry as a whole, and for leading competitors. Surely that would be valuable evidence helping you make shrewd agenda-setting decisions.

The trouble is that a technique is not a sensible technique just because it has desirable objectives. It is only of any use if it also includes plausible means for getting somewhere near the objectives. How are you going to find out the spend-per-head on IT in your industry as a whole? In practice, only by relying on statistics from certain consultancies. Will consultancies allow you to audit their database of statistics to check whether they have surveyed *enough* companies in your industry, whether they are *representative* companies, whether the figures all cover the *same time period*, and are worked out on the *same basis*? Very, very unlikely.

There are other problems too. Even with reliable benchmark data, it can still be difficult to draw rational conclusions about the particular case. For a briefing-length discussion of metrics and decisions, see O'Brien (*Demands*), Briefing 26.

CONNECTIONS

4. Business Modelling	*Pure modelling*, with value chain analysis as the representative example
5. Generic Strategies	*Pure generic analysis* of business strategies; and of the alignment of IT and business strategies
6. Agenda-setting Logic	*Extended generic analysis*, with the strategic grid as the main example
7. Agenda-setting Procedures	*Modelling-procedure* and *combination* techniques, with CSF and CRLC as representative examples
8. Culture, Mission and Vision	Making more tractable some concepts that are often too vague
9. Stage Theories	*Less tractable material*; the question is how — if at all — this can be applied to decisions about actual cases
10. Learning and Historical Themes	Ditto

4. Business Modelling

TOPIC

In the early stages of an IM planning process it is often helpful to draw a model of the activities of the business, that is technology-independent and, where useful, also independent of formal organisation structure.

Many such models are presented as the product of value chain analysis, and thus associated with the ideas of Porter who invented both the term and a certain diagram format. But some quite important points about value chains are understood by different people in different ways; confused assumptions about the meaning conveyed by a model can easily arise.

This briefing has two objectives. One is to explore the field of business modelling in general to see how styles of modelling differ and thus suit different circumstances, and to discuss how a business model can assist decision-making. The other is to demystify value chain modelling. These two objectives go well together: untangling the issues around the value chain provides general insights that will help in clarifying any modelling technique you come across or invent for yourself.

REPRESENTATIVE IDEAS — SUMMARISED

Before confronting the potential confusions of the value chain it is best to establish some general points about business modelling by looking at a couple of relatively simple techniques.

Plain Hierarchy and Anthony Models

Any business model provides a list of activities within an organisation, arranged and organised in some useful way.[1]

Perhaps the simplest method has no particular name: call it the *plain hierarchy*. The model might break down a certain bank into ever more detailed levels: the bank consists of a number of business units, 'loan placements' for one; loan placements consists of (say) four functions, one of them 'identify assets for resale'; identify assets for resale consists of several processes, including 'request credit approval'; request credit approval is made up of. . and so on.

Another technique is the *Anthony* model. Here all activities are arranged into three groups: strategic planning, management control and operational control. Thus 'making five-year plans' is likely to be in the first group, 'suing a supplier' in the second, and 'accepting a customer order' in the third. For a more striking effect, the three groups of activities are often depicted as three layers in a pyramid; however this makes the model more difficult to read and to work with.

A good model in either of these styles can usually assist IM agenda decision-making. At a minimum, managers can look at each activity shown by the model in turn, and ask how much IT investment should be devoted to it relative to the others.

Different styles of modelling sort out activities in different ways, each according to their *underlying theses*. The plain hierarchy model rests on the unassailable thesis that activities can normally be decomposed into several levels of detail. The Anthony model rests on two theses: first, that every activity can be located somewhere along a scale from the thoroughly mundane to the rarefied strategic; second, that it is invariably best to divide this scale up into three regions, rather than (say) two or five. Plainly, it would be possible to agree with the first Anthony thesis but not the second.**2**

Value Chain Analysis: Underlying Theses

If this seems pedantic the payoff comes when a more complicated form of modelling is examined. In general, the more elaborate the underlying theses of a modelling method are, the higher the stakes are raised: there is more chance of confusion about what a model signifies, and the theses are more vulnerable to objections; but there is also more chance of generating subtler insights.

With value chain modelling the first underlying thesis is a distinction between *primary and support activities*:**3**

- If you make a list of specific activities in any business whatsoever (eg 42 activities in a business that manufactures copiers), they can always be divided into two large groups: primary (eg 15 of them) and support activities (eg the other 27). In a different copier business, there might be (say) 41 activities, split 22-19; and in a bank there might be 78 entirely different activities — but in all organisations activities can be split into these two invariable groups.
- Primary activities are the activities involved in the physical creation of the product and its sale and transfer to the buyer, as well as after-sale assistance; for a copier company, order processing will be a primary activity. Secondary activities are all other activities, eg recruitment of staff.
- But primary and support activities also differ in another way. The

primary activities are technologically and strategically distinct; in other words, they can, if required, be treated, discussed and demarcated more or less in isolation — at any rate most of the time. Support activities can't easily be kept distinct in this way; eg recruitment of staff is related to practically every other activity for which staff are needed.

This raises the question: Could not an activity involved in the physical creation of the product (a primary characteristic) have very complicated interconnections with other activities (a support characteristic)? Or is that a contradiction in terms? The answer is that the first criterion is the one that really distinguishes a primary from a secondary activity, and that in practice, by and large, the second criterion tends to reinforce it.

The second underlying thesis is the concept of *nine invariable categories of activity*:

- The set of primary activities in any business — copier manufacturer, bank or any other — can always be analysed into five invariable categories: inbound logistics; operations; outbound logistics; marketing; and sales and service. The set of support activities can always be analysed into four invariable categories: firm infrastructure; human resource management; technology development; procurement.
- Allocation of each company-specific activity to the appropriate category is often straightforward (eg advertising obviously belongs under marketing and sales), but sometimes there is a choice that can carry significance. Should order processing be categorised as part of outbound logistics or marketing? If the customer's order is for 100 tonnes of sugar from a refinery, outbound logistics seems the natural answer; if the order is for a new class of aircraft carrier, then marketing. Between these extremes will fall more tricky cases.
- The number of activities placed in these categories will vary considerably from business to business. For a restaurant it may be difficult to find much to put in the outbound logistics category, since customers carry the product away themselves in their stomachs. Nevertheless, every business will always have *some* activity to place in each one of the nine invariable categories.

Those are the main theses, but they need some clarification:

- There is no further breakdown within each of the nine categories. You may identify 300 activities within your business, and put 100 of them within (say) operations, but there is no thesis about breaking down these 100 into further categories or organising them in any other way.
- There is no thesis that the primary activities are more important and deserve more attention than the support activities. They are just different in the way described above.
- There is no strong thesis about the recording of sequence. Any model, based on any conventions, will be read from top to bottom or left to right, and it would be confusing to arrange categories in a bizarre order; eg one with inbound logistics followed by service, followed by operations, from

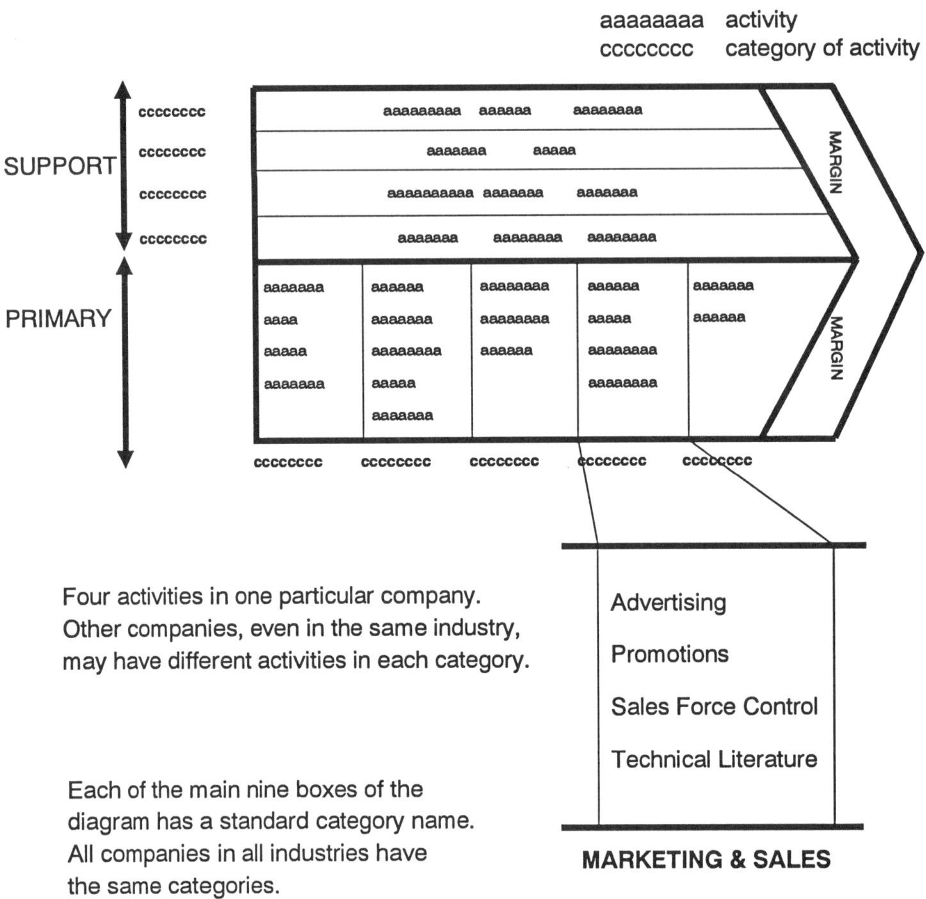
Value Chain - Typical Format
aaaaaaaa activity
cccccccc category of activity
SUPPORT
PRIMARY
MARGIN
MARGIN
Four activities in one particular company. Other companies, even in the same industry, may have different activities in each category.
Each of the main nine boxes of the diagram has a standard category name. All companies in all industries have the same categories.
Advertising
Promotions
Sales Force Control
Technical Literature
MARKETING & SALES

left to right across the page. But avoiding the bizarre is a mild objective. The model does not set out to record sequence in any firm, meaningful sense; it does not assert (for example) that in the manufacture of a copier every single activity in the inbound logistics category is entirely finished before the first activity in the operations category starts.

The diagram gives a representative example of the graphic form usually given to a model based on these theses.

Using a Value Chain Model

How might a model of a business based on these theses be used? In his book Porter mainly uses a diagram with nine boxes for the nine categories (rather than a more detailed one with a box for each company-specific activity):

- A diagram can show quantitative data, such as a breakdown of costs or of assets; eg operations has 46% of the assets, while inbound logistics has only 8%.
- A diagram can show non-quantitative data. Each box can be shaded in certain patterns to show which department or combination of departments has responsibility.
- A diagram can be used to sort out other detailed material besides activities. The 19 cost drivers in a consumer durable manufacturing firm can be arranged with each category-box holding at least one; eg 'regional scale' is one of the cost-drivers within outbound logistics.
- In a variant of the previous use, a diagram can sort out material that does not necessarily fill up every box. For a company making wine, nine sources of cost advantage are identified and arranged in appropriate boxes; eg 'high speed bottling lines' is one of the two items in operations. For this material it is quite reasonable for some of the category-boxes to be empty.
- If several nine-box diagrams are used for different businesses or units within a business, lines drawn between boxes can show links, such as how one firm's outbound logistics is linked to its customer's inbound logistics.

Though Porter depicts no examples, it is plain that any of the above can be done with a diagram at the specific activity level too; eg, for a copier company, the operations box could be divided into four or any other number of parts corresponding to the activities in that category, in order to show information about costs, assets, department responsible etc.

REPRESENTATIVE IDEAS — ANALYSED

It might seem that one point for debate was whether the underlying theses of these modelling methods were *true* or not. But in practice, it is best to concentrate on clarifying some implications, and then assessing how *useful* the resulting models are to decision-making.

Format and Content

A useful preliminary step is to distinguish the precise *graphic form* of the diagrams of any modelling method from the *meaning* conveyed. As the first line of the next diagram shows, any number of different formatting conventions (if clearly defined) can be used to represent what is essentially the same model.

With that impetus it becomes easier to see the similarities and differences of the plain hierarchy and Anthony models (second line of diagram).**4**

From there, value chain modelling can be fitted into the comparison too. As the diagram shows (third line) the format used by Porter and adopted with minor variations by thousands of consultants is not the only possible one for a model based on the underlying premises of value chain

Graphic Form and Model Content

1 The same model content can be presented in any number of forms

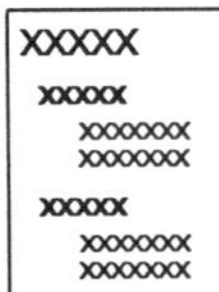
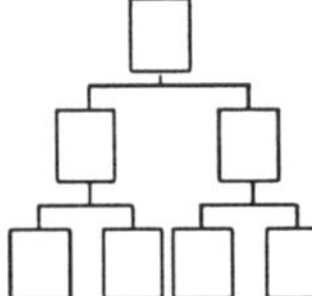
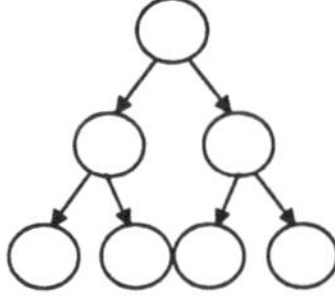
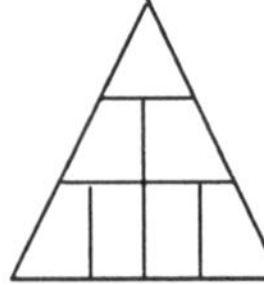
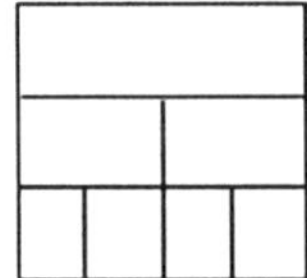

2

Plain Hierarchy Model

The firm can be broken down into as many levels as you like; there are no invariable, standard breakdowns

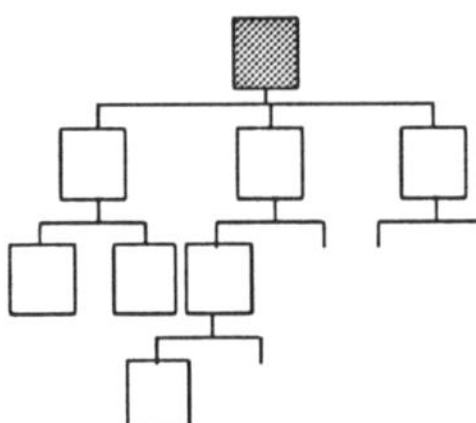

Anthony Model

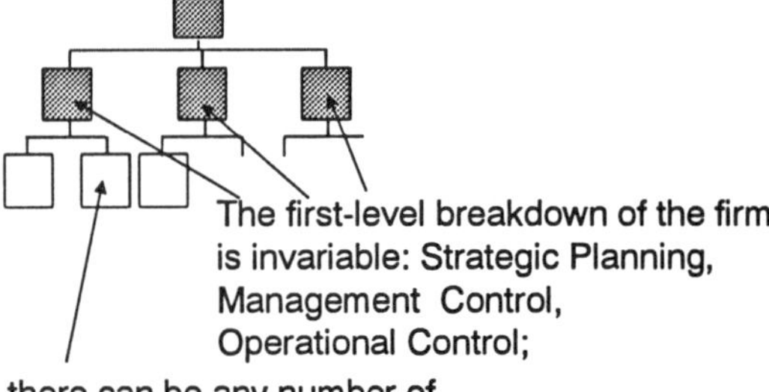

The first-level breakdown of the firm is invariable: Strategic Planning, Management Control, Operational Control;

there can be any number of firm-specific activities at this level;

there are no lower levels.

3 A Value Chain Model, usually like this . .

. . can be represented just as well like this:

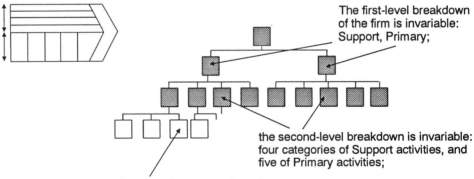

The first-level breakdown of the firm is invariable: Support, Primary;

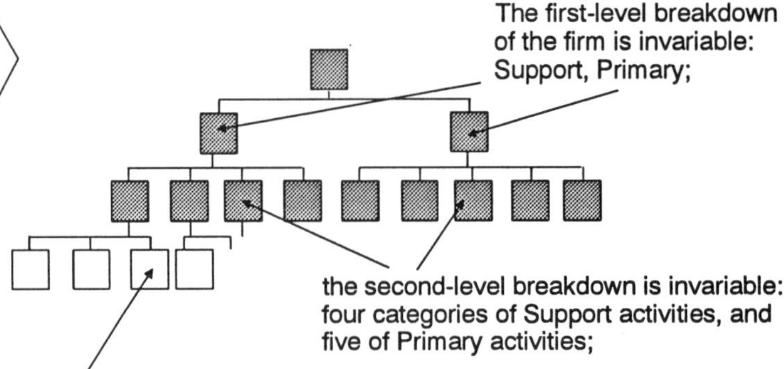

the second-level breakdown is invariable: four categories of Support activities, and five of Primary activities;

there can be any number of firm-specific activities at this level;

there are no lower levels.

analysis. The information that a value chain model contains could be conveyed just as logically (and, some may find, less confusingly) in a hierarchical format.

Links between Activities

Much of the benefit of any business model comes from its intelligent sorting out of activities. A model based on hierarchy makes certain relationships very obvious. But some important links (relationships, associations etc) between activities cut across the hierarchy. That is the problem for any hierarchy-based model.

Porter's text stresses the indubitable fact that it is often important to recognise links between activities (eg if activity A is done badly, this will have bad consequences for activity G), and people sometimes talk as if the value chain were a particularly useful way of *modelling* such links. There are four kinds of link to discuss:

- Links between two or more activities within the same category (out of the nine). The value chain model has no underlying thesis about these links and does not show them.
- Links between primary activities in adjacent categories. By and large, most links from a primary activity to another one outside its category will be to one in the adjacent category. There is no thesis that *all* such links are to an activity in an adjacent category, and the actual links between specific activities are not shown.
- Links between primary activities not in adjacent categories; eg the quality of inspection of finished goods (an activity in the outbound logistics category) may well be linked to (ie have some effect on) repair (an activity in service, which is not the adjacent category). A value chain model does not record this link.
- Links between support and primary activities. If an activity is designated as support, this means (on the whole) that it has a richer pattern of linkages with other activities than if it were primary. But that is all. A value chain model does not claim to show *which* other activities a certain support activity is connected with.

It is, of course, entirely possible to draw a line between two activities whose linkage you want to stress, but then you can draw such lines between activities on any lind of model — plain hierarchy or Anthony or any other. There is very little substance to any claim that value chain modelling is *particularly* concerned with recognising and modelling links.**5**

The Role of Business Models

How can a value chain model or any other type of business model assist IM decision-making? Though Porter's book doesn't show this specifically, it is easy enough to draw analogies with his uses. The boxes of a model (either corresponding to specific activities or to the nine categories) can be used to convey:

- **hard quantitative** information on each activity, such as the amount of current IT spend, or the IT spend per employee, or IT investment in currently running systems, etc;
- **soft quantitative** information, such as the extent to which each activity is automated (inevitably an impressionistic assessment, but in some circumstances useful), or the scoring of users' satisfaction with the existing IT systems associated with each activity, etc;
- **verbal** information, brief phrases recording perceived weaknesses or key factors in the way IT is associated with each activity;
- **ideas**, especially for new uses of IT associated with each activity.

In summary, the typical business model, whether a value chain or not, serves two main, overlapping roles: as a base layer on which other detailed information can be superimposed; and as a stimulus for new ideas. These are both useful ways of furthering decision-making, but trouble can arise if their force is exaggerated.

For one thing, it is usually not valid to argue very forcefully: 'This model, shaded to show IT spend on each activity, proves that we *must* . .' That shaded model may provide one piece of evidence pointing in a certain direction, but then another version of it shaded to show some other variable may suggest a different conclusion. Again, it seems naive to expect that having a model will make all the difference between finding many creative ideas for use of IT and finding hardly any.[6]

Variant Modelling Methods

The plain hierarchy method of modelling can scarcely vary, without turning into something entirely different, but a non-standard variant of an Anthony model is easily possible: it could accept the first premise about ranking activities from mundane to strategic, but, varying the second premise, it could divide the ranking scale into four bands rather than three. It is difficult to see how anyone could credibly maintain that this was *never* a sensible thing to do; there must surely be some conceivable situations where the four-way analysis could be more useful.

The most obvious way of making a non-standard variant of a value chain is to accept all the premises and clarifications given above, except the concept that there must always be nine invariable categories to contain the specific activities of the business. A model of a night-club (or lifeboat service or monastery or art gallery etc) might be given (say) three support and seven primary categories, all defined in the way that seemed most natural for the organisation. Such a model might well be a more convenient base layer for further information and a better stimulus for ideas. This does go directly against Porter's claim that his nine categories are invariable for all businesses. However, since he gives no evidence for the claim and there is no apparent penalty for ignoring it, this need be no problem.7

Other variants of the underlying premises of value chain modelling can be found. For example:

- People sometimes make models with a variant interpretation of the primary-support distinction. Primary is interpreted directly as more important, roughly in the sense of 'has a bigger potential for triumph or catastrophe'.
- Another more sweeping approach is to set up the categories (or perhaps only the primary categories) so that each category's bundle of activities is as discrete an entity as possible. The network of links between categories is made as sparse and neat as possible. Moreover, it should be possible to assemble financial information (such as a profit and loss account) about each category as if it were a formal business unit, without making too many arbitrary assumptions about allocations of overheads, transfer prices etc.8

Variants of this kind will illuminate different facets of the organisation. To advocate one specific modelling method (Anthony, classic value-chain or any other) as *generally* applicable is to claim that the particular facets of an organisation that the method is good at describing are those which are *usually* the most helpful as a base layer for further information and as a stimulus for ideas. This is not credible.9 Any of the methods and variants above could be the best way to go in any particular case. Moreover, if you really need a model that concentrates on (say) how data flows and is shared between activities, or how activities happen in parallel, or how they happen in cycles, or how feedback occurs between activities, then you need some modelling method entirely different from those described in this briefing.

NOTES & ARGUMENTS

1 'Business' and 'organisation' pose a minor problem. 'Business' is a briefer and more vivid word, but 'organisation' confirms that whatever is said applies to government ministries, charities, professional societies and other bodies that are not commercial enterprises. The 'business modelling' discussed in this briefing is generally meant to be relevant to any kind of organisation. This book (like most others on IM) chooses whichever word seems best in context, but, on any occasion when it really matters, makes the distinction explicit.

Also, the entity being modelled may be a business unit (eg a hotel chain) rather than strictly a whole business (eg a conglomerate with interests in hotels and many other industries). This rider, too, should be understood, except where it is specifically modified.

The example of a plain hierarchy model is from Synnott (pp. 234-5).

2 The account given in the briefing text coarsens the ideas RN Anthony set out in 1965. An Anthony model is really supposed to include only management activities (planning, controlling etc), not those activities that *are* managed. But management consultants often interpret the notion of operational control so broadly that it includes such activities as taking customer orders or issuing stock from stores. Hardly anybody goes quite as far as treating the activities of cleaning the floors or serving in the canteen as operational control, but then these things are not normally needed in a model anyway. Thus in practice, and particularly in insurance companies, government ministries and such places, an 'Anthony model' usually does include all activities of any interest. There is nothing to stop the purist adopting tighter criteria and excluding many activities from the model, but this is unusual. The point is discussed in Lewis's book, pp. 111-4.

3 Michael Porter, inventor of the value chain, is currently the most honoured management thinker in the world. But it does not necessarily follow from this that he is a *clear and careful* thinker.

● *Competitive Advantage — Creating and Sustaining Superior Performance* (The Free Press, 1985) talks a great deal about value activities. What other kinds of activities exist then, besides value activities? None; at one point the text makes it plain that all the activities of a business are value activities. Thus the value in value activity is a meaningless noise-word.

● Any intelligent student of Porter's work is bound to wonder what is meant by competitive advantage as opposed to any other type of advantage. Is competitive a noise-word like value or not? This isn't made clear, and *Competitive Advantage* doesn't define competitive advantage. The term first appears in a sentence: 'competitive advantage grows fundamentally out of . . ' Soon after, strategies for achieving competitive advantage are presented. But to say that X grows out of something and to give strategies for achieving X are not to define X, nor to explain how X differs from other concepts. In Porter's other main book, *Competitive Strategy — Techniques for Analyzing Industries and Competitors* (The Free Press, 1980) the term 'competitive advantage' seems never to be used; there is a near-definition of 'competitive strategy' (p. xvi), but that is so broad as to make the qualifier 'competitive' redundant.

● Value chain is what Porter calls the whole model of a business. The name has certainly caught on, but, as the analysis in this briefing shows, a nine-part value chain model is not remotely like a chain.

These things matter. It is difficult to follow any book's argument when uncertainties of this sort are constantly hovering, some of them never to be resolved. Moreover, other people, influenced by Porter, do sometimes talk as if there were a distinction between value activities and other types of activities; or assume a distinction, without defining it, between IT systems that bring competitive advantage and those bringing other advantages; or use the term value chain to refer to just one particular portion of the model that is indeed more chain-like the rest.

Competitive Advantage does not claim to be a book about how to make business models. Chapter 2 outlines a method of modelling; the rest of the book discusses in detail how businesses achieve commercial success; models are used in that discussion, but the modelling conventions are not elaborated further. Therefore to work out what a value chain model based on Porter's book signifies it is only necessary to study that one chapter — albeit intensively, working out which words carry meaning and which are mere noise, translating

Harvardspeak into plain language, and so on. The account of value chain analysis given in this briefing differs from that given in any other book. It is offered as the most coherent interpretation that can be made of the text of that Chapter 2. If you don't like it, see if you can make a different summary that is clear, coherent and yet consistent with Porter's text.

4 It could be argued that in the example of plain hierarchy already given the functions at one level are *decomposed* into functions a level below, but with the Anthony model, the names of the three groups really pick out certain *qualities* of the activities they contain. However, this subtle point is difficult to sustain, since anybody who wishes to regard (say) 'operational control' as one large activity to be decomposed into more specific activities can't really be proved wrong. Still, in certain cases a distinction between decomposing into pieces and classifying by qualities could be important. This book refrains from going any further into these subtleties.

5 Neither does a value chain model document the *nature* of links between activities. Some interactions between activities are bound to be stronger than others. Also, a link in the sense that one activity literally receives some *object* from another is different from a link where the quality or the cost of one activity has some *effect* on another. If you really wanted a model that was strong in documenting links, you could set up a typology of links as your underlying theses, and design appropriate graphic conventions to represent links' type and strength.

6 Is a value chain model a more effective generator of ideas for competitive advantage than a different type of model? The rhetoric surrounding it sometimes gives that impression, but its underlying theses are what count, and they don't really justify that view.

Some make implausible claims for the power of value chain analysis. Peppard, p. 89: 'The main benefit of value chain analysis is that it identifies the main information needs and flows that reflect what the organisation actually does . . ' This is not a credible judgement; a value chain is usually far too primitive a map to depict the complexities of information needs and flows.

Another point: any business model is essentially impressionistic rather than rigorous. The diagrams of (say) a data model based on ER conventions can be compared with the actual state of affairs, to determine whether the model is correct or not. The model will show quite precisely whether a part can be supplied by several suppliers or by only one — and that is either true or false. But a business model is not factual in that way. It may be illuminating or muddled, but that is different from correct or incorrect. If someone persists in finding a certain model of a business extremely valuable, while someone else believes that it gives a dangerously confusing view, there may be no factual evidence that can show one side to be right and the other wrong. This fact does not undermine the whole modelling technique, because a broad-brush, impressionistic view of the organisation may be just what is wanted in many situations.

7 'Every firm's value chain is composed of nine generic categories of activities . .' (*Competitive Advantage,* p. 34). Use the Trivial-False Fork:

- Suppose this statement is taken to mean that in every firm the activities can reasonably be analysed in a way that places at least one activity under each of the nine generic categories. This is probably true: if you analyse everything into thousands of detailed activities, then sooner or later you probably will be able to find at least one activity for each of the nine categories. But this is an utterly trivial and uninteresting point.

- A different, much stronger claim might be that in any industry the nine categories will all contain much the same number of detailed activities. But this is just not credible.
- Suppose the statement is taken to mean something less strong but still interesting: that in a list of (say) the fifty most important activities in any business, at least one activity will belong to each of the nine categories. But this too is difficult to believe. Porter himself gives the example of a restaurant having hardly anything to place in the outbound logistics category.

There seems to be no interpretation of Porter's claim that is both true and non-trivial. Therefore it can only cause confusion and is best discarded.

Generalisations, techniques and analyses in management studies are frequently presented as if valid for *any* organisation, and yet are explained and illustrated primarily in the context of manufacturing industry. Distinguish four levels of generality:

- Some generalisations apply (if valid) to any **organisation**;
- some to any **business** (aka firm or company), ie an organisation that has primarily commercial motives;
- some to any **manufacturing company,** ie a business much of whose activity is making things;
- some to any **mainstream manufacturing company,** ie a manufacturing company whose products are mainly objects that can be dropped on a person's foot (thus excluding IBM or a newspaper publisher, where much activity is concerned with the software or knowledge attached to the objects).

It is best to be unenthusiastic about any generalisation where the level of generality claimed by the author is unclear, or clear but not credible.

8 One representative approach, called the Value Process Model, is described by K Hugh Macdonald, in Appendix D of Scott Morton's book. This starts from the idea that: 'A value system is a representation of the movement of goods and services from the sources of raw materials through to the 'final' consumer. Frequently the intention is to represent the progressive addition of value as goods and services flow between and through organizations.'

In summary, the approach is to sketch out 15-30 operation boxes, corresponding to 'process elements', add detail about them, depict the interactions between them, and then simplify very heavily. Thus if, in an early draft, process element 17 has tentacles showing relationships to eleven others, they will be pruned to make a flowchart showing how things move from one box to another in a way as linear as possible.

Then, for each process element, work out costs (interesting costs, not necessarily those that would be produced by professional accounting standards), broken into: investments, input costs, process/operation costs, preincurred and postincurred (eg warranty) costs, overheads.

This approach seems to be meant primarily for a manufacturing operation, and then only if it has a very clear stream of processes: eg from forest to paper. The more a case deviates from one simple stream, the less appropriate the method is, since the more arbitrary judgements are needed about the allocation of costs between process elements. It is probably unworkable in an extreme case, such as Kamaz, the Russian lorry manufacturer, that not only makes every single component itself, but also makes the machines it needs to make and assemble the components, and further, even makes the machines that repair its own machines (cited in *The Economist*, but perhaps apocryphal).

Another problem is: Since you could probably sketch out 300 boxes, even for a simple forest-to-paper case, how do you decide on *the 30* to put in the model? The main criterion is that each box should represent 'the progressive addition of value'. But what does this mean? It could mean any activity whatsoever, since such an activity would not exist unless it added value in some sense (that is why Porter regards all activities as value activities). But then the criterion would be no criterion.

Or the criterion could be that each box should be defined in such a way that it is *practically feasible* to put a figure on the change in financial value that it produces. Suppose that for some important activity in the draft model there were practical difficulties of financial measurement. (For instance, it might be practically impossible to know the quantity, and hence value, of some chemical left over after some process, except by purchasing some specialised measurement equipment, not otherwise needed.) Then, following the criterion above, you would revise the model by splitting the activity or combining it with another, in such a way that financial measurement became feasible. Of course, this raises a number of further issues . .

The question arises: Does this method have any relation at all to value chain analysis? If the above account were analysed to extract the underlying theses they would surely be quite different from those of Porter's value chain. Value chain has really become a name like hoover or xerox: it is applied to practically any business model within a certain very broad type. Though you can tell from the badge whether a certain machine was in fact made by the Hoover company, you may need persistence and tact to determine whether somebody's value chain model is really based on Porter's underlying premises or on some variant.

9 Some business modellers are loth to concede this, but others are all too ready, and take the view that any rough, reasonably plausible business model is as good as any other, since the model is only meant as an initial sketch-map to guide more demanding work.

CONNECTIONS

5. Generic Strategies	Top-level decision-making, to which the business model may be input
7. Agenda-setting Procedures	Approaches such as CSF that mix decision-making with building a certain kind of model
29. Modelling and Deciding	Fitting all modelling (not just business modelling) into a coherent decision-making process
30. Standard Multi-step Methodologies	Fundamental issues with standard multi-step methodologies, that often embrace business modelling

5. Generic Strategies

TOPIC

IM lore offers many generic analyses — of business strategies, of approaches to change, of forms of strategic impact of IT on the business and so on. If valid, such analysis is relevant to agenda decisions.

There seem to be essentially two main kinds of ideas at this level. First, analysis of available generic business objectives may help decide what the business strategy should be, which the IM strategy should be made to support. Thus the organisation's IM strategy might aim to help achieve the overall business strategy of becoming the most efficient, low-cost, best-value supplier in its market *as opposed to* (say) radically changing the product mix, or expanding rapidly at the expense of short-term profit.

Second, there are different ways of fitting together the organisation's IM and business strategies. 'Supporting' business objective X, ie providing whatever automation X needs, may be a different thing from 'spearheading the drive towards' X, ie aiming for objectives that would be inconceivable without the use of IT, and whose shape is considerably determined by the capabilities of IT.

Some pieces of generic advice about IM are clearly of one out of these two kinds; others have traces of both. This briefing unravels them.

REPRESENTATIVE IDEAS — SUMMARISED

One firm had a clear business policy of gaining market share and increasing profits by becoming super-efficient and undercutting competitors on price. But the IT activities were not well co-ordinated with this policy. A substantial investment was made in a complicated system to provide a very flexible range of product variations. As time went by, the concentration on cost-efficiency led to more and more standardisation of product, and made the sophisticated, flexible computer system pointless. In fact, it was harmful, because its complexities added overhead that reduced cost-efficiency.

So, at the very minimum, IM decisions need to recognise business objectives well enough to avoid that kind of absurdity. A good start is to ask: What kind of broad business objectives may be relevant to IM?

The Porter-McFarlan-Parsons Distinctions

Some distinctions have been suggested by Michael Porter, the influential management thinker:1

- **Three generic strategies** are available to a firm: cost leadership (ie, roughly, producing goods or services cheaper than competitors); differentiation (producing goods or services that are different and/or more varied, and superior to those of competitors); focus (producing completely new goods or services, or variations of existing goods, or services for completely new markets).
- Also, there are **five generic forces** of industry competition: threat of new entrants; bargaining power of customers; bargaining power of suppliers; threat of substitute products or services; jockeying for position among rivals.

Plainly IT can be used to reinforce one of the three generic strategies: computer systems can be designed to make production more efficient and thus cheaper, or to allow a wider range of possibilities to customers, or to support the provision of an entirely new product. Similarly, the generic forces of industry competition can be related to IT possibilities. According to McFarlan, another authority, IT can be used to:

- build barriers to entry of new competitors; eg by making business in the market impractical without large-scale investment in computer systems;
- *or* make it more difficult for customers to switch suppliers, and thus reduce their bargaining power; eg by developing intricate IT-based links with customers for maintenance, reordering etc;
- *or* change the balance of power in relationships with suppliers; eg by setting up IT-based links to numerous suppliers, and using clever procurement and quality control systems to get best value;
- *or* menace competitors with new products and services; eg by developing new IT-based products and services;
- *or* improve competitive position relative to rivals by supporting any one of the three generic strategies: cost leadership, differentiation and focus.

Thus, as the diagram suggests, decisions of business policy, based on generic analysis of possibilities, can be tied to IM decisions in a satisfying, coherent way.

Parsons, another authority, takes the Porter framework and adds an extra level to it. IT is said to have three levels of strategic impact:

- **Strategy** level. It may support the (Porter generic) strategy of the firm.
- **Firm** level. It may influence (Porter's five) competitive forces facing the firm.
- **Industry** level. It may alter the nature of the whole industry fundamen-

Generic Strategy and IM Strategy: Decision-making Logic

Analysis of generic strategies,
forces of competition etc
- relevant to organisations **in general**

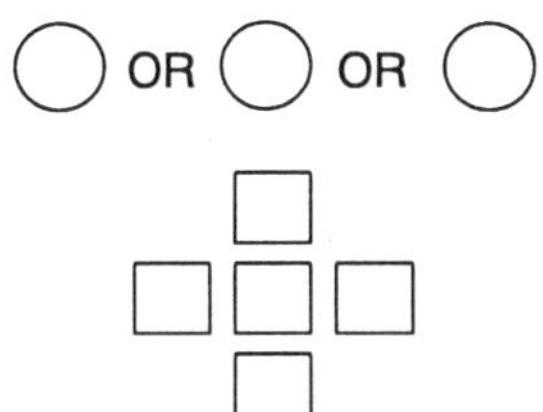

Conceivable computer applications
for this specific organisation

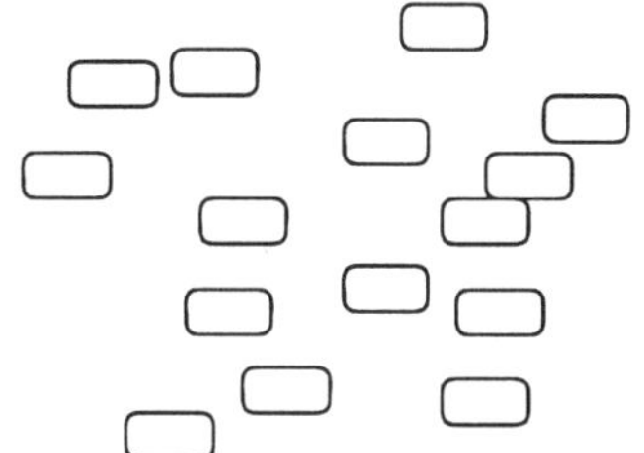

Making whole applications portfolio consistent with broad strategy,
and specific applications consistent with specific business objectives

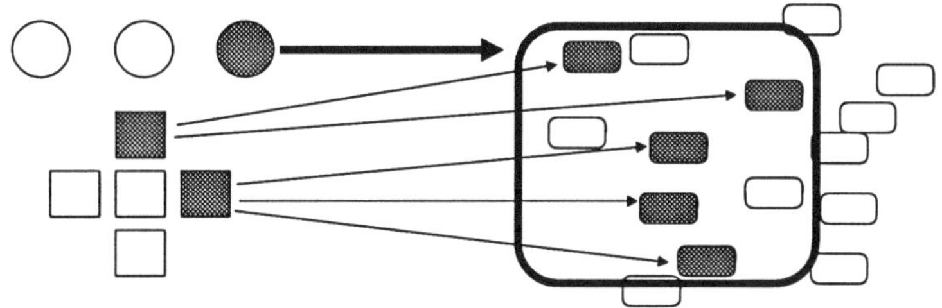

tally. Within this level, IT may cause changes to products and services; or to markets; or to production economics.**2**

REPRESENTATIVE IDEAS — ANALYSED

The main question to ask about a theory of generic strategies, or any similar analysis, is whether knowing about it will help anybody make better decisions. But an important preliminary question is whether allocation of real-life examples to one category or another is straightforward or so tricky as to become arbitrary.

Issues with Categories

Presumably one person's classification of generic possibilities can be better or worse than another's. What tests determine the quality of any proposed classification? Here are two broad criteria:**3**

● **Clarity.** The categories need to be defined so that the differences between them are fairly clear. This is a necessary but not sufficient condition. The categories must also work in practice: if many actual cases have a mix of the characteristics of several categories, then the allocation of cases to categories may become arbitrary.

- **Utility.** Even if the clarity test is passed, there must also be some point to the categorisation, such as providing insights or knowledge that are of practical benefit.

To examine Porter's generic strategies, take these examples given in one textbook:

- **BMW** integrates its computer systems for customer orders and for production control, and is able to deliver the product earlier than otherwise. Cost leadership, because more efficient scheduling means lower production costs? No, differentiation, say the authors.
- The **Caesar's Palace** casino uses IT to analyse data on gamblers, in order to identify those who spend most and offer them special free services. Differentiation relative to other casinos? No, this is classified as cost leadership, because it saves wasting money on free services to less profligate gamblers.
- **American Express** uses IT to provide corporate customers with a detailed analysis of financial transactions analysed by customer employee or other category. A completely new service and therefore focus? No, this is classified as differentiation.

As these examples suggest, the Porter distinctions don't always fare very well on the clarity criterion.

The analysis by Parsons seems to score poorly on the utility criterion. Suppose a bank is considering how to use ATM devices, or a publisher is considering policy towards authors submitting scientific manuscripts on computer disks, or an airline is deciding on the next generation of reservation systems. Why should any of these spend time wondering if the impact of the technology is occurring at industry, firm or strategy level? How could that help any of them make better decisions about the issues facing them?

Practical Utility of the Categorisation

Porter seems to assert, and others have understood him as asserting, that to be successful you must choose one of the three generic strategies to the exclusion of the other two.**4**

If true, this would make the analysis of the three generic strategies extremely valuable; you could settle on one of the three at an early stage, and thus set the agenda for IM decision-making. Subsequent extraction and comparison of options would be greatly simplified, and the whole set of decisions could be made coherent.

But why should this strong claim about the three generic strategies be accepted? Is it really unthinkable for a sensibly managed firm to adopt a set of policies, that could be analysed as 50% cost leadership, 30% differentiation, 20% focus?

Porter gives very little justification for the strong claim. It amounts to little more than saying that if you have a confused idea about what you want to achieve, and keep changing your mind, and make no attempt to do things that are consistent, then, experience shows, you probably won't be successful. This, though true, is nowhere near adequate to support the conclusion that you must choose one and only one of the three generic strategies. It is like arguing that you should always stick to one TV channel for the entire evening, since, if you switch between a dozen channels every few minutes, experience shows, you won't enjoy any programme very much. Or like pointing to some Victorian building in a ghastly mixture of styles, and saying that this kind of thing proves that a good building is always in one and only one style — thus writing off almost every English cathedral.

But if the strong claim for the generic strategies is unacceptable, what more modest claim can be formulated that will be both defensible and informative enough to be worth having?

Suppose the claim is merely that the strategy of every successful firm *can be* allocated to one out of the three categories — not because a strategy is always 100% one or the other, but because it is always *somewhat* biased towards one of the three over the other two. This claim is certain to be valid: with sufficiently microscopic analysis, some slight bias towards one of the three is bound to emerge eventually. Thus the claim is so weak as to be worthless. It won't help anybody reach better decisions.[5]

Tim Congdon pointed out in a disdainful but very convincing review of one of Porter's books that this kind of analysis is like saying that troops can be moved either by land, or by sea or by air, or saying that ships can sail in either a northerly, or an easterly, or a southerly or a westerly direction: true but scarcely likely to bring any insight that will help decide anything useful.[6]

Stimulation of Ideas

It may seem pragmatic to reason as follows: 'Admittedly, categorisation X (Porter's or any other) is quite puny, vacuous even, when examined with any care. But so what? It works. It does stimulate managers to come up with good ideas and to notice factors they might otherwise miss. Therefore you should use categorisation X — just as you should use astrology or geomancy or stroboscopic lights or even Edward de Bono's six coloured hats, if experience showed that they had the effect of stimulating managers to good ideas.'[7]

There is nothing illogical about this argument. It raises the important generic question: Does categorisation X in fact *work* in the practical sense described?

The next table gives details of two cases from Sir John Harvey-Jones's *Troubleshooter*, a sort of entertaining management consultancy TV show. Assume for the argument that this analysis is good.[8] Do the strategy options shown for these cases fit Porter's categories? Maybe that is a

Two Troubleshooter Cases

Case 1: A shirt manufacturer that seems to be in steady decline.

Option A: Refresh the main household-name brand of shirts, redesigning to acquire a new image with customers as a fashionable rather than mundane product.

Option B: Refresh the main household-name brand of shirts, by being innovative in its manufacture (using latest fabrics etc), so that retailers will recommend it to customers as a well-made, excellent-value product.

Option C: Don't alter the nature of the product (as the previous two options do), but concentrate on making it and distributing it more efficiently and profitably — even though this means downgrading service to thousands of (relatively unprofitable) small retailers.

Option D: Give up the main product line altogether. Attach its brand name to a different line of products, industrial clothing, that is smaller but more profitable. Expand and market this line hard.

Case 2: A diary-publisher, badly needing investment.

Option A: Carry on much as before — hoping to do better, of course; make profit and thereby generate capital for investment spread over all activities.

Option B: Sell the printing division; use the capital realised to invest in other activities, and thus do them better.

Option C: Sell the book-publishing division; use the capital realised to invest, and thus do other activities (mainly publishing and printing diaries) better.

Option D: Sell a stake in the whole company to someone else, to raise capital for investment spread over all activities.

question worth debating, but another one is much more pertinent: Would Sir John Harvey-Jones, or anybody else, arrive at this analysis of strategy options any more quickly or lucidly, by consciously applying Porter's categories?[9]

It is very difficult to answer 'yes' to this because of the following catch. Anybody who is qualified to operate effectively at this level is likely to find Porter's analysis far too superficial to stimulate awareness of strategy options that would otherwise go unnoticed. On the other hand, anybody who does need the guidance of Porter's analysis at the moment of decision-making is probably too inexperienced to be trusted with this kind of work.

REPRESENTATIVE IDEAS — SUMMARISED

What does it mean to say that an organisation's IM strategy is *aligned with* its business strategy? Plainly it means that the two are not grossly inconsistent. But beyond this minimum condition, there may be considerable variations. One firm might decide on a certain business strategy and work out consistent measures in many areas — including IM, along with production, distribution, marketing, human resources etc. But another might decide that IT should be the *prime instrument* for making sweeping changes to the means of production and all other activities. In other words, IM strategy may be aligned with business strategy to different degrees, or in different senses, or through different mechanisms. **10**

Parsons's 'Linking Strategies' and Other Ideas

Parsons describes *six 'linking strategies'* to 'provide the broad management framework to guide IT into and within the business'. Here is a paraphrase:

- **Centrally planned**: a central decision-making unit integrates business needs with IT capabilities;
- **Leading edge**: state of the art IT creates business opportunities;
- **Free market**: users determine needs, IT specialists compete with outside vendors to supply them;
- **Monopoly**: IT specialists have monopoly on supplying needs;
- **Scarce resource**: IT resources allocated by formal procedures, such as return-on-investment criteria;
- **Necessary evil**: IT is not used unless there is no alternative.

Sager distinguishes *six types of role* that IT can play in competitive strategy: *routine necessities*: not strategic necessities, eg payroll; *beneficial strategic necessities*: all firms in the industry benefit, eg ATM networks for banks; *unfortunate strategic necessities*: all firms in the industry are disadvantaged, eg treasury workstations provided by banks for more efficient access by corporate customers; *comparative advantage*: 'something a firm does better than its competitors, but which does not necessarily lead to superior performance'; *temporary strategic advantage*: others can follow, using readily available components; *sustainable strategic advantage*: 'an advantage which cannot be overcome by competitors', eg being preferred supplier of cash management account processing services.

Marchand and Horton distinguish *seven generic information resource (IR) strategies,* that can be paraphrased as: use IR strategically inside the company (ie either for cost leadership or for product differentiation); use IR in new and creative ways; use IR to offer a new product or service; use IR to market and distribute a new product or service; use IR in manufacturing; enter the information business as by-product of what you do; eg instead of just supplying fertiliser as ordered, provide the customer with an information service to help manage use of fertiliser and perhaps other variables to run the farm efficiently; engage in joint venture.

Later the same authors suggest *six information strategies*, divided into passive/reactive (broken down three ways between business-as-usual; defensive; major contraction) and proactive (broken down between modest improvement; aggressive expansion; radical new direction). **11**

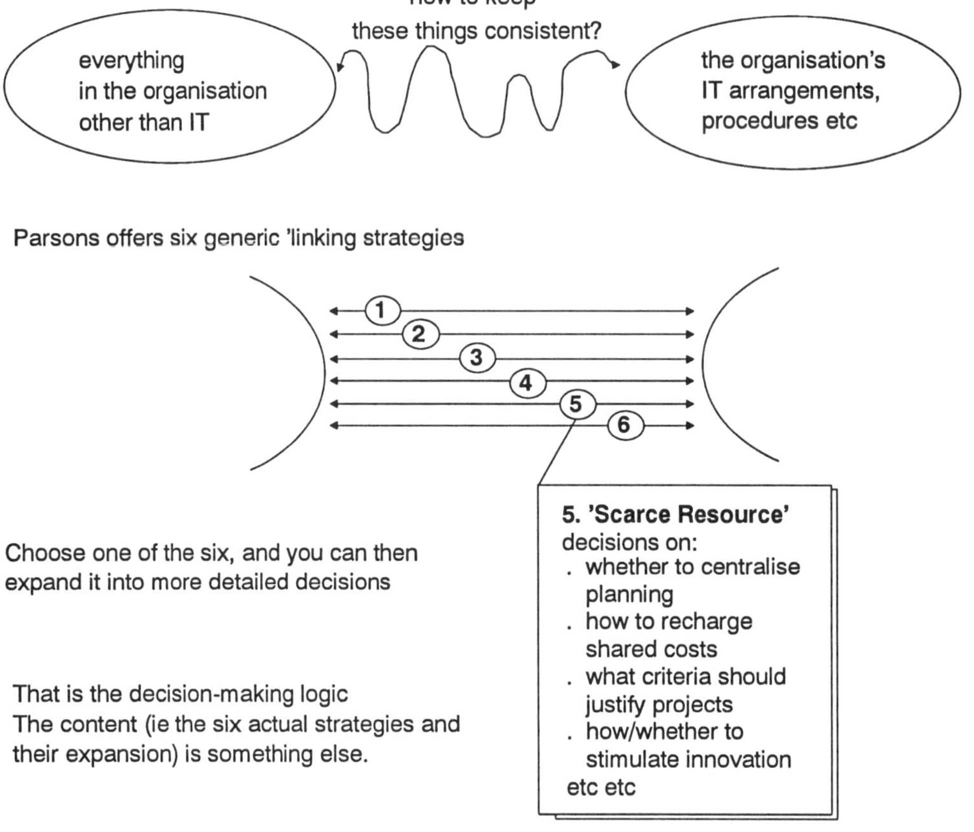
Parsons's 'Linking Strategies': Decision-making Logic
how to keep
these things consistent?
everything
in the organisation
other than IT
the organisation's
IT arrangements,
procedures etc
Parsons offers six generic 'linking strategies
1
2
3
4
5
6
5. 'Scarce Resource'
decisions on:
. whether to centralise planning
. how to recharge shared costs
. what criteria should justify projects
. how/whether to stimulate innovation
etc etc
Choose one of the six, and you can then expand it into more detailed decisions
That is the decision-making logic
The content (ie the six actual strategies and their expansion) is something else.

REPRESENTATIVE IDEAS — ANALYSED

Much of the above analysis fares poorly against the criteria given earlier:

● **Clarity**. In Sager's six-way split, the distinctions between routine necessities, beneficial strategic necessities and unfortunate strategic necessities are obscure. All three seem to share the characteristics of being things that the firm must do as part of its 'cost of doing business', but that don't lead to any particular advantage over rivals. The distinctions between comparative advantage, temporary strategic advantage and sustainable strategic advantage also seem slippery.

The seven generic IR (information resource) strategies of Marchand and Horton don't score highly on clarity either, since many uses of IT cover several of the categories.

● **Utility**. Who needs Marchand and Horton's second analysis? All it says is that there is often a range of decisions available ranging from timid to swashbuckling. Surely that is obvious to anyone.

Parsons and the Coherent Plane

The six-way analysis by Parsons is much the most interesting. The *decision-making logic*, sketched out in the diagram, is sound but the actual content is confused.**12** Still, unravelling it is a good way of gaining insight into the whole problem-area of alignment of IM and business strategies. First, separate out several different issues:

● The application of technology in a firm's systems may (in comparison with its competitors) be **innovative** or staid or anywhere between the two.

● The application of technology in a firm's systems may (in comparison with its competitors or with other industries) be relatively **fundamental** to its existence (eg airline reservation) or much less so (traditional example, a cement manufacturer).

● The **distribution of decision-making** about the application of technology (ie identifying, choosing and planning specific systems) may be highly centralised (eg a central IT planning department) or highly decentralised or some intermediate variant.

● Decisions, however distributed, about individual systems may take place within a detailed, formal organisation-wide **context** (eg organisation standards for ways of calculating cost-benefits, formal rules about procedures for choosing suppliers to meet defined needs) or none or a very limited one.

On each of these four issues choices between options are needed. Many combinations of choices are possible, though not all combinations of choices are equally credible. But the interactions between the issues are of a subtle kind. The first step towards understanding the problem is disentangling these four issues.

The Parsons analysis obscures all this. Its form suggests that one out of the six possibilities should be chosen. But they are not all coherent sets of choices. The *centrally planned* option is concerned with the distribution of decision-making issue and says nothing about anything else. The *leading edge* option is concerned with the innovative issue and says nothing about anything else. The *free market* option combines a certain choice on distribution of decision-making with a certain choice on context. The *monopoly* option is concerned with context and says nothing about anything else. The *scarce resource* option is concerned with context too, and it is unclear why it and monopoly should be treated as mutually exclusive. The *necessary evil* option is concerned with the innovative issue and says nothing about anything else.

Still, untangling this confusion is a fruitful way of gaining insight into the real issues.**13**

NOTES & ARGUMENTS

1 Opening example: Gregory L Parsons, 'Information Technology: A New Competitive Weapon', *Sloan Management Review*, Fall 1983.

Porter's three generic strategies and five forces are introduced in *Competitive Strategy: Techniques for Analyzing Industries and Competitors* (The Free Press, 1980). They are conveniently presented in Chapter 1 of *Competitive Advantage — Creating and Sustaining Superior Performance* (The Free Press, 1985). An influential article by Michael E Porter and Victor E Millar, 'How Information Gives You Competitive Advantage', *Harvard Business Review*, July-August 1985, also anthologised in Harvard (1990), sketches out some connections between the general management concepts and the use of IT.

McFarlan's expansion: F. Warren McFarlan, 'Information Technology Changes the Way You Compete', *Harvard Business Review*, May-June 1984; also anthologised in Harvard (1990).

Parsons's levels: article cited above.

2 Gerstein offers a representative generic analysis of 'competitive positioning': (pp. 43ff., a variation of McKinsey's 'Strategic Battlefield' framework)

- **head-to-head**: meeting competitors on a level playing field;
- **avoidance**: going where competitors are not;
- **specialisation**: seeking niches where one can create advantage;
- **innovation**: creating or exploiting new needs, or using technology to change the rules of the game.

As with the analysis in the briefing text, it is relatively easy to think of applications of IT that would support any of these four.

One of the oldest management consulting generalisations is the Boston Consulting Group's quadrant-diagram. This locates each of a business's *products* in a four-way breakdown:

- **star**: market share high; market growth rate high;
- **wild cat**: market share low; market growth rate high;
- **cash cow**: market share high; market growth rate low;
- **dog**: market share low; market growth rate low.

The book by Ward, Griffiths and Whitmore (pp. 54-7, pp. 182ff.) goes into more detail than most about how this analysis can be relevant to IM decisions. Their logic is that products in the same category tend to call for similar IM decisions and those in different categories for different decisions. But this seems a dubious idea:

- For a star product you might plausibly make a huge investment in improved distribution systems to reinforce its advantage. But you might do that for a wild cat too, in order to challenge the market leader. Or even for a cash cow to earn a higher margin on its apparently assured market share.
- You might well avoid big investment in IT for a dog product, because it has an uncertain future. On the other hand, you might make a big investment to improve it and hope to turn it into a star.
- Many IT investments are not directed at supporting individual products. Many systems for distribution or customer service or management information deal with a product range containing products of all four types, in the hope of improving the

worth to the business of all of them, stars, wild cats, cash cows and dogs.

According to G Johnson and K Scholes in *Exploring Corporate Strategy*, 3rd ed., (Prentice Hall, 1993) an organisation can pursue any of the following *ten generic 'growth strategies'*: do nothing; withdrawal; consolidation; market penetration; product development; market development; diversification (through backward integration); diversification (through forward integration); diversification (through horizontal integration); unrelated diversification. Each of these ten may be implemented in three generic ways: internal, acquisition and joint venture. This gives a 10x3 grid (with the top row null) to map out possible generic strategies.

This analysis raises quite acutely a question hanging over most of the material in this briefing. The analysis may (or may not) be a fine way of summarising what happens in thousands of cases; but, even if it is, would it actually help one particular organisation at one particular moment to take better decisions? How exactly would it be used?

3 These are generally applicable tests of any classification — of investment opportunities, software packages, magazines, ice hockey teams etc.

The examples of BMW and others that follow are from Ward, Griffiths and Whitmore, pp. 199ff.

4 *Competitive Advantage*, p. 12: 'If a firm is to attain a competitive advantage, it must make a choice about the type of competitive advantage it seeks to attain and the scope within which it will attain it. Being 'all things to all people' is a recipe for strategic mediocrity and below average performance, because it often means that a firm has no competitive advantage at all.'

This is made more precise by an argument that one firm might have different strategies in its different parts; eg a large hotel company might own several, fairly independent chains of hotels, and they might follow different generic strategies — but only if each was treated, in effect, as a separate hotel business with its own structure and culture; thus one of them could have everything geared to being cost-conscious, and another to encouraging innovative approaches and services (pp. 17ff.).

But all this seems to be undermined by a passage (p. 19) beginning: 'There are three conditions under which a firm can simultaneously achieve both cost leadership and differentiation: . . '

Some writers on IM have boldly stressed the three-way strategic choice. Sager (p. 72) says that a firm can adopt one and only one of Porter's three generic strategies. This surely can't be meant literally; presumably, the claim is that a sensibly managed firm will adopt one, and only one. Other books (eg Peppard, pp. 54-6; Robson, pp. 50-1) just reproduce the three strategies without any guidance on what they mean for the logic of decision-making; the reader may assume that the successful firm adopts one and only one of the strategies, but the author never quite says that. The treatment by Ward, Griffiths and Whitmore (pp. 197-203) is much superior, and mentions cases where a business seems to have combined generic strategies with success.

5 Another question, easily overlooked, is: Do the three generic strategies in fact cover the strategic possibilities open to a firm? Or are there perhaps some good strategies that just don't fit the analysis?

A company might, under certain circumstances, make an intelligent decision to follow a 'positioning' strategy. Its programme of actions might include a variety of experiments with new products and ways of working, the building up of infrastructure facilities, and the rooting out of manifest weaknesses — all directed towards getting well positioned to make bold moves a few years later, should the situation then warrant it. This could be an astute strategy, with very strong implications for IT activities and organisation, and yet it seems not to match any of Porter's three.

It may be argued that Porter is only concerned with competitive advantage, and a strategy of the sort described does not count as a strategy for competitive advantage. But wait: many books and articles seem to rest on the assumption that any well-run firm is concerned above all with competitive advantage, and a strategy not directed at competitive advantage is *ipso facto* a bad strategy. The example of the 'positioning' strategy seems to show that this is false.

Since the concept of competitive advantage is commonly understood in imprecise ways there is little point in further verbal analysis. The important point to the decision-maker is that it seems not be true that an organisation has essentially three generic strategies open to it at any time.

6 Tim Congdon, review of *The Competitive Advantage of Nations* by Michael E Porter, *The Spectator*, 22 September 1990. This review captures beautifully the frustration leading to fury experienced by anyone who reads Porter's work and tries to think carefully about what it might mean. Congdon is contemptous of the abstractions that 'cavort around each other, in a clumsy verbal gavotte' for hundreds of pages without clarifying anything that really matters.

Another authority is more temperate, but perhaps more damaging: '(Porter's) ideas have had little impact on how big firms go about formulating strategy. One reason is that Mr Porter's work is descriptive, not prescriptive. His vast checklists provide little guide to what firms should actually do, or avoid doing. Every firm would like to be in an industry with high barriers to entry, weak rivals and high profits. But few are so lucky.' in *The Economist*, 20 March 1993, p. 80, and again, *Pocket Strategy* (The Economist Books, 1994), p. 5.

If valid, this criticism is more devastating than its author may intend. The analyst of ethnomusicology or historical linguistics is quite entitled to do descriptive work that is profound, subtle and has no obvious implications for things that people should do; but surely this can't be true of the analyst of management. What is the use of a piece of management science work if it doesn't help managers to manage?

Porter's work has been accorded such uncritical reverence that it is worth introducing yet one more witness: 'Generic Strategies and Congruent Organisational Structures: Some Suggestions' by David Faulkner and Cliff Bowman in *European Management Journal*, December 1992, pp. 494-500. Here is a paraphrase, with notes, of some out of the many thoughtful points made:

- Rather than talk of three generic strategies, cost leadership, differentiation and focus, it is better to identify two distinct issues: *how* to compete (by differentiation or by cost leadership) and *where* to compete (broad or focused). Since there are two issues, each with two options, there are four generic strategies.

Note: the three strategies were introduced in *Competitive Strategy* (pp. 34-41) and became irretrievably famous; the text of *Competitive Advantage* seems to concede that it is clearer to think of four (a quadrant-diagram on p. 12 shows strategies 1, 2, 3A, 3B).

- It is all very well for the academic theorist to identify cost leadership as a major strategy option, but to carry it out seriously in practice a manager needs insight into detailed costing information about the inputs and processes of *competitors*. That is usually not available.
- Porter's examples of differentiation strategy lump together at least two separate things: to offer premium quality at a premium price to a small market is one; to offer quality that is slightly but distinctly better at an average price to a mass-market is something quite different.
- Any of the generic strategies defines a stance *relative to other competitors*. But suppose, as an example devised for this book, the owner of a three-star hotel wants to choose one of the generic strategies. Relative to what group of competitors should a strategy of cost leadership or differentiation, with a broad or narrow focus, be chosen? All other three-star hotels in the same resort? All two-, three- or four-star hotels? All hotels? All forms of accommodation along the same sea-front?

Note: in the two main books this key point seems to be dealt with only in an obscure and unconvincing passage in *Competitive Strategy* (p. 32).

The article by Faulkner and Bowman offers a great deal more besides, but it is about general mananagement, not IM, the subject of this book.

7 *Six Thinking Hats*, Edward de Bono (Penguin, 1985). This identifies six modes of thought or 'hats': white, pure facts, figures and information; red, emotions and feelings, but also hunch and intuition; black, negative judgement, why it will not work; yellow, optimism, positive, constructive, opportunity; green, fertile, creative, lateral thinking, provocation (eg suppose hamburgers were made square); blue, thinking about thinking.

The idea is to switch between modes, consciously and explicitly, thus generating more variety of thought and encouraging the expression of ideas with fewer distractions of personality. For some people this may seem a much more powerful way of generating new ideas that may be relevant to the use of IT in a business than hazy analyses by business-school professors.

There is also the *placebo* argument. If coloured pills containing effectively nothing make some patients feel better, perhaps any theory from a famous business guru, even a meaningless one, will stimulate some managers to thought. The drawback with this argument is . . But no, the purpose of this book is to suggest ways of thinking about IM, not to spell out every possible argument.

8 It excludes several other tempting options for the diary-publisher:

- Scale down other activities to develop new diary-related, printed products, eg calendars, albeit conventional ones.
- Use technology to develop new products not otherwise feasible, such as made-to-measure diaries depending on a person's interests; eg for a firm's employees, individually named diaries with key dates (annual conference, firm holidays etc) already marked in.

9 The following technique is extremely useful in assessing *any* general ideas about strategy found in this part of the book, or in the *Harvard Business Review* or any locale of that sort. Have your own battery of (say) six representative cases; eg the shirt manufacturer, the diary-publisher, the publisher of scientific journals, the CD-library, the dealer specialising in Swiss stamps, and the small insurance company that nevertheless underwrites all kinds of risk other than life. Whenever you read or hear about any new idea, ask: How would that work for each of the cases in the battery? This will reveal pretty quickly how coherent the new idea is. And, if it is coherent, the quality can be assessed too: Would this idea really help the scientific publisher (or the CD-library etc) to recognise its main options and choose between them? Once you have done this a few times it becomes much easier to assess any new ideas that come up.

10 Some writings on this topic of aligning business and IT are so vague as to be worthless. One article by N Venkatraman, John C Henderson and Scott Oldach is entitled 'Continuous Strategic Alignment Exploiting Information Technology Capabilities for Competitive Success' (in *European Management Journal*, June 1993, pp. 139-148). It proposes a '. . strategic alignment model . . based on four basic concepts: business strategy and organizational infrastructure representing the business domain; and IT strategy and IT infrastructure and processes representing the IT domain.' It presents '. . four dominant alignment perspectives, each representing a 'triangle' of three concepts, covering both business and IT domains as well as internal and external domains. Each perspective is unique in terms of the driver — either business strategy or IT strategy and represents distinct management implications.'

The general idea is that an organisation should make sure it is using the right alignment perspective for its situation, and from time to time, if circumstances demand, change from one alignment perspective to another. The trouble is that the article hardly gets any clearer or more specific than that. How would organisations with different alignment perspectives make different decisions about choosing certain types of applications, or about end-user computing, or about data modelling, or about any other IM topic discussed anywhere in this whole book? Anyone can make an abstract model, but to have any value this paper currency needs to be cashable in the coin of insight into specific decisions.

11 References for this section: Parsons ideas: conveniently summarised in Earl, p. 123, and in Ward, Griffiths and Whitmore, pp. 251ff. Sager roles: pp. 75-6. (after EK Clemons & SO Kimbrough). Marchand and Horton: p. 95, and p. 189 (after Gad Selig).

12 An important principle of classifying things ('there are five types . . ', 'there are four options . . ' etc) is that the things should all be on the same plane. The following possibilities might be offered as options on the same plane: go to the cinema, watch television or read a book. But not these: go to the cinema, claim you were watching television at the time of the murder, or buy a house near a library. Issues on the separate planes of evening-entertainment, trial-tactics and housing have been brought together in a thoroughly confusing mixture. Failing to classify on a consistent plane is one particular way of falling short on one of the general tests of any classification: clarity.

13 Isn't it frivolous to knock down ideas that have been confidently published with the full authority of the *Harvard Business Review* or *Sloan Management Review* —

unless something equally solid is erected in their place straight away? Not necessarily. According to Frank Lloyd Wright, the first step towards good architecture is to denounce bad architecture, and as Bertrand Russell pointed out, articulate hesitation is usually an advance on inarticulate certainty.

CONNECTIONS

4. Business Modelling	Modelling that can provide a useful basis for debates on business and thus IM strategy
8. Culture, Mission and Vision	Concepts awkwardly mixed up with strategy, that have repercussions in several directions
9. Stage Theories	Theories about developments of the IT-organisation relationship over time
10. Learning and Historical Themes	More general themes and theories that may affect business and IT strategy
40. Strategic Systems and Competitive Advantage	More about competitive advantage

6. Agenda-setting Logic

TOPIC

In their notable book, Cash, McFarlan and McKenney describe a 'strategic grid' representing four generic situations that an organisation and its use of IT may be in. The idea is that recognising which of the four corresponds to your own situation can lead you to sensible, coherent decisions on a variety of specific matters: kinds of application system to develop, ways of organising IT, and so on. Thus, on determining that you are in (say) the 'turnaround' situation, you can apply more specific advice: 'A company in the *turnaround* situation needs to link IT planning to corporate planning in a two-way dialogue; a company in the *factory* situation, by contrast . .

The strategic grid in combination with supporting material can be quite a powerful generator of rational, consistent agenda decisions. Other authorities have suggested similar mechanisms. This briefing looks at the issues that arise.

REPRESENTATIVE IDEAS — SUMMARISED

A theory that identifies a number of classic situations in which an organisation's IT may be found can be called a *states theory*. A book by Kraemer et al describes one. Here is a paraphrase:

- Distinguish **three types of manager** involved with IT decisions: IS, departmental and top managers.
- Now distinguish **four possible management states**. IS management may be dominant in decision-making; (therefore) decisions are determined by their needs and desires; eg to use advanced technology (this is the **skill** state). Departmental management may be dominant in decision-making; (therefore) decisions are determined by their needs and desires; eg to improve the efficiency of particular departments (the **service** state). Top management may be dominant in decision-making; (therefore) decisions are determined by their needs and desires; eg to set up a company-wide database transcending department boundaries (the **strategic** state). Or none of the above may apply: eg top management is

A 'States' Theory: Decision-making Logic

An organisation and its IM are normally in one out of a certain number of generic states.

1. Decide which state your organisation is in,

2. Take the decisions appropriate to that state, on a variety of issues: eg whether to have an innovation department, how to recharge IT costs to business units, etc etc.

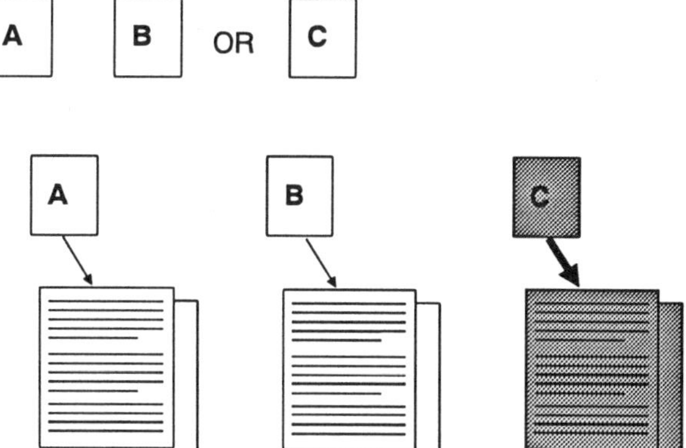

Note. It is easy enough to define a few plausible generic states.
Spelling out sensible generic decisions for each state is the difficult part.

dominant psychologically in decision-making, but the decisions actually taken are what you would expect if IS were dominant (the **mixed** state).

- At any given time, the organisation is in one of these four states. Over time it may (or may not) change from one to another. Note: the mixed state is relatively incoherent, and thus likely to change into one of the other three.
- This theory *does not* assert that an organisation changes from one state to another in any particular sequence, nor does it make any other general claim about how changes of state occur.

REPRESENTATIVE IDEAS — ANALYSED

Leave aside the question of how true this theory is. If true, how could it help with decision-making? Kraemer et al don't address the Decision Question directly, but here are some ideas about how their theory could affect decisions:

- You could take the view that strategic is normally the most desirable state and take decisions to move towards it. But this seems to make the whole thing rather trivial.
- Or you could assess the state you are in, decide whether it was the most appropriate one, and, if necessary, take decisions to shift to whichever of the other states was most appropriate. But how should you decide the most appropriate state? That is unclear.
- Presumably an organisation doesn't flip over in a moment from one

classic state to another. The current state might be (say) essentially service, with some relics of a previous skill state and growing deviations suggesting change to a strategic state. You might concentrate on making your situation as pure and regular an example of a certain state as possible, rather than a mixture. But why? What reason is there to believe that this is, in principle, a good thing to do? In any case, the authors themselves specifically reject this interpretation.

This particular states theory doesn't support decisions very clearly, but as the diagram suggests, the general idea of a states theory to drive decision-making logic is attractive.[1]

REPRESENTATIVE IDEAS — SUMMARISED

The most influential states theory is the *strategic grid* of Cash, McFarlan and McKenney.[2] The definition of four states shown on the strategic grid rests on two ideas:

- Some applications of IT have high 'strategic impact' on the business, ie are very important. Other applications are not quite so important.
- Also, some IT applications are already running and playing their intended role, whereas other IT applications are under development, being planned, under consideration or still vague possibilities.

These two concepts allow the organisation as a whole and its applications of IT to be allocated to one out of four possible states:

- **Support**: importance of present application systems low; importance of future application systems low.
- **Factory**: importance of present application systems high; importance of future application systems low.
- **Turnaround**: importance of present application systems low; importance of future application systems high.
- **Strategic**: importance of present application systems high; importance of future application systems high.

The names of these four states can cause confusion; it is best to regard them as arbitrary labels. Here is an expression of just the same ideas over again in different words:

- Technology changes affect different businesses in different ways. If there is a sudden spurt in the capabilities of (say) artificial intelligence technology, then companies in some industries will be presented with glittering opportunities for new application systems, but this won't apply to all industries to the same extent. It is naive and inadequate to talk as if IT were constantly becoming more and more vital to all organisations at the same explosive rate.
- Therefore to understand where the business is now, assess two separate things — how important IT currently is to the business, and how important IT will be. Don't assume the second follows on naturally from the first.

The Strategic Grid: Decision-making Logic

1. Determine which of these four generic states corresponds best to your situation

Importance of present application systems

		Low	High
Importance of future application systems	Low	'Support'	'Turnaround'
	High	'Factory'	'Strategic'

Note. The names of these states ('Support etc) are mere labels - and not very clear ones

2. Use that as input to decision-making about specific matters:

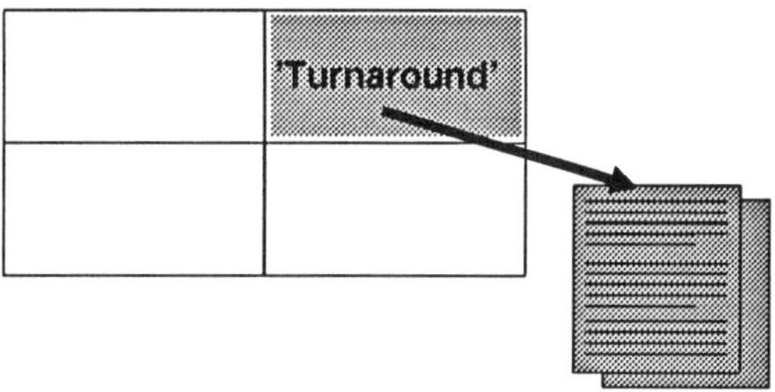

Here are some examples from Earl's book, published in 1989: a typical company in the cement industry will probably be in the *support* state; a typical steel works in the *factory* state; a typical retailer in the *turnaround* state; a typical credit card company in the *strategic* state. Since the grid is so fundamentally concerned with change in technology relevance over time, it would be very surprising if this analysis remained valid in 1999.

As the diagram suggests, the strategic grid can be a starting point for recommendations about more specific matters. A company in the support state (it can plausibly be argued) should have quite tough, internal charging systems for IT, since cost-efficiency is a dominant objective. On the other hand, for a company in the turnaround state, short-term cost-efficiency probably should not be dominant; the charging system should encourage, even subsidise, innovation and experiment.

Whether these views on charging seem plausible or not, the key point is that the strategic grid is a tool for generating decisions on agenda or context issues that transcend individual projects: whether to have a charging system, what the status of the IT director should be, how to organise end-user computing, whether to have an innovation department etc.

States, Issues and Policy Choices

State	*IT Planning Mode*	*Nature of IT Organisation*	*IT Control Mode*	*Technology Policies*
Support	Ad hoc	Back room	Project	Eclectic
Factory	Resource	Department	Budget	Conventional
Turnround	Directional	Budget	Programme	Rethink
Strategic	Strategic	Conventional	Mixed	Architectural

Decision-making Logic:

1. Determine what your state is: Support, Factory etc.

2. From that, decide your general policy on four different issues: IT Planning Mode etc.

The table shows part of a piece of logic suggested by Earl.[3] Of course, several pages of text (and, above all, simple examples) are needed to clarify the terse terms here: the differences between IT organisation and IT control, between ad hoc planning and resource planning etc. But irrespective of the value of these particular recommendations, it is clear that the strategic grid is a powerful means of giving structure and coherence to a body of ideas.

REPRESENTATIVE IDEAS — ANALYSED

The strategic grid defines the state of IT within one company (or other business unit).[4] There are two main problems:

- The whole thing is rather crude. There are only four states and one has to be chosen to represent a global, averaged view of dozens of different applications.
- The grid doesn't explicitly take account of relative position in the industry. You may correctly assess your state as (say) turnaround. Your two main competitors may be turnaround also. One is two years ahead in use of IT, the other two years behind; but the grid doesn't record that.

In later editions of their successful book the authors proposed detailed guidelines to determine the location on the grid — distinguishing firm from industry levels, production from marketing applications, and the industry leader from the individual company. Whether this produces a model whose complications topple over into incoherence, or one that is just as coherent and far more powerful, is a tricky question.[5]

This concept of using states as the first link in a chain of logic only works well if most organisations most of the time can be located in one clear state, rather than on a boundary. Otherwise the chain of reasoning can't proceed smoothly. But there is no strong reason why things should always, or even often, be that clear. Some situations may be too heterogeneous for any single-point plotting on the grid to be sensible.

One big advantage of using the strategic grid as the first step in developing recommendations on more detailed matters is that the links in the chain of reasoning are well exposed. Of course, clarity, though a virtue, doesn't guarantee sound reasoning. Still, at least there is an argument there to examine, rather than worthy-but-dull laundry-lists of points to remember, or (at another extreme) bombastic pronouncements about megatrends and the information society.[6]

REPRESENTATIVE IDEAS — SUMMARISED

The strategic grid is primarily a way of defining the state of a certain *organisation*. Another possibility is to operate at a higher level: determine the state of the *industry* the organisation is in, and go on from there to take decisions.

Earl suggests that the use of IT in any industry sector at any time is in one out of four states: *delivery* (eg financial services, airlines); *dependent* (eg automobiles, textiles); *drive* (eg food); and *delayed* (no example given).[7]

This set of four states differs in form from the strategic grid, since it is not a quadrant-analysis, but a four-degree ranking of gradations of the *current* importance of IT to the business: in the delivery case exceedingly important, in the delayed case not very, and in the other two somewhere between.

Having established which of the four states corresponds to the industry you are in, you can follow decision-making logic analogous to that shown earlier. You read off from a table which choices seem appropriate on each of many issues. On the issue 'technology management', the recommended style for a company whose industry sector is in the delivery state is 'architectural'; for dependent, 'pragmatic'; for drive, 'enabling'; and for delayed, 'ad hoc'. Of course, to be of value this would have to be supported by careful explanation and (above all) simple examples of the difference between (say) a pragmatic style of technology management and an enabling style.

REPRESENTATIVE IDEAS — ANALYSED

Earl's analysis is, in one sense, interchangeable with the strategic grid: the definitions of the four states could be used just as well for analysing individual companies as sectors.

It raises a new issue of general interest — smooth gradations. Most classifications of possibilities identify discrete items: either go to the cinema or read a book. This one has four gradations along a continuous scale. If the scale is continuous the gradations can't mark out discrete categories. So why not three gradations or five or seven along this scale? It would be easy enough to find abstract words to label each. It may be that in this case four gradations are best (ie most convenient and illuminating), because actual cases, though spread along the scale, do in fact form four fairly clear clusters. Or maybe not. At any rate, the question has to be considered.

There is another associated issue. Locating your industry sector or your own company along a four-point scale isn't like taking a measurement such as a patient's temperature. In practice, any location has an awkward, relative character. There are no recognised units of measurement of 'importance of IT to the business'. It seems unavoidable that judgements will form something like this: 'I am tempted to call our industry, magazine publishing, a delivery case, since IT really is very important. On the other hand, IT probably doesn't play quite the role in magazine publishing that it does in (say) banking; therefore I will concede that we are a dependent case.' This raises a large practical, as opposed to logical, problem. If you work in magazine publishing you probably can't justify spending time to gain an acute insight into how all the other main sectors of the economy apply IT. But if you don't, how can you use the scale?

NOTES & ARGUMENTS

1 Accepting the main three states of Kraemer et al merely for illustration, here are some plausible (though debatable) warrants that might be developed.

Should you have a separate innovation department? If in the skill state, you should have a large separate innovation department. If in the service state, you should have no innovation department; rely on the main business units to develop their own innovations. If in the strategic state, you should have a small innovation department, monitoring and co-ordinating innovation work done in the main units or by task forces.

Should you recharge IT costs to business units? If in the skill state, you should have a recharging system that effectively subsidises advanced new services until they catch on and attract critical mass. If in the service state, decisions about new system developments should be dominated by a keen, realistic charging system. If in the strategic state, then you need detailed long-term plans; therefore recharging systems for work to build predetermined systems won't affect major decisions, and are merely a matter of financial hygiene.

2 Cash, McFarlan and McKenney, pp. 24-6 and *passim*. Also summarised and used by Earl, pp. 5-8 and *passim*. Examples and recommendations mentioned in the briefing text are mainly from these sources. Earl uses the strategic grid and related styles of reasoning even more extensively and explicitly than Cash, McFarlan and McKenney.

3 Earl, p. 194. Why not discuss whether the recommendations in the table are good or bad? The trouble is that Earl's book doesn't give enough explanation and examples to show what the pregnant words and phrases exactly mean.

4 The grid has generated a fair number of confusing statements:

- 'Clearly support and factory systems can be easily bought in from software or system houses while strategic and turnaround systems cannot.' (Remenyi, p. 63). At first sight this seems an arbitrary assumption. But it is worse than arbitrary; it is nonsensical. The categories of the grid don't deal with individual *systems*.
- 'Generally the organisations (included in a certain study) tended to be in the strategic quadrant of the grid, *or moving in that direction.*' (Sager, p. 223, stress added). 'Individual firms . . are identified as *progressing* through particular quadrants: support (low, low), factory (low, high), turnaround (high, low) and strategic (high, high).' (Angell and Smithson, p. 41, stress added) Both these statements misrepresent the strategic grid. It defines four states, and asserts that at any given moment an organisation will be in one of them; that is all. Cash, McFarlan and McKenney don't say that an organisation *will necessarily* move from one state to another, and neither do they urge that an organisation *ought to try* to do so.

5 Cash, McFarlan and McKenney (pp. 18-23, 252-61). Here is an outline, showing the *kind* of approach it is:

- Assess the importance IT has to the specific business in two large areas: marketing and production. This can be done by answering standard questions: Is accurate, quick, customer confirmation essential? Are consumer tastes volatile? Does the product require a long, complex design process? Are direct and indirect labour levels high? etc etc.
- Carry out the same exercise with reference to the industry as a whole, and particularly to the leading firms. The results can be shown on a quadrant-diagram with the two dimensions: marketing — IT has high or low impact on success; and production — IT has high or low impact on success. The book, published in 1992, gives some examples: leading (not necessarily typical) airlines and banks are high-high; leading companies in the defence industry have marketing low, production high; in the retail industry marketing high, production low; in paper low-low.
- The quadrant-diagram will thus show answers to the questions: How big is the gap between this firm's use of IT and the industry leader's: with respect to marketing, and with respect to production?
- Now go through two detailed questionnaires. One is for portfolio analysis: What percentage of the development budget is spent on projects involved in cost displacement or cost avoidance productivity improvement? Do tangible benefits of systems amount to 10% of after tax profit or 1% of gross sales? etc etc. The other is for operational dependence: What are the costs of IT as a percentage of total corporate costs? Are critical systems all at one location or several? etc etc.
- The results of all the above steps taken together should suggest the position of the business on the strategic grid.

6 Silk's 150-page book closely follows the structure of a 60-question checklist. You are meant to give your own organisation a score out of 10 on each question. Then, for those questions with lower than average scores, you should devise remedying actions, and list them in an action-plan (in the terms of this book, a set of mainly agenda and context decisions). The text explains each question's import, and suggests the kind of actions that may be appropriate. Representative questions are: 'Do top managers relate IT/IS to their business thinking?' 'Do you have an integrated portfolio for IT/IS?' 'Do you know what threats your people perceive from IT/IS?'

The 60 questions are arranged as six groups of ten, but this grouping plays no role in the decision-making logic. You are not asked (say) to compare the total scores for the different groups and draw conclusions. There is no concept of a *chain of reasoning* (as with the strategic grid, or the six alignment options in the previous briefing), nor (with some minor exceptions) of an arrangement of ideas at several *levels of detail* (as with some of the techniques in the following briefing).

Solzhenitsyn's *August 1914* shows, according to one cheeky critic, what *War and Peace* would have been like if Tolstoy had not been a genius. Similarly, this checklist-based procedure is interesting because it illustrates how inadequate agenda decision-making will be if the reasoning and decisions are not bound together by some plausible unifying concept such as the strategic grid.

A flat, laundry-list structure can raise issues one by one, but is of little help in promoting a coherent set of good decisions. Take these three questions: 'Do you have the necessary formal arrangements to control IT/IS?' (group 1, question 9); 'Is your investment culture the same for IS as for other resources?' (group 4, question 8); 'Do you consciously practice benefit management for IT/IS?' (group 5, question 7). These are not three independent things: if you decide on an action to change formal control arrangements, that may well affect the way investments and benefits are regarded too; and the decision on the most appropriate control arrangements may itself be influenced by issues such as your type of applications (questions in group 2) and perhaps your views on future trends in IT (group 6). A flat list can't come anywhere near capturing this richness of structure in IM issues.

7 Earl, p. 35, p. 195.

CONNECTIONS

4. Business Modelling	Modelling that can provide a useful basis for debates on business strategy
5. Generic Strategies	Less formal approaches to top-level decision-making
21. Regular Projects	Theories analogous to the strategic grid have been used to suggest decisions at the level of individual projects
30. Standard Multi-step Methodologies	More detailed, multi-step, often multi-month procedures
31. Checklists and Weighted Criteria	More abouts checklists and structuring

7. Agenda-setting Procedures

TOPIC

This briefing focuses on two representative techniques that both imply a certain step-by-step procedure for agenda decision-taking.

The product of a *Critical Success Factors (CSF)* exercise is a certain type of model. The classic business model of Briefing 4 is normally just an input to decision-making, but the CSF model, with its choices about what is more and less important, at several levels of detail, itself represents some fairly explicit decision-making.

The *customer resource life-cycle (CRLC)* of Ives and Learmonth is representative of a number of techniques that apply a certain generic analysis of situations and possibilities — but in a more explicitly procedural style than the material discussed in Briefings 5 and 6.

REPRESENTATIVE IDEAS — SUMMARISED

The term Critical Success Factors (CSF) can cover a variety of approaches, differing in stress and in elaboration.1 This section summarises one typical, extensive version.

CSF: Representative Elaborate Approach

It is not uncommon for a CSF study to work through steps of ever-increasing detail to produce a six-level model in the form summarised in the table.2 All this detail can be drawn together into one coherent, *consolidated statement* of business information needs.

The working out of the earlier levels is bound to entail decisions about what is and is not important, but the final step of consolidating all the detail may seem, at first glance, to be mere high-grade clerical work. But that is not so:

- The six levels don't necessarily form a pure hierarchy: certain CSFs may be relevant to several objectives; several objectives may depend on the same CSF; some CSFs may share some of the same business information needs (BINs).

Critical Success Factors, One Representative Version

The entire **Organisation** is made up of several **Organisation Units**
eg finance

Within each organisation unit there are one or more **Functions**
eg manage treasury

For each function there are one or more **Objectives**
eg obtain funding on most favourable rates and terms

For each objective there are one or more **CSFs (Critical Success Factors)**
eg clear forward picture of company expenditure plans

For each CSF there are one or more **Performance Measures**
eg ability to carry out investment plans

and for each performance measure there are one or more **BINs (Business Information Needs)**
eg investment project plans and proposals

- More tricky: one CSF may call for almost but not quite the same BIN as another; one BIN may actually be the same as another, though given a different name or described differently (since a number of people will be involved in the process, and they may not use a consistent vocabulary).
- A representative BIN might be: 'marketing data covering all products, plus competitors' activity and economic factors: including data from external sources and from field staff.' But some of the BINs generated by the process may be more, and others less, detailed than this. They need to be condensed or expanded to roughly the same level of detail.
- Extra content is poured into the consolidated statement: each BIN is classified qualitatively, as strategic or control or operational; and some decisions on relative priority are made and appended to the model.

The consolidated statement together with the six-level analysis that generated it can together be seen as a model of the organisation in terms of information requirements.[3]

REPRESENTATIVE IDEAS — ANALYSED

The idea behind CSF may seem nothing but a banal injunction to decide what is important in a general way before getting on to more detailed matters. This is like saying that the way to play the flute is to blow at one end and move your fingers over the holes: true but it scarcely gets anybody

Agenda-setting Procedures: Decision-making Logic

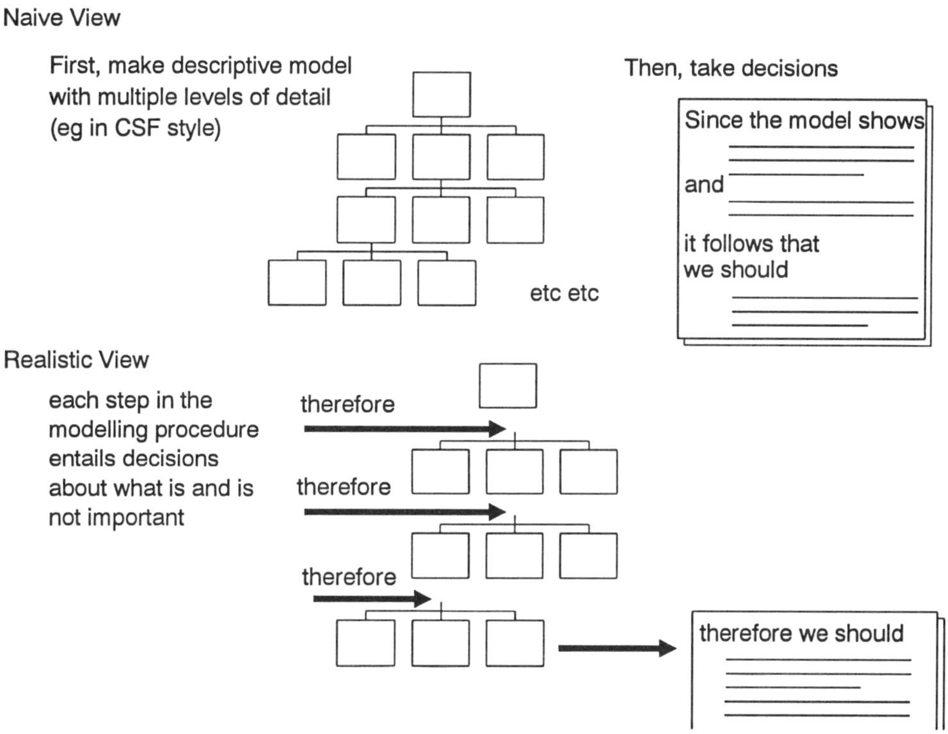

Naive View

First, make descriptive model with multiple levels of detail (eg in CSF style)

etc etc

Then, take decisions

Since the model shows

and

it follows that we should

Realistic View

each step in the modelling procedure entails decisions about what is and is not important

therefore

therefore

therefore

therefore we should

very far. CSF only becomes worth discussing when it takes a fairly elaborate form, as just described. But then some potential problems arise:

● The procedure generates 'information needs' without explicit regard for constraints. The items defined, expanded and consolidated may not necessarily be feasible, or, worse, may be feasible but a long way from a pragmatic 'best buy' choice.

● Not all information needs can be derived reliably as logical consequences of business factors, defined level-by-level; eg the information needed to support completely new products and services will be far less clear than that relating to existing activities.

● The approach generates 'information needs' but a model of information needs may not be the most useful thing for the agenda decisions required in the situation. For instance, the key issue might really be end-user computing; this isn't normally a matter of deciding what information people need, but, rather, what facilities and how organised.

● The CSF model, though detailed and not false, may still miss the main points. Perhaps there already is a marketing database corresponding to the brief description above, but it needs to be much better; eg the present analysis of competitors' activities is based on an out-of-date scheme for classifying different types of products and competitors; also it is only updated quarterly; also, it only uses general available market intelligence etc. Spelling all this out — and operating consistently at this level of detail everywhere else — could make the whole process too elephantine to be workable.

- A crucial ambiguity is difficult to exorcise. Are you uncovering and clarifying the CSFs and BINs that follow more or less inescapably from the indisputable aims of the enterprise — and therefore, in principle, would be revealed by any competent analyst? Or are you actually exposing alternatives, forming judgements, rejecting options, assessing risks and making tricky decisions about changes to the company? If the latter, then this top-down, multi-level procedure may not be the best approach. Under some circumstances, it could be best to identify *alternative* strategies, and consider them in a detail that extends over several levels of the CSF hierarchy before choosing between them. In other cases, a good approach might be to start by stimulating all *middle* managers to come up with bright innovative ideas, then sort these ideas out, and only then firm up the broad, top-level, policy-like statements to give coherence to the firm's activities.

The diagram conveys some of the impact of these points by pointing out that CSF modelling is not a neutral descriptive activity; it is itself a procedure for agenda decision-making. Sometimes that is just what the situation requires, but not necessarily always.[4]

REPRESENTATIVE IDEAS — SUMMARISED

The CSF technique normally leads to a hierarchical model. A number of other approaches also entail a multi-step procedure, but are more concerned with some *a priori* generic analysis of possibilities as the working framework. The customer resource life-cycle (CRLC) of Ives and Learmonth is an interesting example.

The CRLC of Ives and Learmonth

Here is a paraphrase of the logic and claims of the CRLC:[5]

- Any business supplies products to customers. The customer carries out various actions in relation to the product: eg deciding it is needed, ordering it, receiving it, etc.
- These customer actions fall into a pattern of 13 generic categories: 1 establish requirements; 2 specify requirements; 3 select source; 4 order; 5 authorize and pay for; 6 acquire; 7 test and accept; 8 integrate; 9 monitor; 10 upgrade; 11 maintain; 12 transfer or dispose of; 13 account for. Since these have a clear sequence, they can be regarded as stages in a cycle.
- Given the willingness to interpret terms like 'product' and 'supply' and

'customer' broadly, this model can be applied to a wide variety of organisations — not only those making goods in factories, but those providing services as well.

This thirteen-way generic analysis, dominated by the viewpoint of the customer's relations to the business, can be used as the basis for a multi-step procedure. To some degree, the procedure models the present situation, but, above all, it can generate new ideas:

- Sketch out a model of the business by giving a brief description of what happens in each of the 13 stages.
- In rather more detail, see how the scope of present IT systems relates to the model. Very likely this mapping will be rather messy; eg System A covers part of stage 3, part of 4, and part of 5; System B covers different parts of stages 4 and 5, as well as part of 11, etc.
- Apportion the weight (eg running costs and past investment) of the present IT systems over the 13 stages.
- Consider whether the material so far reveals anomalies and inadequacies: an unnecessarily complicated mapping of systems to the 13 stages, or relatively too much attention to some areas at the expense of others.
- Go further to consider each of the stages in turn as an area for innovative opportunities: 'At present we aren't involved with our customers in stages 1-3. We wait until stage 4 (order from retailer to the factory for our products). Why not get into stage 2 by notifying the retailer we think he is probably running out?'
- Bring together the ideas generated by the last two points, and hammer them into coherent agenda decisions.

Related Varieties of Model

Other people have devised generic models based on specific broad activities, that don't claim to be as general as the CRLC, but apply to a particular industry.[6]

One *logistics* model identifies eight generic activities involved in most wholesaling and retailing operations: 1 inbound transport; 2 warehouse storage and materials handling; 3 customer order; 4 order entry process; 5 packaging and shipping; 6 outbound transport; 7 inventory management; 8 inventory location. This is proposed as a basis for a procedure to develop agenda decisions in the ways just described for the CRLC.

Another model in seven steps is offered as generic for a *manufacturing* company: 1 obtain product specification; 2 design a method for producing the product; 3 schedule to produce; 4 purchase raw materials in accordance with the schedule; 5 produce in the factory; 6 monitor results for technical compliance and cost control; 7 ship the completed product to the customer.

The author of this model introduces an interesting nuance. Of course, there are more than seven activities or steps within a manufacturing company; there can be hundreds if the analysis is fine-grained enough. But this seven-way split is claimed to be the most convenient approach to *grouping* activities. Thus step 2 (design a method for producing the product) contains both 'design engineers specify the precise geometry of different parts going into the product' and 'manufacturing engineers program numerically controlled machine tools that will make these parts'.

One of the key IM issues in any business, but particularly in manufacturing, is this: Is it feasible (and if so, is it advisable) to use IT to increase the degree of *integration* between different parts of the business? Once the seven steps of this manufacturing model are seen as seven groupings, each containing many naturally related activities, two different questions can be asked about integration:

- Can two or more activities grouped within the same step be better integrated together? For instance, within step 2, perhaps the design of a part, once complete, could go on to generate the program for the machine tool (semi-) automatically. This would make work *within one step* more integrated.
- Can two steps be better integrated together? Perhaps step 3 could produce a schedule in such a format that it went straight into step 4 to generate orders; and (probably more ambitious) perhaps feedback about delayed or defective raw materials arising in step 4 could go back to (semi-) automatically update the schedule owned by step 3. This would increase the integration *of two steps*.

Besides being industry-specific, the generic logistics and manufacturing models given here differ from the CRLC in another way. They are relatively conventional: they model the things that go on within the organisation. The CRLC is more like a model of activities within the customer's organisation, in so far as they are relevant to your own organisation.

REPRESENTATIVE IDEAS — ANALYSED

This section concentrates on the CRLC, but it raises issues common to many other related approaches.[7,8,9]

CRLC: Problems and Ambiguities

Agenda decisions have far-reaching consequences. Any proposed technique for assisting agenda decisions ought to be appraised critically. Here are some problems that spring to mind with the CRLC:

- Some things don't seem to fit the model at all. What about new products? Suppose a new product entailing extensive use of IT is conceived and developed in the labs. There is a massive marketing campaign, including lavish provision of free samples to convince potential customers of its worth. Where in the CRLC do these things belong?
- Some things can only be accommodated if the definition of the 13 steps

is extremely elastic. Suppose a pharmaceutical company offers a service which checks that drugs ordered for a patient are compatible with those already in use, and have no unfortunate side-effects. Ives and Learmonth allocate this to step 7, test and accept. But this interpretation stretches step 7 from 'test that the goods delivered are what were ordered and are of acceptable quality' into 'test that the order itself is a sensible one — something that can be done without any physical delivery of goods or any checking of the quality of actual goods.'

- The claim that the 13-step model has wide general applicability suggests that it applies just as well to a customer buying a hamburger on impulse as to a government specifying and acquiring a nuclear-powered submarine. This seems rather implausible.
- Even if the 13-step, naturally sequential model works for businesses that supply physical objects, is it valid for service industries? Plainly, it is always possible to make a list of all the things that happen in a supplier-customer relationship, but why should they fit a 'life-cycle' of sequential steps — 13 or any other number? Take the insurance industry. How do straightforward, annual policy renewals fit in? What about sporadic, unpredictable claims? Recalculation of motor premiums based on previous year's claims?
- The industry may not lend itself to a model based on simple, two-way customer-supplier relationships. Any decent model of the insurance business, for instance, would expose relationships between four parties: insured, agent, insurance company, reinsurance company. Similar multivalent business relationships exist for a motor manufacturer, an engineering consultancy, a publisher, an employment bureau, and so on. **10**

Real and Convenient Distinctions

The above problems can be clarified by a certain key concept in critical thinking. If something is broken down into a specific number of separate things, there are two different possibilities:

- The analysis could be offered as factually correct: 'The European Union contains 12 countries.' This is true at the moment of publication of this book, but will very likely cease to be true soon after.
- Or the analysis may be merely convenient; 'There are fourteen main dialects of Italian.' This cannot be true or false in quite the same way, since dialects vary continuously from village to village across the landscape. Anyone who preferred to analyse this linguistic variety into five, 17 or 31 dialects could not be proved wrong; the analysis might be awkward or eccentric or inconvenient, but that is different from false.

'There are nine departments in this company' is a factual statement that may be true or false. But 'there are seven fundamental functions in this company' means no more than 'a convenient way of looking at this company is to divide it into seven parts.' This is true *a fortiori* of claims like 'there are seven (or thirteen or any other number of) fundamental functions in *every* company.'

The CRLC and similar analyses are candidates as *convenient* ways of describing a business. How should convenience be assessed? As with all types of classification, there are two main criteria of quality:

- **Clarity**. Since the distinctions proposed are not factually verifiable, almost any apparent difficulties of classication can be handled by contorting the categories; 'You say that giving out free samples of a new product isn't covered, but if you interpret step 6 (acquire) or step 2 (specify requirement) in an extremely broad sense indeed, then . . ' But in general a classification that requires relatively few contortions, and is unambiguous about which categories most things should be placed in, is more valuable than one where many contortions and much seemingly arbitrary allocation are required.
- **Utility.** A classification that provides relevant knowledge in an elegant way, and stimulates good ideas on relevant topics, is plainly more useful than one whose content is irrelevant, cumbersome and opaque.

Both these factors have to be judged from case to case. An insurance company might give the CRLC a low rating for clarity and utility. So might a manufacturer of confectionery—in a certain situation, but not, perhaps, under some other circumstances. Much depends on the kind of decisions to be taken. On the whole, the more important expansion of links with customers is, the more relevant the CRLC is likely to be. The more crucial an issue integration of factory systems is, the more appropriate is the manufacturing model. If you have already decided that developing new products should be top of the agenda, you may prefer to ignore both.

NOTES & ARGUMENTS

1 Here is a relatively simple version, described in Peppard's book (pp. 83-7):

- A number (typically 6-10) of business **objectives** are defined for the organisation; eg 'to increase market share by 6-10%'.
- For each objective, a number (perhaps four per objective) of critical success factors (**CSFs**) are defined; for the objective above, the CSFs might be: 'by improving market penetration'; 'by better identifying customers'; 'by providing a more efficient distribution system' and 'by making it easier for customers to do business with us'.
- The CSFs of all the objectives are brought together. Then an assessment can be made of what computer **systems** might support the CSFs and thus the objectives; eg 'marketing database', 'distribution system', 'access to external database', 'order management system'.

2 This comes from Tozer (example on p. 43). Unfortunately, that account is confused by use of other terms too: 'corporate goals', 'specific goals and strategies', 'key performance indicator', 'performance objective', 'quantified operational goal'. It is a sound rule to use as few such terms as possible, and to delineate thoroughly the connections between them. On the other hand, there is little point in agonising about the choice of specific terms. The key thing about the representative approach in the briefing is that it sets up a six-level hierarchy; whether its fifth level is called 'performance measures' or 'key performance indicators' or anything else is of trivial importance.

3 The procedure described results in a strongly hierarchical model. There is actually a great deal more variation in CSF-like techniques than the main briefing text, or accounts in other books, suggest.

One possibility is to be less concerned with having many levels of hierarchy, and to devote more attention to the *nature* of the CSFs; eg place every CSF in one of six categories: factors critical to all companies in the industry; issues related to the company and its position in the industry; environmental factors, eg political and social trends; company activities providing short-term problems; procedures for monitoring; building for transition through changes in business environment. This analysis might be used as a start towards modelling the *interactions* between CSFs or between other components of the model, which (the real world not being simple) probably won't fit neatly into a hierarchy. Thus a certain CSF in the environmental category might be generated by, or might be nullified by, or might itself nullify one or more CSFs in the category of 'critical to all companies in the industry'.

There is another possibility with quite a different stress. One purpose of a CSF study is to get managers to think about their organisation and discuss things with colleagues. Even so, the approach described in the main briefing text will work best (or perhaps only work at all) if each item in the model is decided by a reasonably small group of people; thus the CSFs for the treasury function are decided at meetings attended by a small group of people who know about the treasury — not by a 30-person team that sweeps across the entire company examining each piece in turn. But suppose you are less interested in getting a multi-level model agreed than in studying the *diversity of opinions* among managers about CSFs, objectives and the like. An article by A Pellow and TD Wilson in the *Journal of Information Science*, Volume 19, number 6, describes such an approach applied to a university. It shows how organisation goal A scored 12 votes out of 16, goal B 8 votes etc. It gives a matrix of eight goals against 20 CSFs, showing that six people thought CSF 1 to be relevant to goal A, two people thought CSF 3 to be relevant to goal E etc. In effect, this is a version of the Delphi technique. The natural question is: How can you move on from such statistics to arrive at decisions? There may be a good answer to this in particular cases, but it is difficult to believe that any *standard* procedure could work.

Few textbooks point this out, but a CSF study directed mainly at building a multi-level model is quite a different thing from one that focuses on analysing different generic types of CSFs and their interactions; and a study that sets out mainly to analyse the diversity of opinions is different again. These three aspects of CSF can, of course, be blended in any proportions that suit the circumstances. The important thing is to *know* that the term CSF covers a variety of possibilities, and to *decide* for yourself on the approach that best suits the particular circumstances.

4 IBM has long had a multi-step, CSF-like procedure called *BSP*. According to Robson (p. 150) BSP asks: What are the major problems in accomplishing the purposes of this business area? And what are 'good solutions' to those problems? And what role does information play in those solutions? CSF, by contrast, asks: What are the CSFs of this business area? And what information is required to ensure the CSF is controlled? But surely this is what lawyers call a distinction without a difference. The vocabulary may be superficially different but much the same issues will be examined with either approach. If you don't agree, can you describe some example case where a certain issue would probably come up under BSP but not CSF, or vice versa?

Ends-means analysis, on the other hand, is very different. For each process (eg stock management), this modelling technique identifies: *ends*, eg low stock level, subject to various qualifications; *means*, eg forecasting future needs etc; *measures of efficiency*, eg number of orders placed etc; *measures of effectiveness*, eg frequency of running out of stock. (The examples are from Robson, p. 147.) This is more involved than any hierarchical CSF approach. The four items about each process are subtly interrelated; they are not just at different levels of detail.

5 B Ives and GP Learmonth, 'The Information System as a Competitive Weapon', *Communications of the ACM*, December 1984; anthologised in Somogyi and Galliers; summarised by Earl (pp. 48-9) and (sometimes misleadingly) by other authors.

6 Logistics model: LF Pitt and RT Watson, 'How Information Technology Can Put Logistics Back into Marketing' in the Clarke and Cameron anthology, p. 223. Manufacturing model: Koenig, p. 6.

7 Wiseman's approach is widely known (see Ward, Griffiths and Whitmore, p. 212ff.; Earl, p. 58; Robson, p. 118; etc). Distinguish: three generic strategic *targets*: supplier, customer, competitor; and five generic strategic *thrusts*: differentiation, cost, innovation, growth, alliance. This gives a 15-cell grid for classifying applications of IT; eg Ford introduces quality control systems into the companies that supply its components; this has supplier as strategic target and differentiation as strategic thrust.

Wiseman's grid is usually regarded as a means of stimulating ideas about new uses of IT, rather than of analysing the whole portfolio of application systems, including the least glamorous.

8 Wright and Rhodes (pp. 82-85) describe an approach to developing agenda decisions based on ten questions: 'Question 1: What business are you in?', 'Question 6: Is your organisation capable of handling IT and the changes it infers?' Each question is meant to generate further debate; eg Question 1 leads to determining how strongly integrated systems should be. The vulnerable points of this kind of method are the jumps from answers to standard questions across to specific decisions, that consider and choose between options.

9 Keen (1992) (pp. 247ff.) describes an elaborate *Catalyst* methodology:

Step 1. Rate your organisation from 1 to 5 on each of seven *factors* (examples of the factors: senior management awareness; understanding customers' motivations and behaviour; management climate to support change). For each of the factors (if the score is low), employ three or four suggested *vehicles for change*; eg for the senior management awareness factor, one vehicle is to look for exemplars; for the understanding customers factor, one vehicle is to build customer relations databases.

Step 2. Go through a checklist of about 40 items, organised under four headings: *increase business management awareness and action* (example items: build and communicate the business vision to drive IT; provide management education for awareness and action); *(re)define business process*; *develop IS organisation and skill base*; *resolve competitive and technology uncertainties.* Score each of the 40 as follows: 1 not priority; 2 desirable; 3 urgent and vital.

Step 3. Go through the same checklist again, to answer the question: 'How can we accelerate the pace of change in effective design, delivery and use of springboard initiatives?'

'Springboard initiative' seems to be just a fancy term for 'something important and urgent'. Examples are: for an oil company, get into POS; for an insurance company, improve agency automation; for a bank, redesign demand deposit accounting system. Such possibilities exist along a spectrum, ranging from operational necessity, through competitive necessity and competitive opportunity, up to breakaway.

The weakness of this Catalyst methodology is the feeble logical structure linking the different activities together. It is not at all clear how the findings in one part of the methodology can be carried forward to help generate conclusions and decisions in another part, so that the products of the whole methodology are bound together coherently.

10 Should the CRLC properly be described as a life-cycle? The seasons of the year form a genuine cycle because winter is always followed by spring; the ages of man don't form a cycle because people aren't born again immediately after death. Talk of a cycle implies that, after purchasing one hamburger or one submarine, a customer will inevitably purchase another — and that may not be so.

If that seems pedantic, consider the following: ' . . customers perceive a company's products differently over time and . . this perceptual change is locked into a life-cycle of eleven stages', and ' . . (the) model traces how customer needs change over time. It is a means of structuring the way in which a company can optimise its investments in IT in order to be of most benefit to its customers in meeting their changing requirements' (Hochstrasser and Griffiths, pp. 11, 80). But the CRLC doesn't do those things; the confusion arises from slack use of language.

CONNECTIONS

6. Agenda-setting Logic	Milder version of multi-step procedures for agenda decisions
9. Stage Theories	More elaborate theories defining possible states and changes of state over time
30. Standard Multi-step Methodologies	More detailed, multi-step, often multi-month procedures

8. Culture, Mission and Vision

TOPIC

Vision and mission seem irritatingly vague concepts. Can they be firmed up sufficiently to provide inputs to an organisation's decision-making about IM? If so, what distinguishes a useful high-level statement of this sort from one that is futile?

The culture of an organisation may be more difficult to capture in words than its mission or vision. Moreover, culture can be a more complex factor. An organisation's IM decisions should presumably be *consistent* with its mission or vision, but with culture the case may be different; perhaps, in some circumstances, IT should be instrumental in *altering* culture. Also, mission or vision should no doubt be slotted into the decision-making process as factors at appropriate points, but culture may affect the very shape of the process.

By discussing these and similar points this briefing tries to make some progress through a thicket of abstractions.

REPRESENTATIVE IDEAS — SUMMARISED

The table offers statements taken from a variety of books and journals. How can they be sorted out?

Some writers imply that a mission or a vision or both are obviously good things to have, and avoid analysing the concepts critically. In a rare piece of analysis, one academic study recommends that an organisation should have a *corporate vision*, made up of two distinct components — its *mission* and its *guiding philosophy.* **1**

On this view, the mission defines broad, large-scale but finite objectives (once Yamaha is crushed that mission is accomplished), preferably challenging to achieve, and typically with a five- or ten-year timespan.

The guiding philosophy, by contrast, has a more enduring character; it sets up aims and purposes that have no real finishing-line (eg Disney's 'to make people happy'); this statement should last for a number of decades, a century even.

Visions, Missions and the like

A	**Vision Statement** of an insurance company	'To be the easiest in the industry to do business with'
B	**Vision Statement** of another insurance company	'To offer the customer the best value for money'
C	**Mission Statement** of a bank's IS department	'To optimise the investment across the group in systems, information management, computing and technology, while supporting the individual needs of group companies and business sectors in pursuance of business objectives'
D	**Vision Statement** of the chief executive of Otis	'Any sales person in the organisation should be able to order an elevator within a single day'
E	**Mission Statement** of Honda	'We will crush, squash, slaughter Yamaha'
F	**Guiding Philosophy** of Disney	'To make people happy'
G	**High Concept** of a film	'Giant man-eating shark terrorises island resort community'

REPRESENTATIVE IDEAS — ANALYSED

There are tedious problems of vocabulary; most people would call items A and B mission rather than vision statements. But this isn't the key issue, and, to minimise confusions, this briefing will use the broad general term HC (high concept) for all such broad, summarising, encapsulating, direction-setting statements. The interesting questions are: How can you judge the quality of an HC? Are there distinct types of HC? If so, how are they relevant to IM decision-making?

Test of Quality

First of all, a simple test distinguishes a meaningful HC, that could affect IM and any other specific areas of policy, from a meaningless HC:

- A meaningful HC could *discourage* some plausible decision that might otherwise be made. Is anyone likely to say the following? 'Options X and Y on this specific matter (such as a possible new computer system or a new way of organising IT) are both sensible options. I had a preference for X, but I now see that Y fits in much better with our organisation's HC. Therefore I choose Y.' If so, the HC has some meaning.
- If there are no *plausible* circumstances under which the HC would affect decision-making in that way, then it is meaningless.

Out of the examples above, A and B are HCs that, if taken literally, pass the test quite well:

● A could well lead to decisions on substantial investment in IT to support new kinds of insurance policy, designed to be easier for the customer to understand, or convenient, though expensive, new arrangements for taking out a new policy or making a claim. It might discourage otherwise attractive systems to invest funds more profitably or to assess risks more keenly.

● B, if serious, discourages anybody from concentrating on lavish customer service, investing in branch networks in overseas markets, developing new products, setting up a cartel etc. On the other hand, an innovative application of artificial intelligence aimed at assessing risks more shrewdly, in order to offer lower premiums to many customers, would presumably have high priority.

By these standards C is meaningless. There are no plausible decisions that it will discourage anyone from taking; a plausible decision that is not 'in pursuance of business objectives' is a contradiction in terms.

D is not so obviously lame, but it is still difficult to say with any clarity what kind of things are, relatively speaking, to be discouraged or given lower priority. And if none has lower priority, how can any have higher priority? Still, if taken seriously, D can hold some meaning: that the company will, if necessary, spend an enormous amount on computer systems and other investments to achieve the goal about ordering — as opposed to applying cost-benefit criteria to find the 'best buy' in this area.

Of course, 'meaningful' isn't the same as 'good' or 'wise' or 'shrewd', but unless an HC is meaningful the question whether it is good or bad is never even reached.

Types of HC and Situation

At first sight it may seem that HCs can be placed on different levels of generality as suggested above: finite (mission) and enduring (guiding philosophy). The longer the term and the less specific the objectives, the higher the level, and vice versa. And if two levels of HC don't suffice, then perhaps more can be used.

But at what level is A, 'to be the easiest in the industry to do business with'? This could be on the level of F, 'to make people happy' — the company's past and future immutable aim. But it could be an expression of the view that right now there is an excellent opportunity in the market for a company that competes in that particular way, and an immediate effort is needed to change the business in that direction; though, in five years time, no doubt, the market will have changed. If so, A is arguably an HC at a lower level than E, 'we will crush, squash, slaughter Yamaha' — timescale much the same, but content more specific. On the other hand, A might be intended as a kind of guiding principle through the decades, like F, 'to make people happy'.

There is a divergence of interests here. The scholar developing theories about generic types of HCs has to cope with the complication that you can't necessarily tell the level of an HC from the words it contains. But the practical decision-maker in a business can simply steer clear of generic analysis of types of HC. What really matters is that any particular HC should be meaningful and sensible; moreover, if there are several HCs, they should be coherent.[2,3]

REPRESENTATIVE IDEAS — SUMMARISED

Here is one definition of culture: 'Organizational culture is the enduring pattern of assumptions that develops as a result of successful attempts, over a long time, to cope with key problems in the external competitive environment and within the firm.' Most other definitions are also concatenations of vague abstractions.[4]

One author puts forward the following propositions:

- There are four types of culture: tough guy, macho; work hard, play hard; bet your company; process.
- In certain industries, certain of the four types are particularly prevalent, respectively: advertising; computer; mining; and banking.
- The culture of any given company is not necessarily a pure case of one type; it may be a mixture.
- Leaving aside the way a company's culture may be analysed, the strength, identity and impact of culture may be greater in one company than in another.
- It is better to have a strong culture than a weak culture in a company, because a strong culture leads to a sense of sharing in a company's mission, and that is beneficial.

REPRESENTATIVE IDEAS — ANALYSED

The ideas about culture in the previous section are vulnerable to critical analysis: What reason is there to believe that most companies in a given industry have a similar culture? Why aren't (say) a tough-guy-macho computer company or a bet-your-company advertising company normally found? What precisely distinguishes a tough-guy-macho culture from a work-hard-play-hard culture? Aren't the second and third points contradictory? If many companies have a mixed culture (according to the third point), what is the use of the four-way breakdown? And how can such general theories help anyone make better decisions about matters of IM?[5]

SUGGESTED WARRANTS

The main issue with the relation of culture to IM decision-making can be made fairly precise. Some people express the view that the culture of an organisation is: a, fundamental to many IM decisions; b, specific, complex and (therefore) immune to general principles; c, inherently intractable to the demands of rational debate. This might be called the anti-rational position. How valid is it?

Distinctions between Strong and Weak Culture

Compare any manufacturing company with any bank, and there are many differences: one has premises in busy shopping streets and the other does not; the staff wear different styles of clothes etc. But these differences follow reasonably well from the simple fact that they are in different businesses. More interesting differences are those that don't follow from some large objective factor; eg between two companies making similar products with similar success. In *company A* managers are always attending conferences and becoming known throughout the industry, while in *company B* (same industry, same turnover) the managers are withdrawn, even secretive, and hardly ever leave the factory. This is a cultural difference.

But now suppose that in *company C* (same industry etc) some managers are very outgoing, others very withdrawn and others in-between. This is a fair reason for saying that company C doesn't have a very strong (ie homogeneous) culture, whereas companies A and B both do.

Some writers assume, as if it needed no justification, that a strong culture (no matter what its nature: zany, brutal, charitable, timid etc) is a good thing, and a weak (ie not strongly pronounced) one bad. Others do offer supporting argument — roughly, that a strong culture is good, because it causes people to work together coherently, without the overheads of many formal controls and co-ordinating machinery, or the friction of bitter disagreements.

That is too simple. A strong culture may help everyone pull together strongly in the same direction — but the direction itself may be one of either success or failure. If the direction turns out misguided or no longer appropriate, or if flexibility rather than one set course is desirable, then the strong culture can be a great handicap — as with, some might say, IBM or General Motors.[6]

Examples of Defining Culture Factors

If culture covers such awkward things as attitude, prejudice, irrational bias, disposition, atmosphere, climate, ambience, psychology etc, how, if at all, can it be analysed and allowed for? Or are intuition and instinct to replace reasoned discussion?

One lurking assumption is that, just as there are two sides to the brain, so there are only two possibilities about any factor relevant to IM: those you can analyse and reason about it, and those you can't. But that

Culture Factors, Representative Sample

Company D is very commercially driven and sales-oriented. One of its competitors is also commercial, but far more people have a deep interest in the nature of the company's products and services themselves.

Company E encourages people to take gambles and, if necessary, lose money on failures; in fact, boldness is regarded far more highly than method. One of its competitors is much more cautious; there it could be fatal to a manager's career to be associated with a failure.

In **Company F**, every manager is only as good as the latest monthly results. Managers in a competitor, by contrast, take pride in being ready to spend money on things with difficult to quantify, long-term benefits.

At **Company G**, the Birmingham factory is accorded high prestige by everyone; this is far out of proportion to its actual importance or performance. At one of its competitors prestige is awarded on much more objective criteria.

At **Company H** there is always great tension between people in staff functions and others at head office on the one side, and bosses of subsidiaries and branches on the other. At one of its competitors, these relations are far more harmonious.

At **Company I**, despotic board-members all have timid, mediocre managers below them, and both sides know this, and know the others know. At one of its competitors, gradations are far smoother.

Company J is keen on creative tension between managers and between organisational units; people relish a hard bargaining session whenever resources have to be allocated, and enjoy the feeling of being in a toughly run company. One of its competitors, on the other hand, encourages a more relaxed, collegiate atmosphere.

Company K sets great store by measuring and quantifying as much as possible — far beyond merely keeping basic accounts. One of its competitors is sceptical of that kind of thing.

Company L prides itself on investing far more than the industry-average on infrastructure items such as smart, spacious offices and lavish training facilities. Another company in the industry is proud of being a lean operation that never wastes a penny.

At **Company M**, there is a strong tendency to do things by consensus. One of its competitors, on the other hand, tries to keep the credit or blame for everything as narrowly focused as possible.

At **Company N**, people move between departments a great deal, and build up connections with others outside the formal structure. At one of its competitors, the patterns are much neater and more stable.

At **Company O**, there is kudos to be gained by proposing something that is wayout, up to the minute or the latest craze. At one of its competitors, it is just the opposite.

isn't so; there is really a continuum. At one extreme are questions that can be analysed rationally in detail (eg what it really means to say that two systems are integrated, as opposed to merely connected together); at the other is a massively vague concept such as the 'work hard, play hard' culture mentioned above. But, as the table suggests, most of the cultural factors relevant to any particular case fall between these extremes, and therefore can be discussed. (A valuable technique is to clarify the definition of any culture factor with a simple example of what it is not.)

Charting Factors, Problems and Approaches

Once defined, how can such factors affect agenda decisions? As a start, ask three basic questions. Is the state of affairs represented by the factor a good or a bad thing? Can it be accentuated or reduced? Should it be accentuated or reduced? Other more involved questions spring to mind in specific cases.

If, for instance, *company D's* sales-driven culture seems a good thing, that is a strong reason for making strategic decisions about IT systems that reinforce it; maybe this cultural factor will even suggest new IT opportunities not open to other companies with different cultures. But perhaps the more balanced approach of competitors seems better, and perhaps company D managers are beginning to realise this; then it is time for a change of emphasis, and IM agenda decisions can speed up that change.

That is a relatively easy case. Suppose *company E's* risk-taking culture is actually harmful on any objective view — and yet it certainly can't be changed overnight. Then the shrewd way may be to use the politician's trick of saying one thing while doing the opposite: give publicity to some glamorous but low-cost, high-tech projects, while quietly making the main agenda a consolidation of existing systems.

Suppose that at *company F* the bias towards short-term performance measurement happens to be directly contrary to effective use of IT. The firm needs to make a commitment that runs counter to its culture — investment in a telecoms infrastructure, with no short-term payback at all. De Gaulle with Algeria and Nixon with detente were able to lead their followers through radical changes of policy. At company F the best way to push through the right policy may be to put somebody in charge of it who has hitherto been noted for infuriating short-termism. That is still a decision that can be taken rationally by weighing up the factors.

But there can be a more subtle difficulty. At *company G* it can fairly be said that the high prestige of Birmingham is one factor and the irrationality of that prestige is a second factor. But suppose a consultant's presentation includes a slide listing these two things, among others, as relevant factors in the decision-making calculus. However convincing the reasoning, the people from Birmingham may become sullen and unco-operative. The same factor applies even more strongly to the *companies H and I.*

Such examples demonstrate an important truth. Cultural factors in IM have an awkward characteristic: they are some of the pieces of the puzzle to be solved (along with others such as market opportunities, the capabilities of certain technologies etc), but they also *affect the shape of the approach* to the puzzle-solving. The decision-making process has to meet two objectives, that may be in conflict: to do justice to all the relevant factors (including the cultural factors) of the situation itself seen as a puzzle, *and also* to do justice to the social and cultural factors that surround decision-making — people's desire to be involved, their sometimes irrational opinions about what is relevant, resentment at being sidelined etc.

Compromise is often needed. Exclusive concentration on sensitivities is usually going too far, except perhaps in cases where the strategy issues themselves are quite trivial. Taking a pure puzzle-solving approach, without worrying much about people's sensitivities, is rarely advisable, except perhaps in certain crisis situations. To be slightly inefficient in solving the puzzle itself, while skating on thin ice a little, socially and culturally may be the least-bad approach in other cases.[7]

NOTES & ARGUMENTS

1 The study, by James Collins and Jerry Porras, is discussed shrewdly in 'The vision thing', *The Economist*, 9 November 1991, p. 75. The examples in the table are from: Keen (1991), pp. 31f.; ditto; Earl, p. 122; Earl, p. 108; *The Economist*, above; ditto; Gerstein, p. 40. For more of this kind of thing, see these sources and also Ward, Griffiths and Whitmore, pp. 153-4, and Robson, pp. 20-22.

2 There is also a kind of simple/subtle distinction between HCs. Compare two countries, A and B, each with a loss-making rail system. Each has the very general objective of becoming a financially healthy rail system, where income and expenditure are at least roughly matched.

- The directors of *rail system A* adopt a strict financial approach: they assess carefully which lines are profitable, what ticket prices the market will bear and so on, using sophisticated financial models. They take decisions about investments, services and prices on that basis.
- But the directors of *rail system B* reason as follows: 'In the long term we will *never* be financially healthy, no matter what services and prices we offer, unless we can get a substantial number of people who own a car to regard the train as a credible means of transport. Obviously, that depends in part on objective factors (having trains go where people want at acceptable prices), but it is also a question of image: people must be led away from the perception that train is less pleasant and less convenient than car. That is our real HC. It will lead to things that the cost accountants at A would never sanction: eg offer phone facilities in trains, at loss-making rates no greater than those of a car phone; spend a

ridiculous amount to ensure spotlessly clean carriages; offer subsidised taxi schemes to link up with trains; even offer a frequent service on many lines at a loss, so that people know that, even if they don't consult a timetable, they will never have to wait long for a train.'

Plainly, A has a very simple HC, to break even financially, and more detailed policies follow from that in a natural way. B has a more subtle definition of aims at HC level, from which detail can follow.

This difference can easily affect IM policy. A will never authorise a new nationwide information system for travellers, unless it can be cost-justified (though its techniques for modelling the costs and benefits will no doubt be very sophisticated). B, on the other hand, will relish the chance to invest in such a system without obvious financial return, perhaps with refinements that are not strictly necessary (high-resolution images of tourist attractions, or integrated information about current theatres and art exhibitions, say), provided the system seems modern and glamorous, and thus fits the HC.

Of course 'more subtle' is not *per se* 'better'; B's HC might still be based on a foolish analysis of its situation.

3 Core competency is a related notion that seems to offer the prospect of determining top-level policy. It was introduced in an influential article 'The Core Competence of the Corporation' by CK Prahalad and G Hamel, in *Harvard Business Review*, May-June 1990. Here is its line of thought, translated from the Harvardspeak.

If the activities of any company are broken down, then many of them are things that the company doesn't do exceptionally well, and/or things where there just isn't much scope for doing things exceptionally well, and/or things that even if done exceptionally well, would gain little advantage. But there will be some things that, provided the company is a successful one, *are* done exceptionally well and *need* to be done exceptionally well, and, if done *even better*, could be very advantageous: these are the core competencies (CCs). Thus for (say) Honda, making engines is a CC, but making car-seats or running an efficient staff canteen are not.

This CC concept may seem an attractive way of firming up high-level policy that will guide IM decision-making. How does it work out?

Obviously, you need to have some CCs, otherwise there will be no reason to expect your business to prosper. And it is desirable that your CCs can't be imitated or surpassed easily. And you should not be dependent on too many CCs, because that is risky and diffuses your effort. And it is sensible to invest in and improve CCs, rather than less significant things. And if one business unit is very strong in a certain CC, it is probably worth getting other business units to profit from that CC too — even, to some degree, at the expense of reducing their autonomy. The trouble is that if you try to go beyond these platitudes to develop implications for IM decision-making, nothing very satisfactory emerges.

Though the CC concept leads nowhere very special, it does provide a good focus for some critical thinking.

First, nobody can get hold of an abstract concept like this without clear, simple examples. The article says that five or six CCs is a good number for an organisation to have, but it only mentions three of Canon's and one of Honda's. Anyone who wants to urge the concept of CCs should offer as illustrations *the* five or six CCs, for each out of (say) six organisations in a variety of industries and circumstances. Many other management fads are vulnerable to this line of criticism.

Second, there is a crucial ambiguity about the authors' assertion that five or six CCs is a good number, while, if you identify 20 or 30, they are not really CCs. To see this, consider the *granularity* of analysis. For a scientific publisher, maintaining a prestigious reputation in the scientific world might be one CC; but this seems so fundamental that it is impossible to find four or five other CCs that are both distinct and of comparable weight. You could perhaps split the prestigious-reputation theme into three CCs: maintaining good relations with scientist-authors, keeping a good portfolio of scientist-referees, and maintaining good relations with academic institutions. But at this granularity, probably more than five or six CCs can be found. In any event, it is clear that the number of CCs depends on the granularity of the analysis.

Does the assertion about five or six CCs mean that you can analyse *any* organisation (no matter how diversified or unified, no matter how well or badly managed), and you can always identify *the* five or six most important things about it? This must be true: you can adjust the granularity of analysis until five or six is the number of CCs you have: merge two CCs together under some broader heading, or split one into two narrower CCs etc. But then, like others that are always bound to be true, the assertion is entirely trivial and uninteresting.

Or is it claimed that CCs are discrete things that a competent analyst can pick out and count (none, three, seventeen, forty-one etc), and healthy organisations usually have five or six, while unhealthy ones have fewer or more? This claim is far from trivial, but is only viable if accompanied by some clear statement of the granularity of analysis that should be applied consistently across all organisations. And it isn't. Many other techniques for analysing businesses, besides CCs, are vulnerable to this line of criticism.

A final complaint: as so often, a new idea in management is introduced with examples from manufacturing industry, and the reader is left to work out how or whether the idea applies to other types of organisation. This is strange since one commonplace of management lore is that manufacturing is becoming ever less important, relative to other sectors, in the information age.

The above notes criticise a concept in general management theory, rather than IM specifically. In practice, those general management theories that are worthwhile usually help with IM agenda decisions, and those that are trivial do not.

4 Gerstein, p. 28. Another, wider, definition is: 'Culture is the collective programming of the mind which distinguishes the members of one human group from another.' (Geert Hofstede).

Here is one way to get a firmer grip on the slippery concept of culture. Treat *cultural differences* as the differences that survive after obvious, *objective differences* are accounted for. The difference between the experiences of eating a hamburger and a pizza are explained by objective differences in their constituents producing different flavours. But compare eating hamburgers at McDonald's in Moscow and New York. Objectively, there may be little difference (same taste), but there is a big difference of another type: in Moscow the experience is a status symbol, and in New York it is a quick way of assuaging hunger. This kind of difference can be labelled cultural.

As Essinger mentions (p. 118), the emphasis in Japan on paying for goods in cash is cultural: there is no decisive, objective reason for it.

Another instance has been done almost to death by French structuralists. There are ample objective features to distinguish boxing from golf, but boxing and wrestling are objectively quite similar: both involve fighting in a ring. However, there are striking cultural differences: boxers try not to show pain, the rules are enforced, and fights are not normally fixed; wrestlers exaggerate pain to thrill the crowd, breaking the rules is normal, and fights are often arranged spectacles rather than straightforward contests.

The four-way analysis of culture in the main briefing text comes from Winfield's book, p. 147.

5 A slightly more coherent analysis of organisation cultures appears on pp. 114-5, *Managerial Decision Making* by Alan J Rowe and James D Boulgarides (Macmillan, 1992). There are four categories of culture: quality (accepts change); creativity (initiates changes); productivity (resists change); co-operation (supports change). Questions flood in. Is it meant to be a neutral account of four possibilities? If so, why are some described in terms that seem more favourable than others? But there is a more fundamental issue: even if valid, how would this abstract analysis help anybody to take decisions about specific matters of IM in any organisation? Something more is needed than vague exhortations to avoid clashes of culture.

You could, in principle, devise a quadrant-diagram of culture possibilities, as a starting-point for more specific decision-making. You might be able to show that type-A companies should handle experimental, innovative projects (or any of dozens of other IM issues) in a certain way, while for type-B companies something else was appropriate, and so on. Unless something of this sort is sketched out, the abstract categorisation of culture has little practical use.

For a brief roundup of conventional ideas on culture, see *Strategic Decision-Making* by Chris Gore, Kate Murray and Bill Richardson (Cassell, 1992), chapter 3. This contains the statement (p. 58): 'Deal and Kennedy . . estimate the cost of a culture change to be between 5 and 10 per cent of the budget.' Isn't this an absurdly precise estimate of something utterly vague?

6 Loyalty is a different strand in this tangle. Some people imply that a strong culture generates loyalty, and thus low turnover of core staff, and is thus beneficial. But this is not an impressive argument. Whether a strong culture generates beneficial loyalty surely depends on the culture. A company with a strong culture best described as 'ruthlessly profit-driven' might for that very reason have greedy, selfish staff, always looking for a chance to leave and make more money. Conversely, with an immensely strong culture best described as ultra-conservative . .

7 At company L, whose managers relish hard bargaining, the ideal production control system, as conceived by the factory's managers, is judged by the IT people to entail an exorbitant level of investment. But a standard package suggested by the IT people is unacceptable to the factory managers. A prolonged series of bargaining encounters ensues, with much moral blackmail, expressions of pique, accusations of lying, pitiful pleading and similar low behaviour.

That is fine within the culture of L, and it leaves no lasting scars. But it would never work at M, where managers set great store by measuring and quantifying as much as possible. They would approach the same problem by setting up detailed spreadsheet models, generating cashflow forecasts for alternative solutions under a variety of assumptions, and using that data to find the most favourable return on investment.

It might be shown that one approach or the other is objectively better, but the debate is rather sterile. Since decision-making problems don't exist in isolation from specific organisations, the requirement in every case is to find the approach which works best within the culture concerned. This is another reason to be wary of standard methodologies.

CONNECTIONS

5. Generic Strategies	Top-level decisions that may interact with culture, mission and vision
30. Standard Multi-step Methodologies	Methodologies that use mission and vision variously in a multi-step structure
35. Change Management	Broad issues of change management — unavoidably associated with culture

9. Stage Theories

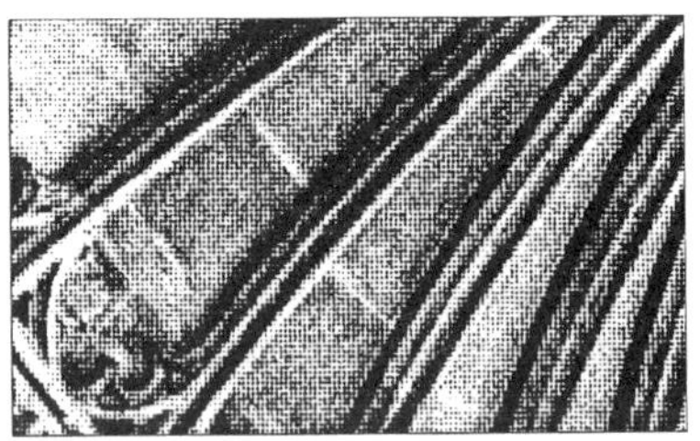

TOPIC

A typical stage theory asserts that an organisation's use of IT develops through a number of definable stages, and describes the characteristics of each stage from a number of angles: the type of systems developed, the organisational arrangements, and so on.

There are two main varieties: general stage theories about any organisation's use of IT as a whole (Nolan's is the best known); and stage theories with similar logic, but specialised — about organisations in a particular industry (say) or about some particular problem area.

These are among the most elaborate theories to be found in IM literature, but to have value to the practical manager or consultant, they should assist decision-making. For example, perhaps knowing that you are at a certain stage can help you take certain decisions appropriate to an organisation at that stage.

Learning the detail of any particular theory is not the best investment of effort. It is more worthwhile to get a grip on the possibilities and pitfalls of this genre of theory *in general*. This briefing summarises and discusses representative theories, in order to suggest how to appraise any stage theory or related form that you may come across.

REPRESENTATIVE IDEAS — SUMMARISED

Nolan's stage theory has appeared in several versions, but its most widely used form was defined in an article in the *Harvard Business Review* in 1979.[1] Here is a synopsis of its main elements:

● To describe the state of an organisation's IT at any time, it is useful to analyse four distinct dimensions (dimension is a less congested term than Nolan's 'growth process'): applications portfolio (roughly, the kind of application systems in action), DP organisation (roughly, how DP people with different specialisms are organised), DP planning and control (eg how formal or lax) and user awareness (eg the feelings about IT, and the degree of accountability for systems of the non-IT people in the organisation).

- Six distinct stages can be distinguished in an organisation's use of IT: stage 1 Initiation, stage 2 Contagion, stage 3 Control and so on . . .
- As the diagram suggests, the six stages can be defined in terms of the four dimensions. Thus an organisation at stage 2 will typically have a certain type of applications portfolio, a certain type of DP organisation and so on . . A typical stage-3 organisation will have a different type of applications portfolio, DP organisation and so on . . Take the dimension of DP planning and control, for example: at stage 1 this will be 'lax'; at stage 2 'more lax'; at stage 3 'formalized planning and control' . . .
- An organisation will move from stage to stage without ever regressing to an earlier stage. It will not necessarily remain for the same length of time in each stage, nor proceed through the stages at any particular speed.

These are the main elements of an elaborate theory. The article itself contains more details and nuances; eg superimposed on the model of the six stages and four dimensions is a curve plotting an organisation's level of DP expenditures; but practically nobody takes this seriously any more.

REPRESENTATIVE IDEAS — ANALYSED

Nolan's theory is given in many books about IM. It is often presented with enthusiasm, as if self-evidently valuable. Even so, the theory can't be said to be well proven. One journal article summarised eight different studies of the theory by other researchers into more than 600 firms in total; the verdict of two of the eight studies was 'partially confirmed' and of the other six 'not confirmed'. The overwhelming impression of these studies is that many parts of the theory are too vague to be either proved or disproved.**2** The question arises: Can the theory be interpreted in a way that is clear *and* sound *and* that could affect the decision-making of a typical organisation — (say) the hypothetical Blue Gum Machines?

Nolan's Stage Theory and the Decision Question

If the Decision Question is posed, a provisional outline answer is clear. The stage theory (if valid) can help the managers of Blue Gum make decisions, because, by knowing that Blue Gum is at a certain stage, they can take decisions that are appropriate to any organisation at that particular stage, on matters related to the application portfolio, DP organisation, DP planning and control, and user awareness.

But giving substance to this plausible outline is not so easy. One author writes: 'By knowing where an enterprise is located in terms of these benchmark scales, and by knowing where it should move to, a planner may formulate a course of action for the ISD (information systems department).' This brief formulation raises what might be called the *determinism* problem. What does 'knowing where it *should* move to'

Stage Theory Logic

A typical stage theory asserts that:

- There are (say) 6 stages.
- Each of stages I-VI is defined by verbal description of (say) four different variables
  (A might be type of applications; B might be way IT is organised, etc)

	I	II	III	IV	V	VI
A	zzzzzzzzzz zzzzzzzzzz zzzzzzzzzz zzzzzz	zzzzzzzzzz zzzzzzzzzz zzzzzzzzzz zzzzzz	zzzzzzzzzz zzzzzzzzzz zzzzzzzzzz zzzzzz	zzzzzzzzzz zzzzzzzzzz zzzzzzzzzz zzzzzz	zzzzzzzzzz zzzzzzzzzz zzzzzzzzzz zzzzzz	zzzzzzzzzz zzzzzzzzzz zzzzzzzzzz zzzzzz
B	zzzzzzzzzz zzzzzzzzzz zzzzzzzzzz zzzzzz	zzzzzzzzzz zzzzzzzzzz zzzzzzzzzz zzzzzz	zzzzzzzzzz zzzzzzzzzz zzzzzzzzzz zzzzzz	zzzzzzzzzz zzzzzzzzzz zzzzzzzzzz zzzzzz	zzzzzzzzzz zzzzzzzzzz zzzzzzzzzz zzzzzz	zzzzzzzzzz zzzzzzzzzz zzzzzzzzzz zzzzzz
C	zzzzzzzzzz zzzzzzzzzz zzzzzzzzzz zzzzzz	zzzzzzzzzz zzzzzzzzzz zzzzzzzzzz zzzzzz	zzzzzzzzzz zzzzzzzzzz zzzzzzzzzz zzzzzz	zzzzzzzzzz zzzzzzzzzz zzzzzzzzzz zzzzzz	zzzzzzzzzz zzzzzzzzzz zzzzzzzzzz zzzzzz	zzzzzzzzzz zzzzzzzzzz zzzzzzzzzz zzzzzz
D	zzzzzzzzzz zzzzzzzzzz zzzzzzzzzz zzzzzz	zzzzzzzzzz zzzzzzzzzz zzzzzzzzzz zzzzzz	zzzzzzzzzz zzzzzzzzzz zzzzzzzzzz zzzzzz	zzzzzzzzzz zzzzzzzzzz zzzzzzzzzz zzzzzz	zzzzzzzzzz zzzzzzzzzz zzzzzzzzzz zzzzzz	zzzzzzzzzz zzzzzzzzzz zzzzzzzzzz zzzzzz

- You will generally find organisations like this:

Stage II Case

	zzzzz zzzzz zzzzz				
	zzzzz zzzzz zzzzz				
	zzzzz zzzzz zzzzz				
	zzzzz zzzzz zzzzz				

Stage IV Case

			zzzzz zzzzz zzzzz		
			zzzzz zzzzz zzzzz		
			zzzzz zzzzz zzzzz		
			zzzzz zzzzz zzzzz		

- You will generally NOT find organisations like this:

					zzzzz zzzzz zzzzz
				zzzzz zzzzz zzzzz	
zzzzz zzzzz zzzzz					
	zzzzz zzzzz zzzzz				

	zzzzz zzzzz zzzzz				
			zzzzz zzzzz zzzzz		
					zzzzz zzzzz zzzzz
		zzzzz zzzzz zzzzz			

Two Key Questions:

- Given any particular stage theory, is this theory true or not?
- How can any theory cast in this form (if true) lead you to make better decisions in any specific case?

mean? Nolan claimed that organisations *do in fact* move through his stages — not that they *ought to* try to move through the stages as quickly as possible, nor that good organisations adhered to the stages, while poor ones did not.

Another book goes into a little more detail about the relation between theory and action, and runs into difficulties: 'Executives can observe where they are in the stage theory. They can make reasonable assertions concerning the future behavior of their organizations. Thoughtful managers can prepare themselves and their organizations for the future according to their observations of the present . . To use the stage theory, management must make an assessment of the posture of the organization or the firm at the present time. Then plans can be based on an extrapolation of the observed trends. For example, if the firm is in the control stage, it would be wise to anticipate and plan for the integration phase (sic) followed by the data administration stage.'

This may sound plausible, but it is still flawed. 'Assertions concerning the future behavior of their organizations' is an ambiguous phrase. It could mean 'assertions about the way Blue Gum will inevitably develop, whatever decisions the managers may take', or it could mean 'assertions about the decisions the managers ought to take in order to make the future of Blue Gum as favourable as possible.'

Here are some awkward quandaries associated with this determinism difficulty:

- If Blue Gum is at stage 3, and if all the evidence shows that it previously passed through stages 1 and 2 in exactly the way the theory suggests, is it inevitably doomed to pass through stages 4 and 5 — no matter what decisions its managers may take?
- If the theory describes the fate of the average organisation, what are its implications for Blue Gum, which (for the sake of argument) is an exceptionally well-managed organisation? Does it go through all the stages quicker, or at the same speed more cost-effectively, or does it spend longer in certain pleasant well-organised stages and less time in those stages characterised by confusion and frustration?
- Suppose the managers of Blue Gum Machines have all made a profound study of the stage theory. Will this organisation follow exactly the same stages in the same way as if its managers had never become aware of the theory, or will awareness of the theory influence developments?

There are difficulties whatever line is taken on these issues, but some clear and convincing answers are needed, if the theory is to deserve respect.

Nolan's Stage Theory and More Problems

There is a more mundane problem: *variety*. Suppose Blue Gum turns out to possess a mixture of attributes that, according to the theory, should not exist. What then? This is no mere theoretical point. In practice, few organisations do present a perfect case of one of the theory's stages.

This is bound up with another problem: *granularity*. Blue Gum Machines finds some evidence suggesting it is at stage 2, but by other measures it is at stage 1 or stage 4. Then somebody suggests that each department should be studied separately; maybe each is at its own stage. This leads to a clearer but not conclusive picture. Then it is suggested that the departments are supported to varying degrees by the central MIS department; if all the factors specific to the MIS department were separated out, perhaps that would produce a result closer to the theory . . In other words, if the definition of the unit studied is varied endlessly, then sooner or later some combination of evidence may be found to fit the theory. But this, to most people, is scarcely satisfactory.

Another associated problem is *abruptness*. Does the theory mean that an organisation jumps abruptly from the characteristic form of (say) stage 2 to the characteristic form of stage 3, as a caterpillar changes into a butterfly? Or does the theory hold that an organisation moves smoothly between stages through very many intermediate states (middle-late stage 2, very late stage 2, early stage 3 . .), analogously to a human being growing up?

A theory asserting the caterpillar-butterfly position will have to be abandoned once any substantial number of non-classic cases turn up. With the gradualist position, the theory is less easily invalidated by evidence, but this immunity is bought at a heavy price. The theory becomes little more than the idea that things develop in a certain direction. There are no longer six discrete stages; the number of stages singled out becomes arbitrary. This makes use of the theory to frame inputs to decision-making rather questionable.[3]

The Stage Theory in Practice

In the face of all the difficulties of principle, people who apply Nolan's stage theory in practice tend to adopt one of two main approaches.

An adherent of the *regularising* approach expects to find that in a given situation there will be factors that don't correspond to any classic stage. The application portfolio dimension may correspond to stage 2 (say) and the DP organisation dimension to stage 3; and the situation may be different in different departments.

With this approach, the differences themselves are regarded as the interesting findings. First, understanding the circumstances that have caused disparities may yield valuable knowledge about key factors that should influence decisions. Second, the whole thrust of policy decisions can be to regularise matters; if investigations of most areas suggest stage 3, then decisions can be made in other areas to produce a more-classic stage 3 state.

This approach rests on the view that each classic stage represents a coherent state of affairs and that coherence, in this sense, is desirable. One drawback is that there may be cases where the apparent lack of coherence is beneficial and perhaps ought to be increased. Unless that point is accepted, the approach comes dangerously close to saying: 'Our research shows that all swans are white; therefore if we come across a black swan we cure it by painting it white.'

This regularisation approach is also a long way from the original theory, which claims that companies do *in fact* pass through six clear stages that are frequently found in the real world. The position here has shifted to the view that companies ought to try to conform as closely as possible to one out of six ideal situations that are rarely found in the real world.

The *moving-on* approach is almost the opposite: assume that at any given time an organisation is *mainly* at a certain stage, and any discrepancies are unimportant; concentrate on moving efficiently on to the next stage, rather than taking measures to make the present stage more coherent. If an organisation appears to have a complete mixture of features from stages 1, 2 and 3, then either the analysis has been done wrongly, or the organisation is in a freak situation. Since this approach just ignores all the problems of determinism, it can't be regarded as a very satisfactory basis for rational decisions.

REPRESENTATIVE IDEAS — SUMMARISED

Nolan's theory is very old; it says nothing about personal computers, for example. In the nineties others have suggested different six-stage theories, but without making any impression on the difficulties inherent in this kind of theory.[4,5] However, some stage theories of more restricted scope are interesting.

A CIM Stage Theory

A less ambitious approach is to develop a stage theory for one particular sector of industry; eg the stages in an organisation's use of CIM (computer-integrated manufacturing) technology. With narrower terms of reference it may be easier to give worthwhile insight into specific matters. Here is a paraphrase of one four-stage theory of CIM:

- **1 Initiation:** several single-function, unconnected systems (eg drafting, numerically-controlled machine-tool programming, engineering analysis); software purchased as packages; largely automation of functions already well understood.
- **2 Expansion:** packages extended with additional bespoke software, in order to achieve better integration (since a fully integrated set of comprehensive systems can't normally be bought from one supplier); this, however, is done on a piece-by-piece basis and (inevitably) leads to failure.
- **3 Formalisation:** people now recognise the integration problem and

attempt to tackle it explicitly: functions are re-analysed and systems redeveloped, using database technology more effectively, to give a much better integrated set of systems; however this is achieved at the price of being over-controlled and over-analysed, and long lead times.

- **4 Maturity:** there is now a reasonably integrated set of systems resulting from stage 3; methods of system development are improved, so that future developments achieve both integration and speedy cost-effective development.

This model offers no new insight into the problems of decision-making logic raised earlier. Its authors say ruefully, but enigmatically: 'The only consolation is that, by recognizing this process over time, a company will learn how to more effectively manage the introduction of technology in general . .'

A Stage Theory of End-user Computing

Another approach is to concentrate on a particular IM problem area, rather than the whole of the organisation's use of IT; eg the growth of end-user computing (EUC).

One such theory suggests five stages: 1, isolation; 2, stand-alone; 3, manual integration; 4, automated integration; 5, distributed integration. For each of these stages a cluster of attributes is described under five headings: planning and control procedures; support activities; end-user training arrangements; attitudes and feelings of information centre (ie technical support) staff; users' attitudes and feelings.

As with Nolan's theory, the implicit logic is that if you know which stage you are at, you can take decisions on a variety of matters.

REPRESENTATIVE IDEAS — ANALYSED

Leave aside the question of whether the CIM model is basically true or whether some other model would be better. This model does have the advantage of being focused much more narrowly than Nolan's. In fact it is obsessed by one particular theme, integration — plausibly enough in this particular application area. Therefore even if Blue Gum Machines isn't clearly at any of these four stages, the model's exposure of the issues, problems, options and consequences of integration might — in an impressionistic way — still lead to better decisions.

The end-user computing model is so close in format to Nolan's that all the same questions of decision-making logic arise, and they remain just as difficult to answer.[6] But by tackling a narrower area, it can express its analysis in more concrete terms. This means that, as with the CIM model, you may decline to accept the underlying logic, but still use some of its concepts.

Suppose Blue Gum is faced with one or more of the following matters for decisions: Who should have the authority to invest in PC hardware?

Who should have the authority to set up new systems on PCs, separate from the main data centre? How should users of PCs be supported by specialised expertise? Should there be an approved list of software products, and if so, what sanctions should there be if someone is caught using (say) Xywrite instead of WordPerfect? Should certain chosen users in each department be given extra education in IT matters? How should integration between data or programs on different PCs be organised? What about documentation of systems designed by inexperienced users? What about data security and integrity? Should there be regular user satisfaction surveys?

A stage theory of EUC can in principle give fairly clear guidance on such questions — if its dubious logic is accepted. But it is safer to reject a stage theory's explicit claims, to treat its content just as a quarry for extracting aspects, distinctions and gradations of possibilities, and to fashion them into your own decision-making logic.

NOTES & ARGUMENTS

1 Richard L Nolan, 'Managing the crises in data processing', *Harvard Business Review*, March-April 1979, pp. 115-126. This article is reproduced in many anthologies.

2 Enthusiasm: eg Wright and Rhodes, pp. 56-61; Sager, pp. 40-47. Article: Izak Benbasat et al, 'A Critique of the Stage Hypothesis: Theory and Empirical Evidence', *Communications of the ACM*, May 1984, pp. 476-485.

Naive quotes in the section following: Remenyi, p. 49, and Frenzel, p. 20 and p. 113.

3 Some of the problems mentioned and some others have been raised in learned journals; eg John Leslie King and Kenneth L Kraemer, 'Evolution and Organizational Information Systems: An Assessment of Nolan's Stage Model', *Communications of the ACM*, May 1984, pp. 466-475. This is quite a rare instance of authorities on IM engaging in genuine controversy; too often they merely preach in favour of virtue and against sin.

4 A recent general theory: 'Striving for Sustained Competitive Advantage', CNG Dampney and T Andrews in Clarke and Cameron, p. 203.

CIM theory: Bray, pp. 255ff.

End-user theory: Sid L Huff, Malcolm C Munro and Barbara H Martin, 'Growth Stages of End User Computing', *Communications of the ACM*, May 1988, pp. 542-550.

5 Theories about progress through stages over time are not always labelled as such. One analysis of 'management decision-making activities' sets up a classification matrix with 18 cells; eg 'project costing' is in the cell on the row 'management control, structured', and in the column headed 'sequential'; 'task scheduling' is in a different cell and 'scheduling management meetings' is somewhere else. (The Center for Information Systems Research, MIT; in Gunton (1990), p. 93.)

This analysis is accompanied by the claim that within an organisation *over a period of time*, there will be movement from one category to another according to a predictable pattern. Thus the automation of 'sequential' activities (those in column 1 of the matrix) is followed by automation of more and more 'independent' activities (column 2) and then more and more 'pooled' activities (column 3). This is really a classification on which a stage-like logic is superimposed. The essential problem remains: If the theory claims to describe what *in fact happens*, how can it suggest what you *ought to do*?

6 This EUC theory raises a few more problems of its own:

● Roughly speaking, the five stages differ in what the authors call 'extent of interconnectedness'. In stage 5 'end users operate in a world in which shared databases exist at desktop, departmental, and corporate levels — a three tiered environment.' Should that kind of thing count as being EUC? If EUC is defined as widely as that, what is *not* EUC?

● Does the theory assert that any organisation's EUC *as a whole* is in one of five stages at any time? Or does it assert (less dramatically but more plausibly) that EUC *applications* can be categorised under five headings, and any organisation's applications at any time may well be a mixture? Or is the theory more subtle than either of those interpretations? It is difficult to know. The authors say confusingly: 'The *maturity* of applications developed by end users is . . adopted as the prime indicator of the stage of advancement of EUC in the organization.'

CONNECTIONS

6. Agenda-setting Logic	Ideas for states an organisation may be in, without implications for progress between states over time
10. Learning and Historical Themes	Concepts of organisational learning — often associated with stage theories
37. End-user Computing	Discussion of ideas — stages and other — about the whole field
38. Decision Support Systems	Discussion of ideas other than stages about management decision-making activities
42. Unifying Theories	Broad generalising theories about the nature of IM

10. Learning and Historical Themes

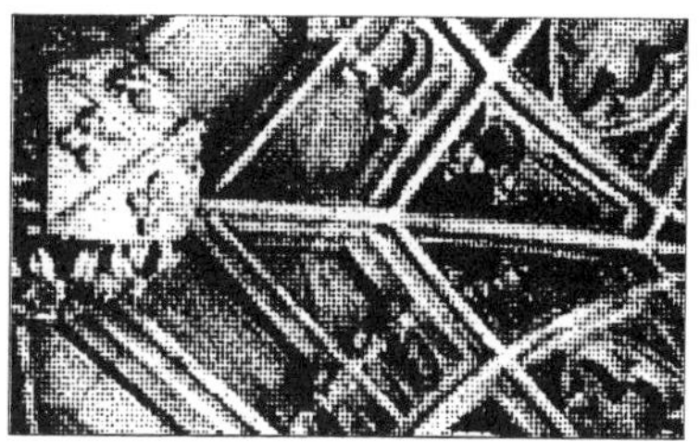

TOPIC

Books and articles sometimes enunciate broad, impressionistic themes: the history of computers can be split into a few distinct eras; there are megatrends in society as a whole; management of IT is essentially a 'learning process'; and so on.

Some of these are too sweeping, speculative or vague to pass the test of the Decision Question — even if they could be supported by any evidence. On the other hand, others may be valuable. It is worth examining some representative themes, but assessing the merit of any particular one is less important than tackling a more central issue: presented with *any* such theme, how should you decide whether to use it or discard it?

REPRESENTATIVE IDEAS — SUMMARISED

A whole group of theories can loosely be called historical, and arranged in four somewhat overlapping categories: theories splitting the history of automation into *eras*; theories that certain *megatrends*, wider than IT itself, exist and will go on developing; *analogies* between the development of IT and historical developments in other fields; theories that the history of any given technology always follows a certain *cycle*.

Eras

One book suggests that the use of IT by organisations can be divided into three eras: data processing (1960s), management services (1970s) and information processing (1980s). Each era is defined by properties in each of four areas: characteristic technologies; main reason for using the technology; basis for justification; and people most directly affected. Vocabulary aside and with some differences of detail, much the same three-era theory has been given by quite a few writers.

Another book makes a stronger claim: 'The history of business computing can be described as occupying four phases, each neatly fitting a decade, and each determined by the current 'state of the art' in the field of communications.' The blokeishly named eras are: 1960s incubation; 1970s corporate invasion; 1980s customer-supplier invasion; 1990s computer mating season.

Occasionally a more speculative claim is made: eg that there are five eras; the world is currently in the third era, 'management of corporate information resources'; and the fourth, 'business competitor analysis and intelligence', is just coming up; and the fifth is still in the future.

Probably the most common era theory is the one that simply asserts a distinction between the *IT era* (which began during the eighties and is still in progress) and the *DP era* (everything before that, the first 30 years of computing). This theory is virtually impossible to state neutrally, since it amounts to: 'DP boring, IT exciting'. For example: 'the product of MIS-EDP is the program', while 'the product of IT is business use of programs.' In the DP era 'computers and communications are not strategic tools', while in the IT era 'IT is a strategic weapon.' Again, in the DP era the business role of IT was 'mostly support', but in the IT era it is 'often critical'. In the DP era the applications orientation of IT was 'tactical', in the IT era 'strategic'; in the DP era the economic context for IT was 'neutral', in the IT era 'welcoming'; in the DP era the management posture to IT was 'delegate, abrogate', in the IT era 'leadership involvement'; and so on.[1]

Megatrends, Historical Analogies, Technology Cycles

Some books start out with assertions such as: 'Human societies generally evolve through three stages . . agricultural . . industrial . . information or service . . Two-thirds of the UK workforce are now engaged in providing services.' The presentations of American management consultants often use figures from the US Bureau of Statistics which forecast that by 1995 93% of the American workforce would be in the service-information sectors, as opposed to the industry or agriculture sectors (in 1945 the figure for the service-information sectors was 57%).

Here is an interesting analogy on a different subject. Steam was the great force of the *Industrial Revolution*. At first it was used to power ships. This technology reached a certain peak, but by that time it had already been overtaken by a new form of steam power, trains. Steam trains, the younger form of technology, rapidly overtook steam ships in importance during the nineteenth century. This corresponds quite closely to the pattern of the *Information Revolution*: if steam corresponds to computer, then ships are mainframes and minis, and trains PCs.

Other theories find a common pattern in the development of any technology: word processing, local area networks, pen-based computing etc. One gives seven stages for the development of a new software technology in the world in general (not in any particular organisation): 1 emergence of basic idea; 2 concept (eg conference papers); 3 testing in

Historical Themes: Decision-making Logic

How can we stimulate people at the four regional offices to use PCs imaginatively, without creating problems of inconsistency and incompatibility?
The Information Revolution is analogous to the Industrial Revolution. Mainframes and minis = steam ships, and PCs = steam trains
I'm sure you're right, but how can we stimulate people at the four regional offices to . . . .
For this, substitute any other IM issue that a real organisation may face. If the historical theme is no help in deciding any such issue, then it is worthless.
For this, substitute any other theory about eras of IT history, megatrends in society, technology life cycles etc

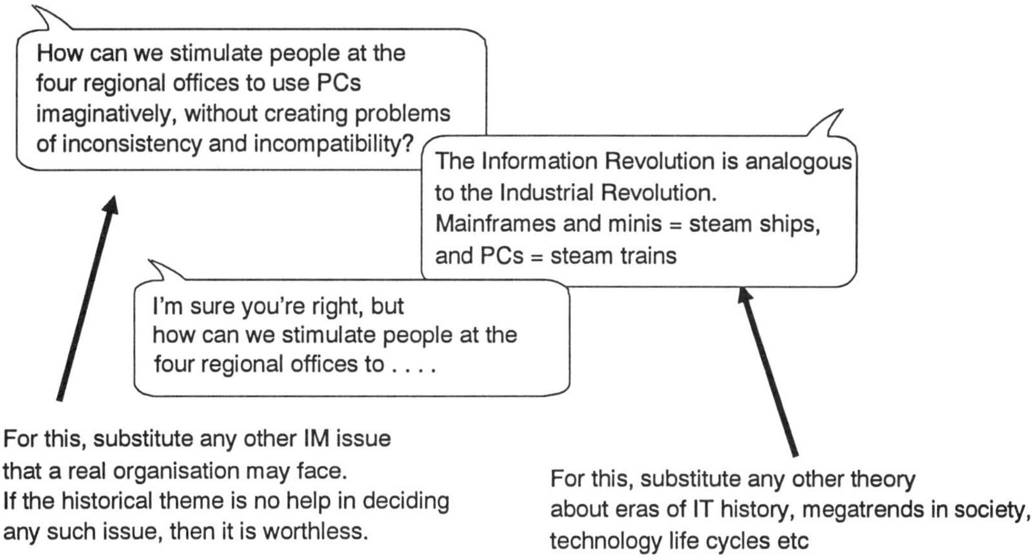

laboratory; 4 used outside lab; 5 beginning of general use; 6 used by 40% of users; 7 used by 70%.

Another gives a four-stage cycle for the status of a new technology within a certain industry: 1 emerging technology, under development, not yet used in the industry; 2 pacing technology, experimental applications in the industry; 3 key technology, leaders in the industry implement major systems; 4 base technology, widely used in the industry.2

REPRESENTATIVE IDEAS — ANALYSED

As the diagram insinuates, all these theories seem vulnerable to the charge of not being directly relevant to decision-making in a particular organisation, and thus, however true, scarcely worth knowing about.

Eras

There is plenty of scope for critical thinking about era theories. Here are a couple of lines of thought:

● Any convincing breakdown of a piece of history into eras needs to show that each era is a relatively homogeneous period, followed by a period of rapid change, succeeded in turn by a new period of relative stability. If this isn't so, and change proceeds at a steady pace or at random, there is no basis for claiming that there are (say) three eras rather than five or seventeen. Yet few advocates of an era theory present evidence of such patterns of change, or even claim that it has occurred.

- To claim that 'technology' or 'the IT community' has developed through certain eras is not necessarily to say that each (or even any) individual organisation will develop in the same way. Dividing up the earth's fossil record into eras says nothing about the development of any one animal during its lifetime. Yet few advocates of an era theory deal with the relationship between the general and the particular.[3]
- In a complex field, it can easily happen that several possible analyses have distinct merits. Scholars dividing up Romance languages and dialects on the map of Europe find that an east-west division is the best way of understanding phonetic variation, but a centre-periphery division is best for analysing vocabulary. Might there not be similar complexity in the history of IT? Could not (say) a three-era analysis be best for technology change, but a two-era analysis for organisational impact, and a four-era analysis for type of applications?

These are relevant points if you take any particular era theory seriously. But should you? It is only worth thinking carefully about an era theory if (assuming it does turn out to be clear and valid and justified) it will help in reaching decisions better or more quickly in particular cases. Otherwise, unless perhaps for a doctoral thesis, there is no point knowing about it. Most theories of IT eras are too vague and general to come near passing that test.

Megatrends, Historical Analogies, Technology Cycles

One problem with some assertions about megatrends is that they slide in the idea that information-service employment is one meaningful category. Service workers such as taxi-drivers and waiters and jugglers are lumped together with obvious information workers such as librarians and authors and computer programmers, as well as intermediate cases such as dentists, vicars and bank counter-clerks.

The difficulties of setting up employment categories that will produce meaningful statistics are immense.[4] This would matter if any IM decision-maker was really likely to be influenced by data about the trend to the information society. Of course that is not so. The concepts are just too vague and crude to affect particular decisions in any organisation.[5]

Alluring historical parallels usually melt away under scrutiny. Bertrand Russell remarks on Hegel's *Philosophy of History*: 'It was an interesting thesis, giving unity and meaning to the revolutions of human affairs. Like other historical theories, it required, if it was to be made plausible, some distortion of facts and considerable ignorance. Hegel, like Marx and Spengler after him, possessed both these qualifications.' Very similar comments apply to parallels intended to bring unity and meaning to the revolutions of IT.[6]

Theories about technology cycles are not quite so vulnerable, but it is still difficult to find a confident answer to the question: How could knowing about such a theory help a decision-maker in a specific organisation reach better IM decisions?[7]

REPRESENTATIVE IDEAS — SUMMARISED

Proponents of historical theories (and also stage theories discussed elsewhere) often introduce the idea that the eras or cycle-stages are manifestations of an underlying 'learning process'. Indeed, people have been known to abandon the specific detail of such theories in the face of awkward evidence or other difficulties, while maintaining that the underlying learning process was what really mattered. In any case, it could be quite reasonable to hold that the idea of a learning process in the application of a technology within an organisation had merit, without accepting any particular historical or stage theory.

The S-curve of Learning

The learning process is a concept that rings true among those with experience — albeit in an impressionistic way that can be difficult to firm up. People often talk of a learning *curve* and depict this graphically as an S-curve (S for sigmoidal and also for its shape).[8] In learning (say) a foreign language, there is a tough initial period; then a time comes when you get noticeably better almost by the day, but eventually this progress peters out. An organisation's learning about the way to use and manage IT, so it is sometimes claimed, resembles this process.

Any curve needs two axes to be meaningful: if the x-axis is time or effort expended, what is the y-axis? What is the thing said to be developing in an S-curve over time? Here are some candidates that have been suggested (or at any rate implied): an organisation's cumulative IT financial investment; *or* 'proficiency in controlling IT', eg based on studies of the relations between projects' estimated and actual spend; *or* subjective satisfaction of non-IT people with the use of IT; *or* 'lessons learnt' from past use of IT, eg learning not to write software organised like spaghetti; *or* opportunities for using IT in business.

Since some of these are more appropriate to describing the development of IT in general than within an individual organisation, there are really two types of theory: one asserting that learning within any individual organisation follows an S-curve (or has some similar property); one asserting that learning within the whole community of organisations using IT follows an S-curve (or has some similar property).

Learning Curves and Learning Stages

Nolan's and other 'stage' theories give descriptive detail about certain generic stages in the development of IT *within an individual organisation.* But stage theories are ridden with difficulties. This raises the idea: Why not eliminate specific detail about particular stages, and concentrate instead on insight into a broad, underlying learning process? This line of thought has in fact been followed. A four-stage version of Nolan's theory came out in 1974. In 1979 came the well-known version — in six stages, more elaborate in other ways too, but subject to numerous objections. Nowadays the more thoughtful books on IM ignore the six-stage version and give a modified four-stage version.[9]

One shift of emphasis is away from verbal descriptions of four stages towards the idea that there are four successive parts to an S-curve that represents learning. Another improvement is to get away from a learning process describing the *whole organisation's* use of IT towards a separate process for *any particular technology* within an organisation. Thus an organisation might be at an early point on the curve for neural network, proceeding tentatively, with little return as yet for effort expended; but much further on for document imaging, already employing the technology widely and effectively, with new and even better applications being discovered all the time.

The book by Cash, McFarlan and McKenney takes this approach, with some refinements. There can be a stagnation block after each of the stages. Just as a person's ability to speak German might be stuck at a certain very moderate level, so an organisation's mastery of a certain technology might be stuck at a certain level far below the maximum too. Also, being at a certain point in the process has implications that can be spelt out: the right structure for a certain project (how to split it up into phases, how to organise team members etc) should be largely determined by the learning stage of its technology within the particular organisation; an organisation might even have different departments for developing systems, depending on the technology stage involved.

But, as the implications are worked out in their book, the four-stage learning process tends to collapse into two. On many issues, the advice amounts to: for stage-1 or stage-2 cases, do this . . (generally something to stimulate learning by experience, without causing too much havoc or discouragement); for stage-3 or stage-4 cases, do this . . (generally something to ensure that substantial developments are efficiently managed).

REPRESENTATIVE IDEAS — ANALYSED

The question to be raised about any theory concerned with learning is, as usual: If valid, how could this general theory help somebody take decisions in a specific case?

Problems with Learning Curves

Any curve whose two axes are obscure is of dubious value. If the x-axis of

The Learning Process

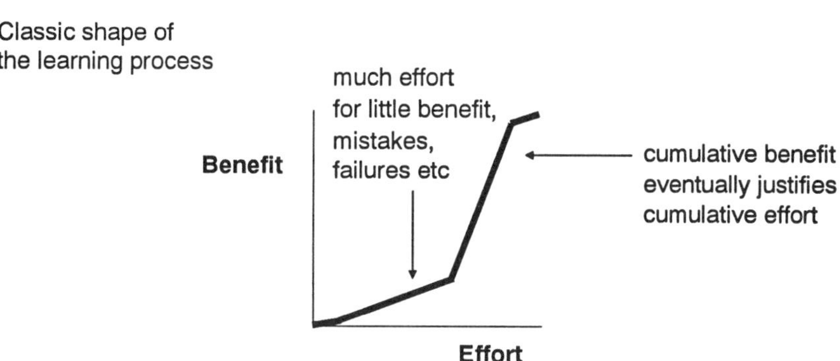

relatively arduous learning, but eventually explosive gains

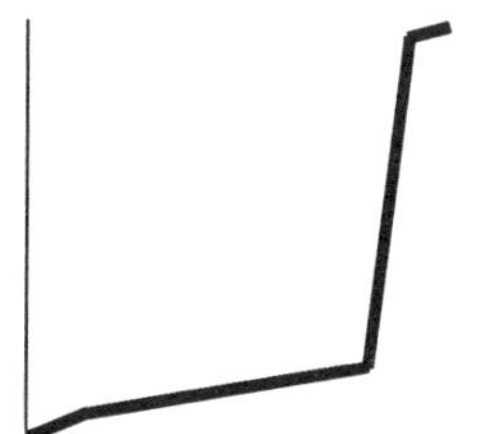

Or in some cases may be entirely different, eg

small increments of effort may bring corresponding increments of benefit; here there is no need to make a large investment in learning

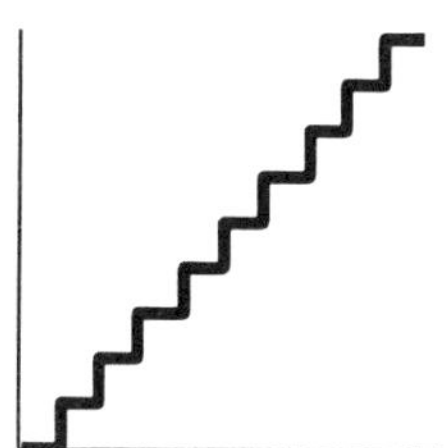

the learning curve is time or effort, what does the y-axis measure? Cumulative financial investment in IT is measurable (albeit with difficulty), but is only vaguely connected with learning. Nobody would document success in learning a language by plotting time against money spent on tuition fees. 'Lessons learnt' is relevant but practically impossible to quantify. Other candidates for the y-axis of learning bring similar difficulties.[10]

To avoid questions that have no good answers, it is much better to talk of a learning *process*, rather than a curve that suggests a spurious precision; to regard the learning process as having two or perhaps four phases; to draw diagrams with simple lines rather than curves; and to accept that different features of the organisation (different departments, technologies etc) will be at different points of the process. But now what force remains in the concept?

It does conveys an essential truth. Using IT effectively is *often* like learning to acquire a skill such as fluency in a foreign language — rather than solving a problem such as a crossword puzzle; or getting through a pile of work at a steady pace, such as addressing a pile of Christmas cards; or manipulating a complex machine, such as a naval vessel into harbour; or inventing something original, such as the spinning-jenny. But 'often' is not the same as 'always'; in some cases, the classic contours of the learning process are more pronounced than in others; and, as the diagram suggests, at times, a different pattern altogether may apply.**11**

Using the Notion of Learning Process

The learning-process concept can well withstand the test of the Decision Question. It might be used to support the following lines of argument:

- 'We are faced with the opportunity of using groupware, a technology new to us and relatively new to the IT industry. If we take it up seriously, we shall probably be committing ourselves to all the frustrations of the early period of a learning process. We can expect that, over perhaps the next two years, there will be big problems, wasted opportunities, targets missed by dramatic margins and so on. We hope, though we can't be sure, that eventually we shall enjoy explosive growth in the effectiveness of applying this technology. I am convinced that we can't afford *not* to embark on this learning process. But don't approve my plans unless you agree that the inevitable learning troubles are, on balance, worth accepting.'
- *And / or* 'I can accept your idea that an on-line service for access to text databases, using keywords and the like, will be subject to the classic learning process, while people get to know the possibilities and constraints. But this proposed system for the board of directors has to prove its worth right from the very start; otherwise it will do more harm than good. I am not prepared to accept a lengthy learning process in such a sensitive area. Therefore I am turning down your proposal. Can you find some less prominent area for our learning about text databases? The marine claims document archive perhaps? If we take time to learn hard lessons there, then perhaps in (say) two years time we shall be able to set up a system for the board in a fairly painless way.'

NOTES & ARGUMENTS

1 The era theories cited in this section come from: Gunton (1990), p. 91; Grindley, p. 45; Marchand and Horton, pp. 112ff.; Stark, pp. 3, 8ff.; Earl, p. 21.

Ward, Griffiths and Whitmore (pp. 10, 17-8) define three eras in terms of five aspects: nature of technology, nature of operations, issues in system development, reason for using technology, characteristics of systems. Another example (among others) is in 'The Evolution of Information Systems and Technologies', David R Lee, *SAM Advanced Management Journal*, Summer 1988, p. 17ff. This identifies three successive phases: DP, MIS and IRM. For quite a lot more of this kind of thing, see also Synnott, pp. 8ff., pp. 28ff.

2 The four theories set out in this section come from: Knight and Silk, p. 4 (also Marchand and Horton, chapter 1); RL Nolan and AHJB Schotgerrits, *Informatie*, 31/12, pp. 991ff.; annual report for 1988 of CAP Gemini Sogeti; Ward, Griffiths and Whitmore, p. 409.

'American business is at a crossroads. We find ourselves in a global marketplace, from the Pacific Rim to the third world, from a united Europe to the former Soviet Union. Our challenges and opportunities have intensified. Our customers' expectations are constantly rising. We are expected to do more with less — and do it smarter, better and faster. Information systems (IS) and IS professionals hold the key to corporate competitiveness in a global economy. We already have many of the tools and approaches that can enhance strategies and cost-effectiveness. We are only beginning to scratch the surface of what information technology can contribute to the business environment's evolution.' 'Business and Systems Planning: Building a New Alliance', Douglas W McDavid, *Database Programming & Design*, October 1992, p. 29. This is all very well, but how does knowing it help anyone make better decisions about using IT in a specific organisation?

3 Grindley (p. 56) sets out what looks like a four-stage theory about the experience of IT in any one typical company. But by Stage III (which begins 'During the 80s . . '), it has turned into an era theory about changes in the IT scene considered as a whole.

Grindley's book (p. 8) contains another theory that falls somewhere between era theory and historical theme: that 1985 was a 'Watershed' year. Suddenly the pragmatists took a stand against the enthusiasts; companies invested less in computer systems, and examined what they were spending more carefully. Suppose this historical analysis is entirely valid. How is anyone better off for knowing about it? Will it help in taking better decisions? It is difficult to see how.

4 *The Economist* pointed out that the work of regular journalists on its staff ended up in the UK Government figures for *manufacturing* (since, in a sense, they help make magazines), but work done by freelance journalists was counted as *service* output.

The statistics for the countries of Western Europe, North America and Japan differ tremendously, and this must surely be due in part to different definitions of what counts as manufacturing and what as service.

5 In a widely cited article Peter Drukker, a management theorist, argued as follows: knowledge workers are becoming the dominant portion of labour; knowledge workers resist the command-and-control form of organisation; therefore new forms are needed, in which knowledge specialists direct their own performance through feedback from colleagues, customers and headquarters; IT is a stimulus for this change. This thesis can be criticised for a couple of reasons:

- Even if entirely valid, it is too broad-brush to help anybody decide anything about IM or anything else in any specific case.
- The argument rests on shifting senses of the term 'knowledge worker'. The first premise is certainly true, if by knowledge workers you mean all those not working in factories. The second premise is very plausible if by knowledge workers you mean something different: people like teachers or librarians, who literally work

with knowledge. But what about non-factory workers such as waiters, bus conductors, supermarket workers, insurance clerks, garage mechanics etc? The argument doesn't show that they . . But the rest of this rebuttal is easy enough to fill in.

To see whether the above paraphrase and criticism are fair, check out 'The Coming of the New Organisation' by Peter F Drukker in *Harvard Business Review*, January-February 1988, pp. 45-53, one of the journal's most reprinted articles ever.

Poppel and Goldstein organise their book around five 'infotrends': content, interoperability, disintermediation, globalisation and convergence. But these five are not all on the same plane: content surely can't be a trend in the way that (say) globalisation is; and the convergence trend is defined as the convergence of the other four trends. This makes a rather messy model that achieves very little.

6 Here are some awkward facts for the Industrial Revolution analogy:

- It is true that steam ships preceded steam trains by fifty years, but these were relatively primitive vessels compared to the great iron steam ships which came much later.
- The main technological features of steam trains were established by 1850, but the key to the success of steam ships was solving the problem of marine condensers — and this was done some time after the main issues in steam train design had been resolved.
- Steam ships were only really accepted as better than sail in the 1860s, when steam trains had already been accepted for years as better than stage coaches.
- Fixed steam engines (eg in mines, factories, ironworks, pumping stations etc) are not mentioned in the analogy but they were introduced long before steam ships and trains. Probably the greatest steam-based project of all was the making of the Manchester Ship Canal by fixed steam engines as late as 1893.

Some other historical parallels are more interesting and less easy to knock down. One put by Thomas W Malone and John F Rockart, appeared in the September 1991 issue of *Scientific American*. The replacement of horse-transport by trains and cars had a first-order effect (people made the same journeys quicker); a second-order effect (people made journeys not hitherto feasible, eg daily commuting, and visits to distant relatives); and a third-order effect (transport-dependent suburbs and shopping malls developed). Similarly, IT has had:

- first-order effects, eg automating routine clerical work;
- second-order effects, eg a plethora of airline ticket options not hitherto feasible;
- and third-order effects, eg IT-dependent structures, with decision-making by area and district managers rather than head office; also, alliances of independent textile firms near Prato, Italy, co-ordinating their production.

Yes, but how is any decision-maker better off for knowing about this attractive analogy?

7 Technology themes are a related form. Often they assert 'X has widespread and ever-increasing implications', where X is some broadly defined technology. Williams (pp. 27-8) gives numerous examples of the benefits of telecoms. So what? You could just as well cite numerous examples of the benefits of electricity, or roofs on buildings, or a written language etc.

In a more subtle form, X is some *aspect* of technology. The claim might be that the ability to access the same data from different software products (say, word processing and spreadsheet) was a theme increasing in importance all over the IT world. The trend to ever more graphic, mouse-using interfaces might be another. Or the theme of separating things into *compartments* might be picked out: eg keeping the technical design features of a database strictly distinct from the logical design; separating an underlying operating system (eg Unix) from its interface and presentation features; structuring a database system into the client-server architecture; designing a telecoms setup in the seven distinct layers of the OSI model. Even so, studying and thinking about this kind of theme probably doesn't assist decisions in any direct way.

8 A real-life instance of S-curve development is the growth of a colony of bacteria on an uninhabited medium. If population is plotted on the y-axis against time on the x-axis, an S-curve results. During an initial period, population is increasing rapidly, but from a very small base; once a substantial population is reached, cell division every twenty minutes results in explosive growth. Eventually the growth tapers off and stabilises at a certain level. See Eugene P. Odum, *Ecology* (Holt Rinehart and Winston, 2nd ed., 1975).

9 Cyrus F Gibson and Richard L Nolan, 'Managing the four stages of EDP growth', *Harvard Business Review*, January-February 1974, pp. 76-88.

Cash, McFarlan and McKenney (pp. 27-31, 115-9) and Earl (pp. 27ff.) give the four-stage version. A good test of any similar book is: Does it give the six-stage version (bad) or the four-stage (good)?

10 People often talk of a '*steep* learning curve' when they mean that there is a long initial period of relatively little gain, ie there is a *shallow* curve, before achievement begins to rise steeply.

11 Is it really true that all new technologies of any moment introduced into an organisation are subject to a very similar learning process, analogous in pattern to learning a foreign language? Do you always have to make a substantial investment in learning without much benefit in return, but eventually reach a point where additional effort expended brings noticeable improvements in competence and benefit?

Assume that pattern applies to technology X. Then it may be quite rational for somebody to say: 'I don't wish to get myself (or my company) involved in technology X, because I don't want to make that initial investment of time, money and psychic capital. The return on that investment is too long-term and uncertain. Moreover, even if I were convinced that it would be a good investment, I can't make every single good investment that may exist; other things have a prior call on my resources.'

This is the logic many managers give for not learning to use a PC, and remaining dependent on a secretary for even the simplest typing. But in their case, the argument is usually fallacious. If technology X is 'using a PC for simple office tasks such as word processing', it just isn't true that the learning process must take the classic shape, characteristic of learning a foreign language:

- A manager could spend two hours learning how to switch a PC on, type simple text and use the backspace key for simple deletions. Printing the document out and everything else could be left to a secretary.
- A month later, having gained enough benefit from simple typing to recoup the initial investment in learning, the manager could spend two more hours,

learning how to move a paragraph from one part of the document to another, and how to make headings bold. Everything else could still be left to a secretary.

- After that investment is recouped, the next step could be to learn how to indent a paragraph . . and so on.

This is quite a different pattern from the classic learning process; there is no substantial investment in learning that will only be recouped much later. In fact, when considering the use of any technology in a certain organisation at a certain time, there is a distinction to be made between three cases:

- where the early stages of a classic learning process apply (investment with speculative returns later);
- where the later stages of a classic learning process apply (exploiting previous learning to recoup investment);
- where the classic learning process doesn't apply, and an incremental learning pattern is possible.

In most organisations use of technologies such as distributed database or text database is probably subject to the classic learning process; early, crude beginners' systems have little real benefit or even negative effects. But this is not necessarily true of expert system or spreadsheet; as with word processing, proficiency can develop in small, useful steps.

Another question is: What kind of thing is being learnt about? There is a fundamental two-way distinction:

- learning how to use a certain type of technology effectively; ie learning how to choose the right options, get good value for money, recognise possible applications, make realistic assessments of what is easy and difficult, design good systems, match applications within your organisation to the possibilities offered by the technology; etc.
- learning how to manage technology (a specific technology or more likely technology in general) in a wider sense; ie learning how to organise the interaction between departments and IT experts to define requirements well, how to structure project teams, how to control the quality of work on development projects, how to fit IM planning together with wider business planning; etc.

CONNECTIONS

9. Stage Theories	More elaborate and specific theories that may influence top-level decision-making
22. Evolutionary Development	Giving a structure to learning-driven projects
35. Change Management	The complications of development by learning and other issues in managing change
42. Unifying Theories	Other generalising theories about the nature of IT management

11. Untangling Matching Decisions

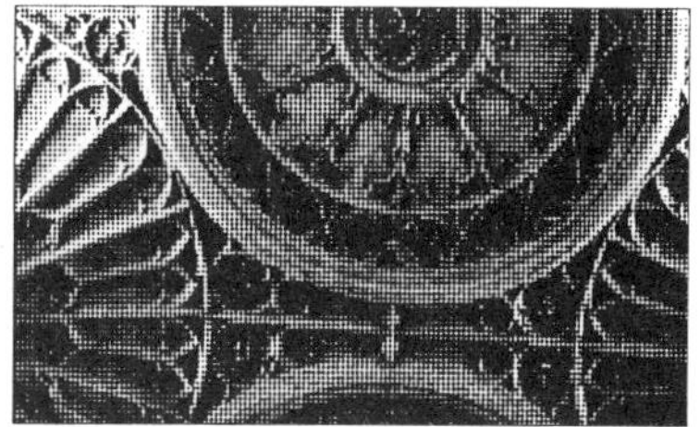

TOPIC

Matching decisions differ from most decisions on the other four planes, because they refer directly to specific technologies. This poses a problem.

Suppose a book's topics include (among much else) critical success factors (CSFs), end-user computing, and the possibilities of expert system technology. There is something unsatisfactory about that mix: any advice about CSFs or end-user computing is potentially relevant to any organisation in any sector, using any technology at any time; but advice about expert system technology, however shrewd, will be relevant to the matching decisions of different organisations in different degrees; moreover, it may well become outdated within a few years. Worse, advice about expert system technology is arbitrary in a way advice on CSFs is not. Why give advice about one technology rather than dozens of others that people may need to use?

This being obvious, most books about IM say little about specific technologies, and concentrate on generally relevant topics, such as CSFs, end-user computing and so on. But this, though natural, means that little is said about a very important class of IM decisions: matching decisions. But how can anything helpful be said about matching decisions, without being technology-specific?

To get into this problem, contrast a book about stock exchange investment. This will contain advice about how to pick shares likely to do well and suit a portfolio; concepts such as the PE ratio, dividend cover and so on will be discussed, but not specific shares. The reason is evident: the PE ratio is a concept that will help anybody appraise any share in any market at any time; Unilever shares may be a good buy today, but not tomorrow (or perhaps not even a good buy today for certain investors). If comments on expert system or any other particular technology are analogous to tips about Unilever shares, what is analogous to the PE ratio and dividend cover? What general concepts and tools can help you appraise any technology for your particular application portfolio, and take good matching decisions? That is the question tackled by this briefing and the six that follow.**1**

Corkwood Bank, Warrants and Decisions

Warrant Form and Representative Warrant	*Representative Matching Decision*
Comparison 'The tradeoffs between CD-ROM and WORM as storage media for high-volume databases are . . '	'We will use CD-ROM (rather than WORM) for a new application system to distribute to our branches a high-volume database of texts about banking law.'
Distinctions 'This table classifies the different ways of using expert system technology to support different styles of computer-assisted instruction . . '	'The category of expert system we need to train our mortgage broking staff is . . '
Gradations 'Here are four main varieties of ATM systems, in ascending order of sophistication of technology and the facilities provided for customers . . '	'We choose to have a new system, using advanced ATMs to provide the following new facilities for customers . . (as opposed to these other possible, more advanced and expensive, facilities . .)
Chart 'Videotex is a *technology* with several variants. Prestel is one particular videotex *service*. Some other services use the same variant of videotex technology as the Prestel service does; others don't . . '	'We will set up a videotex service for our branches abroad, that will support several different variants of videotex.'
Aspects 'Word processing packages have five main aspects, under which all the more detailed features can be bunched: presentation; content; manipulation; essential interface; and advanced interface.'	'We will choose the word processing package for our back-office staff primarily on the quality of its essential interface (as opposed to the other aspects).'
Example 'One company profited from a sophisticated PABX device to prioritise incoming phone calls and thus improve service to favoured clients; here are details of that case . . '	'We will acquire a sophisticated PABX device to prioritise incoming phone calls and thus improve service to favoured clients.'

SUGGESTED WARRANTS

The essential problem with technology knowledge is seeing the wall rather than individual bricks. A survey in a magazine of word processing packages may give a vast matrix, comparing hundreds of features against dozens of products. However good, this material is too detailed for effective use in decision-making. But there may be a pattern to be found in the detail. Perhaps 40 of the 250 features can be grouped within one broad aspect of *presentation*, ie the variety and refinement of printed output; several other features (eg thesaurus, spell-checker, glossary) can be considered as part of one *content* aspect. This leads to a warrant in aspects form such as: 'Word processing packages have five main aspects, under which all the more detailed features can be bunched: *presentation; content; manipulation; essential interface;* and *advanced interface* . . '

This warrant can assist decision-making. It suggests assessing the issues in any particular case under these five aspects. If Corkwood Bank is choosing a software product for the back-office staff only, and if the word processing required is very limited, then a plausible decision could be to choose the product primarily on essential interface (eg use of function keys, menus, mouse etc), rather than the other four aspects.

In other debates it could be more convenient to use a comparison or gradations rather than an aspects warrant. Different tools suit different cases. The table shows the possibilities of approaching technology in this style. All six examples share the general form shown in the 'Decision-making Logic' diagram.[2]

The warrant-form tools can be used in a variety of contexts. As just described, you can process an otherwise unmanageable set of facts from a publication into a useful pattern. You can also encourage experts in a certain area to synthesise their knowledge into one of the six warrant forms, so that others involved in debate get a clear view of what is essential. You can assess the quality of advice given by specialists by seeing if it can be fitted coherently into a warrant form or not.

When reading or listening, you don't need to accumulate a large quantity of material before wondering: 'How on earth can I make sense of all this?' You can try from the start to fit material into the warrant forms. If you are being briefed by someone knowledgeable but prolix, you can break in now and again, with comments like: 'Just to check that I understand what you are saying: there seem to be four main gradations of PABX device . . ' Or even: 'All these facts about ISDN, optical fibre, frame relay and other advanced telecoms are very impressive, but I'm not clear how they affect the kind of decisions our bank might take. Can you help me by summarising the material into some neat generalisations — comparisons of main options (say), or key distinctions between possibilities . . '

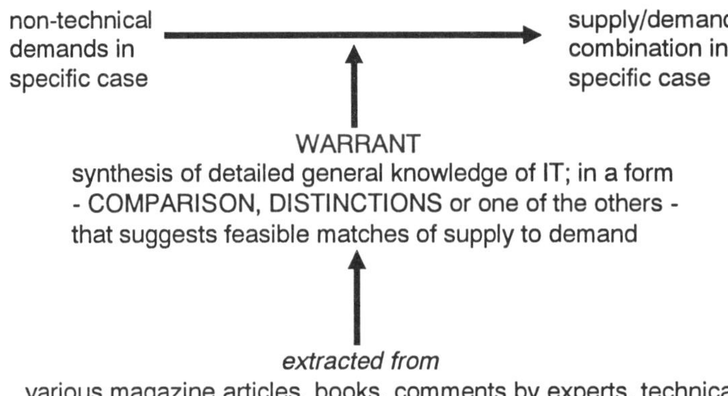
Using Warrants for Matching, Decision-making Logic
non-technical demands in specific case
supply/demand combination in specific case
WARRANT
synthesis of detailed general knowledge of IT; in a form
- COMPARISON, DISTINCTIONS or one of the others -
that suggests feasible matches of supply to demand
extracted from
various magazine articles, books, comments by experts, technical
documents, sales brochures, gurus' pronouncements etc;
often dominated by technology jargon without clear relevance

The briefings that follow give examples of the different warrant forms in action. This shows their power and raises issues of detail about the way to use them.[3]

Relation of Matching to the Other Planes

If an organisation's decisions are to be coherent and rational, its matching decisions will be related in numerous ways to decisions on the other four planes. To take an extreme instance, decisions to redevelop most of a bank's systems, matching many new, hitherto impossible, features with new object-oriented database technology, ought to be consistent with other large decisions of agenda, scope, context and approach.

This may seem self-evident, but it needs stressing, because most books and articles on IM either leave out matching decisions altogether, or limit themselves to technology-specific platitudes: 'expert systems can be a good thing, and telecoms can bring competitive advantage too; oh, and don't forget document imaging . . '[4]

NOTES & ARGUMENTS

1 This seems a pretty fundamental question, and yet nobody else seems to have tackled it — or even formulated it. You may find this as odd as if all books about economics ignored the phenomenon of inflation, or books about pottery never mentioned that earthenware had to be glazed to be waterproof, or books about windmills avoided the fundamental design problem of how to change the plane of the wings when the direction of the wind changes.

Or you may not find these comparisons persuasive. Some people do believe that business requirements should always be finalised before any technology factors are even considered. To hold that view is to deny that matching decisions are IM decisions at all, and thus to obviate the need for any tools for matching warrants. But this ignores the truth that the most rational choice is normally the *best-buy match* of technology supply to business demands — and that is often a very different thing from the unquestioning supply of *ideal* demands that have been defined in isolation. Once that point is conceded, the challenge of decisions on the matching plane is unavoidable.

2 The briefing text almost slides in the assumption that technology facts are *only ever* relevant to decision-making if they are cast in one of the six warrant forms. This is not so. The book by Angell and Smithson contains many facts and judgements about technology that are not in any of the warrant forms:

'Users often fail to appreciate the cost of keeping data online . . their files are out of sight, out of mind' (p. 79); 'It has been estimated that 90 per cent of all organizational information travels less than 0.5 miles' (p. 131); 'Further acceptance (of EDI) depends on the achievement of a critical mass of users and this seems to rely largely on major organizations exerting pressure on their partners' (p. 134); 'Compared to telephone calls, E-mail cannot incorporate intonation and emphasis, and it may actually reduce social interaction; messages lack the verbal 'padding' used to maintain a working relationship' (p. 136); 'Although expensive, video-conferences potentially save travel time and money; it is probably short-sighted to aim solely at travel savings as this may be unpopular where travel is seen as a 'perk' of the job.' (p. 138); 'The idea of distilling the knowledge of experts into an expert system is misconceived for all but highly formalized knowledge' (p. 152).

Plainly, simple statements can sometimes assist decision-making, and thus count as warrants. But the material above would become much more powerful if expanded into one of the warrant forms: eg the point about e-mail could be part of a comparison, setting out the pros and cons of e-mail and other forms of messaging; the point about video-conferencing also; the judgement on expert systems might contribute to a distinctions warrant that showed how different applications of expert system technology have different objectives; and so on.

3 A set of tools for processing technology possibilities can't be demonstrated without bringing in specific technologies. The technologies in the following briefings are *not* the most significant anybody should know about. They are just handy examples. The facts given are meant to be accurate as at Summer 1994, but if there is any value in the tools, it should survive the specific facts.

The warrant forms are the main tools used to construct the book O'Brien (*Database*). Knowledge about the broad field of database technology is organised as briefings containing warrants. The 31 briefings contain 181 warrants, each in one of the six forms.

4 Some books and articles describe cases of the application of technology in an anecdotal, eulogistic way — but do they really help anybody to take better matching decisions?

The book on telecoms by Williams describes how the retailer Wal-Mart made innovative use of VSAT satellite technology (pp. 59-63). With this technology Wal-Mart set up a private network, transmitting data between stores and other locations, for sophisticated, integrated systems to monitor stock, control supplies etc. This network is said to have only one-quarter the operating costs of alternative arrangements.

At 2000 words, this is the longest of the many examples of the beneficial use of telecoms technology contained in that book, but once the enthusiastic rhetoric is stripped away (about how innovative it all was, and how Wal-Mart managers gained the just rewards of their bold vision and so on), the summary in the previous paragraph is about all that remains.

How does this equip anyone to take any IM decisions? The one useful fact contained in the piece is that VSAT technology (whatever that is) can bring cost advantages relative to alternative technologies (whatever they are). Therefore VSAT is a way of doing things very cost-effectively, *but not* of doing certain things that would be *impossible* with other technologies. If true, this piece of general knowledge could help shape decisions in a particular case. But even this fact is never explicitly stated; it is simply the residue that survives after the rhetoric and the case-specific detail are crossed out.

If the cost-saving characteristic of VSAT technology is indeed a true fact, do you gain anything from reading a specific case? Surely not. The details about Wal-Mart just get in the way. 2000 words would be better invested in a comparison warrant showing the pros and cons of VSAT and whatever the rival telecoms possibilities are, including generalisations about costs, appropriateness for different patterns of traffic, risks and other factors. For example:

'(VSAT) is especially well suited to industries with large amounts of light data traffic generated over a wide geographical area. It is best suited to applications requiring short transmissions into a host and full-screen transmissions back to the users; retail, shipping, and reservation applications are examples.' (John P Slone, 'An Introduction to Data Communications' in Umbaugh's anthology, 2nd ed., p. 351.) This one paragraph contains more useful knowledge about VSAT technology than five pages by Williams.

If Wal-Mart did make intelligent use of the technology, a good example warrant might bring out such points, by showing how Wal-Mart's applications matched the general characteristics of VSAT technology. It might perhaps relate that Wal-Mart never thought that full-screen transmissions back to users were important, but VSAT technology made them very cheap anyway, and, as it turned out, they were surprisingly valuable.

An example warrant that eschewed rhetoric to bring out such points could assist decision-making in all kinds of other situations:

- 'Our applications don't call for large amounts of light data traffic; we have small amounts of heavy data traffic. Therefore VSAT probably isn't appropriate.'
- 'Our new systems will probably call for great *up-front investment* in software and database. Therefore the question of which telecoms technology brings the lowest *operating costs* is not the most crucial one.'
- 'Our requirements seem to form the classic pattern where VSAT technology is most appropriate from a *theoretical* point of view. Let's move on quickly to the more practical aspects: Are there reliable sup-

pliers of the technology? Are we strong enough in telecoms experts to handle it?'

The Williams Wal-Mart case isn't unusual. The majority of case studies cited enthusiastically in books and articles are open to the same kind of criticisms. Like many others this case provokes questions without answering them:

How do the low operating costs (which seem to be the point of the whole thing) relate to capital costs? Are the relatively low operating costs perhaps distorted by the transmission of large quantities of data of low marginal value, at low or zero marginal cost?

Did Wal-Mart have to design its own satellite and hire an appropriate rocket to launch it, or did it just sign a contract with some other body that handled all the technicalities — or where between those extremes did its involvement fall? Does Wal-Mart have to run its own team of equipment maintenance engineers, for example?

Was Wal-Mart making a big investment that could conceivably have been a complete failure? Did Wal-Mart have to develop some piece of hardware or software that could be patented or at least would be difficult to develop again? Is VSAT the kind of enterprise a company can enter into gradually with experiments and prototype services?

Is Wal-Mart perhaps relying on a technology that is inherently more vulnerable than other options? Does the choice of VSAT perhaps bring disadvantages in communicating with those outside the network — suppliers, say? Does VSAT carry a price for the future in isolation from other technical standards? Does it give Wal-Mart greater or less flexibility in adapting to future needs — if Wal-Mart sets up a home-shopping service with people ordering through PCs, or if it takes over a financial services firm?

Finally, the most basic question of all is: What were the difficult to assess, finely balanced tradeoffs facing Wal-Mart managers when they decided to use VSAT? Surely the decision *was* finely balanced; if it was an obvious and straightforward one, it would not be singled out for praise in a book.

The importance of such questions goes far beyond the Wal-Mart case in Williams's book. A good case study raises and discusses such questions; unfortunately, many don't.

CONNECTIONS

12. Matching through Comparisons	How supply-demand matching material can be arranged as a comparison of pros and cons that goes a long way towards reaching a decision
13. Matching through Distinctions	The technique of drawing distinctions between possibilities for consideration, that are neutral rather than decision-forcing
14. Matching through Gradations	The important variety of the distinctions warrant where gradations are used to define the options
15. Matching through Charts	Ways of using chart warrants for orientation in an area of technology, to reduce confusion in debate
16. Matching through Aspects	Ways of using the less decision-forcing aspects warrants for orientation in an area of technology
17. Matching through Examples	Examples with less explicit decision-making force, that can still be useful in arriving at matching decisions

12. Matching through Comparisons

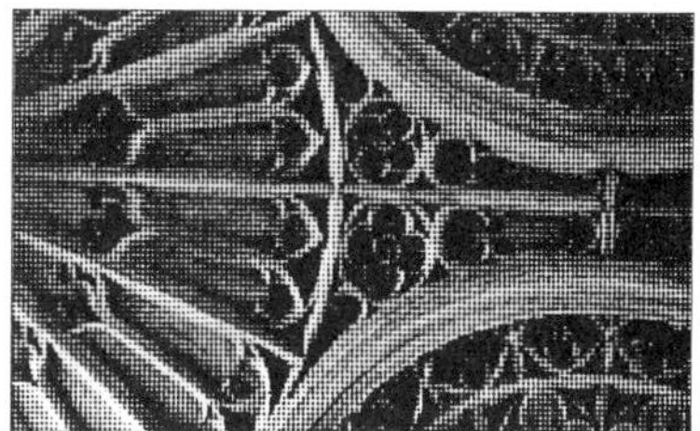

TOPIC

A firm matching decision amounts to a choice between several generally available technologies for achieving something in a particular case. A comparison warrant spells out the pros and cons of two or more different possibilities in general terms.

By seeing how heavily the various general factors mentioned by the warrant weigh in your particular case you can go a long way towards making a choice between the possibilities. That may sound fine in theory; this briefing uses examples to see how it works in practice.

SUGGESTED WARRANTS

Here are three examples, fabricated but offered as plausible, of decision-making through the use of comparison warrants.[1] Putting the straightforward before the complex, the comparisons are between: CD-ROM and WORM as storage media; different types of input device as interface for a database system; and different architectures for office automation.

CD-ROM and WORM: Possible Context

Grey Gum is a manufacturer of diesel engines — expensive and complex products. There are only six distinct models, but each engine ordered can consist of a unique combination of choices on thousands of options. Product documentation runs into dozens of thick volumes — containing many engineering drawings and photos. Here is a rough outline of a possible application:

- Maintain in a computer system the body of documentation about each of the six product models in all variants. Update it as minor changes are made, particularly new problems and solutions.
- When a new engine is sold, deliver its documentation, tailored to the options chosen, on some high-capacity disk that can be read by the customer's PC.

- As changes of documentation occur, send out new information on disks to existing customers.
- Thus allow the customer's engineers or Grey Gum's own engineers to access the documentation electronically rather than on paper or microfilm.

Given those *demands*, a number of issues of *supply* arise. Concentrate on just one of them: disk storage technology. Storing thousands of pages of text would be no problem, but these pages contain graphics too, and that calls for a disk of fairly high capacity. Grey Gum's main choice is between two different technologies for high-capacity disk: CD-ROM and WORM.

The choice can't be made simply by calculating which one will store the required quantity of data most cost-effectively. CD-ROM and WORM differ in much more interesting ways than that. To help decide which of the two is the better supply factor for the demand described, Grey Gum managers need a comparison warrant.

CD-ROM and WORM: Comparison-form Warrant

CD-ROM and WORM can be compared on three main counts: production economics; updating; versions.

- **Production economics**. As with an audio CD, it costs a lot to make the first copy of a CD-ROM and much less to make the second and subsequent copies. By comparison, writing information to (say) 100 WORMs, costs about a hundred times as much as writing to one.**2**
- **Updating**. By comparison with conventional magnetic disks, both technologies store much data, very cheaply on small disks. The drawback is that data once written to a CD-ROM or a WORM can't be overwritten by amendments.

  With a WORM disk, nothing written can ever be changed, but empty parts of the disk can be filled in over time with new data.

  With CD-ROM you could do the same thing, but you probably wouldn't. The economic logic of CD-ROM is to have one relatively expensive device producing many copies of disks for distribution, and many relatively cheap, read-only CD-ROM drives attached to PCs. So, in practice, a CD-ROM, once distributed, is not updated, however much room may be left on it. Should its data become out of date, then a completely new version of the disk can be made centrally and distributed.
- **Versions**. Suppose you want to distribute slightly different versions of a body of data: 90% (say) might be the same on most disks, but 10% might be variable. As the previous two points imply, the WORM approach can handle this reasonably well, without much adverse effect on costs. With CD-ROM, however, different disks (whether different by 10%, 1% or 50%) have to be treated as separate items, without economies of production.

CD-ROM and WORM: Possible Decision-making

With this warrant comparing the two technologies Grey Gum is well placed to make decisions about its own case. Suppose more careful examination of Grey Gum demands showed:

- Thousands of copies of disks will need to be produced.
- When information changes in any important way, the changes are usually sweeping; therefore throwing one disk away and replacing it by another is the natural, neat approach.
- Though products exist with many different combinations of options, it is still acceptable (in fact better for engineers who go from engine to engine) to have standard, rather than customised electronic documentation.

Were all that true, then CD-ROM would be the obvious choice. But careful examination of the demands might give a different picture:

- The company sells hundreds rather than thousands of engines every year, and each engine needs very few disks of documentation. Therefore economy of scale in disk production is not an issue.
- But incremental amendments, additions of hints etc come out almost every week. It would be nice to send out this information on diskette to each customer, who could use it to update the main documentation by some simple procedure.
- Everyone agrees that it would be a fine thing if a section of each documentation disk contained data unique to the particular engine — including material added by the customer's engineers at their own initiative.

This is an extreme set of factors where the decision in favour of WORM is virtually forced. Of course, real-life cases are usually more tricky. The point is that, however intricate, any case will be much easier to debate rationally if there is a good warrant available.

The warrant given is general enough for use in many other situations. Grey Gum might consider some quite different demands: eg storing the master price book, with information, both graphic and textual, enabling sales staff, dealers and engineers to configure new engine orders or to order replacement parts . . .

Interface Device: Possible Context

The Yertchuk Documentation Centre is a combined library, museum and gallery for the history and culture of its region. There is already a computer system storing information about the collection, but it is used only by staff and academic researchers. The demand now is to open up this system to ordinary visitors. Since (it is assumed) many are not computer-literate, interface is a big issue. Should a visitor to the centre enter commands at the keyboard, or communicate with the system in some other way — touch screen, for instance?

To help in this decision it would be good to have a warrant summarising the points of comparison between four different interface devices: keyboard (excluding of course its use for typing data in bulk), mouse, touch screen and tablet.3

Interface Device: Comparison-form Warrant

Interface devices can be compared on five main counts:

- **Naturalness**. This is the point on which touch screen scores best. Nothing could be less formidable to a nervous user than just touching the screen. Of the other three devices, the tablet comes last since it is least familiar and most elaborate. But this is the touch screen's sole success; it comes far behind or doesn't compete at all on the four counts that follow.
- **Ergonomics**. The mouse and tablet score over the keyboard — requiring less effort and getting things done faster. Keyboard input is still much pleasanter than touch screen, which is tiring, slow and error-prone.
- **Instruction-giving**. Most people find it easier to select an option from a menu on the screen by pointing with the mouse, than by pressing arrow keys on a keyboard. For systems with a rather small range of instruction possibilities, the mouse is certainly the neatest and for more complex systems too, many (though not all) people prefer it. For systems with a very wide range of intricate instructing possibilities the tablet is best of all. (Among other reasons, you can get far more options arranged legibly over the area of the pad than on a normal screen, and avoid going through levels of menus.) But for many systems that are not all that complicated, choice between keyboard, mouse and tablet as an instructing device is a matter of taste.
- **Rich access**: ie using the system's functions for access in ways that go beyond the predefined; eg to find all texts containing any of the words 'tower', 'towers', 'towering' etc. The keyboard scores highest; the other devices can't compare with it as a way of inputting text.
- **Manipulating**: ie altering things on the screen; eg splitting the screen into two windows and then resizing one, so that it only occupies a quarter of the screen. If the interface demands include the ability to manipulate graphics in any sense, then the mouse or tablet is essential.

Interface Device: Possible Decision-making

Decision-makers at Yertchuk might use this warrant to develop decisions in many conceivable ways:

- 'We think it will be a struggle to get most visitors even to consider using the system. Therefore we can't afford *not* to make touch screen the interface device. Therefore we will accept all the ergonomic disadvantages, and all the limitations it imposes on the sophistication of what the user can do with the system.'
- *Or* 'Our typical user will be someone interested enough in the subject

to use simple instructions through a keyboard, and will be looking for information best accessed through rich textual access.'

- *Or* 'The big feature of this system will be the images it displays. We choose a mouse. It will enable visitors to click from image to image and — having learnt the system — to bring several chosen images together on the screen for comparison. The more forbidding tablet would bring no advantage.'
- *Or* 'This will be a powerful system rich in functions, used to access many different types of information — texts, paintings, maps, documents etc. The best way of helping people exploit the possibilities is to provide two devices — keyboard and tablet.'

Office Systems: Possible Context

A large legal practice, Blackbutt and Bloodwood (B&B), intends to set up completely new office automation systems. Since there are thousands of legal firms in the world that need automation, it is not surprising that certain supplier companies specialise in marketing systems for the legal sector. Typically, the general-purpose office automation facilities (eg word processing) are combined with specific legal functions, such as time-recording for fee-earners. Within B&B one party puts the following argument:

- All specialist suppliers of systems for legal practices build their systems in one of two ways. *Either* they take a general office automation system (eg DEC All-in-One), that runs on a mini-computer, providing access through terminals, and they add onto it specially written software for legal administration; *or else* they use personal computers linked together in a LAN (local area network) as the hardware, together with a mixture of several general-purpose PC software products and specially written legal software.
- B&B should first decide between these two approaches (call them the mini and the PC architectures). Only after that should B&B invite firm proposals from suppliers — and then only from those with systems based on the chosen architecture.

Some partners disagree, saying that B&B should simply find the best system in terms of functions provided, cost, reliability etc without worrying about technology architectures. But they are persuaded by the following arguments:

- Only present needs and present offerings can be compared in detail, but B&B needs to make a long-term decision. The best chance of meeting the challenges and exploiting the opportunities of the future is to decide which of the two architectures seems *intrinsically* the most appropriate.
- B&B wants freedom to break loose from any system supplier and extend systems in ways it chooses. It will be more confident of doing that if it has positively rather than passively assented to the architecture its system is based on.

● There are numerous possible suppliers — too many to examine in detail. Deciding between the two architectures is the best way to narrow the field and advance debate.

To make a decision between the mini and PC architectures for legal office systems, B&B needs a warrant that compares the general characteristics of the two.

Office Systems: Comparison-form Warrant

Here are six points of comparison between the mini and PC architectures:

● The mini architecture is longer established and better proven. The PC architecture (if at all substantial) requires more expertise to get right. There is more chance of terrible blunders with the PC architecture if the specialists who set it up are not really expert.

● This general point applies *a fortiori* to one specific function: making data (eg in the accounts database) accessible and updatable for many users. This doesn't mean that the PC architecture can't provide what is required — only that it requires more expert people, taking more time.

● When the system is in operation the mini architecture is less demanding to control. With all data stored on the disks of the central mini, it is relatively easy to design and carry out foolproof backup procedures. The PC architecture is less centralised, and this makes system control more complicated. You therefore need a higher-calibre system manager, spending more time.

● The PC software market is a more vital, competitive place than the mini software market. Through natural evolutionary forces, the best of the PC software for such things as presentation graphics, spreadsheets, desktop publishing and so on is generally better than the best of the mini software, in terms of quality and range of functions — and much cheaper too.

● The PC architecture is more flexible, in that it is far easier to arrange for different people to use different software; eg one person uses Excel version 5.0 and another an earlier version, and another some other spreadsheet software entirely. That kind of flexibility is also worthwhile if the software of the system is often upgraded. Then the keenest users can be getting to know the latest version while the majority are still at the old.

● The PC architecture is more flexible than the mini in another way. If a few people in the office become interested in (say) heavyweight statistical analysis or a database of photos, they can experiment on their own PCs without disturbing anybody else. But with an architecture based on one central mini, it could be a tough task to add such facilities without causing any complications for anybody else.

Office Systems: Possible Decision-making

Given this warrant, here is one way the B&B partners might react:

● 'We give great weight to choosing an easy way over a difficult way. Therefore we think there is a prima facie case for choosing the mini architecture over the PC. Therefore the onus is on a supporter of PC to show it has overriding advantages.'
● 'We don't care if the features on our system are less good than the absolute state-of-the-art PC software. We are happy to accept that; it seems a trivial point compared to the main issues.'
● 'We prefer not to have the kind of flexibility brought by the PC architecture in various ways. Control is of more interest to us than flexibility. Even if we had the flexibility to do complicated things we'd prefer not to use it.'
● 'Therefore we choose the mini architecture.'

But it is easy to imagine that the reasoning could go quite differently:
● 'The whole warrant really amounts to a comparison between the mini architecture, which is safe and ordinary, and the PC architecture, with the opportunity to take trouble to have a better than average system, albeit with attendant risks.'
● 'We value very highly the chance the PC architecture offers to have an exceptionally good system. It fits our whole business policy of being an upmarket firm.'
● 'We also want to stimulate people to use IT on their own initiative rather than just use what they are given. Several of the points show that PC architecture is much superior on that score.'
● 'The only question then is: Is the PC architecture too risky? Given the people we have in the firm and our experience to date with IT, we think we have less need to be cautious and follow safe paths than most comparable firms.'
● 'Therefore we choose the PC architecture.'

Using this Warrant Form

These three comparison warrants display minor varieties:
● CD-ROM v WORM is a simple two-way comparison.
● The warrant on interface devices compares four possibilities on five points. On some of the five points of comparison one or two of the possibilities scarcely compete.
● The comparison warrant on office systems is two-way. Instead of straightforward, well-bounded possibilities such as alternative disk technologies, the contenders are architectures — that have to be compared on rather slippery criteria such as risk and flexibility.

These instances of matching warrants and those in the following briefings raise some implications for the structure of decision-making. As the diagram suggests, the warrants permit computer-literate but non-specialist managers to participate in decision-making. If you are not in favour of that, then you won't need such warrants, but then it is unlikely that your organisation will consistently arrive at rational decisions.

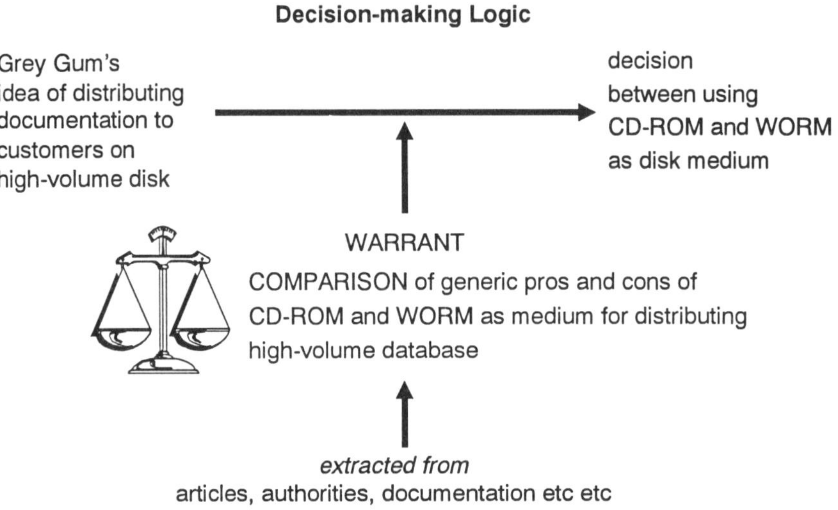
Decision-making Logic
Grey Gum's idea of distributing documentation to customers on high-volume disk
decision between using CD-ROM and WORM as disk medium
WARRANT
COMPARISON of generic pros and cons of CD-ROM and WORM as medium for distributing high-volume database
extracted from
articles, authorities, documentation etc etc

The presentation of the three examples may seem to suggest a rather orderly procedure: first, define demands carefully; second, study a warrant about supply/demand matching possibilities; third, arrive logically at a decision on supply choice. But this depends on the simplifying assumption that the original demands include all the points which, the warrant subsequently shows, are critical to choice of supply.

In practice, things are usually less clearcut. It could be that, to begin with, the people at Grey Gum never considered the idea of the documentation disk being updated by the customer. Perhaps they only began to consider the idea seriously when the warrant revealed that this was a key point in choosing between two supply choices. Perhaps this even ended up as one of the most important features of the system. Thus a far more realistic and fruitful decision-process could be:

- define demands roughly, but covering points that seem likely to be critical;
- study relevant warrant;
- go back to reconsider demands, concentrating on those points of demand mentioned in the warrant as relevant to determination of supply;
- identify several different matches of supply and demand, each consistent with the warrant and each a plausible option;
- do detailed work to choose between the options.

In other words, matching warrants are best used within the *iterative* process that is characteristic of most problems in most fields where the aim is to find the best buy.

NOTES & ARGUMENTS

1 The examples of decision-making in all the briefings about matching decisions are fabricated, thought-experiments, rather than the models to be emulated found in many other publications.

2 There are actually two ways to produce CD-ROMs: use a specialised bureau service, or buy equipment to master and copy the disks yourself. If you want (say) a dozen copies, the latter will probably seem more cost-effective on paper, but it may cost a great deal of specialist effort. According to the feature 'Roll Your Own CD' in *PC Magazine*, 13/9, pp. 137ff., desktop CD-making is 'not yet suited to casual users'. Such veiled warnings are usually to be heeded. Either way, the comparison with WORM given in the briefing remains valid.

3 The touch-screen product is actually a transparent frame that fits over the front of the standard screen hardware.

A digitising tablet has two main components. One is a pad, usually at least the size of an A4 sheet, sometimes much bigger; hidden in the pad are various electronic elements, so that when pressure is applied at any point, the exact location can be sent as a message to the computer. The component used to press on the pad can be a pen or stylus or mouse-like device, called cursor or puck. Often a card or sheet of plastic with a printed template of application instructions is placed on the pad; then moving the stylus across the pad is a convenient way to select options.

CONNECTIONS

13. Matching through Distinctions	Less decision-forcing forms of warrants for matching supply and demand
14. Matching through Gradations	Less decision-forcing forms of warrants for matching supply and demand
15. Matching through Charts	Less decision-forcing forms of warrants for matching supply and demand
16. Matching through Aspects	Less decision-forcing forms of warrants for matching supply and demand
17. Matching through Examples	Less decision-forcing forms of warrants for matching supply and demand
36. Business Process Re-engineering	Should a legal firm want to re-engineer all its business processes, the PC architecture will offer more flexibility — arguably
37. End-user Computing	The PC architecture offers more room than the mini for private end-user initiatives

13. Matching through Distinctions

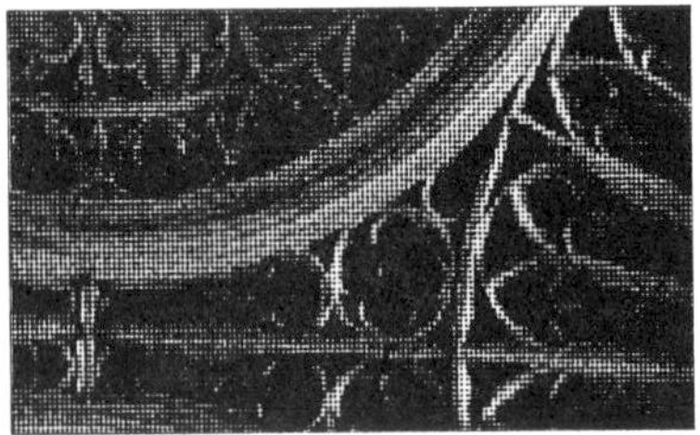

TOPIC

The comparison warrant discussed in the previous briefing exposes certain possibilities, and also provides information that helps in the choice between them. A distinctions warrant attempts less. It clarifies a range of available options, and highlights the key points that make them distinct, but it does not set out all their pros and cons.

Making a useful distinctions warrant calls for more than just knowledge. In any complex field, distinctions may be drawn in many different ways. Judgement is needed to pick those distinctions most likely to be relevant to reaching sound decisions. The examples in this briefing show this idea in action.

SUGGESTED WARRANTS

Here are three examples of decision-making through the use of distinctions warrants. The distinctions are between: different types of expert system application; different types of computer-aided instruction (CAI) system; and different technologies concerned with human speech or language.

Expert System Roles: Possible Context

Expert system technology is potentially applicable to most problems where complicated rules can be applied to facts. Some people at Smoothbark Assurance have the idea of an expert system to process claims:

- Whenever a new claim on a policy comes in, the company sets a reserve for it — a provision made in its accounts for money it may eventually have to pay out to settle the claim. An expert system could determine automatically an appropriate reserve for each claim, applying rules to details known so far; eg (for an employer's liability claim) nature of injury suffered by employee, probability of employer's negligence being proved, trends in court awards for this type of disablement etc.
- An expert system could also judge whether a claim seemed plausible

and should be paid without question, or whether it should be investigated. It might use rules based on factors such as: Is this a relatively low claim for the loss of a suitcase? Does the insured have a record of making frequent small claims for lost suitcases? If so, were any of them investigated thoroughly?

● Every single claim can't be handled completely automatically, but a system could also apply rules to spot delicate cases, and pass them over for handling by humans.

All this sounds promising, in fact too much so; it gives the people on Smoothbark's IT steering committee a decision-making problem:

● Smoothbark can almost certainly find *some* sensible use for an expert system in processing claims. It would be easy to describe a dozen more plausible possibilities to go with those above. They would differ in sophistication, in objectives and in underlying assumptions, and they would overlap and contradict each other in various messy ways. The steering committee needs to impose some coherence on the sifting of possibilities.

● One way is to set up a work group for a feasibility study, but then (experience shows) it might develop a momentum of its own, and report back after months of work with a huge document — describing, recommending and justifying a proposed new system or set of systems, but saying very little about fundamental assumptions that have been made, or about the multitude of conceivable variants that have been rejected.

● Therefore before initiating any such work, the steering committee intends to get a better grip on some of the fundamental distinctions and options that arise. Once some policy decisions have been taken about them, the detailed study of particular systems can be far more effective.

● But what kind of fundamental options can be extracted from all the literature that exists about expert systems? A distinctions warrant is needed.

Expert System Roles: Distinctions-form Warrant

One fallacy about expert system applications is that they usually distill the knowledge and experience of authorities into rules — as when the knowledge and experience of a great heart specialist are expressed as rules within a system that helps a lesser doctor make diagnoses.**1** But, though the essence of an expert system application is rules-based logic, these rules may come from *any* source — from railway timetables or legislation about unemployment benefits or tourism guides, just as well as from authorities.

Not only can the rules come from a variety of sources, but the role played by the system can vary. The various possibilities can be worked up into a six-way distinctions warrant:**2**

● **Authority rules, expert user.** The system's rules codify the expertise of an authority in the field. The main user of the system is the same person or another of similar status. The advantage is that (say) a medical consultant can work faster and with less mental energy for most of the time, and save intense concentration for really tricky cases.

- **Authority rules, shrewd user.** This is the classic medical case mentioned above. The system's rules codify the expertise of an authority. The main user of the system is somebody who would otherwise not be able to do the work, or would do it much less consistently and effectively. However, this user is still far from being a complete novice in the field.
- **Published rules, shrewd user.** The system's rules don't come from an authority, but are based on an intelligent analysis of voluminous, confusing, published material, eg the range of optional features when ordering a combine-harvester. The main user of the system is someone (eg a sales rep), who could, if necessary, manage without it and in some circumstances will ignore it — but is saved much time and possible error by the system.
- **Published rules, uncritical user.** The system's rules represent the content of published material, eg the conditions attached to employment benefit. The main user of the system is someone (eg a clerk in a benefits office), who lacks the knowledge and authority to do anything other than follow the rules.
- **Derived rules.** The system's rules come neither from authority nor from published material; they are derived automatically by mathematics or logic from experience; eg a system helps an advertising agency decide where to advertise, using rules developed by processing statistics about past adverts and their results. Normally, the main users will be a mixture of the shrewd and uncritical.
- **Teaching.** Unlike the previous cases, the system is not (or not primarily) a means of doing work or solving a problem. Rather it is a way of training people, eg how to diagnose and repair defects in a machine. It needs two types of rules: rules about the thing being taught (analogous to the rules in the categories above), but also rules to govern the teaching process itself.

Expert System Roles: Possible Decision-making

Prompted by this warrant the decision-makers at Smoothbark start to recognise some of their options. Here are four different ways the analysis might go:

- *Either* 'Out of the six cases given in the warrant, handling insurance claims is closest to 'authority rules, shrewd user'. Somebody already experienced at assessing claims is a rather modest kind of authority, from whom we can extract appropriate rules. Ours is not a classic case, because the rules extracted from the 'authority' will probably be only a bit more clever than the rules that any intelligent person could think out anyway. We will set up a work group whose terms of reference are to design that kind of system (as opposed to any of the other five).'
- *Or instead* 'Though an expert system certainly can handle the claims

application and may be worth having, once you allow for the necessary involvement of the shrewd user, the net operational benefits are not very exciting. However, perhaps there is a different benefit. What about an expert system in the 'teaching' category — for *training* junior staff in the branches to assess most claims, rather than passing them on to more senior people? Make a work group concentrate on that kind of system.'

- *Or instead* 'We ought to concentrate on motor claims and forget the others. Develop a system in the 'derived rules' category to handle all those thousands of claims — not aiming primarily to save administration costs, but rather to produce claim estimates more keenly calculated than any human could achieve. Get a work group to develop that idea.'
- *Or instead* 'Tell a work group to devise three small, separate applications: one 'authority rules, shrewd user', one 'teaching', and one 'derived rules'. That seems the best way of taking the organisation through the learning process in this technology.'

Computer-aided Instruction (CAI): Possible Context

Turpentine Tours (TT) is a large travel company, offering its own range of packaged holidays as well as normal travel agency services. Attention here is already focused on the teaching category of expert system — aka computer-aided instruction (CAI).

Suppose TT used CAI to train new staff in the procedures for handling bookings (eg how to handle the refunds when a Cairo-Sydney single flight is changed to Cairo-Athens return), and the skills of giving travel advice (eg how to advise someone who wants a holiday collecting butterflies). Perhaps such a system could also train existing staff in new procedures whenever TT introduced new types of packaged holiday.

The potential advantages from improved teaching systems — if successful — are fairly obvious in outline. But before any commitment to detailed work, decision-makers at TT need a better view of the main options open to them.

Computer-aided Instruction (CAI): Distinctions-form Warrant

Possibilities within CAI can be analysed by drawing distinctions on each of three topics: the thing being taught; the teaching technique; and whether the teaching system is stand-alone or embedded in some other type of system (eg an operational one).

Within *thing taught* there are three main distinctions:

- First, there is the case where an expert system is teaching some **well-defined task**, eg how to fill in a tax form or how to carry out a certain medical test.
- But another type of system may be less concerned with teaching how to

do something very specific, than with imparting **knowledge**: eg knowledge of the principles and standards of accounting practice.

- Third is the case where teaching a task or imparting knowledge is a lesser aim than helping someone acquire a **skill**; eg a system can monitor the progress and control the curriculum of somebody learning to play a musical instrument.

Within the *teaching technique* topic there are also several distinctions to be made:

- **Straightforward.** The classic teaching technique of an expert system presents new facts to the pupil, and exchanges questions and answers in a pattern of statement-question-answer.
- **Explanation-dominated.** In some systems much of the learning value comes from the system's explanations of the correct answer, showing the reasoning leading up to it (eg in a system teaching the subtleties of cost accounting). It is even better if the system can take an alternative or incorrect answer and explain why it is not the best answer.
- **Mixed initiative.** A predictable one-to-one interaction can be enlivened by allowing the student to take the initiative. Besides giving a straight answer to a question, the student might be allowed to respond with: 'don't know', 'why do you ask?' or 'don't understand the question' etc.

If a system is largely concerned with teaching people to apply rules that it can and does apply itself, eg calculating the refund on a cancelled ticket, then the teaching facilities can be embedded in the operational system. There are distinct varieties of *embedding*:

- A teaching expert system can be embedded in an **operational expert system** (eg refunds on cancelled tickets); it teaches how to do the same thing the system itself does.
- An expert teaching system can be embedded in an **operational but not expert system**. It teaches how to do something related to the operational system (eg how to key in the data for a new booking). In effect it is a powerful improvement on the 'help' screens of the operational system.
- The expert teaching system can be completely **separate** from the operational system.

Computer-aided Instruction (CAI): Possible Decision-making

Given this warrant, here is one way the decision-makers at Turpentine Tours might work through their options:

- 'Do we want a CAI system where the **thing taught** is a well-defined task, or mainly pure knowledge, or a skill? 'Well-defined task' seems to be the answer; this covers things such as changing a Cairo-Sydney flight to Cairo-Athens and other generic procedures. It is true that advising about butterfly-collecting holidays seems more like knowledge or skill.

But we think we can devise rules for that kind of thing too, if we invest enough effort.'

● 'Next, **teaching technique**. A system with explanation or mixed initiative facilities is bound to be more complex than one with only straightforward techniques. But if the material is tricky enough and the person is studying alone, the more sophisticated techniques may be essential. However, our people will be under skilled mentors at our training centre or else with experienced colleagues in the branch office. Straightforward teaching technique will be adequate — if well designed of course.'

● '**Embedding** is a tough issue. Should the teaching system be embedded in our own operational but not expert system, or should it be a separate system altogether? It is undesirable for the operational system to bear unpredictable overheads; on the other hand, an embedded system could be a better way of introducing novices to steadily more complex procedures. More facts are needed before the choice is made.'

● 'The decision? Set up a team to design a system based on these decisions about thing taught and teaching technique. Tell the team to study and assess both options — embedded and separate.'

That is only one possible line of reasoning. If TT managers held the firm conviction that many rebooking procedures were so perplexing that powerful explanation facilities were vital — even for trained, experienced staff — then the debate would take quite another course.

Speech and Language Technologies: Possible Context

The conglomerate ABC is keen to exploit opportunities for advanced technology wherever possible. By co-ordinating projects in its innovation portfolio it tries to reduce technology risks and profit from experience. Thus if (say) its travel company has a bad experience with CAI technology, its publishing division can learn from this, and do better with its own ventures in that field.

ABC also co-ordinates plans for the use of telecoms by its subsidiaries. This is a separate matter from the innovation portfolio. Or is it? The IT sub-committee of the board is becoming increasingly confused by overlaps between things that once seemed separate. Some technologies associated with speech or language seem to be humdrum-telecoms when seen from one angle, and innovation-with-telecoms-connections from another. For instance, a recent discussion of telecoms planning lurched from voice mail into state-of-the-art voice recognition and from there into text translation. When that kind of thing happens, it is difficult to have confidence that any decisions made are cogent and consistent. The sub-committee asks an analyst to set out the main distinctions in the hazy region of speech and language technologies. That will help in keeping a sense of direction whenever individual projects and opportunities are debated.

Speech and Language Technologies: Distinctions-form Warrant

The prime distinction to make is between technologies associated with artificial intelligence (AI) and those that are not. If a computer can respond in different ways to an utterance made in natural language by a human, that seems to be a fair case of AI. On the other hand, storing a human utterance in some efficient compressed form, transmitting it and replaying it later to another human is really just telecoms technology, not AI. To distinguish possibilities further within these two main areas, a few more concepts are needed:

- Each technology is concerned in some sense with taking something that is **input**;
- and transforming it into something else, **output**;
- and it operates at a certain degree of **granularity**; eg one technology treats a whole utterance as a piece of input or output, while another works at the level of the individual sounds making up words.

These ideas can be used to distinguish the seven technologies listed in the table.

Speech and Language Technologies: Possible Decision-making

The warrant doesn't pose immediate either/or choices, but it should promote better decisions, by prompting confusion-clearing debate:

- 'This proposed innovative project will allow a customer to speak an order into a phone and have it accepted automatically without human intervention. Let's be clear that, as proposed, it entails *two* rather bold steps: use of speech recognition technology to decide what words the customer actually speaks in normal English, and use of natural language interface technology to recognise what they mean, ie deciding which words are verbs and nouns and so on. For the project to succeed these two technologies have to work successfully. Would it not be wiser to design the project somehow to be dependent on only one bold innovation — at least in its early stages?'
- 'This telecoms plan breaks down usage in various ways but it seems to combine stored voice and voice mail in the figures. Since they are two entirely different things, could you please separate them out?'
- 'In some places this project proposal. reads as though information will be output by stored voice, and in other places by speech synthesis. Surely there is a big difference. With stored voice you are limited to a prerecorded repertoire of phrases, but the voice is obviously human and the technology is well-proven. With speech synthesis your system can communicate a much greater range of information, but the voice is humanoid and the technology is still fairly innovative. Without knowing which approach you want to take we can't even consider your proposal, still less approve it.'

Speech and Language Technologies, Map of the Region

Little or no artificial intelligence

Phone conversation: interactive conversation;
input is a human voice;
output is a human voice;
granularity is an utterance.

Voice mail: storing a one-off message;
input is a human voice;
output is a human voice;
granularity is a whole message.

Stored voice: repeated, perhaps automatically edited, delivery of a pre-recorded message;
input is a human voice;
output is a human voice;
granularity is a word or phrase.

Associated with artificial intelligence

Speech recognition: one-off input to a computer system;
input is human voice (usually unnaturally careful);
output is natural language as coded text;
granularity is a word or phrase.

Natural language input interface: one-off input to a computer system;
input is natural language as coded text;
output is one-off input to computer system, formatted according to required conventions;
granularity is a word.

Speech synthesis: tailored output from a computer system;
input is natural language as coded text;
output is humanoid voice;
granularity is a phoneme (technical name for a separate sound within a word; eg 'tin' contains three phonemes).

Natural language translation: changing a text from one language to another;
input is natural language as coded text;
output is natural language as coded text;
granularity is a document.

Using this Warrant Form

The three warrants given as examples display minor variations within the distinctions form:

- The first warrant makes a six-way breakdown of expert systems. It does

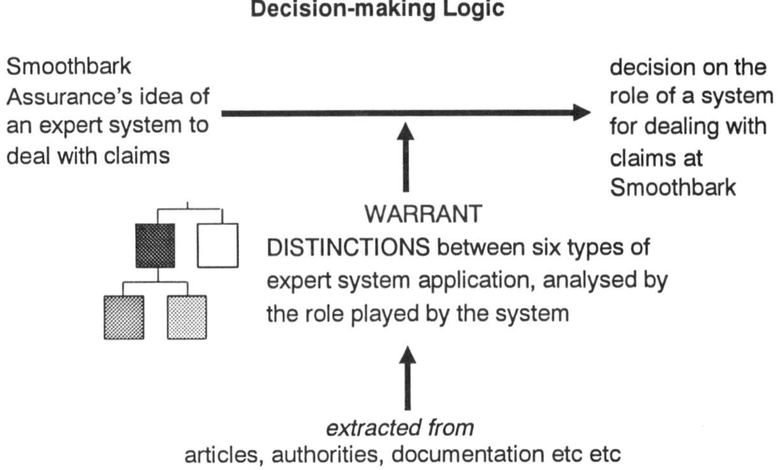
Decision-making Logic
Smoothbark Assurance's idea of an expert system to deal with claims
decision on the role of a system for dealing with claims at Smoothbark
WARRANT
DISTINCTIONS between six types of expert system application, analysed by the role played by the system
extracted from
articles, authorities, documentation etc etc

this largely by identifying two variables — the source of rules and the role of the system — and describing the most important combinations of them.

- The warrant about different types of computer-aided instruction (CAI) system is somewhat different; three main variables are picked out, and each is then broken down further.
- The last warrant about technologies concerned with human speech or language starts with a distinction between two categories and breaks each down further. This warrant is to the other two as a map of the Middle East region including Egypt, Syria, Turkey etc differs from a map of one continent. Its great value is in showing the *adjacent* countries from different continents.[3]

As the diagram suggests, a good distinctions warrant can pass the test of the Decision Question quite well. Though a comparison warrant may be intrinsically more decision-forcing, one in distinctions form can sometimes be the more useful. On some topics a warrant that both defines and compares all the main possibilities adequately would be too complex to be practical. Moreover, the really demanding task in a certain situation may be to understand what the different possible options are; once that is done, the implications of each may be fairly obvious, or it may be safe to delegate the detailed working out of the options. Or an area may be so complicated that it is best tackled in several pieces: first, draw distinctions carefully to expose the main possibilities; second, after narrowing things down further, use a comparison warrant to help choose between the most relevant options.

NOTES & ARGUMENTS

1 For example: 'An expert system is generally defined as a computer program that relies on knowledge and reasoning to perform a difficult task usually performed only by a human expert.' Kamran Parsaye, Mark Chignell, Setrag Khoshafian and Harry Wong, *Intelligent Databases, Object-Oriented, Deductive Hypermedia Technologies* (Wiley 1989), p. 162.

2 The starting-point for developing this warrant was the article by Dorothy Leonard-Barton and John J Sviokla: 'Putting Expert Systems to Work', *Harvard Business Review*, March-April 1988, also in Harvard Business Review (1990).

An expert system maven might very well prefer to make a five-way distinction warrant, or seven-way, or six-way with distinctions defined differently. This doesn't matter. The purpose of the example is to show that *any decent* distinctions warrant can break open a subject to stimulate informed debate. This rider applies to all the examples in these briefings about matching.

3 A 'speech and language' region of the world of IT where AI and telecoms abut excludes some areas of AI technology (expert system, neural network etc) and some of telecoms (eg electronic mail, bulletin board, on-line chat, whiteboard software, videoconferencing etc). If that seems unsatisfactory the region mapped in the briefing can be extended to include the various forms of messaging and conferencing. But then videoconferencing includes shared amendment of documents, and that in turn is closely related to standards for technology-independent documents, text database organisation and multimedia hardware . . . Any map that doesn't cover the entire world is bound to have awkward edges. The important thing is to have a clear map of whatever region is most relevant. What is most relevant will vary from case to case.

CONNECTIONS

12. Matching through Comparisons	More decision-forcing forms of warrants for matching supply and demand
14. Matching through Gradations	Equally decision-forcing forms of warrants for matching supply and demand
15. Matching through Charts	Less decision-forcing forms of warrants for matching supply and demand
16. Matching through Aspects	Less decision-forcing forms of warrants for matching supply and demand
17. Matching through Examples	Less decision-forcing forms of warrants for matching supply and demand.
38. Decision Support Systems	Expert systems are not classic decision support systems, but some are close to that territory

14. Matching through Gradations

TOPIC

Sometimes a range of possible matches of supply and demand falls into the pattern of a distinctions warrant — but of a special kind. The possibilities form an evident pattern of gradations — the higher the gradation, the more extensive the functional demand, and the more substantial its technology supply.

This kind of warrant, like a distinctions warrant, exposes options, without directly indicating their pros and cons. Nevertheless, as the examples in the briefing show, the scale of gradations can be a great help in reaching decisions.

SUGGESTED WARRANTS

The three subjects analysed as gradations warrants are: electronic meeting support; bridges, gateways and other ways of linking together networks; and systems for the production of documents by a collaborating workgroup.

Electronic Meeting: Possible Context

Cedar Wattle City is a go-ahead place that welcomes stylish modern businesses. One of the mayor's many ideas for taking advantage of advanced technology is to set up electronic meeting facilities. When the directors of a corporation considering relocation to Cedar Wattle come to the town hall to discuss local infrastructure and subsidies and so on, they will be shown into a special conference room. There people use terminals to key in contributions to a meeting; they brainstorm through ideas, vote electronically and follow the progress of the debate on a large screen at the front; they can draw and display diagrams to show their ideas, or access data held in spreadsheets and generate pie-charts to support their arguments.

Some visitors may have difficulty with a terminal and prefer to get back to the mayor's office, but they will be encouraged to attend meetings of the education or the public works committee, where councillors use the system fluently, to debate projections of pupil numbers or rerouting of sewers, generating colour bar-charts and maps on the large screen. This, it is felt, should convey a favourable impression of the city's state-of-the-art administration.

Though a great salesman of his city to the outside world, the mayor of Cedar Wattle can recognise hype when other people are selling to him. Most of what he hears and reads about systems for electronic meeting support is long on rhetoric and short on relevant facts. Before going any further he needs to demystify the subject and recognise the issues that differentiate possible applications.

Electronic Meeting: Gradations-form Warrant

Electronic meeting systems typically encourage brainstorming, exchange of opinions, and debate among a group of people. They may allow many people to key in data simultaneously (sometimes anonymously), hold secret ballots on proposals, represent ideas in symbolic diagrams, access databases or spreadsheets of detailed figures, present multi-colour business graphics (bar-charts, pie-charts etc), and provide displays on a large cinema-like screen at the front. The best way of sorting out such possibilities is to focus on the role of the facilitator (or moderator) of the electronic meeting, who co-ordinates everything. Here are four gradations:

- **Gradation 1.** The facilitator has control of all the technology. The participants communicate with the facilitator by speech, not electronically. The facilitator's workstation drives the data appearing on the big screen. This need not be as tame as it sounds. Suppose the meeting is organised around some technique of representing ideas on symbolic diagrams; eg with different shapes for objectives, constraints, influences, interconnections etc. Then it may be far more efficient for a facilitator, fluent in the conventions of these diagrams, to draw them. Arguably though, this gradation is not genuine electronic meeting support, since the participants are not all connected up.
- **Gradation 2.** All participants communicate with the facilitator through workstations, but the facilitator has a much more powerful one, that controls what appears on the screen and co-ordinates the contributions from the others. As with the previous gradation, the facilitator directs the debate — perhaps asking everyone to key in imaginative solutions to a problem, and then picking the most interesting to display on the screen for general debate.
- **Gradation 3.** All participants have quite powerful workstations, capable of accessing spreadsheets or displaying data on the big screen. But the facilitator's workstation has the facilities to control the debate, as if chairing a conventional meeting; the facilitator might nominate one participant to key in ideas at the workstation that will appear straight

away on the big screen. After a while, the facilitator's workstation might interrupt and call for a vote on the proposals expressed.

- **Gradation 4.** All participants have quite powerful workstations and the facilitator's is no different. The facilitator plays a minimal role. The meeting develops in a free, organic, brainstorming way, without a detailed agenda structure or many procedural rules. The facilitator doesn't get involved in the content of the meeting and is mainly concerned with mundane things such as getting things started, ensuring data is properly saved at the end, and helping people master the facilities; eg showing them how to generate a pie-chart from a set of figures.**1**

Electronic Meeting: Possible Decision-making

This general warrant sharpens awareness of the main options. The mayor and his colleagues at Cedar Wattle City might well go on to reason as follows:

- 'Naturally, one of our aims in having electronic meeting support is to have more efficient meetings.'
- 'But another part of our motivation is to do this because it is advanced and up to date. Even if a system were not particularly efficient, it might be worth having, if it impressed only one large business enough to relocate here rather than in some other town.'
- 'Nobody is going to be impressed by seeing a system in operation that is based on ultra-modern technology, but leads to chaotic meetings. In fact if we seem to make Nkrumah-like investments in trendy technology, it may harm us. Therefore we should adopt an approach that is unquestionably go-ahead, but minimises embarrassing anarchy and confusion.'
- 'Gradation 2 is the obvious choice. It is modern and impressive (unlike gradation 1), but safer than gradations 3 and 4 — provided that at least a few people possess the skills and receive the training to act as an effective facilitator.'

Conceivably though, somebody with a different appreciation of the relevant factors might use the warrant to argue like this:

- 'Distinguish two quite different types of meeting: fairly formal debates between opposing political factions (eg about the proposed annual budget and taxes), and more free-ranging, brainstorming sessions, less predictably confrontational, though perhaps still passionate (eg how to improve Cedar Wattle as a centre for the arts).'
- 'It seems undesirable to start with technology for the first type of meeting: whenever it suits them, speakers will claim that the technology is being used unfairly to favour the other side, or that they haven't been given as much training in the intricacies of the technology as their opponents, and so on. It is far better to start off with the less formal, brainstorming meetings, and then only if the people concerned are keen on the idea. Then, if the system catches on, it can gradually be extended to other debates.'

- 'For this policy gradation 4 seems the right choice.'

Of course, the warrant could be used to support a number of other lines of argument too.[2]

Bridges and Gateways: Possible Context

Ironbark is an insurance company of moderate size. Its main departments at head office each have a local area network (LAN), and a separate organisation-wide network provides access to database systems for core administrative functions.

This *does not* mean that any workstation in the building can communicate with any other for any purpose. The telecoms manager now wants authority to invest enough to achieve just that, so that, for all practical purposes, there is just one network, with any joins between its different parts entirely irrelevant to the people using it. The difficulty for even the most computer-literate director of Ironbark is this:

- When presented with an investment proposal, it is normal to ask: What other options exist? After all, however attractive the investment proposed, it may be that some other option would be even more attractive.
- These directors don't know enough about telecoms to see all the main options. The choice seems to be between accepting the telecoms manager's plans as they stand and rejecting them entirely, and thus leaving telecoms arrangements just as they are.
- But this is an unacceptable state of affairs. Why should they abandon the shrewd business-like habits of comparing options just because the subject under discussion is IT?

The most computer-literate director resolves to find out something about the main varieties of technology that exist for linking several LANs and other networks together.

Bridges and Gateways: Gradations-form Warrant

To make sense of the range of possibilities for linking networks together, see how the linking devices form a pattern of gradations:

- Gradation 1. The **repeater** is the most simple. It is used when two networks have exactly the same technical characteristics: same cable medium, same protocol, same network operating system and so on. It links the two networks so that they behave in effect as if they were one network — when the repeater is switched on, that is.
- Gradation 2. The next step up from this, the **bridge**, also turns two networks into effectively one, but is more advanced. It works even if the two networks don't have identical technical characteristics — subject to the proviso that the difference lies in the type of cabling used; one network might use twisted pair and the other optical fibre. The bridge doesn't go as far as handling other differences: different formats for data passed around, different protocols for error correction and so on.

Connecting Networks: Knowledge and Logic

General Problem:
connecting together
two networks

?

General Answer:
The more different the networks, the more sophisticated the connecting technology needed.
There are many gradations: repeater through bridge to gateway etc

From this it follows that another option is to change the networks themselves, and thus reduce the complexity of the connecting technology needed.

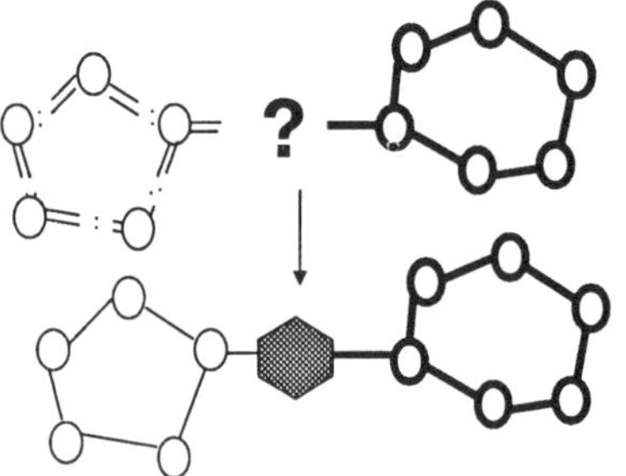

It is far more useful to know that this is the general shape of the whole problem, than to know the precise details of the connecting technology: repeater, router, brouter, bridge, gateway etc.

● Gradation 3. The **router** also links two local networks, so that a workstation on one can send a message to a workstation on the other — as if all were one network. But it has more intelligence: for those cases (maybe the majority) where a message is being sent from a PC to another PC on the same local network, it will avoid troubling the other local network at all. This makes things more efficient.

● Gradation 4. Then a big step further up comes the **gateway**. This links two networks which may or may not have dissimilar cabling, but — more awkwardly — have dissimilar data formats and protocols. A gateway might link a LAN of PCs to a company-wide network including terminals attached to mini-computers and mainframes. As well as carrying out any necessary conversions, the gateway has to be intelligent like the router, in order to send on only those messages from the local network that are intended to go that way.

As the diagram shows, the key variable with these gradations is connection of progressively more dissimilar networks, with progressively more intelligence. Roughly, the higher the gradation, the greater the need to tune and tinker with telecoms hardware and software, the more expensive the linking devices, and the greater the overhead they impose in operation.[3]

Bridges and Gateways: Possible Decision-making

Armed with this knowledge, the Ironbark director, if of feisty temperament, might put the following line of reasoning:

'As I now understand your proposals, you want to leave most of our existing departmental networks intact, with their variety of technology features — different wiring, different protocols and so on — and build in gateways and routers at numerous places, providing all the necessary intelligence to smooth over technical differences and ensure that, to all intents and purposes, everything is on the same network, linked to everything else.'

'Just to state this proposal is to imply that there are other options. For all I know, they may be vastly inferior options, but I can't approve your plans unless I know that you have thought about the options and can show that they are inferior.'

'For example, why not achieve this 'same network' effect a different way? If you replaced the wiring or maybe some other components of some of the departmental networks, then their variety would be greatly reduced. That would save you from setting up baroque configurations of gateways; some would be completely unnecessary, and in other cases a simple bridge might replace a gateway that was expensive to buy or develop, and imposed heavy overheads when in use.'

'Take another conceivable option. Suppose I accept that none of the local networks is to be tampered with. Why should I make the assumption that more or less everything has to be seamlessly connected to everything else? Who says that (say) the household policy department must have the technical facilities to transmit full-colour photos tagged with voice annotation to the accounts department that, as it happens, is on the same floor? Suppose you had to take the most miserly possible approach to providing only those links between department networks for which there was a proven need. Please show us which of your proposed gateways and routers could be replaced by repeaters and bridges.'

Plainly, these are just provisional notions to be refined or perhaps smashed to pieces in further debate. The point is that the gradations warrant at least makes such debate between non-technical managers and technical experts feasible.

Workgroup Document Production: Possible Context

Murray Pine is a huge publishing organisation. One of its divisions publishes 40 monthly newsletters on a variety of specialist subjects, each with a circulation of one or two thousand copies, but a high subscription price. The managing-editor of the division explains to colleagues the decision-making problem they face:

'Every piece in our newsletters is the result of collaboration, discussion and editing between at least three and maybe six people. There must be a way of using technology to make that collaboration far more efficient.'

'I am happy to invest in more PCs, a local area network and some appropriate software.'

'But what should our system for shared document production actually do? The more experts we talk to, and the more brochures and articles we collect, and the more demonstrations we attend, the more confusing the range of possibilities gets, and the more worried I am that any decision will be quite arbitrary. Whatever we decide, we will never have much confidence that we have made anything like the best choice out of the possibilities.'

They agree to stop studying detail and look for some neat way to clarify the most fundamental options for this kind of system. Once they have that, then all the second-, third- and fourth-order details should be easier to snap into place.

Workgroup Document Production: Gradations-form Warrant

The concept of sharing facilities for producing documents in an office embraces a wide range of possibilities, best analysed as gradations:

- Gradation 1. **Device sharing.** Hardware is shared for economy; that is all. It would be absurd to give every PC its own laser printer; PCs can be connected in such a way as to allow access for everybody to a couple of printers. This doesn't imply that people share the work of producing documents in any other sense.
- Gradation 2. **Red-lining.** In this simplest form of collaboration one person (or more) can amend a document prepared by someone else, without obliterating the original; eg additions are shown in reverse mode, deleted texts are kept but in bold face to show that they are not really part of the document any more; and so on. This is a rather limited facility: if the document is passed around a circle of many people, changes may be made, amended back and reinstated *ad infinitum*.
- Gradation 3. **Document sharing**. A system with real document sharing facilities allows amendments, deletions and additions (also comments: 'Let's not get too cute!'), from any number of people, and holds them all

separately — perhaps displayed in different windows on the screen. Later an editor consolidates them, deciding which to action and which to ignore.

- Gradation 4. **Simple document management.** The next gradation introduces the idea of regarding the document as made up of elements that can be produced separately and then brought together; eg one article in a newsletter may consist of a text, a wordchart and two diagrams. The drafting and editing of each element are done in parallel, before the elements are made up together on the newsletter page.
- Gradation 5. **Factory document management.** At the next gradation up, the system monitors parallel and successive activities — rather as if the office were a factory. A schedule defines all the work to be done on all the elements of each issue. Dates are planned and progress recorded. The system can tell a journalist: 'Today you are scheduled to review the article for the September issue of *Sporting Sociology* on 'The Epistemology of the Relay-Race', but it is delayed; the article on 'Why Gold, Silver and Bronze?', planned for October, is available for editing already; do you want its text sent over the network to your PC?'
- Gradation 6. **Content management.** With the last main gradation, the system provides for multiple use of individual elements of content (textual or graphic). Part of the article 'Why Gold, Silver and Bronze?' in *Sporting Sociology* may be reused in a book on metallurgy in Ancient Greece, and another part stored in a general database about sociology for on-line public access through a terminal. This can be quite complex to arrange; the newsletter and book may have different typefaces, line widths and so on. Typically, special codes have to be embedded in the text to ensure that it appears correctly formatted in each medium. But the issues here are moving away from the sharing of document production within one department.

Workgroup Document Production: Possible Decision-making

The managing-editor soon homes in on the idea that gradation 4, simple document management, is the natural choice for the department. Document management is important to a newsletter, because each issue contains quite a few items of various lengths to be fitted together; also material often has to be juggled between issues, to avoid one month's issue being much fatter or thinner than average. Thus anything below gradation 4 is inadequate. On the other hand, gradation 5 would be overkill; it seems more appropriate to a newspaper with tight deadlines, or the documentation department of an aircraft manufacturer.

Choice of gradation 4 doesn't solve everything by any means, but it makes more detailed discussions more efficient. It is now possible to process all the knowledge already collected, by going through and asking of each brochure and each article: Will this really help me make decisions within the context of a gradation-4 system? This could lead to analysis of further gradations *within* gradation 4, exposing more subtle differences. On the other hand, a warrant exposing firm distinctions or comparing different possibilities could be more fruitful.

Moreover, armed with a provisional choice based on the gradations warrant, the managing-editor can listen to anybody who talks about workgroup computing, or document production groupware, or workflow control, or the like, and soon decide whether that person really has a good grasp of the subject, and is offering any relevant input to the specific problem.[4]

Using this Warrant Form

The three warrants given as examples show the variety of possibilities within the gradations form:

- The warrant about electronic meeting facilities has four gradations defined primarily in terms of one easily grasped factor — the role of the facilitator.
- The warrant about bridges and gateways is rather less pure. The factor determining the gradations is roughly the complexity of the network-linking task to be done, but this has two components: mainly how different the networks are, but also how much intelligence in routing messages is desired. As this example suggests, it may be unnecessary to know the names of things — bridge, router etc — provided you understand the driving factors that make them different gradations.
- In a similar way, it could be shown that the gradations of shared document production were determined by one roughly defined factor, consisting of a couple of more specific components. But this is probably getting too abstract. Here it may be better simply to say that the main possibilities technology currently offers correspond to six broad options that manifestly are steps of increasing ambition and complexity.

As the diagram suggests, a gradations warrant often has one particular advantage: it puts you in a good position to judge whether a particular requirement is right up on the cutting edge of technology, perhaps dangerously so, or extremely modest, perhaps too modest.

A number of points of logic associated with the use of *any* warrants in decision-making arise in particularly acute form with gradations:

- Why have six gradations of document production? Why not have just four radically different possibilities, by merging the second with the third and the fourth with fifth? This might well be sound from a purely logical or technical point of view, but it would result in some very wide jumps between the scope and complexity of the gradations. The point of any warrant, whatever the form, is to assist decision-making; in the case of a gradations warrant that means having practical, as opposed to logically rigorous, gradations. Of course, if the purpose of the analysis were to win a prize for computer science, the matter would be entirely different.
- What about progress over time? Would a system based on (say) grada-

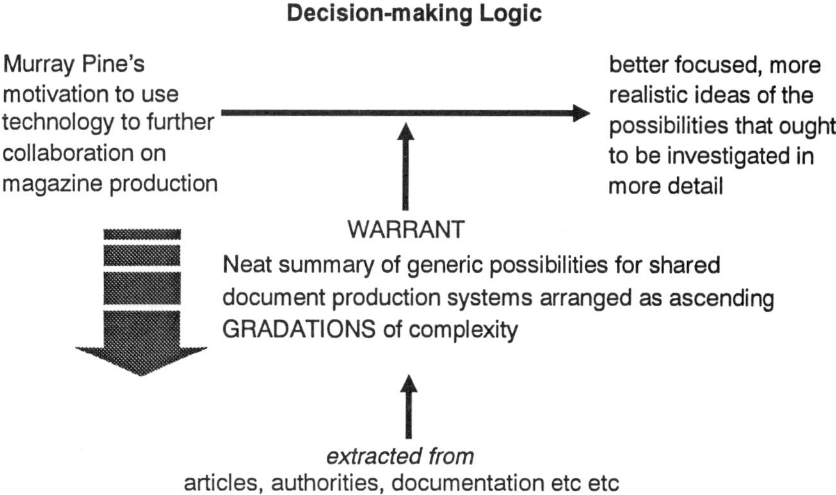
Decision-making Logic
Murray Pine's motivation to use technology to further collaboration on magazine production
better focused, more realistic ideas of the possibilities that ought to be investigated in more detail
WARRANT
Neat summary of generic possibilities for shared document production systems arranged as ascending GRADATIONS of complexity
extracted from
articles, authorities, documentation etc etc

tion 2 typically develop into gradation 3 after a while, and later arrive at gradation 4? Not at all. A gradations warrant is only a device for clarifying possibilities to be chosen between; it makes no greater claim than that. If you were thinking of buying a new camera or a new cooker, you might well set out the main possibilities in a similar way; but that need not imply that you expected to trade up from one to another at any later stage.

● The warrants given as examples seem to imply that each gradation provides all the same facilities as the one below, plus something more. Of course, this is convenient, but isn't it an over-simplification that leaves out some relevant possibilities? Sometimes that is so. When it is, gradations is the wrong warrant form to use. You should use the warrant form that depicts the relevant facts most effectively; at times, that will mean preferring (say) a distinctions to a gradations warrant form.

NOTES & ARGUMENTS

1 This warrant — like every useful matching warrant — simplifies by excluding some variants; eg you can also have a rotating facilitator approach (gradation 3.5, perhaps).

The starting-point for developing the warrant was the article: Alan R Dennis et al, 'A New Role for Computers in Strategic Management', *Journal of Business Strategy*, September-October 1990, pp. 38ff. The July 1989 issue of *I/S Analyzer* also describes a case. The article 'Meeting Makeovers' in *PC Magazine*, 13/11, pp. 205ff., reviews four software products.

It is a general rule that a good article comparing products in field X will be useful mainly for the criteria it uses to make sense of field X rather than for its opinions about particular products. Product choices can be out of date in a week, but insights into the main categories of X product or the main features found in X applications stay relevant far longer. The *PC Magazine* article distinguishes three main aspects of a meeting support system: facilities to set up and structure the meeting; tools for idea processing within the meeting; production of reports of the content of the meeting. This analysis oddly omits another aspect: facilities for accessing external material (documents, spreadsheets, databases etc) during the meeting. Adding that in gives a handy four-aspects warrant, that is complementary to the gradations-by-facilitator warrant.

2 A possible exercise for the keen analyst of IM decision-making is to think out a couple more plausible arguments that are consistent with the warrant and the context. This applies to all eighteen of the examples in these six matching briefings.

3 This warrant is largely based on information in: Frank J Derfler Jr 'Connectivity Clinic', *PC Magazine*, 8/20, p. 383; 9/5, p. 387. Strictly, a router links two technically identical networks (like a repeater), while a brouter links two networks with dissimilar cabling, but otherwise identical characteristics (like a bridge).

4 The warrant given does not cover all the issues that may be relevant; few matching warrants do. Its gradations really measure the complexity of the structure of information held by a system. In some cases, the technical problems of linking up the participants in the workgroup could be a more dominant issue. A gradation-3 system where the participants use different operating systems, network technology and word processing software may well be a greater challenge to set up than a gradation-4 system where these technical features are common.

The *Seybold Report on Desktop Publishing* is a good source of expert, level-headed information on this topic; eg issues 6/11 and 7/1.

CONNECTIONS

12. Matching through Comparisons	More decision-forcing forms of warrants for matching supply and demand
13. Matching through Distinctions	Equally decision-forcing forms of warrants for matching supply and demand
15. Matching through Charts	Less decision-forcing forms of warrants for matching supply and demand
16. Matching through Aspects	Less decision-forcing forms of warrants for matching supply and demand
17. Matching through Examples	Less decision-forcing forms of warrants for matching supply and demand
36. Business Process Re-engineering	A publisher reorganising the sharing of work in document production may be said by some to be re-engineering business processes
38. Decision Support Systems	Electronic meeting systems are never called decision support systems, but they support decisions nonetheless
39. Inter-organisational Systems	Bridges and gateways are part of the technical side of systems that link organisations together

15. Matching through Charts

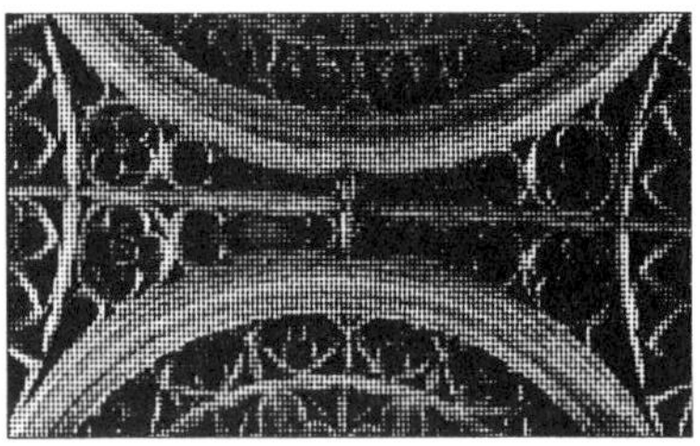

TOPIC

In the early stages of debate, ideas about possible functional demands and possible supply technologies may be too vague and insubstantial for firm matching decisions. Too many confusions and ambiguities may be present for immediate use of comparison, gradations or distinctions warrants to be appropriate.

A warrant in chart form provides a sense of direction by 'charting out' the main concepts in a field: showing what they are and how they relate to each other. To think clearly about something, it may be essential first to grasp that term A stands for some broad concept, of which term B is a specific example, while term C is almost but not quite synonymous with term B. Or it may be impossible to have a useful discussion unless everyone is aware that the choice of technology component X is not an isolated decision, since it is inevitably related to the choice of Y. Getting these things charted out is an intellectual task; whether you actually draw a chart-like diagram is a minor issue.

In short, the example warrants in this briefing are intended as convenient charts for navigating some of the trickier corners of the world of technology.

SUGGESTED WARRANTS

In other briefings the warrants are generally arranged with the more straightforward before the more complex. Here all three charts are of much the same degree. The areas charted out are: on-line database services; videotex and intertwined technologies; electronic forms software.

On-line Database Service: Possible Context

A publicly available on-line database service is one that anyone can access by dialing up from a PC to extract information — statistics on the economy of Paraguay, news items about endangered species, abstracts of recent articles about geology, etc etc.

Within Hill Banksia, purveyors of accountancy, consultancy and allied trades, some individuals make sporadic use of on-line database services. There is no company-wide policy on this matter, since there has never been any need for one. Now a new possibility is under consideration: perhaps Hill Banksia could be a *supplier* of information for such a database service, as well as just a customer accessing it. The company already devotes considerable resources to carrying out surveys, undertaking research and publishing guides to its areas of expertise — an *Annual Survey of the Environmental Policies of Multinationals*, a *Guide to Cross-Border Joint-Ventures*, an *Index of Trends in Leisure Industries*, etc. Why not make this material available in an on-line database? This would yield some income, but the main point would be to build the company's reputation as the natural source of knowledge and expertise in certain fields.

Unfortunately it is difficult to move from the initial bright idea to an understanding of the possibilities a level deeper. There seems to be a bewildering variety of players in the game: hosts, vendors, disk-spinners, information providers, database publishers, value-added networks, information utilities and so on. Should Hill Banksia aim to become a host or an information provider or something else? Are these even different things or just different names for similar things? The Hill Banksia people need a chart of this field, before they can make any decisions about it.

On-line Database Service: Chart-form Warrant

To chart on-line database services start with these four things:

- **Database:** the set of information itself, eg economic data including the gross national product, actual and forecast, of Paraguay over the twenty years starting 1980, together with much else.
- **Information provider**: the organisation that has prepared the information in the database. Sometimes the provider simply makes its database by replicating material published on paper anyway; sometimes the database has no printed version at all; and some cases are between these two extremes.
- **User**: the person accessing database information.
- **Host** (the term 'vendor' is also used): the organisation offering the service that provides access to a variety of databases from different information providers. Thus the information provider does the intellectual work of assembling database information; the host provides the technical service so that users can access it.

In this setup, the host bills the user according to the time spent and information accessed. Part of this payment goes to the information provider as a royalty. Just as one host provides access to a variety of databases from different information providers, so one database may be provided by its information provider to several different hosts. And of course, any user may have accounts with two or more hosts. Thus you might access ERIC (a database provided by the Educational Resources Information Center) on the BRS host service today, and on the Dialog host service tomorrow.

Now complicate this four-item chart by adding in two more practical elements:

- **Information retrieval software and interface.** The host service typically provides access to the database by the use of keywords or text searching. Most have their own conventions for formulating search requests. To make a search (eg find all references to 'hooliganism') on ERIC, the user has to key an instruction in one format on BRS and in another on Dialog.
- **Telecoms and the VAN.** The host may allow the user to dial into its own network to reach the host computer where the databases are stored, but, more likely, another party is involved — a VAN (value-added network). The VAN is a general-purpose provider of telecoms services.

To round off the chart, it is worth recognising several main varieties of host:

- **Information utility:** offering access to many on-line databases, as just one service along with others, such as electronic mail or bulletin board or mail-order shopping facilities.
- **Disk-spinner**, sometimes called an information supermarket: a service whose primary aim is to provide access to a wide selection of databases, with less attention to other types of service.
- **Specialist**: an information utility concentrated on one particular industry or branch of knowledge, offering relevant databases in depth, as well as appropriate ancillary services; eg a service for the entertainment industry might contain advertising and booking facilities as well as database access.

On-line Database Service: Possible Decision-making

Using this chart to take their first steps into the field, decision-makers at Hill Banksia might react in a variety of ways:

- *Either* 'Contact the biggest disk-spinner host. Say we want to be an information provider. Show the host all the printed material we produce already. Let the host choose from this what it thinks would make a suitable database. Get started as quickly and simply as possible. After about a year of this we will have a much better understanding of what the business is all about. At that point, decide what to do next, if anything. This is a low-risk strategy.'
- *Or, more bold:* 'One of our current strategic aims is to become *the* recognised authority on the business economics of sports sponsorship. We should search very carefully for an appropriate specialist host (eg specialising in sport or in marketing or something of the sort) and strike a deal, perhaps taking a stake in a joint-venture. One condition would be

that all database information on sports sponsorship would come from us and none from our rivals.'

● *Or, bolder still:* 'We could easily become an information provider to a host — but then so could any of our rivals. We ought to find a way of doing something that others can't quickly copy. Suppose, for example, we set up an arrangement with one of the information utilities so that users could both access a database provided by us, and also use related services for which we developed the software. For instance, as well as accessing our database of knowledge on cross-border joint-ventures, the user could use a special piece of computer-aided instruction software we would develop; it would give problems and answers to teach anybody how to finance such deals most efficiently, how to avoid legal blunders and so on. That is only an example; perhaps some other area of knowledge would be much more suitable. The key point is that we should do far more than just provide a database.'

● *Or, even bolder:* 'Why not be our own host as well as information provider — offering access to databases made out of all the information we produce. We could start by restricting the service to in-house use. After that, allow selected clients to use it — thereby tying them to us (as the business-school professors are always suggesting), so that they can't easily switch to our competitors. After that we could market ourselves to possible new clients by offering (say) three-months free access to our on-line databases . . .'

Videotex: Possible Context

The Acacia Authority is a government agency that regulates a number of environmental matters. It needs to set up an internal information service, providing access to a reference database. Bureaucrats could use their terminals to look up scientific data about various chemicals and their effects, texts of environmental laws and regulations, locations of main waste disposal sites in an area, schedules of forthcoming events and conferences relevant to environmental concerns, and so on.

The director of the authority asks one of his computer-literate colleagues to look into the matter, saying 'Presumably you'll be using videotex.' The director is amazed when his colleague remarks that he doesn't know what videotex is. But then, his colleague points out, not many people do know what videotex is — at least, not in any useful sense of knowing:

'Almost everybody has *heard of* videotex and has some rough idea of what it is. But is that knowing what it is — in any useful sense?'

'Suppose somebody claims to know what a battleship is, but cannot explain confidently how the concept of battleship is related to at least some of the following: warship, capital ship, cruiser, battle cruiser and monitor. Is a battleship just one type of warship or is it a synonym for warship? What is the essential difference between a battleship and a battle cruiser? Somebody who can get nowhere with questions like this doesn't know what a battleship is — not in any useful sense of knowing.'

'Somebody who claims to know what videotex is ought to be able to explain how the concept videotex is related to the concepts of viewdata, Prestel, teletex, teletext, Teletel and Minitel. Unless you can do that, you don't know what videotex is — not in any useful sense of knowing.'

Plainly, one step towards well-informed decisions in this situation is to chart out the different concepts in the general area of videotex.

Videotex: Chart-form Warrant

This charting is best tackled in two stages. First, sort out the relations between certain terms that are easily confused:

● **Viewdata**. Whatever videotex is, viewdata is too. Viewdata is a synonym of videotex.

● **Prestel and Teletel services.** Videotex is the name of a *technology*. In the UK the name of the national, public videotex *service* is Prestel. The French PTT's national videotex service is called Teletel; other countries have services with other names.

● **Prestel and Teletel technologies.** Next some careful charting is called for. Videotex is the general name of the technology, but there are some variants of videotex. The British Prestel service happens to use one variant and French Teletel another. Sometimes people say 'We have a Prestel service' when what they really mean is 'We have a videotex service, and it adopts the same technology variant as the Prestel service.' Thus to avoid confusion, you may have to say carefully: 'Australia has several videotex services; some are Prestel-like and some are Teletel-like variants of the technology.'

● **Minitel**. One more complication: Teletel (the French videotex service) uses a special terminal called the Minitel. Therefore people sometimes say that there is a Minitel-based service in Australia, when they really mean that the service uses the Teletel-like variant of videotex technology, one of whose features is use of the Minitel terminal.

● **Teletext, Ceefax, Telex and Teletex.** Teletext (with a final t) is the name for another technology, related in some ways to videotex but still separate. Ceefax is one particular service using teletext technology. Telex and teletex (without final t) are two technologies concerned with sending messages, sufficiently different from videotex and teletext to be comparatively clear from confusion.

This is only a start towards the second stage of charting out what videotex actually is. In its most classic form, as set up for the original Prestel service, videotex has three very distinctive traits: first, use of a TV set plus a simple keypad, rather than a computer terminal or PC; second, a crude interaction based on hierarchical menus (choose the next menu screen by pressing a number between 1 and 9, *but not* search the database on the term 'hooliganism'); third, distinctively crude colour graphics.

But there has been considerable movement away from this; the more successful French Teletel uses a special terminal, which in turn permits better search possibilities, thus leaving relatively crude graphics as a surviving distinctive feature of videotex. So how far away from the classic videotex model can a service be and still be called videotex? In fact, the term is now used in two quite distinct senses:

- Some people regard videotex as essentially a **technology**; ie the technology that characterises the Prestel or Teletel services.
- Other people regard videotex as *any* interactive, electronic information **service** that is easy-to-use, mass-market and consumer- or novice-oriented — irrespective of its technology.

These two overlap but are far from identical. You could have an easy-to-use, mass-market, interactive, electronic information service using technology entirely different from Prestel or Teletel. Or you could have a service based on Teletel technology within one organisation (ie not mass-market) and for use by specialists (ie not novice-oriented).

Videotex: Possible Decision-making

With this insight the careful thinker at the Acacia Authority might easily develop the following reasoning:

- 'One essential characteristic of the internal information service we are considering is that it will be used by a great variety of people, many of whom are not very computer-literate. From this it follows that Acacia certainly needs a videotex service in the 'videotex as service' sense — easy-to-use, novice-oriented, etc.'
- 'Another essential point is that access requirements will be extremely varied; one person may want to search on a keyword in order to find and refer to a large chunk of text of environmental health regulations; another may be looking for one discrete fact: (say) the melting point of lead. Therefore Acacia probably doesn't want a videotex service in the 'videotex as technology' sense, since Prestel or Teletel technology seem too primitive to meet the whole range of requirements.'
- 'If this reasoning is valid, one option is to design an in-house system based on an information retrieval software product, capable of storing texts and allowing a great variety of access methods — both sophisticated and novice-oriented. This could easily be quite a substantial enterprise. Preferably, to avoid confusion, don't call this a videotex system.'
- 'But another option is to partition the problem. Have one system for naive users, based on ready-made components of Teletel technology, deliberately avoiding any types of information and any types of access method that don't fit neatly with this technology. Have another system for a different class of users. It will allow sophisticated access techniques,

but based on the assumption that the user is fairly computer-literate and able to formulate access requests carefully and logically.'

Electronic Forms: Possible Context

Sydney Peppermint is a printing firm, known as a skillful, reliable and cost-effective supplier of complicated forms for local businesses: sales order forms, stock requisition forms, employee address change forms and the like. Now one of the proprietors comes back from a computer exhibition with news of what seems to be a threat, but may possibly be an opportunity: *electronic forms software*. Soon, the salesmen enthuse, companies will do without paper forms. This new kind of software displays an electronic facsimile of a form on the screen, the clerk fills in the form on the screen from the keyboard, and the data goes off to update the database — without the need for any printed forms at all.

This seems to be something worth knowing about. But as they study the glossy brochures of the various software products, the Sydney Peppermint people become increasingly confused. Most products claim to have sophisticated printing facilities, with special techniques for maximising throughput when printing out forms at a laser printer. Some brochures boast about facilities for all kinds of typographic subtleties in form design; but surely DTP software and illustration software products are already quite adequate for that. Some products seem so powerful that it sounds as if they take over most of the work of a database management software product; but surely that can't be so.

If they are to conduct any rational debate the Sydney Peppermint directors need an intellectual chart to expose the main different elements in an electronic forms application, and show how these relate to each other and to other technologies.

Electronic Forms: Chart-form Warrant

The best start is to chart out six possible functions within an electronic forms application:

- **Form design**: design a new form for (say) recording customer orders of some complicated product with numerous options.
- **Print blank forms**: print out many blank copies of a form (intended to be filled in later by hand).
- **Screen-form input**: key data in at a screen using the graphic format of a complex form.
- **Crude input**: key data in at a very simple screen without using the graphic format of a form (eg keying in masses of relatively simple transactions, such as order cancellations).
- **Print filled-in forms**: print out form documents each containing a set of previously keyed-in data (either form-guided or crude).

Electronic Forms: Chart of Functions

Electronic forms system

Six main functions of a full system;

▬ fundamental

— optional

Form design	fundamental	could be done by DTP instead, but then not integrated
Print blank forms	optional	maybe cheaper than photocopy or external printer; also minor variants easier
Screen-form input	fundamental	rather than conventional database input screens; these can be much more stylish; but complex validation can be problem
Crude input	optional	
Print filled-in forms	optional	
Update database	fundamental	rather than conventional database system; but integrity, concurrency control etc are problems

This chart:

. breaks down the technology into six pieces;

. makes rough distinction between fundamental and optional pieces;

. relates some pieces to alternative technologies.

This is not a complete account of the technology by any means but, how could you take ANY decision, unless you possessed AT LEAST this basic knowledge?

● **Update database**: use data (either form-guided or crude) to update a database.

Which of these six are indispensable in an electronic forms application and which optional? How do they relate to each other and to other technologies?

● An electronic forms application always includes the **form design** function. You can do just the same design work (eg giving boxes with rounded corners and drop shadows, allowing a variety of typefaces and letter sizes, including a scanned-in logo etc) with an illustration program or DTP program. However, that produces an isolated document; here the form is automatically used in the other functions.

● **Print blank forms** may be irrelevant to many applications, where all data is by screen-form input. However, if you do need blank forms to be filled in manually this could be a better way of producing them than by photocopying or going to a printer, especially if you need many minor varieties (eg different colours or a few boxes already filled in with standard entries such as department number).

● **Screen-form input** is the heart of a classic electronic forms application. This is really an alternative to using the data entry screens offered by a conventional database system. It is a superior approach for an attractive screen design, with several fonts and different point-sizes and wordwrap etc. If you don't need such things, then you can stay with a database system. There is a big submerged issue here: interaction with the database itself, especially for input validation. The more you need complex validation (eg checking whether an order is valid by examining other information already in the database), the less well forms software competes with a conventional database system.

● **Crude input** happens, if at all, outside the forms application but is relevant because the data may need to be channelled to the function that prints filled-in forms.

● **Print filled-in forms** may be of interest in some applications where hard-copy of transactions has to be kept on forms. It includes the possibility of automatically routing different documents (or several copies) to different departments, depending on their content.

● **Update database**. The problem here is that updating a serious industrial-strength database entails quite a lot of (mainly hidden) complexities: checks to ensure database integrity (eg avoiding the case where a product mentioned in the customer order doesn't actually exist in the product file), concurrency control (eg handling cases where two people want to update the same data simultaneously), recovery (ie automatically in the event of hardware failure). An electronic forms system doesn't contain that sort of thing. Therefore you either have to sacrifice all those update complications (probably unacceptable) or get the electronic forms part of the system to mesh into the update complications of the normal database system (which could be messy).

Electronic Forms: Possible Decision-making

Using the knowledge charted in the diagram, the Sydney Peppermint people might well come to conclusions like these:

● 'Two different dangers are facing in. First, our customers may carry on using just as many paper forms as before, but stop coming to us for them, because they make their own more cheaply, using the two functions of form design and print blank forms. Second, our customers may start using electronic forms applications in which far fewer paper forms from any source are needed, where screen-form input is a key function, with little or no use of a print filled-in forms function. Or perhaps half our customers might take the first course and half the second.'

- 'To deal with the first danger we should invest in electronic forms software ourselves, and use it to replace our more traditional printing techniques for some jobs. With our extra design skills and experience, as well as precocious mastery of this new technology, many customers would find it easier to come to us than design and print the forms themselves.'
- 'The second danger is less easily dealt with. If people want electronic forms rather than paper forms the best thing we can do is make a radical change to our business profile, replacing one sort of revenue by another. Instead of selling forms we should become experts on electronic forms technology, sell consultancy and system design services and perhaps even install turnkey systems.'

On the other hand, the knowledge contained in the warrant might just as well set the debate on a different course:

- 'The weak point of the electronic forms concept is the part where the data keyed into the electronic form goes to update the database of the operational system. This can be a very tricky interfacing problem.'
- 'Electronic forms software products are fairly new, but if that updating point can't be resolved adequately by releases of mature software products, the technology will remain a rather peripheral one, and, very likely, the technology market will take some other direction.'
- 'Therefore we shouldn't do anything very radical at the moment, because that could lead to a big investment in something that peters out. On the other hand, we should certainly dabble in this field, to get to know it better and keep well placed to understand how the market develops.'**1**

Using this Warrant Form

As the diagram suggests, a chart warrant can be the key to making sense of the confusing tangles of detail found in real-life. The three chart warrants used as examples in this briefing show some variety:**2**

- In the warrant about on-line database services, many of the elements charted are role-players, and the warrant is largely concerned with who does what.
- The warrant about videotex and intertwined technologies is in two parts: the first is a brief logical analysis of overlapping concepts and terminology; the second differentiates two common but incompatible meanings of the confusing term 'videotex'.
- The chart warrant about electronic forms software gives six main functions making up a hypothetical system — even though a real system need not have all six. The crucial part is the charting of how the functions are related; eg you are bound to have function A, but not necessarily function B; if you do have B, you may or may not have C too . .

Sometimes there is a question whether a piece of charting is con-

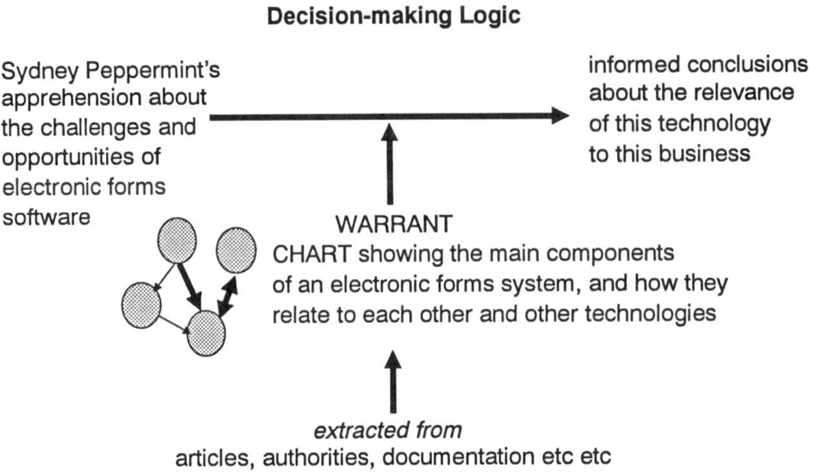
Decision-making Logic
Sydney Peppermint's apprehension about the challenges and opportunities of electronic forms software
informed conclusions about the relevance of this technology to this business
WARRANT
CHART showing the main components of an electronic forms system, and how they relate to each other and other technologies
extracted from
articles, authorities, documentation etc etc

cerned with knowledge or merely nomenclature. But often it isn't possible to keep things clear in the mind without getting nomenclature straight. Progress in debate can come from asking in which of two possible senses somebody is using a term, or from showing that a certain broad term is used inconsistently in different parts of the argument.

Chart warrants also combat imprecision about the way different matters are related to each other. If someone proposes that decisions X and Y and Z be taken, you can scarcely debate that in an intelligent way unless you cope with such questions as: Do the three things belong inevitably together; ie if X is decided, does that predetermine decisions on Y and Z? Or are these three more or less independent decisions? Or are they related in some more complex way?

NOTES & ARGUMENTS

1 This warrant was originally constructed in late-1991 from information in 'Form and Content: Five Electronic Forms Packages', *PC Magazine*, 10/19, pp. 379ff. The magazine reviewed the field again in 1994 with 'Filling (in the) Blanks', 13/6, pp. 149ff. and also 'Go With The Flow', 13/11, pp. 253ff. Those three reviews taken together exemplify some interesting *general* features of the struggle to make sense of technology knowledge.

First, the 1994 reviews deal with more powerful software products, but they don't invalidate the original warrant. By their nature, matching warrants last longer than product surveys.

But the 1994 reviews redefine what an electronic forms system is *relative to other types of system*. In many forms systems screen-form input (one of the six functions of the chart) includes some 'routing' capability: if A fills in an expenses form at a workstation, the system automatically displays it on the workstation of B for authorisation. The rules for this routing of information are built into the system. They can become quite complex: perhaps the expenses claim goes to different people according to its value and/or the status of the claimant; perhaps different types of claim have different priorities, and perhaps these depend on the accounting period. Taken at all far, this workflow logic can become a bigger part of a system than the forms functions; in fact, the vogue term 'workflow system' may creep in. To reduce confusion use this simple chart warrant:

- **Electronic forms**, aka low-end workflow, system: consists of the functions in this briefing's chart; usually includes modest rules-based routing.
- **High-end workflow** system: based on complex routing rules ('automates the administration manual'); includes electronic forms functions, but often others too, eg scanning restaurant bills that go with expense claims and storing them as images.

This exemplifies the challenges of organising technology knowledge. A torrent of hype about a new technology, workflow software, suddenly sweeps in and seems to submerge existing knowledge and understanding, but then a careful chart warrant can be made to bring detail to order again.

2 This book recommends six warrant forms, but there is plenty of room for a more extensive armoury of intellectual weapons. The chart warrant form, for instance, could easily be elaborated and subdivided: you could systematise the generic relationships typically found between items: 'is a component of'; 'is used for'; 'is an example of'; 'is a type of'; 'is characteristic of' etc. Early English *is a type of* Gothic; Salisbury Cathedral *is an example of* Early English style; the pointed arch *is a characteristic feature of* Gothic; a transept *is a component of* a cathedral etc.

CONNECTIONS

12. Matching through Comparisons	More decision-forcing forms of warrants for matching supply and demand
13. Matching through Distinctions	More decision-forcing forms of warrants for matching supply and demand
14. Matching through Gradations	More decision-forcing forms of warrants for matching supply and demand
16. Matching through Aspects	Equally decision-forcing forms of warrants for matching supply and demand
17. Matching through Examples	Less decision-forcing forms of warrants for matching supply and demand
34. Sociotechnical Design	As electronic forms and workflow systems become sophisticated they raise possibilities for new roles for office workers
36. Business Process Re-engineering	Workflow software is a prime technology for supporting re-engineered processes
39. Inter-organisational Systems	Videotex defines one area of the possibilities for systems that link organisations together

16. Matching through Aspects

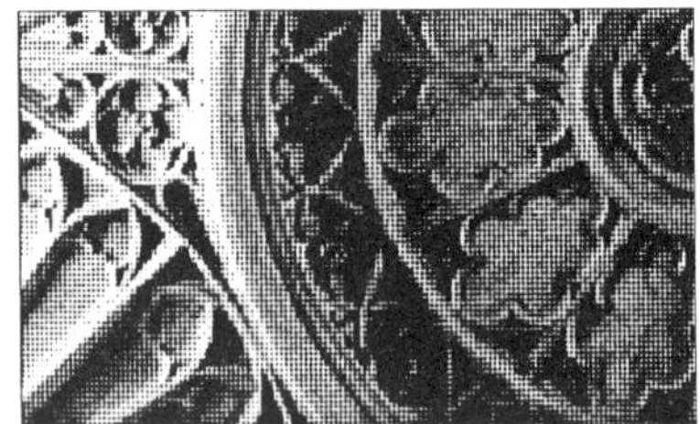

TOPIC

If debate is still at the stage of taking bearings and untangling confusions, a warrant in chart or aspects form may be the most useful. An aspects warrant is less ambitious than a chart warrant. It typically shows *what* the main concepts or components are in a certain area, without approaching the (perhaps complex) question of *how* exactly they relate to each other. This can be particularly beneficial when a certain field seems to contain dozens of interrelated matters, and you need to make sense of them — by sorting them out under four or five broad headings or themes or, better, aspects.

Thus the aspects warrants in this briefing are primarily tools that do the groundwork to prepare for decisions; each makes sense of confusing detail within a certain sector of technology.

SUGGESTED WARRANTS

The three areas of technology analysed into aspects here are: presentation graphics; value-added network; and groupware. They come in ascending order of the difficulty of marshalling their detail.

Presentation Graphics: Possible Context

Coachwood Consultants, the management consultancy firm, has hundreds of consultants. All make presentations to clients in their work, and nearly all use PC-based presentation graphics software to prepare their slides and transparencies.

Coachwood is not the kind of organisation where people at head office feel that if something *can* be standardised, then it *ought* to be. If some consultants want to use the Persuasion software product, others Freelance Graphics, and others something else, that is fine. But this doesn't mean that there is no room for any policy at all on presentation graphics. Perhaps, for instance, there are some valuable, advanced features that many people don't use because they have never had time to discover them. Perhaps there should be a company library of widely applicable images and slide formats — though that might entail some degree of standardisation. Coachwood wants to consider having a policy on presentation graphics, but it is not obvious what subjects the policy should pronounce on, and what it should leave deliberately undefined.

As with most well-established categories of PC application, it is easy enough to find a magazine article comparing available software products, with a matrix to show where each stands on hundreds of different features and topics. But that kind of material is not much use as a basis for policy-making. Something more incisive is needed to separate out the main aspects of presentation graphics technology.

Presentation Graphics: Aspects-form Warrant

Think of every feature of a presentation graphics software product as part of one of these four aspects:

- **Presentation structuring.** A typical product provides an *outliner* facility to help you get your ideas clear — organise concepts into hierarchies, reshuffle them and so on — until satisfied that the sequence of slides (or transparencies) is in the most telling possible order. Later, when many have already been drawn, you may want to recheck and possibly reorganise the planned sequence. A *thumbnail* option displays tiny images of many slides in sequence together on the screen; you can easily use the mouse to drag slides from one place in the sequence to another. You can also review the logic of the presentation by using the *slide show* facility; this displays slides on screen in sequence, changing automatically every five seconds (or whatever time is set).
- **Presentation consistency.** A good product allows definition of *templates*, to ensure that (say) all slides have the same frame, all titles are 18-point Helvetica and so on. Slides can also be constructed in *layers*: if six successive slides all comment on a different part of a certain table of information, the table can be set up as a common layer with the comments on different layers. A product's tools for *spelling-checking* and *search-and-replace* help ensure consistency of terms through a presentation — avoiding arbitrary variants, such as 'IBM' and 'I.B.M.', or 'Proposals' and 'Recommendations' and 'Advice'.
- **Presentation content.** A typical product provides tools to *draw shapes* such as ellipses, rectangles and so on. They can be *manipulated* with techniques such as rotations and graduated fills. *Text* can be *formatted* with attributes such as font size, bullet style, colour and alignment. Another feature is *business graphics* — generating pie charts, bar charts and so on, usually from spreadsheet data.
- **Presentation product.** Once designed, the presentation material can be made into *hardcopy* or overhead *transparencies* or *slides* via normal office laser printer, colour laser printer, plotter, film recorder or slide service bureau. Most products can generate supporting printed materials

too; eg *audience handouts* might consist of reduced images of all the slides printed three to a page; *speaker's notes* could be produced at one reduced slide per page, supplemented by a hundred words of text.

Presentation Graphics: Possible Decision-making

With this insight into the different aspects of presentation graphics, decision-makers at Coachwood might come to the following conclusions:

- *Perhaps* 'Presentation consistency is a key aspect for us. We want to ensure that all slides and transparencies produced by Coachwood have a house style: eg with the heading always in a certain typeface and point-size; with a reference number in a certain position; with one out of a small selection of approved formats for the frame etc. We can enforce these standards without making everybody use the same software product. For each of the main products found in the company we will prepare standard slide templates and layers, and insist that they are used. In exchange for accepting these constraints, we will allow people to do whatever they like on the other aspects.'
- *But perhaps* 'Of the four aspects it is plain that presentation product is the one that deserves our attention. Mainly through ignorance, people are making too little use of speaker notes and audience handout possibilities. To tackle this we will do three things: one, discourage use of certain products that are rather weak on this aspect; two, for each of the products used that to do have rich features, offer a half-day course on using them effectively; three, for anyone unsure of which product to use, recommend one particular one as best — at any rate as far as the presentation product aspect is concerned.'
- *Or maybe* 'We want to develop a central library of slides and transparencies illustrating many of the concepts we apply to our work, including results produced on one project that may be relevant to others and so on. Since different people use different software products for their presentations, we want it to be possible to *convert* an item produced by one product into an item within a presentation produced by another. Of the four aspects, presentation structuring and presentation consistency and presentation product are not very relevant to this objective; the problems arise with presentation content. We will lay down standards to outlaw problematic designs with dodecahedrons or subtle shading effects, that may be easy to draw with one product, but next to impossible to replicate with others.'**1**

Value-added Network: Possible Context

Buloke is a large organisation that owns plantations, forests and mines, and also trades in and distributes commodities. The CIO calls in the telecoms manager and raises an apparently simple point. Buloke has a large investment in company-wide telecoms facilities — linking offices and depots in Europe, North America and other continents. It also has an enviable body of expert telecoms staff. Why not take advantage of this capability to offer VAN (value-added network) services to outside customers? For example, another company might open a new office in Palembang, Sumatra and need to send electronic mail to head office in Europe. Buloke already sends hundreds of messages to and from Palembang every day. Surely the other company could easily be linked into Buloke's system. There might be many such situations where outside customers could use Buloke's telecoms facilities. The marginal costs for Buloke might be relatively low but the income considerable.

Initially the telecoms manager is appalled by the CIO's naivety. The root of the problem is that 'VAN service' is such a vague and confusing term. Before the matter is discussed any further, some analysis is needed.

Value-added Network: Aspects-form Warrant

Terminology in this area can easily become confusing. From now on, 'VAN' will stand for 'the *organisation* that offers use of its own network to customers'. The *services* that a VAN may offer its customers can be analysed from seven aspects:

- **Bearer** services. From the customer's point of view the VAN merely provides a basic facility for transmitting data from place to place. The facility is basic in the sense that the customer takes care of many technical details, eg working out how to interface telecoms equipment to the network, handling data conversion and protocol conversion and so on.
- **Carrier** services. Here the VAN deals with all the purely technical issues involved in moving data from place to place, but it is not concerned with the applications that use the data at each end. They are the customer's own or those of some third party, eg a database host.
- **Information** services. These are interactive applications where the user looks up information in a database without (normally) updating it. There is a range of possibilities including varieties of videotex, with access through a hierarchical structure of menus, as well as text databases with search possibilities on any word anywhere in the database.
- **Off-line messaging** services. This is the general class of applications where messages are passed to users without accessing or updating any database (other than perhaps a 'mailbox' database of outstanding messages). The main examples are electronic mail, bulletin board, teletex, fax and voice mail.
- **On-line messaging** services. This covers straightforward phone conversations as well as sophisticated variations such as teleconferencing and videoconferencing.
- **Transaction** services. These are applications that enable transactions between different customers of the VAN. The difference between a transaction and a message? A transaction has a precise structure and implies commitment, eg a purchase order transmitted in some industry-standard

format: a message much less so, eg 'I might be interested in ordering a hundred tonnes of jute if you are sticking to last month's prices.' Thus EDI (electronic data interchange) services come in this category, but so also do home banking services (not correctly called EDI).

- **Non-telecoms** services. A VAN may also offer additional services that, unlike all the above, have no obvious need for telecoms facilities. There might be a facility for keying in data at a terminal to solve linear programming problems on the VAN's own computer. In principle, this could be done on a PC alone, given appropriate software, but for anyone already using several other VAN services, a 'one-stop shopping' approach can be attractive.

Value-added Network: Possible Decision-making

Given this insight, the CIO of Buloke, being an eager but shrewd individual, can suggest a number of things. They may not survive detailed scrutiny, but neither are they absurd. So this warrant does help to promote intelligent debate:

- 'I suppose there is no point in just using our network to supply bearer services. That is done by national telecoms authorities and other huge companies whose prime business is telecoms. If it was just a sideline for us, there is no reason to think we could be more competitive than them. Or have I missed something?'
- 'We already have internal information services allowing units all over the world to access our central databases of industry and general economic data. It sounds as if there would be negligible costs attached to allowing outside customers to access non-confidential database information — assuming that what we can offer is competitive with what is available elsewhere.'
- 'We have been discussing ways lately of improving our own infrastructure for facilities which, in the terms of the warrant, are on-line and off-line messaging services. That debate bogged down when we found that any major improvements would call for large investment with dubious returns. Suppose we made deals with a select group of medium-sized companies that, because of geographical location and/or business relationships, seemed natural partners. That would help spread the costs; as a by-product, it would be a discipline in controlling the quality of our services, since the partners wouldn't stay with us if they could get a better deal on the open market.'
- 'We could plausibly set up some kind of transaction service in one or two of the industries we dominate. I now see that this would be far more than just a way of recouping investment already made in our telecoms infrastructure. A more correct way of looking at it is this: having made that investment in telecoms, we have acquired the opportunity — which may or may not be worth having — to go on and invest a great deal more

in services that depend on it — if we believe it would be in our business interests to do so.'

- 'Presumably the warrant is describing *aspects* that help in describing the profile of any VAN's services, as opposed to firm *distinctions*. In other words, any VAN will normally offer a variety of services that can be analysed into these aspects. We, for example, could concentrate on the information services aspect with some rudimentary electronic mail (off-line messaging aspect) as an extra, and, if somebody begged us, allow a little of the carrier services aspect too.'

Groupware: Possible Context

Sassafras Magazines is a publisher of magazines about medical equipment, agricultural machinery and various other areas of technology. The company has expanded greatly in recent years and is always on the look out for ways of overtaking less vigorous competitors. The chairman of Sassafras has seized on the idea from a management journal that 'tomorrow's successful business will be one that knows how best to leverage the creative energies of workers loosely organised into ad hoc teams.'

The IT people are currently enthusiastic about a new category of software products called groupware, intended for this very purpose of leveraging creative energies etc, whether in ad hoc or other kinds of teams. They invite a number of software companies to make presentations about their groupware products.

After these sessions they are certainly in a good position to compile lists of buzzwords. Groupware software (aka workgroup software), it seems, provides or ties together any or all of many facilities: electronic mail, group (aka meeting) scheduling, teleconferencing (aka online chat), electronic meeting support (aka electronic conferencing), whiteboard software (aka document conferencing, but not the same as data conferencing), videoconferencing, voice mail, fax, mainstream database (whether distributed database or not), document content retrieval, personal information management, progress tracking, shared document production, compound (and/or portable) electronic documents, shared contact management, bulletin board, gateways to external databases, document image management, electronic forms and rules-based workflow control — to name only a few.

Now everyone at Sassafras is thoroughly confused. The more detail they hear, the less manageable the whole concept becomes and the less confident they can be of recognising the real issues and options that should influence any rational decisions. They decide to start again, studying the subject in a less hype-driven way. The first requirement is an analysis, summarised but incisive, to expose the main aspects of groupware applications.

Groupware: Aspects-form Warrant

To make sense of groupware it is best to pick out four different aspects of activities that may be performed by groups:

- **Project-document.** This is project-like (ie one-off as opposed to ongoing) work by a group, usually temporary, and leading to production of a document (in the widest sense); eg a design for a car, a tourism authority's detailed plans, a management consultancy report. The work is characterised by collaboration, interaction and iteration that doesn't fit any pre-defined structure. It is centred on an intellectual product that gradually emerges and is steadily refined, rather like sculpture from a block of stone. Maybe IT can help the interaction between workers on this kind of project become richer and more efficient.
- **Project-decision.** This is also project-like (as opposed to ongoing) work by a temporary group. But the product is less an elaborate intellectual product than a decision; eg OPEC deciding levels of production and prices, or a toothpaste manufacturer choosing a new advertising agency. Some structure needs to be imposed, albeit one that is not too dictatorial. Maybe IT can help make this kind of project more orderly.
- **Ongoing-formal.** This is ongoing work by a group that exists on the organisation chart (as opposed to a temporary project team). Its members collaborate in a definable workflow; eg journalists and editors in a newspaper; or the administration of a printing business with estimates, customer invoices, supplier invoices, complaint letters etc to be dealt with. Maybe IT can make the workflow more efficient in a factory sense, while remaining adequately flexible.
- **Ongoing-informal.** This is ongoing (as opposed to project-like) work within a group defined on the organisation chart—but where people work individually, and unpredictable interactions and informal links are dominant; eg people in the advice-to-members department of a trade union, or the help-line department for a computer games supplier. Maybe IT can help individuals do their work better and interchange tasks more flexibly.

Groupware: Possible Decision-making

The four variants of groupware application given in the warrant are really aspects, as opposed to categories resting on sharp distinctions. A large organisation may well be best analysed into a complex of interconnected groups, with a different aspect or mix of aspects dominant in each.**2**

The diagram sketches out some of the ways in which this warrant can help Sassafras to match demand (aspects of group work that may plausibly be automated within Sassafras) and supply (specific products most clearly directed at aspects of group work relevant to Sassafras). A number of different decisions are possible:

- *Either* 'The most natural approach seems to be to stress the ongoing-

Groupware: Using the Aspects Warrant

Recognise four aspects of groupware applications

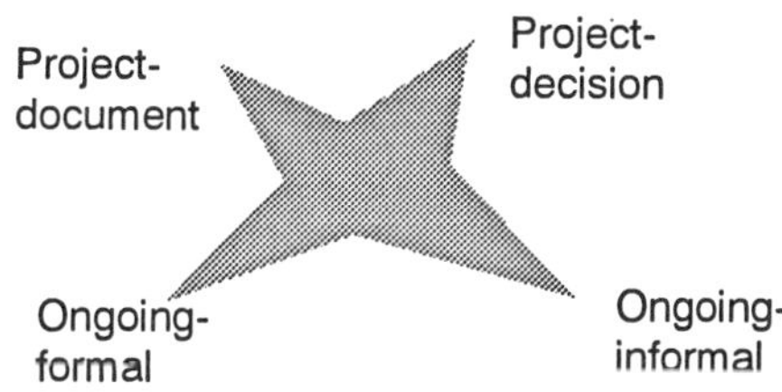

This helps make sense of:

dozens of different groupware functions

	Project-document	Project-decision	Ongoing-formal	Ongoing-informal
progress tracking			■	
document imaging			■	■
electronic meeting	■	■		
voice mail				■
etc				

possible applications in your organisation

	P-Doc	P-Dec	O-For	O-Inf
A1	■			
A2		■		■
A3			■	
A4	■			■

possible products on the market

	P-Doc	P-Dec	O-For	O-Inf
P1	■			
P2	■	■		
P3			■	
P4		■		■

This in turn helps in reaching decisions:

'We will develop THIS application with THAT software product'

We will concentrate on applications stressing THIS aspect (as opposed to the other three)'

We will choose a product strong in THOSE two aspects, and experiment with it' formal aspect. We will plan such a system and choose appropriate software to control production in one magazine. After that, if it goes well, we will extend the system to other magazines.'

- *Or* 'We think the two project (as opposed to ongoing) aspects of groupware offer the most exciting possibilities for our organisation. We will select the software product that seems most powerful in those aspects; then demonstrate it all over the organisation, in order to stimulate people's ideas for the kinds of things that might be possible.'
- *Or* 'We will first select a well-balanced software product, offering reasonable facilities on all four aspects. Then, as an experiment, we will apply it in two or three contexts that, assessed in terms of the aspects, are as different as possible. This will give us very rich experience of the possibilities of groupware; after that we shall be very well placed to make shrewd decisions and plan much larger investments.'

Using this Warrant Form

Considered from the viewpoint of their place in decision-making, these three aspects warrants can be sorted out as follows:

- The warrant about presentation graphics says in effect: since there are hundreds of points that could be discussed on this topic, the need is to define a small number of aspects as headings to impose order on debate. The debate may lead to a decision to emphasise certain aspects over others, but not necessarily: it could be that the main requirements or issues were spread smoothly over the aspects.
- With the other two aspects warrants, by contrast, there is a stronger implication that the way towards rational decisions is to decide which aspect or aspects should have priority over the others. They come closer to being distinctions or gradations warrants, but they don't go as far as setting up clear either-or options.

A good warrant in aspects form rarely shows more than seven or eight aspects at most. A set of a dozen tends to become a laundry list, where it is difficult to keep things in proportion. Worse, it is unlikely that a dozen aspects will be independent of each other; several items will probably turn out to be subdivisions or special cases of other more general items.

As the diagram suggests, the aspects warrant form is less decision-forcing than most of the others. Rather than identify specific options, it offers a way of looking at the situation more carefully, to pick out the relevant issues for decision. For intance, a sharp aspects warrant can cut through the glossy brochures of a product like a hot knife through butter, to show where the product stands, if anywhere, on the issues that matter.

On the other hand, aspects is a relatively crude warrant form. If it seems feasible to impose some firmer structure on the material within an aspects warrant, then it is worth considering whether another warrant form — chart, gradations or one of the others — would be more powerful.

Decision-making Logic

Sassafras Magazines: vague, confused notions about the possibilities of groupware technology → sufficient awareness and sense of direction to analyse possible applications and possible products

WARRANT

Analysis of four distinct ASPECTS of groupware applications, that help sort out the multitude of functions, uses, types of group, product features etc

extracted from
articles, authorities, documentation etc etc

NOTES & ARGUMENTS

1 Analysed with the decision-breakdown tool some of these are decisions on the scope and context planes as well as the matching plane. This is common. It is convenient to call a warrant that brings together supply and demand possibilities a matching warrant, but such a warrant can still be valuable to debate on other planes too.

For more detail about presentation graphics, a good source is 'Presentations With Style, Substance and Splash', *PC Magazine*, 11/19, pp. 245ff.

2 Systems that concentrate on the ongoing-formal aspect of groupware often have the vogue term *workflow* attached. The designer of a large-scale workflow system generally faces a fascinating challenge: how to structure (ie make into a formally defined workflow) processes and activities that seem varied, complicated and informal, and also do it in an enlightened way that enriches rather than diminishes workers' jobs.

The warrant given is based in part on ideas in 'Groupware, are we ready?', *PC Magazine*, 12/11, pp. 267ff. In mid-1994, recognising the interest in groupware and confusion about it, the magazine returned with an extensive feature that included an 80-box decision-chart (13/11, pp. 178-9). By asking questions such as 'Do you need a structured path for documents to move along?' and 'Do you need to track multiple versions of documents?' the chart guides you through to a short list of software products worth considering to meet your needs.

This raises the question: How useful is *any* pre-defined chain of logic made from boxes and arrows? On examination, these decision-charts seem to be of two types. The one in *PC Magazine* is really a complicated distinctions warrant — a way of *classifying* groupware functions and types of products; it can be judged as an aid to understanding options by the same standards as any other distinctions warrant. The other type, in much the same format, provides an answer to a specific question: you don't know what type of cabling is appropriate to your network; by answering certain questions on a decision-chart you will arrive at a clear answer. This is certainly decision-forcing; even so, this type of warrant is relatively unimportant, because it generates little *understanding* of the issues involved along the way. Thus it can only be used with safety for decisions where the problem and its factors can be defined very precisely.

CONNECTIONS

12. Matching through Comparisons	More decision-forcing forms of warrants for matching supply and demand
13. Matching through Distinctions	More decision-forcing forms of warrants for matching supply and demand
14. Matching through Gradations	More decision-forcing forms of warrants for matching supply and demand
15. Matching through Charts	Equally decision-forcing forms of warrants for matching supply and demand
17. Matching through Examples	Less decision-forcing forms of warrants for matching supply and demand
34. Sociotechnical Design	Groupware tends to prompt new roles, rather than automate old roles, for the workers in a group
36. Business Process Re-engineering	Groupware is a prime technology for supporting re-engineered processes
37. End-user Computing	Presentation graphics is one of the clearest examples of an end-user computing application to be found
39. Inter-organisational Systems	Most value-added network services set up inter-organisational systems in some sense

17. Matching through Examples

TOPIC

It is usually worth trying to coax technology knowledge into one of the five warrant forms discussed in previous briefings. Nevertheless, there is also a place for a warrant of less rigorous character. A description of some representative example (whether actual or fabricated) of technology being applied to good purpose can be a valuable stimulus towards understanding of how supply and demand interact.

There is a possible confusion to forestall here. In discussion of any general issues in IM, some abstractions and generalisations arise, and, to keep their meaning clear, examples are generally needed: sometimes a noun phrase, sometimes a couple of paragraphs. Also, in making up a warrant in distinctions or any other form, it is usually best for clarity to stir in some traces of example. In this loose sense, examples should come up all the time in discussions of IM.

But this briefing is devoted to something more specific: the example warrant. Here the content of the example doesn't merely clarify the meaning of some general statement. The impact of the warrant is the example itself, which (if a good one) helps convey an instinct or intuition for how certain supply factors match up with certain demand factors — and in a richer, more powerful way than any analysis in general terms. That is the rationale of the three examples in this briefing.

SUGGESTED WARRANTS

The three example warrants in this section describe: how expert systems solve problems by the technique of backward chaining; how neural networks, a rather new branch of artificial intelligence technology, can be applied; and how the seven 'layers' of the OSI telecoms standard bring certain advantages.

Backward Chaining: Possible Context

Angophora Mining often enters into complex legal arrangements with national governments and joint-venture partners. There is now talk of raising the level of IT that supports the negotiation of new contracts and provides access to details of existing contracts.

The methodical but naive approach would be to start by defining specific requirements: 'We need to ensure that certain standard clauses are included in every contract, except where specifically overridden' or 'We need to pick out from the database all contracts concerned with tin (or any other given metal)' or even 'We need a way of highlighting contractual conditions that are not legally enforceable'. With these demands agreed you could then choose technology to supply them.

But things are more complicated than that. An Angophora task force discusses the kind of requests for information that a system might meet. Ought it to handle a question such as this: 'If the recent devastating volcano in Bolivia ruins all our current joint-venture projects in that country, how much money will we lose — bearing in mind the sums contracted and already spent, but also the wording of the *force majeure* clauses in the different contracts, and the cover provided by various insurance policies and also any relevant legal precedents?'

This seems a very ambitious requirement to stipulate. And if you do insist on it, ambitious or not, why stop there? Why not define some more demanding requirement still? Where will the ambitious requirements ever end? And if you tone down requirements to make them less ambitious, where should the toning down end? The essential problem is this:

- Certain types of access requirement that are plausible (and less ambitious than the above) still go well beyond normal database applications, and very likely call for use of expert system technology.
- The task force needs to concentrate on discussing *realistic* requirements, as opposed to ideas so wayout that they entail systems of hitherto unparallelled sophistication. But judging what is realistic requires some awareness of the kind of things technology can do easily, with difficulty and not at all.
- But it isn't acceptable to exclude from the deliberations those people who don't know about expert systems; they are the people who will have to use the systems.
- These pressures can only be resolved by ensuring that all the decision-makers possess or quickly acquire some awareness of both the potential and limitations of the technology. But how can this awareness be generated?

In getting to know a cultural field — Chinese porcelain, Islamic architecture or rococo furniture — a handy technique is to study a few representative examples of particular styles, ignoring more individualistic works, however brilliant. This principle can be applied to technology too.

Rules for Backward Chaining

Rule A
If bank code not 8631
then card not issued by our bank

Rule B
If card not issued by our bank
then identification is negative

Rule C
If PIN keyed in differs from that on card
then identification is negative

Rule D
If identification is negative
then transaction is invalid

Rule E
If not sufficient cash in account
then transaction is invalid

Rule F
If withdrawal requested greater than $500
then transaction is invalid

etc etc etc

Backward Chaining: Example-form Warrant

Here is a simple example to show how an expert system uses backward-chaining logic to solve problems.1 A bank's automatic teller machine needs to apply some checks before giving out cash to somebody who inserts a plastic card. As the table shows, an expert system would store all the validation logic needed as a set of rules, each consisting of a premise and a conclusion: 'If X is true, then Y must be true.'

The system uses these rules in an interesting way: it sets itself the goal of proving that the requested transaction is *invalid.*

Among the rules are several that conclude 'then transaction is invalid' — rule D, for instance. The system tries to find some other rule where the *conclusion* is the same as the *premise* of rule D: 'identification is negative'. There are several other rules which conclude 'then identification is negative' — rule B, for instance.

Now the system tries to find some other rule where the *conclusion* is the same as the *premise* of rule B: 'then card not issued by our bank.' Rule A has that conclusion.

Now this chain of reasoning can go no further; the *premise* of rule A is a matter of verifiable fact. Either the content of the magnetic strip on the card contains the right bank code or it doesn't. If it doesn't, then the goal of proving the transaction invalid has been reached.

But if that particular test is passed, then the system will try again with all other avenues that may yet prove the transaction to be invalid; eg it can go back to consider rule D, and look for another rule whose conclusion is rule D's premise — rule C, for instance.

If the system exhausts all possible chains of logic that may prove the transaction invalid, then it can conclude that the transaction is *valid,* and authorise the requested cash withdrawal.

The analyst developing such a system just assembles all the relevant rules, in no particular order; rule A is first in the list only because some rule has to be first; there is no other significance. The expert system itself is clever enough to dart about linking rules' conclusions and premises in the way described.

This technique of starting with a hypothesis and working back through chains of rules until the hypothesis is fully proved or disproved is known as *backward chaining*. If your particular problem can be organised in the style of this example, then off-the-shelf expert system software can use backward chaining logic to solve it. Many problems can be put in this way, but not all.

Backward Chaining: Possible Decision-making

With this example, the Angophora people are much better placed to judge how readily their own queries about legal agreements can be handled by expert system technology.

They begin to consider how a system might assess the implications of volcano damage, bearing in mind *force majeure* clauses in existing contracts. The first insight is that a contract clause is itself a rule or set of rules in text form. Therefore it seems feasible to translate a contract into a set of rules on the model of 'if X, then Y'. But to do this every time a new contract with a different *force majeure* clause was negotiated would require a disproportionate amount of work — if the sole purpose were to answer certain queries that might never occur.

Another constraint soon emerges. Backward chaining attempts to prove or disprove a certain proposition, eg either a transaction is valid or invalid. But a question about a volcano's effects is more open-ended; it can't be reduced to an either/or answer. Therefore they conclude that this type of query doesn't fit the backward chaining of an expert system well.

But increased awareness brings an instinct for other types of query that are more manageable, and stimulates ideas that otherwise might never have come up; some information queries fit the backward chaining style well:

- Does this proposed new contract conform to the guidelines Angophora sets itself for joint-ventures in this area of the world?
- Will any of the investment made under this contract qualify for a government subsidy?

Other queries are recognised as probably feasible in principle (ie the problem posed could be solved by backward chaining through a body of rules), but too complicated in practice:

- Will the side-effects of this mining violate international agreements about environmental pollution?
- Could any of the clauses in this proposed contract be unenforceable, because they contradict some law or agreement that has a superior status?

The Angophora task force can assess very many possible information requests by these standards. As they progress, it may reasonably be hoped, their judgements about what is realistic should become more fluent and more reliable. Of course, it is conceivable that, having seen what backward chaining can and can't do and how much effort it entails, they conclude that, on balance, it should not have any place whatsoever in a new system.

Neural Network: Possible Context

Wild Cherry specialises in one particular line of property business — furnished apartments for foreigners staying in London, usually for between three months and three years. A substantial portion of the apartments let are the property of British people going abroad temporarily. This business can be very profitable to Wild Cherry if all goes well and efficiently, but there can be substantial costs and hassle in a minority of problem cases. Any use of IT to avoid the hassles might be said to have strategic importance to the business.

Wild Cherry is now considering a consultant's idea for the use of neural network technology. This, it is claimed, can make shrewd, powerful judgements:

- **Capricious clients.** Clients often cause hassle by starting out with certain requirements, and after viewing dozens of properties, choosing something totally different. A neural network could compare client characteristics with a database of property characteristics and judge for itself which apartments will *really* be the most appropriate.
- **Destructive clients.** The minority of tenants who leave behind a trail of wreckage are a great source of trouble. A neural network could spot tell-tale signs of awkward tenants at an early stage.
- **Bad debts**. The same applies to tenants likely to incur bad debts.
- **Guaranteed letting.** At present, Wild Cherry takes a percentage of the rent paid to owners who go abroad; if there is no tenant, then there is no income. Many tenants would prefer a guaranteed income — even if much lower. If Wild Cherry could offer this in cases where it was very sure of success in finding tenants (and not in other cases), this could be very profitable. A neural network could make such judgements automatically.

The directors of Wild Cherry agree that this would all be marvellous if successful. But all they know about neural networks is that the technology is rather esoteric. Technical jargon about 'weights for middle layer neurodes, and middle- to output layer-weights corresponding to elements of the feature patterns' brings no insight at all.

Perhaps the wisest decision would be to set up some limited experimental project in just one of the four areas above, in order to get a better understanding of the possibilities, snags and pitfalls. But at the moment the Wild Cherry directors aren't even in a position to judge what would be a worthwhile experiment to set up. They lack any instinct for the kinds of requirements that neural networks are good at handling. The best way to gain that awareness is to study some representative example of the technology in action.

Neural Network: Example-form Warrant

When a credit card is lost or stolen the owner notifies the bank and the card is blocked. That is fine if the bank knows within five minutes, but suppose a long period elapses during which somebody else tries to use the card fraudulently. In some banks the system that authorises or rejects credit-card transactions is intelligent enough to say, in effect: 'This card has not been reported missing by its owner, but even so the transaction should be rejected or scrutinised very carefully (or the customer should be called to check if the card is missing), because it seems *very likely* that the card is being used fraudulently.'

How can a system make such a judgement? Mainly by examining the pattern of card usage, seeing if that pattern meets certain criteria believed to suggest fraudulent use, and if so, signal that the transaction is dubious. For instance, if a certain card is rarely used more than once a week, but suddenly used fourteen times in one afternoon, that is a little suspicious. If all fourteen transactions are for purchases of electronics goods in some sleazy downtown area, that is even more so. This notion has a couple of interesting features:

- What distinguishes a good customer on a spending spree from someone using a stolen card? It is very difficult to devise appropriate criteria in advance and program them into a system. Instead, the automated system itself analyses a large body of cases, valid and fraudulent, and works out the criteria that, on average, provide good predictions of fraudulent use.
- It is even better to make this happen on a continuous basis. The system receives feedback — especially about its mistakes — and uses this automatically to tune its own criteria. This is desirable because the relevant factors can change over time and place. Gangs of credit-card thieves may move from town to town. Police may begin or cease special drives on crimes in particular areas. Thieves may buy different things with the cards according to the season of the year. The system can automatically change its criteria as it detects changes in the patterns of good and bad transactions.

The technology for all this is called *neural network*. Its characteristic features are to apply criteria that it derives for itself from raw data, and to tune the criteria continuously through feedback.

The criteria generated are usually concerned with weightings and probabilities, rather than either/or choices. The postal code of the shop where the transaction takes place may be one factor; each postal code will have some numerical risk rating. The number of transactions with the card in a day could be another; the age of the owner of the card another. The system brings values for these and other factors together in some

Neural Network: Knowledge and Implications

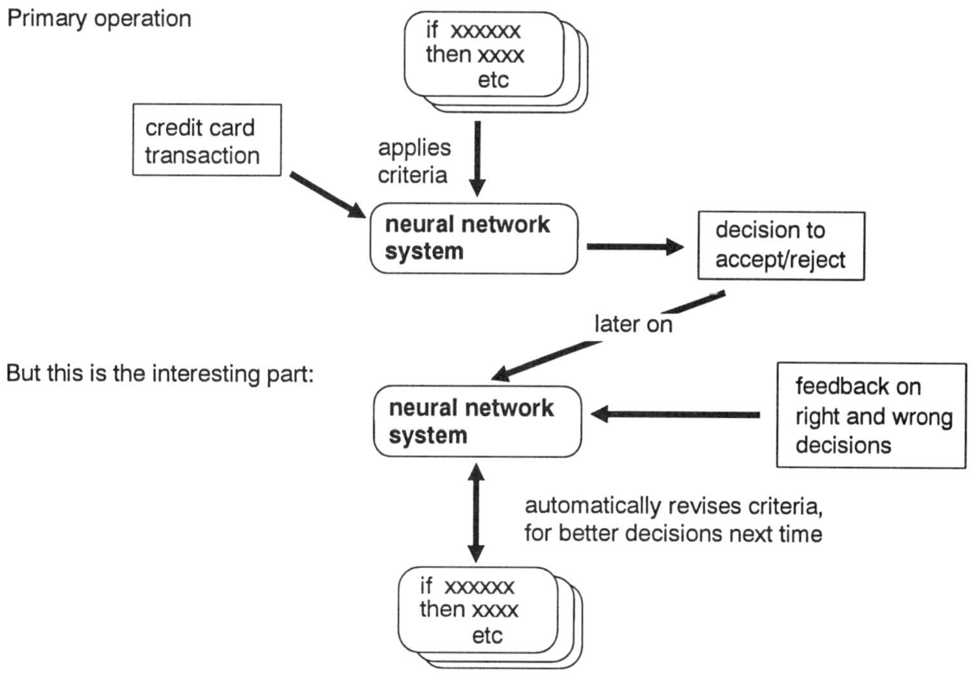

Primary operation

if xxxxxx
then xxxx
etc

credit card transaction

applies criteria

neural network system

decision to accept/reject

later on

But this is the interesting part:

neural network system

feedback on right and wrong decisions

automatically revises criteria, for better decisions next time

if xxxxxx
then xxxx
etc

Implication

To make good use of this technology, you need a healthy volume of transactions to provide the feedback.

formula. If, for any transaction, the formula gives a result higher than a certain cutoff figure, a possible problem is signalled; if not, not.

The system's formula doesn't give equal weight to all factors. If feedback shows that postal code is a more powerful predictor than age of owner, then postal code will automatically acquire more weight. If more feedback shows that age is even less relevant, then it may disappear as a factor from the calculation altogether. New factors — day of the week (say) — may force themselves in. The vital point is that this happens automatically through analysis of feedback.

The name *neural network* is best treated as a meaningless label for this technology. It originates from the idea that the judgement through the feedback of experience mimics the way the neurons in a human brain work when recognising faces, or deciding whether it is safe to cross the road, or performing other judgemental activities.

Neural Network: Possible Decision-making

Once they separate out the essential features of that example from the incidental, the decision-makers at Wild Cherry are much better placed to assess the match between their own possible requirements and the general characteristics of the technology. Here is a line that one of the directors might put:

● Of the four Wild Cherry problems given at the beginning — capricious clients, destructive clients, bad debts and guaranteed letting — at least the first three fit the style of the example warrant well. With the model of the credit card application before you, it isn't difficult to visualise how things would work. If patterns of characteristics in credit card transactions can be discovered, so can patterns in awkward tenants . . . and so on. Admittedly, the fourth possibility — about properties for which a tenant must be found — is more questionable, because that depends on *future* states of the housing market, and a neural network isn't really a forecasting tool.

● 'Since the requirements fit the technology so well neural network is certainly a feasible possibility — except for one thing.'

● 'This technology comes into its own when, as in the example warrant, it is applied to vast quantities of data. There are two reasons. One, if volumes are high an automated system may well spot subtle patterns that would escape any human analyst. Second — as the diagram shows — the idea is to react automatically to feedback. The greater the volume of feedback, the better; with small quantities, the random fluctuations of individual cases will have excessive influence.

● 'But Wild Cherry's portfolio is only about 3000 properties, changing at the rate of 5-10 per day. That seems unlikely to be a critical mass. This point really disqualifies neural network as a credible possibility for Wild Cherry.'[2]

If wise, the neural-network consultant will accept the truth of this conclusion and profit from it — perhaps by approaching the housing ministry with the idea of a national system to monitor all public rented housing.

OSI Layers: Possible Context

PTR (Pink Tea Rooms) is a large chain of fast-food restaurants. It already has a telecoms infrastructure for centralised control of the management of each outlet. The telecoms manager presents a proposal to the board for substantial new investment in a redesigned network:

'The proposed new infrastructure will be expensive, but the justification for it is very strong. Some of its benefits are in the 'can't do without' category, while others are quantified on a five-year basis, suggesting that, all in all, this is an attractive investment.'

One of the directors speaks for all:

'Fine, but that all rests on the premise that the plans and forecasts and assumptions in the proposal document work out as expected. Suppose they don't. Suppose that two years from now somebody has an idea for some new system with radically different patterns of telecoms traffic; or some new technology comes on the scene, that PTR can't afford to ignore; or there is suddenly a much greater need for security against industrial espionage; or PTR takes over another chain of restaurants. If any such things happen you will probably have to redesign much of the network, scrapping some of the investment already made, and calling for new investment on other things. This vulnerability to changed circumstances seems to be the main weakness of the proposal.'

'Admittedly, the changes you mention could occur; we can't plan with absolutely certainty. But the design of the new infrastructure is based on the industry-standard OSI model, and that in itself gives some assurance that changed requirements can be handled easily.'

'How come?'

'Any design based on a widely accepted standard is likely to be a more robust basis for change and expansion that one that it is not. Moreover, the OSI standard in particular is noted for its *layered* architecture; something can be bolted on, or switched in or out, at one of its seven layers, without awkward, consequential changes in the other six.'

'If these *layers* of the OSI model are of such importance, we need to know more about them. Are they like the layers in an archaeological site, or the skins of an onion, or the hierarchy levels in an organisation, or the classification tree of a genus of animals, or the sub-assemblies of a product? Unless we understand what kinds of things the OSI model and its layers are, we can't assess any claims about the flexibility they bring.'

But at this point the telecoms maven plunges into explaining how layer 4 is the transport layer, and contains such things as X214, VTAM and point to point transmission monitoring (data integrity), and the cause is lost.

Innumerable articles and books describe the OSI model, but hardly any provide useful matching warrants that pass the test of the Decision Question. Like the telecoms manager they pick the wrong things to explain. How many layers there are in the model, and what kind of technical matters are handled in each layer are not the most important things to know. You can't discuss the flexibility and robustness of telecoms designs based on the OSI model, unless you understand *what kind of things* the model and its layers are. The best approach to this is through an example warrant.

OSI Layers: Example-form Warrant

Suppose you wanted to set up a videotex service based on the French Teletel variant of videotex technology. To do this it isn't compulsory to take any notice of the OSI model, but suppose, for the sake of example, that you do.

The diagram shows the essential logic of the OSI model. In this videotex example, following the OSI model, that part of the system concerned with the formats of videotex images will be at layer 6 (although layer 6 contains other things besides). This neatness brings valuable flexibility. Changes can be made in one place without fear of repercussions elsewhere. There are corollary benefits:

- You can design and build all the aspects of the system that correspond to the other layers without making any assumptions about the videotex image standard to be used for layer 6. In fact the people working on those layers don't need to know anything about videotex image standards.
- If a non-videotex telecoms network based on the OSI model already exists and it has spare capacity, you may be able to make it support videotex just by tampering with the appropriate layer.
- You may well be able to use ready-made software from elsewhere. If somebody else has an OSI-based videotex system — even if different in many technical characteristics affecting layers other than layer 6 — it should still be feasible to take its layer 6 software and plug it into your own system.

OSI Layers: Possible Decision-making

Once the board members have grasped the message conveyed by this example and have a good appreciation of the sense in which the OSI model provides flexibility, an interesting debate ensues:

'The example shows or hints at the *kind of* changes that can easily be made to a telecoms infrastructure based on the OSI model. Thus if you change from the French to the British standard for videotex images, your worries are confined to layer 6. It would no doubt be possible to imagine thousands of other changes that were confined to one layer. But I don't see how all changes can be handled in that way.'

'What other changes do you have in mind?'

'What about a change in volumes? The standard for videotex images remains the same, but the number of people using the videotex facility increases by a factor of a thousand. What layer do we change then, if any?'

'There is no particular layer corresponding to volume of traffic.'

'Right, there can't be — given the kind of thing the model is, as illustrated by the example. But it is entirely possible that when usage goes up by a factor of a thousand the performance of the network becomes quite unacceptable. Then you may have to make quite extensive changes — perhaps changing the type of terminals used and the type of cables, perhaps adding intelligent multiplexers to optimise throughput, perhaps using different error correction protocols that impose less overhead with the changed pattern of usage, perhaps changing the format of packets of

OSI Model: Layers and Flexibility

In a large-scale telecoms network, dozens of different functions, features and components have to be fitted together:

eg checking for and correction of transmission errors,
splitting a message into separate packets for transmission,
reformatting data for display on a certain hardware device etc.

Don't structure all these things in a messy way like this:

Do it in clear LAYERS like this:

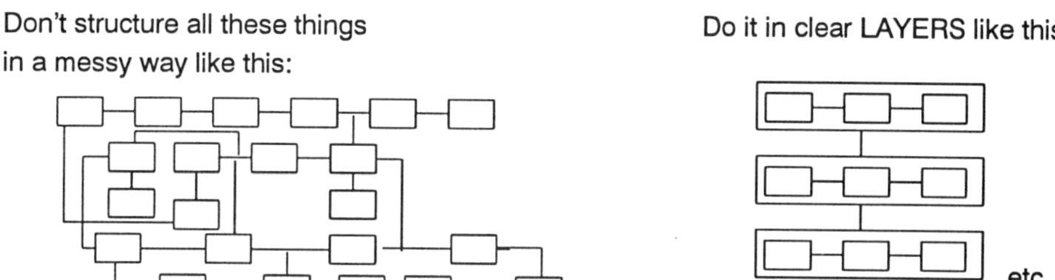
etc

In fact, always do it in the same seven STANDARD layers

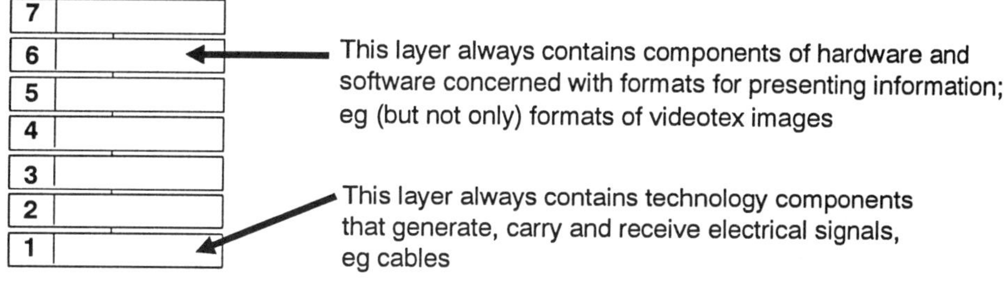
7
6
5
4
3
2
1
This layer always contains components of hardware and software concerned with formats for presenting information; eg (but not only) formats of videotex images
This layer always contains technology components that generate, carry and receive electrical signals, eg cables

Flexibility advantages:

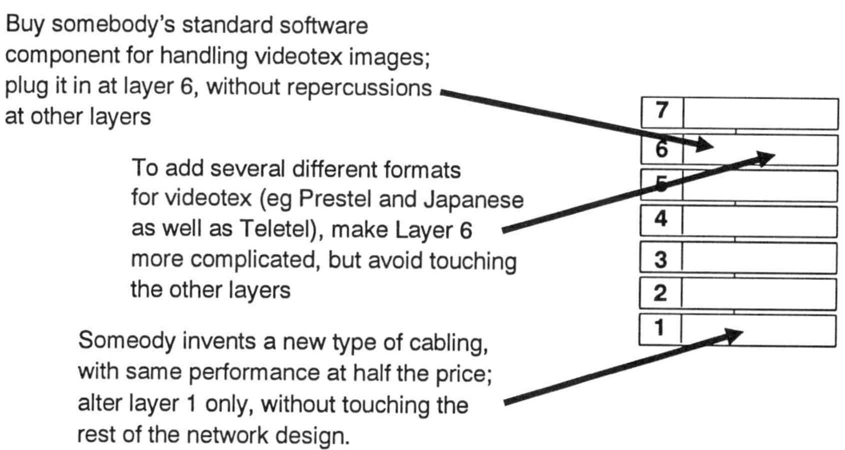
Buy somebody's standard software component for handling videotex images; plug it in at layer 6, without repercussions at other layers
To add several different formats for videotex (eg Prestel and Japanese as well as Teletel), make Layer 6 more complicated, but avoid touching the other layers
Someody invents a new type of cabling, with same performance at half the price; alter layer 1 only, without touching the rest of the network design.
7
6
5
4
3
2
1

data across the network that is most efficient in the new circumstances, perhaps making dozens of changes over all seven layers.'

'Perhaps.'

'Now, if I understand the example correctly, the OSI model helps you be neat and methodical once you have *already* decided to change a specific thing, such as the standard for videotex images or the type of cabling — preferably something contained in just one of the seven layers. The model doesn't immunise you from the possibility that one awkward change, simple but radical, such as a large increase in volumes, may trigger off changes all over the layers.'

'All right. That's true.'

'Then perhaps we could consider this issue of flexibility more realistically if we try and decide the following: Do we expect the changes and developments in our telecoms use over (say) the next five years to have an easily compartmentalised character and/or a kind of evolutionary, organic character? If so, the OSI approach is very attractive and worth pursuing, even if more expensive than some other option. Or, is it fairly likely that there will be some (though we don't know what) radical changes of patterns of usage in that period, calling for reappraisal of the features of the whole infrastructure? If so, and if I understand the example correctly, the fact that we may be following the standard OSI model will not be very relevant.'[3]

Using this Warrant Form

As in the briefings on other warrant forms the examples given above can be differentiated:

- The example of the technique of backward chaining, though not really technical, is detailed. Examples are given of actual rules. The implicit challenge is: given some completely different application, could you envisage analogous rules being processed in analogous ways?
- The example of neural network is more broad-brush. It doesn't describe how the technology works at quite the same level as the backward chaining example. It concentrates on describing the nature of the example problem, in a way that shows the typical characteristics of problems that the technology fits.
- As the diagram suggests, the *classic* example warrant describes an application of a certain technology, in such a way that it helps you judge whether any other problem you encounter can reasonably be handled in a similar way. The example about the layers of the OSI telecoms standard shows how the example warrant can be taken as far as conveying the signficance of what might otherwise remain obscure technical concepts.

There are a few common-sense rules to follow with example warrants. They need to be as short as possible. Distracting, situation-specific detail should be filtered out. But there is no point simplifying the whole thing so much that the essence of the problem disappears. Possessing a large

Decision-making Logic

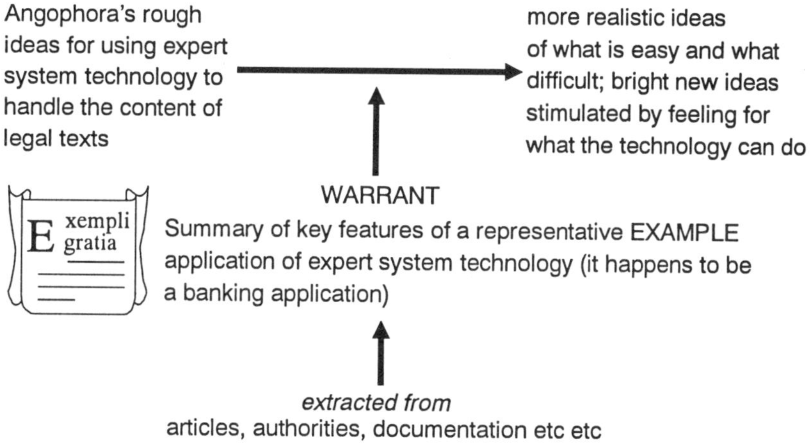

Angophora's rough ideas for using expert system technology to handle the content of legal texts → more realistic ideas of what is easy and what difficult; bright new ideas stimulated by feeling for what the technology can do

WARRANT

E xempli gratia

Summary of key features of a representative EXAMPLE application of expert system technology (it happens to be a banking application)

extracted from
articles, authorities, documentation etc etc

gallery of example warrants about a certain technology area is counter-productive; it is better to have a small number, each carefully honed to demonstrate the key, generally relevant points as neatly as possible.

Sometimes reference to an example warrant will make it obvious that a certain problem falls naturally into (say) a backward chaining format. Other times this isn't so, but, inspired by the example warrant, you may find that the problem can be expressed quite satisfactorily in that form — even though nobody had previously looked at it that way.

NOTES & ARGUMENTS

1 This warrant is based on that given by Kurt Christoff in 'Expert Systems', *Information Center*, March 1988, pp. 10-11. This brief article provides more insight into expert systems than the entire case-filled book by Feigenbaum, McCorduck and Nii.

2 An anticlimax, but this book is about real-life decisions, and many of these are (or ought to be) decisions *not* to do something that sounded promising initially. The credit card application is discussed in 'New Business Uses for Neurocomputing', *I/S Analyzer*, February 1990.

3 This isn't meant to be a complete account of the implications of the OSI model for IM decision-makers — merely a discussion around the topic of flexibility.

As with technology standards in many fields, there can be tricky tradeoffs: if (say) your top priority is cost-efficiency in handling enormous quantities of data, and flexibility and other advantages of standardisation are relatively unimportant, then it may be quite rational to design a network that is not organised neatly into the seven OSI layers.

CONNECTIONS

12. Matching through Comparisons	More decision-forcing forms of warrants for matching supply and demand
13. Matching through Distinctions	More decision-forcing forms of warrants for matching supply and demand
14. Matching through Gradations	More decision-forcing forms of warrants for matching supply and demand
15. Matching through Charts	More decision-forcing forms of warrants for matching supply and demand
16. Matching through Aspects	More decision-forcing forms of warrants for matching supply and demand
39. Inter-organisational Systems	One of the main purposes of the OSI model is to facilitate interconnection between different networks, perhaps those of different organisations
40. Strategic Systems and Competitive Advantage	A neural network application forms a useful starting-point for discussion of competitive advantage, innovation and related topics

18. Untangling Scope Decisions

TOPIC

Decisions on the scope plane don't propose any particular match of supply and demand. They set the scope *within which* supply and demand are to be matched. For instance, the following question calls for a scope decision: 'Should each department of the bank try to find the best match of supply and demand for its text database requirements taken in isolation, or should the bank try to find the supply solution that matches best (or least badly) the demands of all the departments taken together?

Failing to consider all the scope options available, or even to realise that scope issues exist, are common features of poor IM decision-making. Many books and articles about IM ignore matters of scope or make glib assumptions about it. Some terms, such as infrastructure and integration, are used portentously and ambiguously, for lack of attention to the issues of scope that they raise.

Such observations, however valid, are rather abstract. This briefing aims to clarify the concept of scope, giving examples and untangling the main issues it contains.

SUGGESTED WARRANTS

The table gives some representative examples of scope decisions. Even so, the intertangled characteristic of decisions on this plane is not too obvious from a simple list. For this reason, the following section looks into one hypothetical case.

Aspects of Scope

The department of Rosewood Bank that appraises the risks of loans to the governments of foreign countries often applies statistical analysis techniques: regression analysis and the like. It is now selecting the most appropriate software package for its future needs.

The previous sentence contains a scope assumption with three different aspects that can be challenged:

Rosewood Bank, Representative Scope Decisions

'We will pick the most cost-effective technology solution to the text database requirements of the bank's legal department; ie we won't take account of other departments' requirements for text database.'

'The new geographic information system will be carefully designed to contain all the main pieces of geographic information needed by all the head office departments.'

'We will make all our office automation systems strongly integrated with all our DP systems — except for the systems of our travel agent subsidiary.'

'This innovative system to allow customers to view images of transaction documents will be developed in a prototyping (as opposed to experimental) style. The difference between the prototyping and experimental styles is . . '

'Work on designing systems for our two new overseas banks will proceed independently, subject only to the stipulation that they both retain compatibility with the following industry-wide standards . . '

'Since the key challenge of this customer analysis project is getting the detailed requirements defined reliably (as opposed to solving difficult technical problems), it will be structured as a regular, step-by-step project, but with even more weight than usual on the functional specification stage.'

'We will plan application systems A-F together within one database and telecoms infrastructure, and G-P together within another infrastructure, and Q as a quite separate item.'

- **Common-separate dilemma.** Other departments have or may have requirements for statistical analysis software. Should the bank aim to select one software package for common use — the one that seems most appropriate on balance, given the whole body of requirements, even though it may not be first choice for every single department? Or should each department be encouraged to make its own separate choice?
- **Broad-narrow dilemma.** But is it right to think of statistical analysis as a separate application to decide about? Perhaps the bank (or the department) should have an integrated policy, including compatible technology choices, for a much wider area including (say) spreadsheet, linear programming and Monte Carlo simulation. Or, conversely, perhaps statistical analysis is too broad a problem area; maybe two or three different forms of statistical analysis should be separated out for separate decisions.
- **Definite-trial dilemma.** What status should a decision matching supply and demand in the statistical analysis (or some broader or narrower) area have? Should you commit to a definite choice of the technology that, on balance, on paper, best meets carefully defined long-term needs in this area? Or, alternatively, aim for flexibility, by selecting (say) the

Dilemmas of Scope

One possible scope:
decide the best match of functions (demand) and technology (supply) for one application in one dept.

statistical analysis
in
risk appraisal dept.

Common-Separate Dilemma.
But perhaps a better scope is: decide the best match for several (or all) depts, taken together, weighing all the tradeoffs

statistical analysis
in
dept. A, dept. B, dept. C, etc

Broad-Narrow Dilemma.
Or perhaps a better scope is: decide the best match for statistical analysis and related applications, taken together, weighing all the tradeoffs

statistical analysis	spreadsheet	linear programming
in risk appraisal dept.		

Definite-Trial Dilemma.
Or perhaps a better scope is: decide how to try out possible matches of functions (demand) and technology (supply)

statistical analysis
in
risk appraisal dept.

Or perhaps some combination of the above

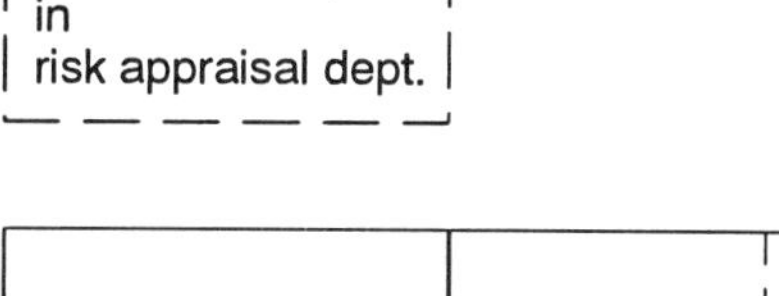

two most promising software products for use during a trial period? Or somewhere between these extremes?

The diagram shows these three dilemmas impressionistically. Intelligent scope decisions avoid the seductive assumption that the greater the scope of a decision, the better. To see the absurdity of this, suppose you tried to plan every detail of every application of every department, all together in one decision-making process of huge scope. The question would immediately arise: Why not include also full detail about all external factors — customers, suppliers, the world economy, government, society? For five five years ahead, or maybe ten, but why not twenty? There is no *logical* place to draw a line. A useful warrant about scope exposes arbitrary assumptions or clarifies vague aspirations, and helps you set the most *sensible* scope, given the circumstances.

Relation of Scope to the Other Planes

Of course, the main decisions on various planes made by an organisation ought to be coherent, or at least not contradictory. Take the scope decision: 'We will make all our office automation systems strongly integrated with all our DP systems — except for the systems of our travel agent subsidiary.' A bank deciding that might well have decisions on the other planes such as:

- **Agenda**. 'We must have a standard interface for all systems throughout the whole company, except in very special cases.'
- **Matching**. 'We will automate these office procedures . . (but not these . .), using this standard office automation software, which is particularly adept at linking up with database software, . . '
- **Context**. 'Each of the nine business units (except the travel agent) will have one systems manager, and together they will form a co-ordinating committee with the following wide powers . . '
- **Approach**. 'Our strategic planning procedures will produce a fairly detailed enterprise data model before any work starts on individual projects.'

Plainly, you couldn't make a radical change to decisions on the scope plane without at least raising questions about the validity of decisions on the other planes. But then the scope plane is not unique in this respect. **1**

NOTES & ARGUMENTS

1 One feature of this plane of decision-making is that some *warrants* are primarily, but not only, relevant to scope decisions.

Take a warrant: 'There are five types of project risk: . . ' Identifying the main risks helps define a sensible scope for a particular project. But the warrant could also assist an agenda decision, such as: 'We will adopt the following drastic measures to get out of this disastrous situation . . (based on shrewd analysis of what has really gone wrong)', or a context decision such as: 'We will divide responsibility for authorising new projects between the following people and committees . . (an organisation structure carefully designed to minimise the main types of risk).'

CONNECTIONS

19. Project and Infrastructure Scope	Generic tradeoffs associated with the common-separate and broad-narrow dilemmas
20. Integration and Connected Matters	Fundamental concepts pervading most scope decisions but particularly the broad-narrow dilemma
21. Regular Projects	Options with regular projects (ie methodically developing definite rather than trial systems)
22. Evolutionary Development	Options with evolutionary projects, where systems are developed in an iterative, less obviously methodical style

19. Project and Infrastructure Scope

TOPIC

A certain fundamental tradeoff, often ignored or underestimated, is of the first importance.

It is plainly foolish to carry out a whole string of projects, producing separate systems, databases and networks, without any attempt at co-ordination.

It seems an attractive notion first to set up an *infrastructure* of database and telecoms, with perhaps certain application systems of a very fundamental kind. Once that is done, subsequent system development work can occur in separate projects consistently and cost-effectively, within the environment of the infrastructure.

But to determine the shape and content of a durable infrastructure, that has a realistic chance of supporting all the systems of the next (say) five or seven years, you have to bring together many factors and issues, assumptions and forecasts, as intricately meshed components of one very large problem.

The more ambitious the aims of the infrastructure, the more difficult and speculative its design; and the more exposed it is to uncertainty factors likely to invalidate forecasts of future requirements; and the greater the penalty if the infrastructure turns out inappropriate for the projects to be supported in the years ahead; and the more bureaucratic the planning process will have to be; and the less opportunity will remain for individual initiative, once the infrastructure design is signed off.

An infrastructure (aka platform, architecture etc) is a good thing, but then retention of flexibility, minimising dependency on vulnerable forecasts, avoidance of arbitrary assumptions, and encouragement of initiative on projects are also good things. Somehow the tradeoff has to be resolved. This briefing argues that this topic is usually discussed in books and articles much less carefully than it should be.

REPRESENTATIVE IDEAS — SUMMARISED

The best way of uncovering the real issues of project-infrastructure scope is to start out with some apparently straightforward ideas and then see how they stand up to analysis.

Some Straightforward Ideas

One article describes with considerable scorn a company whose IT decisions were so little co-ordinated that its departments contained personal computers from eight different suppliers, maintained from five different sources, and used seven different spreadsheet packages. This, it is suggested, is self-evidently bad; a well-managed organisation would co-ordinate choices of products and suppliers much better.

Another article criticises an organisation where several divisions conducted separate feasibility studies, in part employing expensive consultants, into the application of desktop publishing technology.

The common thread linking these criticisms is that things will be much more efficient if a few one-off, organisation-wide decisions are taken, rather than many piecemeal decisions spread out over time or over different units.

One author takes the concept of up-front, co-ordinated decision-making much further, by describing the 'core system' as 'the most important development in IT management's thinking to have emerged so far'. By this account, the core system consists of three main elements: high volume, *transaction processing systems* that update the company's common *databases*, together with the company's *communications infrastructure*. The logic is: the decisions are taken, design made and development done to lay down the core system first; application systems are 'subsequently hung onto this core (sic)'. All basic transactions are handled by the core system. The core system is common to many applications and is supra-departmental. Thus most of an organisation's design and software skill and effort goes into the core system rather than the applications.**1**

A More Subtle Idea

The book by Cash, McFarlan and McKenney also contains examples similar to those just given, but with an entirely different interpretation.**2** It uses a case to explore the notion of tradeoffs. A department within a manufacturing company takes the initiative and acquires hardware and software to experiment with CAD (computer-aided design). The IT people complain because the technology chosen is not compatible with other technology within the company, and it will therefore be impossible or very difficult to achieve integration between the CAD system and (say) bill of materials and costing systems.

As the authors point out — whatever the exact details of this particular case — it is naive to criticise the CAD people on the ground that nobody should ever invest in anything that might turn out later to be incompatible with something else. With that approach to decisions about technology new to the organisation, you will never do anything, because you will never become knowledgeable enough about the issues (both technical and organisational) to be able to make well-informed decisions. This suggests that the best approach in a certain situation can be:

- Plan systems based on established technology, eg bill of materials and costing and inventory control, carefully together in one decision-making process.
- Treat decision-making about new technologies, CAD (say), as separate problems — difficult enough in themselves without the additional complications of somehow achieving coherence with other matters.

Of course this crude distinction is an over-simplification, since there can be *degrees* of coherence, and also degrees of subordination of parts to whole. As Cash, McFarlan and McKenney frequently stress, you have to find the right balance for the situation.

Keen's Platform

An interesting book by Keen devotes considerable attention to the concept of the 'platform'.[3] The underlying argument is that fragmented decentralisation of decision-making and monolithic centralism are both undesirable extremes, and the best compromise is to firm up centrally an IT infrastructure, also called corporate IT platform, separate from the specific applications to be built on it.

Left there, the argument would pack no more punch than the core system idea above. But the interesting point made is that a decision has to be taken about the *scope* of the platform, and to assist this decision, two separate aspects can be picked out:

- **Reach.** Suppose Pink Gum Products has a very powerful platform that makes it feasible to *reach all* suppliers in its industry; but a lesser rival's platform can to reach only some suppliers (very likely those with similar or related technology); another rival's platform reaches no suppliers at all. Similarly, a platform can be described in terms of how well it allows Pink Gum's own departments or divisions to reach one another.
- **Range**. Whatever their reaches may be, the platforms of companies may also differ in the range of information that can be exchanged. For example, Pink Gum's platform (though its reach is extensive) is limited to the exchange of plain-vanilla transaction data. Another company's platform allows, in addition, exchange of texts such as e-mail or word processing documents (with some, but not all, formatting such as different letter sizes, paragraph indentation etc). Another company's platform is sophisticated enough for CAD graphics of products and components to be exchanged. Another company's platform ranges further and allows all this and full-colour images to be exchanged too.

This concept of the platform is a more limited one than that of the core system above, which could embrace a substantial proportion of all the hardware, software and information in the organisation. The logic of this platform seems to be:

- In one major decision-making process you take the decision to make a large investment in a platform of *technology* — that is computer hardware, basic software (such as operating system, database management and telecoms software, and any specially written software to enable these things to fit together) and telecoms lines and devices.
- But you exclude from this decision-making *as far as you can* any detailed consideration of the nature of processing, or the structure and content of databases that may be required.
- When you consider any new application of technology, you already have the facilities of the platform available, and you won't normally build anything that is detached from the platform; you will live within its constraints. However, this still leaves open a great-many application-specific options.

REPRESENTATIVE IDEAS — ANALYSED

The point made by Cash, McFarlan and McKenney is entirely sound. They don't work its implications through in much detail, but at least they avoid the shortcomings of most others who touch on this subject.

Core Systems: Objectives and Problems

To think carefully about X (a proposed approach, a piece of advice etc) it is often good to ask: What would be an example of the bad thing that X is aiming to avoid? The core system concept aims to ensure that, when the time comes, desired application systems can be 'hung onto' the core without great problems. So, what would an *unsuccessful* core system be like?

Suppose the sales director at Pink Gum asks for a new report analysing mail-order sales of kitchen equipment by customers' sex. There are plausible reasons for the request: customer sex may be correlated to the success of certain types of advertising, or to the choice of certain options in the product. But the sex of a mail-order customer is not a data element in the database of the core system. Therefore if the requirement is to be met, changes must be made to the format of the main database; and to some of the software that processes it; and the input forms and screens procedures associated with new customers.

Even the shrewdest analysts and designers in the world are bound to fall foul of this kind of problem. How could it be otherwise? 'Man is no Aristotelian god contemplating all existence at one glance.'[4] There has to be some boundary to the scope of the investigation and planning of an infrastructure; some assumptions have to be made about what is and is not relevant; otherwise nothing will ever be decided. Thus there is always the possibility that somewhere beyond the boundary awkward new possibilities may lurk.

To describe an ideal core system approach, with the implication that it is, on the whole, quite a feasible thing to achieve (given competent designers, shrewd managers etc) does nobody any service. The vital point to grasp is the tradeoff: the more all-embracing and detailed the core system is made, then the greater the benefit if it is successful, but also (as with many ambitious enterprises) the greater the chance that it won't be.

Compromises can be made in various ways: have several smaller core-like systems with tenuous links between them; or deliberately leave out of the design calculations anything concerned with experimental innovative projects; or intend in any case to scrap and redesign one part of the core system three years later; etc. Then the benefits attainable are less, but the chance of achieving them is greater.

Decisions on how far to aim towards the (usually) unattainable ideal, and where to strike the balance, are rarely obvious; they can be vital, difficult decisions with tremendous repercussions.

Choices and Feasibility Studies: Co-ordinated or Dictatorial

Matters such as standardisation on spreadsheet packages, and efficient investigation and investment of desktop publishing provide another twist to the same generic problem. On the bare facts given above, it is not fair to condemn a company for having seven different spreadsheet packages. This may seem terribly untidy to a bureaucrat, but if all seven departments are happy and they don't need to exchange data (or can do so in some simple format), where is the harm? There are very likely benefits: some people may well have positive feelings of pride and commitment about the package they chose; in some departments there may even be sound objective evidence that the features of a certain package do match certain special requirements. There is a dilemma:

- *either* treat choice of spreadsheet package for the whole organisation as one decision to be taken in one decision-making procedure — with ample consultation procedures no doubt, but still in one procedure;
- *or* treat choice of spreadsheet package for different departments as a number of separate decisions to be taken in separate decision-making procedures.

At Pink Gum, a medium-sized manufacturing company, the advantages of co-ordinated choices may seem decisive: perhaps the research department, design department, finance department etc frequently exchange large spreadsheets, containing intricate formulae, not easily translated from one package to another. But, then again, perhaps the balance of factors goes the other way: maybe the spreadsheets are not that complicated, and the whole culture of the organisation is against the imposition of unnecessary diktats.

It may be silly to have two separate feasibility studies about desktop publishing or, then again, it may not. Circumstances vary. Consider two extremes:

- Suppose there is a certain well-defined problem to solve: eg how to connect up a desktop publishing system to the corporate network, so that texts and graphics can be exchanged between locations. Then having two independent studies of this problem will probably be wasteful.
- But suppose the issues in question are more wayout: inventing a completely new type of publishing product, or trying out new work-patterns for collaboration on the production of documents. Then it could be quite astute to set up separate, weakly co-ordinated groups. This improves the chances of bright ideas striking, gives more room for zany notions to survive without being killed by the scepticism of the majority, provides room for experiments with rival, contradictory approaches, and so on.[5]

Commitment and Flexibility in Platforms

Keen's book provides a stimulus for critical thinking about IM matters: careful examination may reveal shortcomings in the ideas presented, but the process of examination itself can produce insights.

First, neither Keen's reach nor range are scales on which *simple* measurements can be made. Pink Gum might conceivably choose to have the platform's reach very great for all intra-company communications, but relatively feeble for customers and suppliers — or the reverse. Or relatively strong internationally, though a little weak nationally. Or with a range that differed by location, eg colour images could go to some outside advertising agencies but not to internal departments. This is not criticism of the concept, merely clarification.

How might the concepts of reach and range in platforms aid decision-making? The two dimensions seem helpful in defining the scope of any number of hypothetical platforms for your own organisation, and can thereby expose the key options that you have to choose between. But Keen doesn't suggest that; he seems to recommend extending the reach and range of the platform as far as possible, giving reasons such as: to avoid blocking an important business initiative; to avoid blocking imitation of a rival's initiative; to permit alliances and consortia; to allow adaptation to reorganisation and acquisitions; etc. Yes, by all means — if the cost is trivial. But definitely not — if the cost of a super platform is greater than the company's annual turnover. As with many decisions the real challenge here is surely to find the best buy.

The trouble is that often you can't analyse a variety of reach and range possibilities against cost in order to calculate the best buy; there may be too many uncertainty factors. If Pink Gum has an absolutely definite need

Pink Gum Products, Possible Scenarios

The organisation-wide technology infrastructure set up in Year 1 excludes any facility for transmitting colour images. What can happen?

Scenario A	In Year 4, you find that you simply must have the facility of transmitting colour images, in order to compete with innovative rivals. Very luckily, it turns out that you can extend your platform in this direction without any awkward repercussions.
Scenario B	In Year 3, you find that you simply must have the facility. Very unluckily, this proves so complicated that you have to scrap the whole platform and redesign and rebuild it.
Scenario C	Only in Year 7, as it turns out, is the facility really needed — and by that time much of the technology for colour images has changed completely. You are delighted that you decided in Year 1 to exclude the facility from the platform built at that time, since its marginal cost would simply have been wasted. By Year 7 you are quite happy to redesign the whole infrastructure in any case, since numerous other unforeseeable developments have occurred.
Scenarios D etc	Any number of other possible outcomes to the development of requirements and technologies . . .

Implications for decision-making logic

Infrastructure planning can't normally be based on a set of entirely firm requirements.

Neither is it rational to cram in everything you might ever need.

There is no clear principle to follow, except the principle of assessing tradeoffs.

This is real decision-making under uncertainty.

for a platform that can deal effortlessly with the transmission of colour images, then that will be one determinant of its platform range; conversely, if the need as good as certainly won't ever arise, then it can be left out. But suppose Pink Gum managers just can't know whether transmission of colour images will ever be needed; after agonising, they exclude this requirement from platform planning. Several possible scenarios could then arise, as the table shows.

Infrastructure decisions entail investment in extensive facilities — but in the face of inevitable uncertainty about which facilities will truly be needed and what will be the best way of providing them in the future.

Simply pouring into your platform as many facilities as you can possibly think of at this moment is not rational.

Different Kinds of Infrastructure Elements

The trouble with the core system described above is that it comprises almost the whole fruit, leaving hardly any room for flesh. Keen's platform concept escapes from that absurdity by concentrating on technology arrangements and leaving out applications and their databases. But merely to ignore these factors is no answer. Certain application elements have an awkwardly fundamental, infrastructure-like character too. Analogous scenarios that turn out well or badly could be sketched out in this application dimension too.

For instance, a tough issue, affecting almost every system, could be the format of Pink Gum's product number: should the fourth digit be used to indicate whether this is a special export product? Another generally relevant matter could be the standard routine accessed by any system needing to know the number of working days between any two dates (bearing in mind that the factory is closed on most, but not necessarily all, public holidays, and also on some days adjacent to public holidays)? A firm, long-term decision is needed on archive data, too: if all stock movement transactions are to be stored for ever in summary form, how should they be analysed and summarised?

It is no answer to say that Pink Gum should decide these things once and for all as part of its infrastructure planning. Suppose that, three years on, some industry-standard format for product-numbers emerges; or four years on, Pink Gum enters a joint-venture with a foreign company (with different public holidays), or five years on it has to generate statistics from archive data to meet some industry regulator's capricious requirements. Here too, there is no avoiding a difficult decision about the scope of up-front design work on application and data features.

This line of thought offers a new dimension for choice in infrastructure decisions. At Pink Gum the apt decision could be to invest heavily in technology infrastructure, and as far as possible leave decisions about the characteristics of application systems and their databases to other decision processes at different times. But in another company (or Pink Gum at a different moment) it could be prudent to concentrate on making the company's database infrastructure more coherent (eg standardising formats of commonly used data elements, bringing logically related items together, and so on), while leaving any decisions about reach and range across a network to decision-making at some later point.

NOTES & ARGUMENTS

1 The three references in this section: J Daniel Couger, 'E Pluribus Computum', *Harvard Business Review*, September-October, 1986; also in Harvard Business Review (1990); Hochstrasser and Griffiths, p. 120; Grindley, p. 98, pp. 135-9.

2 Cash, McFarlan and McKenney, pp. 134-5.

3 Keen's book (1991) is one of the first to attempt a serious discussion of infrastructures (pp. 39-40, 179-209), but the more you study it, the more you wonder what it is and is not recommending.

- The platform (1) is said to be *built on* the architecture (2), ie it isn't the same thing as the architecture. (p. 193)
- Also, the architecture is said to be in effect (puzzling qualifier) the firm's technology strategy (3); and an architecture is a blueprint (4) rather than a facility. (p. 200)
- The architecture is the *blueprint for evolving* a corporate resource (5) — a contradiction in terms, since to evolve is *not* to follow a predefined blueprint; and the firm without an IT architecture does not have a real IT strategy (6). (p. 239)

Working out the relations between these six entities and others is like keeping track of all the characters in a Russian novel. The account given in the briefing text is one possible interpretation.

Briefings 15 and 16 of O'Brien (*Demands*) are less concerned with suggesting a method than with exploring the tricky points of infrastructure planning.

4 Walter Lippmann; the epigraph of *Knowledge and Decisions*, Thomas Sowell (Basic Books, 1980).

Synnott (chapters 8 to 10) devotes more than 100 pages to the organisation-wide architecture, but ignores one fundamental issue: What matters should be dealt with on an organisation-wide basis (ie regarded as part of an architecture) and what should be excluded and left for decision at department and project level? Synnott's description and procedures rest on the unspoken assumption that there is a straightforward, general answer to this question, and therefore most well-run companies will have an architecture of much the same scope. But if the *scope* of the architecture is itself an issue for decision, to be answered in different ways in different organisations at different times, then detailed procedures along the lines: 'develop your architecture this way . . ' are likely to be naive.

5 Another author (Gunton (1988), pp. 147-151; and also (1990), pp. 232-5) describes enthusiastically the idea of planning a large programme of system developments as a *four-course meal*: 'Having decided what functions and features the system should offer to end-users, you serve those up course by course according to a predetermined plan.' The four courses are: hors d'oeuvres — make life easier; main course — solve real problems; cheese course — cement (sic) onto company procedures; and the sweet — lower the barriers to wider use.

This raises the question of the relationship between a whole development programme and its stages — a variation of the infrastructure-project debate in a different key. If by deciding beforehand 'what functions and features the (whole) system should offer' you mean firming up and getting everyone's agreement to a 300-page document, then all the big decisions about functions and features (and thus presumably about technology and work redesign too) are made in one decision-making procedure at the beginning. You are defining one unified project to be carried out. Then the question of whether there should be four, five or 68 courses is a second-order, tactical matter.

But if your definition of the whole meal is as short as a lunch menu — one page, with a paragraph on each of four intended courses, then the situation is quite different. Then you have really decided that there should be four separate projects (albeit successive, with each building on the product of the previous ones). You have decided *not to decide* very much at the beginning, but rather that many important decisions should be taken within the decision-making for each project.

Plainly, there are tradeoffs and it is a challenge to find the right balance between these extremes. If you go too far in making each course a separate project, then the third course (say) may be unduly constrained by the way the first course was carried out; eg data is stored in awkward formats or hardware has been chosen that won't support the functions of the third course. Then it may be necessary to go back and revise decisions taken and work done on the first course, a procedure both embarrassing and messy. The way to avoid that is to take all the main decisions up-front and downgrade the flexibility left to the four stages. But then you still run risks: you are less able to react to the unexpected and, in particular, there is much less room for those creative ideas for using IT that only occur to people when they have already started using a system.

As it stands, the 'four-course meal' is an arbitrary solution to a poorly defined problem. The kind of questions calling for decision on the scope plane are: How firmly or slackly should you determine the whole menu in advance? Which parts of the menu are meant to be fixed from the start and which mere possibilities? To what degree will guests be allowed to ask for extra courses and dishes? And so on.

CONNECTIONS

20. Integration and Connected Matters	Analysis of integrity, compatibility and other terms affecting the scope of an infrastructure
24. Centralisation and Distribution	Concepts associated with context decisions that can influence project scope

20. Integration and Connected Matters

TOPIC

Surely every organisation should set up a meticulously planned technology platform, to provide complete integration of all systems, ensure that the different system elements are fully compatible, and based on open system standards, making software portable from any installation to any other, and . . .

But this is empty talk. Apart from anything else, it rests on the idea that integration, compatibility, portability and others are all reasonably coherent, unambiguous terms. This is far from being true. To have a chance of discussing things rationally, you need to distinguish several different concepts sheltering under the term 'integration'; then see how some kinds of integration are associated with 'compatibility', which itself covers several different concepts. And so on.

The main point of this briefing is to analyse such terms and concepts into warrants — essential tools for probing the tradeoffs of major decisions of scope.

SUGGESTED WARRANTS

What does it mean to call something an integrated system? Anything whatsoever (a bicycle, a country's laws, a factory, a marketing campaign) can be analysed down into distinct components almost as far as you like. But the word 'integrated' suggests that, whatever components are identified separately, they all fit together closely and neatly. This is the start of analysis from 'integration' through 'compatibility' and 'portability' to 'open system'.

Distinctions between Two Senses of Integration

Confused or unrealistic IT policy decisions sometimes result from an ambiguity about *integration*:

● For some things it is reasonable to say 'the more integrated the better'. For instance, the more closely and neatly the parts of a bicycle fit together, the more efficiently it converts effort into progress; and the more integrated a country's set of laws, the less chance of injustices through contradictions and anomalies.

- But with other things it is by no means necessarily true that 'the more integrated the better'. You might abstain from integrating a factory's production schedule closely with that of one key supplier, and prefer to have crude, even ad hoc links with a variety of suppliers. A marketing campaign might be deliberately organised in a rather inconsistent, diffuse way — to avoid making assumptions about which type of media were best and which type of consumers most promising, and to allow scope for opportunistic exploitation later.[1]

Plainly, the second sense is only relevant in cases where a degree of integration less than what is possible is still a valid, and conceivably preferable, option:

- To talk of a very basic word processing system being an integrated system is to talk only in the first sense; it simply means that there are no pointless, awkward inconsistencies. There is no case for having such a system less integrated.
- A more advanced word processing system may include spell-checking and thesaurus facilities. But these things can also be provided by separate systems. In recent years word processing, spell-checking and thesaurus have often been integrated within one package without any great disadvantage. Therefore this also is usually a case where the more integrated the better. Still, in some circumstances, a less integrated approach could still be sensible: a writer on medical ethics might use a word processing product from one supplier, a thesaurus strong in medical terms from another, and a legal reference work on compact disk from a third.
- But what of an advanced word processing system that has integrated facilities for drawing diagrams? It is entirely plausible to prefer to avoid this particular form of integration and stick to two different systems for the two distinct tasks. Here, greater or less integration is a real choice.

Even within these simple examples there can be gradations and varieties of integration: word processor and thesaurus facility might be integrated to the extent that you can select the thesaurus facility from a menu (you don't have to stop the word processor program and start up a separate thesaurus program) — but not entirely integrated, because some details of the interface are different (eg to request help in the main system you press a certain function key, but in the thesaurus a different one).

Real-life decisions on integration involving an organisation's own application systems and databases are invariably far more intricate than those about word processing. With a naive view that the more integration the better, the only task is to try and make everything fit together, but if degree of integration is seen as a genuine variable for decision that is subject to tradeoffs, then certain aspects of integration and associated topics need to be separated out.[2]

Three Aspects of Integration

Context integration

Viewpoint: Person using the computer facilities.

Rough explanation: Different things can be done in the same context.

Simple example: Using a library's information system, you can find out what books the library possesses, and at the same terminal you can also key in a message that you have lost your borrower's card.

Advanced example: You can also access the computer systems of several other libraries, and use exactly the same instructions (keyword search facilities etc) to search their information.

Data integration

Viewpoint: Data administrator.

Rough explanation: Data is input and stored to minimise data capture work, avoid inconsistency problems and to be available wherever needed.

Simple example: Customer data is held once in one place, for access by both the sales order processing people and those in the accounts department.

Advanced example: The text of a railway timetable is held once in such a way that it can be used both for typesetting the printed book, and for access in an on-line information system for travel agents.

Process integration

Viewpoint: Efficiency consultant.

Rough explanation: Different automated processes succeed each other and the output of the one is the input to another without human intervention.

Simple example: Once the material requirements plan for a factory has been produced by one sub-system, it becomes input to another sub-system, that automatically generates orders to be sent to suppliers.

Advanced example: The same, but the system also picks up input about the quality of each supplier's deliveries from the goods inwards department, and makes a statistical analysis of suppliers' reliability record on delivery dates and quality tests, and uses this analysis to decide, without human intervention, how much to order from each of several competing suppliers.

Chart of Topics related to Integration

As the diagram shows, there are three broad aspects of integration worth keeping distinct: context integration, data integration and process integration. These three are a starting-point for charting a variety of other themes:

● **Uniformity of interface.** If you can do several things from the same terminal that is already context integration to some degree. But the context is far more integrated if you always give commands by using the same combinations of function keys, by choosing from menus in similar style, and by using the mouse according to the same conventions.

- **Context switching.** If you can (say) do some word processing, switch to spreadsheet work, send an e-mail message and then, with just a key stroke, come back to your word processing document, exactly as you left it — while continuing to see the e-mail message in one window of the screen — that is a much stronger form of context integration than simply doing one thing after another in the same context.
- **Consistent file formats.** If data is scattered around the organisation without much attempt at overall co-ordination, but nevertheless all in (say) the standard dBase file format, that is a weak form of data integration. It doesn't guarantee that data will be suitable for multiple uses, but at least any future attempt in that direction will be much easier than it would otherwise be.
- **Consistent data formats.** If an organisation observes consistent guidelines for the formats of supplier numbers, date fields, sales analysis codes etc this can be a big step towards data integration, since it makes combination of data from different sources much more feasible.
- **Hot links.** If a piece of data is only held in one place then, of course, it need only be updated once. But it could be held in two places (eg the name of a new product under development might be held in both the marketing database and the R&D database), with arrangements that, if updated in one place, it will *automatically* be updated in the other — there is a 'hot link'. This is a form of data integration.

The essential purpose of this analysis is to point out the kind of options that will need to be considered in typical decisions about integration, once the facile assumption is discarded that the more integration the better.[3]

Chart relating Integration and Compatibility

The theme of integration is associated with, but distinct from, that of *compatibility*. To start with, there are two main kinds of compatibility:

- **Technology compatibility** exists, in its simplest sense, when two pieces of general-purpose technology can work together, without any special modification; eg a Compaq PC can drive a LaserJet printer. The two pieces of technology need not both be hardware; for example, the FrameMaker software product can read in and use text files produced by WordPerfect.
- **Application compatibility** exists when the design of the data or the processing of two application systems is consistent. For example, a sales analysis system can read in and accumulate the data from an order processing system, because both use the same classification codes for analysing types of product.

On these definitions, technology compatibility can exist without application compatibility — if (say) the sales analysis system can read in the sales order data technically, but project group '34' is understood inconsistently in the two systems. Conversely, two systems might use the same coding system and therefore be potentially application-compatible, but be isolated on completely incompatible hardware.

Compatibility has its gradations. A certain PC may be entirely compatible with a certain laser printer — as long as you don't try to print a full-page half-tone graphic. The sales analysis system may be application-compatible with all other systems in the organisation — except that it just ignores the eighth and least significant digit of the customer location code.

How are compatibility and integration related? The three *aspects of integration* defined above refer to three different facilities or demands that you may try to achieve in systems. The *two types of compatibility* just defined refer to different factors that can make integration either easier or harder to achieve, eg:

- Context integration presupposes that the different things integrated in the same context are implemented on the same or on technology-compatible hardware and basic software. Otherwise no common context is possible. But application-compatibility may or may not be an issue. It depends whether the different applications in the same context are interdependent, and (as with two different library systems accessible in the same context) they may not be.
- Data integration entails application compatibility, by its very nature. If (as is usually the case) a variety of people need to access the same information at any time, a considerable degree of technology-compatibility is a practical necessity.
- Process integration entails application compatibility. There must be some technology-compatibility otherwise the links between processes can't be maintained. But this may be a fairly trivial requirement — if one process only takes the output of another after it has finished.

In short, compatibility considerations define the constraints and the opportunities that have a large effect on how ambitious a degree of integration is realistic.

Chart of Compatibility and Portability

Portability is a concept closely associated with technology compatibility. Any given piece of general-purpose technology (word processing package, laser printer, mouse etc) will be technology-compatible with some other things and not with others. Similarly, a piece of application software will run on one computer, perhaps others, probably not all. But that is under your own control; you may deliberately develop application software to be technology-compatible with more than one type of hardware, though perhaps at the price of considerable extra effort.

If a technology item (usually a piece of software) is compatible with several different technology environments (computers, operating systems etc), it can be called portable. There are several different reasons for wanting portability, and they are worth separating out:

- **Efficient design.** In designing a new system it may be most efficient to have different hardware at different locations; eg one type of hardware in a small branch, and a different type at a large branch, that also serves as a regional office, has much higher data volumes, and many extra functions. But some functions may be common to the locations that use different hardware; eg all branches need software to accept a new order. It is plainly desirable to develop such software so that it is portable between the different types of hardware.
- **Flexible technology components.** System requirements and data volumes change; the hardware available on the market changes. It is advantageous to preserve freedom over the years ahead to switch hardware about or to choose completely different hardware, perhaps from a different supplier. That is an argument for developing software to be reasonably portable from the start. Analogously, it may be desirable to retain flexibility to fit in general-purpose software products as yet unknown that may emerge over the years. That argues for use of (or compatibility with) those technology environments for which products are most likely to be developed.
- **Flexible software development.** Even if your planned operational hardware were uniform, and you never expected to change any feature of your system in any way, it could still be an attractive idea to program a system on a PC, test it out there, and only then take that software to run on larger-scale operational hardware. That is only possible if the software developed is portable between PC and (say) mainframe.[4]

Adding Open Systems into the Chart

During the first few decades of computing, incompatibility between technology products was considerable, and portability was difficult and limited. Nowadays more and more products are marketed with claims that they are widely compatible with numerous other products — or more exactly, with established industry standards. The fact that a certain laser printer is (say) a Kyocera is rather trivial; the key point is its compatibility with the LaserJet or PostScript standard or both. That a workstation is (say) an Intergraph may be almost as trivial; what counts is that it is based on the Unix standard, and therefore (subject to some ifs and buts) should run software written for other Unix-based systems. Technology products based on established industry standards (particularly hardware based on Unix) are generally labelled as *open systems*.[5]

In principle, the great advantage to the decision-maker is that software developed with an open system technology is by definition portable. There should be no need for any special effort or expertise to

Analysis, Warrant Forms and Decision-making

Analyse complex terms, such as Integration, Compatibility etc
using warrant forms, such as Distinctions, Aspects and Chart

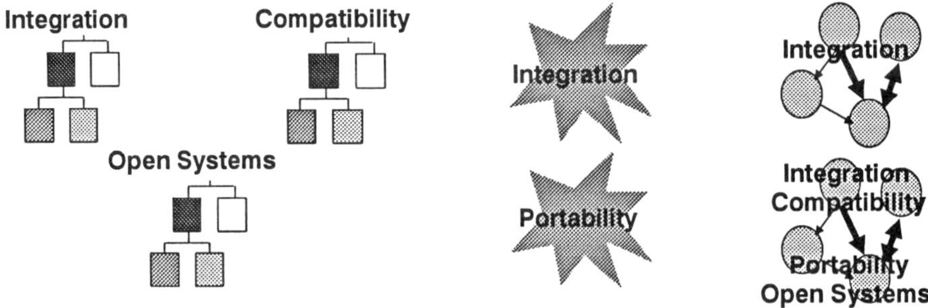

Keep these analytical weapons ready,
and choose the right ones for each problem

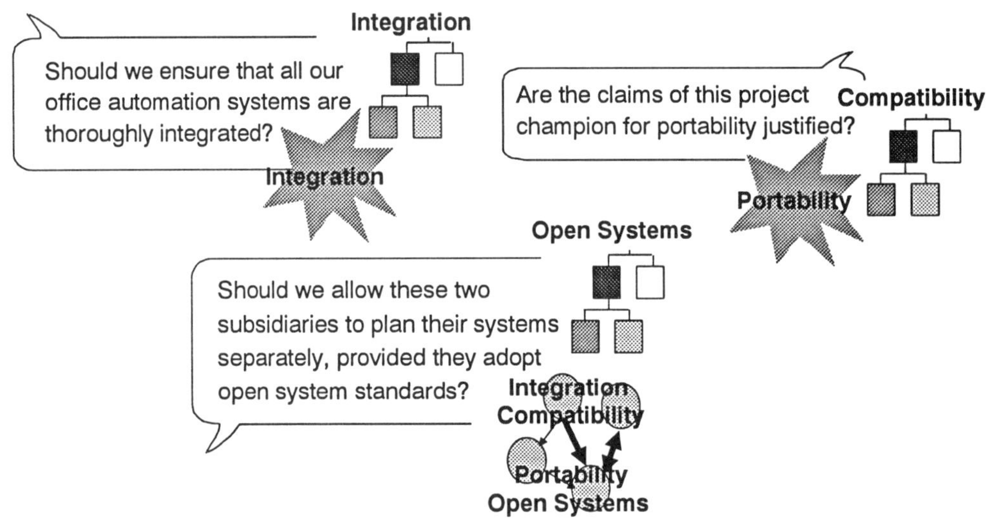

take account of the differences between (say) Intergraph and Sun and DEC hardware.

But just as with suitcases and overhead projectors, there are degrees of portability, even between open systems. A certain geographic information system may be portable between a great variety of hardware configurations, except that on a tiny, monochrome monitor its most complex maps are unreadable. This particular limitation need not be very troublesome, since nobody could expect things to be any different. But suppose a piece of software written in a certain language is intended to be portable between many technology environments — and will be, but only provided that one or two obscure but occasionally useful instructions are never employed. This kind of incompatibility, if noticed too late, could devastate a system, and even if recognised from the start, it could pose awkward constraints.

It is too facile to assume 'open system good, anything else bad'. Different options may provide open systems and portability to subtly different degrees. Moreover (since it is easier to ensure openness by ignoring complex refinements), an option that is less open may, in compensation, permit more sophisticated possibilities. Do you necessarily want to develop a system less efficiently, ignoring some of the most attractive possibilities, in order to achieve perfect portability, just in case some day different hardware might perhaps be used?[6]

Like the other warrants in this briefing, that is a mere sketch of the tradeoffs that can arise. The diagram shows how the warrants are meant as analytical weapons. It is still quite a task to wield the weapons effectively in any specific case.

NOTES & ARGUMENTS

1 Wright and Rhodes (pp. 61-73) provide an interesting but over-complicated analysis of different types of integration. The essence is a distinction between *hard integration*, where events and decisions in one area can be made to generate events and decisions in another area more or less automatically, and *soft integration*, where things are much less automatic.

- For *manufacturer A* — a maker of flameproof electric motors — relatively hard integration would be appropriate. Why? Though there is product variety (of sizes and power ratings), the company not the customer defines them. It is reasonable to expect to deliver customer orders from stock. A diagram of the stages of production flow, though not trivially simple, nevertheless has far fewer feedbacks and interactions and uncertainties than with many other types of manufacturing.
- But for *manufacturer B* — a maker of special steels — relatively soft integration would be appropriate. There is great product variety and it is defined by the customer. A standard manufacturing and stocking process is not practical; delivery dates are negotiable and in turn affect production batch sizes. A great variety of production processes is required: eg each batch may require any five out of 20 possible finishing processes. A flow diagram of all possible paths would be very complex.

The same criteria apply in other contexts. A retail bank might call for hard integration, like manufacturer A (no great product variety; not many or very complex processes), while a hospital might exceed manufacturer B in complexity factors suggesting soft integration. There are millions of possible combinations of diagnosis techniques and treatments that may be needed, and they can't be predefined, since the results of one diagnosis or treatment determine the next.

2 'Modular' is a related term that has its tangled variations:

- To claim 'This modular system has six modules: order processing, sales forecasting, material requirements planning . . ' is to claim, *at a minimum*, that the system is made up of six parts ('modules') that fit together (ie they are not completely separate).

- This straightforward sense of modular may be all that is claimed, but there is also a *strong sense* of the term: the claim may be that the six modules of the system fit together so neatly and simply, that they can be treated as interchangeable components: if unhappy with (say) the sales forecasting module, you could throw it away and replace it by one that forecast sales in an entirely different way, and (this is the vital point) you would not have to alter any of the other modules.
- There is also a *very strong sense*: the claim may be that the six modules can be mixed and matched: you could choose any four of the six to implement for the system at one factory, and then at a different factory (or the same one at a later date) have a system consisting of any five of the six, and (this is the vital point) you would not have to alter any to make them fit together into a coherent system.

Decisions about modularity need to be both clear and realistic. If you do want the six parts of your system to be modular in a very strong sense, make sure everyone knows exactly what that means, and also (since strongly modular usually means more costly) have a good reason for it.

'Modularity' is related to 'integration' because . . . But no, the purpose of this book is to suggest ways of thinking about IM, not to provide a complete set of ready-made thoughts.

3 To illustrate this, here is a brief problem, albeit without an answer — stimulated by Ernest M von Simson, 'The Centrally Decentralized IS Organization', in Harvard Business Review (1991).

A large conglomerate is very decentralised. Each unit has very different markets, with separate computer arrangements and little apparent need for integration. However, there can still be overlap of suppliers; both a travel agent and a sugar refinery might need to buy a photocopier or a security system.

It would be pleasant if the travel agent and the sugar refinery could order individually but achieve quantity discounts appropriate to the size of the entire group. But can each supplier be expected to know that all the companies with different names belong to the same group? And how can the travel agent know that the sugar refinery ordered a photocopier last week? How can anybody check that the full discount has been applied on every order? How can anyone decide how to rationalise and select preferred suppliers? How can one unit negotiate special terms on the strength of the whole relationship?

Some form of integration of purchasing system is clearly desirable, but the whole policy of the group is that as far as possible the travel agent and the sugar refinery and all the others should be freed of the burden of agreeing standard systems together. Thus the need in this case is to find the leanest, most elegant mode of integration to achieve worthwhile benefits. The 'best buy' will be an approach that achieves a few straightforward things fairly simply and avoids the snares of one uniform, integrated purchasing system for the whole group. Finding the best buy means exploring options, and to do that you need to distinguish between different types and gradations of integration.

4 There can be rather complicated loopbacks from portability to the other themes:

- To achieve portability of software you may have to recognise that not all hardware environments can support the graphic user interface you would ideally like. This could pose a dilemma: *either* define a standard interface for all systems (thus contributing strongly to context integration) that *can* be portable, but is relatively crude; *or else* have a much easier-to-use interface for some applications on some hardware, which, however, can't be standard, because it is not completely portable.

- If the different technologies handle data in fundamentally different formats, there may be an awkward choice: *either* aim for complete portability and data integration by adopting some super-format of great complexity and overhead; *or else* keep things simple, with the intention, should it ever be necessary, of using special utility software to reformat and transfer data from one environment to another.

5 An open system, by its nature, rests on a certain industry standard, but there are several *varieties of standard*:

- a standard set up by some standards body, not associated with any particular supplier, eg X.400 for electronic mail;
- a standard originally developed by a certain supplier (typically through some successful product), but whose details are fully documented to the outside world, eg the Unix operating system, originally developed by AT&T;
- a standard originally developed by some particular supplier and still to some degree under its control, or providing the supplier with a favourable position, perhaps because certain fine detail has not been fully documented for the rest of the industry, eg (some people allege) Microsoft's Windows.

Another theme often comes up in discussions of open systems: avoiding dependency on one particular supplier. Anybody regarding this as the most important thing of all would develop systems based on Unix rather than Windows. But this aim may well conflict with another: flexible technology components. If this is the prime concern, then Windows may be preferable to Unix, since there is (and arguably will continue to be) a more lively market in software products based on Windows.

6 In many of the most important areas, truly open systems, based on fully accepted standards, don't exist. SQL is a standard language for accessing a database, controlled by an independent standards body. Hundreds of suppliers offer SQL among the facilities of their software products, but innumerable dialects of SQL can be found: many offer special extra instructions that may well be useful but don't belong to the common standard; the way the system reacts if an SQL access finds an error condition is another source of variation.

This is probably inevitable. Consider the supplier of database software (or any other relevant technology) as a rational economic agent. The supplier has to offer an open, standards-based product, because practically every customer demands it. But to compete with rivals in the market most suppliers will try to offer a better product — and that very likely means a product with extra, ie non-standard, features. Moreover, many customers demand certain features for which no recognised standard yet exists. And again, a supplier in any industry has an interest in discouraging customers, once captured, from going elsewhere; discrepancies in the interpretation of standards — if not too blatant — can be very effective in this.

In other words, you probably can't have *both* a lively, competitive market, with suppliers constantly developing more advanced features, *and also* perfectly open systems.

CONNECTIONS

19. Project and Infrastructure Scope	Setting the scope of an organisation's IT infrastructure
24. Centralisation and Distribution	Concepts and jargon that, unless you are careful, merge confusingly into integration issues
28. Decision-making as Process	The shape of the decision-making process, something that interacts strongly with the degree of integration desired

21. Regular Projects

TOPIC

The regular way to manage system development is in a methodical, step-by-step fashion. The full detail of this, though important, is usually placed outside the boundaries of IM. Moreover, many principles of project management, when starkly exposed, amount to little more than platitudes: 'review the product of one step before starting the next', or 'work out which activities are dependent on which others.'

What kind of IM decisions, if any, remain once the general scope of a possible project has been identified, and a choice has been made for regular development, rather than the evolutionary development discussed in the next briefing? Briefing 6 explores the idea of identifying certain generic states an *organisation* may be in, in order to develop recommendations about organisation-wide matters. Can there be an analogous piece of logic, that identifies generic types of project in order to guide decisions at *project* level?

If a sound generic analysis of regular projects can be established, then perhaps it can be shown that project-type should influence some detailed scope decisions about the shape of the project. After all, it is plausible that, even among projects organised in the regular, methodical fashion, some ought to be more rigidly controlled than others, and the importance of certain aspects may well vary from one type of project to another. This briefing examines how ideas about generic types of project, or generic variables affecting a project, work out in practice.

REPRESENTATIVE IDEAS — SUMMARISED

This section sets out several ideas that have been proposed for classifying projects or systems, trying as far as possible to show how the classification can help decisions about the way any particular project should be handled.

Gerstein's Four Types of System

Gerstein suggests an interesting quadrant-analysis of systems, that does have some decision-making force.1 For any application, ask two questions: What is the degree of operational dependency involved (little or great)? To what degree does the application provide competitive advantage? Thus any application can be assigned to one of four quadrants.

Take a bank: ATM systems represent high operational dependency (ie if they go wrong that is a serious matter); back in 1979 they represented high competitive advantage, but nowadays low competitive advantage (since most banks have them). Many of a bank's PC systems (eg word processing) are low both in operational dependency and competitive advantage. An executive information system, by contrast, is low in operational dependency, but may be high in competitive advantage.

As with most quadrant-analysis, the payoff comes in the logic that follows. Applications in different quadrants, it can plausibly be recommended, should be planned and run in different ways:

- **Low-low** applications. On the one hand, it is difficult to justify investing much high-quality management effort to optimise planning and control; on the other hand, this can be a substantial portion of the whole portfolio of applications, and there can easily be problems in co-ordinating several systems. The challenge is to manage this tradeoff economically.
- **High** operational dependency, with **low** competitive advantage. Issues of performance, reliability, security and the like are vital. There is no great need for planning to favour boldness or for project management to stimulate great creativity. This is the quadrant where intensely methodical, step-by-step control is most appropriate.
- **Low** operational dependency with **high** competitive advantage. These applications are generally innovative, and not manifestly essential to the business. Therefore creativity and flexibility should be encouraged, both in planning and in carrying out the project. An important management problem at both stages may be winning over sceptics to the new system.
- **High-high** applications. In planning and evaluating the project there is a tradeoff between unavoidable risk on the one hand, and missing competitive advantage through caution on the other. Risk may lie not only in trying something new, but perhaps in doing so urgently, when a safer course would be to develop in careful stages. Once the decisions are made on the nature of the system and its phasing, the work of building it may call for management control as rigorous as for the other quadrant with high operational dependency.

Four Types of System: Another Analysis

Ward et al propose a four-way analysis of systems, and give examples based on a manufacturing company:

- **Type A**: applications which improve management and performance, but are not critical to the business, eg word processing, cost accounting;
- **Type B**: applications which are critical to sustaining existing business, eg accounts receivable, computer-aided design of products;

- **Type C**: applications which may be of future strategic importance, eg manpower planning, electronic mail;
- **Type D**: applications which are critical for future success, eg quality control, sales forecasting.

Here are some representative generalisations that are then developed as the next reasoning stage:

- **Development approach.** For a type-A system, use a standard package; for a type-B, traditional life-cycle with some CASE (computer-aided software engineering); for a type-C, prototyping; for a type-D, CASE and information engineering.
- **Management style.** For a type-A system, caretaker style (ie pragmatic, economical); for a type-B, controller style (ie cautious, methodical, minimising risk); for a type-C, entrepreneur style (ie risk-taking, egocentric, impatient of procedure); for a type-D, developer style (ie long term, central planner).
- **Management and team structure.** For a type-A system, cross-functional, multi-skill structure; for a type-B, functional structure with task separation; for a type-C, individual initiative-competitive structure; for a type-D, matrix-team structure.

Types of System for Evaluation

An analysis by Farbey et al concentrates on identifying generic types of system for a more narrow purpose. It argues that proposals for new systems should be *evaluated* in different ways according to the type of system; it doesn't go into the question of how a system, if approved, should be managed differently depending on type.

A ladder of eight types of application system is proposed, ranging from 'mandatory change' at the bottom rung, via 'infrastructure' (rung 5) and 'inter-organisational system' (rung 6) to 'business transformation' at the top rung. The bold and interesting thesis is that as you ascend the rungs of the ladder, four different variables keep in step with you:

- **Benefits.** The higher up the ladder a system is, then, in general, the greater its benefits — if completely successful.
- **Uncertainty.** The higher up the ladder a system is, then, in general, the more uncertain its outcome (in the sense of unforeseen synergies, forecasts over- or underfulfilled etc).
- **Failure risk.** The higher up the ladder a system is, then, in general, the greater its risk of failure.
- **Imprecise case.** The higher up the ladder a system is, then, in general, the less precisely a case for undertaking it can be made.

The argument is then that projects for systems at different rungs on the ladder call for different evaluation techniques. Though the decision-making logic of this advice is clear, its content is rather sparse. The world of IM is very poor in evaluation techniques.[2,3] By rung 3 the authors are already recommending prototyping and experimentation, which (though often apt) are really alternatives to formal evaluation techniques.

Types of Project Failure

Another idea is to analyse from a different angle. Here are *five generic areas for failure of a project*:**4**

- The project had sensible objectives, that for **technical** reasons were not met; eg the telecoms network was inadequate for its workload.
- The project had sensible objectives, but for **data** reasons they were not met; eg people were undisciplined about keying in all transactions on time, and this caused chaos: payments were not matched against customer orders properly, goods were not recorded as delivered and therefore were delivered twice etc etc.
- The project had inappropriate objectives, mainly at the **user** level; eg people ignored many of the advanced facilities that had cost so much to develop.
- The project had inappropriate objectives, mainly at the **organisational** level; eg the budgetary control system (designed by central accounts) did not meet the needs of line managers in the organisation who had to use it.
- The project had inappropriate objectives, mainly at the **business environment** level; eg the order processing system developed for a mail order company was still seriously inferior to that of competitors.

The justification for this kind of analysis is presumably that it could help in spotting potential causes of failure or major risks in a given project, and thus assist decisions on how best to organise it, or indeed whether to undertake it at all.

Project Risks and Organisation

Cash, McFarlan and McKenney are, as usual, more concerned than most with showing how different situations call for different solutions. They identify three main dimensions of project risk:

- **size** of the project;
- whether the technology is **familiar or new** to the organisation;
- how great the challenge is of getting a reliable, **agreed definition** in non-technical terms of what the system should do.

Plainly there can be gradations along each of these three dimensions, but if, for simplicity, each is seen as a high-low choice, then there are eight combinations, each representing a project with a different kind of risk-profile.

There are perhaps twenty or thirty generic issues of project organisation: what kind of person should be project manager; how many and what kind of team meetings there should be; how rigorously bureaucratic the procedures for change control should be; what kind of steering committee there should be; and so on. A good rule for settling such issues is to make choices calculated to reduce whatever risks are most relevant to the particular project. Thus, it can be reasoned, a project with a certain risk-profile, as measured by the dimensions defined above, should take a certain choice on the issue of (say) kind of project manager, whereas a project with a different risk-profile should take a difference choice; and so on. This style of decision-making should produce sound choices on each issue, but, more than that, they will also probably form a *coherent set* of choices.**5**

REPRESENTATIVE IDEAS — ANALYSED

The analysis by Cash, McFarlan and McKenney contains some cogent recommendations about organisational choices for types of project, but the most striking feature is form rather than content. In a field where others define categories that lead hardly anywhere, or offer bland, undifferentiated platitudes, these authors tie ideas together with a plausible chain of reasoning. That point made, this section concentrates on some interesting difficulties that arise with the ideas of the other authorities.

Problems with Classifying Types of Project

The analysis by Ward et al seems incoherent. For instance: Couldn't a system be critical to both present and future success? If so, is it type-B or type-D or both? Suppose the impact of a certain system lies in the future (like a type-C or type-D system), but it will not be critical to the business (like type-A). How is it classified? Suppose a system is definitely (ie not just 'may be') of future strategic importance, but not critical for future success. Is it type-C or type-D? Or are 'of future strategic importance' and 'critical for future success' synonymous? If so, how do type-C and type-D differ? Plainly, if the four-type breakdown is flawed, the succeeding recommendations on how to manage each type fall by the wayside.**6**

Difficulties arise too with the eight-rung classification of Farbey et al. The rungs of the ladder don't correspond to discrete, realistic categories. A project might be mainly concerned with 'mandatory change', but partly concerned with more exciting things; or partly concerned with infrastructure-like, general-purpose database facilities, and partly with more specific facilities; deciding whether a project counts as 'business transformation' or merely 'inter-organisational system' could be fairly arbitrary too.**7**

Gerstein's analysis of applications, by contrast, sets out four reasonably neat categories, and goes on to say something about each that could indeed have sound decision-making force. The only trouble is the high level of abstraction. Expanding this work to generate more specific recommendations would probably entail recognising more variables about

Types of Project and Decision-making

Concept:

Define several generic types of project.

For each type, define
generic ways of of justifying
and organising a project.

For any particular project:
determine what type it is,
and thus decide how to justify
and organise it.

Difficulty:

The possible types of project, and
possible ways of justifying and organising
projects don't fall into neat patterns.

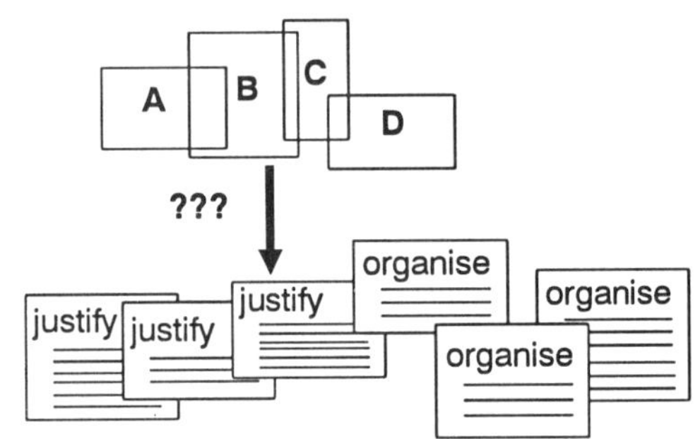
A
B
C
D
???
justify
justify
justify
organise
organise
organise

More Fruitful Approach:

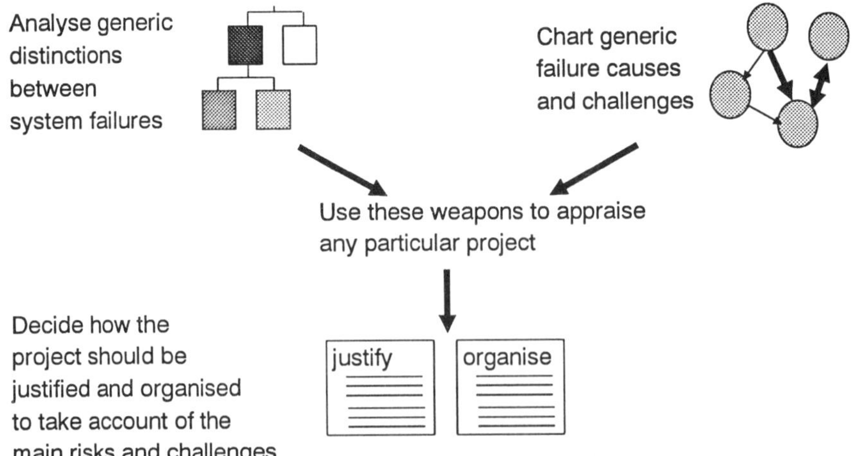
Analyse generic distinctions between system failures
Chart generic failure causes and challenges
Use these weapons to appraise any particular project
Decide how the project should be justified and organised to take account of the main risks and challenges
justify
organise

projects, and perhaps run into the difficulties found with the classification by Farbey et al.[8,9]

In discussion of failure it is important to remember that project is to system as process is to product. A *project* is a process consisting of numerous activities over time directed at producing the software and other components of a system. A *system* is the product of a project. The five failure reasons above mix up problems of system product (ie things wrong with the system) and problems of project process (ie things wrong with the original decision-making and/or the work done). For example, a system might have chaotic data, as a matter of indisputable observable fact; the reason could be that the project had good objectives that were badly implemented, or it could be that the objectives were always unrealistic, or there could be any number and combination of causes.

SUGGESTED WARRANTS

As the diagram suggests, the idea of setting out generic types of project and reasoning from there does not work very well. This section suggests a variation on the line taken by Cash, McFarlan and McKenney: using a generic analysis of things that can go wrong as impetus for decision-making.

Distinctions between System Threats

One book says: ' . . the major cause for failure of office systems is not technical problems, but failure adequately to consider human and strategic issues during the design and implementation process.'[10] Others say much the same thing in different words. But this is a bad start to any clear thinking. Suppose someone says: 'The major cause for failure to hit the tennis ball was not my poor shot, but failure adequately to consider the trajectory of the ball.' The truth is that either you get a *good match* of shot and trajectory or you don't.

Unsuccessful systems are produced when a *poor match* between technology supply and business demand arises during the project process. Poor matching takes certain generic forms that can be identified after the event.

- **Incoherent aims**. In this case, the match of supply and demand adopted must be bad, because the definition of demand is itself incoherent. If you try to summarise it carefully, clear of major ambiguity, and consistent with all the work done to date — you find that you can't. Often ambiguity and incoherence arise over such matters as certain parts being 'integrated' together, or 'compatible' with each other, or having a 'common interface'. Note: coherence implies clarity and consistency — not necessarily wisdom or realism.
- **Gross mismatching**. The demand is essentially coherent, but the matching to supply is unrealistic; eg the demand is for access to a database

through a sophisticated graphic interface, and the chosen supply includes VT100 terminals, which simply can't be used that way. One person may say that the demand is sensible but the supply ill-chosen; another that only with this form of supply is the system financially viable, and, anyway, a graphic interface is quite pointless in this application. However you look at it, there is a gross mismatch that affects the success of the whole system.

- **Second-order mismatches.** The project builds a system with a coherent demand matched by a sensible supply. But there are so many second-order mismatches that the whole system is compromised; eg the inventory software is full of minor bugs, response time is sometimes unacceptable, there are irritating aspects of the user interface, 1% of special products cause enormous trouble etc etc.
- **False premises.** Demand is coherent and well matched by supply, but, it turns out, the expected benefits don't ensue. Perhaps the whole system is justified as a way of meeting orders more quickly, but it actually takes longer. A clear, coherent demand isn't necessarily an intelligent one. It may rest on false premises about what is appropriate for the business.
- **Superseded premises.** The match at the heart of the project is fine and based on reasonable premises — except that they have since been overtaken by external events; eg the company has been taken over, or a competitor has made some dramatic innovation. As a result, unfortunately, the system achieves little.

These are not mutually exclusive, though a system may be so badly flawed on one count that it is pointless even to discuss how bad it is on the others. These five generic cases of poor matching can be thought of as *aspects of threat.* Decide for any given project which of them are the most threatening in the circumstances; decide how to plan and evaluate, and (a different thing) how to structure the project to minimise those threats.

Charting Causes and Challenges

Malaria is a *disease*, sweating a *symptom* and mosquito-bite a *cause.* Roughly, without full philosophical rigour, the breakdown of threats above is of different diseases that generate all the familiar symptoms of system failures — crisis meetings, hours of overtime, problems that never seem to get solved, estimates to completion that get greater rather than smaller etc. Here is a very brief outline of the causes of these diseases.

The causes may be primarily psychological weaknesses in the people concerned, or their failures of performance, or a mixture of both:

- **Psychological** weaknesses may be divided into **demand-drive** (concentration on defining business objectives and requirements with too little interest in the technical implications that are the other half of the match), and **supply-drive** (concentration on achieving a technically competent or stimulating system, at the expense of attention to the business needs the system is meant to serve).

● **Performance** failures are simply shortcomings in execution or in judgement. The many possibilities can be swept into two vast categories: failures to get **demand** defined correctly and precisely and carefully enough, and failures to solve **supply**-side problems.

In organising decision-making about the project and in outlining project structure, the *psychology* of the people concerned is relevant. If there is a danger of excessive demand-drive or supply-drive attitudes, compensating measures can be taken.

The distinction between demand-side and supply-side *performance* can be generalised into two types of challenges that distinguish types of project:

● In the majority of business applications, the demand-side challenge is dominant. The most likely failure of performance is failure to firm up clear, complete, realistic user demands. Once sensible demands are firm, it is relatively easy, even if laborious, to supply them technically.

● In a minority of cases, the most likely failure of performance is failure to meet certain technical challenges; eg it is relatively easy to define what a system for comparing fingerprints must do, but great brainpower and expertise may be needed to develop an effective system.

If you assess where any given project stands on these two challenges — relative to other projects — you are well-placed to make wise decisions on such matters as what proportionate effort to allot to the various stages, how strictly or flexibly to control different stages, or which software house to engage for the work.[11,12]

NOTES & ARGUMENTS

1 The first analysis given in the main briefing text is from Gerstein (pp. 13-18), with the examples and conclusions edited and reworked.

The second is from Ward, Griffiths and Whitmore, introduced on pp. 30-1, and referred to at numerous points thereafter; for the three more detailed recommendations: pp. 366-70, pp. 272-3, p. 290. The authors don't talk of types A, B, C and D; they use the terms support, factory, turnaround and strategic, borrowed from the strategic grid of Cash, McFarlan and McKenney. But these four generic categories of project don't map properly onto the four generic states of an organisation shown by the strategic grid, and so the identity of names is conducive to confusion.

The third is from the book by Farbey, Land and Targett, pp. 121-133.

2 There is often a problem in defining the benefits of any new system or other investment, beyond the obvious things such as staff savings, lower inventory costs and so on. This subject is discussed at briefing-length in O'Brien (*Demands*), Briefing 12.

A substantial part of the 500-page book by Strassmann is about the assessment of systems' benefits and costs, and related matters such as risk assessment, benchmarks, strategic investments etc. It contains both original ideas and much critical (but interesting) discussion of the techniques of others. Recommended.

Warrants about cost-benefits (and

about estimating, next note) have a slightly unusual status: they don't belong naturally on one particular plane of decision-making. Advice about a technique for assessing cost-benefits may affect *matching* decisions (because it helps in deciding whether a certain match of technology and functions makes a viable project), or *context* decisions (because it helps in devising a standard evaluation method to be used for all projects in the organisation), or *approach* decisions (because it affects choice of one method or some other as part of the approach for reaching decisions).

3 If you can't estimate the software development work of a project, then, logic suggests, you can hardly reach a rational discussion on whether or not the project is justified. But the field of ideas about estimating is almost unbelievably barren:

The *Cocomo* technique analyses projects retrospectively, taking account of the number of lines of program code produced, various factors describing the complexity of the system developed, and the amount of work actually done. From this data you can derive a formula relating these variables together. To make an estimate for a new project: first, describe the system in terms of complexity factors; second, estimate the number of lines of program code that will be produced; third, apply the formula to produce the estimate of the work required. Yes, but how do you estimate the lines of code (the second step)? Ah, therein lies the weakness of this method.

Function point analysis rests on the idea of ignoring internal matters, such as the number of lines of code, and measuring only what the system achieves. Thus, in principle, a system that produces (say) ten different reports will require twice as much work as one producing only five — if everything else is equal, each report being equally complex etc etc. With this principle, each new system can be given a score in function points; through comparison with past projects, this score can easily be translated into an estimate of development effort. But there are some problems:

- First, the 'if everything else is equal' clause: suppose one system produces ten different reports and another produces only one — but this one is a very flexible report; it analyses sales in any number of different ways, according to the choice of the user. Does this count as one report or 1734 reports (which happens to be the number of variations that a user could conceivably generate)? One way to approach this difficulty is to give different reports different weights, but then on what basis do you determine the weights?
- Second, the technique rests on an out-of-date model of first defining what you want from the system, then estimating the software work entailed, and then developing the software. But 4GL or other modern approaches to software development shatter this distinction between defining and developing: you define (say) a desired report on the screen, and the software to create it is generated automatically.
- Third, the basic distinction between things produced or achieved by a system, that are measured, and its internal workings, that are not, is problematical. Take the case of a system to control ambulance services: the number of reports produced, number of screens displayed or numbers of interactions with other systems are no measure of the software development work involved, since a large part of the software (if it is a decent system) is concerned with such things as ensuring that, if one ambulance depot is overloaded because of a local disaster, or if one piece of computer

hardware fails, the system can reorganise itself in a smooth, non-disruptive matter. That is, admittedly, an extreme case, but most substantial systems have some processing of the sort, that won't be well handled by a function point approach.

● Fourth, the technique doesn't capture the quality or depth of the work required. One system might need to be tested very, very carefully because any software bug could endanger human life, and need copious documentation because it would be used by very many, widely differing people. Another system without these features could have just the same function point score.

4 Ward, Griffiths and Whitmore, pp. 240ff., reworked with some examples added. This analysis is better than most on this subject. Frenzel (p. 236) records a survey of reasons for failure; eg 'Inadequate definition of project scope 22%', 'Lack of communication with end users 14%', etc. But surely these two are much the same thing expressed in different words.

Hochstrasser and Griffiths (p. 155): 'The current study has found four main reasons why systems implementations often fail to be successful: . .' But all four reasons given are minor variations on the case of the system that is technically adequate but not appropriate to business needs. Banal conclusion: avoid technically adequate systems that are inappropriate to business needs.

5 Cash, McFarlan and McKenney, chapter 10. This includes (with some disclaimers) extracts from a questionnaire used by one company to measure the risk of any given project. There are 42 multiple-choice questions: What is estimated project elapsed time? Is the hardware new to the company? How committed is upper-level user management to system? etc. The answers are processed in a formula to give a total risk score.

Perhaps the most interesting feature is that the score is used, in part, to decide *how* decisions about the project should be taken. If the risk score is low, a low-level committee has authority to approve the project. The higher the score, the higher must be the corporate level of approval. Really high-scoring projects must be authorised by the executive committee.

6 Ward, Griffiths and Whitmore construct a more ambitious edifice on these shaky foundations (pp. 265-73). The argument is that the four types of *application system* can be overlaid on the four classes of *product*, contributed to management consulting lore by the Boston Consulting Group. Type A goes with dog, type B with cash cow, type C with wild cat, and type D with star. Then, the argument runs, management decisions appropriate to the type of product are likely to be appropriate to the corresponding type of system. For instance, the accepted wisdom is that you should disinvest in *dog products*. This might suggest that you should cut down on *type-A systems*, such as word processing or cost accounting, but Ward, Griffiths and Whitmore only go as far as saying that you should use a bureau service or a package for a system of this sort.

Value judgement and neutral classification seem untidily mixed here. A dog product is usually regarded as a definitely bad thing, of which the fewer the better, hence the name; but type-A systems are just one category of system, that you may quite reasonably invest in. Thus the assumption that dog products and type-A systems should be managed in similar ways is a perilous one. Many other criticisms of this analysis might be made.

7 The claims of Farbey, Land and Targett are really too bold to survive scrutiny. They assert that their four variables normally go in step together: if a project promises relatively high benefits, then the other three variables of uncertainty, failure risk and imprecise case will be relatively high too. This, if true, would mean that you almost never found projects where a very precise case could be made for high benefits, and that extremely risky and uncertain projects nearly always yielded high benefits. Since these things are not so, it follows that the premises about the four variables moving in step are false.

The concept might perhaps be rescued by some less sweeping formulation, but there are difficulties. One is how to be more cautious without making the claim so weak that it no longer carries much decision-making force. The other awkward point is this: since the aim is to help people decide how to evaluate a given project, you can't tell them to evaluate a project with high benefits or high risks in one way, and a project with a different profile of benefits and risks in another way. That would be to assume that they had already evaluated these things.

8 The ideas of Gerstein and of Ward, Griffiths and Whitmore raise an important general problem: the notion of a certain application either being critical (vital, fundamental, integral etc) to the business or not. What does it mean to judge that (say) cost accounting is not critical, but accounts receivable is? If two people disagree about the criticality status of system X, what kind of considerations might be brought into the debate? Any of these?

- 'If we had no computer system performing the functions of system X, or if system X was of truly appalling quality, then the organisation literally couldn't function. Therefore system X should be counted as critical.'
- *Or* 'We must have a system X of decent quality in order for the organisation to function at all. Moreover, the higher the quality of system X, the more the business will benefit. In that sense system X should be counted as critical.'
- *Or* 'We don't literally need to have a system X at all. We could function without it. But with it we gain large advantages. In that sense system X should be counted as critical.'

Unless there is agreement on what 'critical' and its synonyms mean in the categorisation of applications, any chain of reasoning will be unreliable.

Is the term 'mission-critical system' worth having? One magazine article talks of 'the applications that absolutely must be developed for an enterprise to survive and prosper'. It gives the examples of Citibank's system enabling it to sell information about consumer purchasing trends to wholesalers, and a Northwest Airlines system that calculates revenue directly rather than rely on traditional statistical sampling methods. Can it be literally true that the bank will go out of business unless it can sell information about consumer purchasing trends as a sideline? Is the airline really dependent on changing its previous accounting procedures, in order to become a profitable enterprise? On this showing, the notion of a separate category of mission-critical systems only brings confusion, without insight.

Strassmann (pp. 105ff., 127) rescues the term by distinguishing between *embedded systems* (eg robots and computerised products), *mission-critical systems*, 'immediately essential for the production of customer revenues' (eg point-of-sales devices, warehouse automation etc), and everything else, *management in-*

formation systems (eg payroll, sales analysis, electronic mail).

9 Here are analyses by some more authors.

Tozer (p. 22, p. 25) distinguishes five types of system. The first four are: administrative support (eg office automation, CAD/CAM); transaction processing (eg sales order processing); operational control (monitoring and exception processes that result from transaction processing systems; eg invoicing and receivables; payroll); planning and analysis (eg sales forecasting; material requirements planning). The fifth category, strategic, includes any system that would normally belong in one of the other four categories, but is exceptionally critical or has some other special features, eg interaction with suppliers or customers.

The breakdown is offered as a way of making a map of all an organisation's systems by business area and type. There is no analysis of how projects might be managed in different ways according to type of system.

It is suggested that the breakdown can influence decisions of 'technical environment' (pp. 108-110). Application systems should be grouped by type, with each group supported by an appropriate technical environment. 'The technical environments are intended to act as containers into which the desired applications are mapped, according to their technical characteristics.' But are these environments literally separate databases and telecoms networks? Or just intermediate ideas in the working papers of the planning process? Suppose two systems of different types in different technical environments have to be strongly integrated. Or is this possibility excluded, by definition?

Keen (1992, pp. 187ff.) identifies four categories of project (or 'moves' in the business game) — radical, innovative, incremental and operational: the closer to the radical end, the more risky. This comes close to tautology. However some (rather common-sense) ways of appraising and justifying possible investments according to these categories are given.

Could this analysis be a starting-point for reasoning about how to organise different types of projects? The trouble is that the four categories suggested are on a scale with gradations of risk. But in deciding how to organise a project, *type* of risk is usually a more interesting variable than *degree* of risk. A project may have a certain risk with respect to the difficulty (technical, human etc) of setting up the system correctly and on time. But the risk inherent in project failure is another type of risk; if the project produces the system a year late and way over budget, what then — bankruptcy or a shrug of the shoulders? A third type of risk is the impact of a successfully achieved system on the outside world; provided the system is developed as envisaged, what are the chances of great commercial advantage — 10%, 50% etc?

Lewis (p. 120) suggests another classification. Three questions are asked of a system: Where does the activity the system supports stand on a continuum ranging from operational through to strategic? Where does the system stand on a continuum from very slight support for the activity to full automation? Where does the activity stand on a continuum measuring the structure of its context (a somewhat obscure concept)? Any system can be assessed in these three dimensions and thus located at a point somewhere in the space of a conceptual cube.

One objection is that a system may well support numerous activities, produce many different answers to the three questions, and thus be impossible to plot at one point in the cube. A graver question is: Why should anyone bother to ask these questions and plot systems in the cube? The book gives no indication of any conclusions this might lead to, or any other benefits that might ensue.

10 Long (1987), p. 182.

11 The (surely sensible) notion that projects with different characteristics should be justified and organised in different ways can menace a concept regarded by some as almost sacred: the standard life-cycle for all projects in an organisation — a standard breakdown into phases containing standard activities. Frenzel (chapter 8) describes one such life cycle, and the natural reaction is: 'How obvious and straightforward. Work is just split up and done in a methodical, step-by-step fashion.' This is because Frenzel ignores all the challenging parts of the problem. Here is a list of six key issues; judge any proposed standard project life cycle by seeing whether and how it deals with them:

First, near the start, there is the problem of identifying and evaluating widely varying options for a project — something difficult to standardise, particularly (but not only) since it is interlinked with the problem of difficult-to-quantify benefits.

Second, the problem of estimating software development work.

Third, the problem of fitting together a project, a fairly self-contained thing, with wider things, eg a database infrastructure serving numerous projects.

Fourth, the complications of feedback, iteration, change control and so on, arising from the fact that it may not be possible or desirable to establish firm breakpoints after each development stage.

Fifth, the role assigned to CASE (computer-supported analysis and software development facilities), since it seems implausible that the most appropriate life cycle for work based on pre-CASE concepts is still optimal, whatever CASE techniques may be used.

Sixth, the procedure for recognising different characteristics in different projects, and from this, going on to justify and organise them by different standards.

12 Some software houses are exceptionally strong technically but less skilled at discussing requirements with users; others are the reverse. The same applies to consultants. When buying in computer services, it is wise to ask: What is the main challenge of the task? Is this company (or person) one whose main strength is in meeting that kind of challenge?

CONNECTIONS

22. Evolutionary Development	The opposite of regular, methodical development
35. Change Management	Wider issues of managing change in the organisation, but closely associated with project organisation, and thus project risk
40. Strategic Systems and Competitive Advantage	Discussion of types of system raises the question whether strategic systems deserve to be a special category

22. Evolutionary Development

TOPIC

The natural, traditional approach to a system development project is to define functional requirements in successive levels of detail, at a certain point handing a specification over to technologists, who proceed in a similar top-down way. However many hundreds of activities may be involved, the underlying logic of this approach is very simple.

The main snag is the difficulty of visualising *beforehand* how a new system can best benefit its users and the organisation as a whole. Even projects methodically carried out by very competent people often prove *with hindsight* to have been imperfectly focused, missing opportunities or wasting effort on trivial features.

Prototyping and related approaches to project management shift the emphasis away from prior design in the abstract. If a crude version of a system is set up early on, tried out and revised several times, the people it is meant for are more likely to understand what they are agreeing to. Then the commitment to building the complete system to high professional standards can follow.

But an iterative, feedback-laden structure is harder to control. Moreover, once you decide against a methodical, top-down style, many variants of project structure present themselves. The literature of IM contains some vaguely approving comments about this type of approach, but there is little warrant-quality material to support decisions about giving a project one particular structure rather than some other. That is the central issue for this briefing.

SUGGESTED WARRANTS

When a project drifts off course, the reason is often that the term 'prototyping' has been used to embrace several different concepts that may at times be in contradiction to each other. This briefing uses 'evolutionary' as a fresher, less hackneyed term for the general approach to project structure outlined so far.

Two Fundamental Aspects

Modern windmill engineers can arrange to mimic evolution quite closely: they can breed good designs. Several designs are tested with wind tunnels and computer simulations; the most successful design is chosen; small random variations are then applied to variables, such as shape and angles of wings, to produce a new generation of designs; these are tested out; the most successful is chosen . . . and so on. The beauty of this approach is that the engineer can avoid staking the success of the design on the correctness of difficult calculations made in the abstract beforehand. This illustrates both the benefits and the potential drawbacks of an evolutionary approach to developing technology. There are two main challenges to be faced:

- **Curbing prodigality**. Evolution may be very costly, since effort is expended on many versions of the product which are subsequently abandoned. (Evolution on earth leaves a fossil record abounding in life forms that were superseded by others.) The prodigality of versions inherent in evolutionary development has to be kept within bounds.
- **Achieving progress.** The price of expending effort on many versions may still not buy success unless there is some way to make evolution proceed in a desired direction. Arbitrary changes to successive versions offer no guarantee that the very last version will be any better than the very first. Some disciplining principles (analogous to biological natural selection) are needed for genuine progress.

These two challenges are considerable when an application system has to evolve. Certain software tools (eg fourth-generation languages) make it relatively easy to develop simplified versions of systems quickly. Also, many features of a system destined to run on a main-frame with hundreds of users at terminals can be tested out by one person at one PC. Careful use of these tools can help curb prodigality. But the real challenge is to find the disciplining principles for genuine evolutionary progress. The warrants that follow are directed towards that.

Distinctions between Types of Evolutionary Project

In evolutionary development it is particularly desirable for everyone to have a clear view of the terms of reference of the project, and to guard against objectives shifting imperceptibly over time. Before dismissing this advice as hopelessly bland, examine some specific distinctions between project objectives. There is no generally established usage for terms such as 'prototype', 'pilot', 'R&D', 'trial', 'experiment', 'market test' and so on, but there is a basic distinction to be drawn:

- The classic **prototyping** project starts from the decision to have a system, and is a way of deciding its scope and detail.
- The classic **experimental** project is a way of deciding whether to have any system at all.**1**

Two Types of Evolutionary Project: Decision-making Logic

Prototyping

'We decide definitely to have a system with roughly this kind of shape'

'Our project will be organised to help us decide more precisely what the system will and won't do.'

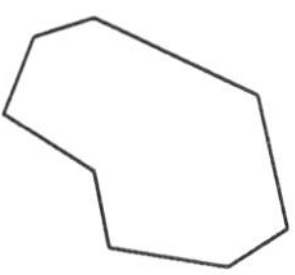

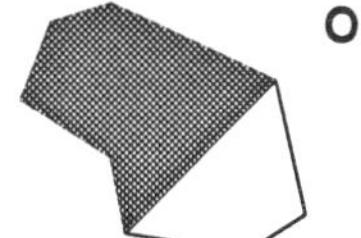

OR

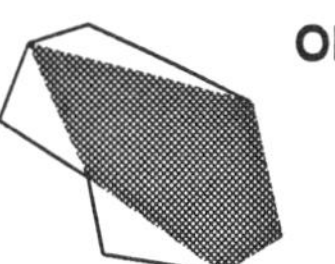

OR

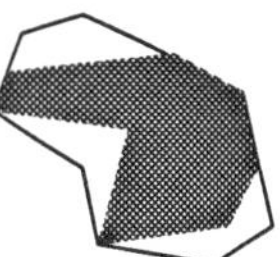

Experiment

'A system with roughly this shape seems an interesting idea, but we just don't know enough about its implications to decide.'

'The purpose of our project is to help us decide:'

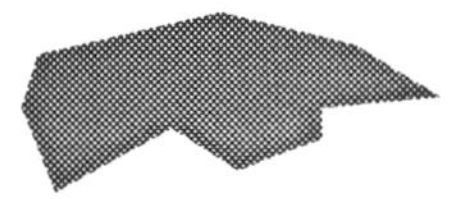

This distinction, shown in the diagram, is complemented by another. To follow the analogy with biological evolution as closely as possible, you would start by trying out a simplified version of the system, and as it went through successive versions, add in more and more refinements, so that at a certain point, it would emerge as a genuine full-scale operational system, optimised to serve numerous users, with security arrangements and fault recovery features and so on all built in. This may well be appropriate in certain cases, but there is no intrinsic merit in following such a *literal evolution* approach. Sometimes the *throw-away* approach may be better. After all, the motivation of this type of development is to generate knowledge of what an effective system should be like. Having generated sufficient knowledge, it could be quite rational to throw away the limited, small-scale version and begin work constructing a robust, industrial-strength system. This produces a three-way distinction warrant:

- *Either* the project is planned from the start on a **literal evolution** basis. The evolving system will become the final system (if any, in the case of an experimental project) eventually.
- *Or* the project is planned from the start on a **throw-away** basis.
- *Or* the choice between literal evolution and throw-away is deliberately **left open** at the start; but the decision point where this choice will be made is explicitly defined in the initial project planning.

It is good to know which of the three you are engaged in. Unless this choice is clearly made, certain work may be done that turns out later to have been pointless or too limited or too elaborate.

This analysis cuts across the distinction between prototyping and experiment: a prototyping project can adopt any one of the three options of literal evolution, throw-away and left-open; so too can an experimental project.

Distinctions between Motivations

Somebody using evolutionary development to arrive at (say) a better strain of wheat will breed successive generations selectively, to optimise the desired characteristics (size or nutritional value or resilience to extremes of temperature etc). The clearer the goal, the less prodigal development will be. Similarly, to guide the evolution of an application system effectively through successive versions, you need to be constantly aware of the main uncertainty factors that motivated the decision to adopt evolutionary rather than traditional development methods.

Suppose a project is based on the idea of using artificial intelligence in the booking system of a travel agency. There are two main uncertainties: How much of the work can current artificial intelligence technology sensibly do? Will the counter clerks find working with an intelligent machine a stimulating or a frightening experience? Successive versions of the evolving design should be organised to obtain insight into those two matters as elegantly as possible, while the temptation to investigate other matters should probably be avoided.

Many possible uncertainty factors could be the drivers of evolution in this way, but two generic ones can be illustrated by example. A piece of evolutionary development results, after many iterations, in a system for accepting travel bookings, with extremely sophisticated graphics on the screen and very slick ways of using a mouse for input. But there is still a potential ambiguity. Was the purpose to evolve by trial and error a graphic user interface that would delight the counter clerks and save them substantial effort? Or was the purpose to find out whether a particular combination of programming language and operating system and hardware could feasibly be used to meet certain (already known or assumed) challenging requirements for a graphics-based interface? As this suggests, there are two classic possibilities:

- Evolutionary development for better understanding of what features a system ought to provide to its users: that is, firming up **non-technical requirements**. This is really based on the working assumption that, whatever the requirements turn out to be, they will almost certainly be technically feasible; the primary task is to clarify them, so that they can be implemented. If this is not a reasonable assumption, then the project is on thin ice. It would be deplorable to devote considerable effort to evolving a design that afterwards couldn't be implemented at any reasonable cost.

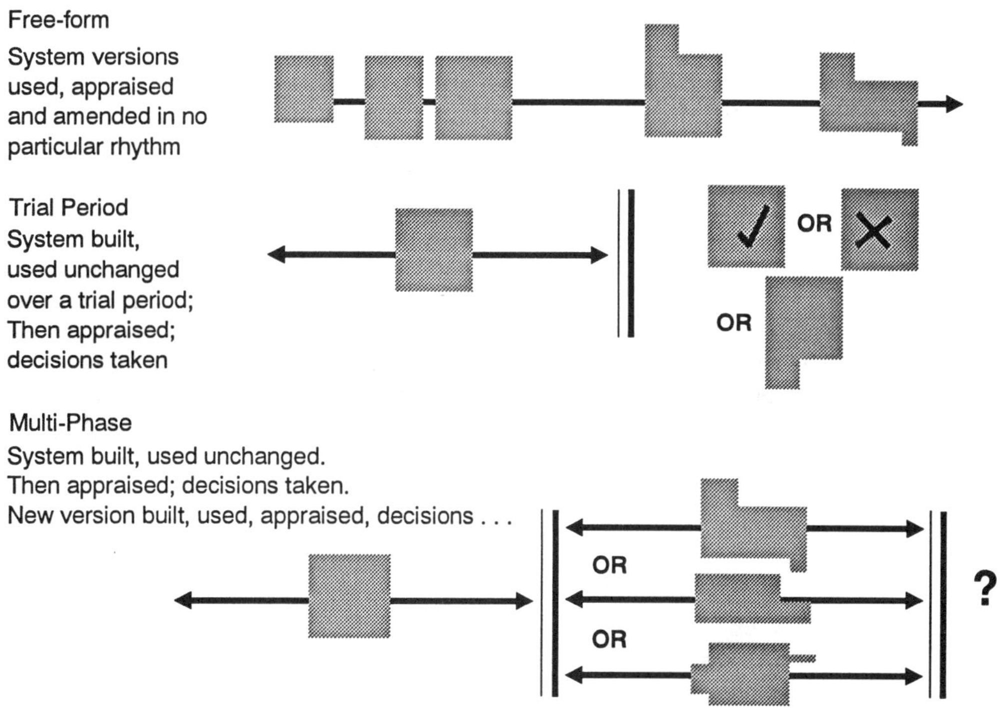
Three Types of Evolutionary Structure: Decision-making Logic
Free-form
System versions used, appraised and amended in no particular rhythm
Trial Period
System built, used unchanged over a trial period; Then appraised; decisions taken
OR
OR
Multi-Phase
System built, used unchanged.
Then appraised; decisions taken.
New version built, used, appraised, decisions . . .
OR
OR
?

● Evolutionary development for better understanding of the way certain **technology issues** should be dealt with (or of the extent to which they can feasibly be dealt with). Here the working assumption is that the technology issues do matter — in the sense that they affect the non-technical features that it may or may not be feasible to provide. If that is not so, accusations of technological self-indulgence may be in order.**2**

These two possibilities are not mutually exclusive, but if you try to make progress on too many fronts at once, it may be hard to keep a sense of direction. Successive versions of the system may be prodigal of effort and yield only oscillations in a steady state of partially acceptable designs, rather than genuine progress.

Distinctions between Styles of Project Structure

The diagram distinguishes three possible macro-structures for an evolutionary development project

An appropriate case for the *free-form* structure might be prototyping a personnel modelling system for a large corporation. A team of four —

bureaucrats and computer people — might work together part-time for (say) three months trying out the practicalities of a variety of possibilities.

The *trial-period* approach could be a natural way for a manufacturing company to try out an EDI (electronic data interchange) system. It might ask twenty customers to use a simple version of the system for a month, and then assess their reactions.

The *multi-phase* approach can become quite complicated. A publisher might experiment with a service for customers to access information through terminals. In phase 1 the audience for the experiment might be some of the publisher's own staff, in phase 2 some potential customers invited to the publisher's offices, and in phase 3 potential customers using terminals in their own offices. For this kind of approach, the decision points should be defined from the start of the project: 'At the end of phase 1, we intend to concentrate on the question: Is the interface (ie what the user has to key in to ask for information) convenient enough? At the end of phase 2, the main issue for assessment will be: Are people using the advanced facilities that, we believe, make this service superior to competitors, or are they ignoring them?' The pre-definition of these decision points makes this a genuinely different project structure.

Distinctions between Justifications

There is one more big distinction. An evolutionary project may be justified as valuable in itself or, *on the other hand*, it may be justified in the context of other projects in the organisation.

The latter possibility is mainly relevant to experimental rather than prototyping projects. When a variety of innovative possibilities seem to deserve experiment (eg if there are many bright ideas for using IT to offer new products and services to customers) then the *portfolio principle* may apply. This affects decision-making in two main ways:

- If there are ten experiments in the portfolio, then that which turns out tenth best is unlikely to be implemented as a full-scale system — because, however attractive it is, the other nine are even more attractive.
- Second, the point of a portfolio is to spread risk or to cover a field. Therefore any new idea is more likely to be allowed into the portfolio if its scope and objectives are significantly different from those in the portfolio already. This in turn means that anyone struggling with the first inklings of an innovative idea ought to be influenced by the fact that, in order to survive, it will soon have to find its own ecological niche in the portfolio.

As the discussion above suggests, an evolutionary development project that isn't based on firm decisions may well fail to curb prodigality and make little real progress. The warrants presented help clarify the options in decision-making.[3]

NOTES & ARGUMENTS

1 Some projects seem evolutionary only through verbal confusion. For instance, projects organised on evolutionary lines tend to use software tools that make it easy to develop simple systems quickly; sometimes a project that is structured quite conventionally is falsely described as evolutionary (or prototyping) development, merely because it uses similar quick-development tools. This is like saying that, since ginger can be an ingredient of a curry, any dish made with ginger can be called a curry.

Sometimes a system is developed in the traditional way, but runs into trouble, and fire-fighting is needed to keep it going. Among the excuses may be such assertions as: 'It was only ever meant to be a prototype'; 'Of course, we always recognised that the system would have to evolve . . ' Such pseudo-evolutionary cases are not considered further here.

2 This is a very basic distinction. Often a more detailed analysis is worthwhile. For instance, if a company is developing innovative products and services in an evolutionary way, drastic changes to its own internal processes too may be required. It might identify four aspects — product, market, technology and organisation — and ask of any evolutionary project: In which of these four aspects is innovation being tried out?

3 At times there may be a case for interpreting these warrants fairly flexibly, eg by having a project that is like prototyping in some respects and is experimental in others. The important thing is to use the ideas in the briefing to clarify what you are trying to do, and find the best structure of project to achieve it. For a longer treatment of this subject, with more detailed examples, see O'Brien (*Demands*), Briefings 30 and 31.

CONNECTIONS

10. Learning and Historical Themes	General theories of learning about IT possibilities, as opposed to prior abstract design
21. Regular Projects	The opposite approach to flexible, iterative development
35. Change Management	Wider issues of managing change in the organisation
36. Business Process Re-engineering	Special structures and challenges for projects that make radical changes

23. Untangling Context Decisions

TOPIC

A decision to set up a special department to stimulate and foster innovative use of IT throughout the organisation is a context decision. It sets up a management context within which future decisions (mainly of matching and scope) about systems and technologies as yet unknown will take place. More generally, most decisions about how to divide IT-related responsibilities between MIS, operating units, staff departments, steering committees and so on are also context decisions in this sense.[1]

Most context decisions are strongly affected by human factors, but that doesn't mean that they can only be arrived at through intuition and feelings. Reasoning about other definable factors is relevant too. This briefing takes a first step towards untangling the awkward mass of context issues, such as those in the table.

SUGGESTED WARRANTS

There are two separate warrants here, each offering a different way of analysing context decisions.

Distinctions between Ways of Dividing Things Up

The representative context decisions in the table mainly deal with variations on one basic problem:

- Given that a certain activity or responsibility exists, or maybe should exist, should it be treated as one separate, *distinct thing* to be done by one person or one group dedicated to that thing?
- If yes, then how should that person or group fit into the rest of the organisational structure?
- If no, then the responsibility or activity concerned will have to belong to persons or groups who have other, possibly conflicting, interests too. How should that be worked out into a viable organisation?

This analysis allows types of context decisions and the warrants

Ribbongum, Manufacturers of Pharmaceuticals
Representative Context Decisions

'We will carry out an urgent action to establish a cadre of hybrid managers. (By hybrid manager we mean . .)'

'Software development will be divided between MIS and user departments in the following way: . . '

'We will have two data centres in different parts of the country — one for the R&D division, one for everything else.'

'The responsibilities of the Data Administration department are defined as . . . and of Database Administration as . . '

'The manager of the main data centre will not have ultimate responsibility for data centre security; instead there will be a higher body concerned with all IT-related security, organisation-wide.'

'The central IT function will recharge its costs to departments at commercial rates.'

'The head of IT will be one step away from the main board.'

'We will have a separate innovation department, with these terms of reference . .'

'We will have a staff department to co-ordinate IT strategy organisation-wide.'

'We will have commercial service agreements between IS and user departments.'

'We will have a separate quality assurance department (but it will concentrate on functional quality rather than technical).'

'We will have a separate computer auditing department (which, among other duties, will check all documentation submitted to the authorities on new drugs . .).'

supporting them to be divided into the four categories shown in the second table.

Gradations of Human Factors

These matters can be viewed from another angle. Decisions about context are (or at least, often should be) influenced by consideration of human factors. The relative weight of human factors in these decisions will vary. This offers the prospect of developing a gradations warrant:

- **Gradation 1.** 'To support our 20 main systems with acceptable security (ie security required by the relevance to the business of those systems), we will have two data centres (rather than one or three).'
- **Gradation 2.** 'The responsibilities of the Data Administration department are defined as . . . and of Database Administration as . . .'
- **Gradation 3.** 'We will have commercial service agreements between IS and user departments.'
- **Gradation 4.** 'We will have a staff department to co-ordinate IT strategy organisation-wide.'

To justify any one of these decisions you would probably try to show that it made sense, given the types of applications concerned, the

Analysis of Context Warrants

Subject of Decision	*Representative Warrants*
Division of Responsibilities	'The top IS man should report to a board member for companies of the following type . . . and be on the board itself for companies of the following type . . ' 'Telecoms infrastructure issues require expert decision, rather than consensual decision or decisions diffused over several parties.'
Division of Human Forces	'The tradeoffs between allowing development work to be done by users freely, or under certain strict conditions are . . ' 'Some companies have a separate 'IT quality assurance department' independent of both the main IT department and user departments. Pros and cons are . . '
Division of Material Forces	'In deciding whether to have one or more data centres, there are generally the following tradeoffs between cost, security and other factors . . ' 'In discussing whether to have one company-wide database or several department-level databases, there are several intermediate options to consider . . '
Rights and Constraints	'The gradations of stringency in commercial service agreements between IS and user departments are . . ' 'Computer people require a more relaxed approach to control to work effectively.'

organisation's general aims and other fairly concrete matters. But you would probably also allow some weight to factors such as the *feelings* of user department people towards the data centre, or the *aspirations* of people in the IS department, or the *psychological needs* of user department managers to feel in control, and so on.

The logic of these four gradations is that decisions at each are likely to be based on a mix of clear reasoning and sensing of human factors, but the higher the gradation, the greater the weight of the human factors. This continuum of gradations is not easy to be sure about in general terms, because the power of the human factors varies from case to case. In deciding how many data centres to have, the unquantifiable 'feeling of owning your own installation' might be important in one case, but irrelevant in another. Therefore, though it doesn't help in structuring a book, this is a handy warrant for working out what is important in specific cases.

Relation of Context to the Other Planes

Sometimes it is hard to identify a context decision, or to separate out the context elements from some very general decisions. To minimise semi-theological verbal analysis, think of context as analogous to a country's constitution: a definition of powers and procedures for handling whatever specific issues come up. Major decisions to alter this context are fundamental but rare, since a constitution, by its very nature, is meant to be ongoing, reasonably permanent, issue-independent and party-independent. That is why in most countries changes to the constitution require more extensive procedures than changes to specific laws. When the post-Gorbachev Russian constitution was changed by the parliament every week, in accordance with fluctuating political tactics, it really lost its character as a constitution altogether.

A scope decision, by contrast with a context decision, is more like a government's decision to set up a task force on a certain policy matter (eg health care or education), with certain terms of reference, that entail a clear beginning and end.

NOTES & ARGUMENTS

1 Procedures for recharging departments with costs incurred centrally or jointly with other departments are an important part of an organisation's IM context. For example, if recharging procedures are designed to recover data centre costs in a very strict cost-accountancy fashion, it *could* happen that the charges for use of the data centre included a large weight of depreciation of investments made in previous years. Some departments might therefore decide to avoid heavy data centre charges by switching as quickly as possible to PC or departmental systems. Those who remained with the data centre would have to pay even heavier charges, motivating them in turn to find some way of avoiding use of the data centre. And so on in a vicious spiral. This subject is discussed at briefing-length in O'Brien (*Demands*), Briefing 29.

CONNECTIONS

24. Centralisation and Distribution	All four categories of context decision: clarifying the issues
25. Functions, Responsibilities and Skills	Two of the categories: division of responsibilities, and division of human forces
26. Operations and Decisions	Two of the categories: division of material forces, and rights and constraints

24. Centralisation and Distribution

TOPIC

It may seem at first glance that a choice must be made between a very centralised IT setup, a very distributed one, or perhaps something between the two. Some writings on IM give the impression that this is so.

But in reality the options are far more complex: you might decide to be fairly centralised in some respects, but distributed in others. This briefing develops that insight.

REPRESENTATIVE IDEAS — SUMMARISED

Several different issues and factors are intertwined here, and it is interesting to look at different ideas for breaking the area down. This is a good start towards recognising what options are open, and choosing between them.

Plain-Vanilla Advantages and Disadvantages

One representative book presents a list of points comparing 'centralised and decentralised structures for information technology and systems'.

The advantages of *centralisation* are given as: economies of hardware scale; concentration of scarce skill resources for new systems development; control over security and audit standards; management information from sharing data corporate-wide; and better prices, maintenance and general treatment as one major account with a limited range of suppliers.

The advantages of *decentralisation* are given as: cost-effectiveness through extensive use of PCs (which are good value for money); faster development of software by the users themselves; better location of systems, data and computing where most needed; management information from sharing data corporate-wide through a network; and decentralised development providing solutions to the real needs of users.

This analysis introduces most of the themes that come up in discussions of this area, albeit only in a primitive way.**1**

A Three-way Breakdown and Four Policies

Several people have suggested more analytical views of this area. One article suggests distinguishing three separate things:[2]

- the way **decision-making authority** is distributed; eg all major IM decisions within (say) the Forest Oak energy utility might be taken by one central steering-committee, *or*, alternatively, responsibility could be much more distributed than that;
- the way **software development** is distributed; eg each of the main units within Forest Oak Energy (customer services, technical, planning etc) might have its own group of analysts and programmers, *or* the work could be more centralised, *or else* more distributed than that;
- the way **hardware** is distributed; eg each head office department and each branch-office of Forest Oak might have its own minicomputer, *or* hardware could be more centralised, *or else* more distributed than that.

To a fair degree at least, these are independent matters. For instance, decision-making could be centralised in one steering-committee, but the committee could still decide that hardware should be distributed to each head-office department and branch office. However, not every single possible combination of choices on these three issues will be cogent. The article identifies four main ones and gives them twee names:

- **Big brother**: all three things centralised;
- **Helping hand**: decision-making authority decentralised, software development centralised, hardware decentralised;
- **Watchdog**: decision-making authority centralised, software development decentralised, hardware centralised;
- **Network**: all three things decentralised.

Three-way Breakdown: Variation and Expansion

Another author gives a comparable three-way breakdown but with an important difference:[3]

- **Direction**: the way decision-making authority is distributed;
- **Development**: the way software development is distributed;
- **Operations**: not merely the way different items of hardware are physically distributed, but the broader matter of the way responsibility for day-to-day control is distributed: backing up databases, trouble-shooting (eg sorting out the problems if a whole day's batch of payments of energy bills is processed twice at Forest Oak), and tactical decision-making (eg keeping things running smoothly while upgraded hardware is installed and tested).[4]

Another book concentrates on the way *decision-making* is distributed, leaving aside the other two dimensions of development and hardware (or operations).[5] It proposes what is in effect a gradations warrant. Here, in paraphrase, are three ascending levels of centralisation of decision-making responsibility:

- **Gradation 1:** optimising supply. 'Given that the departments of the organisation need certain things (hardware, personnel resources etc) *anyway*, we will provide them as efficiently as possible by central planning. For example, economies of scale can come from purchasing PCs in bulk, and scarce resources (eg people skilled in AI technology) can be rationed. But this central planning to optimise *supply* will not influence what departments *demand*: We won't try to persuade them that they don't need what they think they need, and really need something quite different.'
- **Gradation 2:** as 1, but with the notion of optimising the provision of resources taken much further. 'It is in the interests of the organisation as a whole that certain choices and practices are standardised, even if they are slightly sub-optimal in particular cases. Therefore if a department wants word processing, it must use (say) WordPerfect or if it wants to send electronic mail messages, it must use the organisation-wide network. However, we are still not telling any department what it ought to want. It can still decide for itself how much word processing or electronic mail to have.'
- **Gradation 3:** as 2, but with the further principles: 'It is in the interests of the organisation as a whole that departments participate in certain integrated systems, so that data relevant to several departments is accessible to them. Therefore the planning and development of many systems and databases will be done centrally rather than in individual departments. This means that one department can't always persist in deciding what it needs irrespective of the views of the central planners.'**6**

REPRESENTATIVE IDEAS — ANALYSED

As the previous section shows, there are several distinct categories of distribution issue, and on many, the options form gradations rather than an either/or choice. It is essential to separate out categories of relatively separate issues, as the better books do, but there can still be *some* interactions between them: centralised hardware with decentralised software development is a possible choice, but this can't be taken too far, since the developers will probably need *some* local hardware to do their work efficiently.

The notes on representative ideas above concentrate on ways of dividing things up, and thus recognising options. Most writers also give some account of the pros and cons of choices and options, but these usually amount to very little other than the generic tradeoff that applies to this kind of question in any field of management:

- If things are scattered and unco-ordinated, then many opportunities for doing things more effectively are not seen or difficult to achieve . . .
- so by centralising things you gain the chance of doing what is best in the interests of the organisation as a whole . . .

• except that if you centralise too much, you suffer such familiar ills as bureaucratic delay, lack of motivation for those meant to follow instructions from the centre, lack of flexibility to respond to changes in local needs etc . . .
• which can be so damaging as to be worth avoiding even at the expense of trying to optimise things in the theoretical interests of the organisation as a whole . . .
• although, of course, this shouldn't be taken so far as to lead to anarchy.

Whatever the specifics of the case and the vocabulary used, this tradeoff analysis is practically inescapable. However, finding the right balance for the particular circumstances is not something on which generic advice can easily be given.

SUGGESTED WARRANTS

There is benefit to be gained from a warrant that provides a more detailed analysis of the different issues tangled together. After that, one issue can be used as a representative example to suggest the range of choices that may be available.

Distinctions between Distribution Issues

Suppose that Forest Oak is considering how centralised its IT should be. To mark out the area of decision-making start off with a basic distinction between two types of decision: about distribution in system design and about distribution of role. Then analyse each a level deeper.

Within *distribution in system design*, distribution of hardware can be distinguished from distribution of data. Within *distribution of role*, distinguish the three roles of direction, development and operations, and also staff (as opposed to line) roles.

As the table shows, this turns the three-way breakdown of the previous section into a six-way breakdown.

Gradations of Software Development

The examples given in the table are plainly extremes (though not necessarily absolute extremes). With most issues in most categories there are gradations. Here is one representative set of distribution possibilities within the *development role*:
• **Gradation 1.** 'All software development will be done by the staff of Forest Oak's MIS department.'
• **Gradation 2.** 'Software development will be done by IS professionals permanently attached to each of the main business units in the company.'
• **Gradation 3.** 'Development of software can be done by anybody at all in any part of the organisation — but, if done by non-professionals, only

Forest Oak Energy, Types of Distribution Decision

Distribution in System Design

Hardware 'We will provide word processing facilities through terminals attached to a mini-computer in each department' — as opposed to 'Word processing will be done on separate personal computers.'

Data 'As far as it possibly can be, all operational data (but excluding eg word processing documents) will be stored in the central database' — as opposed to 'As far as it possibly can be, all data (operational and other) will be stored at a department's own computer, with only a small quantity of extracted data sent to the head office database.'

Distribution of Role

Direction 'All proposals for projects budgeted at more than $50,000 must be approved by the board' — as opposed to 'All proposals for projects budgeted at more than $500,000 must be approved by the board.'

Development 'All software development (ie writing programs in a programming language) will be done by the staff of the organisation's MIS department' — as opposed to 'Each department will make its own arrangements for software development for its own systems; this may include calling on the staff of the organisation's MIS department, but also any other approaches too.'

Operations 'Departments will be able to call up a hot-line to the data centre in the event of anything faulty or strange occurring' — as opposed to 'Each department will have its own system controllers who are meant to be capable of handling all day-to-day matters for themselves.'

Staff 'There will be organisation-wide staff functions to lay down project standards and check the quality of software development work' — as opposed to 'Each department will make its own arrangements, if any, on such matters as project standards and quality control.'

---

subject to the following constraints: the resulting system must not process operational data and it must not affect any other part of the organisation.'

- **Gradation 4.** 'In general, all software will be developed in whatever way the managers of the department concerned think best — but they must accept a certain discipline with respect to any software that updates the corporate database; eg follow certain standards, fit into certain organisation-wide information planning etc.
- **Gradation 5.** 'Each department will make its own arrangements for software development for its own systems. Cases where software

developed in one department can affect data or systems outside that department will be resolved by ad hoc negotiation.'

To show the richness of the possibilities here is an ingenious policy that might be called a gradation somewhere between 1 and 2. Each business unit has its own group of software professionals and the bulk of software development is done by these people; central IS handles entry-level recruitment of IS professionals, provides their training and arranges short-term experience in a number of business units; after three years, the candidate is placed definitively with one particular business unit. Thus in an indirect way, without any formal mechanisms, central IS can instill a standard approach to designing and developing systems.[7] As this shows, you can't assess a policy just by its explicit rules; indirect effects can be strong too.

NOTES & ARGUMENTS

1 The analysis given is from Sager, pp. 211-2. But could you not (say) combine the advantage of being one major account with a limited range of suppliers (a centralised advantage) with faster development of software by the users themselves (a decentralised advantage)? If those are two objectives you are particularly interested in, surely it must be possible to devise some setup with a plausible chance of achieving them both.

2 John J Donovan, 'Beyond Chief Information Officer to Network Manager', *Harvard Business Review*, September-October 1988; in Harvard Business Review (1990), p. 141. Forest Oak examples added.

3 Earl, pp. 131-3. The book contains another attractive piece of analysis (pp. 135-8), paraphrased as follows:

- In deciding how to distribute decision-making power and how to design the contextual arrangements associated with it, recognise *two tensions*: one is centralised or decentralised; the other is user or technology specialist. How you resolve these tensions is something to be decided according to the case. Crude prescriptions are worthless.
- Recognise **five ideal types** of context arrangements, each a different resolution of the two tensions; eg decisions completely unified at whole firm level; each business unit taking its own separate decisions etc.
- Take account of **four variables** that may affect your context decisions: what kind of organisation you are in general; what kind of applications you have or will have etc.
- Now which of the five ideal types (or variant thereof) you choose depends on the four variables; eg if the whole organisation is decentralised, then IM context arrangements should be too; if you have lots of new strategic applications on the way, then user involvement in decision-making should be favoured.

This seems a good logical structure for a powerful warrant, but unfortunately the five ideal types, the four variables and the interactions between them are sketched out far too vaguely. This remains an outline for working out a warrant, rather than one that will carry decision-making force as it stands. Even so, the thought behind it is in a different league from most ideas on the subject.

4 One variant along a different dimension is *outsourcing* (aka facilities management). This rests on the following idea: Many large companies sub-contract the running of staff canteens to a specialist caterer, with (in principle) advantages that any student of economics could explain. Why not apply the same logic, and sub-contract the running of your data centre to a specialist firm? Obviously, all kinds of issues arise, but there are really two opposite motivations to recognise:

- The more common one is this: 'Processing huge volumes of customer billings and payments doesn't call for tremendous flair or expertise — just very great efficiency (in keeping costs down, while avoiding foul-ups). We could continue to do it ourselves, but it might be even better to sign up with a data processing firm that has a good reputation and offers a cheap fixed-price contract based on vast economies of scale (because it does similar work for many other customers).'
- The other one is this: 'To set up and look after a really sophisticated telecoms network for this energy company we would have to employ a considerable number of very expert technologists. We could do that, but it is rather undesirable: we would be vulnerable to a few key people leaving, and that might very well happen because there would inevitably be peaks and troughs in the amount and interest of their work. But suppose we signed a fixed-price deal with a firm whose main business was providing telecoms facilities to large corporations. Then we could avoid the problem of needing to maintain much specialist expertise in house.'

From this logic it seems to follow that you should outsource those things that are straightforward and also those that are excessively demanding, and do for yourself whatever remains.

5 Ward, Griffiths and Whitmore, p. 416-7, considerably reworked.

6 Another book (Gunton (1990), pp. 148-9) gives an analysis from a somewhat different angle:

- First, distinguish **enabling** policies (eg negotiating quantity discounts from suppliers) from **restraining** policies (eg preventing people from using a word processing package other than that chosen as organisation-standard).
- Then distinguish four policy areas within which central policy decisions (both enabling and restraining) may operate: **financial and commercial** (relations with external suppliers, such as a software house); **technical and infrastructure** (eg organisation-wide telecoms network); **standards** (ie standard ways of doing certain activities); **human resources** (developing skills).

The resulting 2x4 matrix is offered as a 'checklist for the responsibilities of a central information management group, which can be varied according to the size of the organisation'. This is fine, if understood neutrally as a way of sorting things out to help decide what should be centralised and what should not (eg perhaps no restraining policies at all), but dangerous if the assumption arises that all eight cells of the matrix need to be filled in.

7 Ernest M von Simson, 'The Centrally Decentralized IS Organization', Harvard Business Review (1991), p. 83.

CONNECTIONS

8. Culture, Mission and Vision	Relatively vague, top-level concepts that nevertheless have some effect on IT centralisation or otherwise
20. Integration and Connected Matters	Concepts and jargon that sometimes merge almost inextricably into centralisation issues
25. Functions, Responsibilities and Skills	Matters that have to cohere with any centralisation and distribution decisions
37. End-user Computing	A field rich in centralisation and distribution issues

25. Functions, Responsibilities and Skills

TOPIC

There is no need to discuss here the exact job description of the organisation's information analysts or of the head of the data preparation department, because these are matters too detailed to fall within the subject of IM. But some questions of responsibilities and functions probably do deserve to count as IM issues: What should be the status and powers of the most senior manager responsible for IT? How powerful an organisation-wide steering committee for IT should there be (if there is one at all)? Should there be a separate quality assurance department monitoring all system development work? Should you aim to have many managers who possess both IT and business knowledge, with responsibilities to match? These and similar choices are context decisions with wide implications for subsequent decision-making.

Rather than discuss all the interesting issues in this field, this briefing attacks a more basic problem. In contrast to most other IM topics, ideas about responsibility and function don't fall very obviously into warrant forms that help define options, expose interactions and so on. The main objective here is to take some representative issues, and illustrate how critical thinking can indeed promote IM decisions.

REPRESENTATIVE IDEAS — SUMMARISED

This section introduces three issues in turn: the organisation's IT steering committee(s), the CIO (chief information officer) and the hybrid manager.

Recommendations on Steering Committees and the like

'To enable strategic management of IT, the Kobler Unit recommends the setting up of a corporate planning group (not a committee) led by a senior executive, reporting to and being responsible directly to the Board. It is recommended that this group be staffed by secondees of merit drawn from a variety of individual business divisions. The members should be able to spend at least six to nine months, if not longer, in the group, where this is feasible. The group should further include a small number of full-time representatives from the IT division experienced in corporate planning or quantitative methods.'[1]

Now move on to the recommendations in another book (in paraphrase):

- You should have (1) a management steering group which is able to recognise IT strategic potential, and exploit IT as a business weapon, and influence business management, and hold the confidence of senior management.
- You should also have all the following: (2) several functional or business planning groups; (3) several application management groups; (4) one IS/IT planning group; (5) several service management groups; and (6) several technical management groups.
- These six different genres of group are all committees that meet regularly. They are not departments or units that appear on the organisation chart. Nobody's main job is to be a member of any of these groups. Everybody has some conventional job function within the organisation (finance director, systems analyst, administration manager etc), and devotes a minority of work-time to attending these committee meetings and doing tasks associated them — preparing discussion papers, writing up recommendations etc.

The CIO? On the Board?

Much has been written about the concept of the chief information officer, who, to sketch out the argument in primary colours, should look after the organisation's information in the same way that the chief financial officer looks after its cash.

Well, why not? How could anybody quarrel with that? The trouble is that the issues are rarely put in more concrete terms, so it is difficult to find anything worthwhile to discuss or to decide.[2]

A more tangible issue worth discussing is: Where should the highest manager with responsibility for IT (whether called CIO or not) fit into the organisation? This issue is often summarised as: 'Should the IT director be on the board?'

Some writers tend to suggest that the answer must always be yes, since information is such an important thing. But one book says: not always, it depends on the situation. However, the only analysis it gives is that if the application of IT is absolutely fundamental to the business, then the IT director really should be on the board; and if not, then not necessarily.[3]

The Hybrid Manager

The *hybrid manager* has become a popular topic, at any rate in the UK.

Suppose you came across a manager with the following hybrid qualifications: knows about your business, has knowledge and experience of IT, possesses strong interpersonal skills (outgoing but sensitive, good at influencing people and so on). Would it not be attractive to employ such a person in a key information management role? Yes, very probably. One writer sees such people as 'islands of true business/IS understanding', and these islands as catalysts for using IT to better advantage.

Well then, argues the British Computer Society, since these people are scarce, efforts must be made to develop them — in fact, by the year 2000 30% of British managers ought to be hybrid managers.

Earl provides a more subtle analysis of managers that play a part in the management of IT. 'Hybrid' is his label for only one type out of four; the others are called leader, professional and impresario.[4]

REPRESENTATIVE IDEAS — ANALYSED

The representative ideas summarised in the previous section are, by and large, so feeble that their main utility is as targets for critical thinking practice.

Critical Thinking about Committees

The Kobler Unit's recommendations are excessively dogmatic:

- *You should have a permanent planning group, as opposed to a committee.* But some organisations, by the nature of their business and their culture, have a tiny head office and hate any kind of staff departments; other organisations are different in these respects. Aren't such factors relevant variables?
- *The group should be staffed by temporary secondees from business divisions* — as opposed to staffed by people who work only or mainly for the planning group. Surely this too should depend on the situation. Maybe the great problem is a general lack of expertise in planning skills (especially on questions such as how to control innovative projects) throughout the business divisions; or maybe the crux of the matter is getting rival business divisions to collaborate even on simple things; or maybe . . . Surely the design of the planning group should depend on assessment of the types of challenge.
- *There should be representatives from the IT division experienced in corporate planning.* Most IT divisions possess few such people. In situations where massive co-ordinated changes are necessary, perhaps every single one of them should be shifted into the planning group. In other situations, perhaps they should be saved for assignment to business units that have major problems of their own.

This doesn't exhaust the analysis. Thinking critically about over-prescriptive advice is an excellent way of becoming aware of the real issues. Of course the same applies, multiplied by an enormous factor, to the second prescription, which lays down an elaborate structure of six kinds of group. One way of starting is to raise the following argument.

In some situations the plain need is to increase co-ordination and integration between departments and their systems. But this is not the overwhelming challenge in every single case that ever comes up. Sometimes a more crucial aim is to stimulate end-user computing and experimental projects out in the departments, encouraging creativity and minimising control from the centre. That being so, any elaborate management context that anybody puts forward as being generally or even usually the best way of doing things is vulnerable to the ripost: How can one particular suggested way of organising things reasonably claim to be a generally valid prescription, when it takes no account of the fact that the need for co-ordination and integration varies greatly between different cases?**5**

Critical Thinking about the Board

The 'IT director on the board' issue raises another point. To say: 'Under these generic circumstances the IT director should be on the board . . and under these other generic circumstances . . should not' only has value if the term 'on the board' has a reasonably constant meaning. But it doesn't; cases vary considerably.

Suppose Company A is run by a four-director board; each director has several portfolios, defined in terms of both function and market segment. Company B (same industry, same size, similar problems) has a ten-director board, each with one clear functional portfolio: finance, distribution etc. If the IT director is not on the board of Company A, that may be justifiable — even if IT is fairly important to the business. But the exclusion of the IT director from the board of Company B implies that ten other functional portfolios are more important than IT — something true of few businesses.

Thus any advice about the 'IT director on the board' issue needs to be at least elaborate enough to allow both that the importance of IT differs between firms, and that board structures differ too.

Critical Thinking about Hybrid Managers

The notion that 30% of all managers should be catalytic islands seems bizarre. But critical thinking about this subject is practically impossible if there are only abstractions and metaphors to work with. Examples are essential.

First, concentrate on the notion of a person possessing knowledge and experience of IT. Discussion of this subject often seems to rest on the idea that a person either has this knowledge and experience or has not, ie is either computer-literate or is not. This is an appalling over-simplification.

Levels of Knowledge About IT

How much do you know about distributed database?	How much do you know about text database?
Level A: 'Though computer-literate, I am not really sure when a database counts as distributed and when not. I use the term, if at all, loosely and perhaps sometimes incorrectly.'	**Level A:** 'I know that a text database stores texts that you access by searching on specific words, but I can't name any of the issues that typically arise with that kind of system.'
Level B: 'I know the essential points that determine what is a distributed database and what is not. This helps me grasp, though without knowing much of the detail, why it is that distributed database is quite an advanced, and hence sometimes risky, technology. That is as far as my knowledge goes.'	**Level B:** 'I can sketch out some of the main problems with a text database (eg synonyms, difficulty of allocating keywords etc). I could make some shrewd comments on somebody else's ideas for a system, but I would not claim to be able to find the most effective choice of options myself.'
Level C: 'I understand, in outline not detail, the key concepts in distributed database: horizontal fragmentation, vertical fragmentation, replication, distributed updating etc. This means I can make a reasonable judgement whether any given distributed database I come across is a relatively simple or relatively complex case.'	**Level C:** 'I have a good awareness of all the main concepts and possibilities in the logical organisation of a text database (thesaurus, SGML, automatic indexing, hypertext etc). I can apply these concepts to any particular case to suggest the most effective way of handling the requirements.'
Level D: 'I have designed the technical part of a distributed database system. Also, I could explain in detail the relative merits of the routing optimisation features in the rival software products DB2 and Oracle.'	**Level D:** 'I have designed the technical part of a large-scale text database system. Also, I could explain how the indexing structures need to be different, depending whether you are using the Status or BRS/Search software products.'

As the examples in the table show, there are gradations of IT-knowledge along quite an extended scale.[6]

What is the right level of IT knowledge for a hybrid manager? Not D, of course, but what about the other three? To ask this question is to show that it is misguided. There is no right level that 30% of British managers should attain, and there is no one definable catalytic-island role they should all play. In any large organisation, people with knowledge at levels A and B and C, if well organised, can very likely all play roles in deciding about and designing systems that use IT. Moreover, some quite different policies on knowledge and roles are available:

- One organisation might build up a team of roving internal consultants, people with level-C knowledge of many technologies, to work together with line-managers, most at level A.

- Another organisation might have prefer to have few level-C people, but strive to bring as many level-A people as possible up to level B.

A variety of other policies are conceivable. Choosing between them could be quite a far-reaching decision. Impressionistic verbal tokens such as 'hybrid manager' are no help at all in debates on this issue.

Earl defines four categories of manager but presents them without examples of the kind of knowledge each should possess, and thus makes discussion of his ideas practically impossible. If it were claimed that (say) a person in Earl's 'professional' category should possess level-C knowledge about most relevant technologies, and (say) someone in the 'impresario' category should have level-B knowledge, then it would be easier to appraise the analysis, and think through its implications. The same applies to examples of business knowledge and of inter-personal skills.**7**

SUGGESTED WARRANTS

This section puts forward three example warrants to suggest how matters of responsibility can be discussed rationally: one clarifies the CIO issue, one analyses quality assurance tasks, and the last is a kind of master chart of the main areas where tricky decisions about allocating responsibility typically arise.

The CIO: Distinguishing the Rational and the Diplomatic

Whether the top manager is called 'CIO' or 'infogeneralissimo' or anything else is a rather trivial issue. From now on the term CIO will be used for the senior manager with responsibility for IT — but merely as a label. Whether the person is literally on the board is relevant but difficult to generalise about. So what kind of useful warrant can be produced?

First, the the job description of the CIO is really part of a larger issue: What kind of organisational apparatus (directors, managers, planning committees, staff departments at head office etc) should there be, charged with managing the use of IT for the good of the organisation as a whole?

In most organisations, most people will work within terms of reference, such as getting their particular department to use IT sensibly, or ensuring their particular data centre processes data efficiently, and so on. That is more or less inevitable in any sane management context. But from time to time, issues arise where the terms of reference lead to boundary-crossing; eg to get one department to use IT effectively, some sharing of data with other departments may be needed. There must be some arrangements for recognising such issues and handling them.

The CIO and any associated staff department, and any committees drawn from multiple sources, really have two distinct objectives:

- **Rational:** ensuring that intelligent decisions are taken on all matters that span individual departments or installations.
- **Diplomatic:** combatting any ignorance and prejudice that may impede intelligent decisions, by developing good relations with non-IT managers *in general*, and by charm and force of personality that persuade people to accept particular things they find unpleasant.

There can easily be a conflict between these things, and judgement has to determine the tradeoff:

- As CIO, you might allow some system development to go ahead that wasn't particularly in the interests of the business, if the cost of opposing it seemed to be making a fool of a manager whose goodwill you needed, to make a success of some other developments.
- On the other hand, you might decide that all the unpleasantness caused by some new method of recharging IT costs to departments was a price worth paying, because this method of charging was an essential precondition for effective decisions about IT in the future.

That said, it is difficult to generalise much further about diplomatic matters since they are largely concerned with personal skills rather than reason and argument.

Quality Assurance: Distinctions

Most people agree that some quality assurance of system development work is desirable. From there the discussion easily degenerates into the assumption that the more quality assurance the better, and from there to lists of obvious things to check, mixed with platitudes about how necessary it all is. But where are the decisions? What kind of warrants can be devised to help take good decisions about quality assurance (from here on QA)?

A good start is to draw distinctions between different forms of QA, and the best way to do that is to analyse the generic types of quality test that might be applied to any product (system analysis, database design, program code etc):

- **Generic compliance.** Does it comply with certain pre-defined standards for this kind of product? Example test: Is this functional specification document in the format that is mandatory in this organisation?
- **Generic quality.** Does it pass certain pre-defined qualitative or quantitative tests that are standard for this kind of product? Example test: A reader ought to be able to tell from a functional specification alone (excluding any previous documents) how the system will work functionally (not technically); does it pass that test?
- **Specific compliance.** Does it comply with any previously agreed or understood requirement for this specific product? Example test: It was previously agreed that the design of this system would take account of a possible merger of two divisions in the future; does it?
- **Specific quality.** Does this specific product pass tests of intrinsic

quality? Banal example test: There should be no inconsistent cross-references, such as 'see the description of the sales ledger file', when the latter does not exist.

All four of these can be broken down further.[8] But what value does such analysis have? If the full range of QA tests is to be done properly by a QA department, it will have to be a large department containing a wide range of skills and knowledge — in fact, many of the best people. If that is unacceptable, something has to be cut back. This can be discussed most easily in terms of the classification, eg:

- *Either* 'Our QA department will define and maintain our standards, and have great authority in carrying out the generic compliance tests. For generic quality, the QA department will be only one part of a committee that meets regularly to discuss and devise standards and tests of that sort. The QA department will not be concerned with the other types of tests; they are for the project manager concerned.'
- *Or* 'On major projects a person from QA will be seconded to the team and will become so knowledgeable as to be capable of carrying out the complete range of QA tests.'
- *Or* 'Every senior person in the IT area will do some QA work from time to time, but of a specific sort: only specific quality — in situations where that person's particular expertise is relevant.'

Being in a position to compare such options is surely far better than just assenting to a long list of platitudes about QA.

Chart of Responsibility Issues

The QA issue is one of many posing similar problems. For each the question is: Do you want to centralise and/or co-ordinate decisions, or allow things to be decided locally (ie by individual departments or installations)?

The table shows the main topics on which such questions are asked in practice. Suppose topic T (company-wide databases or any of the others in the table) is under consideration. There can be various answers:

- 'T just isn't a big topic with us; therefore awkward responsibility issues don't arise.'
- 'T is definitely a big topic with us; also a high degree of co-ordination is certainly required; there are several different ways that responsibilities could be allocated to achieve this.'
- 'T is definitely a big topic with us; even so, there is no reason to complicate things for the sake of co-ordination; we can simply make different people responsible for different things, more or less in isolation.'
- 'T is definitely a big topic with us; a high degree of co-ordination would be beneficial in some ways but bring other undesirable complications; we need to set out some options and judge the tradeoffs.'

Responsibility Issues: Boundary-crossing and/or Staff v Line

First, **two potentially huge areas**. Manifestly, they can raise large-scale problems of co-ordination, approachable in a variety of ways:

Company-wide and cross-business-unit **databases**;

Telecoms infrastructure.

Second, **three classic service areas**. For each, one approach is to have a staff department reporting to the CIO. That is not the only possible way. Also, the terms of reference of the staff department can vary a lot:

End-user computing: training, support, advice, standards-setting, control;

Innovation: stimulation and control of advanced, innovative uses of IT, often together with (though it is a different matter) technology awareness of managers;

Technology standards and quality: setting organisation-wide standards, and monitoring compliance, on matters such as security and privacy, choice of spreadsheet software, programming techniques, etc.

There are **four other service areas**, whose outlines are less distinct:

Internal consultancy (technical or management): troubleshooting, problem-solving; infusion of expertise; temporary management;

Planning control and co-ordination: setting procedures for (eg) getting a fixed-price tender from a supplier; collecting IT planning documents from different units and consolidating them, etc;

Decision-support systems: planning and running them;

Residuals: planning and running installations, software development teams or projects, that don't belong conveniently with any particular unit, often of a temporary character.

NOTES & ARGUMENTS

1 Kobler recommendation: Hochstrasser and Griffiths, pp. 161-2; six-group approach: Ward, Griffiths and Whitmore, pp. 301-310.

It seems amazing that these authors could have worked out their recommendations in such detail, without wondering whether different factors in different situations might make different structures of steering committees appropriate.

2 Discussion of the CIO is often confused by sloppy definition-making. 'Simply put, a CIO is the highest ranking executive with primary responsibility for information management.' (Synnott, p. 19). This seems an *objective* definition: it doesn't say (eg) 'In order to deserve to be called a CIO, a manager must . .' But then (p. 23): 'The new breed of information managers, the CIOs, are businessmen first, managers second, and technologists third — in that order.' This seems to be the definition of an *ideal*. So where does that leave the highest ranking executive with primary responsibility for information management, who, it so happens, prefers to concentrate on technology?

However, Synnott does go on to give one interesting piece of analysis (pp. 293-5). How should the CIO be involved in particular development projects belonging to particular departments? There are three generic options: the CIO keeps away from individual projects and concentrates on organisation-wide infrastructure matters; *or* the CIO is involved in key decisions about projects, has considerable persuasive force, but does not directly control the people involved; *or* the CIO is at the top of a hierarchy that contains the systems development staff, and thus has formal control and responsibility. As stated, the middle course seems the most attractive, but the possibilities have only been sketched out; there is plenty of room for debate on the detail.

Strassmann puts much the same point, but in a far more incisive way (pp. 299ff.): The more the CIO acts as a master architect of the organisation's information and systems, then — necessarily — the less responsibility is left over for the managers of business units. Conversely, the more the plausible policy is followed of giving units responsibility for their own IT, the more the role of the CIO will be pushed back into mainly technical, organisation-wide matters, such as telecoms standards. As on many other issues, the real challenge is to find the right tradeoff between the opposing factors *for the particular case.*

3 Earl, pp. 148f.

4 References in this section: Robson, p. 336; Earl, pp. 205-8.

5 As on some other subjects, Earl's ideas on steering committees (pp. 149-156) are in a class of their own. Here is a paraphrase of the argument:

- It is silly to assume that every organisation will need just one IT steering committee to co-ordinate things, since the potential issues are too heterogeneous. It is also silly to prescribe a *generally applicable* structure of several committees with different terms of reference; situations vary too much.
- There are at least 11 different rationales typically found for a steering committee: eg to allocate resources; to co-ordinate while some major change or reorganisation is under way; to make senior managers more conscious of IT; to match the culture of the organisation; etc. (Earl doesn't make this point, but 'rationale' here means both 'some objective management problem to be solved' — the first two examples — and 'some desirable aim in human terms'—the latter two.)
- So you should decide which of those 11 rationales (and perhaps others) apply in your own case, and design the steering committee or set of committees, so that a committee is never asked to serve an incoherent, unmanageable bundle of rationales.
- For guidance, Earl describes (in terms of aims, membership etc) four ideal types of steering committee: Type A is a reasonable way of handling his rationales 1, 2, 3, 5 and 6; Type B can handle rationales 2, 4, 5, 6, 7 and 8; etc. However, this analysis is heavily qualified by the statement that some real-life steering committees don't conform to any of the ideal types, but are still effective.

All this is manifestly superior to the crude prescriptions discussed in the briefing text. But, as in other parts of Earl's book, the strong logic (links between rationales and ideal types) is let down by the fuzzy content (vague, abstract descriptions of the actual rationales and types).

It is interesting to compare Earl's treatment of this subject with that by Hussain and Hussain (pp. 504-7). Earl's book contains intelligent, sophisticated ideas, though the poor typography muffles their impact. The Hussain and Hussain book is beautifully designed, but the content presented so clearly is of feeble calibre. Whereas Earl's account is *all about* the point that different situations call for different types of steering committee, the Hussain and Hussain text smooths away such complications, as if there were just one sensible solution that well-run firms normally adopted. It contains some incredibly arbitrary statements; eg (p. 506) 'Another characteristic of successful steering committees is that they make long-range plans instead of approving projects singly. . . Quarterly meetings that focus on strategic issues work best.'

6 To study the question of IT knowledge further, you could devise (say) 30 of these four-gradation pieces covering different areas of technology (local area network, expert system, optical disk and so on), and use them to establish any person's IT knowledge profile. You would probably find that most people scored at either A or B or C level fairly consistently across the range of technologies, with a higher score in a few particular areas. Nobody could score consistent Ds, because the day isn't long enough for anyone to maintain that amount of detailed knowledge. This is merely conjecture; it is not based on any evidence.

7 This issue extends self-referential tentacles. If *you* express opinions on what knowledge of technology other people need in order to play certain roles in IM, then *you* should also have a clear position on what knowledge of technology *you yourself* need for whatever role *you* choose to play in IM—management consultant, business school professor, author, information analyst, CIO etc.

8 Tests of *generic compliance* can be broken down further into three main things where standards for compliance may exist:

- **Structure and format:** eg 'It is mandatory for a data model to use the following conventions to depict the main kinds of relations between data items . . '
- **Content:** eg 'It is mandatory for a proposal for a new system to contain a definition of the exact hardware configuration to be used.'
- **Method:** eg 'In estimating clerical staff savings it is mandatory to include indirect salary costs (such as pensions) in the savings, but not office overheads (costs of desks, office building etc).'

Tests of *generic quality* can be quantitative or qualitative. A quantitative test, or rather norm, might be: 'No software module should be more than 300 lines of program code.' This could be tested, perhaps on a sample basis, analogously to the way a factory part may be tested against some defined tolerance. However, for most products, qualitative, even impressionistic, tests of generic quality are likely to be the more fruitful; eg:

- 'Does this proposal document propose a system attractive enough to gain the commitment of all the different departments involved?' (This, it may reasonably be argued, is a requirement that every system proposal should meet.)
- 'Does this request-for-tender document provide enough information to enable a

competent supplier to prepare a fixed-price quote?'

Tests of *specific compliance* can be divided two ways:

- **Explicit requirement**: eg 'Does this piece of software do exactly what is specifically described in the textual specification?'
- **Implicit requirement**: eg 'It is clear that this system is being championed by one manager against the scepticism of others. Therefore it is essential that there be some early, 'quick strike' benefit that the champion can show the others. Does the project plan under review provide that?'

Tests of *specific quality* can be broken down four ways:

- **Intelligent-mechanical.** An intelligent person, with little knowledge of the subject, can make certain checks of a mechanical kind: eg finding inconsistent cross-references and terminology, grammatical errors, unintelligible diagrams etc.
- **Intelligent-thoughtful.** An intelligent person, using little knowledge of the subject, by thinking about matters carefully can come up with comments such as: 'Fifteen main requirements of the system are listed, but some of them overlap, some are just specific cases of others that are broader, and some are really ways of achieving others. Moreover, I don't see how they follow naturally from the two policy objectives given at the very beginning.'
- **Knowledgeable-factual.** A product may seem intrinsically perfect, but be vulnerable to checks that can only be made by someone with prior knowledge of the field; eg 'In this report you recommend use of the PageMaker software product rather than Quark Xpress. Why don't you even mention rivals such as FrameMaker and Interleaf?'
- **Knowledgeable-intuitive.** 'The document gives certain quantities: customers, products, transactions etc. As an authority on manufacturing systems, I find them very strange. In fact I would guess that you have made the mistake of counting every conceivable combination of minor variations in a product as if it were a separate individual product.'

CONNECTIONS

24. Centralisation and Distribution	Centralisation and distribution decisions that have to cohere with decisions about responsibilities
26. Operations and Decisions	Warrants rather than platitudes in operational management
28. Decision-making as Process	The place of managers' technology knowledge in the decision-making process (as opposed to the organisational context)
35. Change Management	Roles and responsibilities in the process of change

26. Operations and Decisions

TOPIC

A great deal can be said about the management of operations — about managing the data centre, ensuring security throughout the organisation, performing audits, measuring and managing capacity, and so on. Much too can be said about the management of software development departments.

But a large part of the advice people actually give is platitudinous: it is vital to have security that is good (as opposed to bad); it is crucial to have auditing that is effective (rather than ineffective); it is essential to schedule use of the mainframe carefully (not fecklessly) etc. Of course. Moreover, specific advice often seems to lie outside the borders of IM, being so detailed that it scarcely addresses any matters with great implications. Waste paper and old punched cards and tapes and the like should be disposed of, not left about. People should not be allowed to eat sandwiches in the computer room. But won't any competent data centre manager know these things already?

The central question for this briefing is where to draw the line between those matters counting as IM, and calling for debate between people with different responsibilities, and those that lie within the competence of one specific manager. This leads to discussion of an arbitrary but representative selection of topics to show how, in this area too, difficult decisions can be supported by genuine warrants that expose real options.

REPRESENTATIVE IDEAS — SUMMARISED

The table lists some topics that may seem disparate, but turn out to have something in common. They are covered in many textbook-like books about IM. Often the format is: 'Well-managed companies always manage (say) physical security as follows: . . (long list of straightforward, sensible details).'

For example, it is a good idea to have passwords for access to certain types of information. The general advice 'passwords formed from a mix-

Management Topics, but are they IM Topics?

Topic	*Representative issue*
Physical security	Precautions against fire in the data centre
Data security	Having passwords and encryption and levels of access entitlement
EDP audit	Designing control reports that bring together figures from different systems
Data centre scheduling	Ensuring that all systems do their work within agreed deadlines
Technology reliability	Having backup arrangements in case of hardware failure
IT staff management	Arranging that there be a natural career path for someone who joins as a trainee programmer
Software maintenance	Having procedures to specify changes and control successive versions of a piece of software

ture of letters and numbers are the most secure' could lead to the specific decision to have passwords in the format of A2GJ3B, P5RJ4F etc. The advice that having people wear special badges is a useful security technique could lead to the decision to introduce badges for data centre staff.

One article on security, analysed for the payoff behind all the anecdote reduces to a set of simple maxims: 'beware of disgruntled employees'; 'keep all personnel records and privileges up to date'; 'keep security codes strictly secret'; etc.

Another book states: '. . waste materials should be properly disposed of, paper can easily cause fires; all commercially sensitive documents should be shredded; all unguarded doors and windows should be closed (or preferably be self-closing); the position of panic buttons ought not to be at elbow height; cigarette smoking should be restricted; and food and drink should be kept well away from electronic hardware. Such self-evident precautions are all too often ignored.'1

REPRESENTATIVE IDEAS — ANALYSED

If the Decision Question is posed, then much of the advice in the previous section does support specific decisions. But should they be called IM decisions? Surely the board of directors should not have to debate about arrangements for waste-paper disposal or choice of secure windows. If IM is to have any convenient boundary, it probably won't include the specific details of passwords and security badges.

It may be that for some of the topics above there really is nothing more to be said. If so, there are no real decisions of IM to be taken; all you need is somebody competent who will do the straightforward, sensible things. But could it be that sometimes there really are important options that ought to be exposed?

This briefing isn't particularly concerned with giving direct advice about security or any other topic. The real task is to practice thinking about those subjects characterised by bland lists of straightforward measures, in such a way that relevant options can be recognised.

REPRESENTATIVE IDEAS — SUMMARISED

Cash, McFarlan and McKenney, in contrast to most others, sketch out some of the *tradeoffs* between desirable objectives that can occur in real life, and give rise to genuine IM decisions, where senior managers in a company may very well be involved with choices between options.**2**

Warrants about Data Centre Security

It is too easy to write about how vital security is, and to give long lists of measures to increase security. But how far should this go? A large organisation with a huge data centre may consider investment in bomb-proof bunkers, surveillance cameras, desert sites accessible only by private road or helicopter, and so on, but where should it stop? At some point the question must arise: Should you increase investment in the security of the data centre or spend the same funds improving the quality of the systems that run there? There must be a balance to be struck somewhere.

That is a rather brash tradeoff; things can easily become more complicated. Should you have one data centre or two?

- The option of two widely separated data centres seems better from the security angle. Terrorists are unlikely to attack both. If anything unfortunate happens at one (not necessarily as dramatic as terrorism), the other can be organised to provide backup arrangements.
- But having two widely separated data centres is probably more costly, since a single data centre enjoys economies of scale. Probably the two-data-centres option also entails more telecoms traffic. Worse, some of the databases may have to be split between the two sites, or replicated and kept consistent; this can bring great technical complications, and thus costs.

Warrants about Data Centre Objectives

Here is another tradeoff from the same source, albeit heavily edited.

Anyone can write to the effect that the performance of a data centre should be good (as opposed to bad), and that there should be some regular measurement of performance, particularly of things like terminal response time for online systems and reliability in meeting deadlines for batch processing systems.

But worthwhile discussion only starts with the recognition that such aspects may well *conflict* with each other, and thus raise the need for making tradeoffs. Take the following six things:

- performance of online systems (best simple measure: terminal response time);
- performance of batch systems (best simple measure: meeting deadlines);
- ability and speed in handling the unexpected; eg five-times the usual volume of transactions in a certain week, sudden requirement to list out the entire customer file etc;
- reliability; ie frequency and damage of major blunders, such as updating the database with the same tape of transactions twice;
- service quality; ie all aspects of performance not covered by the above; does everybody who phones to discuss a problem get through to a person with appropriate knowledge, courtesy and competence?
- total cost.

Plainly, one or two of these can be optimised, but not all; you can't have ample slack to cope with the unexpected, and at the same time keep costs to a minimum. This simple point can be quite powerful in generating issues for decision:

- 'The mainly online requirements of division A conflict awkwardly with the mainly batch requirements of division B. If you tell people at division B that their work has been delayed, not through any incompetence on our part, but for the sake of division A, it makes them even more angry. This is an argument for giving each division its own installation.'
- 'Our research shows that this data centre is among the most efficient in the industry by measures such as costs per on-line transaction or costs per megabyte stored. But there are complaints about the service. Which do you want: a lean, finely-tuned production facility, or service with a smile but a 10% rise in the costs recharged to user departments?'
- 'The amount of unexpected work at the data centre has grown tremendously and caused all kinds of problems. Get the data centre manager to work out proposals for investing more, in a way that will build in flexibility at the tightest corners in the installation — but without trying to improve performance or service or reliability on the regular systems.'

REPRESENTATIVE IDEAS — ANALYSED

As in many other areas, Cash, McFarlan and McKenney offer genuine warrants where others do no more than state the obvious. They recognise that two or more factors may well conflict, and the decision required is to find the best tradeoff in the circumstances.

SUGGESTED WARRANTS

The rest of this briefing suggests some more warrants to assist decision-making on some of the topics listed at the beginning. This has a dual purpose — partly to convey practically useful warrants, but mainly to suggest how apparently unpromising ground for IM warrants can still yield fruit.

Charting Competence Control and Policy Control

'Measures to protect information should be implemented where they are necessary and can be shown to be effective.' This advice is impossible to dispute but it hardly helps anyone make a better decision. The following statement also seems unsatisfactory, but in a way less easy to capture: '. . just as executive-level management should concern themselves with, say, embarking on a new venture, so they should concern themselves with formulating an overall security policy which would minimize the degree of loss . . '[3]

There is an ambiguity in saying that executive-level managers should *concern themselves* with matter M. This could mean either *competence control* or *policy control*. As the diagram shows they are very different things.

If M is so important, isn't policy control essential? But that raises the question: What are the key decisions that determine the outlines of the company's policy on M? 'We will follow good (as opposed to bad) practice in our management of M' doesn't count as policy decisions. Neither does: 'We will take the following 28 specific measures to improve the quality of M . . . '

If a certain decision determines the outlines of the company's policy on M, it must be the case that some other plausible policy options were considered and rejected. If the executive-level managers don't do that, they can't seriously claim to be making policy, no matter how emotionally concerned they may be about M.

Many IM topics do permit and at times demand policy control: organising end-user computing, using IT as the basis for new products, co-ordinating (or not) databases of different divisions, etc. But suppose the topic is security. What are the radically different policy options for decision that can exist here? If, for a certain organisation at a certain time, there are none, then the natural course is to appoint reliable managers and exercise competence control.

Competence Control and Policy Control

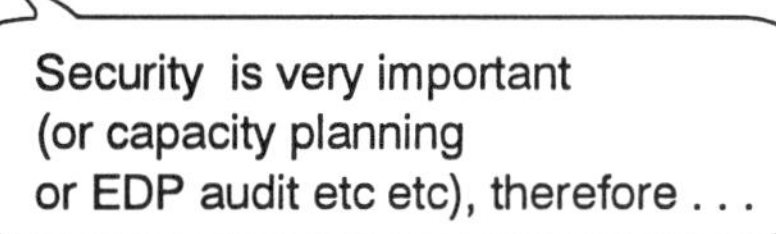

Security is very important
(or capacity planning
or EDP audit etc etc), therefore . . .

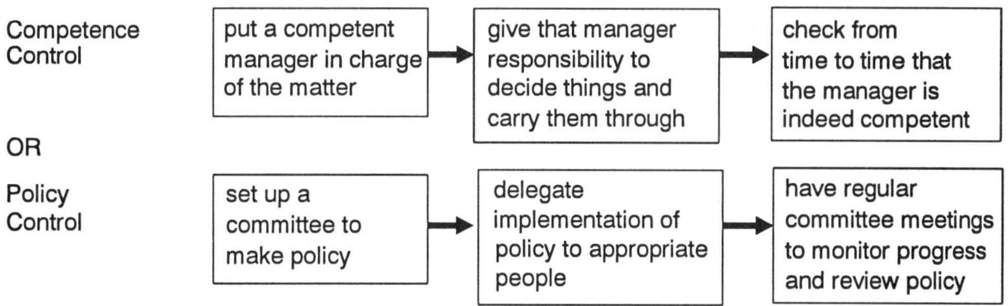

put a competent manager in charge of the matter
give that manager responsibility to decide things and carry them through
check from time to time that the manager is indeed competent

set up a committee to make policy

have regular committee meetings to monitor progress and review policy

Therefore, decision-making logic:

Decide which is best for each matter in your particular situation:
pure competence control OR pure policy control OR some shrewd mixture

Gradations of Vulnerability Factors

One way to open up the subject of security to generate options is to analyse the concept of vulnerability. What are the generic factors that determine how vulnerable a system is?

First of all, there is an underlying factor. As a general rule, the more complex a system is, the more vulnerable it is. Complexity for a computer system is a product of factors such as volume of data, variety of data, level of integration of data, level of integration of processing and various other features that are easily recognised when seen.

This is analogous to saying that, as a general rule, the more complex a piece of choral music is, the more chance of disasters in performance. In itself, it doesn't say what can cause the disasters. But most likely factors (mistakes by conductor, distractions from audience, bad layout of choir on stage etc) are such that the more complex the piece, the greater is the chance that they will apply.

Similarly the more complex the system, the more chance of certain factors being decisive. These vulnerability factors could be set out in a laundry-list format, but they come to life better when organised along a scale of gradations, ranging from shortcomings in your own competence, via external, impersonal forces, such as earthquakes, through to malicious sabotage by others:

- vulnerability to design and implementation flaws, eg software bugs, contradictory procedures;
- vulnerability to accidental mishap in the use or control of the system, eg wrong data input, data input twice;
- vulnerability to accident occurring to the system, eg hardware failure, operating system failure;
- vulnerability to natural disasters, eg earthquakes, lightning strikes;
- vulnerability to broadly directed, external, human actions, eg national strikes by energy or water utilities;
- vulnerability to actions of others, specific but not malicious or dishonest, eg supplier or outside bureau letting you down;
- vulnerability to dishonesty, eg people accessing data and transactions for financial gain;
- vulnerability to malice, eg a disgruntled employee introducing a virus.

This warrant makes it easier to take decisions, or at any rate to discuss options:

'Everything is just too complex and integrated here. To reduce vulnerability through specific factors we should attack the underlying factor: decentralise and simplify links between systems. But can that be done at reasonable cost?'

'We can reduce our vulnerability to other people letting us down if we prepare the monthly compact disks sent out to the branches ourselves, instead of relying on a bureau. But is the extra cost worth the reduction in vulnerability?'

'We don't want to be vulnerable to dishonesty or malice. But if we tried to protect ourselves against everything conceivable, our entire system development staff would do nothing but devise ingenious security features. Where is the best tradeoff?

'This is ridiculous: we have invested a fortune guarding against vulnerability to earthquakes, but we are practically helpless against the risk of those obsolete tape-drives breaking down.'

As the above suggests, there is great scope for making any classification of factors much more detailed and thus raising many more options for decision.

Making a Distinction and a Chart Warrant

Sometimes it is possible to build option-defining warrants out of quite limited material. One book says: 'The choice of location is another obvious source of trouble: a glamorous location diverts major funding from other projects, it may be costly and politically destabilizing for the company, and it identifies and advertises the centre as a target. On the other hand, camouflaging a computer centre in a drab run-down area near social unrest increases the likelihood that staff will be attacked on the way to work.'[4]

This does compare two options although the second is a rather uninteresting one: a drab though stable, low-cost area seems a more credible possibility. From this start, a distinctions warrant might be made to expose the main generic options for siting a data centre: glamorous downtown area of a large city; drab though stable, low-cost area of a large city; deep suburbia or countryside adjacent to a large city; smart, central location in a small, low-cost town; business park or industrial estate; *or* remote green field or yellow desert site.

For each of these, the pros and cons can be defined fairly easily. The same book says: 'Companies are often totally dependent on key (computer) personnel, and so staff motivation, via training and retraining schemes, is fundamental to any sensible personnel strategy.' But on the same page companies are urged to stamp out the playing of computer games, because this is 'symptomatic of sloppy work practices, which can lead ultimately to safety dangers for personnel, or to financial risks for the company'. This suggests a warrant to chart the tradeoffs along the following lines:

- One way to keep computer staff well motivated is through investment in training. But if new knowledge and skills are required in the near term for a particular project or job, training is needed anyway. There is no kudos in that; to make a manifest investment in a person and thus encourage commitment, give training that is not obviously relevant straight away — even at the expense of time that could be worked on urgent projects.
- Another way is to encourage a happy, civilised environment: eg avoid issuing edicts that nobody must ever play computer games; trust people to keep the time spent within reasonable bounds.
- The obvious problem with encouraging commitment in these and other ways is the cost of time wasted on playing games, and on training that turns out not strictly relevant.
- The result could even be the worst of both worlds: incur the costs, without raising motivation, and produce a complacent, over-indulgent, low-productivity environment.
- You just have to judge the relative weights of all these factors in your case and take decisions accordingly.

NOTES & ARGUMENTS

1 Much of the material in the books by Frenzel and (still more) Hussain and Hussain rests on the implicit assumption that every well-managed company normally does things in a certain way. Time and again, a topic cries out in vain for analysis along the lines of 'Here are the main *different* ways of handling the security (or auditing or capacity planning etc) issue, and here are some of the factors that help determine what is best in a specific situation: . . '

Article: William Atkins, 'Jesse James at the terminal', in Harvard Business Review (1991). Waste materials etc etc: Angell and Smithson, p. 98.

2 Cash, McFarlan and McKenney, chapter 11, and specially pp. 212-6.

3 Ward, Griffiths and Whitmore, p. 348; followed by Jackson, p. 215.

4 Angell and Smithson, p. 97 and p. 104.

CONNECTIONS

5. Generic Strategies	Agenda decisions aligning IT with the rest of the organisation, perhaps affecting data centre location and objectives
20. Integration and Connected Matters	Matters that can set the requirements for installation planning
25. Functions, Responsibilities and Skills	Questions of job description, associated with the choice between competence and policy control

27. Untangling Approach Decisions

TOPIC

The value of creative ideas, rigorous analysis and subtle reasoning may be greatly reduced if they arise within some arrangement for decision-making that starts in the wrong place, or rests on false assumptions, or prevents the right people getting involved, or is inadequate in some other way. That is why decisions defining the *approach* to decision-making can have far-reaching consequences for good or for bad.

An approach decision decides how to go about tackling some specific matter that can be given reasonably clear boundaries. Whether the matter is large (an information architecture aligned with business strategy) or small (a choice of software package), the decision-process has a beginning and an end. That is what distinguishes *approach* decisions from decisions (eg about steering committees, innovation departments, quality assurance procedures and hybrid managers) that establish the management *context*, within which decisions on matters as yet unspecified will be taken.

The range of general advice about approach decisions runs from abstract principles through checklists for very specific tasks to firm recommendations on multi-step methodologies. It is no small challenge to keep a sense of direction in this field.

SUGGESTED WARRANTS

The issues of IM are often awkwardly structured.[1] The table gives some representative examples of decisions about how to *approach* the issues. This briefing suggests how to sort out the decisions and warrants typically found on the approach plane.

Chart relating Principle and Method

Decisions about matters of approach can exist at different levels of abstraction. The decision to go for a step-by-step approach intended to make plans for using IT to support a given set of business activities more

Alpine Ash Airlines, Representative Approach Decisions

'We will now make a process model of our engineering maintenance division; that will help us divide the division up into a few manageable pieces; then we will look at each piece in more detail and take decisions about it.'

'We will use the Arthur Andersen Method/1 methodology to produce an organisation-wide information architecture.'

'We will send out questionnaires to all the financial analysts who produce the figures needed for negotiations with IATA and with governments. We will choose the new spreadsheet package by weighting their preferences by their amount and type of use.'

'The approach we will take to designing the new system for scheduling in-flight meals is committee-laden and inefficient — when considered purely as a problem-solving mechanism. But that is the only way to reach another goal: gaining everybody's commitment to the changes that will ensue.'

'We must set up new systems for this small airline we have just acquired in a ridiculously short time. It is rather like planning a major paratroop assault at a week's notice. Therefore every major decision, once taken, won't be altered. There is no time in this case for improving the quality of decisions by feedback and iteration.'

'We have devised an approach to developing our entire IM policy, by fitting together six of the best established ideas and techniques from the business school books: first, Porter's generic strategies, then the strategic grid of Cash, McFarlan and McKenney, then . . . '

'Since we have taken the agenda decision to do the main things we already do more efficiently (as opposed to doing completely new things, such as new types of tickets and 'frequent flyer' schemes), we will approach decision-making and planning in a way fitting that policy; eg modelling the current business (as opposed to working with visions of how IT can transform the organisation).'

effectively (as opposed one meant to generate plans for doing entirely new things) is a decision at at one level. The decision to use some particular methodology (eg Method/1) rather than another (eg IEF) is at another.

General advice about decisions can be offered on two main distinct levels:

- **Method**: 'Use this generally applicable methodology for information planning (or technique for discovering innovative opportunities, or standard checklist for selecting a software package etc)';
- **Principle**: 'There are these generic types of model . . . and they can be fitted into a decision-making process in the following different ways . . ' *or* (more abstract) 'A good decision-making process has to find the right balance between methodical, step-by-step progress and the generation of fresh, structure-defying options.'

Advice about principle, if of reasonable quality, is generally far more use than advice about specific method, however good. Much advice about method doesn't encourage rational decision-making about approach decisions. To take an informed decision to follow (say) methodology A rather than B, you often have to chop your way through hundreds of pages of documentation undergrowth. A good warrant about principle can serve as an intellectual machete, promoting judgements such as 'methodology A uses the following generic types of model in the following ways . . . and balances step-by-step progress and structure-defying options as follows . . . methodology B, by contrast, . . . '

Distinctions between Complex and Simple Approaches

Approach decisions may deal with specific matters that are large, small or in between. Nevertheless, there is a pragmatic distinction to be made:

- **Simple** approach. The nature of the decision required (eg 'which spreadsheet product?'), the options (four rival products) and relevant implications (costs, ease of use etc) are well defined or can readily be discovered. The whole decision-making process is therefore like a clock: essentially one piece of machinery consisting of interlocking parts, producing one result. Any intermediate products will be working papers of little permanent value. To say an approach is simple in this sense is to say nothing about the amount of work entailed, the importance of the decision or the difficulty of reaching it.[2]
- **Complex** approach. The one-off decision-making process inevitably requires a number of separate decision-making steps: eg 'We will conduct this exercise to plan our information needs for the next five years in a process containing these main activities, linked together in these ways . . ' During the steps of the process itself the decisions needed, options and implications develop and change. Intermediate products (eg a business model) may be valuable in themselves.

This analysis provides a distinction warrant of principle. It is a start towards clarifying the nature of any particular approach decision. Most useful warrants of principle — though not all — address the issues of complex approaches.

Chart of Factors in Complex Approaches

Here is another warrant of quite a general character. Several generic factors that typically affect a complex approach:

- **Problem-solving.** Plainly, any approach needs to be adequate from a purely problem-solving point of view. If certain tradeoffs are intrinsic to the problem, then the approach needs to ensure that they are raised and not glossed over; if certain factors should influence things, those factors should be introduced explicitly, rather than simplified out; and so on.

With certain types of problem in other fields, where all the relevant data can with competence readily be assembled and examined, there may be no more to be said, but here there may be additional complications . .

● **Options and levels.** Thousands of different options on hundreds of matters could be worth considering — if the time allowed were infinite, and the participants had superhuman capacity for mastering interconnected detail without getting confused. In practice, though, a good approach must not only produce good solutions to problems but do so efficiently. Therefore work (discussions, investigations, designing and the like) must be arranged into some methodical structure, with different matters at different levels. The complication is that the structure must not be *too* methodical and too rigidly divided into levels — otherwise there won't be room to expose a rich range of options and pursue their implications adequately. Getting the right balance of options and levels is tricky.

If the entire set of decisions were being taken by one person, the account so far might suffice: the challenge would be to use options and levels efficiently to solve the problem . .

● **Degrees of awareness.** In real life, any approach must cope with the fact that different people will be involved in overlapping ways, and they will have different levels of awareness of relevant factors — in particular, but not only, awareness of the facts of information technology. Any approach must also pass the test of allowing for this factor.

The account so far might be complete if it were true that everyone involved in decision-making and affected by it behaved in a selfless, robotic way . .

● **Human factors.** In practice, an approach also needs to allow for another complication: the purpose isn't only to find the objectively best decision. People's involvement in the decision-making process itself (whether happy or unhappy) may influence their performance in carrying out the decisions; that may in turn affect the success or otherwise of the decisions. This factor too may influence the approach.

This still leaves one more complicating aspect of the problem of devising an approach . .

● **Standard methods.** If standard methods exist for tackling a problem, you need to decide to what extent you will use them. In theory, a standard method may save considerable labour in working out the details of an approach; also it may inspire credibility and confidence in some of the people involved. But, again in theory, even the best standard method may still be too crude or too detailed or wrongly focused for the issues of a particular case; also, some of the people involved may have negative feelings about being constrained to do things a certain way, just because that is the standard method. These tradeoffs need to be weighed.

The above is not just a list of five things to get right: it is a chart pointing out that five factors interact in awkward, complex ways, posing a variety of tradeoffs. The general challenge is to design the best decision-making process for the situation. This chart also provides a framework for seeing where the more detailed discussions in subsequent briefings belong within the whole problem-area of approach decisions.

Relation of Approach to the Other Planes

In a strict sense, any decision on any subject whatsoever is taken by following some approach or other. This seems to mean that any decision (as opposed to instinctive impulse) must be preceded by a decision about how to approach it; that decision must itself be preceded by an approach decision, and so on. This line of thought, if taken very far, descends into futility.

On the other hand, it is surely necessary to point out sometimes: 'You are implicitly assuming that a certain approach to deciding this matter is the surest route to sound decisions. But there are other plausible approaches available. Shouldn't we decide the approach first?' The trick is to isolate approach decisions for consideration when it really counts, but avoid an infinite regress of decisions about decisions.[3]

NOTES & ARGUMENTS

1 'Awkwardly structured' is not the same as 'difficult to solve'. Many problems are complicated and difficult without being awkwardly structured: optimising an oil-tanker's route, or developing an alloy with certain desired properties, or finding a cure for a certain disease, or deciding whether to close a factory, for instance. With such problems there is relatively little difficulty in agreeing criteria for success or failure; it is fairly easy to see what kinds of matters are relevant to the problem and roughly how they fit together; and (though not entirely) it is possible to lay down generally valid methods of approach.

Here are some problems that are quite awkwardly structured: allocating money for the maintenance of a country's ancient monuments; designing a country's education policy; deciding the funding of different kinds of medical research; planning the most enjoyable possible tour of Egypt; deciding how to restore works of art; resolving the ethical issues of euthanasia; taking many of the decisions related to IT within an organisation.

Mapping Hypertext by Robert E Horn (Lexington Institute, 1989) is an excellent, stimulating book that ranges much wider than the title suggests. It gives (pp. 204-6) nine somewhat overlapping characteristics of awkwardly structured problems as opposed to tame ones: no definitive formulation of what the problem is; no single criterion to determine correctness; solving the problem is synonymous with understanding it; the problem is ongoing and continuously changing; no list of operations for solution; different explanations of phenomena available, implying different solutions; each problem and solution unique; a solution cannot be undone, because it changes the nature of the problem; and lastly (all one item) no agreement on distinctions between causes, symptoms and problems, level of detail difficult to choose, disagreement on setting problem boundaries. (Horn uses the term 'ill-structured', but 'awkwardly structured' is better, since 'ill-structured' can be misunderstood as 'incompetently structured'.)

Some of Horn's features will be fairly apparent to the systems analyst making the case for investment in an innovative system, the consultant persuading a client that the current plans for using IT are over-ambitious, the specialist in a certain technology translating knowledge into factors relevant to a specific organisation, the CIO working to harmonise IM policy with the board's mission statement, the chairman judging whether a proposed 30% increase in the IT budget is a sound business proposition . . .

If IM problem-areas are awkwardly structured, then *detailed generalised procedures* for IT decision-making and planning are likely to be inadequate. If persisted with, they may produce arbitrary simplifications, make unjustified assumptions, ignore important options and generally do more harm than good. But difficulty of finding standard approaches is no reason to avoid *thinking about* procedures and structures for decision-making. On the contrary, it becomes all the more necessary to do so carefully.

The list above of nine traits of awkwardly structured problems is a general list, and some items are more relevant to IM than others. This briefing dissects IM decision-making to expose its most awkward features.

2 Search the catalogue of a university library on a term like 'decision theory' and you will probably find at least a hundred books. Most fall into one of three categories:

- about human decision-making in general; descriptive, from a psychological or sociological viewpoint; without judgements of whether any one way is better than another; snag — yields little that helps in taking better decisions, particularly on awkwardly structured matters;
- about quantitative methods for management decision-making; eg how to route tankers, optimise production etc; does recommend useful methods; snag — only relevant to solving problems that, though difficult, are not awkwardly structured;
- about management decision-making in general; often a mixture of descriptive analysis and suggested techniques; snag — since practically every single thing in every course taught in a business school can be said to concern decision-making in some way or other, it is difficult to give coherence to such a book; *Decision Making, An Integrated Approach* by David Jennings and Stuart Wattam (Pitman, 1994) includes discussion of value chains, leadership styles, green issues, flat organisation structures, stock control, stimulus-response theory, Jungian personality types . . .

Most existing decision theory helps, if at all, only with IM decisions where a simple approach (in the sense given in the briefing text) is adequate. There is little on the most interesting and difficult challenges in IM decision-making:

- How do you discover the right options to decide between?
- How do you process large bodies of ill-organised material about the specific organisation and about technology in general, in order to extract what is relevant to defining options and assessing their implications?
- How do you structure a whole decision-making process for making a number of interrelated decisions, so that the resulting set of decisions will be good ones, and coherent and economically reached?

Probably these challenges exist in many other fields of real-life decision-making too, but this book is only concerned with IM decisions.

3 This interesting issue is not discussed much in the literature of decision theory. In *The Adaptive Decision-maker*

(Cambridge University Press, 1993), John W Payne, James R Bettman and Eric J Johnson say (pp. 107-8) that people usually approach a decision without much reflection about choice of method. However, there are certainly *some* cases where choice of decision-method is itself a decision with options to be consciously weighed, and this does raise the problem of infinite regress. Having got that far, these authors say lamely that conscious decisions about decisions don't happen very often, and they leave it at that.

CONNECTIONS

28. Decision-making as Process	Complex approaches: the two themes of options and levels and degrees of awareness — describing what is tricky in much more detail
29. Modelling and Deciding	Complex approaches: options and levels; the specific problem of modelling
30. Standard Multi-step Methodologies	Complex approaches: typical multi-step approaches; assessing how well any ready-made standard approach, offered by (say) a consultancy company, meets the challenges
31. Checklists and Weighted Criteria	Simple approaches: including all the themes in mild form
32. Standard Approaches and Contingency	Both complex and simple approaches: the interaction of the two themes, human factors and standard methods
35. Change Management	Human factors in *any* kind of planning and developing process, from deciding a business strategy through to designing a form

28. Decision-making as Process

TOPIC

The first difficulty with approach decisions is to see why they are difficult. Won't common sense guide you most of the way to finding a multi-step approach that is reasonably methodical and comprehensive?

But the things that make a difference between a good and bad approach may require quite subtle judgement. For instance, methodical, top-down planning is certainly a good thing — up to a point; but if top-down principles are applied too firmly, decisions taken at the top may be wrong or imprecise, for lack of lower-level information about their implications. Getting the balance right depends on judgement of the particular situation. And that judgement should probably be influenced by another complicating fact: that the participants in decision-making will have differing degrees of knowledge — of IT, and also of other relevant matters.

Only a few of the books about IM recognise the trickiness of structuring a large-scale decision-making process. This briefing charts out the main challenges that invariably arise. By suggesting options and pointing out dangers, it can promote realistic debate about the structure any particular process should be given.

SUGGESTED WARRANTS

IM poses slippery, awkwardly structured problems. This briefing adopts the technique of starting out from a simplified version of the way things are, and then relaxing certain assumptions and building in more complications to make the account more realistic.[1]

Distinctions between Product and Process

At the outset, it is vital to distinguish product from process. To say 'the quality of this planning is excellent' could mean either or both of the following:

- 'The quality of this planning **product** is excellent' — because the things proposed in the plan fit together well, they are consistent with some clear general objectives, the estimates for the various activities and investments seem plausible etc.

● 'The quality of this planning **process** is excellent' — because all those people who should have been consulted were consulted, the key issues were covered in an intelligent order, and the organisation of the discussions avoided blind alleys etc.

A document containing a set of decisions and plans and designs is a product. It may say nothing about the process that developed it. Managers could have started by agreeing on some very fundamental matters and gradually built up the product very methodically from there. Or they could have begun with a simplified, outline skeleton of the whole thing and then added detail in each area in a rather arbitrary sequence. Or they could have worked out some parts in great detail, become dissatisfied, scrapped them and worked them out all over again. In assessing the plans as product you are not directly concerned with such things.

This product-process distinction is potentially relevant whenever there is talk of 'planning', 'decision-making', 'reasoning', 'argument' and the like. Sometimes it helps avoid confusion or expose unnoticed issues.**2**

This briefing is concerned with process. Clearly, a good process is one likely to generate a good product efficiently. What, in general, are the challenges that arise?

Charting the Options and Levels Themes

The most obvious challenge is solving the problem, ie taking account of all the relevant factors and possibilities to arrive at the best answer; but practically all the other briefings are about that in one way or another.**3** What generic factors apply to the process itself?

Recognise two opposing forces that affect the form of any large-scale decision-making process:

● One force leads towards the definition and comparison of **options**. This is natural because any genuine decision usually entails adopting option X, rather than Y or Z. If not, its status as a decision is doubtful.

● But on the other hand, it is also natural to impose order on any complex decision-making by breaking it up into **levels**: 'Now that we've finalised our decision at Level 3, we will go forward and develop further detail at Level 4.'

There is a potential conflict between working in neat, methodical levels and examining a rich range of options — as the diagram shows by a *reductio ad absurdum.* Careful structuring into many separate levels promotes order, sense of purpose and coherence; but the fewer levels there are, the more substantial each level will be, and thus the more room it will give to explore options and their implications thoroughly.

This isn't just a matter of deciding *how many* sub-divisions the process should have. There is another variable: the *rigidity* of their

Levels and Options

A 100-Level Approach to Decision-making

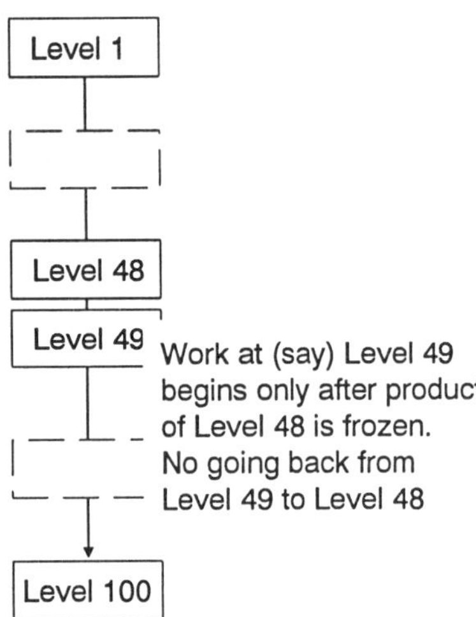
Level 1
Level 48
Level 49
Work at (say) Level 49
begins only after product
of Level 48 is frozen.
No going back from
Level 49 to Level 48
Level 100

A 2-Level Approach to Decision-making

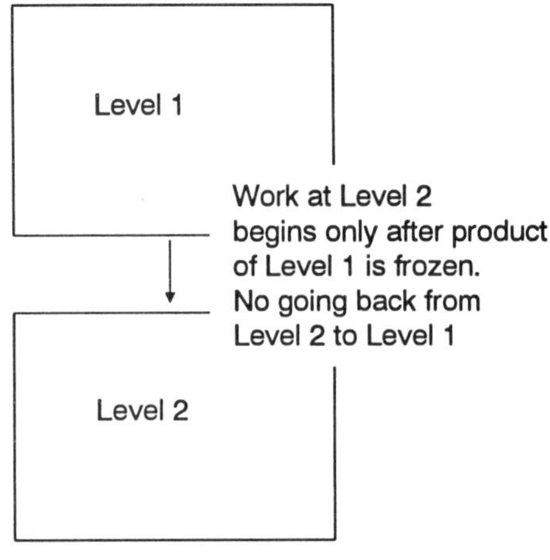
Level 1
Work at Level 2
begins only after product
of Level 1 is frozen.
No going back from
Level 2 to Level 1
Level 2

Problem

At each level options will arise for decision. How can you decide between the options at Level 48, when their implications only become clear from the work done at Level 49 and subsequent levels?

Problem

Plenty of room within each of the two levels to expose options and investigate all their implications - but there may be so many, and interrelated in such complex ways, that chaos may ensue.

So try to
divide decision-making into plenty of levels, with each small enough to be manageable;
but
ensure each level is a large chunk of the problem, with enough room to explore options and implications, without having to go up or down between levels.

boundaries. You may want to permit (perhaps encourage) some feedback leading to iteration between levels, but the more that happens, the more the orderly, methodical character of the whole process is undermined.[4]

Resolving this option-level tradeoff is one fundamental challenge for any complex decision-making approach.

Adding Degrees of Awareness to the Chart

The option-level tradeoff exists because decisions generally have to be taken on the basis of imperfect knowledge; it is not practically feasible to set out all the conceivably relevant facts and possibilities like neat exhibits on a table, before deciding anything. This would be so even if one intelligent dictator carried out all investigations and took all decisions.

But in practice the problem of imperfect knowledge has another twist. An IM decision process often brings together a variety of people with different responsibilities and backgrounds, and different degrees of awareness of relevant matters (of marketing techniques, of optical disk storage capacity, of government regulations, of expert system possibilities, of financial modelling etc). This complicates things considerably. It raises a new challenge that has no real parallel in genuine 'single intelligence' situations, such as solving a chess problem, calculating a tax liability or marking a history essay.

Many IM decisions require a realistic understanding of the way business demand and technology supply possibilities interact to offer options of varying degrees of cost, risk and other factors. Since it is unacceptable to restrict decision-making to a tiny few who are both experts on IT supply factors and deeply knowledgeable about the specific organisation, it follows that the process has to be so organised that people with overlapping areas of knowledge and interest can collaborate.

This isn't just a matter of bringing together two sorts of people — IT and business. There are different types of IT people with different degrees of interest in wider business matters, and non-IT managers range from those that boast an aggressive ignorance of IT through to those possessing a more realistic understanding of IT's capabilities and constraints than many IT specialists themselves.

Somebody solving a chess problem has a complete knowledge of the rules of chess and a perfect view of the whole board. But suppose that a group of people had to work together to find good moves. Suppose one was a great expert on the rules governing the movement of pawns, had a rough idea of the possibilities of bishops and rooks, had always been thoroughly confused by the movements of knights, and couldn't quite see the top left corner of the board. Another person had a different awareness profile, and somebody else a different one again. All the knowledge required to solve the problem might be present in the group as a whole, but finding a mode of working to co-ordinate their contributions would be a formidable task. That is a close analogy to this awkward challenge in finding a good decision-making process for IT.[5,6]

Example Case: Angophora Mining

Suppose Angophora Mining is considering a database system for storing legal texts and related information. The diagram shows the main role-players in decision-making. They have different profiles of IT knowledge. Also, some, such as Colin, will be strongly affected by any decisions, while for others, such as Dora, this is quite a small matter.

It would be absurd to expect that all six should fully understand and vouch for every detail that plays any part in arriving at Angophora's

Angophora Mining, Decision-making Process and Role-players

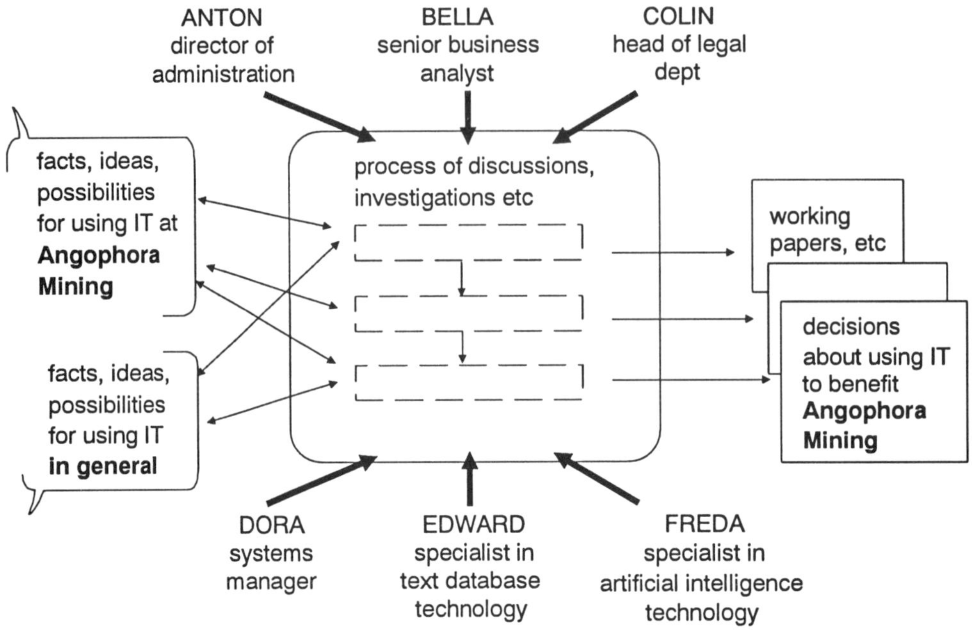

ANTON
director of
administration

BELLA
senior business
analyst

COLIN
head of legal
dept

facts, ideas, possibilities for using IT at **Angophora Mining**

facts, ideas, possibilities for using IT **in general**

process of discussions, investigations etc

working papers, etc

decisions about using IT to benefit **Angophora Mining**

DORA
systems
manager

EDWARD
specialist in
text database
technology

FREDA
specialist in
artificial intelligence
technology

decisions. There has to be some division of decision-making into separate compartments inhabited by different people, and this may be done in any number of ways.**7**

The second diagram suggests two possibilities. The first is the more economical. (A leaner approach still would probably not be feasible, since it would leave no room for the overlapping knowledge of the participants to be exchanged.) This might well be the most efficient way of arriving at rational decisions about the main features of the new system.

But not necessarily. There are arguments for the other approach too. One problem is that people's knowledge and concerns have no sharp boundaries; they shade off gradually. Therefore the crisply, compartmentalised approach that seems efficient in theory may fail to capture odd, unforeseeable details that turn out afterwards to be material. Also, the fewer the boxes in the process, the higher the stakes. If there are relatively many boxes, progress may be more laborious, but each decision taken is a relatively smaller step forward, and the need for bold, painful, perhaps wrong, decisions is reduced. And again, the more thoroughly people are consulted, the greater their commitment to the decisions reached — at least in theory, unless they take up irreconcilable positions, and ruin the whole decision-making process.

Of course, an excessively complicated decision-making process, with

Role-Players and Decision-making Process - Extreme Alternatives

How should Anton, Bella etc organise their discussions?

Discussions organised into a few carefully devised compartments

OR

Almost everybody involved in discussing almost everything

AC
BC
BEF
BDE

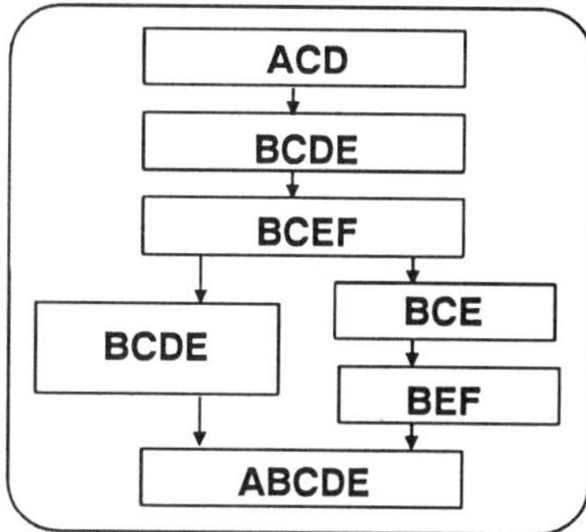

(say) twice as many boxes again, might go too far, and suffer from the familiar evils of excessive bureaucracy. There is no *generally* valid solution. There are general factors that typically have some relevance, but how they are best traded off depends on the particular circumstances.

How does this example pass the test of the Decision Question? It exposes some factors that are real and important, and yet are rarely discussed explicitly. Thus it may help you make better decisions about the decision-making approach to be adopted for any specific case.

NOTES & ARGUMENTS

1 This is analogous to the way economists define a state of perfect competition, study it, and then refine it with ever more elaborate factors, or engineers study a mechanical system first as if it were without friction, and then gradually add in the complications.

In terms of this book's general approach, this briefing sets out an extensive chart warrant identifying factors related to approach decisions and showing how they are inter-related; it does this by starting with a sketch and adding complicating detail.

2 For instance, Frenzel (pp. 85ff., 100ff.) claims to describe a planning cycle. But it seems very vulnerable to the following charge: 'This describes a desired *product*, a set of documents containing decisions and plans. That is just the easy part; the real problem is finding a *process* to arrive at that product, so that: a, its parts are consistent with each other, and b, it represents somewhere near an optimum set of choices.'

3 The factors relevant to the problem are both hard and soft. Hard factors include such things as the capabilities of various items of technology, the months' work required to develop certain software, the financial savings through more efficient inventory control, the estimated time for a person to handle a certain transaction, and so on. Some factors are fairly hard, even though their values can only be estimated — the price of suppliers' goods, growth in the national economy, exchange rate movements and so on.

But soft factors have to be bought into the calculus too, even though they don't lend themselves to quantitative assumptions; eg shifts in consumer tastes, or government attitudes, and (primarily) human reactions to new systems.

Suppose that, based on hard factors alone, it is estimated that a certain project will yield a certain return on investment through more efficient inventory control. This is not achieved, because of soft factors: the people in the inventory area feel that the new system deskills their work; they work less hard and take less trouble than they ought. Or perhaps, instead, the soft factor is that the new system frees people of hated drudgery; they feel motivated to use every ounce of skill and judgement to optimise inventory; the return greatly exceeds estimates.

The first step is to accept that such soft factors exist and will affect the outcome of decisions. But accepting that a soft, human, in a loose sense irrational, factor exists shouldn't mean assuming that the factor is completely unpredictable and impossible to allow for. The factor may be hard to capture, but not immune to assessment. In any discussion of the process of IM decision-making, it should be understood that the factors to be processed include both hard and soft factors.

4 For a great deal more discussion of options and levels, see O'Brien (*Demands*), particularly Briefings 4, 7, 17 and 25.

5 There can be other repercussions too. The option-level tradeoff may be affected. If many of the people involved tend, by temperament, to veer away from clear chains of reasoning, it may be best to maintain coherence with quite a rigidly structured process — even if that is not best from the point of uncovering and brainstorming through creative ideas. But if the people concerned have an exceedingly bureaucratic, hierarchical outlook, then it may be best to go the other way.

Other personality attributes may make it best to vary procedures from what would be the theoretical ideal. Some people are eager to get into detailed design work that a coldly rational person might say was based on unproven assumptions. To avoid antagonising or demotivating people, it could be best (ie least bad) to permit a certain degree of reckless plunging into detail.

Also, the accurate assessment of soft variables may be more or may be less difficult to make in a group. More people *may* mean more insights, but perhaps extra complications too: eg the manager of a department may not make sound predictions of how its staff will react under new conditions, but others in the decision-making group may feel inhibited about claiming that they know better.

6 Probably there is nobody in the world who knows all about how to make a simple lead pencil, in the sense of knowing how to mine the graphite, grow the wood, produce the rubber, design factory machines, manage a factory, raise the capital for investment in a factory, and so on. Pencils are produced only because people with different specialised knowledge interact successfully.

How about with IT? There seems to be a definite difficulty in arranging that knowledge of facts about technology be applied efficiently. Many writers ignore the issue; others who raise it, say little of interest and just confirm that it is a problem. Keen (1991) (p. 136, p. 209) is a rare exception to the 'more business-oriented than thou' attitude of many books: 'If IT planning was overtechnical and ignored business priorities through the 1970s and early 1980s, the pendulum swung too far back in the late 1980s . . It is time to put the 'T' back in IT and competitive advantage.' See also O'Brien (*Demands*), Briefings 1-4.

Suppose an organisation allows the most fundamental, agenda-setting decisions to be taken by people who possess only a vague knowledge of technology. Isn't this rather like generals drawing up plans for campaigns, with arrows on maps, not knowing or caring about practical matters, such as how the terrain will be affected by the rain of the last two weeks and whether the standard anti-tank gun can pierce the armour of the enemy's new tanks? If IM decisions are not grounded in an appreciation of those technology matters that can make a difference, they may be no more than neat, unrealistic patterns on paper.

In practice the majority of people involved in decision-making will know *something* about both business and IT, albeit skewed perhaps heavily one way or the other. The problem is really to structure the decision-making process so that people with different knowledge profiles can collaborate.

7 This rather obvious point is associated with another more subtle one. Some argumentation analysts claim that there is no such thing as an inherently good argument, since an argument's quality depends on how well it matches the specific audience it is addressed to. Thus it might be quite sensible to debate the same matter in different ways with different premises, arguments and evidence for different audiences. Another corollary is that it may be impossible to argue effectively with an audience that is extremely varied in knowledge, values and motivations. From this it follows that a complex decision-making process should be divided up into compartments, such that, within each, there is a *coherent* audience, with a reasonable overlap of knowledge and interests.

CONNECTIONS

29. Modelling and Deciding

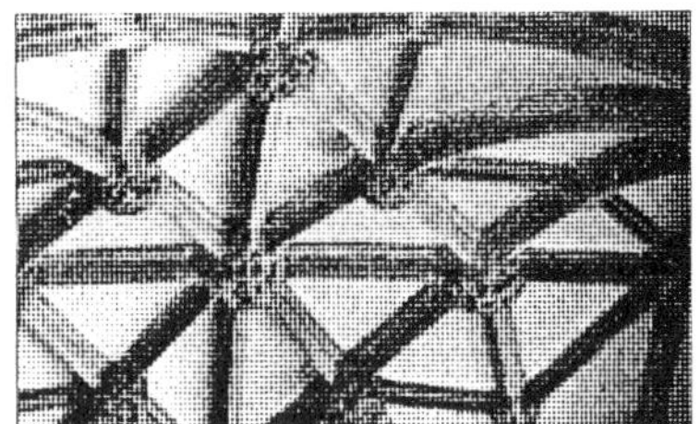

TOPIC

A decision-making process is rarely just a sequence of arguments and decisions. *Descriptive* activities are mixed in too: if decisions are to be based on facts about the present situation, then some work must be done to describe the present situation; again, a decision to invest in some new system normally requires that there be some description of the features of that system.**1**

Finding a structure to fit together descriptive activities, debating activities and explicit decision-making may not seem particularly hard. However, one trouble is that many modelling (ie descriptive) activities associated with IT systems can be inordinately time-consuming. Worse, sound reasoning based on the careful comparison of options may be swept aside by the momentum resulting from the sheer effort entailed by modelling. For such reasons it can be a serious mistake to commission (say) a detailed value chain analysis or an entity-relationship model at the wrong point in the decision-making process.

How can you decide what kind of models to use at what points in decision-making? The literature of IM, database and system development contains much about how to make particular types of models, but far less about how to decide what kind of model will assist what kind of decisions. That is the central issue for this briefing.

SUGGESTED WARRANTS

The briefing starts by distinguishing models from other things, and goes on to provide warrants that analyse in much more detail the relationship between modelling and deciding.

Distinctions between Models and Other Things

Many a business architecture, logical roadmap, conceptual blueprint, information plan or functional flow diagram is best swept into the broad category of 'model'. But sometimes documents with these titles or even documents labelled as models are better thought of as something other than a model. A cluster of three distinguishing features helps distinguish the model from other styles of planning and development documentation:

- A model is a **description** of something — of a body of data or a business, for instance. Neither a schedule of actions for a project nor a report comparing alternative strategies counts as a model.
- A model is a more **explicitly structured** description than a piece of prose. Usually it consists of diagrams, employing certain conventions for brevity and precision: a single-headed arrow in one place in the model and a double-headed arrow somewhere else may convey valuable nuances that would otherwise need a whole paragraph of explanation.
- A model has a relatively **non-technical** character. A diagram of the activities of a business is generally called a model; the technicalities of the computer systems may also be described in diagrams, but they aren't normally called models.

Distinctions of Model Content

Once demarcated, this modelling territory can be divided up. As the diagram shows, models may differ according to what it is their content describes:

- A **data model** concentrates on describing the items of information relevant to an organisation.
- A **process model** concentrates on the steps of procedures.
- A **business model** operates with concepts such as 'function' or 'activity', whose definition can't easily be pinned down; however, this doesn't matter very much since a business model is usually impressionistic rather than precise.[2]

It is certainly worthwhile to ask of any model: 'What exactly is this a model of?' If the model is an ill-defined mixture of several different types of content, then it probably won't be a very reliable basis for decision-making.

This three-way breakdown is valid and important, but in practice is not as clear-cut as might at first appear. A process model often gives considerable detail about data too — otherwise its description of the processes would be unintelligible. A classic business model is highly summarised, but if the detail of its content is steadily expanded, then sooner or later it will have to describe specific items of data and specific processes. Thus distinguishing between data, process and business models is a help in getting a grip on modelling activities, but it is by no means sufficient.

Aspects of Model Role

One banal truth is fundamental: detailed modelling is very laborious. It costs a great deal in skilled effort and psychological resources to make a

Mannagum Machines - Representative Fragments of Models

Business Model

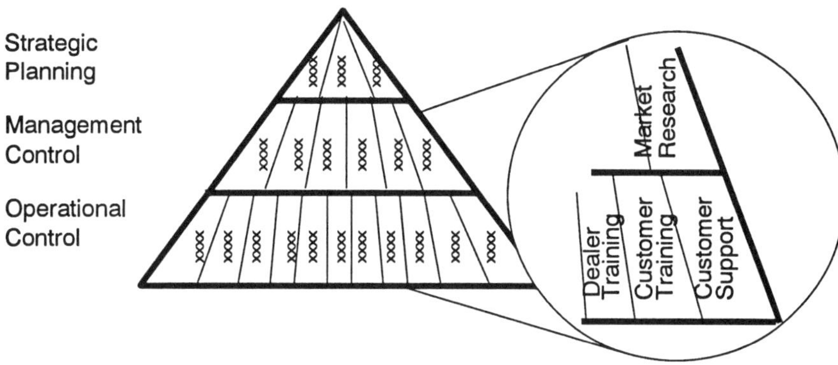

Data Model

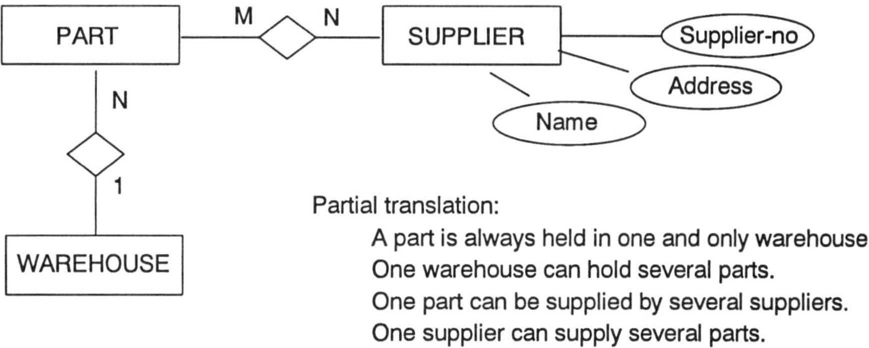

Partial translation:

A part is always held in one and only warehouse.
One warehouse can hold several parts.
One part can be supplied by several suppliers.
One supplier can supply several parts.

Process Model

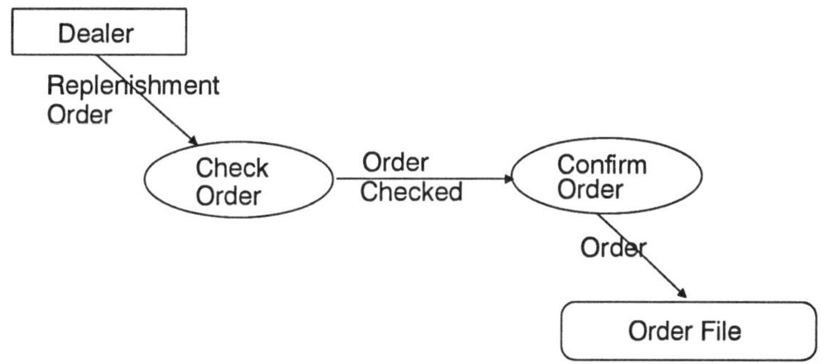

good data model or process model of one department, let alone a whole organisation. This truth is at the root of two typical problems that turn up in case after case:

'Everyone said we needed an enterprise model as the basis for our IM planning. But now we have this massive intellectual construction, we are none the wiser about the decisions we should take.' Connoisseurs of fallacies may analyse this as the result of a bad argument *ad verecundiam* (literally, being too bashful to question accepted wisdom).

The second common problem exemplifies the fallacy of an argument *ad misericordiam*: 'It cost us so much energy to make this 200-page model, we just couldn't bear the thought of not using it. We will press on and develop the software for all the systems it describes.'

To avoid these pitfalls, you need to be firm about the *role* of any model you decide to build; then you can avoid elaborating detail in directions the role doesn't require. There is no established way of categorising models by their role, but since the matter is so important, an analysis is needed. A model always describes, but it may or may not help very much with decisions; moreover different models help with different kinds of decisions. Three related aspects help clarify a model's *role*:

- What assumptions is the model based on? That is, what kind of decisions should have already been taken when the modelling started?
- Does the model describe whatever it describes in order to support better-informed decisions, or alternatively, in order to build up solid detail for the development of systems or databases?
- (If it is meant as an aid to decision-making) What kind of decisions does the model assist?

This analysis helps firm up the role any particular model plays in a decision-making process.

Charting Model Roles in Detail

All this may seem rather abstract but it yields results quite readily. One classic role for a model is providing input to IT decision-making at an early stage, before attention shifts to individual systems. In other words the model helps with agenda decisions. A model can show the main functions of Mannagum Machines, a hypothetical manufacturer of sewing machines. The functions are broken down in the most natural possible way, quite independently of the structure of any computer systems, present or future. Managers discuss the relative importance of each function shown in the model and perhaps shade them in on the diagram accordingly. The resulting model is one input to debates about priorities for new IT investment.[3]

Agenda-setting is a handy term for this role. The relationships between the model and the three aspects of model role given above can easily be charted:

- The model depends on few if any preceding decisions about IM policy.

- The model's whole purpose is to assist decision-making; it doesn't build up detail for the development of systems or databases.
- The decisions the model can assist have a fundamental character — determining priorities, recognising new opportunities for investment, setting total IT budgets etc.

A second classic role is that of the *masterplan*. A model playing this role comes in after a decision has already been made to invest in IT developments in a certain well-defined (though perhaps quite extensive) area. Given that decision, the expense of building a detailed model can be justified. For example, after deciding to have new systems in the purchasing department, Mannagum commissions a data model, that describes in detail the different items of information relevant to the department. It is the foundation for the work of setting up a database and developing software that will follow.

The information in most databases is shared — by several systems or sub-systems or departments. Bodies of data often have to be split over several locations or several databases. Most development projects are split into several phases. The classic masterplan model is built *before* decisions on any of these things are taken. The model itself is the main basis for taking the decisions on these 'dividing, sharing and linking' matters. The relationships between the model and the three aspects of model role are:

- Modelling begins after the decision has been taken that a certain substantial area of an organisation should be subject to intensive new development.
- Modelling is more concerned with building up a detailed description as an essential step towards developing new systems or databases, than with promoting major decisions.
- Nevertheless, one main purpose of the model is to be the basis for 'dividing, sharing and linking' decisions.

Third is the *development* role. This arises when a discrete project has already been set up with well-defined terms of reference, and links between phases, between systems, between databases and so on have already been decided. There are no more major decisions to be taken — except perhaps some of a mainly technical character. The remaining work is to pursue the expansion of non-technical detail into software. For example, Mannagum models in precise detail exactly what happens when dealers place orders for new stock to be supplied from the factory, taking account of all exceptional conditions that may arise. Though this model is non-technical, it becomes so detailed, so precise and so well-organised that it may be turned into software with relatively little more intellectual effort. Here the relationships between the model and the three aspects of model role are:

- The main decisions have already been taken.

● The model is a means of carrying through the process of building new systems, not a basis for decision-making.

In summary, this charting of roles is based on a three-way distinction:[4]

● **Agenda-setting model:** relatively succinct; applicable when fundamental decisions have yet to be taken.

● **Masterplan model:** can be very detailed; natural step towards building systems and databases in a certain area; basis for 'dividing, sharing and linking' decisions.

● **Development model:** also very detailed; part of system development; little connection with decision-making.

Charting Model Role, Model Content and Modelling Method

How do the three roles of agenda-setting, masterplan and development relate to the three types of model content — business, data and process?

● **Agenda-setting** models, if effective, are almost always **business** models. In principle, a very selective data model or process model can play an agenda-setting role by focusing on key relationships between certain information items or processes; but in practice it is difficult to be succinct without being arbitrary.

● The **data** model fits the **masterplan** role very naturally. Nevertheless, in certain cases, a carefully summarised process model may be more appropriate. Also, a business model is sometimes expanded into such detail that it no longer forms a basis for discussing policy and plays the masterplan role.

● A **development** model is normally a **process** model.

So far three kinds of content and three kinds of role have been distinguished, but there is certainly a large number of different modelling methods and conventions to be found. How can they be brought into the overall chart?

First, *business models.* There are many different ways of making a business model, just as there are many possible cartographic projections of the globe. An Anthony model (shown as a simplified fragment in the diagram) arranges the activities of an organisation into three levels: strategic planning, management control and operational control. By contrast, a classic value chain analysis model (though many are far from classic) rests on the idea that all activities of all businesses can be analysed into nine standard categories. Other standard methods exist, and it can also be quite sensible to invent your own technique to suit an individual case.

Just as different projections stress and distort different features of the Earth, so different styles of business model inevitably stress and distort different features of the organisation. You need to find the right style for the case; otherwise, decisions may be based on a distorted view of the relevant factors.

With *data modelling* the situation is rather different:

- The classic data model uses some version of a technique known as *ER (entity-relationship) modelling*.
- Most approaches to database development entail the creation of a *conceptual schema* — still a non-technical model, but carefully edited to ensure that its requirements fit neatly onto the technical features of a particular database software product (DB2, Informix, Ingres etc).
- Some people make a clear distinction between these two models; others work the one into the other through many tiny steps. However developed, these models describe a database, that generally serves several systems or at least several development phases.

Apart from this, it is fair to say that the various techniques for both *data modelling and process modelling* are much more homogeneous than those for business modelling. Some authorities may argue strongly that the Chen conventions for modelling data are superior to the conventions of Bachman or Howe or Elmasri-Navathe (shown as a simplified fragment). Process modellers may dispute about the merits of Backus-Naur, Gane-Sarson and Yourdon-DeMarco (shown as a simplified fragment). But most such arguments are about little more than notation: perhaps one modelling method uses an arrowed line between boxes where another prefers a line with a thick dot at each end. Differences of substance, as opposed to notation, do exist, but are generally of a rather esoteric character, unlikely to affect IM decision-making.

Aspects of Model Status

One further issue cuts across distinctions of model content and role. It is worth asking of any model: Is this a view of the way things are now, or of the way they might be in the future?

This is not necessarily a simple distinction. Perhaps a model could have timeless character? One line of argument runs like this: An organisation's operational procedures and IT arrangements are inherently mutable; they may be changed at any time if better ways of meeting the organisation's objectives are found. But a truly valuable model (of business or of data) should represent the essential nature of the organisation, that will persist through any superficial changes in the way things are done. Therefore the distinction between modelling how things are and how they might be is irrelevant and misleading.

This is a fallacious argument (Can any data model seriously be expected to survive unchanged for the next hundred years?), but thinking about a fallacy can often yield insight:

- In some agenda-setting situations, an outline model sufficiently general to represent the situation both now and in (say) five years time may be both feasible and appropriate.

- But if you are keen to stimulate radical innovation, you may make several different models — describing both the present and several different possible futures.
- However, if you are in a very volatile industry indeed, you may prefer to refrain altogether from modelling future scenarios, since, if in any detail, they are almost bound to be wrong.

A masterplan model is normally too elaborate to permit the luxury of having more than one version. The best advice here is to formulate the model's terms of reference carefully (how stable the model is meant to be, what assumptions are to be made about the future, and so on), to explain them to everyone involved and to stick to them. In fact, these are good general principles for keeping any kind of modelling activity under control.

NOTES & ARGUMENTS

1 In most fields there is a clear distinction between decision-making and doing. Planning inventory requirements for a factory is obviously a very different kind of thing from using a spanner on the production-line. Planning the logistics of a military campaign is a different thing altogether from firing a rifle. Designing a shopping mall is a different thing from mixing concrete. There may be border-line activities, but in most fields this is no great problem.

With IT the distinction is more awkward. Of course, working out a cost/benefit analysis for a new project is different from changing the disk packs for an operational system. But what about programming? Presumably that counts as doing, but then where should the boundary of decision-making be located? What about program design? Screen layout design? Database design? Data modelling? Can you do data modelling without making decisions of principle? That depends in large part on where you start from and how you organise it.

These are not just theoretical questions. Distinguishing between decision-making and work that implements decisions is a good way of maintaining coherence in any process. It can reveal that (say) a document entitled 'IT Strategy' leaves out some things that really should have been decided, and confuses the picture by including some things better regarded as doing rather than decision-making.

2 There is one striking difference between business modelling and data modelling. For data modelling some quite rigorously defined conventions exist, and it is possible to have detailed arguments about whether a certain model is correct or wrong. Moreover subtle errors in the modelling (eg drawing a double-headed arrow somewhere instead of a single-headed) can lead to serious difficulties. With business modelling the conventions are much looser; if one person believes that a certain model should depict a business in one way, and somebody else thinks the business ought to be modelled differently, there is little basis for showing that one way is correct and the other is not. Since the modelling conventions are not very subtle, neither are the opportunities for subtlety of interpretation, valid or invalid.

3 The same company might well make a different business model, in the style of value chain analysis (say), to compare the operating costs and the assets employed in different parts of the business. The effort of producing this additional model might be justified by the extra insights provided for debates on organisation-wide IT policy.

For a great deal more on the relationship of modelling to decision-making, see O'Brien (*Demands*), pp. 205-286.

4 The breakdown by role suggests incisive ways of appraising any particular model; eg:

'This document is clearly an agenda-setting model, and you suggest that it *proves* we should give priority to new systems for the customer support and training functions. But an agenda-setting model — like any other model — is a description, not a piece of reasoning. It can't prove anything; it merely supplies material for debate. Other evidence may point to other conclusions.'

'Your masterplan model of our whole production process rests on the unstated, undebated premise that all our systems in that area should be redeveloped. Now I either have to authorise enormous investment over the whole area you have modelled, or accept that most of the two man-years work that went into the model was wasted effort.'

'This detailed model shows what happens when we receive an order from a dealer in a foreign country where we don't market our sewing-machines, and we pass the order on to another company that has a licence to make a version of our products under a different name. It is really a development model. But we haven't firmed up our project planning yet. It might be three years before we need such a detailed model of that portion of our procedures.'

'This is a fine, detailed model of our organisation, but I don't know how I can use it. Some parts are stimulating and provocative, like an agenda-setting model. Other parts seem to be a non-technical design for a database, in the style of a masterplan model. Other parts are at the level of a model for detailed development. I'm not keen to use such an incoherent mixture as a basis for taking decisions.'

CONNECTIONS

4. Business Modelling	Business modelling — one of the three main varieties
7. Agenda-setting Procedures	Variety of business modelling mixing debate with description
28. Decision-making as Process	Analysis of the general problems of fitting activities together into a structure
30. Standard Multi-step Methodologies	Standard methodologies that generally contain modelling activities at several levels, and usually produce a masterplan model

30. Standard Multi-step Methodologies

TOPIC

Many consultancies and companies in the computer services industry offer standard, multi-step methodologies for strategic planning of IT. Some of these methodologies have copious documentation, though it is rarely accessible for outsiders to examine. Some multi-national companies have developed their own standard multi-step approaches. Some books describe the detail of a proposed generally-applicable approach.[1]

Much of this material makes quite opaque reading; by generating a fog of detail it may even put you in a worse position to make good decisions about the use of a standard methodology. The warrants in this briefing are offered as tools that help in scrutinising any particular methodologies that may be on offer.

SUGGESTED WARRANTS

The briefing tackles the issues that confront any organisation considering use of a standard methodology — Hill Banksia, for instance, the large accountancy firm with interests in many other professional services besides. To start with there seem to be two main issues: How can any particular methodology be related to others by allocation to a broad *category*? What tests can help assess the *quality* of a methodology?[2] Relatively little has been written about these issues, but when they are tackled, some handy warrants emerge.

Gradations of Starting-points

A methodology largely concerned with the work of developing one system of well-defined scope is plainly in a different category from one that tries to develop a policy for the use of IT in an organisation, beginning with questions such as 'Why are we in business?' This point is easy to state but can be surprisingly difficult to apply when you are faced by marketing brochures of particular methodologies.

A good way of clearing a path through the brochureware is to plot the relevance of any methodology on a continuum of activities ranging from the most high-level reflections about policy through to really detailed programming work. Usually, it is easy to see where a methodology leaves off; the difficult and interesting question is: What decisions does the methodology start by assuming to have been taken already?[3] A gradations warrant, based on the six most typical starting-points, is introduced most easily at the *second* gradation:

- **Gradation 2** Some methodologies *claim* to start off with no assumptions at all, and yet, in fact, do rest on certain assumptions that the methodology doesn't examine. Typically, the examples given in the methodology handbook are 'green field' cases, without any awkward constraints. The business goals formulated lead naturally to the design of entirely new patterns of systems and databases. The methodology itself does not contain procedures for testing such assumptions and taking a different course if constraining factors apply: eg Hill Banksia might be short of money for investment in IT systems, because it has just invested in an expensive head office building; its current systems for billing and debt collection might be in a desperately vulnerable state etc.
- **Gradation 1.** Therefore a truly searching methodology avoids 'green field' or expansionist assumptions, and is applicable to any combination of circumstances, no matter how messy. This is, of course, a very difficult thing for which to make standard procedures.
- **Gradation 3.** Some methodologies, like many at gradation 2, devote much attention to drawing matrices of data and functions, and generating outline system or database designs from them. The difference is that a gradation-3 methodology starts out after the decision has already been taken that some defined area (maybe the whole of Hill Banksia or maybe just part of it, eg human resources administration and planning) should be the subject of analysis, leading more or less inexorably to a database design that integrates everything as neatly as possible.
- **Gradation 4.** Some methodologies pay a lot of attention to procedures (eg what exactly happens when an employee works on an overseas assignment, and receives various allowances for accommodation and transport, that to some extent have to be recharged to a client), as well as data (eg recording the skills of professional staff). The starting assumptions may seem similar to those of gradation 3, but, since the modelling becomes very detailed, the range of the exercise will probably be defined quite strictly at the beginning. Despite this, there is no starting assumption about individual projects or systems.
- **Gradation 5.** With some methodologies the concept of the individual project or system appears at the starting point. The decision has been taken that there should be a new system (say) to produce better statistics analysing revenue by client industry, type of assignment etc, and its scope is reasonably well defined. However, some quite important matters are

still open; in particular, there is no assumption yet about the technology to be used.

● **Gradation 6.** Here there is already a well-defined project to develop a certain system based on certain technology. This is a methodology for system development (as opposed to IM) and outside the scope of this book.

Gradations from Tangible through to Intuitive

A different variable that helps categorise a methodology is the tangibility or vagueness of its content.

● **Gradation 1.** At one extreme are approaches that collect facts and work hard to quantify: 'the organisation's hardware costs have declined from 27% to 21% of total IT expenditure' and 'half the systems analysts have less than three years experience in their work' and '63% of departmental managers are dissatisfied with their IT systems' etc.

● **Gradation 2.** Next come methods with strong fact-based content, but without much quantification. This covers fact collection such as detailed inventories of installed hardware, descriptions of existing systems, analysis of the characteristics of products and services, narratives of marketing history and so on.

● **Gradation 3.** A step along from this comes the concentration on things that are definable but not factual. This includes the breakdown of a business into functions, analysis of data into structures, and so on. The purpose of much of this high-level analysis is to clarify and generate insight, rather than to convey facts that are provably correct.

● **Gradation 4.** Then there are the intuitive, difficult to define factors. This covers items of evidence such as 'I suspect many of the younger accountants will leave soon if they don't get experience of other things besides auditing' and 'The enthusiasm of this manager is the MIS department's biggest asset' and 'Everyone says the interface between the data modellers and the project teams works well; I doubt it.'

Very many methodologies contain something of all these elements, but when you look through their documentation and gauge the way their advocates approach problems, significant differences in emphasis can emerge.

Gradations of Status

Besides starting-point and character of content, there is another way of classifying a methodology objectively. *Status* is a concept best shown by its gradations:

● **Gradation 1.** The methodology is one integrated approach, without much scope for variation. You would normally start at the beginning and work through to the end. Either the whole thing suits you or it doesn't.

● **Gradation 2.** The methodology is one integrated, beginning-to-end approach. But in many places it specifically points out different ways of doing a certain thing, and it contains explicit advice on how to decide which of these ways is most appropriate for your particular case.

- **Gradation 3.** The methodology is a family of tools, based on common underlying principles. They don't form a firm beginning-to-end approach. Some tools overlap; they are so varied that you would never use them all, or even most of them, on one case; you could combine these tools with other tools from other sources.
- **Gradation 4.** The stress of the methodology is on defining certain *general principles* that should underlie methods. This does lead to some actual tools, but the principles are what really count — because they can help you develop your own tools, and appraise those of other people, and design one-off methods for particular cases.[4]

Expressed this way, gradation 2 may sound the ideal. Unfortunately, its requirements are so onerous that hardly any actual methodologies qualify.[5]

Distinctions of Content Planes

As the diagram shows, the documentation defining a methodology may contain material on four distinct planes:

- How to **structure and organise the planning process**; ie identifying discrete activities, and showing how they are related, and also covering associated matters such as who does what, how the planning process is managed and monitored, etc.
- How to carry out the work within each **discrete activity** that is identified in the structure.
- What the nature and format should be of the **products** of the activities (mainly documents — models, matrices, barcharts etc).
- **Advice** on how to make good rather than bad decisions or designs.

The difference between the second and third is sometimes blurred but can be crucial. To define how an end-product should look (eg a data model based on subtle conventions) is to say nothing about the work of arriving at it: perhaps you should make a very rough version first, deliberately ignoring certain complications, and then refine it with successive levels of detail; or perhaps you should start by concentrating on certain key areas; or perhaps you should organise the work in some other way.

The difference between the fourth, advice, and the others is considerable. Take the topic 'productivity improvement'. The methodology may define where in the *structure* this topic is dealt with, describe how to perform the *discrete activity* of dealing with the topic, and may describe the format of a *product* document to contain whatever is decided. But there is no place on any of these three planes for specific *advice*, such as 'use high-level languages, use standard application packaged software, encourage physical exercise at midday.' That is material on a different plane altogether, the fourth.[6]

Standard Methodology: Four Planes of Definition

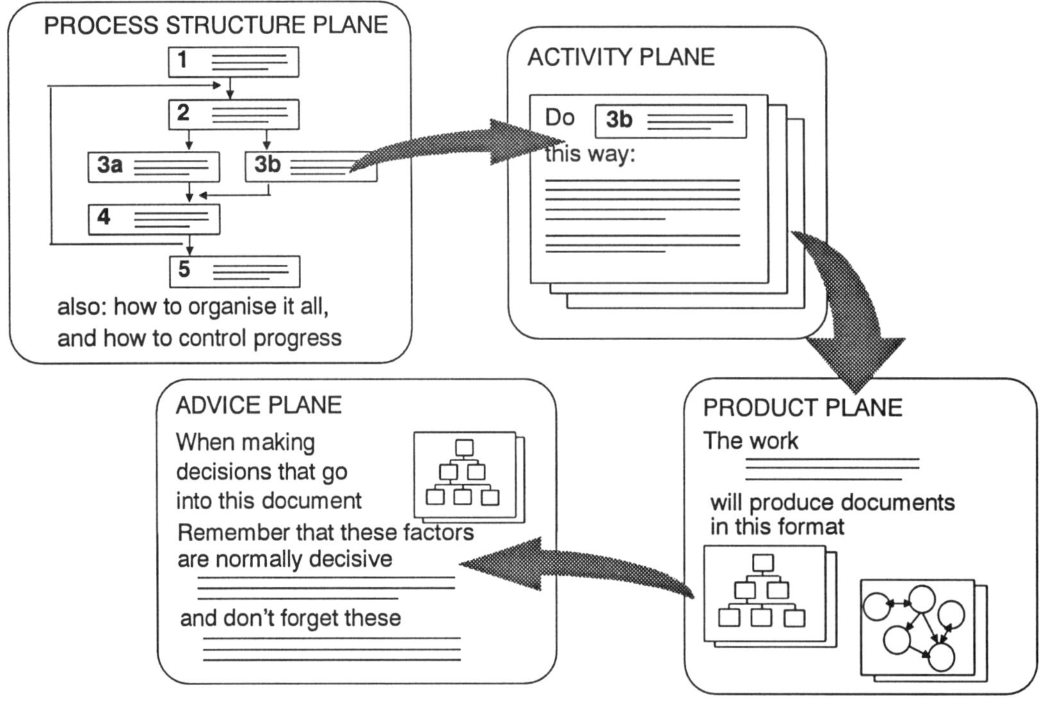

To clarify all this PRESCRIPTION there may well be EXAMPLES

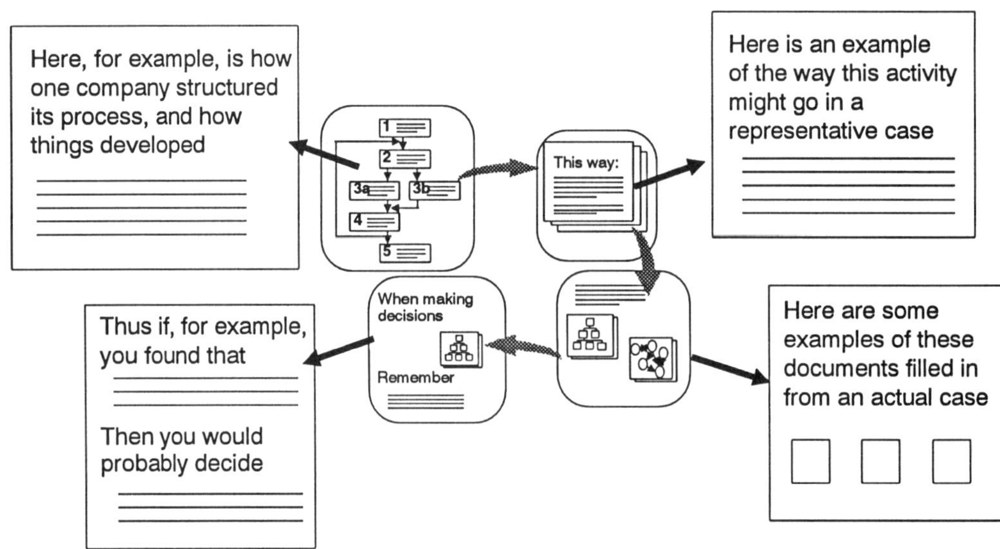

The above distinctions of content provide a further way to categorise a methodology objectively; eg 'This methodology concentrates on products, saying very little about the other planes' or 'This methodology is mainly about process structure.'[7,8]

At this point a fresh idea comes into play. The previous three warrants have suggested ways to categorise any methodology without having to make judgements about its quality. Whether the documentation is lucid and elegant or opaque and confusing, it should be feasible to locate the methodology objectively in the appropriate categories. But this warrant about planes offers both a further way of categorising a methodology and a powerful test of quality.

A prescriptive document that jumbles up material on these four different planes has the weaknessess of any other badly organised document. The reader has to work harder to be sure of what is being said, and not every reader may have the time and energy to work hard enough. People may get the wrong message through confusions of plane: it may seem to one reader that (say) designing a client-server architecture is an essential part of the methodology, on a par with (say) drawing a project scheduling chart, when the author of the methodology really introduced client-server as one example of the kind of issues to be handled at a certain point.

Moreover frequent, ill-disciplined jumps between different planes often turn out, once recognised, to obscure weaknesses that would be apparent if the documentation were more coherent.

Distinctions between Driving Forces

The next warrant is another that helps both in categorising and in assessing a methodology. Most standard planning methodologies include a recommended structure for the planning process. Stage 4 of a methodology might seem a sound enough procedure, as might stages 1, 2, 3a, 3b and 5 taken in isolation *as discrete activities*. But what about stages 1-5 taken together as a whole process? Do they make sufficient provision for free-form brainstorming, weighing of fundamentally different options, prototyping and the like? But how can you compare two or more methodologies in a holistic way, when each is described in perhaps hundreds of pages of documentation? If one methodology offers (say) a six-step approach to developing an organisation's IT strategy and planning its activities, starting from mission statements and working through data models to outlines of required projects and so on, how can you compare it with another in six different steps or another in five steps or in seven steps?

One way is try and find certain driving forces, or underlying assumptions, or principles implicit in a methodology. There are perhaps three main different driving forces that can be detected deep down — most simply expressed as imperatives:

- 'We must carefully model the essential characteristics of the organisation and then move on to work out the most appropriate use of IT for that organisation.'
- 'We must stimulate ideas for new ways the organisation might be structured and do business — rejecting the idea that many characteristics are essential (ie unchanging), and regarding IT as the catalyst for that kind of change.'
- 'We must reject previous mechanistic ways of looking at systems and plans, and take a whole new look at the deeper, human aspects of systems — so that, whatever plans are developed, they generate assent and enthusiasm, and lead to systems rich in human values.'

These may seem to be objective distinctions of methodology character rather than tools of qualitative appraisal, but the practice is different. First, exposing the underlying driving force is skilled work and generates controversy; many will claim that their methodology is excellent on all three of the above, implausible though that may be. Second, this is really a test of *coherence*. A poor-quality, incoherent methodology can often be exposed because its components don't really add up to a mechanism for following any one of these three imperatives, or any other that can be formulated.**9**

Aspects of Structure Clarity

Since the structure offered by a methodology is so fundamental, it seems amazing that many methodologies fail to define properly the structure they are proposing. Here are three sources of obscurity, or, more positively, three challenges to be met:

- **Iteration.** Is it the intention that you complete step 2 definitely, freeze its results, and then start step 3, or is feedback from 3 to 2 allowed? If so, how is it meant to work? Does it only happen if some kind of mistake is discovered? Or is it a compulsory activity? Or what?
- **Transition.** It may seem obvious from diagrams and everything else that step 4 is meant to follow on from step 3. But will the work of steps 1 to 3 put you in a position where enough has been decided to do the work of step 4 properly, ie without taking arbitrary decisions on incomplete information?
- **Parallelism.** You would like to judge whether step 7 is indeed the right place to handle end-user computing as the methodology proposes, but does it really follow steps 1-6 as the numbering implies? Or after 1-4 but simultaneously with 5 and 6 as several diagrams strongly suggest? From its description, step 7 needs to build on some decisions already taken in steps 5 and 6. Perhaps the people working on 5, 6 and 7 are meant to be interchanging ideas every day? Or perhaps the sequence and relations of 5, 6 and 7 are meant to vary from case to case? If the parallelism of activities is left obscure, that should seriously undermine the credibility of the methodology.

Notorious and Inevitable Problems

How does this **torpedo targeting system** deal with the notorious and inevitable problems of:	How does this **standard methodology for IT planning** deal with the notorious and inevitable problems that:
• a shoal of fish in the shape of a submarine? • jamming devices from the enemy? • safeguards against attacking your own side?	• changes of mind or realisation of impossibilities may invalidate decisions previously firmed up, and thus require **iteration beween levels**? • many managers asked to define their requirements have no **informed understanding** of their feasibility? • a **detailed model** of (say) information requirements can depict either the present situation or a future system, but not (except confusingly) both at the same time? • different activities and planning structures are appropriate to organisations in **different circumstances**?

Plainly, it is a necessary but not sufficient condition that all such things should be clear. Only then can the question be reached: Is this an efficient, practical structure, likely to do justice to real IM issues?

Examples of Notorious and Inevitable Problems

If a methodology does have a structure that is clear, then the question is reached of whether the structure is of good quality.

The most obvious test of quality is: Do things get decided in appropriate places? A methodology might deal with the organisational arrangements for end-user computing in (say) step 7. Is step 7 the appropriate place for those decisions? It could be too late, given that the work of steps 1-6 will have already produced decisions that constrain what happens in step 7; or it could be too early, given that the work of steps 8-12 has not yet been done. Or it could be, on balance, just about the right place. Splitting data over databases held at different locations occurs in step 8; is that sensible, given the content of steps 1-7 and 9-12? And so on.

Such questions of appropriate place in the process often turn out more tricky than at first appears. The question whether end-user computing is best handled in step 7 may be unanswerable unless you take account of iteration, ie the arrangements for revising decisions taken in earlier steps.

In many fields an efficient mode of assessment is to step back from the detail and raise certain notorious and inevitable problems: iteration between levels is one. As the table suggests, just as with a torpedo targeting system, it may be effective to ask early on how the methodology stands up to a small battery of tests.[10]

Of the four tests shown, the most exacting is the last — contingency. Does the documentation spell out which parts can be bypassed and which cannot? Does it show clearly how certain parts can be done in several different ways? Does it explain (or at least make apparent) typical circumstances that would cause you to decide which parts to leave out or do differently?

NOTES & ARGUMENTS

1 The books by Tozer, Martin, Long (1982), Gallo, and Burk and Horton are each primarily concerned with describing one specific, general-purpose methodology for decision-making and planning. The books by Remenyi, Keen (1992), Daniels, and Ward, Griffiths and Whitmore each contain a description of a particular methodology among other content. Much of this material stands up poorly to critical thinking.

There is more debate about the issues raised by multi-step methodologies in Briefings 7 and 17 of the companion book, O'Brien (*Demands*).

2 The distinction between category and quality is an aid to clear thinking. Classification in any field is best kept objective: a botanist classifying flowers isn't influenced by how attractive they look; a librarian doesn't use concepts like 'boring' and 'exciting' in classifying books. Appraisal of quality is separate from classification.

Given any standard methodology to consider, it is usually best to start by seeing how it can be classified relative to others. Once its category is clear, assessment of quality is easier. And if it belongs to a different category from what you are after, then you are spared the controversy of value judgements altogether.

The above, though right, isn't definitive. Classification and value judgements can't always be entirely separate. Suppose a methodology has on a certain page of its handbook: 'At this point you must decide which hardware to use. This is very important. And now for something else . . . ' In a case like this, you really have to make the judgement that the methodology's treatment of hardware selection is so utterly trivial that it can't reasonably be said to cover the topic at all. However, apart from such obvious cases, it is best to give a methodology the benefit of the doubt at the classification stage.

3 You may know that a hammer and nail can be used for fixing two planks together or for hanging a picture on wall, but to understand the scope of these devices you must also know that they *can't* be used for fixing curtains to a rail, or a light bulb to its socket. This principle applies *a fortiori* to abstract intellectual devices like methodologies. The zealot for a certain methodology is rarely keen to look at things in that way; hence the need for a warrant.

4 Few pure gradation-4 methodologies are ever described, but Burk and Horton come as near as any. They suggest a four-stage approach: identify the organisation's main items of information (here called IREs), eg a mineral exploration company had 74 (including 'drill-log and assay data' and 'geological samples data'); draw large matrices to relate the IREs to the different people and units that use them; work out the cost and the value of each IRE; decide which IREs should count as *corporate* information resources (in their example 16 of the 74 do). The technique of building matrices of information items and their uses is found in many other methodologies, but the other ideas are more original:

- The stress on the cost and the value of different IREs is interesting, but there are obvious difficulties. The valuing suggested is largely a ranking of relative rather than financial value. Burk and Horton offer a variety of plausible and feeble ideas, but they are really advocating the *concept* of this kind of exercise, rather than claiming to offer an entirely viable method.
- The idea of using the matrices, costs and values in order to segregate the IREs into *corporate* information resources and *other* information resources is refreshing. It avoids the assumption, in many other methodologies, that all information identified must form one huge body to be regarded in an integrated way. Burk and Horton make it plain that they are only giving *examples* of the way this analysis might plausibly be done, and not prescribing generally valid criteria. What is the point of distinguishing corporate and other information? Presumably, the corporate IREs should become an organisation-wide database, whereas the other IREs should not; ie this approach will help you take important decisions on the scope plane. Regrettably, the authors don't quite spell out the conclusions of their logic.

It would be dangerous to follow this book uncritically, and the authors do make disclaimers from time to time. However, for anyone already *au fait* with the tricky issues in approaches to information planning, the general principles suggested and illustrated could be a helpful stimulus towards devising a good approach for a particular case.

5 The content of the standard methodologies used by the large consultancies is rarely published in any form other than the glossy brochure. A minor exception is an article in *Information Systems Management*, Summer 1992, pp. 13-20, by Albert L Lederer and Veronica Gardiner, which describes Arthur Andersen's Method/1. This is a reasonably jargon-free account of one representative and widely used methodology, and it provides a stimulus for thinking about some general issues:

- The methodology consists of ten successive work segments — ten plausible and unsurprising steps for proceeding methodically from general statements about the business through to the definition of a number of separate projects for developing systems.
- 'Because every organization is unique, the team must customize the planning process to the exact needs of the organization.' Very well. Does this mean that some work segments can be omitted, some can be merged, some can be done in parallel instead of successively, some can be done in a different sequence, and other completely new work segments can be added in?
- The article says that some work segments can be omitted, but the other questions go unanswered. The dilemma is rather nasty. If a consultancy offers a methodology consisting of ten rather ordinary segments and allows that they may well have to be rearranged and varied and added to in a multiplicity of ways in order to suit circumstances, then what is offered will be neither very special nor very standard. If, on the other hand, hardly any variation is allowed, a thoughtful critic can easily point out many circumstances where the methodology is likely to be inadequate.

• The only escape route seems to be to *standardise the procedures for matching process to circumstances*: eg in step 5 of the methodology, various data might be collected and decisions on various matters might be taken; then rules might determine, based on that data and those decisions, whether the study should proceed next to step 6A or 6B or straight to 7. That is an outline sketch; any credible methodology along these lines would probably be an expert system. As far as can be seen by an outsider, neither Method/1 nor its competitors offer anything like this.

6 For more advice on physical exercise at midday and related matters see Long (1982), pp. 150ff.

Analysed more carefully, there can be *two* types of material on each of the *four* planes: *injunctions* to do things a certain way ('at this point in the planning process decide your midday exercise policy') and *illustrations* ('you might, for instance, decide that energetic music should be piped around the data centre at noon'). To be intelligible the documentation of a methodology should make clear which parts are injunctions (ie part of the methodology proper) and which mere illustrations (ie typical things you *might* do if following the methodology). Otherwise confusions can arise: eg 'The documentation talks here about Porter's three generic strategies. Does it mean that we have to choose one out of those three, or just that we have to define some such broad strategy, by whatever means we like?'

Yet another complication is that some methodologies are supported by software tools that reduce the labour of drawing matrices and diagrams, and also spot inconsistencies between different items. Describing how to use the software to draw a certain matrix can, in poor documentation, get confused with describing the work that goes into the content of the matrix.

7 Zachman's ISA framework for structuring the documentation products of a project has become fairly influential. It divides all project deliverables over six rows; eg model of the business (owner's view) in row 2; model of the information system (designer's view) in row 3; technology model (builder's view) in row 4. See 'A Framework for Information Systems Architecture', JA Zachman, *IBM Systems Journal*, Vol 26, No 3, pp. 276ff. Also, 'The ISA Lightning Bolt', by Barbara von Halle, *Database Programming & Design*, January 1992, pp. 11-12; and the same column for many months after that.

Questions flood in: Why can't the owner have two or more views — with different levels of detail and/or showing different aspects of the business? Why should any particular number of rows (whether it be six, five or twenty-three) be the right number for all projects? Anyway, what counts as a project? Is the whole framework meant to be applicable to a project to develop an entirely new sales analysis system? Upgrade an existing sales analysis system, with dozens of improvements? Amend a sales analysis system because of changes in government legislation? Develop a whole new set of database systems for a business unit? If the claim for the scope of the framework is not clear, how can anybody judge whether it is good or bad?

But perhaps the most weighty point is that this framework only defines a desirable set of *products*, ignoring the question of the *process* of getting to the products. (It just isn't acceptable to assume that you merely complete one row after the other in a methodical way. Why not? See the analysis of issues of process in this and surrounding briefings.) This is not *per se* a defect of the ISA framework; a framework about the product plane alone is perfectly respectable. However, any enthusiastic claims for the ISA framework which carelessly imply that it does say anything about the other three planes (process structure, activity and advice) should be vigorously opposed.

8 One important category of methodology is primarily concerned with defining a process structure that consists of certain standard phases. Each begins with a certain standard input (which is broadly defined) and ends with a certain output (broadly defined), but what happens within each phase (to get from input to output) is left fairly open. If Hill Banksia had a mainly-format methodology, people could say, eg:

- 'Within the format of the seven standard phases we normally use Anthony diagrams for the content of phase 1, and we always apply some special techniques of our own to handle the content of phase 2, and we are currently looking for better techniques for phase 3.'
- 'In this organisation, the corporate planning department is always concerned with phase 1 of the methodology; it then hands over to the business analysis department, which is always responsible for phases 2 and 3. . '
- 'Hill Banksia uses quite different techniques for planning computer systems from one of its main rivals; and yet both of them, whatever the content of their work, always arrange it in the seven-stage format of the same methodology.'

Unfortunately the mainly-process methodology is often badly described and understood. Documentation often describes the kinds of things that may be done within each phase, and confusion arises over what is injunction and what is illustration.

9 There is a related but different issue: quality of documentation. The important nuance here is that the documentation of an intellectual product (eg a methodology), as opposed to a physical product, has a rather special status. Suppose the documentation for a torpedo-guidance system was unclear or even contradictory about how it dealt with the problem of shoals of fish resembling a submarine. It might be that the torpedoes and their electronics were inherently excellent but the documentation was shoddy and could be improved.

With a methodology the situation is different. Excuses like the following are not acceptable: 'Though not ideal, the documentation isn't all that bad. Admittedly, its chapters don't correspond to the stages very clearly, and many issues outlined in one chapter or stage, are dealt with piecemeal in later chapters, but with patience you will find most things are covered somewhere.' *or* 'Everything is documented in much more detail back at our office, but we don't divulge that, for reasons of commercial confidentiality.' Why? Because there is no separate physical object like a torpedo that the documentation exists to describe. The description *is* the methodology and a methodology with incoherent documentation is *per se* a bad methodology.

10 Here is another kind of battery test. The following is a mixed list of examples of twelve things that a methodology may or may not help with:

- designing screen layouts;
- designing decision support systems;
- strategic information planning;

- finding the right structure for a software development team;
- deciding the terms of reference for the organisation's information centre (ie the people who support and advise end-users with PCs);
- deciding the way to recharge central IT costs to user departments (which may be affected by the organisation's culture);
- spotting opportunities for innovative 'competitive advantage' systems;
- designing the structure of a prototyping project;
- assessing the value of office automation that has little direct financial impact;
- deciding policy for R&D (based on both IT and other technologies);
- setting up standards for project control;
- designing dialogues between a user and an AI system.

This is a simple test of the quality of a methodology. If you can tell from the documentation fairly quickly that (say) eight of these twelve are definitely covered and four are definitely not, that is fine. Suppose, on the other hand, you give up in frustration after deciding that five are definitely covered and one is definitely not, while for two there is pseudo-coverage (eg amounting to no more than 'When deciding/designing X take full account of all relevant factors, whatever they may be . . '), and it is unclear how the other four should be scored . . . Then the judgement of quality is obvious.

CONNECTIONS

6. Agenda-setting Logic	Multi-step reasoning, as opposed to multi-step large-scale planning processes
19. Project and Infrastructure Scope	Infrastructure and project scope definitions — typically the end-result of a methodology
28. Decision-making as Process	Challenges in designing any structure for decision-making, whether a standard one or not
35. Change Management	Human factors in development, that should be fitted into a multi-step planning process

31. Checklists and Weighted Criteria

TOPIC

This briefing is concerned with those approaches that are relatively simple, in the sense of providing a self-contained procedure for reaching a discrete decision, such as which software product to choose.

A standard checklist of points to consider in choosing PC software may seem a harmless, uncontroversial thing, but once adopted, it determines the shape of the decision-making process, if only because it mentions some things to be taken into account and excludes others. So, you shouldn't just adopt *any* plausible checklist-based approach; you ought, first, to judge whether it is right for the specific situation, or whether some other standard checklist might be more appropriate. Thus you have to make a kind of meta-decision about the method to be used for making the real decision. Suddenly everything seems far more complicated.

This briefing explores this and other problems that lurk in the application of checklists and in the related method of choice by the weighting of criteria.

REPRESENTATIVE IDEAS — SUMMARISED

Checklists of various styles can be used to cover many different subjects in IM: checklists of all the points to go over before signing off a statement of requirements, or for carrying out a hardware sizing, or for assessing an installation's catastrophe planning; and so on. This section contains a few representative examples of standard checklists, not for the intrinsic interest of their content, but rather as a basis for discussing the checklist approach *per se*.[1]

A Typical Checklist

The checklist illustrated might be used in a large company to guide choice of personal computer software packages.[2]

Like most checklists (apart from the feeble 'laundry list' of items in no particular order or grouping), this one helps decision-making in *two*

Choosing a Software Package for Personal Computer
Outline of a Checklist of 28 Questions

Performance

Does the package perform the job as you have defined it?
Did you see the package running a similar job?

Interface

Does the package use function keys extensively?
How intuitive are the combinations of function keys used for commands?
Is the use of function keys consistent with industry standards or with other software packages?
Are there short-cut commands for high-speed expert users?
Can you use a mouse?
... three more questions

On-line Help

... five more questions

Documentation

... three more questions

Training

... four more questions

Compatibility with other technology

... six more questions

---

ways: it *raises 28 issues* thought to be relevant, and it suggests *structuring* the evaluation and debate under six headings.

Checklists for More Elaborate Purposes

Checklists can play more sophisticated roles; for instance, in IBM's BSP methodology. Here are two noteworthy features of that approach:

- Checklists are used to structure interviews with executives. The lists include items such as: What are your responsibilities? What are your three greatest problems? What is the most useful information you receive?
- The findings of discussions are also summarised in a standard format that is really a checklist too. The interviews are meant to expose 'problems'. Each problem is to be described briefly under six standard checklist headings: 1 problem, eg 'lack of what-if capability on cost sheets'; 2 solution, eg 'Monte Carlo simulation of costs ability'; 3 value statement, eg 'improve profit'; 4 information system needs, eg 'cost system'; 5 affected process, eg 'finance'; 6 causing process, eg 'administration'.

This raises two new ideas not present in the example of the software package checklist:

Outline of Another Checklist of 28 Questions

Performance

Does the package perform the job as you have defined it?
Did you see the package running a similar job?
Have you evidence that the package will perform satisfactorily at your expected quantity of work and information?
How many of your potential users have agreed that the package will meet their requirements?
Are you taking a risk by being a first or very early user of the package?
Do you know of any bugs?
Does the package make you redefine your view of what the job should be?
Does the package offer any extra functions, that may be relevant later on?
Is the package made unnecessarily complex by the inclusion of many features you never ever expect to need?
Have you checked with the salesmen about new features in new releases in the near future?

Interface

Have you allowed different users with different degrees of skill to try out the package and confirm that they are happy with the interface?
Have you any reason for doubts about the acceptability of the interface?

On-line Help, Documentation and Training

. . . six more questions

Compatibility with other packages

. . . five more questions

Compatibility with other hardware and operating systems

. . . five more questions

● use of a checklist not merely to take a certain decision (eg which package to choose), but also to help **discover issues** that require investigation and decision (eg what problems are troubling executives);

● use of a checklist to structure debate and investigation by **standardisation;** organising material about each problem under the same six standard headings is meant to cover what is important thoroughly but economically, and also allow material about different issues to be collated effectively.

REPRESENTATIVE IDEAS — ANALYSED

A checklist is ostensibly a technique for collecting information, that can form the basis for decision-making, rather than a technique for actually making decisions. But this distinction can be illusory, since a checklist inevitably imposes a certain structure on the problem and makes certain assumptions about the kind of material that may be relevant. The danger is that the structure and assumptions, even if appropriate to many cases, may not be appropriate to yours.

Even Simple Checklists Affect Structure

In practice, a decision taken at the beginning to use a certain checklist (rather than some other checklist or some different approach entirely) embodies a judgement about which topics should be studied in depth and which hardly at all.

Even a relatively simple checklist like that for selecting a software package will affect the way the problem is tackled. To see this, consider the second checklist, which also has 28 questions. The author of this one has different ideas about the way work on this kind of decision should be structured. Thus the choice between this and the previous checklist is itself an important decision; it will affect the attention given to various issues — and thus, very possibly, make a difference between good and bad choices of packages.

BSP Structure

The BSP methodology illustrates the point on a larger scale. Items 4, 5 and 6 (information system needs, affected process and causing process) of the standard format presuppose that the information systems and processes are well identified and fairly discrete. This discourages certain ways of looking at the problems: the real cause of a problem might be that two processes, perfectly adequate in themselves, don't interact properly; or perhaps one information system (eg the costing system) is too big, and would be better split in two; or perhaps the idea of finance being a separate process from administration is a source of difficulties.

Analogous objections apply to the idea that issues can always be expressed accurately in the format problem-solution-value statement (items 1,2 and 3). A set of problems rarely fits into a one-dimensional list without distortion or mutilation: some problems are much more fundamental than others; some overlap each other; some are causes of others; some are related by having the same cause; some can't be understood except as the conjunction of other apparently innocuous causes; some may be problems to one part of the organisation, but their existence prevents worse problems elsewhere; some are only problems in the sense that things might theoretically be better; some are problems in the sense that opportunities for doing things differently can be imagined (though whether they would be any improvement is as yet unknown); and so on.

It can be argued that a really alert analyst will always be able to overcome the crudity of the checklist in order to discover and record the most meaningful facts about the situation somehow or other. But that is

Weighted Criteria: Decision-making Logic

Hierarchical Model of Relative Importance of Criteria/Issues/Factors

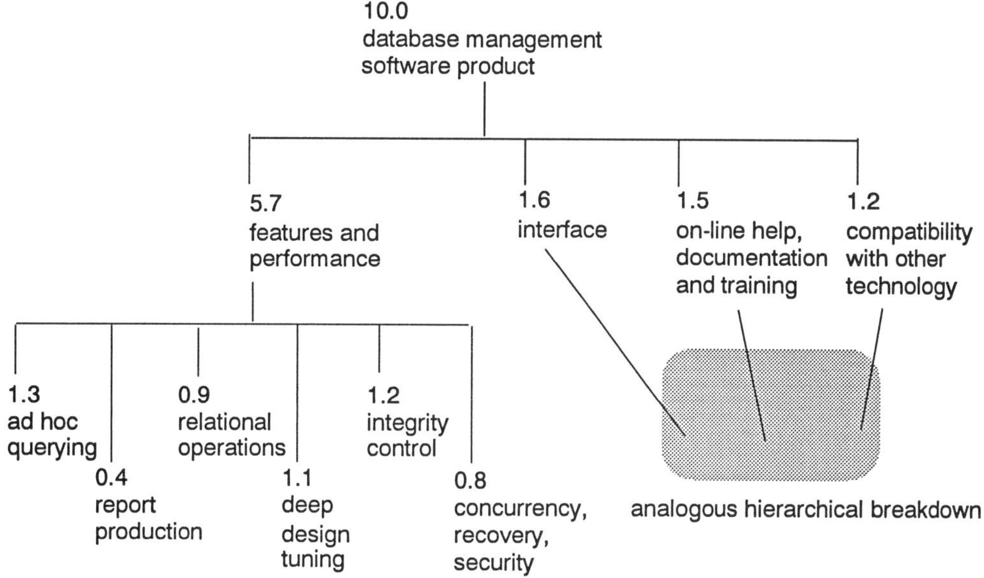

Decision Logic:

1. Score each competing software product out of 10 on each bottom-level item (ad hoc querying, report production etc)
2. Apply the weights (1.3, 0.4 etc), and thus arrive at a score for each product out of 100.
3. Choose the product with the highest score.

Problem

On what basis do you decide the weights? What do they even mean?

---

not the issue; the question to ask of any such checklist approach is whether it will, on balance, make it easier or harder to get hold of the issues that really count.3

REPRESENTATIVE IDEAS — SUMMARISED

Take a different kind of list: of criteria to apply in choosing between several options, with weightings attached to show the relative importance of the criteria. This represents a very explicit decision-making approach.

Weighted Criteria in Software Selection

Mountain Blueberry, a retail chain, is choosing a software product for database management:

- A committee agrees on criteria to take into account. There are four main headings: features and performance; interface; on-line help, documentation and training; compatibility with technology (ie other software products, hardware and operating systems). Under each heading more detailed criteria are defined.
- Weightings are attached to criteria in such a way that the top-level total of all the weightings is 10. As the diagram shows, this produces a hierarchical model defining all applicable criteria and their relative importance.
- Any candidate software product can be marked out of 10 on each one of the criteria at the lowest level of the hierarchy; simple arithmetic then gives an overall score out of 100. If one product's total score is (say) 67.2 and another scores 47.8, the first will be chosen.

Thus, though no product is likely to be better than all others on all relevant criteria, this procedure can suggest the best choice on balance.

Weighted Criteria in Project Selection

Though selection of a software product may be difficult and controversial, the nature of the decision is rather straightforward: given (say) seven candidates, choose the best, on balance. A weighted criteria approach can also be taken to less readily structured decisions, such as deciding which possible projects for new application systems Mountain Blueberry should undertake, and which it should turn down.[4]

- Each project is first scored out of 10 on each of three criteria: *financial benefit, company goals* and *management information*.
- Scores on these three criteria are adjusted by standard weights: financial benefit has a weight of 0.6; company goals 0.25; and management information 0.15. Thus totalling up these three weighted scores gives a score out of 10, the project's *business justification score*.
- Then the project is scored out of 10 on each of two more criteria — *functional risk* (weight 0.6) and *technical risk* (weight 0.4). Totalling these two weighted scores gives a score out of 10, the *technical viability* score.
- Multiplying together the business justification score (out of 10) and the technical viability score (out of 10) gives a *total score* for the project out of 100. The higher the score the stronger the case for the project.

In the previous case of software selection, the purpose was to find one winner. Here the scores are a way of *ranking* projects. A newly proposed project may score (say) 71 and thus be inferior to another scoring 75, but if five other possibilities all score below 71, then (since the company has the capacity for carrying out several projects) that scoring 71 will still have a strong chance of being adopted.

REPRESENTATIVE IDEAS — ANALYSED

There are some awkward problems with the weighted criteria technique. Ignore the matter of whether the issues identified and the weights given them and the marks awarded are sensible or not in any given case. The more fundamental question is: Why should anybody believe that this general format was a valid way of arriving at decisions?

Problems with Weighted Criteria

For convenience, say there are just four main criteria — A, B, C, and D — and one person judges their relative weights to be (say) 5.7. 1.6, 1.5, 1.2. The claim is that a calculation based on the following algorithm will yield a sound decision:

$$5.7A + 1.6B + 1.5C + 1.2D.$$

But suppose somebody else claims that the following algorithm is better:

$$2.9A + 2.5B + 1.8C + 2.8D.$$

How could any arbiter decide which was more appropriate? What kind of evidence could be cited? In practice, all that can be done is to listen to people repeating ever more forcefully that one assessment of relative importance is right and another is wrong. There seems little scope for rational argument here.

This suggests that there is something faulty with the premises of the whole approach, but there is a more radical difficulty. Suppose a third person suggests that the very idea of *adding* scores is unfounded and that an algorithm constructed like this would be better:

$$(3.3A + 2.5B) \times (C + 0.5D).$$

It is difficult to see how anyone could put forward reasoning to demonstrate that this, or any of a hundred other algorithms (simple or complex), was the one most likely to produce sound decisions. If that is so, the logic of the whole procedure is discredited.

Perhaps this argument, however valid in principle, can be disregarded, since the more intricate algorithms are just too fanciful to be credible? But that is not so:

- Suppose criterion C is on-line help, documentation and training. A product that was virtually impossible to learn and use would score very low here, but might score very high on the other criteria. With the classic addition-based algorithm, it could still end up the winner. The way to minimise that kind of anomaly is to *multiply* criteria scores together or divide them or something of the sort.
- Suppose B is interface. It may be thought essential that the product meet some minimum standard (say at least 4 out of 10), but there may also be some level (say 7 out of 10) beyond which a higher quality of interface is relatively unimportant. Therefore any algorithm used should

ensure that a product scoring 5 out of 10 for B gains a great advantage over a product that only scores 3; but a product scoring 9 obtains only a small advantage over a product scoring 7. That can be done but only at the price of considerable complexity.

But once you get into complicated algorithms, it becomes extremely awkward to argue whether one complicated algorithm is better or worse than some other.[5] The question arises whether there may be a clearer and simpler way.

SUGGESTED WARRANTS

A natural response to criticism of checklist and weighted criteria approaches is: But how else could you do it? The best response is to avoid proposing any alternative *standard* approach to decision-making, and to show how different situations call for different approaches.

Distinctions between Checklists

Standard checklists inevitably influence the structure and, being standard, influence it in a way that may fail to do justice to the special features of individual situations. But it is possible to mitigate this problem.

The items in a checklist can be hard or soft. If a checklist is the basis for weighted criteria or any other approach with totalling and calculation, then it calls for rather *hard* answers — ratings on a scale of 0 to 10 (say). But the BSP question 'What is the most useful information you receive?' is merely a heading for a discussion; the response it generates will be a soft piece of data.

Soft checklist items can be divided further between *suggestive* and *neutral*. The item 'Are you taking a risk by being a first or very early user of the package?' has clearly been devised by somebody who believes that being an early user is often a risky, undesirable thing. On the other hand 'Have you checked with the salesmen about features in new releases in the near future?' doesn't imply that anything in particular is good or bad.

Example of a Soft Checklist

One way of reducing the problems sketched in earlier sections is to tend towards the collection of soft information, making the issues raised fairly neutral — but still sharp enough to expose crucial issues. The directors of Mountain Blueberry want to encourage managers in different parts of the organisation to put forward proposals for experimental, innovative projects. The diagram shows how a well-devised soft checklist can shape decision-making.

The checklist does impose a definite structure on the whole debate, but a helpful one, likely to be flexible enough to cover all proposals for innovative, experimental projects quite well.

Mountain Blueberry, Soft Checklist: Decision-making Logic

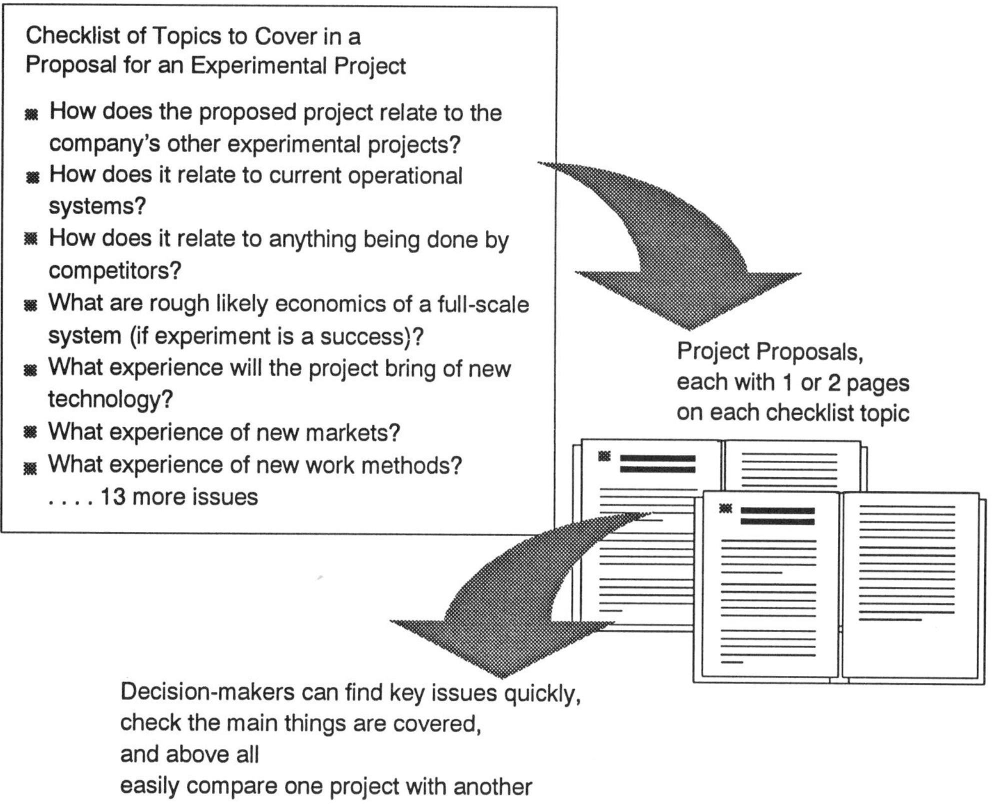

Checklist of Topics to Cover in a Proposal for an Experimental Project
How does the proposed project relate to the company's other experimental projects?
How does it relate to current operational systems?
How does it relate to anything being done by competitors?
What are rough likely economics of a full-scale system (if experiment is a success)?
What experience will the project bring of new technology?
What experience of new markets?
What experience of new work methods?
. . . . 13 more issues
Project Proposals, each with 1 or 2 pages on each checklist topic
Decision-makers can find key issues quickly, check the main things are covered, and above all easily compare one project with another

Example of a 'Narrowing Down' Approach

It is an assumption, and often a false one, that there should be one large process, in which all the issues and possibilities are brought together and processed (with weighted criteria or in some other way) to produce a decision. It is often better to have several decision steps, each narrowing down the possibilities, thus allowing successively more detailed work to be better focused:

● A committee at Mountain Blueberry decides that there is a requirement for a certain broad type of software product: one for managing a text database on PC. This may be an obvious decision to take as a starting-point, or perhaps not: it depends how neatly the requirements within Mountain Blueberry map onto the main categories of package known to exist on the market.

● Next the requirement is defined somewhat more precisely: a product organising texts primarily in hypertext form, as opposed to other styles of text database software. This may be a decision entailing much discussion and assessment of requirements, and analysis of sub-categories of product on the market.

- Mountain Blueberry people then examine some representative products, in order to identify certain key criteria that are *both* vital *and not* a universal characteristic of all packages in the category; it might be absolutely vital that the package read in text prepared in WordPerfect, without loss of formatting (characters of different point sizes, paragraphs with different indentations etc). This decision too may call for well-informed judgement: if 100 million characters of WordPerfect text in complex formats already exist, the formatting criterion is probably truly vital, but in other circumstances it may be too glib.
- The vital-and-not-universal criteria are used to whittle down the range of choice further . . and so on.

The point about this is that you don't always narrow things down in three or five or seven or some other standard number of steps. You have to judge the most sensible narrowing-down approach on the facts of the case.

Example of a Prima Facie Approach

Another way, more appropriate to policy decisions, is to structure decision-making by establishing a prima facie case for one option, that is obvious, plausible and relatively straightforward, and then examine in turn all the main counter-arguments and rival options. The prima facie option may survive or it may be replaced by a better one. Either way, the decision-making approach is reasonably coherent and economical.

Suppose the current systems of Mountain Blueberry run on hardware that is literally obsolete. There is no alternative but to invest in new systems on modern hardware. But how, in slightly more detail, should that be done?

Here is a prima facie case: Mountain Blueberry should install the software of a set of systems already used by another company in the same group, and buy the appropriate hardware. There will have to be some minor changes to these systems. The result will be nowhere near an ideal system. Mountain Blueberry won't be using IT to gain competitive advantage in any meaningful sense. But it will survive. This is the least risky way out of a perilous situation. Make this strategy A, the one other strategies have to beat.

Mountain Blueberry's current system supplier wants to develop a whole new family of integrated systems for the retail business, based on up-to-date hardware. This will provide the ideal system visualised by some Mountain Blueberry managers, and also result in development of a marketable software package, in whose profits Mountain Blueberry will share. Call this strategy B.

Perhaps strategy B will produce systems that bring vast labour savings compared to strategy A? This is investigated and the word 'vast' is found to be unwarranted. Perhaps the hardware costs of strategy B will be much less than with strategy A? No, detailed investigation shows this isn't so. Perhaps strategy B's plan for marketing a package will bring tremendous profits in the long-term? Not proven; the supplier's market projections don't stand up to scrutiny. Perhaps strategy B will bring greater long-term flexibility than strategy A? Dubious; there is no solid argument to support the rhetoric. And so on. Strategy A survives the assault of strategy B.

Then there is strategy C: buy packaged software for some of the systems, but develop specially designed software for the other systems. How does strategy A stand up to that alternative . . and so on.

NOTES & ARGUMENTS

1 The concept 'checklist' normally implies generality. The list is a *standard* list of points likely to be relevant in many different situations. Of course, you can say: 'We are confronted by a really unique situation here. Let us make a list of the points likely to be relevant.' But that isn't really a checklist in the normal usage of the term. The debate around checklists arises from the claim to generality.

2 Inspired by Gunton (1990), p. 200, but greatly altered. The details of BSP that follow are taken from Martin.

3 A third style of checklist demonstrates quite vividly the need to match approach to situation. Some management consultancies will form a judgement on the management quality of a data centre by a method something like this:

- Take a standard checklist of (say) 50 topics: eg backup procedures, capacity planning procedures, financial procedures etc.
- Discuss each of these 50 topics, by raising five standard questions or issues: Quality of the procedure? Adherence to the procedure? Regularity of the procedure? And so on.
- For each of the 50x5 items arrive at a score in the range 1 to 5. The result is a set of scores in a matrix of 250 cells. (For the sake of credibility this tones down reality. In fact, some people produce amazing matrixes with many thousands of cells.)
- The body of figures can then be processed by a spreadsheet to generate an overall judgement on the efficiency of the data centre.

This procedure is meant to help with decisions such as whether or not to change the management of the data centre, whether specific weak spots such as back-up procedures need attention, whether the procedures are good but should be applied more rigorously, and so on.

Apart from any other drawback, this approach may cost so much time and energy that it may not be humanly possible to investigate any other issues specific to the case, or to look from any viewpoint other than the checklist's. Suppose there were an argument (though not an obviously conclusive one) for splitting the main data centre into three regional centres. If so, detailed investigation of current data centre procedures from a monumental checklist might be actively harmful, consuming so much attention that the question of splitting the main data centre never got the attention it deserved.

4 This example for discussion is loosely based on techniques discussed in: Walter M. Carlson, Barbara C. McNurlin, 'Measuring the Value of Information Systems', *I/S Analyzer*, Special Report, 1990.

Anyone who feels sceptical about the example in the briefing text certainly won't like the elaborate weighted-criteria method offered for assessing projects by Sager (pp. 144-150). Similar methods are given by Jackson (p. 105) and Ward, Griffiths and Whitmore (p. 361).

For a typical account of weighted criteria in selecting software, see Rob Gerritsen, 'Selecting a DBMS', *DBMS*, Summer/90, pp. 7-14.

5 Much more could be said against the weighted criteria technique. For instance, what about money? Financial benefit is one element in the project ranking system in the briefing text. One natural approach is for the mark awarded in this section to be proportional to the rate of return after discounting the project's cashflow; a project with a return of (say) 18% should be marked twice as high as one with 9%.

But suppose one tiny project, of five days work, has an estimated return of 100%. If that project is awarded 10 out of 10, then the other two projects will get a mere 1.8 and 0.9 out of 10, respectively. In fact, the marks for almost all substantial projects will probably be depressed in the same way. This in turn means that financial benefit will play hardly any role at all in differentiating projects, and thus it will have hardly any effect on decisions.

Avoiding that absurd result means introducing a more complicated algorithm; eg any return of above 20% scores 10 marks, 15-20% scores 8 marks, 10-15% 6 marks and so on. But this makes things very arbitrary.

A similar difficulty applies to less easily quantifiable factors. Suppose the mark for 'company goals' is arrived at as follows: 10 out of 10 if the project achieves at least three of the 14 company goals, as given in its mission statement (which contains goals such as improving customer service, cutting costs etc); 8 if two goals are achieved and one goal is indirectly assisted; 6 if . . and so on.

But surely all 14 goals can't be equal in importance? What does 'achieve' mean? Suppose many projects aim for the same goals, while others are left out. Why not give extra credit to projects achieving as many as five goals? And so on. The more you try to justify such vague concepts, the more you have to introduce new ones, which also cry out for justification.

Strassmann (pp. 422ff.) discusses some techniques based on the idea of scoring points for various factors, promoted by IBM to help organisations decide between, or to prioritise, possible projects. With laudably clear thinking he points out the shortcomings of such methods that, though elaborate in detail, rest on implausible simplifications and arbitrary assumptions.

In *The Adaptive Decision-maker* by John W Payne, James R Bettman and Eric J Johnson (Cambridge University Press, 1993), chapter 2 contrasts the weighted criteria method with seven variant methods — all in situations where options, criteria and scores are already known. These authors, like many others in this academic field, analyse how human beings do (rather than ought to) make decisions;

they don't discuss whether any particular methods are sensible or foolish. Still, some of their variants could be easier to justify than the classic weighted criteria method; one using the notion of a cutoff score (any option scoring below (say) 4 on a certain key criterion is eliminated, no matter how good it is in other respects) could suit certain combinations of problems, options and scores.

CONNECTIONS

6. Agenda-setting Logic	Multi-step reasoning and techniques at the agenda-setting level
30. Standard Multi-step Methodologies	Full-scale multi-step approaches

32. Standard Approaches and Contingency

TOPIC

Previous briefings suggest ways of deciding the most appropriate approach to decision-making for a particular situation. But they avoid considering one factor. Whatever their intrinsic merits, it may be that approach X is a standard methodology used by 5000 other organisations, whereas approach Y is one that has just been devised. Does that give X the advantage? Or Y?

This briefing addresses two different questions associated specifically with the *standardness* of an approach.

First, how reasonable is it to believe in the concept of *standard* approaches to IM decision-making, that are valid across numerous industries and situations?

Second, a standard methodology can be applied rigidly or flexibly, but almost all proponents of any standard methodology will claim to have exactly the right blend of rigour and flexibility; how can their positions and attitudes be clarified?

REPRESENTATIVE IDEAS — SUMMARISED

This is a contentious area. Some people argue that since strategic decisions about IT are so challenging, you should profit from the lessons of past experience and the investment people have made in thinking ideas through. Others say yes, but there are lots of other human activities where experience and ideas are valuable (running for political office, rescuing a bankrupt business, making a takeover bid etc), but where it is not appropriate or feasible to follow a detailed standard method, so why should it be in this case?

Though the dilemma is plain and important, not much of value has been written about it. The detail of most standard methodologies is not published, so it is difficult to assess their claims and achievements. They are usually presented with rhetoric amounting to no more than: 'This approach aligns IT strategy with the business. It has already been used successfully in hundreds of companies. Let's go.'

A Standard Methodology as Example

A book by Van Schaik presents a detailed account of a approach, which, though untypical, stimulates thought on the question of the status of standard approaches. Here is a paraphrase of its ideas:1

- You could make a generic business model applicable to all companies in a **certain industry.** For example, a generic model for the insurance industry would show how all companies need activities such as deciding a new policy's premium, assessing claims, liaison with agents etc. For manufacturing, a generic model would show the typical activities of ordering from suppliers, making production schedules, issuing components from stores etc.
- Similarly, you could make a generic business model of a **certain function,** such as a purchasing department, human resources department, marketing department etc. This would apply across a variety of industries — insurance, manufacturing, publishing etc.
- Why not make a generic business model of the **I/S function** — valid for insurance, manufacturing, health care, banking or anything else? Such a model need not go into the detail of how software is developed or what exactly a mainframe operator does. It will identify and relate together all the management planning, decision-making and control activities — setting long-range objectives, hardware configuration planning, manpower planning, project scheduling, costing and charging, and many others.
- Van Schaik's book offers such a model — the **ISM Process Model,** developed by IBM. Here is an impression of its scope. The overview chart has 42 processes; each is broken down further into just over 200 process items; charts show how these things are related to each other. There is an inventory of 34 data classes, each of them containing data elements. Within each class, sample (ie several hundred impressionistic, and not complete) data elements are given. For instance, one data class is 'personnel plan'; its sample elements include skills type by organisation, quantity required and when, productivity factors, cost rates, education plan. Within the text the breakdown goes into more detail still.
- Any specific organisation can use this generic model as the basis for its own **I/S management systems**.

This approach is relatively unusual. Most standard methodologies describe activities within a planning and decision-making *process* that has a beginning and an end; to varying degrees they describe the products (models, charts etc) of this work too. Van Schaik concentrates on the documentation *products* of an ongoing management system, with little attention to management processes.

REPRESENTATIVE IDEAS — ANALYSED

Two issues arise: the broad question of how standard any methodology can sensibly be, and the narrower one of how useful one particular variant, the generic business model, can be. Take the narrower first.

Generic Business Models

Any carefully made generic business model can command assent if it consists of just a few boxes on one sheet of paper. But once dozens of items are defined, a quandary arises:

- Does the generic model claim to be a description of the way things really are at some deep level? If so, those companies or departments that are organised somehow differently (ie most of them) do conform to the model *really*. Apparent differences are just trivial differences of terminology and other surface detail.
- Or is the model offered as a prescription of how things *ought* to be in a well-managed business? Then, it isn't surprising that some companies or departments don't conform; some are simply better managed than others.

The trouble with the first is that it gives the generic model a very weak status. Suppose three companies organise themselves in three different ways, but they can all be shown in some vague sense to be *really* carrying out 35 distinct activities identified by the model. What follows from this analysis? It seems to have no decision-making force at all.

With the second, this problem disappears; the implication is that, if a company differs from the prescribed model, then it ought to change to become more like it. But this smuggles in the assumption that a valid generic model containing dozens of activities and hundreds of data elements *can* be reliably prescribed — a large claim surely not acceptable without justification.

Van Schaik hints at the problem here, but statements like 'However, no real I/S organization will have processes exactly like those of the generic model' and 'One approach is to consider the generic model as a target, and migrate the currently installed processes toward the target' only make the status of the generic model more confused.

REPRESENTATIVE IDEAS — SUMMARISED

Almost everybody offering a standard methodology seems to assume that it is a feasible, sensible idea to have such a thing. But this is not self-evidently true. It needs to be justified, and this is practically never done.[2] However, a few writers have taken a more subtle position: standardise to the extent of distinguishing a small number of generic situations an organisation may face, and point out how different standard approaches are appropriate in different generic situations.

Standard Methodology and Contingency

Problem

Situations vary too much, for any standard methodology to be generally useful.

Idea

Define several generic types of situation an oganisation may be in.

Recognise several generic types of methodology.

Decision Logic

Match them up.

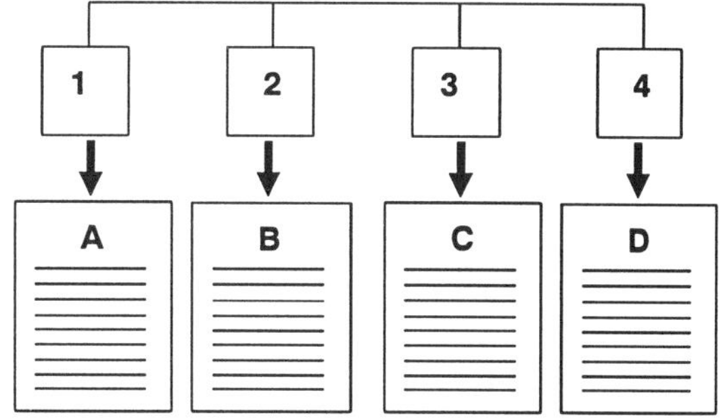

Different Situations, Different Approaches

One article suggests that a company should assess where it stands on two basic issues:

- How fundamental is IT to the business?
- How diffuse is IT in the organisation — in terms of where hardware and other technology is located?

Since the answer to each may either 'high' or 'low', there are four possible combinations. The argument is that the broad approach to planning should depend on which of the four applies: a fairly straightforward, general methodology may well be adequate in a low-low case, but the complexities of a high-high case may need either a non-standard approach or some standard method exceptional in its subtlety. Having established that, this particular article doesn't go much further.

Another article recommends you to start by deciding what the essence of your situation really is out of four generic cases. The key questions are: Is a company-wide (or at least trans-project) view required? (If so) what is the relation between decisions of business strategy and those of decisions of IT strategy?

- **Case 1.** Little integration between application systems is required. The need for decisions that transcend individual IT projects, eg decisions about infrastructures or company-wide procedures, is very limited.
- **Case 2.** The main task is to improve the efficiency of the existing organisation and its structures, products etc — not blindly of course, rather taking advantage of opportunities to automate things better. The key point is that new initiatives of business strategy are relatively unimportant here. The challenge is really: given this complex organism (the business — which will need to be studied in detail), make administra-

tion as healthy and efficient as possible, but don't try and change it into anything substantially different. Improved health often entails increased *integration* of systems and databases, but that is a likely consequence, not an essential feature of the case.

- **Case 3.** A general business strategy entailing a reasonable degree of change and sharp priority-setting can be defined first, and the main task is to develop consistent strategic decisions about IT; eg 'substantially improve customer relations' is translated into 'produce information for quick response to customers' and then 'systems should have interactive ability'. Note that this doesn't entail much interaction or feedback. It isn't intended that anyone should say: 'We've looked into the IT implications of substantially improving customer relations and they are very unattractive; so why not scrap that objective and replace it by one to increase turnover by 30%?'
- **Case 4.** Here, by contrast with Case 3, there is a complicated interaction between business strategy and IT strategy; eg development of new products is a big part of the business strategy, but the new products will be based on advanced information technology. Therefore decisions about technology will feed back and affect business decisions (since any *realistic*, as opposed to trivial, business decisions about new products will have to be based on realistic technology decisions).

It is scarcely credible that any one standard approach will be appropriate for all four cases. Therefore, according to this article and as the diagram shows, the generic type of methodology you choose should depend on the case you are in.[3]

Out of all the books on IM, those that are best on most measures are also those that most stress the need for different approaches under different circumstances. For example: 'Not only do appropriate answers . . vary among companies; different answers and structures are often appropriate for individual units in an organization. In short, there is a right series of questions to ask and there is an identifiable but a very complex series of forces that, appropriately analyzed, determine for each organizational unit the direction in which the right answer lies — for now.'[4]

REPRESENTATIVE IDEAS — ANALYSED

The warrants just given are fine as far as they go. But there is another dimension of the problem to explore. The rest of this briefing discusses people's *attitudes* towards standard methods.

SUGGESTED WARRANTS

Debate about standard approaches is often driven by feelings as much as by reason. It is an observable fact that attitudes differ, and since this matters, an analysis of attitudes is worth having.

Distinctions between Attitudes

Any standard methodology can be applied too literally or too capriciously. If asked outright, almost all proponents of a standard methodology will say that they apply it with exactly the right blend of rigour and flexibility.**5** Since this can't be true, some probing is needed.

To start with, make a broad distinction between *three attitudes*, held by both proponents and opponents of standard methodology:

● **Methodology.** Use a standard methodology — a pre-defined set of actions and techniques. *Claim:* this is an effective way of doing justice to the great majority of all cases where an organisation has to take fundamental decisions about the use of IT.

● **Toolkit.** Have a set of intellectual tools ready: eg the strategic grid, value chain analysis, Elmasri-Navathe conventions for data modelling etc. *Claim:* these tools help with particular aspects of a case; like physical tools, they can be selected for use in any order or not at all according to the case. (A methodology, by this analogy, is more like a complicated piece of machinery that is carried intact from place to place.)

● **Common sense.** Rely primarily on the judgement and habits of experienced people. *Claim:* quality of judgement about the specific case is far away and away the most important thing; generalised ideas are usually of peripheral relevance, or else over-simplify issues dangerously.

This is just a start. The first two attitudes can be subdivided further.

Comparison of Three Variants of the Methodology Attitude

The general **methodology** attitude can be broken down into three:

● The **zealot** works with one detailed methodology, is convinced that it is the best available, is keen to evangelise, and doesn't see much reason to do things differently or do extra things outside the standard approach.

This attitude is only defensible if the methodology concerned really is quite exceptional. If it can't bear all the weight put on it, then the brightest and most creative people will notice the shortcomings and be unwilling to throw themselves into the evangelism. In the long term, only mediocre people may remain.

● Those with the **broad church** attitude are rather like Anglican bishops, prepared to accept almost anyone with almost any beliefs. It is possible to have a standard, detailed step-by-step methodology available and be prepared to preach about it to a receptive audience, but, on the other hand, be quite happy to make almost any far-reaching amendments or extensions, depending on the situation.

The trouble is that if everything about a methodology is negotiable, if there is no way of ever saying that something shouldn't be done because it is against the methodology, or must be done because it is essential to the methodology, then there isn't really any methodology there at all. This can open a credibility gap. People will begin to say that, on the one hand, you are always saying how desirable it is to have a standard step-by-step approach, while, on the other, you are prepared to deviate from your standard at the slightest temptation.6

- The **broker** agrees that every organisation should use a step-by-step IT planning methodology, which is standardised, in the sense that the same basic planning structure is used within the organisation over the years, but argues that there are good and bad things about most of the existing ones. Therefore you should choose the methodology that is most appropriate, and indeed decide whether it should be enforced strictly or flexibly, according to the organisation.

The main drawback here is that to meet the claim of identifying the right methodology for the situation, and recommend how it should be applied, the broker needs to possess a fairly exceptional combination of knowledge and skill.

Distinction among Toolkit Followers

It is worth making a simple distinction between two types of adherents to the **toolkit** attitude:

- The **Swiss army knife** attitude rejects the idea of a methodology with a standard, step-by-step structure, but aims instead to possess a collection of analytic and problem-solving tools, each appropriate to particular types of problems, types of situations and stages in planning. Which tools are used and whether planning is divided into three steps or 31 are matters which depend on the nature of the specific case.

The potential drawback here is the sacrifice of the classic advantages usually claimed for a standardised approach: a familiar structure, defined at the start, so that everyone can easily see how everything fits together; and a breakdown into parts of varying difficulty, so that less experienced people can safely be used to play substantial roles.

- The holder of the **thinktank** attitude goes further and regards tools such as value chain analysis or entity-relationship analysis as relatively unimportant ingredients for success. However, this is not to go as far as the rejection of general ideas inherent in the common-sense position. Rather, it is a choice of a different kind of tool. Generic ways of looking at strategic problems, theories about the role of IT etc (as opposed to specific techniques and procedures) are encouraged. So a fund of semi-codified principles for thinking about IM is built up.

The big drawback with this attitude is that it calls for high-calibre people, and sufficiently subtle management to get the best out of them.

How does this analysis of attitudes to methodologies withstand the Decision Question? Its justification is that it can help you take better decisions on the approach plane, because it will help you process people's claims for their own standard methodologies better. First, there are zealots about; they won't leave you alone, so it is as well to know that other attitudes are possible and to form an attitude of your own. Second, it is good to have some yardstick for gauging the attitudes of other people, that lie behind the words they actually say. Third, it is interesting to assess how successful people are at gaining the benefits and minimising the drawbacks that are inherent in whichever of the attitudes they adopt.

NOTES & ARGUMENTS

1 Van Schaik, whole book (discussion of the status of the generic model around p. 82). The account given in the briefing text is a summary of the underlying logic implicit though not too clearly stated in the book.

2 Nobody seems to have written any journal article along the following lines: 'It is probably not feasible to devise a general methodology for prosecuting any fraud case, or optimising any ecosystem, or making any country's naval policy — except of course by standardising what is trivial and leaving out the tricky parts. Nevertheless, it *is* possible to have a standard methodology for strategic planning of IT, including the tricky parts, in any organisation. Here is why: . . . '

This questioning of premises is relevant too, even against apparently innocuous, standardising generalisations:

- Marchand and Horton, (p. 57, after RH Hayes & SC Wheelwright) advocate that there should be **three** levels of business strategy: corporate strategy; strategic business unit strategy; and (within that) functional strategy, eg market strategy, human resources strategy etc. Why? Why not have two levels? Or four? Or three but with functional above strategic business unit? In fact, why should *any* such structure, however ingeniously contrived, be generally valid?
- Gerstein (p. 37ff.) recommends **four** levels: strategic vision, mission and scope; competitive positioning and strategic goals; supporting strategies; and action plans. He clearly means that these levels should correspond to four main pieces of decision-making that occur in sequence. But why should this always be the best approach in any situation that any organisation may be in?
- Peppard (p. 11) presents **five** 'stages of the strategic planning process': target setting; gap analysis; strategic appraisal; strategy formulation; and strategy implementation. Why should there be any such thing as *the* strategic planning process?

3 Two basic issues: Cornelius M Sullivan Jr, 'Systems Planning in the Information Age', *Sloan Management Review*, Winter 1985, also in Cox's anthology. Four generic cases: Jeffrey E Kottemann and Benn R Konsynski, 'Information Systems Planning and Development: Strategic Postures and Methodologies', *Journal of Management Information Systems*, Fall 1984, also in Cox's anthology. The text of the briefing is quite a substantial reworking of this article. The article mentions particular methodologies for particular cases: Case 2 BSP; Case 3 SST; Case 4 SAST.

4 Cash, McFarlan, McKenney, p. 152. Four corporate environment factors are said to influence the structure of planning (pp. 264-6): the status of the systems manager; the physical proximity of relevant people; the (in)formality of corporate culture; the organisation size and complexity. The interplay of these factors is not discussed in detail, but at least the principle of different planning structures for different situations is established: 'In aggregate these corporate environment items explain why recommendations on how to do IT planning 'in general' almost always are too inflexible for a specific firm. Even within a firm, these issues often force considerable diversity of practice between organization units.'

Many other books, eg Frenzel's, start from the view that well-managed companies generally do everything of importance in one particular way, and all the student need do is to learn what that is.

The methodology delineated by Earl (pp. 67ff.) is interesting because it recognises that different situations call for different approaches. 'Top down', 'bottom up' and 'inside out' 'legs' are to be used in a 'three-pronged attack', where 'each prong interacts with the others'; and 'the emphasis laid on each leg may well vary across firms and over time.' This is a tremendous improvement on the many methodologies based on the assumption that work should always proceed in a top-down, step-by-step methodical pattern. But how you decide the emphasis for the legs appropriate for your case, and how the three prongs interact are crucial questions that Earl leaves obscure.

5 Here is an extract from *Asimov's New Guide to Science*, Isaac Asimov (1987, Penguin), pp. 766-7:

'The spider is born with a nerve-wiring system, in which the switches have been preset, so to speak. A particular stimulus sets it off on weaving a web, and each act in the process in turn acts as a stimulus determining the next response . . The very fact that the complex task is carried through so perfectly and in exactly the same way every time is itself proof that intelligence has nothing to do with it. Conscious intelligence, with the hesitations and weighings of alternatives that are inherent in deliberate thought, will inevitably give rise to imperfections and variations from one construction to another . . The spider builds a beautiful web, but if its preordained web should fail, it cannot learn to build another type of web. A child on the other hand, reaps great benefits from being unfettered by inborn perfection. What human beings have lost in convenience and security, they have gained in an almost limitless flexibility.'

Surely IM too must involve applying intelligence to conscious weighing of alternatives, and require the flexibility to take full account of circumstances. This suggests that an approach depending on preset switches and predetermined stimuli and responses is bound to be inadequate.

The trouble is that people can easily agree with this combination of rhetoric and reason, but still disagree utterly about where the right balance between preset switches and flexibility lies when discussing any specific standard approach.

6 The brochure of one computer services company has a chart showing 24 activity boxes — 'explore opportunities', 'strategic analysis', 'technology strategy' and so on. But if you pick on (say) 'cost-benefit analysis' and ask: 'Why is that box here and not further up or lower down in the chart?' or 'What kind of things are having their costs and benefits analysed here?', there are no direct answers. The response is: 'Well, the cost-benefit analysis box needn't always be there. In many cases it could be somewhere else, or in three different places, or nowhere at all. And the scope of the cost/benefit analysis isn't precisely defined by the standard methodology; you just measure whatever costs and benefits seem appropriate.'

One consultancy has a brochure that starts: 'Good information policy can only come from methodical work. The quality of the method determines the degree of success.' They may do good work there, but the brochure does suggest a certain attachment to standard method over other factors such as personal judgement of situations.

CONNECTIONS

30. Standard Multi-step Methodologies	Tools for assessing any particular multi-level standard methodology
31. Checklists and Weighted Criteria	Separating the specific detail from underlying assumptions in any standard technique, however straightforward

33. Untangling Grand Topics

TOPIC

Stanley Baldwin is supposed to have said that you should never run after a bus or an economic policy, because there will always be another one along soon. He would probably have advised against running after fads in information management too. There are certainly grounds for cynicism: the most fashionable terms are applied so recklessly that they lose any sharpness of meaning.

Even so, untangling the vocabulary of the glossy brochure can still bring positive benefits. What is the difference between change management and sociotechnical design? Is business re-engineering the same thing as process redesign? Could an organisation's IT be highly centralised, yet rich in end-user systems, or would that be self-contradictory? Does strategic information planning lead naturally to strategic systems, or are they two separate topics that happen to have similar names? You will surely be better off for having thought about such questions.

This briefing picks seven grand terms — strategic system, end-user computing, decision support system, inter-organisational system, change management, sociotechnical design and business re-engineering — and untangles them. These are not necessarily *the* seven key terms, but the modes of thought applied to these can help tame any other grand terms you may encounter. **1,2**

SUGGESTED WARRANTS

To start with, most such terms can usually be placed in one of two categories: terms concerned with *application systems* of a particular type, or having particular qualities, eg strategic system, end-user computing, decision support system and inter-organisational system; and terms concerned with *designing and developing* application systems in particular ways; eg change management, sociotechnical design and business process re-engineering.

Charting Four Types of System

In this briefing recognition of the *halo term* — putting a little halo around some concept that the speaker wishes to commend — is essential to careful thought:

- **Strategic system** is a halo term, only used of successful systems. Moreover, the success has to have an impact on other competitors in the market, and some innovation, or at least imagination, is also implied. This may seem rather vague, but, as the term is normally used, the only essential feature seems to be commercial success. Saying that a certain strategic system was a failure would be self-contradictory, like saying that a painting was a masterpiece but trash.
- **End-user computing, decision support system** and **inter-organisational system** are not halo terms, since many organisations, including the mediocre, have them. It would be quite intelligible to talk of a decision support system that was unimaginative and pointless. Unlike strategic system, these three can be defined, at least roughly, by the nature of the application.

Even so, any brief account of the application has to include some *elastic* word or phrase — one that may be interpreted as strictly or idiosyncratically as you please:

- An **inter-organisational system** exists when the systems of two organisations exchange data in any reasonably automated way. 'Reasonably automated' knocks out systems that exchange data entirely by mail, but leaves plenty of scope for debating the question: *how* automated?
- A **decision support system** is one providing information to help managers take decisions — by contrast with a system for routine administration. 'Decisions' is the elastic term. If you key in details of a policy to insure a fleet of tankers and the system responds that, weighing up all the risks, the new policy is very risky, that is surely decision-supporting (eg you may decide to reinsure 90% of the risk immediately). But if you key in details of a new household insurance policy and the system responds that the customer already has a motor policy with your company, that is presumably routine administration (even though you may then decide that the customer would be better off with a 'super-combined' policy, rather than separate household and motor policies). But where between these two extremes is the break-point?
- **End-user computing** is the worst of all. Very nearly everything a computer system does is (or is meant to be) for the *benefit* of an end-user in the organisation. So most interpretations of the term 'end-user computing' restrict it to cases where the user plays some *active role* in the system or (an adjacent concept) has some *discretion* about its use. This narrows things down, but leaves 'active' or 'discretion' as elastic terms.

Ironbark Insurance, Representative Grand Terms

An executive has a personal system storing details of complicated reinsurance treaties on a high-powered PC with fine graphics capabilities — this is **end-user computing**.

The system helps the executive to decide such things as whether to buy more reinsurance on the portfolio of fire policies — thus, it is a **decision support system.**

Having decided, the executive can use the system to send both electronic mail and data about the whole portfolio of fire policies to a reinsurance broker — thus the system is **inter-organisational** too.

The system dramatically alters relations with the reinsurance broker and gains competitive advantage over less progressive fire insurers — it is hailed in business schools as a **strategic system**.

The design, development and implementation of this system were done in ways that conscientiously took account of the feelings and aspirations of all concerned — a fine piece of **change management**.

A human resources expert might praise the system for enriching the content of the executive's job — good **sociotechnical design**.

And this might be cited as a case where imaginative design swept away procedures formerly needing squads of clerks — **business process re-engineering**.

Three Aspects of System Development

The three terms concerned with application system development in general, as opposed to particular types of system, are all halo terms. Each stresses a rather different aspect of the development process. They are illustrated most easily as crude exhortations:

- 'Ensure that the application system you set up is suitable for use by actual humans with all their complex psychology, as opposed to theoretical humans that behave as mechanistic operators.' That is the main stress of ideas about **sociotechnical design**.
- 'Regard the *process* of designing, developing and introducing a new system as a complex one where objective problem-solving interacts with the feelings and motivations of human participants.' That is the main stress of ideas about **change management**.[3]
- 'When designing a new system, be radically innovative and be prepared to make sweeping changes.' That is the main stress of ideas about **business process re-engineering**.

The terms discussed in this briefing can overlap quite readily. As the table suggests, a certain system might even attract all seven.

Relation to Planes of Decision-making

These topics have a richness that usually calls for decisions on a number of planes. The key to rational debate is to see how decisions on the different planes are interrelated. For example, all the following are decisions about the topic of end-user computing:

- **Agenda**. 'We must increase end-user-computing systems (relative to other categories of system).'
- **Matching**. 'We choose this particular database software as the best way of meeting actuaries' needs to access mainframe data for their modelling of life assurance funds: . . '
- **Scope**. 'We will regard the choice of desktop publishing system for our political and economic advisory unit as an issue to be settled in its own right, without reference to any organisation-wide plans.'
- **Context**. 'We lay down the following rules to determine what software development may be done by end-users independently of the data centre: . . '
- **Approach**. 'In our strategic planning procedures we will take the key decisions on end-user computing at these points in the process . . '

NOTES & ARGUMENTS

1 *Downsizing* is another faddish term. If an application system is long-established then it may well be a plausible idea to redevelop it to take advantage of new technology. Nowadays that rarely means getting a bigger and better computer; the attractive approach is to 'downsize' by giving more work to PCs or departmental mini-computers. *Retooling* is an alternative, grander, term for the same concept. Two simple themes are commonly associated with downsizing:

- First, the new system may be more attractive in *qualitative* terms (eg attractive graphic interface with use of a mouse), as well as financial terms.
- But second, there is a danger of underestimating some of the costs or other negative factors associated with downsizing (eg more work, trouble, responsibility and perplexity for the users of the systems).

A good hype-free reference dissecting the subject further is *I/S Analyzer*, January 1990.

2 *Legacy system* is another concept that people tend to agree earnestly is terribly important. First, clear away one distraction. Replacing an old system by one based on up-to-date technology (eg client-server database architecture) may be challenging because the new technology, though bringing great benefits, may be difficult for the specialists to get right. But this can be just as true of green-field cases; it is not inherently a legacy-system question.

There are two characteristic legacy problems of great interest:

- First, a long-established system, based on the technology of a decade or more ago, might plausibly be replaced with one based on up-to-date technology, with much lower running costs (eg lower hardware costs or lower staff costs for data entry). So, if all the most carefully estimated figures show that it is amply cost-effective to go ahead and replace old by new, what more is there to discuss? The problem arises if the system is a huge and fundamental one (eg storing all the policies of an insurance company). The best-guess estimates for a new system may well show a healthy return, but such a great upheaval in such a vital area seems to carry some risk, albeit small, of things going wrong, with disastrous consequences. Is that small risk really acceptable? It is certainly tempting to put it off until next year or the year after.

● Second and different, the functions of any system are usually modified over the years. After every modification, the system becomes less neatly organised, and thus more awkward to modify again; thus successive modifications require ever more work, cost and elapsed time. At some point the system will become so difficult to modify further, that it is unacceptable as a long-term basis to support the work of the organisation. But at what point? You may have to replace an old system by a neat new one at a substantial cost that can't be justified in simple cost-benefit terms, because there are no immediate spectacular savings. The justification is the vague though genuine one that this is the only way of permitting essential modifications, in line with changes to the business in the future, *as yet undefined*. Again, it is tempting to wait until next year or the year after.

These two different problems are often bunched together under the general heading of the problem of legacy systems, but in most cases one or the other is predominant. It is worth being clear about what the problem actually is.

As described, these seem to be particularly tricky questions of project justification. One insight helps tame them: the choice between staying with the old system and replacing it by a new one may be too stark. There may be good intermediate options: alleviate the problem of the almost unmodifiable system by replacing only certain parts: eg only the out-of-date *database* technology, or only the *interfaces* between user and system. A useful article sets out eight generic options: 'What About Legacy Systems?' by Paul Winsberg in *Database Programming & Design*, March 1994, pp. 23-25. In short, the key to a legacy system problem may be to question the *scope* of the problem.

3 Are the definitions in this briefing descriptive or prescriptive? Generally accepted or idiosyncratic? Entirely descriptive definitions of the way these terms are used would be worthless, because they are often used in ludicrously inappropriate ways. That said, most of the definitions do correspond to the usage of these terms by reasonably fastidious speakers.

'Change management' is the exception. This is often defined poetically as 'the ability to see your organisation as a dynamic entity in a constant state of flux', or 'assimilating change into the culture of your organisation'. In the delectable words of the 1992 Body Shop annual report, you should: 'Learn to love change. Feel comfortable with your creative intuition. Make compassion, care, harmony and trust the foundation stones of business. Fall in love with new ideas.' A spoilsport might point out that there could be a contradiction between falling in love with a new idea to raise profits by sacking staff, and making compassion, care etc the foundation stones of business.

Many sensible people avoid 'change management' altogether. However, there is a need for some term that will stand for the management of change in the specific sense given in the briefing, and remain distinct from the adjacent concept of sociotechnical design. Change management is recommended as the least bad term for this role.

CONNECTIONS

34. Sociotechnical Design	Aspects of development
35. Change Management	ditto
36. Business Process Re-engineering	ditto
37. End-user Computing	Types of system
38. Decision Support Systems	ditto
39. Inter-organisational Systems	ditto
40. Strategic Systems and Competitive Advantage	ditto

34. Sociotechnical Design

TOPIC

It is a commonplace that IT-based systems which seemed sensible to their designers often fail in practice through problems connected with human attitudes, motivation and other psychological factors. Some books do little more than repeat this point endlessly in different words, without producing usable warrants to help make better decisions. A good start is to distinguish between issues of *process* — how the planning and design activities for a system are done — and issues of *product* — the nature and effects of the system produced by the planning and design process.

These are separate things. You might have a very democratic consultation process in determining the features of a new system, but the resulting system might still turn out to be unpopular and unsuccessful — for the usual reasons that design by committee often fails. Or you might have an operational system that met the highest human values criteria, even though it was actually designed by just one very shrewd outsider.

This briefing concentrates on the human factors associated with the system as product. Issues of process come in Briefing 35

Any discussion of questions relating to human factors runs the danger of drowning in mere platitudes and exhortations. The briefing concentrates on the issues that are interesting to discuss: those where tradeoffs between conflicting factors have to be resolved.

REPRESENTATIVE IDEAS — SUMMARISED

Much that is written about sociotechnical design is rather overblown for the quality of the analysis offered. This section starts off with a medley of representative problems, themes and issues, as a reminder of what the subsequent, more abstract, ideas are getting at.

A Medley of Examples

'Sociotechnical' factors in system design are roughly those factors that apply because human beings have emotions, motivations and a variety of

Sociotechnical Factors, Representative Examples

Example 1: intrusion into a subordinate's PC or VDU	theoretical gain in control may be outweighed by subordinate's resentment
Example 2: detailed performance recording and analysis	may lead to excuse-recording and neglect of service intangibles
Example 3: multiple functions in one job, for efficiency and job-enrichment	may make people work in ways that don't suit their psychology and talents
Example 4: automate away both drudgery and brain-work	may need entirely new people with the right psychology and talents for the new job

other psychological properties. Here (also summarised in the table) are some examples of typical issues.

First, on a purely rational view, it may seem a good idea for the computer periodically to flash onto the screen of a data entry operator: 'Your work-rate is below average.' Or the screen of a manager's PC might be made to show exactly what a secretary is doing on a PC in the next office, but not vice versa. Or the editor of a newspaper might be able to flash comments directly onto the screen of a journalist: 'Opening paragraph lacks punch.' Any of these might be supported on grounds of control and efficiency — correctly if the people involved were emotionless role-players in an administrative machine. But in real life, people's negative feelings at being subjugated in these ways may have greater weight than any positive advantage.

Second, new systems may generate detailed information about the performance of (say) a technician or salesman who travels about. But this may encourage people to keep private diaries to defend themselves, if the figures are unfavourable: 'There was a traffic jam here; somebody was changing a nappy there; I had to mend a fuse for the customer somewhere else.' Moreover, systems recording such work quantitatively can work against quality of service. Suppose a large retailer of electrical goods measured the work of delivery and installation staff. The way for an employee to maximise throughput would be to hand the VCR over in its box, and only actually install it if the customer asked — as opposed to (say) volunteering to install the VCR, demonstrating how to use it, untangling wires to reinstall the Nintendo already attached to the TV set, explaining patiently why it isn't possible to record Nintendo pictures on videocassette etc.

Third, suppose the current system is as follows: Yvonne takes orders over the phone, and passes the details to Zelig; Zelig keys order data into the computer system to check availability or suggest an alternative; Yvonne phones the customer back to confirm the order. Why not have a system where all three things are done by one person? It seems likely to be more efficient and also job-enriching. Yes, but some extroverted people like Yvonne love talking to people over the phone, and hate working with machines, whereas with some intraverted people like Zelig it is the reverse. Thus it is by no means self-evident that changing the present system would be advantageous.

Fourth, American Express is said to have developed a system for controlling problem accounts, that takes much of the drudgery but also much of the brainwork out of the process. Is this taking a purely rational view, ignoring sociotechnical factors? Won't the account analysts feel that their work is impoverished, over-automated and so on? Not necessarily; the company is hiring different kinds of individuals as analysts — instead of people good at number-crunching and applying complex rules, people skilled at dealing with customers; ie presumably, people good at lulling a customer into acknowledging transgressions, good at explaining very politely that the company may have to take legal proceedings etc.**1**

This last example goes further than the others, because it shows how sociotechnical factors are not merely things it is wise to take notice of (like the weather or the laws of the land). They can be complex variables in the decision-making process that throw up new options for choice.

Pava and Sociotechnical Design

A book by Pava has been quite influential in establishing the place of sociotechnical factors in decision-making. Here is an outline (heavily paraphrased and with added examples) of its most interesting argument:

- In describing any **routine office system** (eg handling straightforward motor insurance claims) you can map out all the different actions and processing steps that normally take place, including any choices or judgements made at various points (eg 'Is there any particular reason to be suspicious of this claim?'). This can be accompanied by fairly firm statements of who is responsible for what. You can describe the present system in this way, but also various possible future systems to choose between. This process of description and decision-making is analogous to planning the configuration of machines in a factory.
- But a **non-routine office system** (eg handling complicated, one-of-a-kind, insurance claims for ships and aeroplanes) can't be described adequately in the same way, because much that happens can't be readily expressed as specific processing steps or defined choices or clear responsibilities.
- You could **try to reduce** non-routine systems to the terms of routine systems. Many IT systems of the seventies and eighties attempted to systematise what had previously been flexible. But in the long run that approach doesn't work, is not necessarily conducive to efficiency, and makes people feel that the value of their job is reduced (causing them to become sullen and unco-operative and so on).

● Part of the solution is to use much **subtler concepts in describing** systems and possible systems; eg mapping out 'deliberations' (as opposed to firm decision-processes) and 'discretionary coalitions' (as opposed to permanently defined hierarchical functions). The analytical concepts can be made quite subtle; eg within any deliberation various roles are available: a person might be responsible, or consulted, or informed, or approve.
● Another part of the solution is to identify specifically the **human values** that seem relevant. Here are six generic features that (research suggests) make most humans feel that a certain job is worth doing well: autonomy and discretion; learning on the job; variety; exchange of help and respect with other people; sense of meaningful contribution; prospect of advancement or at least attractive future. These apply even in routine systems; in less routine cases you can employ more sophisticated analyses of the different values held by role-players.
● In summary then, you should use a rich palette of concepts to describe the systems you are deciding about and to identify the sociotechnical factors involved.

Walton: Compliance and Commitment

A book by Walton introduces an interesting distinction between *compliance and commitment*:
● If a factory employs 500 people, who all perform rather straightforward, unvaried, undemanding tasks, a certain degree of **compliance** is needed, but no more; even if all 500 suddenly became very enthusiastic and committed, the improvement in the factory's performance would probably be rather small.
● If a car showroom employs ten salesmen, then the more **commitment** they have the better. A substantial increase in commitment can lead to a substantial increase in profits. In this context, 'commitment' stands for overlapping factors such as: enthusiasm; keenness to find new angles; hard work; ability and energy to treat each case separately; willingness to make extra efforts.
● Commitment may sound a good thing to maximise, but that isn't so. In the hypothetical factory, workers who are so highly motivated that they keep trying out new angles may be less effective machine-operators than those who merely comply. In the car showroom, excess commitment may lead to an undesirable lack of compliance with company policy about administrative procedures and honesty. You really need to find the **balance of compliance and commitment** that is right for the specific situation.
● All this would be so even if there were no such thing as IT. But **modern IT reinforces the distinction**. It can alter the compliance-commitment balance *in either direction*. IT *can* be used to make work more routine, efficient and cost-effective than it used to be, and reduce the dependency on commitment. But it can also be used to enrich people's work, and

enlarge their scope for discretion, and free them to take on more and more responsibility — things that will only work with increased commitment.

● This **raises the stakes** for decision-makers. It may be quite sensible to introduce more rigorous, closely-defined systems — but only if you believe that people will happily comply with them, and any consequent loss of commitment will have no effect. Or it may be good to introduce systems giving people increased powers to search out information from databases and make their own judgements about it — but only if the people concerned are competent and committed enough to make a success of it.

Mrs Fields Cookies

Mrs Fields Inc, a chain of cookie stores, provides an excellent example of these themes.[2] Here is a five-point paraphrase of the way its managers decided things:

● 'We want to emphasise service factors: friendly staff, cheerful decor etc. Admittedly, everybody else says that too, but we really mean it. To achieve it we will make sacrifices on other fronts.'

● 'We can't afford to hire the best managers (ie, best educated, most experienced etc) for our cookies stores, because they can get higher salaries at fast-food stores, that have a much higher turnover than us — since they sell higher-value items.'

● 'Therefore we will hire store managers who are strong in people skills and thus capable of providing good service — but (since they can't command top salaries in the job market) are probably quite weak in management qualities such as administrative efficiency. These people must have strong commitment above all to customer service; for most of the other managerial functions only compliance will be required.'

● 'Therefore to see that the administration of the business doesn't collapse, we will set up very detailed computer systems that take all the initiative out of administration and monitor each store's progress in a very intrusive manner. Managers must just comply with these systems.'

● 'Some of the brainier existing managers will find the new systems take all the skill and interest out of their jobs. They can leave. Our policy is to have store managers who are strong in people skills and perhaps not much else.'

If this account is true, it shows a company taking account of sociotechnical factors quite intelligently. To see this, imagine how it might conceivably have got the balance of compliance and commitment *wrong*:

● by following the business strategy defined by the first three points above, but then — uncritically following fashionable ideas — building systems that made the job of the manager too 'enriched' for the chosen type of person to handle;

● by developing the systems that monitored stores intrusively, without thinking through the link with policy on hiring managers, and thus missing the key point about finding managers with the right mix of commitment and compliance;

● by carrying through all five points, but also having systems so intrusive that they require compliance, rather than commitment, on the people side too; sending out hourly instructions to stores on how much to bake at a time is one thing; but a system for generating statistics about customer wait-time — in shop or telephoned orders — could well topple over into destruction of commitment towards service quality (for the reasons given earlier).

REPRESENTATIVE IDEAS — ANALYSED

As on many topics, critical thinking about the pronouncements in certain books can be a quite efficient way of deepening insight into the real issues.

Pava: Critical Thinking

As presented in Pava's book the firm distinction between routine and non-routine office systems seems rather odd. Surely even a routine system can benefit to some degree from the richer description and recognition of sociotechnical factors. It seems better to think of a continuum of possible cases, rather than a firm distinction.

This makes it easier to see that Pava is really attacking a straw man. Of course, there is no sense in designing systems that take no account whatsoever of any sociotechnical factors. The interesting issue is *how far* to go in studying them and how much weight to give them. The approach given in the previous section is plausible enough as it stands — because it is only an outline. But how deeply need people's roles in deliberations, and their drives and motivations be analysed? Surely it all depends on the situation:

● Be economical and elegant in whatever descriptive work you do: select and home in on what seem to be the areas fundamental to the system's success; don't be shy to be subtle, but only if it is really necessary.

● But shrewdly allow some margin of extra detail — for two reasons: you may be mistaken about what actually matters most *and* you may want to avoid offending people who feel they should be influential.

Walton: Critical Thinking

Walton's book does totter on the verge of idealism occasionally, but on the whole is far better than others in a platitude-infested field at showing how different factors may have to be traded off.

As the material in the previous section shows, IT can eliminate human drudgery, but things are more complex than this. Sometimes new IT systems deskill people's jobs, making them duller and less satisfying than they were before. But in other cases, IT systems go further than just automating what was drudgery; they actually enrich jobs and thereby increase performance and commitment. There is usually a variety of different ways of designing any new system. Some possible designs are bound to score better than others on the deskilling-enriching scale. Should design *always* maximise job enrichment?

Some books do seem to suggest that you should always design systems to create the absolute maximum of job interest and similar human values, whatever the other factors may be. This seems too glib, because it ignores all other considerations — cost for example. Who wants an enriched job with a company that goes bankrupt because of its extravagant investment in computer systems?

Or can it be argued that there is no conflict in practice, because systems providing the richest jobs are usually the most cost-effective systems too? Such wishful thinking is torpedoed by Walton's compliance-commitment distinction.[3,4]

SUGGESTED WARRANTS

This section provides an example warrant to suggest more vividly how the compliance-commitment distinction can influence decision-making.

Examples of Compliance and Commitment

Two hypothetical companies each set up an electronic mail facility.

- At *company A* a large part of the traffic turns out to be demands and exhortations down through the hierarchy and **compliant** responses in the other direction.
- At *company B* people are encouraged to send spontaneous, **commitment**-enhancing messages all over the organisation, often bypassing direct supervisors; eg sudden claims for a pay rise, or innovative ideas, or invitations to the chief executive to visit a branch.

If you are considering any kind of system for communicating within a certain organisation, it seems prudent to have a view on how much compliance and how much commitment it should further. That may well influence the way the system is designed and run.

Expert system technology is another rich field for such quandaries:

- *Company A* has an expert system that follows certain rules to decide automatically how much of which product to reorder and when. The people who formerly made reorder decisions now switch off their initiative and comply with the system. Any overriding of the system's recommendations is frowned on, even if apparently advantageous. Thus compliance is stressed over commitment.
- *Company B* has an expert system for reordering that is much the same as A's, except for one big difference: the reorders recommended by the system are regarded as a kind of minimum strategy. The person reordering is supposed to take account of them, but is encouraged to try to do

better — modify them by personal hunches and knowledge of factors not allowed for by the system. Since this is felt to be an interesting and rewarding task, commitment is demanded and reinforced.

It is easy to drift into the assumption that B's expert system is better, but that is not proven. Maybe B's system can only work if more-skilled, more-expensive people are employed. Or maybe the beauty of A's system is that it frees people to spend time on other tasks far more satisfying than deciding reorder quantities.

One corollary of all this is that judgements may have to transcend individual systems. If people are encouraged to make hierarchy-busting use of the e-mail system, maybe it is inconsistent to impose tight control on their discretion to determine reorder quantities. Or maybe not; perhaps the first could be a harmless concession with little practical effect, cunningly made so that people accepted the second, the one that really counted. At any rate, that is the kind of factor-weighing called for in decision-making.

That is at the macro-level. There are also interesting ramifications several levels deeper. If the system designers are competent, the expert systems at companies A and B ought to differ in one crucial respect:

- Company B needs a system with a strong 'explanation' facility — the part of the system that explains the logic behind the recommendations. Otherwise a person at B is not well placed to understand, override and improve the system's recommendations. But at A there is no such need.
- An explanation facility can easily be the most complicated and thus expensive part of an expert system to build. It is difficult to program the machine to *select* the parts of the reasoning a human will find most relevant; probably the reasoning has to be displayed on a screen using colour and graphic shapes . . Therefore although B needs to make a large investment here, A does not.
- Therefore when A and B are considering the shape, scope, costs etc of their expert systems, they need to bring sociotechnical factors, such as compliance and commitment, into the same debating process as the feasibility of major system features such as explanation facilities.

NOTES & ARGUMENTS

1 References for the four points in this section: Karen Nussbaum, 'The Case of the Omniscient Organization', in Harvard Business Review (1991), p. 109. Walton, pp. 169-170. Walton, p. 22. *The Economist*, 1 August 1992, p. 53.

These are examples of *tricky* sociotechnical issues. Other matters sometimes raised under this heading, though important, call for little or no discussion. There are two main headings:

- **Design competence.** Some writers point to cases like the infamous system of the London Ambulance Service, where an increased level of automation reduced operators' flexibility in emergency cases, with disastrous consequences. Lewis (p. 163) gives this as an example of 'ignoring human factors during design of the system', since (if the system has been fairly described) it is nothing but an example of *idiotic* system design. There is little to debate about this or similar cases, since the correct policy is obvious: avoid incompetent system design.

● **Detail competence.** David B Paradice and James F Courtney (in Carey's anthology, p. 95) list 15 psychological biases in the way managers use a management-information system: being unduly influenced by data presented first, or by the ease of recall of a piece of information, or by data redundancy . . . and so on. If all managers were truly rational, such things should not occur; but, according to this research, they do. Therefore a design for any such system should not only supply correct, convenient, useful information to the right people, at the right time; it should also allow for these psychological biases. Much similar work has been done on the design of user interfaces to systems. Again, there is little to debate here, since it plainly is a sensible thing to take account of such detail in system design.

It is obvious that you should try to avoid macro-level incompetence and try to design micro-level detail competently. This briefing concentrates on more interesting sociotechnical issues, where confident, general advice is much harder, since tradeoffs are involved.

2 Walton, pp. 26-8 and (case study) pp. 34-46. The examples have been devised for this briefing and the Mrs Fields case study has been reorganised. This is a gem of a case study, far and away the best to be found in all the books about IM listed in the bibliography. It is almost unique in describing decisions that took account of constraints and tradeoffs.

3 It is one thing to judge that commitment (as opposed to compliance) is not vital to a certain task, and therefore need not be stressed; it is something else to undermine commitment as a deliberate act of policy. At one time the British Admiralty took the view that if dockyard workers were too committed to the ships they built, they would take too much trouble, and costs would go out of control. So it was decided that the *Devonshire* should be built at Chatham, Kent; the *Kent* at Portsmouth, Hampshire; and the *Hampshire* at the other end of England, on Tyneside. This policy worked all too well: when the *Kent* could not attain her designed speed, the Chatham people were scathing about the quality of the work done at Portsmouth. The policy was reversed for a later generation of 'County' class ships.

4 A much-cited book by Zuboff develops points similar to Walton's, but much less cogently. If you like the idea of words like 'informating', then this is the kind of book you will like. Its main burden, never quite stated clearly, is this:

● It is natural to use IT to automate certain work hitherto done by people—just as you might replace one machine in a factory by a less expensive or more reliable or faster machine. But people may become distressed under a new, more automated system — feeling more like cogs in a machine, being more strictly controlled either by computer or supervisor, having less scope for human contact, application of skill, exercise of responsibility etc.

● On the other hand, a new system may have pleasing effects. It may bring release from drudgery, better access to wider information, enrichment of work, broadening of responsibilities and more identification with a team.

- A system with strong positive results of the second kind can have quite complex implications. Somewhat anarchic or revolutionary consequences may ensue from an undermining of established patterns of authority; on the other hand, a virtuous spiral of learning and improvement may be triggered off.
- Conclusion . . That is a problem. The *logic* of the book points towards some rather tricky tradeoffs, but they are never spelt out; the *tone* of the writing suggests strongly that you should always try to maximise positive job-enrichment aspects, no matter what other factors may exist.

This calls for application of a certain tool of critical thinking: What is the *status* of an injunction to enrich people's jobs as much as possible?

- Is it an **ethical** injunction? Is it like saying that you should never design systems with multi-coloured data entry screens, on the grounds that this is unfair to potential employees who may be colour-blind, and discrimination against handicapped people is morally wrong?
- Or is it an injunction of **enlightened self-interest**? Is it like arguing that you should have a company crèche, on the grounds that it will bring benefits that, even if only in the very long run, will outweigh the expense and make it a good investment?

If the injunction is an ethical one, then it is meant to be obeyed even if that costs you money; that is the nature of ethical injunctions. Suppose the job-enriching systems cost so much that your business makes losses, and you have to put half your employees out of work; should you carry on obeying it? If that is too absurd, where do you draw the line?

If the injunction is one of enlightened self-interest, then, if valid, it should be capable of justification. How? Perhaps by discussing cases (real or hypothetical) where a company has some perfectly adequate, cost-effective option available, but deliberately chooses a more expensive, job-enriching option, whose extra costs are not obviously justified — in the expectation that this is a better buy in the long term. But this kind of analysis is never presented in Zuboff's book and similar writings.

CONNECTIONS

10. Learning and Historical Themes	Learning and successful sociotechnical design
15. Matching through Charts	Charting the possibilities of electronic forms and workflow systems exposes possibilities for new roles for office workers
16. Matching through Aspects	Groupware, a broad concept best analysed into aspects, tends to prompt new roles, rather than automate old roles, for the workers in a group
22. Evolutionary Development	Ideas for project-structuring to achieve, among other things, good sociotechnical design
35. Change Management	Taking account of human factors to carry out projects effectively — including, but not only, achieving good sociotechnical design
36. Business Process Re-engineering	Job enrichment — one important strand

35. Change Management

TOPIC

This briefing discusses decisions about organising people's involvement in the process of deciding about change.

In the feminist book *You Just Don't Understand* Deborah Tannen advances the thesis that while most men mostly use conversation to give a report, women use it more often to gain rapport, as a bid for understanding or a statement of sympathy. However that may be, a less sweeping point is sure: there is often more to communications between humans than just the explicit content — and this brings complications.

The quality of communications between people engaged in the decision-making process can create or reinforce or destroy *commitment* to the decisions reached. This in turn can affect the *success or failure* of the decisions.

But a decision-making process that maximises commitment (eg by keeping everybody thoroughly involved, and only moving onward when consensus is reached) is often far from the most reliable way of arriving at high-quality decisions. But . . . This briefing grapples with that awkward tangle.[1]

REPRESENTATIVE IDEAS — SUMMARISED

This section summarises a few representative ideas about the management of change. As they stand, some seem vulnerable to the Decision Question. But the notion of tradeoffs can be introduced.

Nine Feelings and Four Factors

One piece of analysis presents *nine different feelings* associated with resistance to change.[2] They are shown in the diagram.

Four broad organisational factors are said to cause some or all of these nine different feelings:

- **Departmental boundaries.** New systems may destroy or weaken the

Resistance to Change: Nine Feelings

'I resist the new computer system because I feel . . .'

'that I shall be replaced by a machine'

'that I shall perform badly with the new system'

'that I shall have less control over my own work'

'that my self-esteem or image in others' eyes is threatened'

'that I just don't understand the new system'

'reluctant to abandon the security of established systems'

'that it is being forced on me by others'

'reluctant to replace established personal relationships by different or fewer relationships'

'afraid of the unknown in a general kind of way'

---

boundaries of existing departments, set up new boundaries and blur and confuse boundaries in general.

- **Informal structures.** Ditto — for informal communication channels.
- **Organisational change attitude.** The organisation as a whole, but particularly top management, may manifest a distrustful attitude to change, perhaps regarding a new IT system as no better than a necessary evil.
- **Method of introduction.** The change may be introduced in a tactless, domineering way causing fairly predictable negative reactions among those affected.

User Involvement Desiderata

Another writer discusses four desiderata for the involvement of user (ie non-IT) people in decisions and design for new computer systems.[3]

- **Typical users.** The people chosen for involvement should be typical — not exceptionally talented or particularly concerned with untypical departments or products.
- **Knowledgeable users.** Taken as a whole the people chosen for involvement should be thoroughly knowledgeable about the business area and its issues — not discovering things about it themselves.
- **User perspective.** The choice of people and the style of procedures adopted should ensure that users retain a perspective as users — rather than adopt the attitudes and viewpoints of IT specialists.

● **Active involvement.** The choice of people and the style of procedures adopted should ensure that users either possess or develop a realistic awareness of the technology's possibilities. They should contribute actively to development of ideas and decision-making; they should do more than just answer questions and check for mistakes in other people's designs.

These seem all very desirable and necessary, but, as the writer points out, in practice they can be contradictory:

● 'Typical users' implies the inclusion of some with limited experience or competence, but 'knowledgeable users' implies concentration on the (untypical) more experienced and articulate.

● 'Active involvement' is not logically incompatible with 'user perspective', but in practice very few individuals will meet both requirements, and one who does may be far from a typical user.

Plainly, the task is to find the approach that, on balance, in the circumstances, forms the best tradeoff between these conflicting desiderata.

Complexity-Commitment Tradeoff

Another book identifies four different general styles with respect to any kind of management, not just IM: exploitive-authoritative; benevolent-authoritative; consultative; and participative. But these are less four discrete options than points across an authoritarian-participative continuum. There is a tradeoff:

● **Problem complexity.** The most efficient way of solving complicated problems, requiring many disparate pieces of data to be fitted together in intricate, subtle ways, seems to be to allow a small group of appropriately qualified people to master-mind the collection of data, and fit it together themselves in a decision-making style towards the authoritarian end of the continuum.

● **Commitment importance.** But the participation, assent and commitment of those outside a core of decision-makers is generally necessary *to some degree*. The greater this degree in any particular situation, then the more reason to push the style down the continuum in the participative direction.[4]

The best way of resolving this tradeoff will vary from case to case.

REPRESENTATIVE IDEAS — ANALYSED

This section suggests some ways of working up the above ideas into a more incisive form, suitable for generating options and producing clear decisions.

Analysing the Nine Feelings and Four Factors

At first glance the nine feelings and four factors seem rather platitudinous: you should try and avoid all these bad things — of course. But critical thinking can yield benefits.

The first item is reasonably coherent — granted that it is possible for one person to have several of the nine feelings simultaneously. The four items that follow stand for threats that may generate any of the negative feelings. But a more fruitful attitude to these four is to see them as factors that may generate *either* negative or positive feelings according to circumstances. Some lively, imaginative, go-ahead people may be delighted that the old departmental boundaries and informal structures are being reshuffled; moreover, if the organisation's attitude to change is coherent, realistic and energetic and the method of introduction is supremely skillful, then these factors may generate and reinforce positive attitudes.

With this insight it is plain that the nine negative feelings can also have positive analogues. Some may feel 'unhappy that I shall be replaced by a machine', but others may feel 'glad that a machine will take the drudgery out of my work'. Some may feel 'afraid of the unknown in a general kind of way', but others may feel 'stimulated by adventure, in a general kind of way'. And so on.

In the four-way breakdown of factors, 'method of introduction' is ambiguous in a different respect too. It could mean:

- *Either* **method of introduction.** 'We have already decided to have a certain system whose scope and budget we have already defined, at least in outline, and whose broad implications for the workforce are already clear, at least roughly. Now, how democratic should we be about the detail of defining people's new job content and organisation, arranging system tests, parallel runs and implementation schedules; setting up training programmes etc?'
- *Or* **method of decision-making.** 'We have to take fundamental decisions about whether to have a new system or to patch up an old one, and, if we have a new system, what its scope and budget should be, at least in outline, and what broad implications it has for the workforce, at least roughly. Now, we could devise a procedure that seemed likely to produce astute decisions quite efficiently. But should we perhaps choose instead some different decision process that, though more time-consuming and even perhaps less likely to produce the best decisions, had the virtue of bringing in many more people and thus strengthening commitment, minimising negative feelings etc?

This distinction results in a much more powerful chart of the factors in play here:

- You need to find an approach to taking fundamental decisions, that has a reasonable chance of both reaching sound decisions and attracting commitment.
- Among the things considered in this decision-making will be the four factors above (including method of introduction in the narrower, detailed sense).

● In deciding about them the aim will be to minimise the nine negative feelings and maximise their nine positive analogues. This may of course entail tradeoffs; eg accept that departmental boundaries will be reorganised and that this will unavoidably generate some negative feelings, but try to build up positive feelings to compensate by showing some people that they will have richer, more interesting work.

Analysing User Involvement Desiderata

The four desiderata for user involvement can also be fashioned into a more powerful piece of analysis. The four — typical users, knowledgeable users, user perspective and active involvement — are desirable in two quite distinct ways. They help to produce a good system (ie one that is based on correct understanding of a department's needs, takes advantage of opportunities etc); and they also help to generate commitment to the system (ie people in the department feel positive towards it). This can be charted in more detail:

● There are four factors, each of which in itself ought to be maximised . .

● . . except that this is impossible, since they usually conflict.

● Therefore you have to find the best compromise . .

● . . but not the best compromise to reach one particular objective (eg a well designed system) . .

● . . rather, the best compromise to reach the best balance between two possibly conflicting objectives: a well designed system and also commitment, confidence, enthusiasm etc.

Refining the Complexity-Commitment Tradeoff

The complexity-commitment tradeoff is fine as far as it goes, but there are usually other relevant variables too:

● **Problem nature.** The problem may be of the 'high jump' type — you either solve it or you don't; just failing by a millimetre has zero value, clearing by a margin of 10cm has no extra value. Or it may be of the 'long jump' type — there is no sharp line between success and failure. These are extremes; many problems have both elements, but to different degrees.

● **Problem centrality.** If the organisation is in a desperate position and the problem is to save it, the approach needs to be simply the best possible for that particular problem. But suppose the task is to set up an experimental, in-company bulletin board service — a minor application. You might reasonably adopt an approach to this problem that was not the most effective for solving it. Perhaps this is one of dozens of experimental applications to be tackled in the near future. Why not approach it in the way that fits best with the broader aim of establishing good procedures for approaching *any* experimental application?

Thus the task of gauging the approach to decision-making about change can be redefined as finding the right point along the authoritarian-participative continuum; and the calculus for doing that will use four factors: problem complexity, commitment importance, problem nature and problem centrality.

SUGGESTED WARRANTS

This section develops the ideas of the previous section to expose a certain fundamental tradeoff between two very broad factors.

Charting Rationality and Commitment

Imagine a game of chess where moves were decided by group decision, but where the people in the group were themselves pieces and the pieces couldn't be relied on to always carry out the moves decided. The group might decide to move a bishop four squares along a diagonal, and this might be far and away the best move by any objective criterion. But the bishop himself might feel upset at lack of consultation on this major decision, and, feeling sulky, move three squares instead of four. This is quite a close analogy to things that typically happen with IM:

- A company decides to set up a new inventory control system. This seems an excellent decision. Assessment of soft factors such as the likely reactions of staff, their supervisors and their managers to their new tasks reinforces the decision; all will have more interesting tasks. But the system is a failure and in retrospect the reason is obvious. The supervisors and managers concerned were hardly consulted about the original decision (mainly because it seemed so obviously right that little consultation was needed). This irritated them so much that they co-operated in the detailed design and testing without enthusiasm. Therefore the system began badly with some design flaws and software bugs it need never have had. Having given the system a bad name, none of the people involved made much effort to rescue it.
- *By contrast*, another company chooses between two possible inventory control packages, A and B. By any objective assessment the choice should be A. Everybody on the committee sees that, except the inventory controller who wants B. The debate is long but respectful; in the end, the choice is B, even though everybody except the inventory controller is certain that A is the better choice. Determined to vindicate his choice of B, the inventory controller takes great pains to see that the new system is a success. Long afterwards, the controller concedes that the arguments for B were bad ones, and A would have been the better choice. Nevertheless, the company does have a successful system.[5]

These representative, though simplified, examples illustrate how in the decision-making process itself there is a *rationality-commitment tradeoff* to resolve:

- You need a process that will arrive at good decisions efficiently in a problem-solving sense.
- But it should also take account of needs for commitment and sponsorship, bids for understanding, statements of sympathy etc.
- There may well be a clash between these two things, and you have to find the best, or least bad, way of resolving them.

The main test of any ideas on change management is whether they help in understanding this clash of desiderata.

NOTES & ARGUMENTS

1 Tozer (p. 3) points out that a large-scale planning process can have beneficial side-effects, beyond its immediate objective of arriving at good plans: the process of interview and analysis of non-IT business plans may stimulate and sharpen management thinking in general; communication between levels of management, and across functional and geographic boundaries, may be fostered; weak areas of business organisation, eg lack of competitive intelligence, may be exposed. Another factor is slightly different: people may acquire feelings of sponsorship and positive attitudes towards the IT systems they plan.

True enough, but tame. The subject becomes interesting when you notice that such desirable phenomena can also have undesirable counterparts:

- The need for careful IM planning can sharpen management thinking about the business in general, but at the same time lead to resentment against bumptious analysts and consultants. 'It is fatal if the IT department is thought to be setting the firm's strategy! However, the IT director often has to lead the clarification process, but as far as possible from behind!' (Earl, p. 73).
- Again, positive sponsorship feelings about a particular system can lead to sly, anti-social or irrational behaviour. '(Project) champions frequently underestimate costs in order to increase the chance of the project being accepted. Underestimates may be deliberate attempts at deception or merely optimistic accounts of potential costs.' (Farbey, Land and Targett p. 13).

2 Claudette and Tim Peterson, 'The Darkside of Office Automation' in Carey's anthology. The nine feelings and four factors of the article have been considerably reworded and reordered in the briefing.

3 Walton, pp. 147-8 (after Dorothy Leonard-Barton). This text goes beyond platitudes and indicates that there are problems and tradeoffs, albeit not quite in the terms used in the briefing.

Here is the outline of a different piece of advice about organising projects with the right mix of people (Kathy Brittain White in Carey's anthology, p. 141). Recognise four different types of project (definable in terms of the main challenge faced), and four main types of activity on any project, and four Jungian types of personality. If all those categories are valid, rules can be developed for which types of personality should be used for which types of activity on which type of project. Formally, this makes a fine, rich decision-forcing warrant. Whether it will work in practice is another matter.

4 Wright and Rhodes, pp. 45-7. These authors take several dull analyses by other authorities, and refurbish them by pointing out that different situations call for different solutions.

'This study identifies several key variables which contribute to the acceptance of change of an MIS by individuals. The variables are individual rigidity, commitment to the status quo, knowledge of the status quo, exposure to the new system, preparation for the new system, and previous experience with the new system in a different environment.' (Carey, p. 204). There are two questions to think about with this kind of generalisation:

- First, is there anything surprising, ie non-trivial, about the list of six factors? In particular, are some plausible factors you would expect to find deliberately excluded?
- Second, are they precise enough to mean anything useful? It may be thought that the first two factors (individual rigidity and commitment to the status quo) are so broad that they are bound to mop up anything not absorbed by the other (more specific) factors.

5 Soft-systems theorists lay considerable stress on a related theme, best shown by example.

Suppose a legal practice is trying to decide its policy on IT. Suppose that most of the firm's 20 partners are habitually treated as inferiors by the five most important. Whether this is resented or accepted or has some more complex effect, it is a factor which could affect the design of a system's functions or the future organisational arrangements for IT.

Now a management consultant investigates the situation, and interviews all the partners in turn. The consultant, if skillful, will discover this inferiority-complex factor (among many others) — but by the very action of doing so through interviews with each partner and a round-table discussion with all 20, the consultant may make the 15 feel slightly less inferior and the five less bossy. Thus the work of finding the factor changes the factor, if only, in this simple instance, slightly and temporarily. This raises two interesting points:

- Simple cases like the above can be claimed as examples of a general principle of change management, operating (so it is claimed) much more powerfully in more complex cases. There is no point in denying that such a principle can be theoretically valid; the issue is whether its effects are strong enough in practice to deserve much attention — except in certain special circumstances.
- If the principle is both valid and frequently strong in its effects, can any general methods be devised to cope with it? Lewis's book lays great stress on this theme of the intervention of the analyst (pp. 157-160), but although a methodology and a case study are described, all they show is that the analyst or consultant has to bear this kind of influence in mind. They don't reveal any unexpected techniques for (say) reducing its force or taking advantage of it.

CONNECTIONS

28. Decision-making as Process	General analysis of problems of finding an appropriate structure for decision-making
34. Sociotechnical Design	Human factors associated with the design of systems, as opposed to their change management
36. Business Process Re-engineering	Radical change — and thus demanding change management

36. Business Process Re-engineering

TOPIC

The synonymous terms 'business (process) re-engineering' and '(business) process redesign' (from now on swept together into BPR) emerged at the start of the nineties, and soon became exceedingly popular with authors of marketing brochures for consultancy or computer services companies. But is there any substance to the rhetoric? Certainly, clever use of IT can have a big effect on an organisation, but that has been true for twenty years or more; certainly, imaginative, clever systems analysis can bring impressive gains to a business with old-fashioned procedures, but that is scarcely a new discovery.

This briefing raises some basic questions that ought to be put more often: How can BPR be established as a clear concept, with characteristic distinctive features? Is it an essential trait of a re-engineered system to be based on up-to-date telecoms and database technology, or is that just a chance feature of many cases cited in articles? Can several different sub-categories be usefully distinguished within the category of BPR? Should decision-making and development for BPR be structured in any special way?

Cutting through the glossy-brochure talk like this produces some warrants to assist decisions about *any* major system developments, whether or not they are labelled as BPR.

REPRESENTATIVE IDEAS — SUMMARISED

Much that is said and written on this subject can be cast aside as glib platitude and naive exhortation.[1] But two early influential articles about BPR provide far more substance than most of the glossy brochures. From now on this briefing refers to the *Harvard* article and the *Sloan* article. A third article in *The Economist* provides a sorely-needed intelligent summary of the case for BPR.[2]

Business Re-engineering, Representative Rhetoric

'Instead of embedding outdated processes in silicon and software, we should obliterate them and start over. We should 're-engineer' our businesses; use the power of modern information technology to radically redesign our business processes in order to achieve dramatic improvements in their performance.'

'In re-engineering managers break loose from outmoded business processes and the design principles underlying them and create new ones.'

'At the heart of re-engineering is the notion of discontinuous thinking — of recognizing and breaking away from the outdated rules and fundamental assumptions that underlie operations.'

'In short, a re-engineering effort strives for dramatic levels of improvement. It must break away from conventional wisdom and the constraints of organizational boundaries and should be broad and cross-functional in scope. It should use information technology not to automate an existing process but to enable a new one.'

'. . one factor that is necessary for re-engineering to succeed: executive leadership with real vision . . Commitment, consistency — maybe even a touch of fanaticism — are needed to enlist those who would prefer the status quo.'

'We must have the boldness to imagine taking 78 days out of an 80-day turnaround time, cutting 75% of overhead, and eliminating 80% of errors. These are not unrealistic goals. If managers have the vision, re-engineering will provide a way.'

BPR: Two Key Articles

As the quotations in the table show, the *Harvard* article indulges in some rhetoric that seems vulnerable to critical thinking. One objection is that some of the claims could apply almost as well to a manufacturing company recording inventory on computer for the very first time in 1968, or to an insurance company using a computer to print out its policy documents and automatically calculate premiums for the first time in 1973. If BPR is some special, new thing, what is special or new about it? The article's two main example cases begin to suggest an answer.

Ford re-engineered its purchasing, goods inwards and accounts payable processes. Formerly, numerous documents such as purchase orders, invoices, delivery notes and so on flowed between these three departments and Ford's suppliers. Much effort was spent on sorting out problems when documents didn't match with each other or with the goods actually delivered. The new re-engineered system makes more use of computers and includes some radical innovations:

- If goods received don't correspond to what the computer says were ordered, don't follow any procedures to investigate the discrepancy; simply send the goods back.

- Tell suppliers not to send invoices (if invoices come, ignore them); simply send out a payment automatically for all goods received and accepted.

The spectacular result was that Ford's accounts payable department, formerly containing 500 people has been reduced to 125.

In the second case, Mutual Benefit Life Insurance re-engineered the process of handling applications for new policies. Previously there were 30 procedural steps, five departments involved and 19 people. Now one case manager is responsible for most of this work. He or she has an expert system on a PC-based workstation, connected to a mainframe. Turnround is much faster, and the same number of people can handle twice as many applications for new policies as previously.

The *Sloan* article is the more thoughtful. It introduces some ideas barely hinted at in the *Harvard* article. The authors sketch out the theory that from the Industrial Revolution until roughly now, the trend has been to break work down into narrowly defined tasks done by different people, with superstructures of management to organise and control everything. Modern IT provides the chance to reverse that trend — having each person perform a more varied range of activities, with fewer layers of management.

It also says more than the *Harvard* article about how to do BPR. It gives seven principles, such as: 'organize around outcomes, not tasks', 'have those who use the output of the process perform the process', and so on. However, some of these overlap and all really amount to saying in different words: 'choose a simple, elegant way of doing something over a complicated, messy way.'

BPR: Essence of the Case

Interesting though those two articles are, some may find a certain lack of intellectual coherence about them. Many of the assertions they contain might have been made at any time in the last thirty years. Can their ideas be bound together to make a case that is coherent and convincing and new? The brief *Economist* article has a quite different tone, and contains the elements needed to express quite a rational case for the concept of BPR:

- Before computers were available, the administration of business was organised rather like a factory. Hundreds of clerks each performed specialised, limited tasks, that in combination made up one intricate system. Things were done like this, because no other way was possible.
- As computers were introduced, administrative systems were improved. Though much labour was saved and new information produced, still the concept of many people performing specialised, limited tasks, within the system survived — not because systems designers were bigoted fools, but because no other way was possible with the available technology.
- At about the end of the eighties, changes in technology capabilities and cost made it feasible — fairly suddenly — to design new systems that

fragmented work far less. Now one person's role in a system could embrace quite a number of different tasks, previously done by separate people.

- In principle, this must be more efficient, because the overheads of interactions between different parts of the system are reduced. It is no longer necessary to fill in five different forms and send them to five different people, if you yourself are now doing all the work the five used to do.
- And there may be softer benefits too: people playing wider, more stimulating roles may be better motivated, may contribute to continuous improvements, and may perform better in unpredictable circumstances.

REPRESENTATIVE IDEAS — ANALYSED

The case just presented offers a defence against any charges that BPR talk is nothing but exhortation to do what is obvious, but is it a sound case? Are its premises true and its inferences valid?

New Technology, New Possibilities?

The key point of the case is that around 1990 — rather than five or ten years earlier — technology become particularly suitable for designing systems where people play wider, far less specialised roles. Is this true?3
Here is some support for the view:

- Several technologies reached a certain maturity during the late eighties.
- These technologies are vastly more powerful in combination than singly. This synergy makes radical change possible.
- For example, take three features of the re-engineered Ford system: information is accessed and updated in the **database** easily and flexibly; information is made widely and conveniently available through a **telecoms** network; the setup is **fault-tolerant**, ie all kinds of recovery and control mechanisms are built in, invisible to the user, to allow work to continue even in the face of technical mishaps or other complications. Only with these three technology features together is it feasible to rely on the concept of information (eg what parts are on order) being held electronically once in the database, rather than on several pieces of paper and their copies. Given that, radical redesign becomes possible.
- Thus it is indeed plausible that the technologies central to the Ford BPR case reached a certain decisive level of maturity and cost-effectiveness in the late eighties.

One other technology factor is less prominent in the Ford case, but fundamental to the Mutual Benefit case: the arrival of cheap PCs. Once it becomes possible to put a powerful PC on the desk of every office-worker, all kinds of new possibilities suddenly arise.

Aspects of BPR

If this gives a reasonable basis for holding that BPR is a respectable concept, how can it be analysed further? From the *Harvard* and *Sloan* articles three distinct aspects of BPR can be discerned:

- Successful BPR cases produce **spectacular quantitative benefit** (eg 125 people do the work of 500) — as opposed to benefits that are merely healthy (500 down to 400, say).
- As the Mutual Benefit Life Insurance case exemplifies, **job enrichment** results too: workers can perform a richer mix of activities.
- The third common aspect of BPR seems to be **simplicity**, or perhaps elegance, in the redesigned system. Any chart documenting the activities and forms of a system will be much simpler.

When anything appears (or is claimed) to have three salient features, it is invariably worth asking, as an almost automatic reaction: Are these three always found clustered together, or not? Is job enrichment (say) always accompanied by spectacular quantitative benefit and simplicity?

The cases described in the *Harvard*, *Sloan* and other articles suggest strongly that the three features given are aspects of BPR, present to varying degrees in any given case. In the Ford case spectacular quantitative benefit and simplicity are very pronounced, but there is relatively little stress on job enrichment. In the Mutual Benefit case the stress is on job enrichment and simplicity, though quantitative benefit is still impressive.

To count as *classic* BPR, it may reasonably be insisted, a case should possess all three of these aspects to a substantial degree, but it seems quite plausible that there can be non-classic cases too. Spectacular quantitative benefit might be aimed for and achieved, without making jobs richer or poorer, on balance. Or an organisation might choose to develop new systems where many people had wider, richer jobs — justifying this by long-term, unquantifiable considerations, rather than immediate financial benefits.[4] In many cases there can be a variety of options available, where the three aspects are given different weights; and awareness of more options should, in turn, lead to better decisions.[5]

SUGGESTED WARRANTS

Further analysis of the flood of rhetoric about BPR can break down re-engineering possibilities further. This may assist decision-making by suggesting or clarifying options, and by showing how different types of system call for different approaches.

More Aspects of BPR Cases

However a case stands with respects to the three aspects of the previous

Streamlining and Enabling

Streamlining

Make a complex but definable administrative process simpler

Replace this | By this

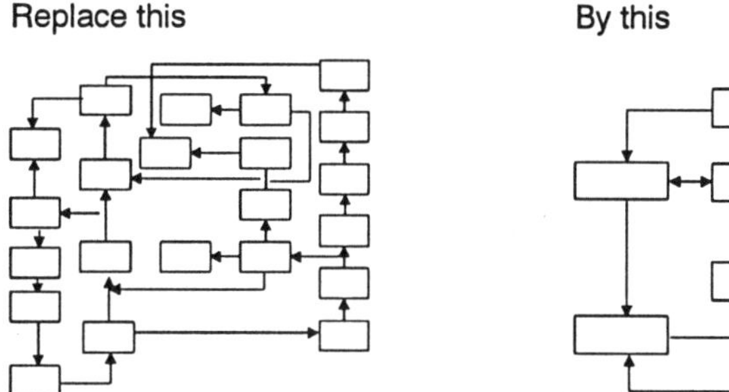

Enabling

Take a process where parties interact with each other repeatedly, in sporadic unpredictable ways, and make their interaction richer, faster, more effective.

Replace this | By this

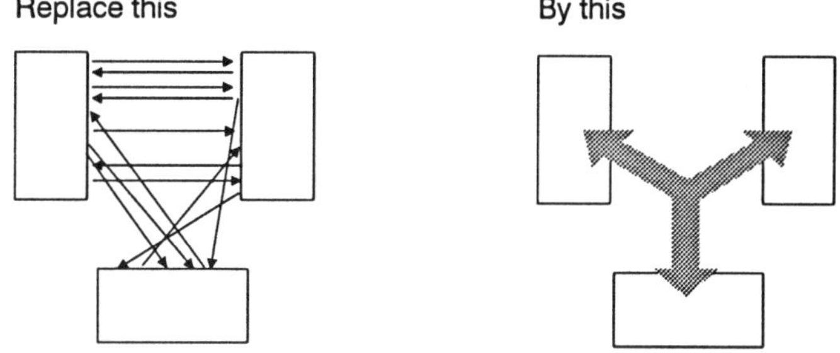

section there is, as the diagram suggests, a difference between two *fundamental types of system* that may be re-engineered:

- A system is redesigned to provide a slicker, crisper, more **streamlined** way of administration that, despite certain complications, does have a definable normal sequence of steps, where the main variations are predictable; eg organising material supply or setting up a new insurance policy. The majority of cases described in articles are like this.
- Arrangements are provided to **enable** people to carry out certain work much more efficiently, but this work isn't really administration and has no definable normal sequence of steps and variations. Moreover the work is split between people working in parallel, who interact in complex, unpredictable ways. Out of two main example cases and seven subsidiary in the *Harvard* article, one of the subsidiary cases belongs in this second category: a system to allow separate units, working in parallel at development of different parts of a new photocopier product, to exchange

diagrams and other information electronically. The *Economist* article gives the case of an energy company that introduced new systems, based on high-powered desktop workstations, to share management information between divisions. Much of the more futuristic writing on the subject of BPR seems largely concerned with this type of system.

In principle, one system could display both aspects to differing degrees; in practice, this often an either/or distinction.6 The broad two-way breakdown fits fairly neatly with another, identifying different *broad technology resources* for achieving the goals of BPR:

- Take advantage of the maturity of large-scale **database and telecoms** technology, as in the Ford case.
- Use any **other well-established** technology, in the context of networked PCs or workstations; eg expert system in the Mutual Benefit case.
- Use the relatively new **workflow** software, that applies rules to control the flow of information between workers, and thus 'automate the procedure manual' — or rather a rewritten one. The interesting challenge here is to streamline and rationalise systems, while in some ways making them more subtle; eg coping with intricate exception conditions, and allowing complex feedback between different people.
- Use the relatively new **groupware** software, that, for the first time, provides integration between technology elements and systems that are essentially separate things: word processing, spreadsheet, access to central or external databases, electronic mail, scheduling meetings etc. This is mainly relevant to enabling cases.

These four are worth identifying separately, even though in certain cases you may opt to use more than one. Of course, if an organisation is infested with obsolete processes, it is also possible to make radical improvements by sheer, straightforward systems analysis, without pronounced use of any of these four technology resources.

Distinctions between Approaches to BPR

According to the *Sloan* article: 'Re-engineering cannot be planned meticulously and accomplished in small and cautious steps. It's an all-or-nothing proposition with an uncertain result. Still, most companies have no choice but to muster the courage to do it.' What does this mean exactly?

The logic of a classic BPR case, such as Ford, is roughly as follows: 'Currently we have (say) 30 main procedural steps. The proposed redesign has only 12 steps: of these, seven are completely new steps, three are heavy modifications of the old system and two are not much changed. The new system has very great benefits and no great disadvantages relative to the old.'

But, experience of systems analysis over the decades shows, any new design that seems, on paper, to be much neater than the old can easily turn out to have irritating minor flaws:

- Perhaps the redesigned system leaves a loophole for a certain ingenious

Magic Square Problems

Magic Square Problem:

Given these seven numbers, fill in the other eighteen, so that each of the five vertical columns, five horizontal rows, and two main diagonals add up to the same total.

-	21	10	-	-
9	-	-	26	15
-	8	-	-	-
-	-	-	-	-
-	27	-	-	-

This seems close to solution, but is it? Maybe you will have to go back and change numbers already filled in. That could continue indefinitely.

19	21	10	-	25
9	18	12	26	15
28	8	13	24	-
17	6	20	15	-
7	27	22	11	-

Business Re-engineering Problem:

Redesign this system to achieve the same things much more efficiently.

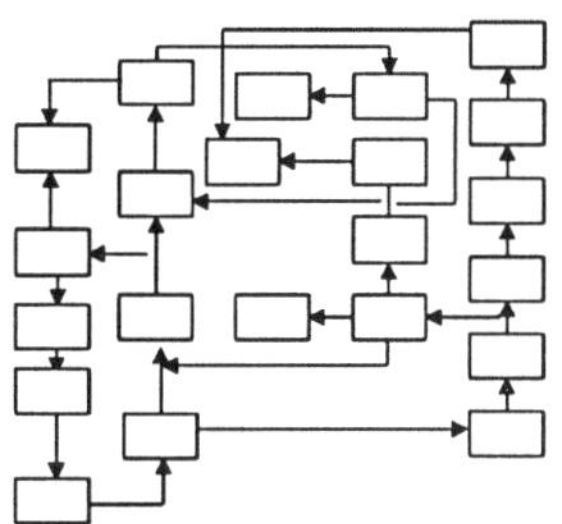

A perfect redesign solution almost complete. Or is it? Perhaps you will have to go back and change processes already designed.

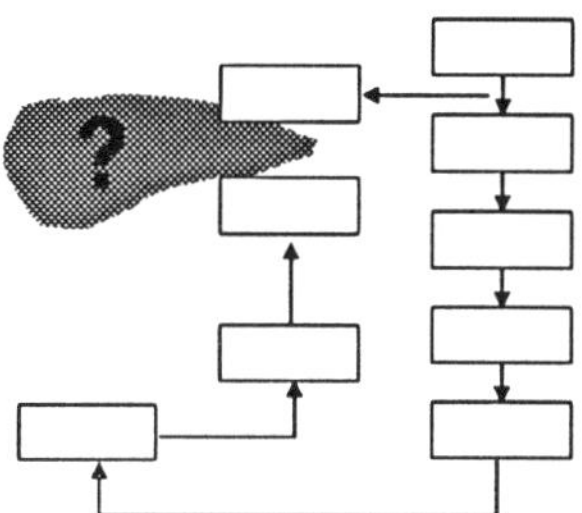

kind of fraud. It is unlikely that a criminal will ever discover the possibility, but it didn't exist at all with the old system.

- Perhaps the redesigned system is unable to produce easily the combination of data in precisely the required format, required by the regulatory authorities of the industry. No doubt any rational person would agree that the reports it can produce are actually superior, but the authorities won't see reason on this point.
- Perhaps the redesigned system has the awkward characteristic that under very exceptional trading conditions (eg Christmas combined with an oil crisis) it will get out of control (eg violent peaks and troughs in reordering motor parts).

Once noticed at the design stage or during system testing, such imperfections can often be remedied at a small price in complication — add an extra report here, introduce a manual override there. But not always. Occasionally, awkward blemishes, minor but quite unacceptable, can't be cured just by altering one localised part of a design.

The new 12-step redesign may be perfect save for one such irritating blemish; but the only way to remove the blemish may be completely to revise seven of the steps and the way they fit together; but this in turn means abandoning other bright ideas and opens up new sources of difficulty.

As the diagram suggests, a BPR task may well be like an infuriating *magic square* problem. You can't ever say that you have *almost* solved this kind of problem. Either you have a complete solution or you haven't. It is worthwhile to judge to what degree any BPR project will have these magic square characteristics.[7]

If the BPR project is essentially *streamlining* you can, in principle, describe a possible new design and demonstrate in a rational way that it is better than another design — by making calculations about staff savings or turnround time or other quantitative factors. Therefore your approach should stimulate and compare possible new designs as efficiently as possible, with the assumption that you can go a fair way by reason, as opposed to trial and error.

With an *enabling* case the situation is different. Suppose you set up electronic communications between Verdi the composer and Boito the librettist, so that they could work together better in parallel. Would they get their operas ready quicker? Or produce higher quality operas? Who can say? They might do worse; increased communication could lead to more arguments, more discarded drafts and so on. It is very difficult to show beforehand by reason that one option for an enabling system will necessarily be better than another. This suggests strongly that the approach to an enabling system should be much more experimental and rich in feedback.[8]

NOTES & ARGUMENTS

1 One consultancy's brochure affirms: 'It is only when integrated changes in the infrastructure are conceived and implemented at the same time, to support new business processes, that the urgently needed step-change in performance can be achieved. We call this Business Re-engineering . . ' Or in clearer language: integrated changes should not be conceived piecemeal, and step-changes cannot be continuous. This is true, but no more interesting than declarations that a triangle certainly *does not* have five sides or that an irascible person really *is* prone to anger.

'Business process reengineering (BPR) (is) an approach for soliciting major business change, in contrast to the non-BPR environment, in which we apply information technology (IT) to existing business processes. In a non-BPR environment, we don't think about why or how these business processes are carried out. (Actually, we *do* think about these things, but nobody wants our opinion!)' from 'The

Tools of Change' by Dan Wahl and Barbara von Halle, *Database Programming & Design*, June 1993, pp. 13-15. This is a version of the straw man fallacy — shooting down a ridiculously easy target in order to show how important your own idea is by comparison.

An office Wall of Shame soon fills up, and at least half the fatuous statements about IM will probably concern BPR. The great challenge is to find the specks of genuine insight among the dross.

2 Michael Hammer, 'Reengineering Work; Don't Automate, Obliterate', anthologised in Harvard Business Review (1991), pp. 18ff. Thomas H Davenport and James E Short, 'The New Industrial Engineering: Information Technology and Business Process Redesign', *Sloan Management Review*, Summer 1990, pp. 11-27. 'Take a clean sheet of paper', *The Economist*, 1 May 1993, pp. 71-2.

'It sounds like a parody of a management fad — no mean feat considering that many people view management fads themselves as parodies of rational thought.' From this entertaining start the *Economist* article goes on to give a very fair view of the sense and nonsense associated with BPR.

3 Many articles about BPR don't really stress this claim. But, without it, the bold rhetoric is little but banal exhortation to do away with pointless work-practices, be imaginative rather than dull, and so on.

The *Harvard* article argues that current organisational processes in an organisation are probably not an optimal design because they are the result of numerous accretions, preserved remnants of ad hoc solutions etc. Thus, an example goes, foreign accounts are sent to the corner desk. Why? Because that is where Mary used to sit and she spoke French. Mary has long since moved on and we no longer do business in France, but we still send foreign accounts to the corner desk. But this example undermines rather than bolsters the credibility of any claim that BPR is something special. It merely makes the trite point that obsolete work practices are a bad thing that should be changed — something which has always been true, and always will be.

An article in the *Harvard Business Review*, November-December 1993, p. 119-131, 'How to make Reengineering really work', by Gene Hall, Jim Rosenthal and Judy Wade features the case of BAI (an Italian bank). When an ordinary customer paid in a simple cheque, the administration used to involve 64 activities, 9 forms and 14 accounts; after BPR, only 25 activities, 2 forms and 2 accounts were needed. The personnel per branch, previously 7 to 9, was cut to 3 to 4. But cases of this sort only prove that if a company's administration is absurdly over-complicated, then it can probably be greatly simplified. That does nothing to establish BPR as a distinct concept.

An impressive BPR case study would show how a business that was already well-run by most standards employed up-to-date technology to allow people to play wider, less specialised roles — with favourable consequences, of course.

4 Job enrichment is closely associated with the megatrend of empowering the intelligent knowledge-worker and doing away with fascist management styles.

The multi-disciplinary team is a related theme. The argument is that if each person has a rich job that also overlaps with others within a team, then people will learn from each other — in a virtuous spiral of ever-increasing effectiveness.

5 The article by Hall et al (cited above) gives the case of an insurance company. Rather than re-engineer everything, it chose between three possible objectives: improved claims processing (a quantitative benefit aspect); more knowledgeable service representatives (job enrichment); offering a broader portfolio of products (probably job enrichment, but perhaps simplicity). After researching customers' wishes, the company made the agenda decision to concentrate on the first of these.

Sometimes it may seem that the real choice is between quantitative benefit and job enrichment, and that simplicity is a superfluous variable, already covered by one of the other two. But simplicity often is a distinct third aspect:

- *Insurance company A* scores high on simplicity: most of the complexities of decision-making, rate-setting and even sending messages to co-insurers are handled by a very sophisticated piece of expert system software. Most of its staff are drudges dedicated to tasks like keying in data and changing the toner in the printer.
- At *company B* a chart of the re-engineered system is far more complicated, because the computer system makes fewer decisions. It leaves more responsibility with the staff, who thus have richer jobs.

6 This analysis ignores another category of ambitious new system development: using IT to offer a new product or service. This seems a different thing from redesigning the administration of current products and services. An agenda decision may well be needed to define which of those two broad objectives should be given more weight. On the other hand, the distinction may not always be sharp: perhaps a certain new service can't be launched effectively unless the company's main administrative systems are also re-engineered.

7 Aren't most designs for computer systems like magic square problems? No, with many applications, you can make a top-level design, tackle each part individually, breaking each down further still, and so on. If the outline design is sound, faults in one part can be rectified without repercussions elsewhere. But that may not be so, if an ingenious redesign aims to reduce 30 steps to 12 and reduce the workforce by 75%. Nevertheless, different projects (including different BPR projects) face the magic square problem to different degrees —and that degree is an important variable in decisions about a project.

If a system can be broken into pieces to be refined and improved separately, then prototyping can be an effective way of doing the refinement in a steady, purposeful way. But in prototyping a system with strong magic square properties (radically re-engineered, and can't be broken into separate pieces), doubts about one part of the system may force suspension of the prototype; and several other parts, which were thought to be already settled, may have to be redesigned. This makes it much more difficult to manage a prototyping process.

8 Further reading? Here are some books:

Reengineering the Corporation, a Manifesto for Business Revolution, Michael Hammer and James Champy (Harper Business, 1993)

Process Innovation, Reengineering Work through Information Technology, Thomas H Davenport (Harvard Business School Press, 1993)

Business Reengineering, the Survival Guide, Dorine C Andrews and Susan K Stalick (Yourdon Press, 1994)

Breakpoint, Business Process Redesign, David K Carr (Coopers and Lybrand, 1992)

Reengineering, Leveraging the Power of Integrated Product Development, V Daniel Hunt (Omneo, Oliver Wight Publ., 1993)

Business Process Reengineering, Breakpoint Strategies for Market Dominance, Henry J Johanson (Wiley, 1993)

Re-engineering Your Business, Daniel Morris and Joel Brandon (McGraw-Hill, 1993)

Making Re-engineering Happen, Eddie Obeng and Stuart Crainer (Financial Times and Pitman, 1994)

Successful Reengineering, Daniel P Petrozzo and John C Stepper (Van Nostrand Reinhold, 1994)

Business Process Re-engineering, Practical Handbook for Executives, Steven Towers (Technical Communications, 1994)

Business Process Reengineering, Current Issues and Applications (Institute of Electrical Engineering, 1993)

Hammer and Champy are messianic and lightweight, while Davenport is much more thoughtful. As *Information Management Decisions* goes to press the storm flood of books about re-engineering is still surging through publishers' catalogues. Their content seems to add little to what is said more succinctly in articles. But that is only a provisional, perhaps unfair, reaction; it is really too soon to make a careful comparison of books on the subject. For this reason the *Critical Bibliography* section has no re-engineering heading.

CONNECTIONS

12. Matching through Comparisons	In any comparison the PC architecture offers far more flexibility than the mini — should a firm want to re-engineer its business processes
14. Matching through Gradations	Reorganising the sharing of work in document production is a form of re-engineering, and there are gradations of complexity
15. Matching through Charts	Workflow software is a prime technology for supporting re-engineered processes, and its possibilities need charting out
16. Matching through Aspects	Ditto groupware, but it is an even broader term
22. Evolutionary Development	Appropriate for some, but not all, re-engineering projects
34. Sociotechnical Design	Job enrichment, a big issue in re-engineering and part of the theme of sociotechnical design
35. Change Management	Getting change understood and accepted — a challenge for dramatically re-engineered systems
40. Strategic Systems and Competitive Advantage	Nearby concepts, sometimes overlapping

37. End-user Computing

TOPIC

End-user computing (from now on EUC) is a topic easy to glimpse but difficult to capture. Different people define it different ways, and this can matter. Some general advice about EUC may be sound if the definition embraces (say) drafting and design systems for architects, but excludes foreign exchange applications running on PCs, and excludes user-defined queries to a central database. But with a different definition, different advice may apply.

Nevertheless, whatever you choose to include in the EUC category, the crucial decisions about EUC are likely to deal with one fundamental tradeoff. EUC can liberate users to employ technology effectively and thus benefit the organisation, but excessive liberation can lead to anarchy and other unpleasantness. Some balance has to be struck.

This briefing suggests that, on the whole, the valuable ideas about EUC are the ones that help in appreciating and exploring the subtleties of this tradeoff.

REPRESENTATIVE IDEAS — SUMMARISED

Sometimes debate about definition can be sterile, but with EUC a convenient way of exposing many of the themes is to start with the different ways the subject has been defined.

Definition: Main Themes

One book opens by contrasting two types of systems:

- **End-user** systems: 'all information systems where end-users have considerable discretion as to whether and how to exploit the computing power at their disposal';
- **Operational** systems which 'process business transactions or control production processes where use clearly is not discretionary'.

This is supplemented with the note that end-user systems include 'office automation and departmental systems as well as personal computers'.

It is easy to sense a difference between the end-user and the operational systems within an organisation, but the dividing-line is not entirely clear. 'Discretion', as above, is one possible distinguishing trait.

Another book offers: 'By end user computing we mean active and spontaneous use of computers by non-EDP-professionals in support of their tasks. It can be both ad-hoc use of computers and user-driven application development.' This formulation has the merit of exposing two separate concepts that are blurred together in the first definition's phrase 'discretion to exploit computing power':

- **Discretionary use:** eg a company sets up an electronic mail facility for general use; use is discretionary, in the sense that anyone can use it a great deal, or a little, or not at all.
- **Discretionary setup:** at its own discretion, ie independently of the IT people, a department sets up new automated facilities: it buys a laser printer to replace a matrix printer, or writes spreadsheet macros to process data in new ways.

Another writer includes only discretionary setup in the definition of EUC: 'the direct assumption of system development and data processing tasks by the user of the service for his own direct benefit.' This definition, like the others, avoids identifying EUC with any particular technology, such as PC hardware. Most people regard the defining characteristics of EUC as relatively soft variables, such as discretion, freedom, flexibility, initiative etc, rather than harder ones such as particular types and locations of hardware. **1**

Issues Summarised

Much discussion of EUC issues can be summarised rather brusquely as being the detail of a certain fundamental problem.

Most organisations have a co-ordinating body of experts (usually called an IC, information centre) to help and to some degree control end-users. There are opportunities for choice about the functions of the IC. Almost any conceivable IC is likely to have certain minimum functions (eg helping when something unexpected happens during word processing); there are other functions it may well have, but not necessarily (eg defining minimum quality standards for EUC development work); and other functions that it may possibly have, though most ICs don't (eg managing the development of end-user systems in a prototyping style). **2**

The possible functions for an IC can be discussed specifically but they really depend on how the organisation treats one basic tradeoff:

- **Control**. On the one hand, there is a prima facie case for co-ordinating the management and use of computing in different departments of an organisation. This seems to be sound, if dull, management practice. Many PC users cry out for guidance and supervision. Moreover, there are anecdotes galore of atrocities perpetrated by headstrong technology novices. The possible problems with unbridled licence are pretty obvious: bugs in programs not tested properly, inadequate validation procedures to reject bad input, lack of system documentation, laziness in making backup copies of data, incompatibility between systems, grotesquely inappropriate choices of technology etc.

- **Freedom**. On the other hand, the less people are supervised, the more they will show initiative, creativity, positive motivation and so on. There are supporting anecdotes for this too.

An organisation has to find the right (or least-bad) balance between these conflicting forces. It might decide to risk some minor atrocities from a few users as the price of liberating the many — or alternatively decide, with a heavy heart, to inflict unnecessary frustrations on some competent enthusiasts as the price of avoiding anarchy.

Most of what is worth discussing about EUC, not just about ICs, but other matters too — investment justification criteria, system implementation strategies, distributed software development and internal charging mechanisms etc — is essentially an elaboration of that tradeoff.[3,4]

REPRESENTATIVE IDEAS — ANALYSED

The interesting management issues with EUC revolve around the control-freedom tradeoff, which is closely bound up with relatively soft factors such as discretion. The notion of discretion deserves further analysis.

Examining Discretionary Use

The distinction between *EUC* systems — discretionary use and non-transactional — and *operational* — transactional and non-discretionary use — soon becomes blurred. First, concentrate on the function any person may have in an organisation, leaving aside for the moment any associated computer systems. Take these four:

- **Alice** works in the claims department of an insurance company keying in the details of an endless stream of simple motor claims.
- **Bernard** is supervisor of ten clerks in the department for health insurance claims. The task is to ensure that this highly predictable work is well organised and to resolve any exceptional problems of procedure that come up.
- **Clare** is the head of the department for claims relating to household contents. If a policy-holder's carpets and curtains are damaged by fireworks, Clare takes the decision on how much to offer in compensation.
- **Derek** is a specialist in complex, marine insurance claims; one claim may entail many days work, entailing negotiations with legal experts, marine repair experts, re-insurers and so on.

Alice's work is classic transactional and non-discretionary and Derek's the opposite, but the other two cases are midway between.

Moreover any number of other gradations can be imagined: a claim tends to become gradually less routine and thus to offer more scope for discretion, the more fraud, police interest, human injury and death enter the picture. Thus the work any person does can be located somewhere along a continuum from transactional to discretionary, but there is no natural breakpoint. Moreover, even for any one person, some activities will be more transactional or discretionary than others.

The work of these four people is supported by IT. Alice only works at data entry; Bernard has access to a database of past claims and payments; Clare also uses some expert system software; Derek has a special database combining the texts of numerous documents with images of maps and vessels. All four use terminals attached to the same computer; the same computer system stores all the databases concerned; all four people use the same electronic mail facilities.

There is another complication too. *Discretionary use* can mean two separate things:

- *Either* use of a facility is discretionary, in the literal sense that you can use it as much or as little as you like; eg electronic mail.
- *Or* to use the facility sensibly you have to exercise discretion. The facility is powerful, but you must decide how best to use it; eg Derek has access to a text database, but must use personal judgement to choose appropriate keywords for searching.

All this suggests that it is really futile to separate out two categories of system: EUC and operational. The most that can be said is:

- In describing a person's job there are any number of possible gradations along a continuum between transactional and discretionary.[5]
- Most people's jobs can be assisted or altered by IT — and in various complex ways. IT could make Alice's strongly operational job more mechanical, and thus push it further towards the operational end of the continuum; but, alternatively, IT could allow Alice to access certain information and exercise a little more discretion. IT could permit Derek to tap into a wealth of information that would support more informed judgements; or IT could be used to impose more standardisation on the way Derek goes about things; or it could do both at the same time.

Discretion in Decision-making and Development

As the previous discussion shows, examining discretion in the *use* of functions and systems leads to rich detail that can be of great value to decisions about what kind of systems to have in the organisation. But as a way of approaching the specific topic of EUC it is a deadend. Discretionary setup, ie discretion in *decision-making and development,* is much the more fruitful branch to explore for advice and options that are helpful to decisions about EUC.

Leave out the nature of the system itself. Ask the question: If a certain department is dissatisfied, can it stop using the system and replace it by

End-user Computing, Issues, Options and Policies

THREE ISSUES	OPTIONS
Decision To what degree may a department decide for itself to purchase outside goods and services?	*either* **A** complete freedom; *or* **B** intermediate, eg free to buy from supplier on a recommended list, subject to MIS blocking major wrong directions; *or* **C** not at all, eg an MIS analyst or project manager decides what is required.
Payment What does a department pay for — either literally or after recharging from MIS?	**A** goods from the outside world, such as PC hardware, software products and external professional services; *and/or* **B** data centre use and associated costs; *and/or* **C** training and support by IS or IC staff. Note: the cost of whatever of these a department doesn't pay for is usually absorbed by the IC or the data centre.
Budget Does a department make a formal annual budget for those things it will have to pay for?	*either* **A** yes; *or* **B** no, it pays as it goes, like a consumer.

FIVE POLICIES	defined as options chosen on each issue	
1. Freedom and responsibility	Decision:	complete freedom (A)
	Payment:	all (A *and* B *and* C)
	Budget:	yes (A)
2. Freedom as consumer	Decision:	complete freedom (A)
	Payment:	all (A *and* B *and* C)
	Budget:	no (B)
3. Guided freedom	Decision:	intermediate (B)
	Payment:	all except IS/IC staff costs (A *and* B *but not* C)
	Budget:	yes (A)
4. Subjugation with cost-awareness	Decision:	none (C)
	Payment:	all (A *and* B *and* C)
	Budget:	no (B)
5. Subjugation without responsibility	Decision:	none (C)
	Payment:	none (*neither* A *nor* B *nor* C)
	Budget:	no (B)

something else? Here are two extreme gradations, posing the control-freedom tradeoff in accentuated form:

- **Genuine liberty (extreme freedom).** At this extreme, the following three things are all true: the department has the *theoretical right*, according to company procedures and general policy; the department has the *effective right*: ie it won't normally be prevented from exercising its practical right by subtle or brutal pressures from other parties; the department has the *practical capability*: it possesses people of its own with adequate skills to arrange for such a change to happen successfully (including (say) skills to get value for money from outsiders such as a software house).
- ***or* Subjugation (extreme control).** None of those three things apply. The department has to rely on either informal lobbying or nasty confrontation to get the change accepted, and even then it will have to rely on the central IT people to carry it out.

Of course, these are extremes bounding a scale on which many gradations can be marked — a handy way of understanding the reality of the EUC situation in any organisation (which may be different from the rules set down on paper), and the options for making new arrangements.[6,7]

SUGGESTED WARRANTS

This section presents a fairly elaborate warrant based on an extension of some of the concepts in the previous section.

Distinctions of Policies

One good way of analysing any set of relationships between parts of an organisation is to seize on how things are paid for. The warrant in the table identifies three *issues* associated with payment, and gives several *options* for each.

It then distinguishes five plausible *policies*: each policy is a coherent set of chosen options. Put another way, these are five different ways of resolving the control-freedom tradeoff.[8]

NOTES & ARGUMENTS

1 Opening two references: Gunton (1988), p. 2; Heikkilä, p. 5. Third: Robert V Head, 'Information Resource Center: a new force in end-user computing', *Journal of Systems Management*, February 1985, in the Somogyi and Galliers anthology, p. 37.

Suppose you have an on-line facility to a database at the other end of the country. You want a new report containing a new selection of information. Then, on the definition given by Head, there are two main possibilities:

- You may use a simple access facility yourself to specify and extract the new report. That definitely counts as EUC.
- You may contact the people at the data

centre and ask them to do whatever is necessary to produce the report you describe to them. That is definitely not EUC.

2 Robson (p. 297) gives a list of 18 candidate services for an IC. This book also asserts (p. 305): 'Many of the problems associated with an information centre will change . . . However, at all stages having an *unclear* role will be a significant problem.' Of course, there must be some truth in this, but the question arises: How clear should the role of the IC be?

It may seem obvious that there should be a firm demarcation of what the IC people do and don't do, but is it? Take some other services. With a lawyer or an estate agent or a vanity publisher, it probably is a good thing to have the boundaries of services and responsibilities very clearly understood. But what about a schoolmaster or a funeral director or a family doctor? There the best arrangement (if it can be achieved) may be for both sides to expect the person giving the service to do *whatever seems reasonable*, without exact prior demarcation. In some cases (by no means all), that may be the better model for the IC. The point is that the clarity of demarcation (lawyer-model or teacher-model) is itself a variable for decision.

3 The treatment by Hussain and Hussain is a kind of exception that proves the rule. Throughout its 600 pages this textbook avoids confusing its students with awkward tradeoffs. This is a grave handicap to intelligent discussion of EUC. 'One of the more important roles of the (information) center is to nurture user awareness of the importance of standardization and integration of resources.' (p. 432) True, but the important thing worth knowing is that these natural aims usually have to be balanced against contrary aims, such as creativity and initiative. 'Job descriptions of information center personnel will vary from one organization to another. Assignment of duties will depend on how the center is organized and what services are offered.' (p. 435) Obviously, but this is scarcely worth writing down, unless you give some account of how different organisations might choose different approaches.

4 Gunton (1988) contains another piece of analysis (pp. 46-50) that is well worth discussion. This is a quadrant-diagram made from the two variables: autonomy and coupling. End-users may have high or low *autonomy* (ie freedom to decide what to do), and EUC systems may be strongly *coupled* to central operational systems (eg directly accessing up-to-date data in a central database) or not (eg using weekly summary data extracted from the database). This gives four combination-possibilities or quadrants.

What do you gain by this quadrant-analysis? Gunton offers a map, subject to disclaimers about it being rough, showing how companies in different industries should tend to have EUC in different quadrants. But this map doesn't seem very credible. In any case, it is undermined straight away by the statement that different units within one large organisation often need their EUC in different quadrants. The book also says that different quadrants have different success factors, and that this quadrant-analysis can guide infrastructure planning and other aspects of the management of EUC. But these things are not spelt out; there is no analysis of (say) how the functions and responsibilities of the IC will be different for each of the quadrants.

In the book the *autonomy* variable seems to refer only to discretionary use;

discretionary setup — surely a very important variable in high-level EUC policy — seems to be left out.

On examination the *coupled* variable seems to confuse a variety of things and thus offer false choices. Each *EUC system* might be allocated to one of the following pigeon-holes:

- One kind of EUC system (eg concerned with decision support) needs to access operational data, such as business transactions (whether summarised or not). For this kind of system there are three main possibilities: one, coupling to a central system serving all departments of the organisation; two, coupling to a modest system concerned only with the same department; three, no direct coupling, data down-loaded from time to time.
- Another kind of EUC system does need data from some external source, but not of an operational, transactional character; eg it may access a database of legal texts, or a library of ready-made, standard CAD drawings. There may be different ways of arranging this, but they are not sufficiently important for analysis at this level.
- The other kind of EUC system doesn't need any data from another source; eg it is concerned with typing letters or solving linear programming problems. Here the question of coupling simply doesn't arise.

This defines five main categories for any one EUC system. One department could easily have a variety of systems, falling into different categories.

Why discuss Gunton's quadrant-diagram at this length, if there is so much to criticise? Because it exposes certain themes of *general* importance in thinking about IM:

- Anybody can suggest a quadrant-diagram; you just think up two questions with yes/no or high/low answers. The real work comes in showing how organisations in different quadrants of the diagram should plausibly take different decisions on each of a variety of more specific issues. That is the real test of analysis on any IM subject.
- The critical thinking of the above notes may seem negative, but look at the result: a much more realistic analysis of the *coupling* variable. It is frequently easier to develop that kind of analysis by working out why somebody else's account seems unsatisfactory, than by starting from a blank sheet.

5 Another handy concept is analysing users into different generic types. Plainly, the actuary who has enthusiastically developed ingenious spreadsheet macros to value pension funds is a different case from the word-processing copy-typist. If the end-users in the organisation fit into a number of categories, reasoning can proceed along the lines: 'Given this particular profile of end-users . . . then the following policy on EUC seems appropriate . . ' This approach is explored in O'Brien (*Demands*), Briefing 5.

6 Most articles and chapters in books about EUC have the merit of exposing options and tradeoffs. This is one of the best areas of IM from that point of view. Even so, there is often a lack of bite to the analysis. Here, to compensate, is an argument. One idea in Robson's lengthy treatment (pp. 288ff.) is that there are two independent variables: the rate of expansion of EUC in the organisation, and the level of control of EUC (by some central body). Since either can be high or low and all combinations are possible, there are four generic policies available.

But these two variables are not independent. There are three (not four) generic policies available: *either* exercise a low level of control (and thus abstain from any attempt to influence the rate of expansion), *or* exercise high control and ensure that the rate of expansion is higher than what it would otherwise be, *or* exercise high control and ensure that the rate of expansion is lower than what it would otherwise be.

The second and third policy options only have any point if you judge that, left to develop naturally, the rate of expansion of EUC within the organisation will be inappropriate. How would you stimulate expansion? Probably by a combination of agenda decisions (eg 'All departments must own on average at least one PC per employee') and financially-weighted context decisions (eg 'Departmental purchases of software are subsidised by 50% from a central fund'; 'Departments get internal consultancy by experts from the information centre for nothing'). The opposite policy (deliberately curbing the rate of growth), though feasible through agenda and context decisions that go the opposite way, may be difficult to carry through without creating resentment — to put it mildly.

7 The issues of EUC may look very different before long. Most discussion of the subject has rested on the assumption that, however awkward precise boundaries might be, end-user systems are entirely different from the main systems handling the basic administration of the business, developed and maintained by the MIS department. But suppose the vogue for *workflow* systems gathers strength. The classic workflow system automates the internal administration of the business, it uses PCs and networks in the departments, and it is developed by translating the organisation's procedure manual into a set of rules for routing information between workers (rather than by programming). Is that EUC or not? Doesn't it call for reappraisal of all the categories and issues associated with EUC?

8 The ideas in this section are an extensive reworking of those in Heikkilä, pp. 59ff.

The *issues-options-policies* format is useful in many decision-making situations. Usually, many combinations of options can be generated. The trick is to weed out most of the combinations, to arrive at the most coherent and relevant; eg (in this briefing's warrant) on the payment issue C without A is conceivable, but it would mean that a department didn't pay the costs of hiring programmers from a software house, but was recharged internally for time spent by the organisation's own IS or IC staff — a rather unlikely arrangement. For much more about general techniques with issues and options, see O'Brien (*Demands*), Briefings 8-10.

CONNECTIONS

9. Stage Theories	A theory of stages of growth in end-user computing
10. Learning and Historical Themes	The learning process — important in end-user computing
12. Matching through Comparisons	In any comparison the PC architecture might be held to offer more room than the mini for private end-user initiatives
16. Matching through Aspects	Presentation graphics, most usefully analysed into four aspects, is one of the clearest examples of an end-user application to be found
24. Centralisation and Distribution	Issues of scope loom large in end-user computing debates

38. Decision Support Systems

TOPIC

Systems meant to provide information that will help managers decide things are notoriously difficult to design, plan and manage. Classification is a good beginning — distinguishing what counts as a decision support system from what does not, and analysing features that distinguish the varieties of decision support system (DSS).

Some ideas for classification already exist in the IM literature; this briefing examines them critically and suggests some elaboration. This leads to some analysis that can drive a variety of IM decisions on the agenda, matching or scope planes.

REPRESENTATIVE IDEAS — SUMMARISED

As this section shows, some ideas that seem to classify different types of DSS or to distinguish DSS from EIS (executive information system) actually turn out to cover wider matters, such as types of managerial decision-making or degrees of maturity of technologies.

Analysing Management Work by Degree of Structure

Many authorities have suggested that some decision-making tasks are more *structured* than others, in the rough sense that deciding how much inventory to reorder or deciding the optimum location for a warehouse are more structured decisions than selecting the cover for a weekly news magazine or choosing a new manager to hire. One claim is that there are *three* broad classes of problem:**1**

- **Relatively structured.** Here IT can take over most of the burden of processing data to arrive at decisions — provided that the initial analysis is done to lay bare the full structure of the decision-making. Of course, for regular decisions (eg inventory reordering), the gain is greater than for one-offs (eg warehouse location).
- **Relatively unstructured.** By their nature, some decisions can't be

taken in any genuine sense by an automated system, though technology can make the decision-maker's task easier in more mundane ways: eg page makeup software makes it easy to try out various designs for a magazine cover; word processing software can store textual notes on promotion candidates in easily accessible form; an expert system may even help in deciding which personal qualities fit a certain job.

- **Moderately structured.** There are management problems midway between these two, and these moderately structured problems are the main target for DSSs. There are different management levels: operational control (eg bond trading), management control (eg setting an advertising budget) or strategic planning (eg capital acquisition).

Distinguishing DSS, EIS, MIS

Another interesting approach presents the following reasoning:

- Make a distinction between **hard and soft technologies**. If a manager is given spreadsheet software, much still depends on how cleverly this tool is applied to solving the particular problem; this makes spreadsheet a soft technology. Set up a teleconferencing system and it could be a great help in reaching decisions, but the managers just use it. It would be rather odd to talk of somebody *cleverly* applying this tool to solve a particular problem; this makes teleconferencing a hard technology.
- Now make a different distinction. At any given moment some technologies are more **mature** than others; taking (say) 1990 as the point of measurement, spreadsheet was more mature than expert system. To say spreadsheet is mature in this context means that people already know how to use spreadsheet effectively, ie which type of problems it suits and how to use it efficiently not wastefully.
- Now use the term **MIS** to denote whatever management-supporting systems and technology are on the frontier between the mature and the immature at a given moment.
- Now divide MISs (ie systems on the frontier of maturity) into two categories: MISs based on soft technology can be called **DSSs**, and those based on hard technology **EISs** (executive information systems).**2**

REPRESENTATIVE IDEAS — ANALYSED

The classifications proposed in the previous section are useful material for critical, not necessarily negative, thinking.

Management Work and Structure

The main problem with analysing by 'structure' is that this is an impressionistic concept bundling together a number of different variables:

- If a task is largely pre-programmed (ie there are clear result-determining rules to follow) it is usually regarded as more structured than one where this is less true.

- If a task is carried out by defined, standard multi-step procedures (not necessarily just rules) it is usually regarded as more structured than one where this is less true.
- If a task is carried out by following defined rules and/or procedures that are very complex it may be regarded as more structured than one where rules and procedures are less complex. But on the other hand, it may not — on the grounds that the more complex the rules and procedures the more scope for judgement, interpreting them according to the situation.
- If a task calls mainly for intellectual skills of analysing facts and reasoning carefully it is usually regarded as more structured than one where interpersonal skills play a large part.
- If the problem tackled by the task is one where cause-and-effect can be defined and studied it is usually regarded as more structured than one where guesswork and intuition are required.
- If a task's product is very clear (eg decision to cut prices by 10%) it is usually regarded as more structured than one where this is less true (eg decision to aim marketing more at upper middle-class consumers).

Of course, these overlap a good deal, but not completely. Moreover, a number of associated variables are still left out: whether the matter is large-scale or small-scale; long-term or short-term; routine or non-routine; done by senior or junior managers. Putting these four variables together with the six bullets above, you might devise a ten-dimensional matrix for classifying management tasks, and then show how different regions of that matrix were, in general, best served by particular types of computer system. But this would be far too complicated to be of any practical use. As in quite a few other areas of IM, the knack required is to analyse deep enough to notice the complexity that is obscured by simple generalisations, but also to focus on just those subtleties that actually count in the particular case you are dealing with.

DSS, EIS, MIS

There is little point having long arguments about terminology, as if a DSS were 'really' a certain thing and an EIS could be shown to be 'really' something else. The question is: Does it help decision-making to distinguish between a system using soft technology (called DSS) and one based on hard technology (called EIS)?

This hard/soft distinction may be too fragile to sustain intensive analysis, since many technologies seem to be located in a broad area midway along the continuum between hard and soft. But can the distinction be employed in this one particular area of systems associated with management decisions? There seems to be a difference between two types of system facilities:

- **Soft facilities.** The aim is to make it very easy to extract data from a

Marking out DSS Territory

At the soft frontier:	*Middle ground:*	*At the hard frontier:*
Information-only system The system doesn't take or suggest decisions; it just provides access on-line or as printout to useful data; eg it shows that sales are down in California.	**DSS (decision support system)** The system comes close to suggesting the decisions to be made *and/or* it presents information in such a keenly analysed way that conclusions and decisions are strongly implied; *and/or* it provides facilities for exploring the effects of possible decisions.	**Decision-generating system** The system itself takes decisions on a routine basis; eg it recommends what adverts and TV commercials to place in California, taking account of relevant factors, such as whether sales are up or down.

body of management information, according to many possible selection criteria, and to display it conveniently, perhaps with a moderate degree of analysis, eg calculating totals and averages. The emphasis is on ad hoc access facilities, in the sense of making possible all kinds of unpredictable requests for information.

- **Hard facilities.** Here there are powerful 'drilling-down' and business graphics features; the system might display a pie-chart analysing sales, allow selection of one slice of the pie, then display another pie-chart analysing that slice, and go on drilling down through further levels. The stress is on allowing the busy manager to analyse quantitative data from the corporate database *in the kind of way such analysis is usually done* — as opposed to providing a general-purpose facility to select any data by any criteria.

This difference is relevant to decision-making. You can use it to firm up the kind of system you want, and that will influence its design, the way it is developed and the technical approach.[3,4]

SUGGESTED WARRANTS

The rest of the briefing is essentially elaboration and variation of the contrast between the hard (ready-made, powerful, less flexible) and the soft (more demanding but more flexible).

Chart of DSS Systems and Technologies

The table suggests a way of marking out the territory of DSS (including EIS and related terms). With boundaries drawn like this, a typical DSS would be one enabling you to work on data in 'what if' mode, to explore the effects of defined assumptions and decisions; eg increase TV advertising 15% in California, assume the whole market is growing at 5% a year, etc. If the system is sophisticated, it may be able to work backwards from some defined, desired result to find out what assumptions and actions are needed to produce the result.

On this analysis, those systems that only present data from *databases*, no matter how cleverly they extract it and format it, are on the soft, information-only frontier of DSS. *Spreadsheet* (and related financial modelling software) is plainly one central DSS technology. The other is *expert system* (or more broadly, artificial intelligence). It is true that expert system technology can form the basis of systems over on the hard, decision-generating frontier, but it can also be used in a less deterministic, DSS way. For instance, a system could possess some rules about the correlation of weather, time of year, TV advertising and other factors with sales, but rely on the manager using it for such things as assumptions about future weather, actions of competitors etc.

This is only a rough chart of systems and technologies; the complication is that, as already glimpsed, the same technology can provide very different types of decision-making system:

'Here is a database and some expert system software. You yourself have to set up whatever rules and inductive mechanisms you need to define and solve your problem.'

'Here is a spreadsheet already filled up with all the data you will need. It has general-purpose what-if facilities. You choose the particular what-if variables to try out.'

'Here is a database and spreadsheet software providing various handy standard formats and algorithms for what-if marketing decisions in our company. There are standard formulae for the marginal impact of extra TV advertising and a standard format for all the main variables to be quantified and the relations between them, when considering a new marketing campaign. Therefore, if you have a given problem to study, it is pretty obvious how to go about it.'

'Here is expert system software complete with rules, formulae and logic, to solve the problem of finding the optimal size and distribution of sales force in a region; it accesses a database too but you don't need to know that. Answer a few questions and it will give a reasonably good solution. On the other hand, you can, if you like, alter the rules yourself.'

NOTES & ARGUMENTS

1 'Decision Support Systems: Promise and Practice' by Sid L Huff in Umbaugh's anthology, 2nd ed. (p. 697).

2 Earl, p. 15.

Synnott (pp. 128-9) suggests a different breakdown. Analyse systems that support management into two categories: those that *solve problems* or simulate scenarios; and those that just provide *access to information*. Now break the second category in two, between: systems that provide *general-purpose* facilities for extracting and combining data from a large database; and systems tailored for very *specific* use, eg offering the chief executive a ten-choice menu, corresponding to ten key quantitative measures chosen for the particular business.

This is not really a *distinctions* warrant; it is better seen as a warrant defining three *aspects* of systems to support management: problem-solving, general-purpose access, and tailored access. Though one system *could* be 100% one of the three, more often the key to defining an effective new system will be determining the relative weight to be given to the three aspects.

Synnott's three-way analysis is essentially a more subtle version of Earl's hard-soft distinction.

3 Different software products are suitable for the two kinds of system. See O'Brien (*Database*), Briefing 17.

4 The breakdowns of DSS contained in this briefing all ignore one facet that, within a few years, may perhaps turn everything upside down. A DSS is usually regarded as a system used by a fairly senior manager to make sense of large quantities of data in a fairly hierarchical organisation. Suppose the trends towards flatter organisations and re-engineered, enriched jobs and groupware software all gather force. Then many more people will have roles that include taking decisions that need to be supported by information. Then many systems will include decision-supporting features. Then the idea of there being a separate class of decision-support systems will have to be re-examined.

CONNECTIONS

13. Matching through Distinctions	Expert systems are not *per se* decision support systems, but when broken down by role, some end up in that territory
14. Matching through Gradations	An electronic meeting system is never called a decision support system, but, whatever its gradation of complexity, it is meant to assist decision-making
22. Evolutionary Development	An attractive way of developing a DSS is by evolution, rather than prior detailed design
40. Strategic Systems and Competitive Advantage	Some count the DSS as one variety of strategic system

39. Inter-organisational Systems

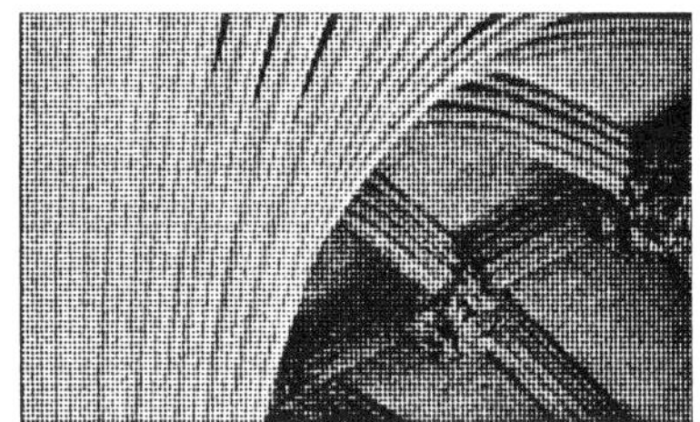

TOPIC

It is easy to come away from reading certain articles and books with the impression that the more use you make of telecoms the better, and the more closely you integrate your systems with your customers and suppliers the better. But things are a good deal more complicated than that.

This briefing takes on a critical-thinking task of a rather general character. People often imply that 'X is a good thing, the more the better'. X may be 'inter-organisational systems' or 'integration' or 'expert systems' or any number of other things. But it is usually advantageous to unpack X and show that it isn't one thing but several. There may be a variety of possibilities, many with both positive and negative features. This makes it apparent that 'the more X the better' is not a good basis for decision-making. With that awareness, you are well placed to take decisions by choosing the most appropriate possibilities, with the most favourable balance of tradeoffs.

In this briefing the concept of 'inter-organisational systems' is examined in that style.

REPRESENTATIVE IDEAS — SUMMARISED

An inter-organisational system (from now on IOS) is a system where the interaction between a company and its trading partners (ie customers and suppliers) is automated to some degree. For example, instead of sending orders on pieces of paper the customer sends a magnetic tape (extremely low-tech) or transmits data across a telecoms network to the supplier's computer (higher-tech). The two main areas to explore are: how to define the possibilities more precisely than this, and how to identify the issues that matter.

IOSs: Characteristics and Importance

One article identifies four key characteristics of an IOS:[1]

- Since the system crosses company boundaries, it raises issues of control (more awkward than with normal internal systems), also planning (ie fitting it into the long-term planning of internal systems), and also day-to-day management (harder than with normal internal systems).

- By crossing company boundaries, the system raises issues of a legal or related character: When does an order become an order? What about new scope for unfair practices?
- Often there is an IOS facilitator, some intermediate supplier of network and related services: an on-line service (eg Compuserve) or perhaps an industry consortium. This introduces a new source of complications.
- Any system is meant to bring its user some benefit, and the majority of new systems change the way an organisation works to some degree, but an IOS probably raises more opportunities for achievement and for organisational change than the average system.

These four points differ in status; the last is essentially a motive for seriously considering having an IOS, while the first three are challenges to be faced in achieving a successful IOS.

In reinforcement of the potential advantage of the IOS, the article points out that a (successful) IOS is a particularly strong weapon for dealing with each of Porter's five competitive forces in the marketplace. For instance, one force is the entry of new competitors threatening existing players; an elaborate IOS linking trading partners may be a strong deterrent to potential new rivals, who would have to make the investment to set up something similar. Another force is the bargaining power of customers; but a customer whose systems work hand-in-glove with your IOS, will find it very difficult to change to a different supplier, and will thus exercise less bargaining power.

Electronic Data Interchange and Related Concepts

Other things being equal, the more elaborate and sophisticated the IOS, the higher the stakes. The problems to be solved will be greater, the investment greater, the risks run greater, and, if the system is well conceived, the benefits of success will be greater. Making informed decisions about such things demands awareness of the different options available, with different mixes of sophistication, investment, risk and benefit.

Sometimes IOS is treated as a synonym of EDI (electronic data interchange), but this is lazy usage. Not all IOSs, ie systems linking a company to its trading partners, are cases of EDI. First, exchanging transaction data on tape or diskette is universally regarded as too primitive to count as EDI; treat this as an extreme point on the scale of IOS systems, but nevertheless still on the scale.

Is every system where data is sent between trading partners by telecoms a case of EDI? Most people involved with EDI find this far too loose a criterion, and assert that, if the term EDI is to have any decent meaning at all, it must include at least two concepts:**2**

- **computer-to-computer** exchange of information (without human intervention);
- **standard** (rather than company-specific) formats for messages.

This definition avoids the dangerous confusion of EDI and videotex. The Datafreight system is well respected as one example of an innovative IOS in the UK. It links up road freight transport companies, to help match loads with available vehicles, but it uses videotex not EDI technology. Videotex technology is based on the idea of exchanging information *between a computer and an operator at a screen*. This is fundamentally different from computer-to-computer transactions without human intervention, which is characteristic of EDI.

Similarly, fax and electronic mail applications don't count as EDI either. Whether you count them as IOS depends probably on whether the content of the messages is structured enough, and the exchange of messages is regular enough to be considered a *system* as opposed to a mere *ad hoc facility*.

Classic EDI

It is often helpful to set up a classic example of some concept and analyse its distinctive traits. One article does this for EDI systems. The four classic traits are:

- **Computer-computer.** Data moves between the computers of trading partners without any human intervention.
- **Standard format.** The messages are sent between computers in an industry-standard format (ie not a format agreed between customer A and supplier B, nor a format agreed between customer A and all its suppliers).
- **Clearing-house.** The whole facility is run by a central clearing-house service. Thus any given company can avoid the problems of linking up with all its separate trading partners; it only need concern itself technically with links to the clearing-house.
- **Mailbox.** The clearing-house provides a mailbox service. That is, once a message reaches the clearing-house, it is stored in a notional mailbox, which the receiving party can access at any time: every ten seconds or twice a day or once a week or whenever it likes. The clearing-house guarantees to keep messages safely in the mailbox until accessed.

The first two of these are really integral to the *definition* of EDI; a system without these traits isn't EDI. The last two are traits of *classic* EDI; a system with the first two traits but not the second two is EDI, but not classic EDI.

Analysing IOS Objectives

A number of writers have suggested ways of breaking IOS (ie including but not only EDI) possibilities down further, by analysing system objectives. What follows is a medley of ideas from several sources.[3]

First, separate two aspects of linking up with customers or suppliers: the objective may be to improve *service quality*, and/or it may be to achieve more *efficient administration*:

- The service quality objective can be split further into two main aspects. A system may provide much the same service as before, but **better** (eg it dispatches the same engineers to repair a piece of equipment — but quicker), and/or it may provide a service that is **different** in kind (eg providing regular status reports on the progress of a made-to-order product).
- The administrative efficiency objective also has two main aspects. There is the straightforward gain from **reduced overhead** of paperwork, accounts clerks and so on. But a different aspect is **flexibility**; a sophisticated ordering system, may bring more scope for revising production schedules from hour to hour in accordance with changes in demand, unexpected mishaps or opportunities, and so on.

Second, after objectives recognise *degrees of ambition*. For example:

- One system whose objectives were mainly *administration-flexibility* might provide managers with reliable, up-to-date information enabling them to revise production schedules frequently. But a more ambitious system, also with administration-flexibility objectives, might receive information from suppliers that certain vital parts were delayed, and then *automatically* amend production schedules.
- One system whose objectives, by the above analysis, were mainly *service-different* might exchange sales forecast statistics along with individual transactions, to help the partner with macro-level planning. A more ambitious service-different system might offer a service for optimising the customer's logistics worldwide, taking account of freight costs, import quotas, national taxation rates and regulations, and so on.

In principle, any number of gradations are possible with this ambition variable, but there is a plausible four-gradation scale:

- **Transactions**: just interchange of transactions.
- **Inventory/availability:** the system provides information on what is available and its pricing, perhaps differentially between customers; ie it provides information that will influence the transactions that will occur.
- **Process linkage:** there is a high degree of functional integration; eg the design process in one organisation is linked to the tooling and production processes of another.
- **Negotiation, dialogue and knowledge sharing**: this is more interactive than the automatic integration of the previous gradation, and deals with more fundamental matters, eg development of product specifications.

REPRESENTATIVE IDEAS — ANALYSED

Most of the ideas summarised above plainly offer some insight into options

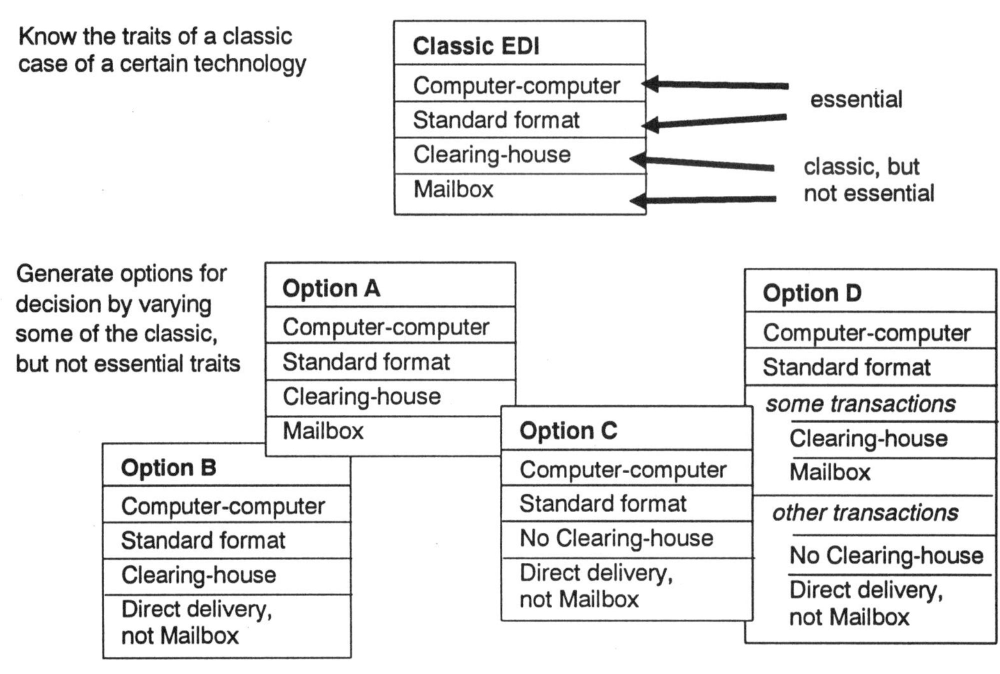

for decision and their implications. This section spells out in a little more detail how they can affect decision-making.

Varying Classic EDI and IOS

As the diagram shows, one great advantage of setting up a classic case is that by varying the classic traits you can generate other plausible, non-classic options for consideration. This 'classic case' technique is potentially applicable to any kind of technology, not just EDI.

The computer-computer trait of EDI is not quite as simple as it may seem at first.[5] The essential point about EDI is that the *exchange* of transaction data (eg to order a part from a supplier) occurs computer-to-computer. The data for the message could be generated automatically by some material requirements planning system, or it could have been keyed in completely by a human, within an internal system, separate from any link to the outside world. Further variations that may be well worth considering count as IOS but not as EDI:

● Suppose a person at *company A* accesses databases of parts and quotes offered by *several* industry suppliers; then decides which to order from; then sends a transaction message. This may well be done through an industry clearing-house, and may well use standard message formats.

Whether it is done on a mailbox or direct basis will depend on the nature of the industry and what is supplied. This may be an innovative IOS, but it is not EDI, still less classic EDI.

● Suppose a trading partner keys in orders online to *company B's* computer, with appropriate prompts for relevant data and validation checks. That describes some innovative systems that became famous during the eighties, but it is not EDI. In fact, it probably doesn't have any of the four classic traits.

● Suppose *company C* exchanges with its partners structured non-transaction messages such as pricelists, production schedules, sales forecasts and inventory data. They may not be in any industry-standard format and therefore not EDI — although they may be sent through the same telecoms facilities as regular transactions that are undoubted EDI.

Analysing IOS Objectives

The breakdown of IOS objectives into aspects is valuable and decision-forcing, if used with care.

First, not every IOS need aim for all the four aspects described: making service both better and different, and achieving administration with both reduced overhead and increased flexibility. It could be perfectly rational to have an IOS intended to make service dramatically better, even if its effect on administrative efficiency was slightly negative.

Some clarification of priorities is usually called for, but this does not mean that a choice must be made between four distinct types of system. There are four aspects that any one system may possess, albeit normally to differing degrees. It could be quite plausible to aim for a system with tremendous stress on one aspect, moderate stress on another, and some, but still slight, attention on the other two.

Understood in this way, the four aspects can help make IOS decisions consistent with broader policy matters:

'Since our general business strategy is to offer a distinctly superior service (as opposed to competing on price or being exceptionally innovative), shouldn't our planned IOS offer specially slick handling of customer orders (instead of just saving money on administration)?'

'The agreed purpose of this IOS is to cut administrative costs. Why then aren't we following the most straightforward route of using the industry-standard system that already exists?

'How can you expect to reach your ambitious objective of an IOS to provide intriguing new services to the customer, and thereby support a general company strategy of competing by differentiation, when your IOS is based on a primitive mailbox approach?' And so on.

SUGGESTED WARRANTS

This section is a consolidation and expansion of the representative ideas already discussed. It provides a warrant charting out the relations between IOS, EDI and some other concepts.

Charting IOS, EDI and Innovation

Most innovative uses of IT found in business-school case studies were not EDI. EDI entails standard message formats. This reduces its room for being innovative, since such standards only develop once a reasonable number of people are already satisfied that they are needed.

It is still not compulsory to follow industry standards for message formats in a new system to link up with trading partners; in other words, a sophisticated IOS doesn't have to be EDI.

In the industries where EDI is most relevant there are now agreed formats for the different types of transaction messages (purchase orders, bills of lading etc), with associated uniform product codes. Therefore the more attention the system pays to industry standards, the more authentically EDI it will be, but the less innovative it will be, and hence the less likely it is to become a business-school case. Plainly, the more aware your industry is of the possibilities of linking trading partners, the more likely it is to have EDI standards already, and the less likely it is that use of EDI will surprise competitors.

Moreover, EDI runs counter to one much-admired theme: using an advanced IOS to lock in trading partners. EDI encourages the agreement of detailed standards within a whole industry and the setting-up of industry clearing-houses; these things make it easier than ever before for a customer to switch to another supplier. Similarly, standards and clearing-houses reduce the barrier of upfront investment for new entrants to an industry. This analysis can expose some high-stake choices:

- *Either* interact with trading partners in an EDI setup, using industry-standard formats, and a clearing-house, and with features comparable to those offered by others in the industry. This is the safe option that does not aim to gain any striking advantage over competitors.
- *Or* have an industry-standard EDI setup for the exchange of information, but intensify the automated processing associated with each message; eg make the generation of new order messages to suppliers or the effect on scheduling of new orders from customers more closely integrated with internal systems.
- *Or* set up a service of your own, bypassing the clearing-house and probably with non-standard formats, intending that it should be superior to the EDI arrangements of the rest of the industry. This option is ambitious and likely to have either splendid or disastrous consequences.

NOTES & ARGUMENTS

1 James I Cash, 'Interorganizational Systems: An Opportunity or Threat?', *The Information Society*, Volume 3, Number 3, 1985, in Somogyi and Galliers (p. 200).

2 *I/S Analyzer*, August 1989. A 12-page introduction to EDI. Recommended.

For Datafreight, see Gunton (1990), p. 45. This is written as if a videotex system (ie a person-to-computer system) could be an instance of EDI, whereas the briefing text suggests that an EDI system is essentially computer-to-computer. Making the term EDI so broad that it includes videotex has a number of disadvantages: it goes against the practice of most who have analysed the subject; it destroys a valuable distinction; it raises a difficult question: What *doesn't* count as EDI?

The classic traits in the following section are from 'EDI — The Competitive Edge' by CM Hill, in the Clarke and Cameron anthology, pp. 63ff.

3 Sources used: P and P Swatman, 'EDI and Its Implications for Industry', Clarke and Cameron, pp. 105ff.; the article on electronic data interchange by David G Robinson and Steve A Stanton in Umbaugh's anthology, 2nd ed., pp. 121ff.; another article, same subject, same anthology (pp. 717ff.) by Richard C Norris; K Hugh Macdonald in Scott Morton, Chapter 6. All these are useful items, though the last is rather pompous.

Careful analysis of this kind is a necessary antidote to sweeping 'Link up or else' exhortations: 'In the next 24 months, mount major partnership projects with 75 percent of your major suppliers/distributors/customers. . . Continually add value-enhancing, ever-tighter links to every member of the distribution channel.' Tom Peters, *Thriving on Chaos* (Harper & Row, 1988), pp. 130, 132. Before following such advice on linking-up systems it is surely worthwhile to clarify possible objectives, and perhaps give some of them greater priority than others.

4 Since this seems better than mailbox, why not do it this way always? Because it usually entails much more sophisticated hardware and software arrangements, and thus higher costs and greater management control requirements.

5 The twists of analysis here raise the question whether the distinction between computer-computer (EDI) and person-computer (not EDI) is really worth fighting for. There is a much more general issue: When is it worth taking trouble to agree precise definitions and preserve subtle distinctions?

Sometimes logic-chopping in the style of St Thomas Aquinas is not fruitful; eg detailed debate about the definition of 'strategy', or the difference between 'information' and 'data'. But here the cause seems worthwhile. The two defining traits given for EDI in the briefing text seem much the best means of preserving EDI as one category of system within the broader category of IOS. If you abandon that position (ie if you accept that EDI is a term with no clear meaning), you are pushed back to allowing that there are a dozen or more variants of IOS, but no incisive way of sorting them out.

CONNECTIONS

14. Matching through Gradations	Bridges and gateways are part of the technical side of systems that link organisations together
15. Matching through Charts	Videotex, when charted and related to other technologies, defines one area of the possibilities for inter-organisational systems
16. Matching through Aspects	Most value-added network services set up inter-organisational systems in some sense
17. Matching through Examples	One of the main purposes of the OSI model is to facilitate interconnection between different networks, perhaps those of different organisations
36. Business Process Re-engineering	Fashionable ideas related to IOS in unclear ways
40. Strategic Systems and Competitive Advantage	Famous case-study systems, most of which are IOSs, though not all IOSs are successful enough to become case studies

40. Strategic Systems and Competitive Advantage

TOPIC

There is a kind of pantheon of systems renowned for their strategic, competitive-advantage use of IT — Sabre, American Hospital Supply, McKesson, and so on. What, if anything, do they have in common?

It isn't good enough to conjure up a vague impression that strategic systems are the ones that are imaginative and successful, and leave it at that. If strategic systems are genuinely distinct, then they probably raise special issues, but to have any chance of discussing the issues properly, you need a reasonable view of what is distinct about them.

There is also the question whether it is advisable to spend time reading about and studying such cases — as some authors evidently think you should. That investment of effort can only be worthwhile if helps you make better IT decisions in your own organisation. Will it? How? What can be learnt from the famous cases?

REPRESENTATIVE IDEAS — SUMMARISED

This briefing follows general practice in using 'strategic system' and 'system that gains competitive advantage' as synonyms, to be chosen according to context. The table shows some of the best-known systems in the pantheon. How can they be analysed?1

Common Features of Strategic Systems

McFarlan, one of the most respected authorities on IM, identifies six characteristics of strategic systems. A strategic system: is *not easily replicated* by competitors; makes a real *difference in the marketplace*; opens up *new markets*; *changes the rules* of competition; *can evolve* (ie acquire more sophisticated functions incrementally, as opposed to being scrapped and rebuilt); has an intense volume of transactions with outsiders, making it *addictive*, ie psychologically difficult for the customers or suppliers to switch allegiance. This analysis carries the disclaimer that not all strategic systems necessarily possess all six attributes.

Strategic Systems, Representative Actual Cases

American Airlines set up an on-line booking system called **Sabre**, that made it easier for travel agents to book flights on American than on other airlines. This led to increased market share and various other favourable commercial consequences.

American Hospital Supply (AHS) provided its customers with terminals, enabling them to send their orders for medical suppplies straight into AHS's own computer system, without any intermediary, such as an orders clerk.

McKesson Drug provided a system similar to AHS's for pharmacists ordering drug products. McKesson went on to build in extra features, such as dealing with the reimbursement for drugs covered by health insurance.

Federal Express built a system that monitored its parcel-delivery service closely to record exactly where any shipment was at any moment. This made more sophisticated logistics possible and, more radically, provided customers with reports on the progress of their deliveries.

Nissan's British factory set up a system that called the factory of its seat-supplier, to interfere in the supplier's own computer systems — drawing up daily production schedules for that factory to meet Nissan's requirements.

Otis built technology into its lifts; whenever repair or maintenance was needed, a call would be made without human intervention to a central computer, that would then dispatch repair staff. This meant that the company provided its customers with a higher standard of service.

The book by Ward, Griffiths and Whitmore offers two different analyses:

- **A four-way analysis.** A strategic system may: set up *links* to customers or suppliers; make internal systems more *integrated*; generate *new products or services* based on information; produce better management *information*. The claim here is that a strategic system always does at least one of these and may do several.
- **A seven-way analysis.** A strategic system may have any of these characteristics: *external focus*, as opposed to using IT to handle internal processes; *'better, not cheaper'*; *benefits shared* with outsiders, eg suppliers; *understanding the customer* (better); business *innovation* (eg new service), but technology used not particularly innovative; development in *pragmatic steps*, ie not as one 'big bang', but not as predefined steps within one masterplan either; *knowledge feedback*, ie the system generates better knowledge about the business (usually customers), and thus puts the company in a position to consider further innovations. These seven are, it is said, features that occur frequently in a study of 150 cases (presumably mainly from the 1980s), but are not common in traditional (eg pre-1980) systems.

Others have given other analyses of characteristics found in strategic, as opposed to non-strategic, systems. James A Senn, a mild maverick, argues that this is a rather pointless thing to do, since *any* kind of system, however mundane its characteristics, *could*, under certain imaginable circumstances, stymie competitors and bring spectacular benefits to the business.[2]

REPRESENTATIVE IDEAS — ANALYSED

Before tackling such issues as whether it is wise to seek to obtain competitive advantage through IT, or whether many companies have in fact done so, or what use it is to study famous cases, there is a prior question: Does the notion of gaining competitive advantage through the use of IT even have any clear meaning?

Defining 'Competitive Advantage'

It is impossible to hold a discussion about the typical characteristics of an X, or about the main varieties of X, unless there is some initial rough, agreement on what the difference is between an X and a non-X. Senn is right to be sceptical. Many writers on IM plainly believe that there is a separate category of systems that achieve competitive advantage, but hardly any explain clearly in what fundamental way such systems are different from others.[3] First, two preliminary points:

- 'Treason doth never prosper; what's the reason? For if it prosper, none dare call it treason.' said Sir John Harington. Conversely, a strategic system is always a great success — because if it isn't, nobody ever calls it a strategic system.
- Even the tiniest modification to the most trivial system only has a point if it is meant to benefit the organisation; that is, bring some advantage; that is, help the organisation compete better. But the phrase 'competitive advantage' is not generally attached to *all* systems that successfully bring benefit and advantage.

When you take a decision to undertake any system whatsoever you hope that it will be successful; and you can only hope; you can't be certain. Thus if the category of strategic system is to be of any use to the practical decision-maker (as opposed to the business-school analyst after the fact), it must apply to systems which, *if successful*, will achieve one special kind of success, generally called *competitive* advantage. (In the following discussion, qualifiers such as '*aims* to achieve' and '*if* successful' etc are often omitted, for brevity.)

Since hardly any writer has distinguished satisfactorily between systems for competitive advantage and the rest, the only course open is to search for key factors that seem *implicit* in the detail of the popular case studies. That is the justification for the following thought-experiment:

- Insurance *company A* introduces a more automated system to produce annual statistics, analysing premiums and claims, in order to determine the rates to be set for different types of risk the following year. The system is neatly designed, but there is nothing very innovative about it. It produces exactly the same statistics as before, but saves ten clerical staff, and is thus an excellent investment.

● *Company B* introduces a system for its statistics. There are no staff savings, but the system uses advanced neural network technology to reveal all kinds of new relations between premiums and claims. This enables the company to calculate its rates on quite new principles: on many types of risk it can reduce premiums by a handy amount and still make a profit. (On a minority of relatively bad risks, it doubles or trebles premiums.) Thus it can seduce many good-risk policy-holders away from other companies, by offering rates that are lower but still profitable.

● Whatever the net financial benefits of these two cases, there is an interesting difference, best expressed in two interlinked themes. First, the effect of A's system is **private** — there is no immediate impact on any other companies; but B's effect is **public** — other companies are directly affected: they lose market share. Second, A makes a bankable **investment** — the savings achieved will be made year after year from now on; B plays a **move in a game** — it changes the situation in a competitive market until somebody makes another move, and that could be next week.

Systems cited as case studies of 'competitive advantage' usually have pronounced public and game-move qualities, like B's system. Moreover, such systems may very well pose special decision-making problems.**4**

Variations of 'Competitive Advantage'

This seems the least-bad way of putting competitive advantage on a firm basis, but things are not that simple:

● Suppose *company C* builds a neural network system similar to B's, but instead of using the improved statistics to set keener rates and gain market share, it prefers to tune its rates in order to make more profit on the same amount of business. Is that a competitive advantage system?

● Suppose *company D*, like A, produces the same statistics as before in a straightforward, more automated way — but not to save staff. It now produces the statistics quarterly instead of annually, and thus benefits by adjusting rates quickly in response to trends in claims. Is that a competitive advantage system?

● Suppose *company E* follows a similar strategy to A's, producing the same statistics as before in a more automated way, and only to save staff — but the old way was extremely inefficient, and the new way is marvellously elegant. The company can pass on its savings in administrative costs by making a 1.5% reduction in all premiums, and thus gain some market share. Is that a competitive advantage system? Suppose *company F* is just the same but the reduction is 0.15%; and *company G* is the same, except that the reduction is 15%.

● Suppose *company H's* statistics system aims for and achieves two effects: it cuts staff by a useful but not spectacular amount, and it also sharpens rate-setting to a useful but not spectacular degree. Is that a competitive advantage system?

This suggests that the idea of a firmly distinct competitive-advantage category, to which any system either does or does not belong, is naive. Possibly, some completely different definition could produce a category with sharper boundaries, but it seems unlikely. Here are some implications for decision-making:

- Think of all systems as located on a continuum (called the competitive advantage continuum or not, according to taste), ranging from extremely private investment across to extremely public game-move. Be cautious about splitting off 'systems that achieve competitive advantage' (aka 'strategic systems') from the rest. That is to draw a line at some point across this continuum, and, wherever drawn, the line may be arbitrary and misleading.
- Take account of this continuum when taking decisions about *any* possible new systems, even unglamorous ones. Investigate ideas for shifting the system up or down the continuum. That will help clarify aims and perhaps suggest new options.

Chart of Strategic Systems, Functions, Themes, Game-moves, Innovation and Risk

This analysis suggests that James A Senn is more or less correct, and associating particular functions (such as those in the four-way analysis of Ward et al) with strategic systems is pointless. Of course, an inter-organisational system, such as one for receiving customer orders, is inherently public, but that need not make it a significant game-move. Moreover, as the hypothetical example shows, even something as intraverted as insurance statistics *can* have public effects and be a bold move in the competitive game.

The seven-way analysis of Ward et al and that by McFarlan are more interesting: they expose game-move themes, on a more general level than application functions. By knowing about these themes and understanding how they operated in particular textbook cases, a person is more likely to find good game-moves in a new situation, just as by reading books about chess and playing over the games of masters . . . But does this analogy hold? Surely a bold game-move in a commercial market has to be original and unexpected. Can reading the results of a survey of 150 cases from the past help anyone get new ideas? This line of thought brings the debate to the concept of *innovation*. Consider two hypothetical cases:

- *Publisher P* switches from publishing art books in printed form to publishing them on compact disk. This is a bold move in the market, but it is a great success, in part because the technical experts develop special software with ingenious compression algorithms for storing and displaying high-quality colour images very efficiently.

● *Publisher Q* introduces new technology and reorganises all its editorial, typesetting, and production processes. The investment is so great that the chairman is virtually betting the company on its success. Q avoids technical innovation: it invests lavishly, but only in proven technology. No other competitor invests so much so fearlessly, or manages change so shrewdly. Q's new systems are so efficient that it can produce high-quality art books so cheaply that it sweeps most competitors out of business.

As this shows, innovation in business and in technology are separate variables. A bold game-move may entail one of them, or both (as with P) or neither (Q).

Surveys of the well-known case-studies make it fairly clear that the great majority were more like Q than P. Significant technology innovation is quite rare among them; almost all used up-to-date but established technology, though more shrewdly or on a larger scale than competitors. Business innovation is more commonly found; sometimes a brilliant new product or service is launched, but very often whatever is new seems a very natural, even obvious, application of technology. As with Publisher Q, the main risks usually seem to have been in doing something on a larger scale than others, and in trusting that, if successful, the system would indeed justify its costs.[5]

Implications for the Decision-making Process

By their very nature, systems with strong game-move characteristics call for tricky decisions at several levels: when discussing the very broad concepts of possible new systems, when defining second-order detail to find the best balance between risk of failure and possible gain, and when planning introduction of the system (eg gradually or 'big bang').

Studying past cases won't help much in any literal sense: what was a bold move in the competitive game five years ago cannot be so today. But cases might help in a more general way by showing the techniques and procedures a bright, resourceful business used to generate options at different stages, and showing how tradeoffs were assessed in choosing between options. But most accounts of the famous systems don't cover this facet. They simply say how marvellous the resulting system was. This is like teaching someone to paint by pointing at a Rembrandt or a Titian and saying: 'try and do something like this.'

The idea for a bold new system — as at AHS, for example — might conceivably arise in various ways:

● *Either:* It was apparent that technology was moving in a certain direction. AHS employed the brightest people. It also had excellent planning procedures, responsive to technology and business opportunities. Given those three factors, it was natural that AHS was first with its system for customer order-entry.

● *Or:* The technology trend concerned was not particularly obvious, and AHS's planning procedures were not a great factor. But a few exceptional people within AHS were inspired by the idea of this system, and persuaded everybody else to back them.

- *Or:* AHS carefully set up a portfolio of a dozen innovative experiments, and pursued them all with impartial enthusiasm. One of the twelve turned out to be a spectacular success.
- *Or:* AHS stumbled into the strategic system by a complete accident, while working on something much more humdrum.

It seems that the last of these is closest to the truth.[6]

One article makes the general claim: 'Case histories often describe pioneers who gained an edge by accident, usually while building systems for more conventional purposes.' If true, this would certainly explain the suspicious fact that books and articles that eulogise certain systems rarely say how they arose. If many such systems do arise by accident, the value of reading or writing books about them is considerably diminished.

NOTES & ARGUMENTS

1 For descriptions of these cases and others established in the pantheon, see Frenzel, pp. 47ff.; Robson, pp. 184-7; Ward, Griffiths and Whitmore, pp. 20-2. Keen (1992); Keen (1991); *The Economist*, Information Technology Survey, June 16 1990 — an intelligent piece. Synnott's survey of examples of the beneficial use of IT (chapters 5 to 7) is more analytical, and thus better, than most.

Like the six in the table at the beginning, most of the systems praised in such sources are inter-organisational, but a minority are not: eg using robots to build cars and to send progress information back to a master computer system, which reschedules the work of the whole factory; using computers to design electronic circuits; using expert system software to advise engineers on how to repair complex machinery; using flexible manufacturing systems to allow many varieties of products to be produced economically in small lots. Any useful defining notes on strategic systems need to cover these *intra*-organisational cases too.

2 References in this section: F Warren McFarlan, 'The 1990s: The Information Decade', *Business Quarterly*, Summer 1990, pp. 73ff.; Ward, Griffiths and Whitmore, pp. 22-6; James A Senn, 'The Myths of Strategic Systems', *Information Systems Management*, Summer 1992, pp. 7-12 — an article that could with advantage have questioned even more premises.

3 'Whereas computers have been in use in business for approximately 40 years, strategic information systems have only been a separate computing issue for about seven years' (Remenyi, p. 131); 'Hundreds, perhaps thousands of firms own and operate information systems that provide advantage for them in their competitive spheres of operation' (Frenzel, p. 56). 'So what good *does* come about? Competitive advantage, no, but improved profitability, yes.' (Robson, p. 202). Comments like these seem to imply that a strategic system is only one kind of successful system, and that competitive advantage is a more specific thing than mere commercial success.

The natural way to establish competitive-advantage systems as a clear category is to contrast two manifestly worthwhile systems, explaining why one belongs to the category, and the other does not. That this is hardly ever done is rather suspicious. Ward, Griffiths and Whitmore (p. 13) do at least attempt it:

- Automation of a warehouse to improve efficiency and improve inventory management, without fundamentally altering the business process (however successful), does not bring competitive advantage.
- A system for the Aalsmeer Flower Auction 'linked the auction transactions to the time critical administration and distribution systems.' Since this better system meant a better service for buyers and sellers it led to increase in the auction authority's market share. This counts as a competitive-advantage case.

The contrast is not entirely clear. If the warehouse is made dramatically more efficient, won't its business perhaps gain market share? And *how* fundamentally was the business process at Aalsmeer changed?

4 The concept of the game-move brings another useful insight.

Synnott introduces an *information-weapon* concept with fanfares about winning new customers and markets with technology. This and many other books, if read carelessly, can leave the impression that, in any go-ahead company, *most* uses of IT will be systems with pronounced game-move qualities — or at the very least that *most important and tricky* IM decisions will be about such matters. Neither of these is a sustainable proposition. In any game, there are good moves and bad moves; sometimes a bold and imaginative move is bad enough to lose the game; at many points the best move is a shrewdly cautious one. Moreover, choosing to make a dramatic move on the basis of its hoped-for results, without a realistic assessment of their feasibility, is a common cause of bad decisions.

Some writers on management have associated competitive advantage with achieving superior profitability (or productivity or some other performance variable) *than competitors*. This may be a useful concept for the academic analyst, but it can promote a fallacious line of reasoning: the prime motivation of a rational manager should be to gain competitive advantage; competitive advantage goes with superior performance to competitors; therefore all important decisions should be directed at achieving superior performance to competitors.

The real-life decision-maker has to decide what to do *in a given situation*. In some circumstances, it may certainly be appropriate to use an IT system as a move aimed at gaining higher profitability than average for the industry; but at other times the only realistic objective may be to keep up with more powerful competitors; and at others to struggle through a desperate situation without expecting to make any immediate profit at all. Policy based on the assumption that a business should constantly be aiming for higher profitability than competitors, and trying to use IT to do it, may be as disastrous as moves based on the view that you must always try to win rather than draw a game of chess, no matter what the position.

5 Successful game-move systems, however ingenious, are rarely based on the IT equivalents of a patented drug, or a secret formula for making a liqueur, or a secret process for putting chocolate on biscuits without it melting. This means that the advantageous effects of the move played are unlikely to last very long. Competitors can also assemble competent people to use the same technology in similar ways. If a competitive edge lasts (say) two years, that may not be time enough to recoup the investment in an expensive system.

A lone innovator may be pursued by competitors, clubbing together to match the innovation in a joint system, at relatively low cost to each. Citicorp innovated with its cash dispensers, but an alliance of the other New York retail banks soon caught up. Thus: 'Being a pioneer in competitive edge is like running too fast in the 10,000 metres. You're out in front for a few glorious moments, then the pack swallows you up.' (Grindley, p. 192). Also, from a survey of opinions: ' . . it is a fallacy to expect long-term competitive advantage from individual systems, whatever their short-term strategic impact. Once the competition catches on, further advantage can only be derived by constant improvements and additional innovations.' (Hochstrasser and Griffiths, p. 34)

At any given moment, the number of companies for which either keeping up or catching up with the leaders is the wisest strategy must necessarily be greater than the number for which forging out ahead is best. For many organisations, the intelligent strategy, most of the time, is to keep up with the leading pack and stay well-positioned to catch up quickly, should anybody take the risk of breaking away. Should not management thinkers devote more attention to case-studies and theories of this kind of strategy?

6 AHS set up a very conventional system for order processing, like that of thousands of other companies; orders received on paper would be keyed in by clerks in AHS offices. One day, a fairly junior person tried out the idea of taking an order-entry terminal over to a nearby hospital; the system worked and everything grew from there; soon AHS was famous in business schools all over the planet. Source: CU Cibbora and GF Lanzara, 'Designing Networks in Action: Formative Contexts and Post-Modern Systems Development' in the Clarke and Cameron anthology, pp. 265ff. These authors also point out that at the time, order entry and straightforward telecoms were generally regarded as dull areas of IT; artificial intelligence and decision support systems were thought to be far more significant.

Even the origin of Sabre, the most famous of them all, was somewhat fortuitous. For a long time, American Airlines negotiated with other airlines to form an industry-wide consortium to offer a booking service to travel agents. Only when these talks broke down, did the company decide to go ahead on its own; it grafted the booking functions onto an existing set of systems called Sabre, that dealt with inventory management of seats, tracking spare parts, scheduling crews and other related functions. And this worked surprisingly well. Source: Max D Hopper, 'Rattling SABRE — New Ways to Compete on Information' in the Harvard Business Review (1991) anthology.

Another example: 'It was an accident. We put in the computer system to speed up the accounting procedures — mainly for chasing premium payments. A side effect was we could pay out small, undisputed claims almost instantly. The marketing boys were onto it straightaway. We captured 40% of the travel insurance business that year!' (Grindley, p. 44).

The general claim about accidental strategic systems is made by Cornelius H Sullivan Jr, in 'Looking for Competitive Advantage' in Umbaugh's anthology, 2nd ed. (pp. 107ff.).

CONNECTIONS

5. Generic Strategies	Discusses the question of what, if anything, the 'competitive' in 'competitive advantage' means
7. Agenda-setting Procedures	Procedures that can help focus on areas for bold game-move decisions
17. Matching through Examples	Neural network is a technology best understood through an example application
36. Business Process Re-engineering	Consultants' buzzwords that have overtaken 'strategic'
39. Inter-organisational Systems	Most of the famous case-study systems belong to this category

41. Untangling Human Factors

TOPIC

It is easy to agree that human factors can be important in the successful use of technology. Yet, for anyone trying to get a grip on IM decision-making as a coherent domain, human factors raise some difficulties: The cry of 'human factors' may impede rational debate. How can such things as feelings and attitudes and motivations be fed into any decision-making calculus? Again, human factors crop up everywhere; there are not many IM topics, where they have no relevance whatsoever to decisions; but neither are there many where human factors can easily be isolated from other considerations.

This briefing helps tackle these two problems. It provides an extended distinctions warrant showing how different types of assertions and advice affect different topics and decisions. This is a help in seeing that any general ideas about human factors are fitted into the most relevant places within a debate. The *CONNECTIONS* section of the briefing provides a kind of index to show which out of all the preceding briefings are most affected by human factors and how.

SUGGESTED WARRANTS

Analysed carefully, most pieces of general advice about human factors typically found can be related to specific planes of decision. The table analyses in a hierarchical way different pieces of advice affecting decisions on different matters.[1]

Human Factors, Representative Advice Categorised by Plane and Subject of Decision

Agenda

ie about impossible-to-quantify human factors in top-level decisions

'A strong organisation culture is advantageous under the following circumstances . . . but dangerous when . . . '

Matching

ie about the human-factors features of a designed system

General characteristics

'Automation brings a characteristic tension between job-enrichment and stultification.'

Specific characteristics

Human-machine interaction

'Most people are prepared to work quite happily with systems requiring many arbitrary combinations of keys — eg ctrl+alt+F7 — providing they only ever use that system.'

Information presentation

'For most textual information, paper is as good a medium as the screen, if not better. The main exception cases are: reference (where any topic may be sought through various keywords); multi-facet (items of interest to different people are unavoidably mixed together).

Documentation and help

'An expert system should generally have, amongst other things, a paper document explaining the underlying logic, its assumptions, and hence its possible shortcomings.'

Scope

ie about how to divide things up and organise development

Infrastructure-project decision

'The degree of centralisation and integration of IT should be influenced in part by the organisation's attitude to centralisation in general.'

Macro project-structure

Problem definition in macro-terms

'There are the following five generic causes of resistance to change . . . '

Approach definition in macro-terms

'There is a Laffer curve for optimum user involvement — not too much and not too little.'

Specific project elements

Human resources
'There are the following four psychological types of people to fit into a team . . . '

Micro-level techniques

Development of user interface
'If, but only if, the user is above a certain minimum level, agree the fields first, then give the user screen-painter software to design the report format personally.'

Development of other detail
'Workshops to finalise details of (say) what should be in the monthly statistical summary report are best organised as follows . . . '

Context
ie about roles and responsibilities of people and units

Division of responsibilities
'The top IS manager should report to a director at board (or equivalent) level for organisations of the following type . . . and actually be a board director for organisations of the following type . . . '

Division of human forces
'Some organisations have a separate 'IT quality assurance department' independent of both the main IT department and user departments. Pros and cons are . . . '

Division of material forces
'People in a department often have a positive feeling of owning the system if its hardware is located in their office; on the other hand . . . '

Rights and constraints
'The gradations of precision in commercial service agreements between IS and user department are . . . '

Approach
ie about the non-rational features of the decision-making process
'The decision-making process should be structured to allow for the different levels of technology awareness of the participants; thus . . . '

NOTES & ARGUMENTS

1 Carey begins with a unifying model as the framework for an anthology of articles on human factors in IT.

CONNECTIONS

8. Culture, Mission and Vision	Mainly agenda decisions
10. Learning and Historical Themes	Mainly agenda decisions
23. Untangling Context Decisions	Mainly context decisions
24. Centralisation and Distribution	Mainly context decisions
25. Functions, Responsibilities and Skills	Mainly context decisions
26. Operations and Decisions	Mainly context decisions
32. Standard Approaches and Contingency	Mainly approach decisions
34. Sociotechnical Design	Mainly matching decisions
35. Change Management	Mainly approach decisions
37. End-user Computing	Mainly scope decisions

42. Unifying Theories

TOPIC

A natural part of thinking carefully about anything is to try to tame detail with generalisations: 'many projects are disastrous in apparently different ways, but the risk attached to any project can be assessed in terms of three generic factors', or 'most of the specific issues in end-user computing are manifestations of one characteristic, dominating tradeoff between conflicting objectives.' Much of this book contains analysis in that style.

Why not go further to look for some general patterns or themes or forces or principles that underlie the *whole subject* of IM, including risky projects, end-user computing, business modelling, matching technology supply to demand, re-engineering, multi-step planning and everything else? Apparently disparate things such as the movement of apples in orchards, tides in oceans and planets in the heavens are all explicable in terms of gravity. Perhaps there are gravity-like fundamental ideas and unifying theories to be found in IM. This briefing discusses some of the more plausible attempts that have been made in this direction.**1**

REPRESENTATIVE IDEAS — SUMMARISED

A number of writers suggest that the tenets of 'systems theory' can be relevant to IM. One representative account explains how every 'system' (roughly, a set of parts that interact with each other) has certain *general properties* — whether the system be biological, like the body of an antelope, social, like the education system of a country, or of any other type. For example:

- Any system has a **boundary**, separating it from its **environment**, but it may be either an open or a closed system, depending on how firm the boundary is.
- Within any system there is a hierarchy of **levels**; eg the cells making up a living organism are at a macro-level relative to the micro-level of the molecules making up the cells. This is pretty obvious, but the important

claim is that things work in quite different ways at different levels: chemistry can't explain biology, and biology can't explain ethology (the behaviour of animals).

● A system changes over time through **feedback**, of which there are several types: *positive feedback* (amplifying processes, that take the system ever further from its original state), *negative feedback* (counteracting processes, stabilising the system) and *feedforward* (anticipating and correcting discrepancies). The feedback may be either *deterministic* or *probabilistic* or *random*.

This is a mere sketch. The analysis of systems can be taken much further, with generalisations about different forms of feedback, or about how different levels of a system fit together, or about different ways in which a system may be related to its environment.

If this is all true of systems in general, what does it have to do with systems that include the use of IT? The claim is that those systems too are subject to the same laws as the body of an antelope or an education service. There are rather few snappy examples to be found to demonstrate this parallel, but here is one: computerised mailing lists and word processing exist at one level of a system; junk mail and junk fax are phenomena at a different, macro, level. One of the features of this macro level is that automation reduces the cost of messages to the sender, but increases annoyance to the receiver.[2]

How does this way of thinking pass the test of Decision Question? Even if valid, how could these ideas be relevant? This is not too difficult to answer in principle, because systems theory has the merit of smooth transition from description to prescription. In describing the general characteristics of *all* systems, you soon begin to analyse why certain systems are *more successful* or *more healthy* than others. The language of feedback and levels and so on can explain why one species becomes extinct while another thrives, or show how it happens that one country has a better education service than another. For example, Ashby's Law of Requisite Variety states, in summary, that to be effective a system must be capable of a variety of responses to match changes in the environment. If the system is the organisation using IT, then these general insights can be translated into more specific recommendations and propositions:

'An IS Manager should ensure that his organisation has enough internal variety of responses to be able to react tactically in an appropriate manner to changes in the business environment.'

'As part of homeostasis (ie stability) and of growth, every system will evolve control mechanisms to protect its integrity. But every change involves risk. Computers give a major opportunity to enhance organizational security, but they also introduce the possibility of far greater security headaches.'

Other books give accounts that vary in specific concepts, but adopt a broadly similar approach.[3]

REPRESENTATIVE IDEAS — ANALYSED

Accounts of systems theory may provide some insights into the phenomena of IT-based systems in organisations, but, whatever the claims, they rarely help much with decisions of *information management*. To see why, separate out three quite different ways in which systems theory might conceivably be used:

- **Application system design.** You might use systems theory to help you design better application systems. Thus the design for a sales order processing system might include pages of diagrams, describing (among other things) various kinds of feedback with great subtlety. Ashby's Law of Requisite Variety might be invoked in decisions about how to deal with changes to customer discount rates.
- **Business modelling.** You might use systems theory to model the business — preferring it to (say) value chain analysis or critical success factors. Such a model would then be the basis for IM agenda decisions, such as 'We will give priority over all else to the problems in our sales office', or 'Our sales order processing system must give the customer a better service than those of our competitors'.
- **IM decision-making as system.** The processes of IM planning and decision-making in an organisation — including the procedures followed and the responsibilities given to different people — might be thought of as a system, and thus designed on systems theory principles. You might analyse different multi-step approaches to organising planning at different levels to which different laws apply. You might analyse arrangements for recharging costs to users in feedback terms. And so on.

Though some writing about systems theory in an IT context muddles these three things together, they are really three separate candidates for the application of systems theory.

Using systems theory for the detailed design of application systems may be a good idea — or it may not. Either way, the matter is outside the scope of this briefing and of the whole book, because detailed design of application systems is not part of IM.

A business model based on systems theory would be a more complex thing than most business models, and would cost more work. Would the model earn its keep by leading to better agenda decisions? The question remains open; nobody seems to have given a clear account of how such a model might assist typical IM decisions: eg which parts of the organisation should have priority for IT attention over others; whether more applications of a certain type should adopted; whether IT should be used mainly to cut costs or to improve service or to do something else.

The idea of applying systems theory to the whole of IT decision-making is the most stimulating of the three. If done successfully, this would be a way of unifying ideas on different planes (agenda, matching, scope etc) of IM. But it would be a large task, and there is no sign that anybody has made any credible attempt at it.[4]

REPRESENTATIVE IDEAS — SUMMARISED

The book by Hopstaken and Kranendonk is in Dutch; its fascination is that it goes further in the direction of abstraction than any in English. It has much the same status as the work of Chomsky or Lévi-Strauss: interesting ideas in rough outline, but there is no great attraction in toiling through the actual text.

Hopstaken and Kranendonk unify their book by four 'models': the searchlights, oval, cross and cycle:

- **Searchlights.** Approaches to IT planning and decision-making are either design-oriented or development-oriented. Design concentrates on factors that are concrete, objective, tangible and quantitative; its style is mechanistic, blueprint-like, model-based, analytic, reductionist, linear and down-to-earth. It is like building a house or making an itinerary or functioning as a sponge. In short, it is using the left half of the brain. Development, by contrast, concentrates on factors that are psychological, subjective, intangible and qualitative; its style is organic, open-ended, incremental, synthetic, holistic, cyclical and imaginative. It is like growing a garden or letting things happen or functioning as a lawn-sprinkler. In short, it is using the right half of the brain.
- **Oval.** An organisation has six elements: activities, products/services, people, means, environment and change process. Each of these six elements can be described at different levels and in different forms.
- **Cross**. Practically every problem falls into one of four categories: cultural (norms, values), communicative (who), substantial (what) and procedural (how). With the cultural and communicative categories the accent is on human problems and the development approach should be stressed. With the substantial and procedural categories, the accent is on technical problems and the design approach should be stressed.
- **Cycle.** Learning follows a cycle, consisting of four modes, in the sequence: concrete experience, reflective observation, abstract conceptualisation, active experimentation, concrete experience (again).

This rich palette of abstractions is used throughout the book in discussing general issues of 'information planning' and, to a limited degree, in analysis of case studies. The authors also explain how their underlying models fit in with some concepts fished out of the clouded waters where management, sociology, psychology and metaphysics flow together; eg one authority's analysis of the three methodological dilemmas in studying social phenomena: subjectivism v objectivism, nominalism v realism and anascopic v catascopic; and the four views of the organisation put forward by somebody else: system-structural view, strategic choice view, natural selection view and collective action view.

REPRESENTATIVE IDEAS — ANALYSED

Here are some critical notes on each of the four models of Hopstaken and Kranendonk:

- **Searchlights.** The analysis is surely intended to be objective and value-free, but it is difficult to avoid the implication that development is good while design is bad. Also, how can the two great clusters of attributes be justified? What reason is there to believe that (say) objective always belongs with linear, and subjective with cyclical? Why should an objective-cyclical or subjective-linear approach be regarded as impossible?
- **Oval.** Why are there six elements and not five or seven? Are they really distinct? If analysing (say) an employment agency, would activities, service and people really be three distinct elements?
- **Cross.** This raises a difficulty common to the whole body of ideas. You can't really tell what you think of the analysis, because you can't see what it entails, because there are hardly any specific examples to show what the abstractions stand for. Will almost all problems fit clearly into one of the categories? Or can there be problems that don't fit any category? Or problems that unquestionably straddle categories? Will problems be spread fairly evenly over the four categories? Or will one category be much fuller than the others? These are basic tests of the quality of *any* categorisation of *anything*. Unless the categorisation is clear enough to help you apply those tests and agree that they are passed, you can't give it any informed support.**5**
- **Cycle.** Is it true? Who knows? Without neat, credible examples to illustrate the cycle in operation, it is impossible to form an opinion about it. Any kind of cycle theory has to take a stand on a certain key point: is the cycle offered as a description of what always inevitably happens, or is it a recommendation of what you should ideally try to make happen? This theory is so vaguely expressed that you can't tell where it stands.

The notion of bringing unity to ideas in this field through a small set of underlying abstractions is an interesting one, but there is a necessary, though not sufficient, condition: the abstractions have to be made sufficiently tangible, and illustrated by sufficient examples, for people to grasp what they mean.

REPRESENTATIVE IDEAS — SUMMARISED

This book has a companion, *Demands and Decisions*. It too discusses many generic issues in IT decision-making. Whereas this book devotes considerable attention to discussing ideas that other people have expressed, *Demands and Decisions* tends to reason about each issue without that distraction. To facilitate this approach it ties ideas together with a unifying model, containing three sources of tension in IT decision-making:[6]

● **Supply-demand interaction.** On the one hand, it may be possible to raise many plausible demands — opportunities for using IT to benefit the organisation. On the other hand, the more ambitious the plans for investing in technology and building the systems to supply the demands, then the greater the financial investment, elapsed time, organisational upheaval, vulnerability to uncertainties and risk of failure. It is often tricky to find the match of supply and demand that offers the best buy. To define demand in isolation and work out supply implications afterwards may be like ordering from a menu without any prices, but to put supply before demand may be like running a hospital for the benefit of the doctors.

● **Commitment-flexibility tradeoff.** In most fields up-front commitment is more cost-efficient than separate investments spread over many small steps. A five-bedroom house is cheaper in the long run than a one-bedroom house extended with new rooms one at a time. Commit to long-term IT plans now and you can invest in hardware and systems far more efficiently than if you are continually adding and replacing things. But it is no use investing cost-efficiently in something that turns out afterwards to be not what you want at all. Starting with a one-bedroom house may well be the best strategy, if there are strong uncertainties likely to invalidate any forecasts of future requirements. In a fast-moving field like IT there is much to be said for retaining the flexibility to change your assessment of what the demands actually are and what the most appropriate supply factors are. You have to find the best tradeoff for the situation between the conflicting forces of commitment and flexibility.

● **Option-level blend**. A useful decision normally chooses one option at the expense of others; so the generation of plausible options is one feature of a good decision-making process. But developing plans methodically through successive levels of detail is also indispensable. Too much concentration on level-based work hinders recognition of options arising from the interplay between supply and demand, and between commitment and flexibility. But excessive discussion of options can lead to muddle and confusion, and long delays in actually deciding anything. For each particular case, a coherent blend is needed with option- and level-based work fitted together to do justice to the issues.

Recognising these three underlying sources of tension in IM decision-making makes it easier to think carefully about many more specific issues:

● Prototyping is an attractive technique for system development, but it can become an expensive luxury, that is difficult to control. To find the right structure for a prototyping project ask whether the objective is to clarify demand possibilities or to experiment with bold supply possibilities or to examine the interaction of supply and demand.

● Some consultants use techniques of 'strategic information systems planning' where large matrices relate together an organisation's main functions and data. When applying such techniques, bear in mind the danger that assumptions about commitment to large-scale architectures and infrastructures can easily creep in unnoticed at the expense of flexibility.

- Finding a rational justification for projects whose benefits are hard to quantify is a notoriously tough problem. It becomes more tractable if the question is seen as one of comparing the marginal costs and benefits of a whole range of options, rather than of taking a yes/no decision.

In similar ways, recognising the three sources of tension can assist discussion of many other topics: deciding where to set the planning horizon, taking account of unpredictable technology change, fitting data and business modelling into the decision-making process, using accounting procedures to recharge IT costs to departments, assessing the value of any standard methodology of information planning, using quantitative measurement techniques as a foundation for decision-making, and so on.

REPRESENTATIVE IDEAS — ANALYSED

The three sources of tension identified in *Demands and Decisions* can be translated into the terms of this book:

- The supply-demand interaction dominates decisions on the **matching** plane.
- The commitment-flexibility tradeoff dominates decisions on the **scope** plane.
- The option-level blend dominates decisions on the **approach** plane.
- Decisions on the **context** plane set the scene for the matching, scope and approach decisions that are likely to come up. Therefore they should be based on a broad assessment of the way these three sources of tension will manifest themselves in the organisation.[7]
- Decisions on the **agenda** plane are essentially high-level judgements resolving one or more of the three sources of tension.

The *Demands and Decisions* reference model is a lunge from a different angle at the same objective as this book's: making it easier to think critically about issues, premises, generalisations, methods, possibilities and so on, and thus arrive at rational decisions in specific cases.

NOTES & ARGUMENTS

1 The outstanding book by Cash, McFarlan and McKenney unifies much of its material by introducing six underlying themes early on (pp. 17-41), and showing how they come into discussions of many more specific matters of IM. A chart shows how, in each of 12 chapters, two, three or four of the themes are prominent. The first two of the six themes have been discussed in earlier briefings of this book:

- the **strategic grid**, which is an original concept;

- the organisation's **learning curve**, which is not original, but is presented in a particular way by the authors.
- the **coming together** of three things: data processing, telecoms and office automation;
- the **make/buy** choice, which is mainly relevant in matters of software acquisition;
- the **life-cycle** of projects and systems;
- the **balance of power** between three parties — general management, user and IS department.

Taken as a set, the six themes vary in status:

- The learning curve is a rather profound phenomenon that — if it does exist and have importance — is presumably more or less inherent in IM and will be prominent still in twenty years time.
- But the coming together of data processing, telecoms and office automation surely can't be an inherent theme analogous to the learning curve. At some moment the three things will have come together and that will be that. The authors don't suggest that the coming together of ever more technologies (whatever they may be at any particular moment) is a permanent theme.
- Most of the themes are general enough to affect decisions in a variety of areas, but the make/buy choice applies mainly (admittedly not entirely) to choices of application software. Even then, only a small proportion of cases call for any difficult decision, in the sense that a plausible case can be made for either approach.

For these reasons, the set of six themes can't reasonably be put on the same level as a model of interacting factors to explain some set of complex phenomena: unemployment in an economy, the properties of the atom, the feats of homing pigeons etc. The plausible claim here is more modest: that most discussions of IM are likely to run into one or more of these six themes, just as most Hollywood films include one or more of a small set of themes (love, war, comedy etc).

This is a less ambitious generalising endeavour than the three others discussed in this briefing. Some may think that this gives it more chance of success.

2 This example, like the rest of the account, is taken from chapter 2 of Angell and Smithson's book. It may seem an inadequate piece of evidence for the strong assertion that biological systems, social systems and IT-based systems are all similar in certain profound, non-obvious ways. Unfortunately, few advocates of applying systems theory to IT provide anything much better.

There is a potential problem. In *Decision Making, An Integrated Approach* (Pitman, 1994), (p. 28), David Jennings and Stuart Wattam analyse the fate of Modern Leisure, makers of aerobics videos: 'The aerobics videos are not given sufficient value by the environment (here the customer) to allow them to be traded for money that can be used to sustain inputs of energy, materials and knowledge. Without adequate resource inputs Modern Leisure experiences entropy. Eventually the components of the business — people, physical assets and financial resources — will no longer form the structure known as Modern Leisure; they will lose that ordered form and return to the environment.'

If you find this analysis a great improvement on the statement that Modern Leisure failed because not enough people bought its products, then fine. But if not, a depressing spectre looms: could it be that other, much longer passages in books about systems thinking are also, in essence, pointlessly complicated statements of the obvious, that manage to survive and gain respect merely because they consume so many pages and use so many abstract terms that no reader has the patience and tenacity to demystify them? One way of deciding your position on this important matter is to study the cases described by Sager (chapter 1) and Lewis (chapter 10).

3 For instance, Knight and Silk (pp. 131-8) offer this analysis: Any system has four *components*: content, structure, communications and decision-making. In the context of each of these four components, there are four *processes* related to information: collection, storage, processing and communication. Any *system* may be either open or closed, either directed or undirected, either fully specified or complex, either a partial system or an entity.

They also suggest subjecting the notion of 'information' to subtle generic analysis (pp. 141-5). Distinguish between stocks of information and flows of information; between residuals and aggregates; between hypothetical and actual information; between knowables and unknowables; between information as stable and unstable measures; between precise and fuzzy information.

There are still other important ideas about systems to be mentioned. Here are four possible positions that can be held: first, you can ignore the kind of theories about systems contained in the briefing; second, you can accept those theories (about feedback etc) as valid for all systems, including IT-based systems; third, you can accept those theories, but add in extra theories that apply only to systems (including IT-based systems) where humans play a significant part; fourth, you can concentrate on theories specific to systems that contain humans, and give little or no attention to theories about systems in general.

It is certainly a plausible claim that there is something peculiar about those systems where humans play a part; after all, humans are more complicated than most other components a system might have (humans behave unpredictably, they have self-consciousness etc). Moreover, as the briefing on change management discusses, things get more complicated still, since the humans contained in the system being studied or designed *interact* with the humans designing it or investigating its problems.

The first of the four positions above need not be one of mere ignorance; you might hold that the theories about systems, though interesting and to some degree true, are only of third or fourth order importance, by comparison with some other less abstract ideas. To maintain the second position, you might very well agree with the point that systems including humans are different, but hold that they are *not all that* different, and that common sense and personal skill are adequate to deal with their special features.

Plainly, it is vital to know which position somebody is advocating, and this is not always clear from the terminology employed. The term 'soft systems' normally implies that the complications of humans in systems are stressed, and thus denotes either the third or fourth position. The books by Angell and Smithson, and by Knight and Silk both set out versions of the second position. Lewis's book, taken as a whole, seems to represent the fourth position.

4 Lewis's book is subtitled 'Systems thinking in the field of information-systems'. It is primarily concerned with investigating problems, designing systems and modelling data. If the issues contained in the tables of all the 'Untangling . . ' briefings of this book are taken as a fair sample of

IM issues, then it is fair to say that Lewis addresses few IM issues in any direct way. This is not a criticism *per se*, merely a clarification of the book's scope.

5 Examples are vital to discussion of abstractions. Admittedly, the cross is used explicitly on *one* case study in the book. There the four-way breakdown (cultural, communicative, substantial and procedural) seems not very useful, and a better split would be between substantial and everything else (eg the organisation's inexperience with IT planning, unclear lines of responsibility, staff reluctance to accept change etc), and then, within substantial, a split between supply (eg forthcoming closure of data centre) and demand (eg change in government regulations).

Much of the detail in the case studies of Hopstaken and Kranendonk is reminiscent of soft-systems themes: how the managers of a certain organisation held meetings with competing consultants, leading to acceptance of proposals for an information planning study; how certain passages from the consultants' reports were edited out for internal distribution, and what this implied about the organisation; how the consultant deliberately wrote a report in a style alien to the culture of the organisation, in order to gain attention; how the consultants reluctantly used a certain methodology insisted on by the client; how the company managers sometimes pushed the consultants forward, but at other times kept them in the background. This is all very well, but it comes at the expense of more straightforward details; eg what issues the people actually faced, what options they considered, why they chose a certain option over another, etc.

6 The account in this briefing is a summary of the *Reference Model* section of O'Brien (*Demands*). That book contains examples: too many, according to one reviewer.

7 For instance: If deciding whether to have a separate innovation department (a context decision), you need to take a view of whether the commitment-flexibility tradeoffs in the organisation are likely to lead to many scope decisions in favour of innovative projects structured as experiments. If deciding on the mechanism for recharging data centre costs to departments (a context decision), you need to take a view of the kinds of systems (ie combinations of supply and demand) the accountancy will be applied to.

CONNECTIONS

1. Untangling Information Management	Fundamental questions about what information management is
9. Stage Theories	Individual theories almost as fundamental as those in this briefing
10. Learning and Historical Themes	Ditto

Critical Bibliography

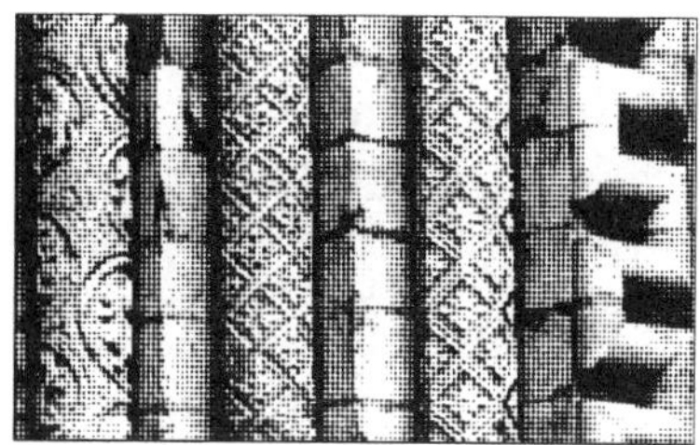

Usually a book's bibliography is a separate extra. Here it is a continuation of the analysis from a different angle.

Some books about IM are aimed explicitly at business-school students, and others at professionals (managers, consultants, information analysts etc), but the majority are potentially of interest to both groups. **1**

The Decision Question is a valuable tool for appraising the quality of any book. It is remarkable how much of what is published proves on analysis to have little or no relevance to practical decision-making. Nevertheless, some of the books criticised in the notes that follow can still help by goading you into clarification of your own ideas: 'This analysis seems too crude; how could it be refined?' 'What unstated assumption has crept into this text?' 'That exhortation sounds too glib, but why exactly?' 'What example would expose that fallacy?' 'Why does this account seem so mixed up?' 'Why exactly is that reasoning unsound?' And so on.

If a book does contain useful warrants, the question arises: For decisions on *what planes* are these warrants mainly relevant? This is a good way of sorting out an otherwise tangled body of literature. It is also a test of quality: useful books contain warrants that pass the test of the Decision Question. In the following list a few that (in the view of this author) do well by that standard are specially marked out: ■.

All Planes except Matching

❑ *Strategic Management and Information Systems, An Integrated Approach,* Wendy Robson (Pitman, 1994)
❑ *Strategic Planning for Information Systems*, John Ward, Pat Griffiths and Paul Whitmore (Wiley, 1990)
❑ *Corporate Information Management*, Ivan F Jackson (Prentice-Hall, 1986)
❑ *Management of Information Technology,* Carroll W Frenzel (Boyd & Fraser, 1992)

The books under this main heading all contain a wide range of mainstream IM ideas, though without the technology specifics needed for matching warrants. These particular four are thick textbooks for business-school students. None of them tries very hard to fit all the frameworks, theories and techniques together in a coherent view of the whole field. Neither do they stimulate much enquiry into the premises or the application of the concepts presented.

Robson's book provides the most thorough roundup of generally taught material. The book by Ward, Griffiths and Whitmore includes more original ideas than the other three, but (if the criticisms in foregoing briefings have any weight) they are not particularly good ideas. The books of Jackson and, particularly, Frenzel are blighted by the prevalent tone: 'Well managed organisations generally do things exactly like this . . ' This is an insuperable handicap to intelligent grasp of IM issues.

■ *Corporate Information Systems Management, The Issues Facing Senior Executives*, James I Cash, jr, F Warren McFarlan and James L McKenney (Irwin, 3rd ed., 1992)
■ *Management Strategies for Information Technology*, Michael J Earl (Prentice Hall, 1989)
❑ *Managing Advanced Information Systems, An introduction to frameworks and experience*, Michael Sager (Prentice Hall, 1990)

These three, also candidates as textbooks for a course, are more thought-provoking and coherent books than the others under this heading.**2**

Cash, McFarlan and McKenney are more successful than any rivals at avoiding the sense of a mere procession of abstract ideas; their discussion of specific issues is unified by certain general themes used in *leitmotif* fashion. They score heavily by pursuing the principle that different situations call for different approaches; this generates many intelligent insights not found elsewhere.

Earl's book too has the rare merit of stressing that many IM issues don't lend themselves to 'best practice' textbook answers. It combines a selection of contemporary ideas with a considerable amount of original (or at least uncommon) analysis, probably more sophisticated than that in almost any other book. But you can't be certain; without examples, many of the abstractions and terse metaphors are sketches for further development rather than clear, definite advice.

Sager focuses on a selection of the best-known ideas, discusses them in detail, and uses case study material. There is a problem with this promising approach: the cases are too real and the discussion is too honest. Though the author probably doesn't intend this, it is all too clear how limited is the value of the general ideas in practice, and how much remains specific to each situation.

These three books are recommended to anyone already well into the subject of IM, and thus able to appreciate what is different about their attitudes, able to spot the limitations in some of the ideas, and able to fill in some outlines that are only sketched.

❑ *The Information Weapon, Winning Customers and Markets with Technology*, William R Synnott (Wiley, 1987)
❑ *The Corporation of the 1990s, Information Technology and Organizational Transformation*, Michael S Scott Morton (ed.) (Oxford University Press, 1991)
❑ *The Management Challenge of IT*, Daniels (The Economist Intelligence Unit, 1991)
❑ *Controlling IT Investment, Strategy and management*, Beat Hochstrasser and Catherine Griffiths (Chapman and Hall, 1991)

Synnott's is one of those enthusiastic books all about the opportunities of the information age and the challenges facing managers. It is better than most in that vein, and covers quite a lot of ground. If you read it sceptically and watch out for glib assumptions, it can help you sharpen up your own ideas. The other three books are less promising, even from that grudging point of view.

Scott Morton's book contains chapters by different contributors, presenting the findings of the MIT90s research programme. This pretentious work will appeal to those who relish high seriousness and concatenated abstractions ('Application of Interrelatedness and Exploitability'; 'Drivers: A Dynamic, Global, Technology-Enabled, Increasingly Competitive Business Environment' etc) — but it is not for anyone who wants clarity and relevance.

The Daniels book, though absurdly expensive, is just a selection of common ideas about IM, skewed towards the themes and methods favoured by one particular consultancy.

Hochstrasser and Griffiths are concerned with presenting the lessons for good management derived from a detailed survey of actual practice, but the result is little more than a collection of representative clichés and arbitrary prescriptions.

❑ *The Information Infrastructure* (Harvard Business Review, 1991)
❑ *Revolution in Real Time: Managing Information Technology in the 1990s* (Harvard Business Review, 1990)
❑ *The New Management Challenge, Information Systems for Improved Performance*, David Boddy, James McCalman and David A Buchanan (ed.) (Croom Helm, 1988)
❑ *Towards Strategic Information Systems*, Elisabeth K Somogyi and Robert D Galliers (ed.) (Abacus, 1987)
❑ *Managing the Information Revolution*, John Lew Cox (ed.) (Industrial Engineering & Management Press, Atlanta, 1986)
❑ *Information Management, State of the Art Report*, Pat Griffiths (Pergamon Infotech, 1986)

The five anthologies all offer a mixture of interesting and pointless articles, mainly in the same style and about the same issues as the other books in this section. None is very much better or worse than the others.

Griffiths combines an anthology of invited papers with selected extracts from well-known articles and books. This is a good idea in theory, but the effect is of an uninspired scrapbook.

All Planes, including Matching

❑ *Information Systems Management, Opportunities and Risks*, Ian O Angell and Steve Smithson (Macmillan, 1990)
❑ *Information Resources Management*, John R Beaumont and Ewan Sutherland (Butterworth-Heinemann, 1992)
❑ *Managing Information, Information Systems for Today's General Manager*, AV Knight and DJ Silk (McGraw-Hill, 1990)
❑ *Management of Information Systems Technology*, Janice Burn and Eveline Caldwell (Van Nostrand Reinhold, 1990)
❑ *IT Strategy for Business*, Joe Peppard (ed.) (Pitman, 1993)
❑ *IT Strategies for Information Management*, David Bawden and Karen Blakeman (Butterworths, 1990)
❑ *Inside Information Technology, A Practical Guide to Management Issues*, Tony Gunton (Prentice Hall, 1990)
■ *Handbook of MIS Management*, Robert E Umbaugh (ed.) (Auerbach, 2nd ed., 1988); (3rd ed., 1991); (Supplement, 1993)

Another important class is the textbook combining an overview of mainstream IM concepts with some facts about important technologies. Though wider in scope, this book is usually no longer (and often briefer) than the textbooks in the previous section. The great difficulty is to cover so much ground and still give the target reader an intelligent understanding of the ideas that will be of some practical use.

The book by Angell and Smithson is the least unsuccessful, because it covers fewer topics and adopts a more argumentative style than its rivals. The Beaumont and Sutherland book exemplifies the problem of the genre: it says a little about many things (some irrelevant, eg anecdotes about the culture of Stirling University or the US-Japan semiconductor agreement) and ends up conveying little useful insight into anything.

The Knight and Silk book is even less successful, since its choice of material seems so arbitrary: seven pages (out of 250) on encryption and related techniques, two on IT in the retail sector, three on fifth generation systems, 15 on a six-phase project life cycle, 15 on basic telecoms technology. Burn and Caldwell also offer an extremely odd selection: six pages on disk hardware (out of 250), five on IT management structures, two on spreadsheets, one on 'What is information?' etc.

Peppard's book has chapters by different contributors, but organised into the structure of a normal book. The topics selected are well-balanced rather than arbitrary, but it is difficult to make any more enthusiastic comment.

Bawden and Blakeman write about 'information services', as opposed to other applications of IT; some chapters on IT fundamentals are accompanied by some very dull writing indeed on such things as planning and implementing IT systems.

Gunton's book is less of a textbook. It really belongs to the large class of 'technology for managers' books, but unlike most such, it mixes in some mainstream IM material and attitudes as well.

The anthologies edited by Umbaugh given above provide 2000 pages of briefing-like articles of about ten pages each. Each is about a certain management theme, type of application or rising technology. Not every single article is brilliant, but there are some good matching warrants to be found, and the general quality of this work shows up quite starkly the shortcomings of most other writing that summarises technology for managers. The second edition contains a great deal of still useful material that was not carried forward to the third.

Several Planes: Ungainly Subsets

❑ *End User Focus*, Tony Gunton (Prentice Hall, 1988)

❑ *New Office Information Technology, Human and Managerial Implications,* Richard J Long (Croom Helm, 1987)

❑ *Competing in Time, Using telecommunications for competitive advantage*, Peter Keen (Ballinger, 1992)

❑ *Competitive Manufacturing through Information Technology, The Executive Challenge*, John Stark (Van Nostrand Reinhold, 1990)

❑ *Managing IT at Board Level, The Hidden Agenda Exposed,* Kit Grindley (Pitman, 1991)

■ *The Business Value of Computers, An Executive's Guide,* Paul A Strassmann (The Information Economics Press, 1990)

Some books choose a portion of the IM field, but treat it broadly and end by covering a rather ungainly subset of the issues and concepts found in the mainstream books. The books by Gunton and Long both ramble into fairly general IM issues well beyond any narrow definition of their subject; Long discusses control of railway marshalling yards, and Gunton brings in CSF, OSI and stage theories.

Keen is concerned with any application using telecoms in any way, no matter how minor. Stark includes just as many examples outside manufacturing as in it. Both set out to spread the gospel about the innovative use of IT, rather than to provide facts that are sufficiently clear to support real-life matching decisions. The material on the context and approach planes is mostly pretty general, rather than specific to telecoms or manufacturing.

Grindley's book is a kind of free improvisation on the results of a survey of managers' opinions. Though of variable quality, the text has the great advantage of being more argumentative than most. Most of the interesting material is on the agenda and context planes.

Strassmann's primary concern is with principles for evaluating, and thus making good decisions about, IT-based systems. By interpreting this theme broadly, he is able to cover a fair selection of IM topics: strategic systems, the CIO, CSFs, etc. The great merit of this book is its refreshingly intelligent style. The author is manifestly an experienced authority, and capable of thinking critically about the subject — qualities all too rare in the literature of IM.

Mostly Agenda Plane

■ *The Technology Connection, Strategy and Change in the Information Age*, Marc S Gerstein (Addison-Wesley, 1987)
❑ *Infotrends: Profiting from Your Information Resources*, Donald A Marchand and Forest W Horton, jr (Wiley, 1986)
❑ *Information Technology, The Catalyst for Change*, PA Consulting Group (Mercury, 1990)
❑ *Managing Information Systems, Change and Control in Organizational Computing*, Kenneth L Kraemer et al (Jossey-Bass, 1989)
❑ *The New Telecommunications, Infrastructure for the Information Age*, Frederick Williams (The Free Press, 1991)
❑ *The Rise of the Expert Company*, Edward Feigenbaum, Pamela McCorduck, and H Penny Nii (Times Books, 1988)
❑ *Deciding to Innovate, How Firms Justify Advanced Technology*, James W Dean, jr. (Ballinger, 1987)
❑ *Information Technology, The Trillion-Dollar Opportunity*, Harvey L Poppel and Bernard Goldstein (McGraw-Hill, 1987)

The first two-thirds of Gerstein's book provide one of the most intelligent surveys available of agenda warrants. The rest forms a summary overview of context issues. This book is far superior to the others under this heading.

Much of Marchand and Horton's material fails to survive the test of the Decision Question. What remains consists mainly of low-grade agenda warrants. The PA book contains a random selection of superficial, agenda-like material, mainly exhorting companies to use IT more effectively and adventurously.

The Kraemer et al book is at least original. It expounds a theory that the management of computing in organisations moves between certain defined 'states'. If you find this theory both valid and useful, that is presumably because it stimulates warrants about companies in certain states taking certain decisions on key issues. However, the book itself contains very little of this line of reasoning.

Williams presents many example cases, described very superficially. In so far as it can have any influence on decisions, this material might be regarded as weak agenda warrants. The book by Feigenbaum, McCorduck and Nii is even worse. It contains much material of the type: 'He sat down at the Apple, spending another hour debugging, until at long last it worked. He was so excited he woke his wife, Jan.' If you didn't previously know that an expert system could (say) help diagnose faults in equipment, this book will tell you that it can. But it won't help you appreciate why one diagnosis system might be more sophisticated or more tricky to implement than another.

The last two books are classified in this section of the bibliography *faute de mieux*. Were anybody to find anything here that could influence a decision, it would probably count as an agenda warrant. Dean uses five case studies in the innovative use of IT in manufacturing industry, to draw some extremely banal conclusions, eg informal contacts between decision-makers are important as well as formal. The opening sentence of Poppel and Goldstein is: 'This book is dedicated to helping readers anticipate and capitalize on information technology (IT) developments.' At the end of the book, after a surfeit of buzzwords, it is still obscure what readers the authors are trying to help and how.

Mostly Matching Plane

❑ *Computer Integrated Manufacturing, Theory and Practice*, Daniel T Koenig (Hemisphere, 1990)

❑ *Computer Integrated Manufacturing, The Data Management Strategy,* Olin H Bray (Digital, 1988)

❑ *Strategic Planning for Electronic Banking, From Human Resources to Product Development and Information Systems*, Dimitris N Chorafas (Butterworths, 1987)

❑ *Electronic Payment Systems, Winning new customers*, James Essinger (Chapman and Hall, 1992)

❑ *Managing Information Technology's Organisational Impact*, R Clarke and J Cameron (ed.) (North-Holland, 1991)

The first two books each devote most of their space to telling you about the possibilities and issues in CIM, and conclude with chapters that address management and planning directly. Koenig's detail is easier to fashion into serviceable warrants than Bray's. Moreover, the specifically management parts by Koenig are still about CIM, whereas much of the equivalent in Bray's book could be applicable to any kind of technology or application. There are some other books about CIM, that don't qualify for this bibliography, because they don't say enough about managing or taking decisions to count as IM.

The Chorafas book is pretty well devoid of any content that would help anybody decide anything. Essinger's book certainly contains *some* content that passes this test, but it is disappointing not to find far more.

Despite the title, the Clarke and Cameron anthology consists mainly of article-length accounts of the way particular organisations apply IT, or of the kind of applications particular technologies can support. This makes it a source of matching warrants.

Mostly Scope Plane

■ *The Mythical Man-Month*, Frederick P. Brooks, jr. (Addison-Wesley, 1975)

❑ *Shaping the Future, Business Design through Information Technology*, Peter GW Keen (Harvard Business School Press, 1991)

❑ *How to Assess Your IT Investment*, Barbara Farbey, Frank Land and David Targett (Butterworth-Heinemann, 1993)

❑ *Professional Systems Development: Experience, Ideas and Action*, Niels Erik Andersen et al (Prentice Hall, 1989)

The Brooks book is very old, but a classic. It provides a string of ideas that are still relevant on problems and issues with the management of software development projects.

Keen writes about issues of IM in general, but concentrates on areas he believes particularly important and insufficiently dealt with elsewhere. The most stimulating material in the book is about the 'platform' or infrastructure that an organisation sets up, distinct from individual applications.

The short book by Fawley, Land and Targett is about the important problem of evaluating and justifying possible projects. Much of the text is rather ordinary, but the last 30 pages do discuss how different types of project call for different methods of evaluation.

The Andersen et al book is primarily about how to structure and manage system development projects (rather than how to design a system, or modularise software, or make use of CASE etc). It misses almost completely what should be its most promising theme — deciding how *different types* of project should be structured and managed in different ways.

Mostly Context Plane

■ *Managing End User Computing*, Jukka Heikkilä (Helsingin Kauppakorkeakoulun Kuvakaitos, 1990)

❑ *Managing Computer Resources*, Donna Hussain and KM Hussain (Irwin, 1988)

Heikkilä's booklet collects together several interesting articles, and focuses strongly on the key issues of freedom and control of end-user computing.

The 600-page textbook by Hussain and Hussain concentrates on the less glamorous parts of IM: running an installation and associated topics. Though well written and designed, it is irredeemably flawed by the policy of smoothing out any awkward options and tradeoffs, to present a composite, generic, 'good practice' approach on every issue.

Mostly Approach Plane

❑ *Planning for Effective Business Information Systems*, Edwin E Tozer (Pergamon, 1988)

❑ *Strategic Data-Planning Methodologies*, James Martin (Prentice Hall, 1982)

❑ *Design and Strategy for Corporate Information Services, MIS Long-Range Planning*, Larry E Long (Prentice-Hall, 1982)

❑ *Strategic Information Management Planning*, Thomas E Gallo (Prentice Hall, 1988)

❑ *Introducing Strategic Information Systems Planning*, DSJ Remenyi (NCC Blackwell, 1991)

The first four are each concerned with describing one specific, general-purpose, multi-step methodology for decision-making and planning. Even the best of them falls short of providing convincing treatment of many fundamental issues. These books should be read very suspiciously; spotting the many unspoken assumptions and glossed-over difficulties is a good way of developing an awareness of the real challenges.

From this offbeat point of view Tozer's book is by far the most valuable: a rich brew of techniques that seem plausible and pragmatic, other procedures that seem far less likely to work, progress by sleight of hand and some structural incoherence. In sum, a stimulating book for the critical thinker.

Martin offers a much smoother view of a step-by-step process that is largely based on data modelling; it deserves careful, sceptical reading, to spot all the tricky points that are glossed over. The books by Gallo and Long are much weaker, and easy targets for even the gentlest critical thinker.

Remenyi's text is just as vulnerable. It presents some typical ideas about multi-step methodologies in a very bland way, and offers a short account of a recommended 20-step structure. This is awkwardly mixed up with material on a quite different topic, the category of systems commonly described as 'strategic'.

❑ *InfoMap: A Complete Guide to Discovering Corporate Information Resources*, Cornelius F Burk, jr., and Forest W Horton, jr. (Prentice Hall, 1988)

❑ *A Management System for the Information Business, Organizational Analysis*, Edward A Van Schaik (Prentice-Hall, 1985)

❑ *Planning IT, Creating an information management strategy*, David J Silk (Butterworth-Heinemann, 1991)

❑ *Informatieplanning in tweevoud*, BAA Hopstaken and A Kranendonk (Kluwer, Deventer, the Netherlands, 2nd ed., 1991)

❑ *Information-Systems Development, Systems thinking in the field of information-systems*, Paul Lewis (Pitman, 1994)

❑ *Information Systems Management: Analytical Tools and Techniques*, Phillip Ein-Dor and Carl R Jones (Elsevier, 1985)

Burk and Horton focus more narrowly on an approach to analysing the broad categories of information in an organisation. This book is better organised than Tozer's, but is worthwhile in a similar way: it must be read critically, but then it can be a handy stimulus for clarifying your own thoughts about the subject.

Van Schaik's book contains little discussion, but sets out an elaborate system for IT management. Unlike most, it concentrates on describing a body of planning *documents* rather than the steps of a planning *process*.

Silk offers an approach to reaching agenda decisions through a 60-question checklist. This primitive structure provides little opportunity for exposing such essential subtleties as how the answer to one question may influence another, or how the actions generated by several answers may need to be kept consistent.

In complete contrast, the book by the Dutchmen Hopstaken and Kranendonk undertakes an extremely ambitious intellectual enterprise. In order to discuss approaches to large-scale information planning exercises, it starts out with a set of abstract concepts, that are then applied to unify the more detailed ideas. However, the impact is gravely reduced by the lack of clear examples.

The first two parts of Lewis's book contain some valid criticisms, albeit in academic style, of established methods of developing systems. This prepares the ground for the description of a better methodology for problem investigation, system design and data analysis. But when this arrives, it falls rather flat.

Ein-Dor and Jones explore the deeply unfashionable approach of using operations research algebra and micro-economics graphs to take decisions — on such matters as how to design chargeback mechanisms, how to upgrade hardware resources, how to plan software development and maintenance, and how to assess whether it is worth investing in systems that will in turn generate information that has a certain value.

Several Planes: Human Factors

■ *Up and Running, Integrating Information Technology and the Organization*, Richard E Walton (Harvard Business School Press, 1989)

❑ *Manage IT! Exploiting information systems for effective management*, Michael Wright and David Rhodes (Frances Pinter, 1985)

❑ *Managing New Office Technology, An Organizational Strategy*, Calvin HP Pava (Free Press, 1983)

❑ *In the Age of the Smart Machine, The Future of Work and Power*, Shoshana Zuboff (Basic Books, 1988)

❑ *Managing the Adoption of New Technology*, David A Preece (Routledge, 1989)

❑ *Facilitating Technological Change, The Human Resource Challenge*, Patricia M Flynn (Ballinger, 1988)

There have been quite a few books in that area roughly defined by the concepts of human factors, change management and sociotechnical design. Ideas on these matters *can* be relevant to decisions on any of the five planes, but in practice some books under this heading are so weak that the Decision Question wipes them out completely.

Walton's is much the best. It is dominated by discussion of the ways IT-based systems may have an enriching or a stultifying effect on the people who have to use them. It minimises the customary platitudes.

Wright and Rhodes offer a number of concepts and models concerned with the management of change at a rather abstract level. Time and again the book seems on the verge of conveying a stimulating idea, but just misses. Still, it easily takes second place in this weak division.

Pava's book from 1983 is fairly well-known. It makes the case for taking account of social factors, as well as the more obvious considerations of efficiency, in designing systems. A multi-step approach is included. Zuboff's is a widely cited book. Unjustly so. It takes longer than Walton's to say less, more pretentiously. The books by Preece and by Flynn are towards the academic end of the continuum. They even make Zuboff's book seem worthwhile; at least that is irritating in a provocative way that could goad you to clarify your own thoughts. It seems amazing that Flynn examined 200 case studies and came up with such insipid findings.

❑ *People and Computers, The Impacts of Computing on End Users in Organizations*, James N Danziger and Kenneth L Kraemer (Columbia University Press, 1986)

❑ *Organisations and Information Technology, Systems, Power and Job Design*, Ian Winfield (Blackwell Scientific, 1991)

❑ *Organizational Structure and Information Technology*, Jon Harrington (Prentice Hall, 1991)

❑ *Motivating and Managing Computer Personnel*, J Daniel Couger and Robert A Zawacki (Wiley, 1980)

❑ *Managing the Human Resource*, John Westerman and Pauline Donoghue (Prentice Hall, 1989)

❑ *Human Factors in Management Information Systems*, Jane M. Carey (ed.) (Ablex, 1988)

❑ *The Management Implications of New Information Technologies*, Nigel Piercy (ed.) (Croom Helm, 1984)

Danziger and Kraemer analyse a questionnaire-based survey of attitudes of system users in a very broad sense — including many who never touch a PC or terminal (ie not 'end user' in the more common sense), but they fail to conclude very much of interest.

The books by Winfield and Harrington both discuss organisations in a hopelessly bland and abstract way, and virtually nothing said passes the test of the Decision Question. The books by Westerman and Donoghue, and Couger are about the application of concepts of human resource management to IT staff. Couger's is based on a quantitative survey of personality characteristics, while the scope of Westerman and Donoghue is broader. Neither produces useful warrants.

The two anthologies are more valuable. Carey's is about the interface between humans and computer systems and related topics; its contributions (some of which are interesting) are co-ordinated by a unifying model of the subject area. About half the articles in Piercy's anthology are about 'human' topics — IT's effect on future work patterns, on industrial relations and so on; the remainder are more disparate.

Books Associated With This One

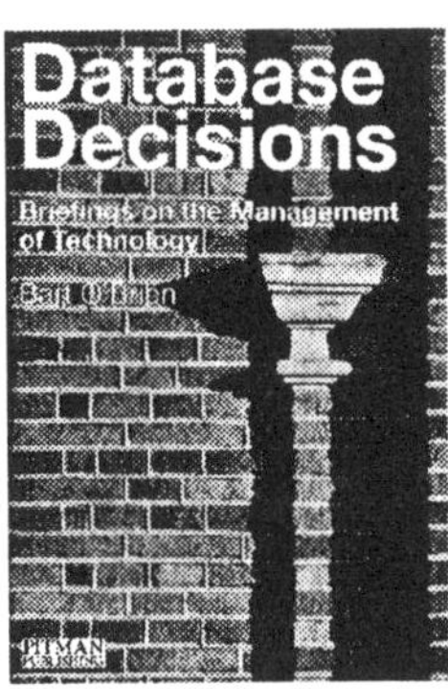

■ *Demands and Decisions, Briefings on Issues in Information Technology Strategy*, Bart O'Brien (Prentice Hall, 1992)
■ *Database Decisions, Briefings on the Management of Technology*, Bart O'Brien (Pitman, 1994)

This book, *Information Management Decisions*, reviews the world of ideas about IM, and suggests ways of thinking about them and the problems they address.

Demands and Decisions operates on a similar level, but concentrates on discussing a range of tricky IM problems and issues, as rationally as possible, *without* the distractions of theories and techniques that others happen to have expressed.

Database Decisions suggests by example how to tackle one specific IM problem: making warrants for decisions on the *matching* plane. It concentrates on one area, database technology, marshalls a body of 181 matching warrants into 31 briefings, and shows how this material can be relevant to practical IM decision-making.

NOTES & ARGUMENTS

1 The *classic academic* style of writing about IM is manifested in PhD theses, conference proceedings and academic journals. This material attempts to establish theories about IM as far as possible in an intellectually respectable, near-scientific way. The hallmarks of this style are:

- *empirical research*, especially questionnaire-based surveys: eg studies of a number of companies to discover how various human or other factors determine the success of projects;
- *intellectual vocabulary* not heard in most businesses from one year to the next; eg 'elements of a paradigm for describing a universe of discourse', and 'syntactic and semantic classification schemas for objects';
- *abstract models:* 'in assessing the quality of any IT system, let O = f (E,M,F,R) represent the relationship between variables such as the existing situation, the model of the system, relevant constraints . . '

The drawback here is that the scientific ideal of developing rigorous theories through research is so difficult to apply to IM. It has been estimated that the trajectory of a pin-ball after bumping 20 posts in a few seconds is effectively unpredictable; the calculations are just too complicated to be done accurately in any reasonable length of time. Since the phenomena in such fields as economics, sociology and IM are presumably more complex still, the whole approach of aiming for semi-scientific abstract models is misguided, or so it can be argued.

In complete contrast are ideas about IM in the *classic consultancy* style. Some see management consultancy as a conduit bringing academic ideas from the business school to the real world. With IM this image only works if you imagine a rather leaky conduit, fed also by other strongly flowing channels from less respectable sources.

Many consultancies and computer services companies promote prescriptive ideas about how to plan IT strategically, make an information architecture or approach other IM tasks. Many of these ideas, when examined thoughtfully, are too primitive to earn respect. Often a standardised method is bought at the price of vast, hidden, simplifying assumptions.

Given the above, it is not surprising that publishers tend to publish mainly books on IM that lie somewhere *between* these two classic extremes.

2 There are at least a dozen contenders as textbooks for a business-school course on IM. Here are six tests for a quick assessment of the quality of any candidate book:

- Does it discuss (not just state) Nolan's stage theory?
- Does it explain the strategic grid of Cash, McFarlan and McKenney clearly, and show how it can be used?
- Does it discuss the relevance of strategic system cases (not just praise them)?
- Does it convey the trickiness of infrastructure planning (not just say that it is a good thing)?
- Does it analyse the use of prototyping (not just say that it is one mode of development)?
- Does it expose the tradeoffs at the heart of end-user computing matters?

The more enthusiastic 'yes' answers, the higher the book deserves to be rated.

Critical Thinking — An Inverted Book

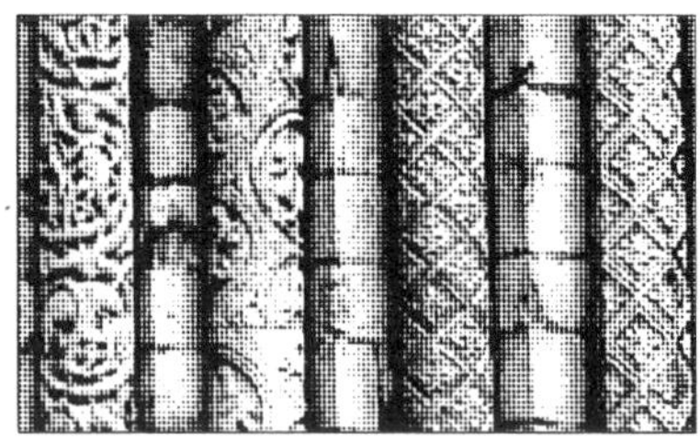

This section is an *inversion* of the rest of the book. The essay at the beginning, *Critical Thinking — Some Basic Tools*, introduces the Decision Question and the six warrant forms as fundamental concepts for critical thinking about IM. The briefings in the main body of the book are organised by topic; within them, many more techniques for critical thinking are employed to discuss particular issues.

For example, the briefing on inter-organisational systems states that a *classic case* of an EDI (electronic data interchange) system has four traits: computer-computer, standard format, clearing-house and mailbox. If a system has the first two traits but not the others it still counts as EDI, albeit a non-classic form. This analysis is meant to convey useful knowledge about EDI, but even for someone with no interest in this topic, it still has value on a different level. It illustrates a certain general thinking technique — *spotting classic traits.*

To clarify your ideas about downsizing or re-engineering or multi-step methodologies or neural network or legacy systems or any other topic, you might identify a small number of traits that characterise the really classic case. Then, you could ask whether your particular case had all the classic traits, or whether some but not all were present, or whether, by picking only some of the classic traits and varying other things, you could generate different options to choose between. To do that would be to use the general thinking technique which the briefing on inter-organisational systems shows in action.

This section lays out a whole set of general maxims for critical thinking, together with pointers back to examples of their use in the rest of the book.[1]

Careful Use of Terms

1. When defining X, make clear what is not X.

   A useful definition of electronic data interchange (EDI) should make it clear that videotex applications are excluded. (Briefing 39)

   Whatever your definition of *information management*, it ought to make clear that certain management activities *do not* count as information management. (Briefing 1)

   Defining end-user computing is tricky, but unless it is understood what kinds of computing *don't* belong in this category, debates about how to manage end-user computing may never grasp the issues effectively. (Briefing 37)

   A useful definition of re-engineering should pack enough punch to exclude *some* valuable projects. Otherwise the term will mean nothing more than 'any new system development that the speaker wishes to praise'. (Briefing 36)

2. When defining X, avoid the confusions of extraneous material. If defining (say) *porcelain*, it only confuses matters to talk about what you believe marks out good porcelain; define the term in a way that includes all porcelain, irrespective of quality. If defining a *shawm*, leave theories about its origin till later. If defining a *pergola*, just define it; keep advice on how to build one separate.

   Definitions of IM as 'aligning IT with strategic objectives' or 'integrating IT and business planning' are really statements of what the speaker regards as *good* IM. It is much clearer to define IM itself first, and only after that go on to discuss what counts as good and bad IM. (Briefing 1)

   It is sometimes thought that the definition of *competitive advantage* lies in a well-known passage by Porter that begins: 'competitive advantage grows fundamentally out of . . ' — but that is no definition at all.

   If discussing the CIO (chief information officer) make up your mind whether to use a neutral definition (eg 'The CIO is whoever is in charge of IT') or a statement of objective (eg 'To deserve to be called a CIO a manager should . . . etc'). (Briefing 25)

3. When deciding what X really means, think out how it differs from other related terms.

   What exactly is a *core competency*? If you use the term, you ought to be clear on whether you regard it as the same thing as a *critical success factor* or not. (Briefing 8)

   Whatever you wish *re-engineering* to mean, you need to have thought about whether the famous *strategic systems*, such as Sabre, McKesson and Otis, count as re-engineering or not. (Briefings 33, 36)

4. Watch out for *halo terms* that imply praise.

Strategic system and *re-engineering* are unavoidably halo terms. *Change management* often is too, but not in this book. (Briefings 33, 35, 36, 40)

So is *integration* as used by some people — but it shouldn't be. (Briefing 25)

5. Watch out for *elastic terms*, that can take any number of overlapping or even contradictory meanings.

End-user computing and *decision-support system* are difficult to define without elastic terms such as '(end-user's) active role' and 'decision'. (Briefing 33)

Videotex is pretty elastic. So is *value-added network*. (Briefings 15, 16)

6. Recognise *broad and narrow concepts*, as in 'the disastrous state of the economy' (broad) and 'lack of food in shops' (narrower). Questions in opinion polls often suffer from confusion here.

Strategic planning (by almost anybody's definition) will include decisions about integration, among other things. So integration decisions (or at least, the important ones) can't be a separate thing, distinct from strategic planning. But strategic planning will probably include other things beside integration decisions. (Briefing 3)

Use *evolutionary development* as a broad term, and keep *prototyping* and *experimental project* as narrower terms within it. (Briefing 22)

7. Recognise *hoover or xerox terms*. They may indicate no more than that the product belongs to some broad generic class.

A business model labelled *value chain analysis* usually has some rough similarity to the model format given in Porter's book, but, on examination, it may well be based on quite different principles and conventions. (Briefing 4)

8. When generalising about X, make sure that X is something sufficiently solid to generalise about.

'Under these generic circumstances the IT director should be on the board, and under these other generic circumstances, not . .' Yes, but different companies have boards with different sizes, styles, compositions, powers, habits etc. 'On the board' is not a solid concept. This makes any such generalisation futile. (Briefing 25)

9. Recognise two things as different but not independent.

End-user computing and the role of the MIS department are two different things. But they are not independent: your decisions on one automatically imply decisions for the other. (Briefing 3)

10. Recognise *house/mansion* cases. How large must a house be to count as a mansion? In what context is belly more appropriate than stomach? Plainly two words can have different overtones without standing for two distinct concepts.

What distinguishes a *hybrid manager* from a line manager who has a fair degree of knowledge and experience of IT? (Briefing 25)

Are 'data as a corporate resource' and 'information architecture' really two separate issues calling for decisions? No, they are probably just different expressions used in slightly different contexts. (Briefing 3)

Where does competent system design end and business re-engineering begin? (Briefing 36)

11. Recognise *irregular verbs*. Here are two examples from *Yes Prime Minister*, by Jonathan Lynn and Anthony Jay: 'I have an independent mind; you are eccentric; he is round the twist'; 'I give confidential briefings; you leak; he has been charged under Section 2a of the Official Secrets Act.' Seriously, it is good practice to scan your draft report to the board for any blatant first-person (positively loaded) or third-person (negatively loaded) forms. Whether you alter those you find is another matter.

I keep up with developments in management science; you read management magazines now and again; he parrots boardroom buzzwords. (Briefing 3)

I have an integrated planning system; you accept some rigidity, inflexibility and bureaucracy to achieve co-ordination and avoid incompatible technology; she has a management approach that Stalin would have been proud of. (Briefing 24)

I have a strategic system; you have a system that made a good return on its investment; he picked an easy target for automation. (Briefing 40)

I expose that report as a farrago of incoherent reasoning, false assumptions, jargon and platitudes; you carefully analyse the logic of the report's recommendations; she indulges in theoretical hair-splitting of no practical importance whatsoever. (CT-SBT and Briefing 2)**2**

Tools and Principles for Debate

12. Clarify any statement, but especially a decision, by asking: *'as opposed to?'* If that is difficult to answer, maybe there is something wrong. After all, any decision worthy of the name is a choice of one option over some other.

'We will use IT to develop innovative products' makes far more impact if it is also clear what plausible IT policies are being excluded by this decision. (Briefing 2)

Deciding to have good security is no decision. Deciding for the sake of security to have two (as opposed to one or seven) data centres is. (Briefing 26)

Get to the heart of any high-level policy, mission or vision by asking: What plausible options, one level of detail lower, will be ruled out by this policy? (Briefing 8)

13. Clarify any material — issues, decisions etc — by analysing from a negative point of view.

A neat way to analyse the key factors distinguishing one type of development project from another is to focus on generic *failure* reasons for such projects. (Briefing 21)

Expose the significance of the important Mrs Fields case study by pointing out the ways the managers might have gone wrong. (Briefing 34)

14. Clarify any decision by asking: 'Can this be broken down into several decisions?'

'We will use software product X as the company standard' is really two decisions: 'We will have a company standard', and 'We choose X rather than Y.' That kind of unpacking may cause you to question whether both the decisions are right. (Briefing 2)

'We will use the Method/1 methodology as the basis for our planning' consists of first: 'We will use some *standard* methodology' and then: 'The particular standard methodology we choose is Method/1.'

15. Distinguish: deciding to do something that is in your power (eg 'I will play the Sicilian Defence against Kasparov') and deciding to attempt something (eg 'I will try and become world champion').

'We will develop a bold new system to gain competitive advantage.' Nobody can stop you developing a bold new system. But whether its effect will be to drive your competitors, or you yourself, out of business is something not entirely under your control.

'We will set up an information centre team and thus stimulate but also control end-user computing.' You can certainly decide to set up the team, but you can't decide that the result will be a beneficial mixture of stimulus and control. You can only hope it will. (Briefing 37)

16. Distinguish between decisions that exist on different *planes* of decision-making. This helps impose order on otherwise perplexing combinations of decisions.

For IM the most useful thing is to separate out these five planes of decision-making: agenda, matching, scope, context, approach. (Briefing 2)

17. Sort out decisions in any policy area by getting them into the format *issues-options-policies.*

Identify three key issues on end-user computing; spell out the options available on each; look at the resulting combinations of choices; knock out the implausible; this leaves you with five generic policies to choose between. (Briefing 37)

In a similar way, identify three main issues of distribution and centralisation; sort out the opions on each, and assemble them into four generic policies. (Briefing 24)

18. Assess the *problem frame* critically. Too narrow is bad, but too broad can be too.**3**

Rather than ask 'What should be the job description of the CIO?', ask 'What structure of steering committees and staff functions and management should there be?' (Briefing 25)

Rather than ask 'How shall we go about replacing this manifestly obsolete legacy system?', ask 'How can we alleviate the disadvantages of this legacy system?' That leaves open the possibility of replacing just *part* of the system. (Briefing 21)

19. Test any statement or document by asking: Is this *description or prescription*? 'Does this new book describe how parliamentary democracy in fact works, or how, in the writer's view, it ought to?'

This is an important tool for making good use of modelling activities within the decision-making process. A model may describe how things are, or it may prescribe how things ought to be — but probably not at the same time. (Briefing 29)

Generic models of (say) the insurance business or the IS function run into difficulties here. (Briefing 32)

Theories about organisations learning to use technology, or about the historical development of the IT industry need careful examination. Is the theory describing the inevitable or is it offering advice on what you should do? (Briefing 10)

20. Distinguish decision-making *product* (eg the laws actually passed by the legislature) from decision-making *process* (the debates, lobbying, emotions and power-struggles that produced them).

Cling hold of this distinction to find your way through the complexities of designing the right decision-making structure for your situation. (Briefing 28)

If the documentation of any standard methodology confuses product and process, give it a very black mark. (Briefing 30)

21. Fit the argument and the information to the *audience*. Terms, facts and arguments depend on context: 'the earth is flat' (context: tennis); 'the earth is round' (context: naval gunnery); 'the earth is an oblate spheroid' (context: astronomy).

Use this principle as the basis for designing the way people with different backgrounds and particularly different levels of knowledge of IT can be brought together in decision-making. (Briefing 35)

If trying to convince the board that use of the OSI model will bring important flexibility, leave out the telecoms detail, and explain how this model is, by its very logical structure, capable of accommodating change in an orderly way. (Briefing 17)

Even if you agree with all the ideas in this book, you don't necessarily have to expound them in exactly the same terms to all your colleagues. Some people respect concepts expressed in a very abstract way; others are the opposite. (Briefing 2)

Untangling Complex Areas

22. Try to convert any text containing general information and advice into *warrants* in clear, standard forms, such as a drawing of distinctions or a scaling of gradations. This makes the material far easier to use in debate and reasoning.

For IM the most useful thing is to work with this set of six forms: comparison, distinctions, gradations, aspects, chart, example. (CT-SBT)

23. In particular, coax general facts about any *technology* into warrants in standard forms. This is the best way to ensure that technology facts take their place in the debate about how to use technology for business ends.

Regard the warrant forms as a repertoire of tools for getting control of technology facts (Briefing 11). When studying an article about technology or listening to a technical expert, choose comparison (Briefing 12), distinctions (Briefing 13), gradations (Briefing 14), chart (Briefing 15), aspects (Briefing 16) or example (Briefing 17) warrants to pick out the points that count.

24. Also, set up warrants in standard forms about less tractable factors, such as human attitudes or philosophies or values. This is the best way to fit such things into general debate.

Use warrants to think critically about: the essentials of an intellectual product beneath the surface detail (Briefing 29, Briefing 30); the meaning of vague words such as 'culture' (Briefing 8); people's responsibilities (Briefing 25); people's attitudes (Briefing 32); objectives of experimental projects (Briefing 22); reasons for project failures (Briefing 21); general theories about the whole subject of IM. (Briefing 42)

25. Get a sense of direction in any complex area by taking some representative problems, generalisations and decisions, and sorting them into broad categories.

Reduce confusion about 'human factors' issues by distinguishing the different planes of decision that may be affected, and breaking issues on each plane down further. (Briefing 41)

Make sense of questions about the organisational *context* for IT, by showing how most issues in this field fall under a few main headings: division of responsibilities, division of human forces etc. (Briefing 23)

Clarify confusing terms such as *end-user computing, change management* and so on, by showing how one representative system may be associated with several of them in different ways. (Briefing 33)

26. Probe a complex area by setting up a *simplified version* and then relaxing assumptions to make it more realistic step by step. Economists define a state of perfect competition, study it and then add in more tricky factors. An engineer may study a mechanical system without friction first and then add in complications.

To understand the issues in structuring decision-making, first analyse the problems that would confront one powerful intelligence taking decisions alone; only after that feed in the complications that arise from the need for group decision-making.(Briefing 28)

To understand the effect of IT on 'compliance' and 'commitment', start by identifying those things even in a world where IT didn't exist. (Briefing 34)

27. Probe any complex area by starting out from a *naive solution* — in order to spell out the problems it gives rise to.

To see the trickiness of tradeoffs within infrastructure planning start out with some examples of advice about *core systems*, about co-ordinating feasibility studies, and about standardising PC suppliers, that quite miss the real substance of the problems. (Briefing 19)

28. Try splitting a broad concept or problem area in two: 'Ethnomusicology has two main strands: musical and sociological.' 'The problem of the twins' birthday really has two parts: what presents and what party.'

Legacy systems seems a topic that is important but difficult to break open. Distinguish two separate problems raised by legacy systems: risk of changing a vital system; difficulty of justifying the right moment for replacement. (Briefing 21)

Outsourcing may seem a rather bland topic, but distinguish two separate motivations: efficiency of huge but straightforward processing; commanding expertise in advanced technology. (Briefing 24)

29. Clarify the issues in any field by asking: Is there really some *essential tension* (eg a tradeoff between certain fundamental factors) underlying all the more specific issues?

Most of the tricky issues in end-user computing come down to the need to balance freedom (that brings creativity but perhaps anarchy) with control (order but perhaps sullenness). (Briefing 37)

Decisions about how extensive to make the scope of a certain project, or how elaborate to make an infrastructure, should be governed by one deep tradeoff between commitment and flexibility. (Briefing 19)

30. Recognise *defining traits*, as opposed to classic traits. In Britain a post-box is normally a red box used for depositing letters; but there can be, and in fact are, non-red British post-boxes.

Classic EDI has four main traits (in brief): computer-computer, standard format, clearing-house and mailbox. If either of the first two don't apply to a case, then it just isn't EDI. Either of the other two can be varied and the result is still EDI, albeit a non-classic form. Getting this clear helps coherent debate. (Briefing 39)

31. Know the *classic case*. Then you can ask: Does this specific case for decision have all the traits of a classic case, or only some of them? Is there room for choice? Can plausible options be generated by varying classic details?

A classic case of re-engineering has three pronounced traits: spectacular quantitative benefit, job enrichment and simplicity. Ask whether your case necessarily has all three, or ought to be changed to have all three, or would be better by stressing one or two of them, and thus being non-classic. (Briefing 36)

A good approach to deciding about an internal information service could be to sketch out a classic Prestel-based videotex service, and then see what shortcomings that might have. (Briefing 15)

It is fairly easy to define the responsibilities of a classic information centre to support end-user computing. Do that. Then consider what features of your own case call for non-classic variations. (Briefing 37)

Testing Generalisations: Broad Techniques

32. Test out and clarify any generalisation with the *Decision Question*: Even if true, how could this generalisation assist a decision of information management in any particular case? *Warrant* is a convenient term for a generalisation that passes this test. These are among the most fundamental ideas in the book.

The notion of a learning process in the use of IT is interesting, and indeed relevant — but only if you think through the following: How might awareness of learning-process theory help in identifying better options and deciding between them more shrewdly? (Briefing 10)

Nolan's stage theory has been widely influential and yet, if you ask how the theory could help anyone make better decisions, it is hard to put together any convincing answer. (Briefing 9)

Textbooks and articles give cases of companies achieving *competitive advantage* through bold use of IT. When reading such material ask: How will awareness of these cases enable better decisions to be made in future cases? (Briefing 40)

A quadrant-diagram defines four possibilities — styles of end-user computing, say. But anyone can devise a quadrant-diagram; what counts is showing that it can be used to generate plausible decisions about specific matters in particular cases. (Briefing 37)

33. Test for *tautology* such as 'a car moves along the road because it possesses motive power', or for statements so bland that they are true but uninformative.

Discussion of the importance of critical success factors often verges dangerously on tautology. (CT-SBT)

Discussion of topics such as culture, mission and vision may escape tautology only at the cost of turning to platitude. (Briefing 8).

Given something as soft as a list of six generic variables that affect an individual's readiness to accept change, ask: Is there anything at all surprising in this list? Are the six items reasonably precise and distinct? (Briefing 35)

34. Test any generalisation with the *Trivial-False Fork*. If some statement can be interpreted several different ways, one may be true-but-trivial and another may be non-trivial-but-false. To be useful, there must be some meaning that is both non-trivial and also true.

Is information a resource? It depends what you mean by that. It is not easy to find a meaning that is both true and non-trivial. (Briefing 1)

Is it feasible to break down any organisation into its major parts corresponding to 'the progressive addition of value'? Yes, if you take that expression in a very trivial sense; probably no, if you are serious about detailed accountancy to measure value. (Briefing 4)

Is it true that there are five generic forces of industry competition? Use the *Trivial-False Fork* to help decide what you think. (Briefing 5)

35. Test any list of general characteristics by asking whether the items are all on the *same plane*. If not, be very cautious with the list.

An article gives four key points about inter-organisational systems (IOSs). One is essentially a *motive* for seriously considering having an IOS (it can bring various benefits), while the other three (eg it raises new legal issues, etc) are *challenges* to be faced in achieving a successful IOS. (Briefing 39)

McFarlan gives six characteristics of strategic systems. Some describe *actual* beneficial results of the system (eg opens up new markets), but some describe things *instrumental* in leading to beneficial results (eg can evolve; is not easily replicated by competitors). (Briefing 40)

36. Clarify any generalisation by asking for examples. 'Perspicacity is a function of reciprocity.' 'You're probably right; now what would be a *good example* of that?' Since obscure abstraction is a frequent enemy of clear thinking, this is one of the more important maxims.

If somebody makes a point about how a company's mission statement should be a different thing from its vision, ask straight away for illuminating examples. (Briefing 8)

'A prototyping project should be regarded as a different thing from an experimental project, with different objectives and different project structure.' All right then, examples please. (Briefing 22)

A method based on the idea that every 'problem domain' has three components, 'domain anchor', 'domain pivot' and 'impacted domain', may be good or it may be bad. Without clear examples to show what these labels stand for nobody can possibly tell. (CT-SBT)

Do you agree with Earl's analysis of four types of manager, each possessing a different degree or kind of knowledge about IT? You can't, unless you are given some specific examples of the sorts of IT knowledge they are supposed to have. (Briefing 25)

What about the use by Hopstaken and Kranendonk of four models (searchlights, oval, cross and cycle) to unify examination of many of the issues in IM? Impossible to assess, since they give hardly any down-to-earth examples. (Briefing 42)

37. Faced with any sophisticated general model or theory, ask: What *kind of thing* is this?

When offered a model that divides things up into stages over time, ask straight away: Are these meant to be stages in any one organisation's development, or stages in the use of IT by the world as a whole? (Briefing 10)

You can't understand anything about the OSI seven-layer model of telecoms, unless you probe by asking: What does 'layer' mean? Layer of what? Is layer different from level? And so on. (Briefing 19)

38. Scrutinise any generalisation that you should always strive for certain goals, or always follow certain principles, by asking what *kind of recommendation* it is: ethical, enlightened self-interest or something else?

Zuboff's book seems to urge you to use IT to make people's jobs as rich and fulfilling as possible. Why should you? Because it is morally right or financially advantageous or what? What kind of injunction is this? (Briefing 34)

Some enthusiastic writers on re-engineering give the impression that if you don't redesign your processes to give people a more varied range of activities, then that is morally culpable. (Briefing 36)

39. Check *independent variables* to see if they really are. A person's age and hair-colour are different variables, but they are not necessarily independent.

A data centre's cost-effectiveness and its ability to cope with unexpected peaks in demand are both desirable variables to optimise, but they aren't independent. The more spare capacity there is to meet unexpected peaks, the less cost-effective the data centre will be. (Briefing 26)

Control of end-user computing may be high or low; its rate of expansion may be high or low; but these are not two independent variables for decision: you can't combine a decision to have low control with a decision to have any particular rate of expansion. (Briefing 37)

40. Use a *battery* of tests or cases to assess the quality of any general idea or simply to make sense of it.

When examining some standard planning methodology that is new to you, get to grips with it quickly by seeing how it fares against a battery of tricky points that typically arise with this sort of intellectual product. (Briefing 30)

Test any technique for generating strategy options by asking: Would it succeed in generating the right options for Harvey-Jones's shirt-manufacturer and diary-publisher, and some others from your own experience? (Briefing 5)

Test any proposed standard life-cycle for software development by seeing where it stands on six key issues. (Briefing 21)

Testing 'X is a good (or bad) thing'

41. Test any assertion along the lines of 'X is a good thing' by asking: 'is X really a *coherent thing* that can be carefully defined and still be unequivocally a good thing?'

Some write as if *integration* were definitely a good thing. But that idea collapses as soon as the notion of integration is examined more carefully. (Briefing 20)

There are problems in finding definitions of *inter-organisational system* or *open system* or *innovation* that leave them as definitely good things. (Briefings 20, 39, 40)

42. Test any 'X is good, not-X is bad' by asking — is not-X a *straw man*? To set up a straw man is to set up and attack an argument or a description of a situation which is not the real one to be discussed, but a poor imitation of it, and thus easier to criticise and denigrate.

Proclamations about the glorious IT Age at the expense of the boring-old DP Age make you feel ashamed to have been around at that time — until you realise that it is only a straw man being set up. (Briefing 10)

Re-engineering is sometimes defined by setting up as a straw man the idea that, in the past, people designed computer systems that did nothing but replicate existing procedures. (Briefing 36)

Anti-rational attitudes often rest on a straw-man view that to be rational is to ignore awkward factors, to structure the problem too rigidly, to refuse to search for new ideas etc. (Introduction)

43. Test any statement that X is a good thing by asking: Is not-X really all bad, or is there perhaps a *tradeoff* to be struck between X and not-X?

Some writers seem to hold that you should design your new systems to enrich job satisfaction and empower the worker as much as possible. Aren't there other, perhaps countervailing, factors to take account of too? (Briefing 34)

Shouldn't a large data centre be expected to cope with unexpected rush jobs from time to time? Not if you insist that it be a highly cost-efficient production facility for regular systems. There is a tradeoff to be made. (Briefing 26)

44. Test any statement that X is a good thing with: 'Yes, but is it *feasible*?' People sometimes urge you to do something and imply that, on the whole, it should be feasible, when in fact they are merely describing a theoretical, ideal state of affairs.

It is easy to agree how desirable it would be to collect quantitative data about your organisation's use of IT and compare it with industry benchmarks. Yes, but desirable doesn't mean feasible. (Briefing 3)

It is easy to describe how you would ideally like to set up a core set of systems, such that other systems can be neatly slotted in later. The first step is to understand the difficulties with this and the kind of compromises open to you. (Briefing 19)

45. Test any statement that 'X is a good thing, the more of it the better' by asking: Aren't there several *varieties* of X, and if so, does it still make sense to say 'the more X the better'?

Should there be thorough *quality assurance* procedures for all systems development and related activities? Before answering, bear in mind that there are an awful lot of different kinds of checks and tests that might be called quality assurance. (Briefing 25)

Some authorities seem to argue that the more inter-organisational systems the better. But this simplicity evaporates when you probe and discover that this concept shelters a variety of possibilities and objectives. (Briefing 39)

46. Test any statement that 'X is a good thing, the more of it the better' by asking whether the *Salt Curve* applies. No salt on food is awful; some salt is good; too much salt is terrible. The Laffer Curve is similar: increase tax-rates and you may reduce tax-yield, through tax-avoidance and reduced economic growth.

Innovation in the use of IT to gain competitive advantage — the more innovative the better? No, many of the famous cases suggest that you should be just innovative enough to make a difference, but no more, because that is too risky. (Briefing 40)

Some people seem to suggest that you should encourage as much user involvement as possible in the development of any new computer system. Wrong! No involvement is awful; some involvement is good; too much is (or can be) terrible. You need to gauge the *right amount* of involvement. (Briefing 35)

47. Test any statement that 'X is invariably the best way to do things' by looking for factors in a situation that might cause X to be not the best way.

'Every organisation should have a management steering committee co-ordinating the business planning groups and also application management groups and . . ' Thinking out the conditions where such over-prescriptive recommendations would fall down is an excellent way of identifying the real issues in the topic. (Briefing 25)

A few writers have sketched out analysis to show how certain approaches, adopted by others as invariable standards, are clearly appropriate for some but not other generic situations. (Briefing 32)

Look at value chain analysis carefully and you soon find that it doesn't suit certain situations. Ditto critical success factors. (Briefings 4, 7)

48. Given a list of 'bad things', make it more useful by turning it into analysis of *tradeoffs* — rather than just assuming that the opposites of the bad things must be good.

A list of nine generic negative feelings people have about new systems, and four factors that cause these feelings, has little decision-making force. It becomes more useful when converted into an analysis of how certain factors can generate either good or bad feelings according to circumstances. (Briefing 35)

It may appear self-evidently bad for different departments in the same organisation to use different spreadsheet software, to buy PCs from different suppliers, and to commission feasibility studies from consultants on overlapping topics. But the sensible aim should be to strike the right *balance* on questions of standardisation and co-ordination, in order to avoid both bureaucratic centralism and wasteful anarchy. (Briefing 19)

Testing Distinctions, Breakdowns and Analyses4

49. Test any analysis by asking: Is this meant to be *factual* (eg 'the USA is divided into 50 States'), or just *helpful* (eg 'there are five main dialect-areas of American English — or nine or 31, depending how fine an analysis you want). Both types can be useful, but you need to know which of the two you are dealing with.

The customer resource life-cycle breaks a company's activities down into 13 pieces. Don't fall into the assumption that there is anything factual here. For many businesses some other breakdown may be more helpful. (Briefing 7)

The Boston Consulting Group put forward a famous quadrant-diagram: a product is either a star, wild cat, cash cow or dog. What kind of a four-way distinction is this? (Briefing 5)

50. Test any classification by trying to *lump* (show how apparently different things really belong in the same class) or to *split* (show how things placed in the same class are actually different).

Many business-school textbooks cover Porter's three generic strategies, but Porter himself later split one of them in two, thus making four. Why stop there? One or two of the categories still seem rather heterogeneous. (Briefing 5)

One way of categorising different standard methodologies is by the starting assumptions of each. On this basis there seem to be six main categories. Or can that analysis be improved by lumping some of the proposed categories together, and/or splitting one of the categories into several? (Briefing 30)

51. Test any distinction to see if the different words amount to any real difference in practice.

One approach concentrates on the information needed to control critical success factors of a business area. Another, by apparent contrast, concentrates on the information needed to solve the problems of a business area. This could turn out to be a distinction without a difference. (Briefing 7)

52. Test any distinction or contrast by asking: Are several things *clustered* together here? Suppose a contrast is drawn between A and B, and A is said to have four distinctive characteristics. This implies that any case will have all or none of the four characteristics — an important claim that needs to be checked.

Debates about centralisation and distribution sometimes suffer because a variety of issues are wrongly clustered together within each of these broad terms. Unclustering (say) issues of software development from issues of hardware location gives decision-making a much sharper edge. (Briefing 24)

There is no such (useful) thing as integration. Even conceding that there can be degrees of integration, the concept is still too broad. You need to uncluster context integration, data integration and process integration. (Briefing 20)

53. Test any classification to see if it should be two classifications, because it mixes categories from *different planes*.

Parsons differentiates six 'linking strategies' to 'provide the broad management framework to guide IT into and within the business'. But they seem to muddle up issues on different planes. (Briefing 5)

Gerstein provides an interesting breakdown of issues within the field of IM, but they are an uneasy mixture of neutral classification and specific recommendation. (Briefing 2)

54. Test any distinction classifying a thing as either an X or a not-X. The interesting issues may lie in the gradations. An X may be merely a case in the region at one end of a *continuum*.

To talk as if any manager is either knowledgeable about IT or is not destroys any chance of useful debate. The important point is that different gradations of IT knowledge are possible. (Briefing 25)

Some people seem actually to believe that there is a definite category of re-engineering projects that 'massacre obsolete work practices' — as opposed to other projects that are too squeamish to do so, and are therefore not re-engineering. But there is an infinite number of gradations along the continuum from pusillanimity to merciless slaughter. (Briefing 36)

'A piece of software is either portable from one technology environment to another, or it is not.' Wrong. As with suitcases, software can be portable to different degrees. (Briefing 20)

55. Test any simple claim that either X or not-X must be true. 'Either agriculture spread across Europe as tribes practising it migrated, or else the idea itself spread between tribes in different places.' (from a BBC *Horizon* documentary). No, this is a false antithesis: the truth could easily be a messy combination of the two explanations.

'Either you have a centralised or a decentralised setup.' No, you could have centralised planning and fairly decentralised software development. (Briefing 24)

'Either you develop a system in the regular, methodical way or else in an improvisatory, prototyping way.' No, there are any number of variants, meshing the methodical with the improvisatory in all kinds of ways. (Briefing 22)

56. Test any analysis that the choice or decision is between doing X and not doing X. There could be *intermediate possibilities*.

Shall we use a standard, multi-phase planning methodology — or not? Confusing choice. A four-phase approach is very different from one with 14 standard phases and 58 sub-phases. Also, how strictly you follow the standard is another variable. (Briefing 30)

Of course, having a perfect infrastructure, capable of accommodating all future needs, is vastly better than having none at all. But the serious decision is about *how far* to go to gain the benefits and minimise the drawbacks of an infrastructure. (Briefing 20)

57. Test any breakdown of a topic to see if it provides *useful categories*, that will promote decisions between relevant different options.

Projects organised on *evolutionary* lines can be categorised as either *experimental* or *prototype*, and from there sub-divided further. This kind of analysis earns its keep because it exposes options that you may well need to choose between. (Briefing 22)

Distinguish between different types of model — business model, data model and so on. But do it in a way that assists the decision: Which type of model do we want at which stage of our decision-making? (Briefing 29)

Signs of Flimsy Analysis and Reasoning

58. Be cautious with vague, loose *analogies*. They can confuse.

Should you structure your system developments like a four-course meal? That depends what you understand by a 'course' and a 'menu'. (Briefing 19)

Is the development of IT within an organisation analogous to the process of an individual learning a language, and/or the s-shaped growth in a colony of bacteria on an uninhabited medium? In some ways. But these suggestive analogies should be just the *starting-point* for examining the matter more carefully. (Briefing 10)

59. Be cautious about substantial conclusions built on *flimsy foundations*. 'A drama set in Spain where people speak and sing in German is silly; therefore Beethoven's *Fidelio* is completely worthless.' 'The dams and dikes of the Mississippi exacerbated the 1993 floods; therefore river engineering should never be done.' Both of these have defensible premises, but unjustified conclusions.

'An incoherent, muddled business policy is a bad thing (true premise). Therefore (shaky conclusion) a company should choose one out of three possible generic strategies, and do nothing inconsistent with that.' (Briefing 5)

'The ball-point pen was originally designed as a pen for pilots at high altitudes, and the typewriter was only meant for blind people. This shows that projects with limited formal objectives can often lead to unpredicted benefits. Therefore (questionable conclusion) we should go ahead with this project, despite all the valid criticism of its design and objectives, since it could still yield completely unexpected benefits.' (Briefing 22)

'That prototyping project ended up costing more and producing worse results than a project done in the normal, methodical way. Therefore prototyping doesn't work and should not be done.' (Briefing 22)

60. Be cautious about arguments with a *dubious starting point*. Charles II is said to have assembled the wisest men in the kingdom and asked them why it was that a fish weighed more when dead than alive. After listening to their theories, he said he doubted if any were valid, because he had just made up the idea that fish weigh more dead than alive, and knew of no evidence for it.

'Touch screen is obviously the best interface for unsophisticated users. Therefore . . ' (Briefing 12)

'If you don't transform yourselves into an organisation for the information age, you will perish. Therefore . . ' (Briefing 10)

'Research shows that most IT directors think that strengthening links with customers and suppliers is terribly important. Therefore . . ' (Briefing 3)

'Most workers want an interesting job, rich in human contacts. Therefore . . ' (Briefing 34)

61. Be cautious about *can-therefore-will* arguments. 'Strict environmental regulations in a country's economy *can* help, rather than hinder, exports, by stimulating cost-saving technology, developing exports in products for environmental control etc; therefore they *will* . . ' If a certain result *can* plausibly follow from something, that doesn't necessarily mean that it *will*.

Heavy involvement by all users in system design *can* lead to strong positive feelings of commitment to the system. But it doesn't necessarily follow that this will be so. (Briefing 35)

Using information technology more adventurously than competitors *can* lead to increased market share and superior profitability — sometimes. But being adventurous is no guarantee of success. (Briefing 40)

62. Be cautious about conclusions drawn from null evidence (aka the *ad ignorantiam* fallacy). 'The pyramids were *not* built by slave labour, because no evidence of slavery has been found.' (from a BBC *Horizon* documentary). This is only a good argument if you can name the kind of evidence of slavery that might reasonably have been found.

'There is no evidence that use of a standard approach to IT planning stifles creativity or over-simplifies issues. Therefore a standard approach to IT planning is a good thing.' This might be a just-acceptable argument — if based on some impeccably conducted research, but not if it merely amounts to: 'We haven't noticed any evidence that . . ' (Briefing 32)

'There is no evidence that using Nolan's stage theory leads to bad IM decisions. Therefore go on using it.' This is not the kind of thing that is easily proved or disproved by collected evidence; it is better to judge by whether the theory seems reasonable, coherent, clear, meaningful etc. (Briefing 9)

63. Be cautious about *can't lose* arguments. In a bid to take over Company X, Company Y has offered to swap some of its own shares for those of X. All share-holders of X should accept Y's offer. Why? Because, if Y's offer *over-values* X, X's share-holders will be receiving an unduly high price. And, if the offer *under-values* Company X, they will gain shares in Y — whose value is bound to rise, because Y will just have acquired X at a bargain price. Since this logic applies to all such bids, irrespective of the details, it seems likely that there is something wrong with it.

'We should develop an innovative system to offer buyers of our cars free parking spaces. Either it succeeds and we gain competitive advantage, or it doesn't, and we can be confident that none of our competitors can overtake us by using that idea.' (Briefings 22 and 40)

'To determine the choice of the new client-server software, we should devise an election-like voting mechanism with a wide franchise of user managers and technology experts. If it succeeds in producing a wise decision, that is fine. If it doesn't, everybody will be strongly committed to the decision, because it has been reached democratically.' (Briefing 35)

Fallacies and Flaws

64. Watch out for elementary logical blunders.

'All prototyping projects use 4GL-style software. This project uses 4GL-style software. Therefore this is a prototyping project.' (Briefing 22)

'Some projects that launch new IT-based services achieve competitive advantage. This project launches a new IT-based service. Therefore this project will achieve competitive advantage.' (Briefing 40)

65. Watch out for *circular*, question-begging arguments (aka *petitio principi*) 'Shakespeare is greater than Robbins, because people with good taste in literature prefer Shakespeare.' 'How can you recognise people with good taste in literature?' 'They read Wordsworth and Milton and (er) Shakespeare.'

'Research shows that the go-ahead, breakaway companies also invest heavily in IT. Therefore we should invest heavily in IT.' 'How can you recognise the go-ahead, breakaway companies?' 'They are the ones always in the news for doing exciting things like (er) investing heavily in IT.' (Briefing 3)

'All successful companies have five or six core competencies.' 'What is a core competency?' 'One of the (er) five or six things most important to any business.' (Briefing 8)

66. Watch out for the fallacy of *equivocation*: using the same word in two senses in different parts of the argument. 'The end (ie goal) of a thing is its perfection; death is the end (ie last event) of life; therefore death is the perfection of life.'

'Management information systems are fundamental throughout the entire business. Management information systems are only effective with expensive workstation hardware providing a powerful, colour graphic interface. Therefore we must have expensive workstations throughout the entire business.' In the first premise 'management information systems' seems to stand for 'all computer systems'; in the second for 'systems providing ad hoc information to high-level managers.' (Briefing 38)

'Knowledge-workers (in the sense of all workers not in factory or farm) are an ever-increasing portion of the work-force. Knowledge-workers (in the sense of people whose work requires deep knowledge) don't work well in a strongly regimented environment. Therefore (unwarranted conclusion) most organisations should change to far more flexible and democratic structures.' (Briefing 10)

67. Watch out for the fallacy of the *irrelevant conclusion* (aka *ignoratio elenchi*): 'This was a terrible, terrible murder. Therefore you should find the accused guilty.' 'This country's schools are in an awful state, and education is vitally important. Therefore my party's education policy is the best.' This fallacy seems risible when set out in the logic textbook, but it is surprisingly potent in real life.

People often assume that a value chain model is particularly powerful at exploring linkages between activities and between organisations. It isn't really. Porter's book *says* a great deal about how important such linkages are, but it is wrong to assume that the format of model that accompanies the rhetoric must be something special. (Briefing 4)

Advocates of soft systems theory say a great deal about the importance of various human factors, and complain that these are too often ignored by designers of systems. But it doesn't follow from this that their own soft systems *methodology* is full of ingeniously contrived tools and techniques to cope with human factors. It isn't. (Briefing 42)

You can find consultants prating about re-engineering on every corner. But those who are most earnest about it don't necessarily have the best skills. (Briefing 40)

68. Watch out for fallacies of *composition*. 'Every ship in the convoy is ready to sail; therefore the convoy is ready to sail.' Not necessarily; what about agreeing signals, formations, tactics etc? 'Every act is entertaining. Therefore the whole show is.' Not necessarily; a show consisting entirely of juggling acts, each in itself entertaining, is unlikely to be an entertaining show.

'We have ten different experimental, innovative projects under way. This big commitment makes it very unlikely that any competitor will develop an innovative use of IT that takes us completely by surprise.' Maybe, but only if the ten products are managed as a genuine balanced portfolio — otherwise each one could be experimenting in the same small corner of innovation space as all the others.' (Briefing 22)

'Every system in this organisation follows open system standards; therefore linking them up should be easy' — not necessarily; they could be using different open system standards. (Briefing 20)

69. Watch out for *confusion of category*. 'Which is the most dangerous: a lion, a tiger or a peril?'

Shall we use CSFs or a consultancy's standard methodology or a sociotechnical design approach? These things are not alternatives; they overlap, but in quite intricate ways. (Briefings 3, 27 and 33)

'Should this system be regarded as a case of end-user computing or competitive advantage or an open system or prototyping?' These things are not alternatives, though they may overlap. (Briefings 18 and 33)

70. Watch out for fallacies of *relevance*. 'If you really spent a whole year studying Dutch seventeenth-century painting, how come you took us to the Amsterdam *Rijksmuseum* on a Monday when it was closed?'

'This analysis is based on a survey of opinions of 500 key directors. Therefore it must be valuable.' Not necessarily — except perhaps to somebody selling to that target group. (Briefing 3)

'Porter's analysis of the way competition operates is based on decades of research into thousands of companies done by some very bright Harvard people. Therefore it must be very useful to managers.' These premises could be true, but the conclusion need not follow. The analysis could be a triumph of insightful, synthesising description of the essence of 10,000 cases, but that doesn't necessarily make it useful to any particular manager deciding what to do next in a particular organisation. (Briefing 5)

71. Watch out for the *ad misericordiam* fallacy. 'We have invested so much in the Concorde project that it would be a shame not to carry on.'

Elaborate multi-page data models or process models can develop an irrational impetus of their own, rather like plans for military campaigns. (Briefing 29)

So can use of checklists. 'We have conducted dozens of interviews and collected thousands of answers to the standard checklist questions. We can scarcely entertain the idea that all this work was ill-focused for this specific case, and that we ought to discard most of our material, and study things from a quite different angle.' (Briefing 32)

72. Watch out for the *ad verecundiam* fallacy: being too bashful to question authority or accepted wisdom, or assuming that if a certain authority says something, it must be right.

Ill-directed modelling activities often arise from accepting vague assumptions that an enterprise-wide data architecture is the kind of thing every self-respecting organisation ought to have. (Briefing 29)

The *Financial Times* of 30 April 1990 said that the MIT90s research programme was marvellous, and it did cost $5m. But you should still look carefully at what it actually produced, and ask the question: Are all these abstract ideas of any practical value to anybody? (CT-SBT)

73. Watch out for the *ad hominem* fallacy — criticising an argument or proposal because of its source, rather than its quality. The *ad hominem* fallacy is the opposite (or better a variant) of the *ad verecundiam* fallacy.

'The salesman says that his standard methodology is exactly what we need. But he is manifestly an uncritical zealot with, moreover, a vested interest in getting a large consultancy assignment. Therefore we should reject his standard methodology.' No. He may be a zealot and biased, but the rational course is to ignore that, and make an objective judgement of the methodology. It could still be worth using. (Briefing 32)

'This book criticises many things taught in business schools and promulgated by consultants. Since the author is neither a famous business-school professor nor the boss of a large consultancy, his ideas can be ignored.' No. The worth of the ideas in the book depends on the worth of the ideas themselves. (This Whole Book)

NOTES & ARGUMENTS

1 A technique such as spotting classic traits need not only apply to thinking about IM; it might help in getting to grips with another technology, eg biotechnology or aerospace, or with anything else, eg labour economics or Thai classical music. In the list, each maxim is presented in a form that seems generally valid, rather than IM-specific. This is followed by examples of application of the maxim within the field of IM, together with pointers back to the body of the book.

The maxims are set out as a kind of intellectual smorgasbord. This is to ignore certain intriguing but tricky questions. Don't some of the items given overlap others? Don't some of them amount to the same thing, but in different words? Is some more subtle style of classification possible? Are all the 'fallacies' always disreputable? But this is a book about IM, not about critical thinking *per se*. The temptation to pursue such analysis is resisted.

Some of the examples here are made up or heavily edited, but they all come close to things that people have said in actual cases, or have written in books or articles about IM.

2 Here is a management consultant's trick well worth knowing. Suppose Arthur points out carefully, step by step and unanswerably that your consultancy report is full of contradictions, fallacious reasoning and arbitrary assumptions. Just hint gently to Beryl, Arthur's boss, that Arthur, though terribly bright, has a rather theoretical approach to life — a luxury that grown-up decision-makers like us can't quite afford in the rough-and-tumble real world. The beauty of this trick is that the more thoroughly and rationally Arthur destroys your arguments, the more ammunition he provides for your insinuations about how pedantic he is.

3 De Bono points out that the 'search frame' should not be too specific or too broad. He gives some different ways of defining much the same problem: 'to encourage people to share cars', or 'to make it advantageous for people not to drive into town in their own cars', or 'to save gasoline and diminish traffic congestion', or 'to increase the seat occupancy in each car from 1.4 to 2.' Edward de Bono, *Opportunities, A handbook of business opportunity search* (Associated Business Programmes, 1978) p. 154. See also *Letters to Thinkers* (Harrap, 1987).

A related point made by De Bono might be called the swamp/desert distinction. To build a new town in a swamp, your main challenge will be to drain the swamp, ie remove a major cause of problems. But to build a new town in a desert, you probably won't try to remove the sand; your challenge will be to design houses that can stand up on sandy foundations.

4 In Briefing 5 two main criteria for the quality of any classification are suggested: clarity and utility. In this set of maxims: 49 deals with the *status* of any classification; 50-53 with basic tests of *clarity*; 54-56 with one particular problem of *clarity*, the tendency of categories to spread into each other, instead of curdling into separate globules; 57 with *utility*.

Concept Index

Ideas, issues, theories, techniques, principles, arguments etc are divided roughly into three sections: 1. Analogies; 2. Concepts (general): ideas etc easily found in other books and articles about IM or other areas of management; 3. Concepts (this book): ideas etc based on critical thinking, and thus fairly original.

1. Analogies

2. Concepts (general)

3. Concepts (this book)

General Index

This index has seven sections: 1. Applications; 2. Authors and authorities; 3. Cases (fabricated); 4. Cases (real); 5. Products and suppliers; 6. Sectors of the economy; 7. Technologies.

1. Applications

2. Authors and authorities
(a reference in bold is to an entry in the Critical Bibliography)

3. Cases (fabricated)

4. Cases (real)

5. Products and suppliers

6. Sectors of the economy

7. Technologies